JOHN HENRY NEWMAN

John Henry Newman was one of the most eminent of Victorians and an intellectual pioneer for an age of doubt and unsettlement. His teaching transformed the Victorian Church of England, yet many still want to know more of Newman's personal life. Newman's printed correspondence runs to 32 volumes, and *John Henry Newman: A Portrait in Letters* offers a way through the maze.

Roderick Strange has chosen letters that illustrate not only the well-known aspects of Newman's personality, but also those in which elements that may be less familiar are on display. There are letters to family and friends, and also terse letters laced with anger and sarcasm. The portrait has not been airbrushed. This selection of letters presents a rounded picture, one in which readers will meet Newman as he really was and enjoy the pleasure of his company. As Newman himself noted, 'a man's life lies in his letters'.

Roderick Strange was rector of the Pontifical Beda College, Rome, from 1998 to the summer of 2015. He was ordained as a priest of the Diocese of Shrewsbury in 1969 and, besides working as a parish priest, he has been the Catholic Chaplain at the University of Oxford and the chairman of the National Conference of Priests. He has written extensively on Newman including *John Henry Newman: A Mind Alive* (Daton, Longman, and Todd, 2008), which was published in the United States as *Newman 101: An Introduction to the Life and Philosophy of Cardinal Newman* (Christian Classics, 2008).

Praise for *John Henry Newman: A Portrait in Letters*

'Highly recommended.'

Church of England Newspaper

'A fascinating glimpse into this extraordinary mind.'

Catholic Herald

'Brilliantly distils Newman's letters, giving readers a rich view of the great convert's charm, integrity, and genius.'

The Catholic World Reporter

'There is much pleasure in this book; and the letters could just as easily be read one or a few at a time as chapter by chapter. It will be a valuable tool for anyone wishing to get to know Newman's character better in the company of a sensitive guide.'

Serenhedd James, *Church Times*

'Roderick Strange has performed a great service to all who would study theology in our own climate and culture . . . This is an excellent addition to Newman studies.'

Stephen Platten, *Crucible*

'The outstanding nature of the editor's achievement . . . a volume which will long remain as an introduction, companion, and guide to Newman's writings.'

Dermot Fenlon, *The Furrow*

'Newman lives again in every page of this remarkable collection.'

Paul Deal, *The New Criterion*

'Reading this book leads one to discover (or rediscover) a rich and fascinating personality, and creates a desire to plunge further into certain exchanges of letters or the development of certain themes and ideas.'

Reed Frey, *Newman Studies Journal*

'[W]hat makes this effort from Roderick Strange exceptional is its deep understanding of the material, which allows him to organize, yes, but also to reveal . . . Roderick Strange set out to create a portrait of Newman and he succeeded. For students and other interested readers seeking perspective on both Newman's personal life as well as his way of thinking during different theological controversies, this volume is indispensable. But more than this, it is an absolute pleasure to read. Strange has done a superb job with the editing: the introductions are insightful, the footnotes after each letter are helpful without becoming overbearing, and the index of Newman's correspondents keeps the reader from getting lost. Most of all, Newman's command of the English language is present throughout the text.'

Joshua Canzona, *Reading Religion*

'No one, to my mind, has ever written a biography of Newman which quite captures him. This book does so, however, in all his paradoxical greatness. Thank you, Mgr Strange.'

A. N. Wilson, *The Tablet*

JOHN HENRY NEWMAN

A Portrait in Letters

Edited by

RODERICK STRANGE

OXFORD
UNIVERSITY PRESS

OXFORD
UNIVERSITY PRESS

Great Clarendon Street, Oxford, OX2 6DP,
United Kingdom

Oxford University Press is a department of the University of Oxford.
It furthers the University's objective of excellence in research, scholarship,
and education by publishing worldwide. Oxford is a registered trade mark of
Oxford University Press in the UK and in certain other countries

Published in the United States of America by Oxford University Press
198 Madison Avenue, New York, NY 10016, United States of America

British Library Cataloguing in Publication Data

Data available

Library of Congress Cataloging in Publication Data

Data available

ISBN 978-0-19-960414-2 (Hbk.)
ISBN 978-0-19-877928-5 (Pbk.)

Printed and bound in Great Britain by
Clays Ltd, Elcograf S.p.A.

In memory of
Charles Stephen Dessain
1907–1976

Acknowledgements

The invitation from Oxford University Press to produce this edition of the letters of John Henry Newman has been a privilege. I owe a serious debt of gratitude to Tom Perridge as the Commissioning Editor who has been a source of unfailing support and encouragement throughout the preparation of this work, and at different times Lizzie Robottom, Karen Raith, and Caroline Hawley have also supplied help that has been invaluable. I thank them and all at the Press who have assisted me.

My brief has been to prepare this work from the thirty-two volumes of Newman's letters that began to be published in 1961 and whose publication was completed in 2008. That is the rich mine which this book quarries. I was asked to select from those letters, their footnotes and introductions, editing and adapting. I am keenly conscious that I have been dependent on the generosity of many people. I, therefore, endorse wholeheartedly the thanks expressed in those volumes to the countless individuals and institutions who made that publication possible. I thank the Fathers of the Birmingham Oratory for their permission to work on this project and I am also much indebted to the Oratory's archivist, Daniel Joyce, who took great pains on my behalf to check a particular portion of the text to ensure, so far as is possible, its accuracy. I thank as well my friend, Father Paul Murray, OP, for suggesting the photograph of Newman that graces the book's cover.

At one stage Father Brendan Callaghan and the community at Campion Hall in Oxford gave me shelter and warm hospitality for an all-too-brief sabbatical that allowed me to concentrate on this project undisturbed, and most notably I thank the members of the community at the Pontifical Beda College, Rome, my friends and colleagues, the staff and students, for their patient support and understanding throughout. In a special way, however, I thank Professor Eamon Duffy whose enthusiasm for this work has been a tonic from the start. Then, during its preparation, he has always been ready to offer promptly, but without pressure, wise and incisive advice on drafts of the particular introductions to the individual sections and to the main Introduction. His guidance has been a gift, encouraging, but also challenging, and he has alerted me to my mistakes. The mistakes that remain are mine alone.

Most particular thanks, of course, must be reserved for those who worked on the original volumes of *Letters and Diaries* for varying periods of time, Vincent Blehl, Edward E. Kelly, Thomas Gornall, Ian Ker, Francis McGrath, and Gerard Tracey. I am also conscious that there will be others, unknown to me, who have assisted and supported them. I thank every one of them. I have been standing on their shoulders. The whole project, however, was most of all the brainchild of Father Stephen Dessain who was convinced that only the publication of all Newman's letters could do him justice. The standard of meticulous scholarship that Dessain established has won widespread acclaim. He had overseen the publication of twenty-one of the volumes before his death in 1976.

It is my personal boast that I am the only full-time graduate student whose doctoral research Stephen Dessain directed. His firm advocacy for the complete edition of Newman's letters and his reserve concerning selections make me aware that he would probably have viewed this present undertaking with misgivings. All the same and in spite of its inevitable limitations and imperfections, I wish to dedicate this volume to his memory with gratitude and affection.

Contents

Abbreviations

~~~~~

The abbreviations used for Newman's works are those listed in Joseph Rickaby, S.J., *Index to the Works of John Henry Cardinal Newman*, London 1914, with a few additions.

References to works included by Newman in his uniform edition are always, unless otherwise stated, to that edition, which was begun in 1868 with *Parochial and Plain Sermons*, and concluded in 1881 with *Select Treatises of St Athanasius*. From 1886, until the stock was destroyed in the 1939–45 war, all the volumes were published by Longmans, Green and Co. They are distinguished from other, usually posthumous, publications by having their date of inclusion in the uniform edition in brackets after the title, in the list of abbreviations below. The unbracketed date is, in every case, the date of the edition (or impression) used for giving references. (Once volumes were included in the uniform edition the pagination usually remained unchanged, but there are exceptions and minor alterations.)

Add.	*Addresses to Cardinal Newman with his Replies etc. 1879–82*, ed. W. P. Neville, 1905.
Apo.	*Apologia pro Vita Sua* (1873) 1905.
Ari.	*The Arians of the Fourth Century* (1871) 1908.
Ath. I, II	*Select Treatises of St Athanasius* (1881) 1920.
A.W.	*John Henry Newman: Autobiographical Writings*, ed. Henry Tristram, 1956.
Call.	*Callista, a Tale of the Third Century* (1876) 1923.
Campaign	*My Campaign in Ireland, Part I* (printed for private circulation only), 1896.
D.A.	*Discussions and Arguments on Various Subjects* (1872) 1911.
Dev.	*An Essay on the Development of Christian Doctrine* (1878) 1908.
Diff. I, II	*Certain Difficulties felt by Anglicans in Catholic Teaching*, two volumes (1879, 1876), 1908.
Ess. I, II	*Essays Critical and Historical*, two volumes (1871) 1919.
G.A.	*An Essay in aid of a Grammar of Assent* (1870) 1913.
H.S. I, II, III	*Historical Sketches*, three volumes (1872) 1908, 1912, 1909.
Idea	*The Idea of a University defined and illustrated* (1873) 1902.
Jfc.	*Lectures on the Doctrine of Justification* (1874) 1908.
K.C.	*Correspondence of John Henry Newman with John Keble and Others, 1839–45*, ed. at the Birmingham Oratory, 1917.
L.D. I–XXXII	*The Letters and Diaries of John Henry Newman*, ed. Charles Stephen Dessain et al., 1961–2008.
L.G.	*Loss and Gain: the Story of a Convert* (1874) 1911.

M.D.	*Meditations and Devotions of the late Cardinal Newman*, 1893.
Mir.	*Two Essays on Biblical and Ecclesiastical Miracles* (1870) 1907.
Mix.	*Discourses addressed to Mixed Congregations* (1871) 1909.
Moz. I, II	*Letters and Correspondence of John Henry Newman*, ed. Anne Mozley, two volumes, 1891.
O.S.	*Sermons preached on Various Occasions* (1870) 1927.
P.S. I–VIII	*Parochial and Plain Sermons* (1868) 1907–10.
Prepos.	*Present Position of Catholics* (n.d. 1872) 1913.
S.D.	*Sermons bearing on Subjects of the Day* (1869) 1902.
S.E.	*Stray Essays on Controversial Points* (private) 1890.
S.N.	*Sermon Notes of John Henry Cardinal Newman, 1849–1878*, ed. Fathers of the Birmingham Oratory, 1913.
T.T.	*Tracts Theological and Ecclesiastical* (1874) 1908.
U.S.	*Fifteen Sermons preached before the University of Oxford* (1872) 1909.
V.M. I, II	*The Via Media* (1877) 1908, 1912.
V.V.	*Verses on Various Occasions* (1874) 1910.

★ ★ ★

Ward I, II	Wilfrid Ward, *The Life of John Henry Cardinal Newman*, two volumes (London, 1912).

A Note on Brackets

Newman used round brackets. Quarter brackets ⌈ ⌉ indicate text he had copied. Angled brackets < > or double square brackets [[ ]] indicate explanatory comments he added later. Single square brackets [ ] are editorial.

Introduction

'A man's life lies in his letters'

John Henry Newman (1801–90) was one of the most eminent of Victorians, an intellectual pioneer for an age of doubt and unsettlement and a Romantic visionary whose teaching transformed the Victorian Church of England. Though nurtured in the deeply conservative ethos of Regency Oxford, Newman was blessed with a startlingly original and questing intellect. He became at the start the energizing force behind the Oxford Movement that sought to revive catholic and apostolic ideas and practices within the protestant Church of England, but found himself gradually compelled by the logic of his own convictions and by the resistance to them of the Anglican establishment to seek admission into the Roman Catholic Church. As a Catholic priest he adapted for England and established a new branch of an Italian religious community, the Oratory of St Philip Neri, founding Oratories in Birmingham and London. He was then invited to undertake a series of demanding projects, the founding of a university in Dublin, the oversight of a new translation of the Bible, and the editorship of a controversial periodical, the *Rambler*; he was also encouraged twice to set up an Oratory in Oxford, to challenge the sceptical, secular age that he predicted was dawning. None of these ventures was a success. They did not receive the official support they needed. Newman was regarded with increasing suspicion by certain Catholics who feared he was importing alien or liberal ideas into the Catholic Church.

Beside these abortive projects, Newman's Catholic years were also marked by a series of controversies, each of which gave rise to major literary or theological masterpieces. In 1863 Charles Kingsley, celebrated novelist, Cambridge professor, Christian Socialist, and 'muscular Christian', accused Newman and the Catholic priesthood in general of systematic disregard for the truth. The ensuing literary dispute evoked some of Newman's most savage satire, but also produced perhaps the greatest religious autobiography in the language, his 1864 *Apologia pro Vita Sua*. Two years later a debate with his friend and former Oxford colleague, Edward Pusey, over Catholic devotion to the Blessed Virgin Mary, enabled Newman to offer a radical reorientation of contemporary Catholic piety and teaching by recalling it to its roots in the early Church Fathers. And in 1875 his response to William Gladstone's outburst about the political implications of the Vatican Council's decree on papal infallibility, prompted by Gladstone's defeat in the general election, allowed him to interpret that doctrine in a more precise way that has remained influential ever since. Then in his old age in 1878 to his delight Newman was elected as the first Honorary Fellow of Trinity College, Oxford, where he had been an undergraduate. He felt able to visit Oxford once more. And the following year to his still greater astonishment he was created a Cardinal by Pope Leo XIII. The cloud of suspicion under which he had laboured so often as a Catholic was lifted. His final years, though still not without their troubles, became more tranquil.

More is known about Newman than about most Victorian writers and thinkers, yet people may still wonder who he really was. In spite of the projects and controversies, his life was more remarkable for inner than outward events. Until 1845 he lived largely in Oxford as an undergraduate and then as a Fellow of Oriel College, and thereafter he lived mainly in Birmingham as an ordinary parish priest. Although one of the critical turning-points of his life occurred during an illness in Sicily, in fact he travelled very little. His life in many ways was hidden. Visited in extreme old age by his bishop, William Ullathorne, he told him, 'I have been indoors all my life, whilst you have battled for the Church in the world.'[1] It was no more than the truth. He was rarely on public display. And so the question remains: who was John Henry Newman? The most promising place for an answer is to be found in his correspondence. Through his letters he helped shape his age and he also, vividly and unforgettably, revealed himself.

It is not possible to calculate precisely how many letters Newman wrote, but he seems exceptional. The Victorians, of course, were enthusiastic letter-writers. Twelve volumes of Charles Dickens's letters have been published and the combined correspondence of Thomas and Jane Carlyle has already filled forty-three volumes, but Newman's correspondence alone has run to thirty-two substantial volumes. It is estimated that 20,000 letters are extant. Bearing in mind that he also destroyed letters and that there are sometimes weeks in his diaries from which no letters survive—which does not mean that none were written during those days—the output is formidable. By any standard, even in the age that invented the penny post when in central London there could be multiple deliveries each day, he was an indefatigable correspondent. The collection that has been gathered in the archives at the Birmingham Oratory bears full witness to that. There are the letters he copied himself, the letters that others have copied for him, drafts of letters, and letters that have been returned, besides letters that have appeared in print and the photocopies of letters that their owners have allowed to be made.

And while some few of these letters, such as those sent to newspaper editors, were intended for publication, the rest were not. They may often have been composed with careful precision, for that was Newman's way, but others were dashed off. A frequent refrain refers to his hand being tired from writing so much. In these letters, whether intentionally or not, Newman's personality begins to appear. On 12 March 1871, for example, he wrote to his friend, Edward Bellasis, to whom he had dedicated his *Essay in Aid of a Grammar of Assent* the previous year. The letter is not particularly noteworthy and is not included in this volume, but it contains a memorable aside. 'I have a pen', Newman complained, 'which writes so badly that it reacts upon my composition and my spelling.' While some people, he noticed, are brilliant in conversation and others shine when speaking in public, there are still

---

[1] Cuthbert Butler, *The Life and Times of Bishop Ullathorne, 1806–1889* (London, 1926), II, p. 284.

others who 'find their minds act best, when they have a pen in their hands'. He included himself in that last category: 'I think best when I write.'[2] And to the end of his life, when he wrote, he used a quill pen. He replied kindly to a lady who had sent him 'a metal pen', but confessed to her that in his hands it was 'nothing else than a skewer', beyond his mastery and 'proportionately fatiguing' (21 August 1874).

Letters fascinated Newman. As an old man, he joked with his friend, Frederic Rogers, by then Lord Blachford, about hobbies and confessed that his was 'a love of order, good in itself, but excessive' (5 October 1886). That certainly was evident in the way he worked on his letters, copying them, filing them, arranging them, and sometimes adding cross-references, notes, or corrections. These comments and revisions can be followed in this collection which has adopted the same protocol as the complete edition. In particular, his interlinear explanations are printed in the text in angle brackets < >, after the word or phrase they explain; sections that he copied are indicated by quarter brackets ⌈ ⌉; and significant additions or notes are included in double brackets [[ ]] or, when this is impracticable, in footnotes. Round brackets, which he generally favoured, are Newman's own, while single square brackets are editorial. His spelling, use of capitals, and punctuation have been left unchanged and the rare typographical errors have been corrected silently.

For Newman, letters trumped biography. In a well-known letter to his sister, Jemima, in 1863 he expressed his conviction that 'a man's life lies in his letters'. 'Biographers varnish;' he told her, 'they assign motives; they conjecture feelings; they interpret Lord Burleigh's nods; they palliate or defend.' And he explained his point of view: 'I sincerely wish to seem neither better nor worse than I am. I detest suppression; and here is the great difficulty. It may be said that to ask a biographer to edit letters is like putting salt on a bird's tail. How can you secure his fidelity? He must take care not to hurt people, make mischief, or get into controversy.' This concern over controversy was a significant preoccupation of his. He was aware that what he called 'party interests and party feelings' persist. People have agendas. And as extensive correspondence will rarely be made available 'by reason of its prolixity', he observed, so half sentences may be lifted from letters and used on one side of a controversy or another (18 May 1863).

This letter itself echoes a memorandum he had drawn up three years earlier on 20 November 1860 in which he referred to letters he had destroyed, but also to those he had preserved. He had kept them, he noted, because they contained 'records of misunderstandings or personal collisions'. He was guarding against the other party publishing their view of the dispute, and he wanted his side of the question to be available. 'In saying this,' he went on, 'I am not implying that I was always right, and my correspondent wrong—but while I have no wish or intention whatever to rake up any one of these old quarrels myself, so on the other hand I have no wish either, though I have some suspicion, that others may rake up one or other of them and lay down the law as to the rights and wrongs of it.'[3]

---

[2] 12 March 1871, *L.D.* xxv, p. 300.

[3] See *L.D.* xix, pp. 424–5.

He returned to this point in 1872 in a further memorandum that he wrote in case his biography were to be written. He emphasized that among the collections of letters he had made those that could be controversial should only be used in defence, in order to correct misstatements or imputed motives.[4] And four years later he wrote a further memorandum in which he objected to people taking initiatives on his behalf that attacked others. If the friends of those with whom he had clashed, like Frederick Faber, his fellow Oratorian, or Henry Manning, his Oxford contemporary who like him had been received as a Catholic and later became Archbishop of Westminster, made charges against him, then there were papers available to correct the facts and explain his views and motives. Otherwise they were not to be used. And he observed, 'Some officious writer on his own hook, implicating no one else, might commit the offence, and it would be hard that through his impertinence others, as Manning, should suffer.' And he added a line on 7 August 1881, 'Since I am now a cardinal, bye gones should be by gones.'[5]

A way of reconciling his care for his correspondence and his apprehensiveness about a future biography was resolved for Newman when his friend Anne Mozley produced her volume of her brother's letters, *Letters of J. B. Mozley*, in 1885. He was impressed, congratulated her, and invited her to perform a similar service for him with respect to his life as an Anglican. He let her have letters, memoranda, and an autobiographical memoir, the material he considered she needed for the work, and left her to herself. She was able to consult his Anglican friends, Lord Blachford and Richard Church, the Dean of St Paul's, but, in spite of some initial fidgeting, he kept himself apart. Her two volumes, *The Letters and Correspondence of John Henry Newman*, appeared in 1891, the year after his death.

These comments to Blachford, Jemima, and Anne Mozley, in the light of remarks from various memoranda, make plain how important his correspondence was for him. The sheer quantity of letters, however, creates a further question. With the passage of time and the publication of much material relating to the issues that concerned Newman, the danger of initiating the kind of controversy that he feared has passed. Personal reputations are no longer at risk, as once they might have been. All the same, a selection of letters remains problematical. It led Father Stephen Dessain in his introduction to the complete edition of the letters to conclude that only such an edition could be satisfactory, partly because Newman was of interest to so many different people whose reasons for reading him would vary. But he identified a more specific difficulty as well: 'to select is to interpret, to give one's own view, when Newman should be left to speak for himself.'[6]

Dessain's word of caution has been a valuable influence on the way the letters presented here have been chosen. They do not pretend to be a representative selection; still less should they be read as a 'Life in Letters'. They have been placed

---

[4] See *L.D.* XXVI, p. 201.

[5] *L.D.* XXVIII, pp. 92–3.

[6] *L.D.* XI, p. xvii. Because so many of Newman's Anglican letters were already available, this complete edition began at volume xi with the Catholic letters.

in chronological order, not arranged thematically, and each section has an introduction that highlights some of the key people and events during the years when the letters were written. That background should be helpful. A life in letters, however, would be impracticable. Too many trails would need to be followed. Indeed a principal challenge in this work has been to indicate a path through such a wealth of material that did justice to detail without being overwhelmed by it. And in any case, Ian Ker's biography, *John Henry Newman*, makes masterly use of Newman's correspondence throughout.[7]

So this is not a life in letters. Instead, what guides this selection is a desire to offer a portrait of Newman himself. Letters are often fragmentary, like snapshots. They do not give a smooth, rounded, complete narrative, but, taken together, they may offer nonetheless a genuine portrait of the writer. They may not all sparkle; some may seem quite ordinary; but they contain gems. They illustrate the man. Letters after all arise from relationships, and relationships are revealing. So there are letters to family and friends, letters that counsel people who approached him about their faith or about crises in the Church, whether Anglican or Roman. Then there are practical letters concerned with projects he was administering, as well as letters prompted by controversies. There are funny letters, tired letters, sad letters, angry letters, tetchy letters, reflective letters, and many more. And an attempt has also been made to include the more famous letters, like the one Newman wrote to William Ullathorne, his bishop, on 28 January 1870 during the First Vatican Council, protesting against the behaviour of those whom he called 'an aggressive insolent faction', people whom he believed were pressing too forcefully for the defining of papal infallibility. All the same, these letters have not been chosen, so to speak, as evidence to make a case for a particular view of Newman. Instead, they offer glimpses. The impression they make on different readers will vary. These letters range so widely that many portraits may no doubt be possible. Nevertheless it is hoped that Newman's personality, the kind of person he was, will emerge so that those who have read them will acquire a feeling that John Henry Newman is someone they have come to know. They will recognize him in his relationships and through the projects he undertook, and they may also come to appreciate his cast of mind.

Newman's Sense of Principle

One consequence of that startlingly original intellect with which Newman was blessed was not only the clarity of his thought, but his firm sense of principle. When he had recognized in an issue a matter of principle, his adherence to that principle was unswerving. One such principle was dogma. 'From the age of fifteen,' he declared in his *Apologia*, 'dogma has been the fundamental principle of my religion'.[8] And the outstanding example of such a principled dogmatic conviction was his belief in the visible Church as one, holy, catholic, and apostolic. It shaped his

---

[7] Ian Ker, *John Henry Newman: A Biography* (Oxford, 1988, 2010).
[8] *Apo.*, p. 49.

life. He sought for its realization while he was an Anglican and, once he had become a Catholic, he worked for its purification.

As an Anglican, he believed that catholicity was realized within Anglicanism which he saw as a branch of the great Church Catholic, along with the Roman Church and Eastern Orthodoxy, and he pursued it through his formulation of the Church of England as a *via media*, a middle way between Roman excess and Protestant error. And while he acknowledged that the Church's unity had been compromised by division, he never wavered in his recognition of its holiness. Even when his own position within the Church of England was becoming increasingly fragile, he clung to the witness of holiness that he found among his friends, most notably John Keble. The crucial aspect, however, was apostolicity, the belief that the Church was to be recognized through its communion with the bishops, the successors of the apostles. Apostolicity was for him the driving force, essential in principle to the Christian Church. The Oxford Movement sought to revive an awareness of its presence within Anglicanism. The challenge was great because in those days the English regarded their Church as Protestant. What was Catholic was dismissed as papist. Newman knew he would be misunderstood. As he joked to one of his friends in 1834, 'tho' I am already called Papist and Pelagian—well, I am neither Puritan nor Protestant at least—what I aim at is to be a-Postolical.'[9] His *Lectures on the Prophetical Office*, delivered in St Mary the Virgin and published in 1837, were his sustained attempt to present this understanding of the Church as founded on apostolic tradition, while following that middle path between Roman excess and Protestant error. He uncovered evidence for his view in earlier Anglican Divines, but he acknowledged at the same time that what he was presenting had never truly been tested as a living system. This middle way, he declared, had only ever existed on paper.

From 1833 to the summer of 1839 Newman was riding high in his prosecution of this way of understanding the Church and was astonished to find how many people supported the case he was making. He was also attacking without inhibition those like the Regius Professor of Divinity, Renn Dickson Hampden, whom he saw as opposed to his position. 'Judging by his writings,' he observed to one friend, Hampden 'is the most lucre loving, earthly minded, unlovely person one ever set eyes on' (3 March 1836). Even allowing for the qualification, 'judging by his writings', the ferocity of the language is hardly Newman at his most attractive. Then, however, he was himself struck a series of blows. In 1839, while reading during the long vacation he seemed to discover a precedent for his middle way in the early Church. It had been a living system after all, not just something that existed on paper. What alarmed him, however, was his realization that the middle way was not orthodox.

He was studying the controversy surrounding the fifth century Monophysite heresy. The Monophysites opposed the accepted belief of the Church that there were in Christ two natures, human and divine, that were united without being confused; they affirmed instead that there was in Christ only a single nature and it

---

[9] 21 August 1834, *L.D.* IV, p. 325.

was divine. At the same time, they opposed the Eutychians whose understanding of Christ's one nature as divine was even more extreme than theirs. As such their position could itself be said to occupy the middle ground between orthodoxy, identified as the Roman teaching, and the Eutychian heresy. Newman's alarm was then compounded by an article written by Nicholas Wiseman, the future Cardinal and Archbishop of Westminster, who argued against Anglican claims to apostolicity by reference to the fourth century Donatist schism in north Africa. Its relevance did not strike him at first; Anglicans after all were not like those African rigorists. Then a friend pointed out to him Augustine's declaration, '*Securus iudicat orbis terrarum*', the universal Church is in its judgements secure of truth: as the Donatists had isolated themselves, so Anglicans had separated themselves from Rome. By these words, Newman stated in his *Apologia* years later, 'the theory of the *Via Media* was absolutely pulverized'.[10] He wrote to his friend Frederic Rogers in the September and remarked that the whole experience had given him 'a stomach-ache' (22 September 1839).

In 1844, in a series of valuable letters to Catherine Froude that described rather than analysed the movement of his mind, and that were written while he was still an Anglican, Newman commented further on the effect that Wiseman's argument had had on him. It seemed to demonstrate to him that 'the English Church was in Schism'. He continued, 'The fact to which the Monophysite controversy had opened my eyes, that antagonists of Rome, and Churches in isolation, were always wrong in primitive times, and which I had felt to be a *presumption* against ourselves, this article went on to maintain as a recognised *principle and rule* in those same ages. It professed that the fact of isolation and opposition was *always taken as a sufficient* condemnation of bodies so circumstanced, and to that extent...the *fact* of separation was reckoned anciently as decisive against the body separated' (9 April 1844). 'I saw my face in [a] mirror,' he was to remark in his *Apologia* years later, 'and I was a Monophysite.'[11] After the summer of 1839, however, as his normal routine was re-established, everything became calm again for a while. But two years later, in 1841, his nightmare returned. He had begun once more his study of the Arian heresy, the subject of the first book he had written, and this time it was the heretical Semi-Arians whom he saw as occupying the middle path between Rome, on the one hand, and full-blown Arianism, which rejected the divinity of Christ, on the other. 'The truth kept pouring in upon me', he was to tell his friend, Henry Wilberforce, in 1848. 'I saw in the Semi-arians the Viamedians, I saw in the Catholic Church of the day the identical self of the Catholic Church now' (30 November 1848).

In 1841, however, Newman had sought to defend his position by writing *Tract 90*. Tracts, initially pamphlets, but later more substantial works, played a vital part in the Oxford Movement. They were the common means by which Newman and his friends presented their viewpoint. In this instance, he wanted to show that the Church of England's Thirty-Nine Articles were, despite appearances, compatible

---

[10] *Apo.*, p. 117.   [11] *Apo.*, p. 114.

with Catholic doctrine. The Articles themselves were popularly considered, of course, to be a bulwark against Popery, Romanism, and superstition, but Newman argued that, as they had been drawn up as part of the Elizabethan Settlement, prior to the conclusion of the Council of Trent, 'with the purpose of including Catholics', of making them feel at home in the Church of England, 'Catholics now will not be excluded'.[12] The intricacy of the case could make the argument seem like sophistry. Nevertheless Newman was concerned at that time to restrain some of his more enthusiastic younger followers from deserting the Church of England for Rome. He realized the Tract might stir up some trouble, but thought it would be slight. He felt people were becoming bored with these controversies. He was mistaken. After some initial correspondence in which he thought he had managed to protect and establish the position he had outlined, the bishops began to attack the Tract. Over the next three years, twenty-four of them condemned what he had said. It was not merely the scale of the onslaught that dismayed him, but the fact that it was the bishops themselves whose very authority as the successors of the Apostles was fundamental to the understanding of the Church that he was advocating, who were rejecting and condemning a position he believed was essential for Catholic Christianity. He was stunned. As he was to remark to John Keble, 'By October next the probability is, that hardly a single Bishop but will have given his voice against it' (14 March 1843). They were making his position untenable. What was he to do? And at the same time a further difficulty was simmering.

A decision had been taken to establish a Bishopric in Jerusalem that would act as a centre for Protestants in the Holy Land, and the bishop was to be alternately Anglican and Lutheran or Calvinist. The idea that the bishop could be indifferently Anglican or Protestant appalled him. It implied that the Church of England was itself a Protestant denomination. To support such a view was to abandon the catholicity and apostolicity that he had sought to secure by arguing for the *via media*. His vision of the Church of England as a branch of the great Church Catholic was falling apart. 'This Jerusalem matter is miserable', he told his sister, Jemima, 'and has given me *great* uneasiness' (16 November 1841).

At this point Newman more or less retired to the parish at Littlemore, a kind of out-station to his University parish of St Mary the Virgin where he was Vicar. He did not hurry. He reflected and prayed. In May 1843, he confessed to Keble, ' I am very far *more* sure that England is in schism, than that the Roman additions to the Primitive Creed may not be developments, arising out of a keen and vivid realizing of the Divine Depositum of faith' (4 May 1843), and by the following January his confidence in the Church of England had so dwindled that he confessed again to Keble his 'uncomfortable feelings' that he 'should not like to die in the English Church' (23 January 1844). He had felt secure before on account of two considerations, one positive, the other negative. The positive had been his conviction about the apostolic succession within Anglicanism. Now, however, that conviction had been undermined as he reflected on the implications of their separation from Rome,

---

[12] *V.M.* II, p. 348.

and the bishops' virtually unanimous rejection of *Tract 90* and their establishment of the Jerusalem Bishopric. The negative had been his view that there were certain definite Roman doctrines 'not to be found in Antiquity'. But his position on this point was changing as well. He had, as he told Catherine Froude in that series of long letters that he wrote her, 'always held a development of doctrine, at least in some great points of theology' (9 June 1844), and so in due course he began to study and review this second issue. He set about writing his *Essay on Development*, which he described as 'an hypothesis to account for a difficulty'.[13] If Anglicanism as a middle way between excess and error had collapsed, where was the Church of Christ to be found? It could not be by alliance with Protestant error, but might it be that what had previously been dismissed as Roman excess was rather to be recognized as the 'keen and vivid realizing' of faith, developed over the centuries? When he became convinced of this second possibility, he acted and was received into the Catholic Church on 9 October 1845.

There are various ways of describing Newman's path from Anglicanism to Catholicism, but this one, tracking his commitment to the Church as in principle apostolic, reveals a key aspect of his personality and way of thinking. Once he had identified a principle, he followed it relentlessly whatever the consequences. And there was a reverse side to this coin.

If as an Anglican his unyielding sense of principle had led him eventually to Rome, as a Catholic that same sense of principle made him critical when he heard appeals to principles that he felt were unfounded. He refused to allow as principles points of view that he regarded simply as legitimate alternative opinions. It was the particular bone of contention between him and W. G. Ward.

Though they had never been close friends, Ward had been one of his most enthusiastic younger disciples at Oxford, preceding him into the Catholic Church. He was an accomplished pure mathematician with a cast of mind that loved to push an argument to its logical conclusion, and that approach was characteristic of his theology as well. He was well known as an Ultramontane, one of those who were exponents of extreme views on papal authority. Newman tried to moderate that extremism. 'The truth is,' Newman told him, 'where you have a number of intellectual persons, where you have a number of schools, a number of orders, you *must* have a number of differences' (13 June 1855). It was not a viewpoint with which Ward could feel at ease. Indeed, even before he accepted the editorship of the *Rambler* in 1859, a position that was to cause him such problems, Newman, in writing to Ward, challenged him by asking what he meant by referring to the *Rambler*'s 'detestable *principles*'. He went on, 'I have disliked its *tone* as much as any one could; but what of its principles?' Ward typically could not immediately recall (10 March 1859). And later Newman complained to him, 'Pardon me if I say you are making a Church within a Church, . . . and in St Paul's words are "dividing Christ" by exalting your opinions into dogmas, and shocking to say, by declaring to me, as you do, that those Catholics who do not accept them are of a different religion from

---

[13] *Dev.*, p. 30.

yours' (9 May 1867). Nevertheless, he and Newman retained a warmth for each other. When their paths diverged, Ward described himself as 'a kind of intellectual orphan',[14] and, although Newman became exasperated with his dogmatizing spirit and his tendency to elevate minor differences into matters of great importance, he described Ward years later as being 'so above board, and outspoken, that he is quite charming'. He appreciated his straightforwardness (4 January 1875).

As a Catholic, what Newman bemoaned in particular was the lack of different schools of theological thought which meant that everything tended to be seen through Roman lenses (9 November 1865). 'As an Englishman,' he once observed, 'I do not like a Romaic religion—and I have much to say, not (God forbid) against the Roman Catholic, but against the Romaic Catholic Church. I have no great sympathy with Italian religion, as such—but I do not account myself the worse Catholic for this.'[15] The schools would have been the antidote to the dogmatizing of people like Ward.

His clarity of intellect and sense of principle, therefore, cut both ways, guiding his path, while brushing lesser matters aside. It was the reason moreover why he could become so indignant when others tried later to explain his move to Rome as motivated by pique or disappointment, rather than as the conclusion to a demanding, sustained intellectual exercise. He became a Catholic, he remarked years later, not out of despair, but out of his study of the Church Fathers (3 July 1871). In 1844 indeed he had explained to Manning, '[As] far as I know myself, my one paramount reason for contemplating a change is my deep unvarying conviction that our Church is in schism and that my salvation depends on my joining the Church of Rome . . . I am not conscious of resentment, or disgust, at any thing that has happened to me. I have no visions whatever of hope, no schemes of action, in any other sphere, more suited to me. I have no existing sympathies with Roman Catholics. I hardly ever, even abroad, was at one of their services—I know none of them. I do not like what I hear of them' (16 November 1844). And the following month he stated starkly to Jemima, that although people might conclude that he had joined the Church of Rome because he must be 'disappointed, or restless, or set on a theory, or carried on by a party, or coaxed into it by admirers, or influenced by any of the ten thousand persuasives, which are as foreign from my mind as from my heart', still as time goes by, 'they will see that all these suppositions do not hold; and that they will be led to see that my motive simply is that I believe the Roman Church to be true' (22 December 1844). It is fair to say that Newman was sensitive, and sometimes hypersensitive. But the course he pursued throughout his long life was not the result of sensitive self-regard that would have made him seek his own comfort, or sulk; it was rather the fruit of a steely fidelity to the truth as he came to recognize it, whatever the consequences might be.

---

[14] Wilfrid Ward, *William George Ward and the Oxford Movement* (London, 1889), p. 81.
[15] 16 June 1863, *L.D.* xx, p. 471.

Catholic Projects

If Newman's cast of mind, the clarity of his thought and his firm sense of principle, was particularly conspicuous during his Anglican years, his Catholic years called into play his administrative gifts. The Catholic authorities, unsure how to make best use of his talents, asked him from the start to oversee various projects, such as the founding of the Catholic University in Dublin, preparing a new translation of the Bible, rescuing the periodical, the *Rambler*, from censure, and on two separate occasions establishing an Oratory in Oxford. All these enterprises called for an array of practical skills, planning and organizing, hiring the appropriate personnel, raising finance, and sometimes purchasing property, and, when the projects collapsed, thwarted by lack of support from those who had initially encouraged them, disengaging from those plans and trying to limit the financial losses that had been incurred. In the circumstances, it comes as no surprise to see Newman's comment in his Journal for 1863 where he observes, 'since I have been a Catholic, I seem to myself to have had nothing but failure, personally'.[16] His letters supply evidence of his exasperation, sometimes openly, sometimes more controlled.

The Dublin project proved challenging for a variety of reasons. There was tension between Archbishop Paul Cullen of Armagh who had invited him, and the other Irish bishops who were suspicious of Cullen's motives. Newman was caught between the two. And, while Newman himself was intent on creating a university, the bishops wanted something more akin to a Catholic Training College. But it was Cullen's treatment of him that Newman found particularly irksome. Less than a month before his final departure he declared, 'He has treated me from the first like a scrub, and *you will see he never will do otherwise.*'[17] He had described Cullen's behaviour to J. M. Capes in 1857: 'I will tell you his *rule* of acting—not once, or twice, but his rule and principle—to let me ask a question in June, to call about it again and again, to let me write to him about it in July, to let me write to his intimate friend to get an answer for me in August, to give up the chance of one in September, and in January accidentally to find he all along has been telling others that he *has* decided it in the way I asked him *not* to decide it, though even now in February he has not, directly or indirectly, answered me. I say, this is his way of doing business— and the sort of confidence he puts in *me*' (1 February 1857). The year before, following a brief conversation about visiting the church Newman had built for the University in St Stephen's Green and fixing a date for its opening, Cullen sent Newman a letter with a series of questions about whether those who attended mass there before its consecration would fulfil their Sunday obligation, about those who would officiate there, about whose the church would be should Newman leave Dublin, and about those who were gazetted to preach there. In his terse reply the same day, Newman could scarcely disguise his irritation. He thanked Cullen for

---

[16] *A.W.*, p. 255.
[17] Letter to Robert Ornsby, 17 October 1858, *L.D.* XVIII, p. 487.

asking those questions, but added, 'I should have been still more gratified to have elicited them some time ago' (12 April 1856).

As his time in Dublin was coming to an end, he accepted a proposal put to him by the bishops of England and Wales to edit a fresh translation of the Bible. He began to gather a team of translators and sent Wiseman a detailed estimate of the costs that he believed would be incurred (7 November 1857). He heard nothing more. He was encouraged to cooperate with a similar American project that was under way, but received no further instructions. The whole enterprise was left entirely to him. In 1860 he received a letter from Archbishop Francis Kenrick of Baltimore who was directly engaged in the American translation. 'I did not know,' he replied, 'what I find by your letter, that your Grace had been in some suspense as to the intention of the English bishops with respect to it. For myself, as you seem to wish me to speak on the subject, I can only say, that I have been in the same suspense myself', and he made excuses for Wiseman's silence by reference to his anxieties, engagements, and state of health (8 July 1860). It would be difficult not to read between the lines his sense of frustration.

Immediately following his return from Dublin, Newman also found himself embroiled in controversy over the affairs of the *Rambler*, the Catholic periodical that had earned the displeasure of the English bishops and was likely to be censured in their Pastoral Letters. Newman too was not uncritical of the *Rambler*, disliking its tone, as he had told Ward, but he still valued it because it supplied an alternative view to people like Ward who championed more extreme opinions. So he was invited to intervene in the first place to persuade the editor, Richard Simpson, who was his friend, to resign so as to deflect the bishops' criticism. He managed that, but when Wiseman then became anxious that Simpson's successor might be just as obnoxious, Newman realized that the only way out of the impasse was for him to take on the position himself. 'I have the extreme mortification of being Editor of the Rambler', he told Henry Wilberforce. 'It is like a bad dream, and oppresses me at times inconceivably' (31 March 1859). All the same, it gave him a platform for explaining the role the laity could play in the life of the Church. Education was Newman's line. Editing such a periodical was an opportunity. His article in only his second number in charge, 'On Consulting the Faithful in Matters of Doctrine', has proved seminal, but at the time there were those who denounced what he said. Disputes were stirring and he had even then already been encouraged to resign. Once more, those who had sought his help when in difficulty had not supplied the necessary support. And it took years before the misunderstanding and opprobrium that the denunciation had aroused in Rome would be explained and resolved.

More fundamental than any of these projects, however, was Newman's responsibility for establishing the Oratory in England. That became complicated from the beginning. When he arrived back in the country he learned at once that the flamboyant and enthusiastic Frederick Faber, whom he already knew from Oxford, wished to become an Oratorian as well and bring with him a group that he had founded, called Wilfridians. There were eighteen of them. Newman was welcoming, but wary. Within days of discovering Faber's desire to have his followers become Oratorians, he wrote him a friendly letter, but even then wondered whether Faber had 'fully mastered *what* Oratorianism is' (31 December 1847). And very soon trouble was brewing. Faber had declared that he and his Wilfridians were coming to Newman unconditionally, 'but as time goes on,' Newman pointed out to him, 'we see more clearly than we did, that there are anxious conditions attached to it' (28 March 1848). These conditions involved particular obligations to the mission at Cotton, that the Wilfridians had undertaken for the Earl of Shrewsbury and which they now left Newman to unravel. Newman felt sympathy for the Earl, but explained that he had been told the Wilfridians were becoming Oratorians with his sanction, that Oratorians work in cities, not the countryside, and that it would in any case be impossible for the Oratory to sustain the expense of the mission (25 February 1848). Nevertheless he continued to take responsibility for that mission for a while longer.

Further complicating factors were the decision about the location of the Oratory, either London or Birmingham, and the size of the community. Once Faber's group had been admitted, it was clear that the community would need to be divided and a second Oratory would have to be opened. Newman discussed these issues particularly in letters to Faber. Dividing the community was no easy task, but imperative. '[Does] not your knowledge of human nature tell you,' he asked, 'that ... in so large a body as we shall be can we possibly hope to get on without dissensions?' And where were they to settle? Wiseman who had been the first to encourage Newman to become an Oratorian, had by now moved from the Midlands District to London. Should they follow him there? Faber's eyes were set on London, but initially he did not want to be separated from Newman. So where was Newman to be? Newman, however, was clear about wishing to remain in Birmingham, because their coming to Birmingham, he argued, 'does *not* depend on the accident of Dr Wiseman having been Vicar Apostolic [for the Midlands] when we were at Rome', and, as Birmingham had been named in their Brief, 'I do not see how the conclusion can be avoided, that I must be here' (16 February 1849). The community divided in 1849, with one group remaining in Birmingham with Newman as Superior, and the other moving to London with Faber. It had been a delicate manoeuvre.

Other issues soon emerged as well. The demands of ministry in Birmingham and London were naturally not identical. The London Fathers in particular wanted to be able to hear nuns' confessions, something that had been excluded from the Brief drawn up by Newman in Rome. Newman, like St Philip before him, had been against it as something that would absorb too much time. Late in 1855, however, he learned by chance that the London House had petitioned the Congregation of Propaganda in Rome for a change in the Rule to make hearing these confessions possible. He had thought at first that they were merely inquiring about Oratorian customs in different places. In fact, the London House was exercising its own independence, while Propaganda took it for granted that Newman had been consulted. When he discovered, therefore, that what was in view was not merely a permission for London, but a change to the Rule without reference to him, creating thereby a possible change also for the Birmingham House, he reacted fiercely. As Oratorian communities are independent and Oratorians do not take vows, the Rule is the basis of their vocation.

Newman then wrote what he regarded as a perfectly reasonable letter, asking the London Fathers to write to Rome to ensure that there was no misunderstanding of 'that fundamental principle of the Oratory of St Philip, whereby its Houses are entirely independent of each other, and what one does is not the act of the other' (8 November 1855). He asked them to act at once and to let him, as founder of the English Oratory, have their response to transmit to Rome. But Newman's letter was read with different eyes in London. It seemed to them unjust and domineering. They felt he was behaving more like a Father General in a religious order, trying to assert his authority. They refused to do as he had asked, stating that they must wait till they had received a reply from Propaganda.

Correspondence escalated without any progress being made. The London Fathers declared their love for Newman, but would not change their position. Both parties felt deeply injured. In December Newman left for Rome with his friend and fellow Oratorian, Ambrose St John, not to secure his own authority over the London House but simply to safeguard Birmingham's independence from the action of the London Fathers. He succeeded, but the quarrel stained his reputation in Rome. More immediately, the relationship between the Birmingham and London communities was damaged. Although the London Fathers sought to heal the breach the following summer, they never seemed to have grasped the seriousness or significance of what they had done: 'We did not in the least look upon our application to Propaganda in the serious light you do.'[18] And they never offered an apology for their behaviour and that failure always rankled with Newman.

From then on, he decided that the only way to avoid such problems in the future was to ensure that each House lived its own life, neither interfering with the other. They became like two houses of different religious orders. To safeguard the principle of independence Newman was unyielding. And he was in the right. Nevertheless it is hard not to see in his implacable adherence to principle something intransigent. It would have been cheering if that penetrating intellect had been able to recognize that the mistakes committed by the less intelligent were not necessarily malicious and then, without condescension, to have made some allowances for them. It was no doubt wise to place a distance between Birmingham and London after their clash because trust had broken down, but did the breach need to be so absolute?

In handling all these matters there is to be seen in Newman a stern practicality that those who see him only as scholarly and intellectual too often overlook.

---

[18] Richard Stanton to Newman, 5 June 1856, *L.D.* XVII, p. 254.

Losing Trust

A) FREDERICK FABER

One specifically complicating factor in Newman's dealings with the London Oratory was his relationship with Frederick Faber. Faber as a young man had come under his influence at Oxford and he was received into the Catholic Church shortly after him. He was later to become W. G. Ward's spiritual director, and he and Ward came to represent the Ultramontane extremism of which Newman was so critical. But whereas Newman, though often exasperated by Ward, retained a certain affection for him because he was open and forthright, he never felt the same warmth for Faber. Temperamentally they were poles apart. Faber was enthusiastic, emotional, extravagant, and in religious terms extreme—in their Anglican days, Newman had warned him against mixing Roman and Anglican ways, against, as he put it, 'decanting Rome into England',[19] while Newman himself, on the other hand, was cautious, reflective, measured, moderate, and self-consciously Anglo-Saxon.

There was as well a narcissistic streak in Faber. He was charming, but self-absorbed and manipulative, intent on getting his own way. After the breakdown in the relationship between the two Houses, it comes as no great surprise to find Newman observing to Ambrose St John, 'As to Fr Faber himself, he now finds himself as he was before he sought the Oratory—independent, with all the additional advantages, which St Philip, extended reputation, and years give' (7 July 1856). In spite of his protestations of loyalty and affection, Faber seemed always to want things on his own terms.

What riled Newman more than anything in his relationship with Faber was Faber's tendency to gossip and the way he spoke openly about the rift between the two Oratorian Houses, stirring scandal. Faber's exuberance was stoked further by Wiseman showing him confidential letters he had received from Newman relating to the dispute which Faber then showed to others. Trust was crucial and it had been lost. In a letter to Mary Holmes with whom he corresponded for years, he remarked of Faber: 'I found that there was that in Fr Faber, with all his good qualities and talents, which made it impossible to trust him' (19 April 1859).

When Faber became seriously ill and was approaching death in 1863, Wiseman wrote to Newman, asking him to make a visit. Newman replied, telling the Cardinal that he had been in touch with Faber to let him know that he wished to see him and informing him 'of the precise time when I hope to have that sad satisfaction' (14 July 1863). There was satisfaction for Newman because he was indeed glad to be able to see Faber; that Faber was so ill and dying made the circumstances sad. Nevertheless there was a coolness in Newman's reply to Wiseman that gives an ironical flavour to his turn of phrase. Once Newman's trust had been lost, it was not easily restored.

---

[19] 1 December 1844, *L.D.* x, p. 443.

B) HENRY MANNING

Newman lost trust in Manning as well. They had much in common. They had known each other since their days in Oxford in the 1820s and had been friendlier than people often acknowledge. Both had been Anglican clergymen and both were fellows of Oxford colleges. Manning had supported the Oxford Movement. Both had been received as Roman Catholics and ordained as priests. But their relationship had broken down later. When Manning approached Newman in 1867 to heal the breach between them and wanting to know its cause, Newman apologized to him if he seemed rude, but then stated bluntly that 'it is a distressing mistrust, which now for four years past I have been unable in prudence to dismiss from my mind'.[20] And two years later, in reply to another letter from Manning who had referred to their 'friendship of so many years, though of late unhappily clouded', he declared memorably, 'I do not know whether I am on my head or my heels, when I have active relations with you. In spite of my friendly feelings, this is the judgment of my intellect' (3 November 1869).

The distance between Newman and Manning is what people tend always to remember, but they had indeed enjoyed a long, though not an especially close, friendship. Reading Newman's letters bears this out. There is no hint of difference between them until about 1860, but after that three issues in particular emerged to separate them. First, there was the temporal power of the Papacy which was under threat as the movement for Italian unity gathered force. For Manning the Pope's temporal power was inseparably bound up with his faith in the Papacy, while for Newman, as he told his friend, Thomas Allies, 'though I have no difficulty in saying that the temporal power is necessary, while it lasts, nothing can make me say that it is necessary, if it be clean taken away' (21 October 1866). Such an attitude was anathema to Manning. Then, hand-in-hand with his conviction about the status of the Pope's temporal power was Manning's extreme view of papal infallibility that he worked so industriously to have defined at the First Vatican Council. And here too Newman's emphasis was different. As a Catholic he had always believed in infallibility, but he saw no need to define it formally. In his famous 'leaked' letter to Bishop Ullathorne during the Council, he protested against the 'aggressive insolent faction' who were pressing so hard for it, and asked, 'When has definition of doctrine de fide been a luxury of devotion, and not a stern painful necessity?'(28 January 1870). Manning would have felt the whiplash of criticism. And thirdly, underlying these differences, were their conflicting attitudes to what was called mixed education, Catholics attending English universities, in particular being allowed to go to Oxford and Cambridge.

For all that Newman could see the benefits of university education in a Catholic setting, which had after all inspired his work in Dublin, he had also come to recognize that it was impracticable at that time. As he observed to William Monsell, 'At least, the leave to go to Oxford and Cambridge should not be withdrawn, till an

---

[20] 10 August 1867, *L.D.* XXIII, p. 290.

English Catholic University is actually provided. As to the question whether a Catholic college in Oxford or Catholics in Protestant Colleges, that is a point for subsequent consideration—but it is a strange act to forbid, yet not to compensate. Are Catholics to be worse educated than all other gentlemen in the country?' (12 January 1865). He could see no more harm from someone attending one of the ancient universities than their enlisting in the Army. He wrote this letter scarcely a month before Wiseman died. By then Manning was highly influential as Provost of the Westminster Chapter, already adamantly opposed to the scheme, and soon to succeed Wiseman as Archbishop. His influence would grow. Although he and Newman were both Oxford men with so much in common, Manning was now suspicious of the Oxford ethos and particularly suspicious of Newman.

If Catholics were to be allowed to go to Oxford, there was a plan for Newman to found another Oratory there to care for their pastoral needs. Twice in the 1860s his bishop, William Ullathorne, had encouraged him to do so. Here was another of those projects where his practical administrative skills were engaged, finding property, raising money, and enlisting the help of old Oxford friends. But the plan was scotched in Rome through Manning's influence. Newman learnt about it from Edward Bellasis. As he reported to Charlotte Wood, Manning 'was more opposed to my going to Oxford than to Catholic youth going there, . . . I was the cause of his opposition' (21 December 1866). Manning was fearful that Newman's presence would act as a magnet. In writing to George Talbot in Rome in February 1866, he famously described Newman's type of Catholicism as worldly. It was, he declared, 'the old Anglican, patristic, literary Oxford tone transplanted into the Church'.[21] Manning was suspicious of that ease with questioning that Newman exemplified. All the same, when John Keble, their friend from Oxford days, died weeks later, it was Newman he found himself writing to, as he put it, 'almost instinctively': 'I have just heard of dear Keble's death: and I feel as if it had put me back half my life to the days when we used to look to him and his Christian Year as the service of our happiest thoughts. Nobody can understand this as you'.[22]

It would be easy to read into these differences personal antipathy and even doubt the sincerity of that letter of Manning's. Nowadays that might be true. But it was not the case between them. On a number of occasions Manning made significant attempts to bridge the gap between Newman and himself, attempts which Newman's mistrust always made him resist. He regarded them as attempts to control him, which may well have been true.[23] Newman, however, insisted to Thomas Allies, who had tried to encourage him to think better of Manning, 'You strangely misunderstood what I said about Manning, and treated it as if it denoted personal feeling on my part. What I said was, that I could not trust him—"confidence" is the

---

[21] Quoted in David Newsome, *The Convert Cardinals: Newman and Manning* (London, 1993), p. 257.

[22] Henry Manning to Newman, *L.D.* XXII, p. 198 n. 1.

[23] See Newsome, *The Convert Cardinals*, p. 371: 'it is probably fair criticism that [Manning's] propensity to offer olive-branches was motivated more by his desire to win [people] to his side than by his sincere readiness to meet them half-way.'

word I used. Confidence is an intellectual habit, not a moral...I never doubted Manning felt kindly to me.'[24] Yet in later years he was never to drop his guard.

Friends

Solitude was not a burden for Newman. People would quote of him the old saying, *nunquam minus solus quam cum solus*, he was never less alone than when alone. Yet he was also blessed with many friends. He recognized the curious combination himself, remarking once, 'I have often been puzzled at myself, that I should be both particularly fond of being alone, and am particularly fond of being with friends' (16 March 1868). His wide-ranging and revealing correspondence with so many of them cannot be fully represented here, but it is possible to offer indications.

His two closest friends from his Oxford days were John Bowden and Hurrell Froude. Bowden and Newman became friends during their time as undergraduates at Trinity. They met the day Newman came into residence and their friendship never faltered. Although Bowden was based in London after leaving Oxford, he was an important member of the Oxford Movement and his premature death in 1844, when Newman was wrestling with his position in the Church of England, left Newman distraught. He made a note in 1862, 'I sobbed bitterly over his coffin, to think that he left me still dark as to what the way of truth was, and what I ought to do in order to please God and fulfil His Will'.[25]

Newman came to know Froude at Oriel in 1826 when Froude became a Fellow. He was like a whirlwind, a man of charm and forceful personality. Piers Brendon has observed that he was remarkable 'not for the startling nature of his beliefs but for the vigour and originality with which he expressed them'.[26] His influence on Newman was profound rather than specific. In the *Apologia* Newman acknowledged that he had taught him 'to look with admiration towards the Church of Rome, and in the same degree to dislike the Reformation'.[27] He died from tuberculosis in 1836. Newman wrote to Bowden the day after hearing the news: 'He was so very dear to me, that it is an effort to me to reflect on my own thoughts about him. I can never have a greater loss, looking on for the whole of life—for he was to me, and he was likely to be ever, in the same degree of continual familiarity which I enjoyed with yourself in our Undergraduate days' (2 March 1836).

Besides these more intensely personal Oxford friendships, there were also others that were vital to Newman, especially those associated with him in the leadership of the Oxford Movement, notably John Keble and Edward Pusey.

When Newman was elected a Fellow of Oriel in 1822, Keble had been a fellow for eleven years. Newman was in awe of him. In a letter to Bowden he described receiving the congratulations of the fellows after his election. 'I bore it', he told him, 'till Keble

---

[24] 4 June 1865, *L.D.* xxi, p. 483. [25] *L.D.* x, p. 343.
[26] Piers Brendon, *Hurrell Froude and the Oxford Movement* (London, 1974), p. 37.
[27] *Apo.*, p. 25.

took my hand, and then felt so abashed and unworthy of the honour done me that I seemed desirous of quite sinking into the ground' (15 April 1822). Although Keble left Oxford the following year to become vicar of Hursley, he and Newman remained in close contact, and a warm friendship grew between them. Keble was to write a number of the *Tracts for the Times*, and he was someone to whom Newman turned for advice, especially later when he was agonizing over his position in the Church of England and wondering about resigning as Vicar of St Mary the Virgin. Keble urged him to stay. And in a later letter, unburdening his state of mind, he concluded, 'How this letter will distress you! I am ever thinking of you, My dear Keble' (8 June 1844).

After Newman's reception into the Catholic Church, there was an exchange of letters and Keble wrote several times, the last on Easter Tuesday in 1846. For reasons Newman could not recall later, he never replied to that letter and there was silence between them for seventeen years. Then in August 1863, at one of the darkest times in Newman's life and shortly before the rehabilitation had begun that the controversy with Charles Kingsley and the *Apologia* were to set in motion, Keble wrote again. It is a distinguished, moving letter. 'I ought to have felt more than I did', Keble confessed, 'what a sore burthen you were bearing for conscience' sake, and that it was the duty of us all to diminish rather than aggravate it, so far as other claims allowed.'[28] In his reply, Newman declared: 'Never have I doubted for one moment your affection for me— never have I been hurt at your silence... You are always with me a thought of reverence and love' (15 August 1863). Contact had been renewed and was not to be broken again. Keble applauded Newman's *Apologia* and the friends met once more in 1865. Keble was to die the following year, but at that meeting Pusey was with them.

Pusey was a year older than Newman and became a Fellow of Oriel in 1823, the year after him. He impressed Newman immediately, but their close friendship developed from 1828 when Pusey moved on to Christ Church as Professor of Hebrew. When Pusey was desolate after his wife, Maria, died in 1839, Newman called on him or met him for a walk every day for five weeks, with only two exceptions when he had other unavoidable commitments. Pusey had been initially apprehensive about the *Tracts*, but later was fully involved and after Newman's conversion he was recognized as the undisputed leader of the Oxford Movement. By contrast with Keble, after only a brief period, he and Newman soon resumed contact, writing friendly letters to each other frequently. During their meeting at Keble's vicarage, Pusey talked about a dispute in which he had become entangled with Manning. Newman was dismissive at first, but later to Pusey's delight was drawn in, writing his formal *Letter to Pusey* that sought to correct Pusey's misconceptions about Catholic teaching on the Blessed Virgin Mary, while tempering the excesses of Catholics like Faber and Ward. In the last letter he wrote him, in August 1882, the month before Pusey died, he criticized the inaccuracies in a memoir his brother-in-law, Tom Mozley, had published about Oriel and the Oxford Movement. Newman remarked, 'It is infamous to make me complain of you, who have always been so careful in your words about me' (4 August 1882).

[28] 4 August 1863, *L.D.* xx, p. 501.

Then in 1843, when Newman's hold on his position in the Church of England was weakening and some friends were distancing themselves from him, he was joined at Littlemore by Ambrose St John. St John, born in 1815, was a good classical scholar and since 1838 had been a Student of Christ Church. For the previous two years, however, he had been curate to Newman's friend, Henry Wilberforce, at East Farleigh. He went to Prior Park to be received into the Catholic Church a few days before Newman and remained his faithful friend till his death in 1875. He went with him to Rome in 1846 to prepare for priestly ordination and accompanied him again in 1856 to clarify the dispute between the Oratories. It was St John too who in 1862 took on the position of headmaster in the Oratory School that Newman had founded when the first head, Nicholas Darnell, had resigned and tried to take the staff with him. Darnell had wanted more control over the school and to distance it from the Oratory. Newman was not to be moved and St John was completely loyal. St John also returned to Rome once more in 1867 to deal with the allegation that Newman was preparing his pupils at the school for entrance to Oxford. And on that occasion he found himself at last getting to grips with Rome's misunderstanding of Newman over his article on consulting the lay faithful in the *Rambler*.

In 1875, St John collapsed from overwork. He seemed at one stage to be recovering when suddenly he died. The first letter of condolence that Newman answered was to another of his dearest friends, Frederic Rogers, by then Lord Blachford. He paid Ambrose tribute: 'From the first he loved me with an intensity of love, which was unaccountable. At Rome 28 years ago he was always so working for and relieving me of all trouble, that being young and Saxon looking, the Romans called him my Guardian Angel. As far as this world was concerned I was his first and his last. He has not intermitted this love for an hour up to his last breath' (31 May 1875). Yet when Newman was on trial for libel because of his allegations against the former Dominican Achilli and then under pressure during his Dublin years, it was St John who often bore the brunt of Newman's temper. When trying to deal with issues in Newman's absence, when he was recuperating after the Achilli trial, Newman let fly: 'Does it not come to this, that I am unnecessary to you?' (10 January 1853). Or again, when he thought St John was being buttered up by Faber: 'Don't send me Fr Faber's letters. I have read *neither* of them. I know they would make me angry' (17 November 1857). Those who are closest can often be targets for outbursts of temper. True friendship can accommodate anger. When St John died, Newman described his death as 'the greatest affliction I have had in my life' (13 June 1875).

The strength and depth of this friendship has given rise more recently to speculation about Newman's sexuality. Society today, obsessed with sex, struggles to imagine 'mature, intimate friendship within a life of priestly celibacy', but once the evidence has been examined, that is the model of relationship that Newman and St John supply.[29] And Newman's letter about St John to Maria Giberne, after his death, places it in perspective. She was by this time a Visitation nun, Sister Maria Pia,

---

[29] See John Cornwell, *Newman's Unquiet Grave* (London, 2010), p. 230; see also Ker, *John Henry Newman* (Oxford, 2009), pp. 746–50.

living in France. They were old friends. She had been staying with the family when Mary, Newman's beloved youngest sister, had died in 1828. Maria was devoted to Newman, was received into the Catholic Church two months after him, and when Newman was accused of libelling Achilli, she had worked wonders on his behalf by collecting witnesses from Italy who could support his defence. On his return from Rome as a Cardinal, while travelling through France, Newman planned to visit her, but his frail health and the poor weather made it inadvisable to break the journey. Their correspondence contains memorable moments. In old age, he told her, 'If you have not teeth, you *cannot* eat hard substances without danger. Unchewed meat is as dangerous to the stomach as brick and stone, or a bunch of keys. You are not an ostrich. I am *very serious*' (5 January 1882). She died suddenly in 1885 without becoming ill. When he had written to her about St John's death, he recalled as well her many kindnesses to him and then he went on, 'Since his death, I have been reproaching myself for not expressing to *him* how much I felt *his* love—and I write this lest I should feel the same about you, should it be God's will that I should outlive you' (4 June 1875). Many people were attracted to Newman and offered him friendship and love.

Besides Maria Giberne, there were numerous other women with whom Newman had an extensive correspondence, the wives and widows of his friends, converts and nuns and devoted ladies.[30] One of these was Emily Bowles, to whom he also wrote a brief, but loving letter after St John's death: 'Don't be surprised that I have written to some others before you—this is because I love you so much and trust you so well, that I have wanted to send you a longer letter than I could now. But I send a few lines' (3 June 1875). Emily was a convert and had a brother, Frederick, who for a time was an Oratorian, but who finally left the Oratory in 1860 and ministered as a priest elsewhere. She was a determined, gifted woman who was also perhaps emotionally rather insecure. Newman's letters to her, however, come to display relaxed freedom. In 1863 he wrote her a long letter in two parts on the way he had been treated by Propaganda in Rome. He likened himself to 'the Persians driven on to fight *under the lash*'. He concluded by commenting, 'Now observe, the letter of which I send you now the remainder is a freer one *than I ever wrote to any one before*' (19 and 29 May 1863).

Another young woman with whom Newman communicated was John Bowden's daughter, Marianne, who had become a Visitation nun at Westbury. She became ill and died when only 36 in 1867. Some months before, answering a letter from her, Newman began, 'Your letter of this morning brought tears into my eyes—first because you spoke so affectionately of me, and said, that, wherever you are, you will not forget me' (15 July 1867). In spite of his reserve, emotion was not far away.

---

[30] This correspondence has been studied perceptively and entertainingly in Joyce Sugg, *Ever Yours Affly: John Henry Newman and his Female Circle* (Leominster, 1996).

Family

When Newman learnt that his brother-in-law, Tom Mozley, was writing his *Reminiscences chiefly of Oriel College and the Oxford Movement*, he was pleased at first. When the book appeared, however, he was horrified by its errors and inaccuracies and told Mozley so (9 June 1882). What angered him in particular was Mozley's account of his parents, littered with mistakes. Newman was a devoted son. On going up to Oxford, he was naturally anxious to make them proud of him, but when he took his degree, he performed miserably. 'It is all over; and I have *not* succeeded', he told his father. 'The pain it gives me to be obliged to inform you and my Mother of it I cannot express. What I feel on my own account is indeed nothing at all, compared with the idea that I have disappointed you' (1 December 1820). His mother replied the following day to reassure him, 'Your Father and I . . . are more than satisfied with your laudable endeavours.' His father was to die four years later and then in 1836 rather suddenly his mother became ill and she too died. She had laid the first stone of the Littlemore Church that was to mean so much to Newman. Newman wrote her entertaining letters, especially when he was travelling in the Mediterranean in 1832 and 1833.

At that time he was also sending letters to his sisters, Harriett and Jemima. There survives as well the scrap of a poignant earlier letter to Harriett in which he declared, 'No calamity, I think, could occur to me here so great, as to lose your love and confidence' (6 February 1828). And yet that was what happened in 1843. She first of all thought her brother had been trying to persuade her husband, Tom Mozley, to become a Roman Catholic and, when she discovered that on the contrary Newman had made every effort to restrain him, she changed tack and attacked 'his spirit and tone' (21 January 1844). It was the start of the estrangement between them that had still not been resolved when she died in 1852.

His letters to Jemima are full of news and often supply entertaining summaries of events, although sometimes Newman's pain and sense of hurt are unleashed in them. Jemima understandably mourned his leaving the Church of England and he equally understandably wished to explain himself to her, but she could not cope with that. In 1846, when wounds were still raw, he chided her for her coldness (16 August 1846). Even nineteen years later, however, when she at last invited him to visit her in Derby because their brother, Frank, was going to be there too, he took the opportunity to write her a dreadful letter, refusing to go, complaining of the way she had treated him, and revealing the hurt he had nursed over the years: 'None have so acted towards me as my near relations and connexions' (31 October 1865). In spite of that outburst, relaxed and friendly letters continued to pass between them. The severe clash did not destroy the relationship. Jemima must have known her brother well. She died on Christmas Day 1879, the year Newman had been made a Cardinal. As he remarked to Anne Mozley twelve days later, 'What I miss and shall miss in Jemima is this – she alone, with me, had a memory of dates . . . yesterday was the anniversary of Mary's death—my mind turned at once to Jemima, but she was away' (6 January 1880). Mary, of course, was the much loved youngest sister who had been taken ill suddenly and died in 1828, and whose memory Newman always cherished. Her name, especially around the anniversary of her death, recurs regularly in his letters.

Newman's contact with his brothers, Charles and Francis, was much less frequent. Frank he had helped through Oxford where he gained a double first and was elected a Fellow of Balliol. Four years later, however, he resigned as his views drifted towards non-conformity which meant he could no longer subscribe to the Thirty-Nine Articles. Later he turned to Unitarianism. That drift alienated him from his brother, but there was in time a kind of reconciliation. And they corresponded also about Charles, who quarrelled with the family after his father's death and for years scarcely settled, although he relied on his family for support for some time. Newman observed to Frank, 'I have so little hope [about Charles], that I do not know what to propose. At one time I was willing to set aside my own money to purchase him some situation. I gave up the notion finally in consequence of things which occurred which made me feel that it might be all lost to him and to me, as his own was lost' (5 May 1840). Charles abandoned any belief in Christianity and became reclusive, settling in Tenby for the last thirty years or so of his life, where his landlady and her daughter cared for him most kindly. When Newman visited him in September 1882, the brothers had not met for more than forty years. After his death, however, Newman acknowledged to Anne Mozley, 'He must have had some curious natural gifts, for eccentric, violent and self-willed as he was, he attached to him the mother and daughter with whom he lodged and, the mother having died, the daughter has refused a nurse and has nurst him day and night through his last illness' (23 March 1884).

Newman's family life was marked by loyalty, love, and laughter, but also by arguments, disagreements, and separations. Like many other families, there was hurt, but there was also healing. It seems fitting that at the very end he was visited by his niece, Grace Langford, Harriett's daughter, who had married and emigrated to Australia. His letter to her is the last he wrote. He had not seen her since she was a small child in 1843, shortly before her mother had broken off relations with him. 'Thank you for your wish to see me', he told her. 'I embrace it readily and I will see you whatever day next week suits you for that purpose' (2 August 1890). She called on 9 August, and he died two days later. 'He was very kind,' she wrote later, 'holding my hand in his all the time.'[31]

---

[31] *L.D.* XXXI, p. 299 n. 3.

Early Years
(1801–33)

On 3 June 1808 Newman wrote to his mother, telling her when he would be home for the school holidays. The letter is brief and simple, typical of letters from children to parents. Newman was seven years old and it is the first of his letters to survive. Other early letters are similar and his letters to his sisters are laced with humour.

Newman had been born in 1801 into a conventionally devout Anglican family, but in the summer vacation of 1816, while he remained at school in Ealing, he became ill. It was the first of three illnesses in his early life that he came to regard as providential. And at this time he experienced his first conversion. He felt over-whelmed by the sense of 'two and two only absolute and luminously self-evident beings, myself and my Creator'.[1] He had come under the influence of one of the masters at the school, Walter Mayers, who was an Evangelical. While Newman's conversion at this time was not typically Evangelical, nevertheless he acknowledged its Evangelical influence and in old age he would pay it tribute.

In June 1817 he went up to Oxford and began to settle in at Trinity, his college, buying his gown and adjusting to college life. Shy, diffident, and earnest, he did not find it easy, recoiling rather priggishly from the drinking culture that he encountered there. He set himself to study hard.

He was expected to do well when he took his degree, but in fact the stress proved too much for him and he failed disastrously. He barely managed a pass and wrote disconsolately to his father: 'The pain it gives me to be obliged to tell you and my Mother [that I have *not* succeeded] I cannot express.' His mother's reply was warm and affectionate and full of confidence that, when the time was ripe, his gifts and hard work would be rewarded. And within the year he had resolved to be ordained and had decided to stand for an Oriel fellowship. Oriel's academic reputation was at its peak at that time. Newman did not expect to succeed immediately, but felt the attempt would be good experience for the following year when he planned to try again. As it happened, he triumphed. Edward Copleston, the Provost of Oriel, remarked of him later that he 'was not even a good classical scholar, yet in mind and powers of composition, and in taste and knowledge, he was decidedly superior to some competitors, who were a class above him in the Schools'.[2]

Newman felt abashed in the distinguished Oriel common room, especially when he first met John Keble who was to become one of his closest friends, but it was Richard Whately, the flamboyant, extrovert philosopher who took Newman in hand

---

[1] *Apo.*, p. 4.   [2] *A.W.*, p. 64.

and helped him overcome his reserve. Although their casts of mind were different, Whately drew Newman out and Newman credited him with helping him 'to think correctly and . . . to rely on myself'. However, in the autumn of 1827, while examining in the Schools, he fell ill again, not seriously, but enough to make him reassess his enthusiasm for the intellectual excellence that the Oriel common room had encouraged. This was the second providential illness of his early years.

In 1824 he had been ordained a deacon and the following year a priest in the Church of England, and his work among parishioners at St Clement's helped him to appreciate their goodness and began to wean him away from the stricter, more Evangelical views that he had adopted before. Then in January 1828 his beloved youngest sister, Mary, died unexpectedly. Newman was heartbroken.

In 1828 as well Oriel needed to elect a new Provost. The main candidates were Newman's friend, John Keble, and Edward Hawkins who was also the Vicar of St Mary the Virgin, the University Church. Newman admired Hawkins and had been helped by him in his early years at Oriel. He believed him to be better qualified than Keble to become Provost. And Hawkins was in fact elected. Newman went on to succeed him as the Vicar of St Mary's. Before long, however, they clashed over their understanding of a college tutor's duties. Newman wished to develop a system in which the brighter undergraduates would receive more individual tuition, while Hawkins preferred the traditional approach in which the tutors concentrated on delivering lectures without discriminating between the abilities of those in their charge. In the event and after protracted correspondence, Newman had to bow to the Provost's will. He did not give up his tutorship, but no further pupils were assigned to him. The consequences were to be far-reaching.

Then in 1829 Newman was drawn into controversy about Catholic emancipation. His devotion to the Church of England made him anti-Catholic, but more particularly he was shocked by Sir Robert Peel's volte-face. Having been returned as the University's MP and opposing Catholic emancipation, Peel had changed his position. He resigned his seat, but offered himself for re-election. Newman voted against him on principle and canvassed support for Peel's opponent, Sir Robert Inglis. To his delighted surprise his campaign was successful.

In 1831 he began a commissioned history of the Ecumenical Councils of the Church, but his study grew to be too detailed for its original purpose. It became instead his first book, *The Arians of the Fourth Century*. And throughout this time his understanding of the apostolic origin and authority of the Church was developing. He valued celibacy more and more as an apostolic state of life, although, as he told George Ryder, 'I think that country parsons ought, as a general rule, to be married'.

By September 1832, however, without pupils and with his book completed, he accepted an invitation from his friend Hurrell Froude, who was already sickening with the tuberculosis that would eventually kill him, to accompany Froude and his father on holiday to the Mediterranean. It was to be a momentous journey for Newman: he would see for himself places that he had known before only from his classical studies; he would visit Rome for the first time; and his travels would culminate in his making a second visit to Sicily on his own where he became dangerously unwell. They set sail in the December.

He wrote long, lively letters to his mother and to his sisters, Harriett and Jemima, which were also often spiced with high comedy, for example, the escape of a duck on board ship or an account of the boat, caught in a storm. Christmas in Malta, however, proved frustrating as they were not permitted ashore for fear of cholera. But Newman's descriptions of what he saw as he travelled are rendered sharply, and when he first came to Sicily, he exclaimed to Jemima, 'Wonderful place, piercing the heart with a strange painful pleasure'. The seeds of his return had been sown.

His reactions to Rome were mixed. He was impressed by the city and was surprised, he observed, at finding it 'so intelligent and liberal a place'; but at the same time he was repelled by 'the unedifying dumbshow' that surrounded the Pope and recoiled from the Roman Catholic system, while confessing himself more attached to the *Catholic* system than ever. During this time news was reaching him from England of the Reform Bill.

On 9 April the Froudes set off to return to England, but Newman was drawn back to Sicily 'by an irresistible attraction'. At the beginning of May, while crossing the island, he became seriously ill, probably with typhoid fever. It was the third of the significant illnesses that mark this early period of his life. In spite of the severity of his condition he was convinced that he would not die because, he believed, God had a work for him to do. After the crisis had passed, he was able to make his way to Palermo and eventually after various delays found an orange boat to take him to Marseilles. Becalmed in the Straits of Bonifacio, he composed his poem, 'The Pillar of the Cloud', better known as the hymn, 'Lead Kindly Light'. From Marseilles he travelled to Lyon, and from there to England, arriving in Brighton on 8 July.

He was too ill to write many letters towards the end of this time, but soon after his return, though over weeks, he composed an account for his friend Henry Wilberforce. Before that, however, he had written an affectionate letter to Provost Hawkins at Oriel. Their clash over the tutorial system had not undermined their regard for each other.

1

Early Years (1801–33)

To Mrs Newman

Ealing, June 3rd, 1808.

Dear Mamma,

I am very glad to inform you that our Vacation commences on the 21st Inst. when I hope to find you all well.

I am Dear Mamma, Your dutiful Son, J H Newman.[1]

[1] Endorsed 'I went to school May 1. 1808'.

To Jemima Newman

Ealing, April 12, 1815.

My dear Jemima,

It is always a great pleasure to me to write to you, for the following reason. If I write to Harriett she always requires a laughable letter, which is by no means suited to the dignity of my character, but you Jemima being conspicuously and wonderfully sedate yourself, always like a serious, sedate, sensible epistle. One thing in your letter disappointed me very much, and this it was. At the end you say, we all send our love with your affectionate sister, J. C. Newman. I consequently very naturally supposed that you were sent to me, as your letter seemed to imply it, and as there was a lumbering *heavy* lump of something or other at the bottom of the parcel, I concluded it must be you, and so I began to unpack this rapidly, to give you (as I thought) some fresh air, of which I did not doubt that you were in want. When to my surprise, having unpacked the said heavy lump, it proved to be a cake! And now I have touched upon the subject I will say two or three things about this said cake. I am very much obliged to Mama that she was so good as to be so punctual, then as to the cake itself I think it rather too much done, and that Mama must know if she has seen it. I liked Harriett's letter to Charles very much, excepting what related to Trusty, the trusty Trusty.[1]

Believe me ever, my dear Jemima, your affectionate Brother.

[1] One of his father's horses.

To Mr Newman

⌈Oxford June 11. 1817

[[To my Father]]

The minute I had parted from you, I went straight to the tailor's, who assured me that, if he made twenty gowns, they would fit me no better... If he took it shorter... he would if I pleased, but I might grow etc etc. He tells me it is customary to pay ready money for the cap and gown—he takes 5 per cent off other things, if paid for directly.

I then went HOME, and had hardly seated myself, when I heard a knock at the door, and, opening it, one of the commoners entered, whom Mr Short had sent to me, (having before come himself with this said commoner, when I was out,) to explain to me some of the customs of the College, and accompany me into the Hall at dinner.[1] I have learned from him something I am much rejoiced at. 'Mr Ingram' said he 'was very much liked; he was very good natured; he was presented with a piece of plate the other day from the Collegians. Mr Short on the contrary is not liked; he is strict; all wish Mr Ingram were Tutor still.' Thus I think I have gained by the exchange and that is a lucky thing. Some time after, on my remarking that Mr Short must be very clever, having been second master at Rugby, he replied, 'Do you think so? *I* think him not *too much* so.' Another proof that he is a strict Tutor.

At dinner I was much entertained with the novelty of the thing. Fish, flesh and fowl, beautiful salmon, haunches of mutton, lamb etc and fine, very fine (to my taste) strong beer, served up on old pewter plates, and mis-shapen earthenware jugs. Tell Mama there are gooseberry, raspberry, and apricot pies. And in all this the joint did not go round, but there was such a profusion that scarcely two ate of the same joint. Neither do they sit according to their ranks, but as they happened to come in.

I learned from the same source, whence I learned concerning Mr Short, that there are a *great many* juniors to me. I hear also that there are no more lectures this term, this week being the week for examinations, and next week most of the members go. I shall try to get all the information I am able respecting what books I ought to study, and hope, if my eyes are good-natured to me, to fag. I expect every minute for three or four servants to knock at my door for their fees, which amount altogether to about half a guinea...

Tell Harriett I have seen the fat cook. The wine has this moment come in. 8⅓ per cent is taken off for ready money. Two things I cannot get, milk and beer, so I am obliged to put up with cream for the one and ale for the other.⌉

---

[1] The commoner was John Bowden who was to become one of Newman's closest friends. Short was Thomas Short (1789–1879), Newman's tutor, who befriended him and whom he met again on becoming an honorary Fellow in 1878.

To Mr Newman

⌈June 16th 1817.

[[To my Father]]

The coach to Winchester goes every morning at 7 o'clock, and gets to Winchester at 3 or 4 PM and the charge inside is £1.8. outside 16/

I was very uncomfortable the first day or two, because my eyes were not well, so that I could not see to read; and, whenever my eyes are bad, I feel low spirited. Besides, I did not know any one, and, after being used to such a number about me, I felt very solitary. But now my eyes are better, and I can read without hurting them, and I take my hour's walk regularly, and have been able to fag pretty well this last day or two . . .

I am not noticed at all, except by being silently stared at. I am glad they do not wish to be acquainted with me, not because I wish to appear apart from them and illnatured, but because I really do not think I should gain the least advantage from their company. For Hollis the other day asked me to take a glass of wine with two or three others of the College, and they drank and drank all the time I was there.[1] I was very glad that prayers hindered their staying together longer than half an hour after I came to them—for I am sure I was not entertained with either their drinking or their conversation. They drank while I was there very much, and I believe intended to drink again. They sat down with the avowed determination of each making himself drunk. I really think, if any one should ask me what qualifications were necessary for Trinity College, I should say there was only one,—Drink, drink, drink.

. . . I ought not to envy them [[(my brothers at home)]] but I feel very much like it. However, I believe I may come home this day fortnight. I shall have kept my three weeks, which is all that is necessary.⌉

[1] George Parry Hollis entered Trinity College in 1815. He became Rector of Doddington near Bridgewater.

To Walter Mayers

[About 12 September 1820]

⌈The quiet of a Long Vacation is profitable to growth in religion, as to progress in learning, unless a person's every thought is engrossed by anxiety for the latter. I am more happy here, than I suppose I ever was yet; for the comparative freedom from temptation I enjoy in having hardly any one near me (I hope I do not speak presumptuously) leaves me at greater liberty to look into my heart, and to keep my thoughts on God. As it is, I make my daily prayer, though I do not feel it as I ought to do, that I may not get any honours in the schools, if they are to be the least cause of sin to me. Yet with all the earnestness I assume, how little does my heart go with my words, or feel their extent. A very distinct thing it is to say so, when the trial is at a distance, and when the temptation comes in full force.

...I fervently pray God, He may not suffer so strong, perhaps so fatal a temptation to assail me. In truth I am in no common situation. The very few honours that have ever been taken by men of our College, the utter absence of first classes for the last ten years,[1] the repeated failures which have occurred, and the late spirit of reading which has shown itself among us, render those who attempt this autumn objects of wonder, curiosity, speculation, and anxiety. Five of us were going up for first classes, this time; one has deferred his examination; one most likely goes up for no honours at all; one is expected to fail; one whom I think quite certain of success (as far as human means go) may before the examination remove to another College;—one remains. 'Unless,' I am told, 'success at length attends on Trinity this examination, we have determined it is useless to read.'

The high expectations too that are formed of me, the confidence with which those who know nothing of me put down two first classes to my name, the monstrous notions they form of the closeness of my application, and the consciousness of my own deficiencies,—these things may create a smile, to think I feared them, in my future life, but they are sufficient to dismay me now. I fear much more from failure, than I hope from success. Still may be [I] continue to pray, 'Let me get no honours here, if they are to be the slightest cause of sin to my soul.'

But, while saying this, I often find that I am acting the part of a very hypocrite; I am buoyed up with the secret idea, that by thus leaving the event in the hands of God, when I pray, He may be induced, as a reward for so proper a spirit, to grant me my desire. Thus my prayer is a mockery.⌉

---

[1] Newman was mistaken. There had been three firsts at Trinity within the last ten years, two in 1812 and one in 1813.

To Mr Newman

⌈Trinity College December 1st 1820⌉

My dear Father,

⌈It is all over; and I have *not* succeeded.⌉ The pain it gives me to be obliged to inform you and my Mother of it I cannot express. What I feel on my own account is indeed nothing at all, compared with the idea that I have disappointed you; and most willingly would I consent to a hundred times the sadness that now overshadows me if so doing would save my Mother and you from feeling vexation. I will not attempt to describe what I have gone through, but it is past away, and I feel quite lightened of a load.—The Examining Masters were as kind as it was possible to be, but my nerves quite forsook me and I failed. I have done every thing I could to attain my object, I have spared no labour and my reputation in my College is as solid as before, if not so splendid.—If a man falls in battle after a display of bravery, he is honoured as an hero; ought not the same glory to attend on him who falls on the field of literature?⌉

Believe me, My dear Father Your dutiful Son
John Henry Newman.

P.S. I am obliged to add that I find a degree costs £15. I take my degree Tuesday, *will* you send me that sum by that time? Unless you hear to the contrary I shall come to Town on Wednesday next by dinner time.

[1] 'He had overread himself, and, being suddenly called up a day sooner than he expected, he lost his head, utterly broke down, and after vain attempts for several days had to retire, only making sure first of his B.A. degree. When the class list came out, his name did not appear at all on the Mathematical side of the Paper, and in Classics it was found in the lower division of the second class of honours, which at that time went by the contemptuous title of the "Under-the-line", there being as yet no third and fourth classes.' *A.W.*, p. 47.

To Mr Newman

Febry 15. 1822

... This brings me to ... my trying at Oriel. I do not *intend*(!) to come-in this year. I want all my friends to know that.[1] I have no chance, and simply stand for the sake both of knowing the nature of the examination for the sake of *next* year, and being known to the examiners. (I have been to the Provost, and he tells me I must get a certificate of my birth)

The same motive which led me to go to the Provost so soon, has also decided me in circulating as quietly as I could my intention of going into the Church; the absence of which qualification would, I am sure, go against me. This year then I hope to spend in reading; and, if I do read, I think I shall stand a great chance of getting in at Oriel next year.

[1] 'It did certainly startle Mr Newman's friends at Trinity to find him contemplating an attempt upon an Oriel Fellowship; and many of them it pained also, for they were sure it would end in a second miscarriage. They had not the shadow of a hope of his succeeding; and they would have thought him wise, if, instead of following an *ignis fatuus*, he had accepted one of the family tutorships offered for his acceptance.' *A.W.*, p. 54.

From Mrs Newman

⌈Febr. 21 1822

I cannot let this 21st anniversary of your birthday pass, without a line of congratulation from me ... As my words flow from the heart of a Mother, I know they will meet a kind reception. I thank God, it is a day of rejoicing to us all; to your Father and me, that it has given us a Son who has uniformly persevered in improving the talents given him, and in forming his character both morally and religiously to virtue. And now that we have no more the dear child, we may boast instead, a companion, counsellor and friend. To your dear brothers and sisters it has given a second father, to whom they are much indebted for the improvement and cultivation of their minds; and, proud and happy am I to say, you are worthy of each other. To yourself, my dear, it is a day of thankfulness and rejoicing, that you have been guided and protect[ed] in this good path to fulfil all these duties so satisfactorily to your nearest and dearest connections, and likewise to form other friendships, which promise to be permanently valuable, and that you are placed in the situation that seems most suited to your abilities and character. These and innumerable other blessings we have all of us to be grateful for, and I rely with humble but perfect confidence in that Almighty Power who has hitherto preserved you, that He will diffuse His blessings on your future years.⌉

To Mrs Newman

⌈March 6. 1822

[[To my Mother]]

Thank you for your very kind letter. When I turn to look at myself, I feel quite ashamed of the praise it contains, so numerous and so great are the deficiencies which even I can see. There is an illusion in the words 'being of age,' which is apt to convey the idea of some sudden and unknown change. That point, instead of being gained by the slow and silent progress of one and twenty years, seems to divide by some strongly marked line, the past from the to-come. When I thought of the years that are gone, and the unknown expanse which lies before me, I felt much affected, and quite shed tears to think I could no longer call myself a boy. Not that I am sorry so great a part of life is gone,—would that all were over!—but I seem now more left to myself, and, when I reflect upon my own weakness, I have cause to shudder....

... What time I have left, I am glad, and am indeed obliged, to devote to my attempt at Oriel,—wishing to prepare for that which will not admit of preparation. I was very uneasy to find, by something in my Father's and your letter, that you thought I had a chance of getting in this time. Do not think so, I intreat. You only hear, and cannot see the difficulties. Those on the spot, and they are likely to judge most correctly, think there is little or no chance: and who indeed will not rightly wonder at the audacity of him, who being an Under-the-line himself, presumes to contend with some of the first men in the University, for a seat by the side of names like Keble and Hawkins?⌉

From Mrs Newman

⌈March 11. 1822

... This subject I have been anxious to begin with, but another is equally pressing on my mind and your Father's, that is, the state of your health and spirits. We fear very much, by the style of your letter, you are depressed; and, if imperious reasons did not forbid us, you would certainly *see* us. We fear you debar yourself a proper quantity of wine ... Take proper air and exercise; accept all the invitations you receive, and do not be over anxious about any thing. Nothing but your own over-anxiety can make you suppose we glance a thought at Oriel. If it had not been from fear of improperly discouraging you, I should have repeatedly said I thought it unlikely you should *ever* succeed among so many candidates. I now tell you my opinion, merely to convince you how far we are from being sanguine, or being likely to be disappointed at your not succeeding. Indeed, your Father began a letter, of which I have promised to write the substance, in which he requested you to give up all endeavours for Oriel, as he saw it was too much for your health and spirits.⌉

To Mr Newman

⌈April 12. 1822 (Friday)

[[To my Father.]]

I am just made Fellow of Oriel. Thank God. Love to all.⌉

To John William Bowden

⌈Oriel College,⌉ Oxford ⌈April 15th 1822⌉

My dear Bowden

I hope you excused the very short letter I gave you on Friday—I had several to write and very little time so it seemed better, since I knew you would be glad to hear of my success, to put you to the expense of postage for two lines, than to delay till Sunday's post. I now sit down to give a detailed account of the whole proceeding—and as in doing this I feel considerable difficulty how to speak of myself without egotism, I must request you to forgive any appearance of vanity or ostentation in my relation, and reckon that I have preferred compliance with your wishes to the praise of modesty.

⌈The examination commenced Saturday week—when on assembling we found there were eleven candidates—Ottley of Oriel, Parker of Oriel, Bullock of Ch Ch [Christ Church], Bosanquet of Balliol, Coleridge of Corpus, Tomlinson of Trinity, Newman of Trinity, Thompson of Wadhams [sic], Williams of Queens, Proctor of Jesus, Chapman of Exeter⌉—Tomlinson, however, soon retired from the competition, and there were left 4 first classes, 4 second, and one under the line—as to Mr. Parker the 10th I cannot make him out, whether of Oriel or Brazennose, what class or any particulars, even his name.[1]—Of Williams of Queens it was predicated (see how logical I am already) that he would certainly succeed—he acquitted himself so well in the schools—the time we went up—that the Oriel fellows it is said without solicitation voted for him when he stood for the Vinerian Scholarship[2]—After getting this, he determined to stand for Oriel immediately (this was last year), and indeed did put down his name as Plumer tells me, but afterwards withdrew it intending to make himself sure by a year's more reading. Ward[3] tells me that at Winchester he had always the fame of a hard reader, and if report, which indeed loves exaggeration, be credited, he has the last year been reading 14 hours per diem and living on pulse and herbs—However, deducting all colouring, that he is a very hard reading man, that he was patronized by the Oriel fellows, that he withdrew his name last time in order to read, is certain—Proctor got his first class this last examination, and Porter was said to have pronounced him the best scholar of the class paper—this, however is contradicted in other quarters, and it is asserted that

Chapman (who was a fellow-pupil with Proctor of Bethel's) was a sounder man, and certainly a mathematician—Ward is acquainted with Chapman's relations and says he has been fagging ever since he could read. Ottley and Thompson tried last year, and thus had some acquaintance with the nature of the examination. ⌈We were kept in 8 hours on Saturday, 9 on Monday, 4 on Tuesday—viva voce Tuesday, Wednesday, Thursday. It was decided on Thursday night, given out Friday morning.⌉ The electors (all the fellows) as I since learn, were kept up to one in the morning and then up again at 6, all through the examination comparing the compositions. ⌈We had a Latin Essay, English Essay, Spectator to be translated, 12 Philosophical and Mathematical Questions, 10 Logical, and were examined in 9 books viva-voce. At first sight it seems as if, being nearly the only mathematician I had an advantage over the rest—I ought to have had, but I am ashamed to say I only answered 4 while some others answered 7—Of the viva-voce passages I had seen two—some Thucydides and Cicero de Oratore. Having begun to think of standing so lately, you recollect yourself I had no practical thought, viz, attempt at preparing myself, last November it is not to be wondered at that I, as well as others, should think myself to have little chance of success—Luckily, however, by an induction of particular instances, I found out Latin composition to be by much the principal thing, and to that I have been giving, particularly to Coplestone's most beautiful prelections, unceasing attention.[4] If I could have but known the success which attended my first day's compositions, *at the time* in how much more correct and superior a manner should I have gone on with the examination—But possessed with the idea that I had all but disgraced myself, and stiff, oh how stiff! with sitting 8 hours on hard benches, I crawled about in the most piteous condition on Easter Sunday, and had so bad a night and felt so uncomfortable a heat and as I thought eruption on *my spine*, that I determined the first thing when up to go to Tuckwell—Morning, however, came and I was better, so I abandoned my midnight measure and went into the examination. Before the day was half over, my weakness was such that I was obliged to lay by, consequently through despair, headache and dimness of the twilight I was forced to send in my Latin Theme uncorrected—and only 4 mathemat: questions.⌉ However, if I go on in this way, it may be justly objected that I am introducing unnecessary boasting: so ⌈I pass on to Friday morning and my surprise on finding myself elected. I had to hasten to the round tower[5] where we had been examined, to receive the congratulations of all the fellows—I bore it till Keble took my hand, and then felt so abashed and unworthy the honour done me that I seemed desirous of quite sinking into the ground.⌉[6] How diffuse and chattering am I! but you provoked it and must suffer for so rash a provocation—⌈I was installed (literally—in Chapel) at one o'clock, and dined at the Gaudy at 6—I have since that time *regularly* for two days dined in the common room, and am abashed to find I must call them 'Hawkins' 'Keble' 'Tyler' etc., Ogle's joy is not to be described⌉—he now looks forward, and I with him, with great eagerness to next November, when we hope and expect to be able to salute you Fellow of All Soul's.—⌈The confusion it excited in Trinity is inexpressible—Echalay [Echalaz], Ward, Tompson, Hamilton, Phelips, could not read a word the rest of the day, Tomlinson has behaved in the most kind and generous manner without showing the slightest feeling of disappointment or pain, and fresh candidates seem already starting at Trinity for the new Oriel and Balliol elections⌉—And now good-bye—I must I fear have fatigued you. ⌈My fellowship is a lay one if I choose—but most likely I shall go into the Church—I own I have felt all along that the assiduity with which I have applied to books must show itself at one time or other, and I fancifully applied to myself the line of Gray concerning the wind

And hushed in grim repose expects his evening prey.[7]

I have great cause of thankfulness—and great cause of fear lest I should grow vain and conceited.⌉

Believe me Yours most sincerely John Henry Newman.

I am afraid you will think this letter very vain.

---

[1] John B. Ottley was one of the two successful candidates. Edward Bullock became a barrister and was Common Serjeant of the City of London 1850–5, dying in 1857; Robert William Bosanquet became a clergyman and died in 1880; Edward Coleridge became an Eton master and was a friend of Newman until his death in 1883; John Wickes Tomlinson was Rector of Stoke-on-Trent from 1831 till his death in 1857, and wrote poetry; William Cookesey Thompson spent most of his life as a clergyman in Devon, dying there in 1866; William Rosser Williams was a Fellow of Queen's College, 1823–35 and a barrister, dying in 1873; Thomas Procter was Michel Fellow of Queen's College 1824–6 and then Chaplain to the Forces in Calcutta until his death in 1836; John Mitchel Chapman was a Fellow of Balliol 1824–38, then Rector of Tendring until his death in 1878.

[2] For law.

[3] John Ward, Scholar of Trinity College in 1822.

[4] Edward Copleston, *Praelectiones Academicae Oxonii habitae* (Oxford, 1813). For their influence on Newman see *Idea*, p. 369.

[5] Above the Oriel gateway.

[6] Cf. *Apo.*, p. 17.

[7] *The Bard. A Pindaric Ode*, ii, 2: 'That, hush'd in grim repose, expects his evening-prey'.

To Mr Newman

⌈August 9. 1824

[[To my Father]]

...So far from this invasion of 'an Englishman's castle' being galling to the feelings of the poor, I am convinced by facts that it is very acceptable. In all places I have been received with civility, in most with cheerfulness and a kind of glad surprise, and in many with quite a cordiality and warmth of feeling.[1] One person says, 'Aye, I was sure that one time or other we should have a proper minister—' another that 'she had understood from such a one that a nice young gentleman was come to the parish—' a third 'begged I would do him the favour to call on him, whenever it was convenient to me' (this general invitation has been by no means uncommon) Another, speaking of the parish she came from said, 'the old man preached very good doctrine but he did not come to visit people at their houses as the new one did.' Singularly enough, I had written down as a memorandum a day or two before I received your letter, 'I am more convinced than ever of the necessity of frequently visiting the poorer classes—they seem so gratified at it, and praise it.' Nor do I visit the poor only—I mean to go all through the parish; and have already visited the shopkeepers and principal people. They it is obvious have facilities for educating their children, which the poor have not—and on that ground it is that a clergyman is more concerned with the children of the latter; though our church certainly intended that not only schoolmasters of the poorer children, but all schoolmasters, high and low, should be under her jurisdiction. The plan was not completed, and we must make the best of what we have got.

I have not tried to bring over my regular dissenter—indeed I have told them all, 'I shall make no difference between you and churchgoers—I count you all my flock, and shall be most happy to do you a service out of Church, if I cannot within it.' A good dissenter is of course incomparably better than a bad Churchman—but a good Churchman I think better than a good dissenter. There is too much irreligion in the place for me to be so mad as to drive away so active an ally as Mr Hinton seems to be.

Thank you for your letter, and pardon my freedom of reply[2]]

[1] Newman reports on his visits to parishioners.
[2] John Newman, Newman's father, died on 29 September 1824.

To Mrs Newman

[November 9 1826

[[To my Mother]]

Pray wish Mary for me many happy returns of this day; nay kiss her (shocking!) for me, and tell her I hope she will grow a better girl every year—and I think her a good one. I love her very much, but I will not say (as she once said to me) I love her more than she loves me. This is fine frosty weather, if Mary does not suffer.]

To Richard Whately

November 14. 1826

From John H. Newman Esqre to the Revd Richard Whately[1]

My dear Principal,

I have just received through Hinds your kind and valuable present, for which accept my best thanks. [[Whately's Logic, on its first appearance]]

On looking through it, I find you have enriched your Treatise with so much new matter, that, compared with the Article in the Encyclopedia, it is in many respects a new work. I cannot tell you the surprise I felt on seeing you had thought it worth while to mention my name, as having contributed to the arrangement of its materials.[2] Whatever I then wrote was written, I am conscious, almost as an Undergraduate's exercise, and consequently of little value, except as regards my own improvement in doing it. Yet, while on this ground I take the liberty of questioning the necessity of your mentioning my name, I cannot regret that in the composition of your work you have introduced it in some sort of connexion with your own. There are few things which I wish more sincerely than to be known as a friend of yours; and, though I may be standing on the verge of propriety in the earnestness with which I am expressing myself, yet you must let me give way to feelings, which never want much excitement to draw them out, and now will not be restrained.

Much as I owe to Oriel, in the way of mental improvement, to none, as I think, do I owe so much as to you. I know who it was that first gave me heart to look about me after my election, and taught me to think correctly, and (strange office for an instructor,) to rely upon myself.[3] Nor can I forget, that it has been at your kind suggestion, that I have been since led to employ myself in the consideration of several subjects, [[N.B. in the Articles in the Encyclopedia Metropolitana]] which I cannot doubt have been very beneficial to my mind.

[[There is scarcely any one, whom in memory I love more than Whately even now. How gladly would I have called on him in Dublin, except that again and again by his friends and my own I have been warned off.[4] He is now pursuing me in his new publications, without my having any part in the provocation.[5] In 1836 he was most severe upon me in relation to the Hampden matter. In 1837 he let me call on him, when he was in Oxford;[6] I have never seen him since. I ever must say, he taught me to think. A remarkable phrase is to be found in the above letter, 'strange office for an instructor, (you) taught me to *rely upon myself*'. The words have a meaning, viz that I did not in many things agree with him.[7] I used to propose to myself to dedicate a work to him, if I ever wrote one, to this effect: 'To Richard Whately D D etc etc who, by teaching me to think, taught me to differ from himself'; of course more respectfully wrapt up—November 10. 1860]]

---

[1] The text is Newman's holograph copy which contains small stylistic changes from the very rough draft. The heading is in the hand of William Neville (who collected and copied Newman's papers), hence the slip 'Esqre'.

[2] For Newman's connection with the earlier article for the *Encyclopaedia Metropolitana* see diary for 1 July 1822 and fourth note there (*L.D.* I, p. 143). For the parts that Newman himself wrote, see letter of 10 October 1852 to William Monsell (*L.D.* xv, pp. 175–8).

[3] 'If there was a man easy for a raw bashful youth to get on with it was Whately—a great talker, who endured very readily the silence of his company,—original in his views, lively, forcible, witty in expressing them, brimful of information on a variety of subjects . . . free and easy in manner, rough indeed and dogmatic in his enunciation of opinion, but singularly gracious to undergraduates and young masters, who, if they were worth any thing, were only too happy to be knocked about in argument by such a man . . . Mr Newman brought with him the first of recommendations to Whately in being a good listener, and in his special faculty of entering into ideas as soon as, or before, they were expressed. It was not long before Mr Whately succeeded in drawing him out, and he paid him the compliment of saying that he was the clearest-headed man he knew. He . . . was soon able to reassure the Oriel men that they had made no great mistake in his election.' *A.W.*, p. 66. In his letter of 10 October 1852 Newman said that it was Whately 'more than any one else' who 'broke' him of his evangelical views. He also taught Newman 'the existence of the Church as a substantive body' and 'those anti-Erastian views of Church polity, which were one of the most prominent features of the Tractarian movement'. *Apo.*, p. 12.

[4] See letter of 15 October 1863 to W. J. Fitzpatrick (*L.D.* xx, pp. 536–7).

[5] See *Thoughts on the New Dogma of the Church of Rome* (London, 1855), pp. 20–3; *The Right Principle of the Interpretation of Scripture considered in reference to the Eucharist, and the Doctrines connected therewith* (London, 1856); *The Scripture Doctrine of the Sacraments* (London, 1857), pp. 24–7.

[6] Newman called on him not in 1837 (so too *A.W.*, p. 69) but 1838, see letter of 21 September 1838 to J. W. Bowden (*L.D.* VI, pp. 318–19) and *Apo.*, p. 11.

[7] See letter of 10 October 1852 to William Monsell for the theological subjects, on which 'I had always differed from him, even to his face': 'I recollect on one occasion he said to me, "I like you, for you do not, as others, only agree with me, but you differ—"' (*L.D.* XV, pp. 177, 178).

To John Keble

[Marine Square, Brighton Dec 19. 1827]

My dear Keble,

[Though I have not written to you on the important College arrangement which is under our consideration at present and in which you are so nearly concerned, you must not suppose my silence has arisen from any awkward feeling (which it has not) or any unwillingness to state to you personally what you must have some time heard indirectly—I have been silent because I did not conceive you knew or understood me well enough to be interested in hearing more than the fact, anyhow conveyed, which way my opinion lay in the question of the Provostship between you and Hawkins. This may have been a refinement of modesty—but it was not intended as such, and spontaneous.—I write now because Pusey has told me that you would like to receive a line from any of the Fellows even though you have already heard their feelings on the subject before us—and I am led to mention my reason for not having written before, (which I otherwise should not have done,) lest you should think my conduct less kind to you than in intention it has really been. I have been so conscious to myself of the love and affectionate regard which I feel towards you, that the circumstance of my not thinking you the fittest person among us in a particular case and for a particular purpose seemed to me an exception to my general sentiments too trivial to need explanation or remark *to myself*—but I have forgotten that *to you* things must appear different—that this is the first time I have had an opportunity of *expressing* any feeling towards you at all, and that consequently it would have been acting more kindly had I spoken to you rather than about you. Forgive me if I have in any way hurt you or appeared inconsiderate.

I have lived more with Hawkins than with any other Fellow—and have thus had opportunities for understanding him more than others. His general views so agree with my own, his practical notions, religious opinions, and habits of thinking, that I feel vividly and powerfully the advantages the College would gain when governed by one who pursuing ends to which I cordially approve would bring to the work powers of mind to which I have long looked up with great admiration. Whereas I have had but few opportunities of the pleasure and advantage of your society[1]—and I rather suspect, though I may be mistaken, that did I know you better I should find you did not approve opinions objects and measures to which my own turn of mind has led me to assent. I allude, for instance, to the mode of governing a College,[2] the desirableness of certain reforms in the University at large, their practicability, the measures to be adopted with reference to them—etc. It is an ungracious task to go on—particularly in writing to you, above others—for you could easily be made believe any one alive was more fit for the

Provostship than yourself—I have said enough perhaps to relieve you from any uneasy feelings as regards myself—the deep feelings of love I bear towards you these I shall keep to myself

Yours ever affectionately⌉ John H Newman

[1] 'I knew Hawkins and he had taken me up, while Keble had fought shy of me.' See letter of 9 April 1866 to Henry James Coleridge (*L.D.* XXII, pp. 209–10).

[2] 'it was a longing on my part for some stricter discipline which was the direct cause of Hawkins's election. He had the reputation of even sternness. "He was just the man we wanted" I said.' See letter of 4 November 1884 to Lord Blachford (*L.D.* XXX, p. 432).

To Robert Isaac Wilberforce

11 Marine Square—January 14. 1828

My dear Wilberforce,

My last sad letter was short, both because I had many letters of a like nature to write, and also because I did not feel I was justified in intruding my sorrows upon you at any length.—Your very kind and feeling answer to it exacts from me a fuller reply; and now I can do it more calmly that I have paid the last mournful duties to all that was mortal of my dear Sister. First however let me acknowledge with many thanks your Mother's considerate suggestion and your offer of coming to me—On the whole I think we have determined to decline it, not without feeling its friendliness to me—we expect the Rickardss today, and Mrs R. is so much attached to my Sisters that I trust her presence may be of great service to them and my Mother, whose comfort of course I must principally consult.

My dear Sister Mary was on Friday week as well as she ever was, having scarcely had an illness of a day since she was a child—we had friends stopping in the house, besides Woodgate[1]—and [Isaac] Williams of Ch Ch [Christ Church], who happened to be here for a few days, dined with us. In the course of dinner Mary was obliged to leave the table under feelings of indisposition—in the course of the evening spasms came on, and advice was immediately had, but no alarming symptoms appeared. It turned out afterwards (or at least it seems highly probable) that in the violence of the spasms some vital part was touched—certainly from Saturday morning till 9 P.M. when she died, she was gradually dying—as if the system continued to work merely from previous impulse, the principle of life being already gone.

We were not aware of her imminent danger till 5 P.M. about 4 hours before her death—and then, knowing well the strength of her religious principle, we hesitated not for an instant to acquaint her with it. She received the news without emotion or agitation, with affecting composure—and, being in full possession of her mind, collectedly turned herself to the consideration of that unseen state to which she was so suddenly summoned She confessed herself quite unworthy of God's mercy, spoke of some imperfections in her heart and conduct (which *we* could not see) of which she deeply repented, expressed her desire to live that she might be with us, and have time for becoming more meet for heaven and more like Christ, yet her faith in Him as her only Savior, and her conviction that to depart and be with Him was far better.—During the whole of Saturday she was in little pain—and told us that during the acuteness of her previous spasms she had received great comfort from being able to repeat to herself Keble's hymns—And so she departed.

I am writing a very rambling and strange letter, I believe—but I cannot collect my thoughts, as I should wish. To us all her sudden death is of course a most bitter affliction—yet it is graciously softened by numberless merciful alleviations, and we one and all feel from our hearts (and have from the very first felt) a strong conviction that it is most good and right and desirable—and we bless God for it—all our recollections connected with dear Mary are sweet—and our sorrow at her loss is borne down by the remembrance of what she was to us, our joy and delight,—and the hope of what she will be when we meet her before the throne of God. Few of course can know what she was—we know her mind to have been rare indeed and intensely beautiful. She was gifted with that singular sweetness and affectionateness of temper that she lived in an ideal world of happiness, the very sight of which made others happy. All that happened to her she could change into something bright and smiling like herself—all events, all persons (almost) she loved and delighted in—and thus, having lived in this world as if it were heaven, before she discovered (as she must in time) that it was not so, she has been translated into the real and substantial heaven of God. For myself indeed, I have for years been so affected with her unclouded cheerfulness and extreme guilelessness of heart that I have be[come] impressed with the conviction that she would not live long, and have almost anticipated her death.[2] Whether these anticipations ought to have been formed or not, certainly they have providentially prepared me for this most sudden event—which is thus rendered for me more tolerable, though still my sufferings as well as others have been most acute. Yet I rejoice and will rejoice—rejoice that God has so schooled me heretofore with his kind chastenings that of *every* earthly good I habitually take more pleasure in the present enjoyment than in anticipations of the future, and so have enjoyed Mary's love and dear society for what it *then was;* not what it might be in years to come—and rejoice again, because whom God loveth He chastiseth, and because I feel I am especially honored by him and cared for, and that he is assuredly training me for usefulness here, and glory hereafter.—More trials have I had and have, than most men and I can glory in them—nay almost boast of them as marks of the Lord Jesus—And why should I say more? for as if God were taking me (so to say) at my word, I think I see more trial in store, and the very death of this dear girl has accidentally disclosed to me (as I think) the elements of future tempests which may afflict me still more bitterly—God's will be done, only may *He give grace*

Yours ever affectionately J H Newman

---

[1] Henry Arthur Woodgate (1801–74) was a Fellow of St John's College. He and Newman were friendly, but lost contact between 1845 and 1864. Their friendship was renewed after the *Apologia* was published.

[2] 'It must have been in October 1826 that, as I looked at her, beautiful as she was, I seemed to say to myself, not so much "will you live?" as "how strange that you are still alive!"' *A.W.*, p. 213.

To Harriett Newman

⌜February 6. 1828

[[From me to Harriett]]

...And we love one another. I cannot say how I love you. No calamity, I think, could occur to me here so great, as to lose your love and confidence. For of all my brothers and sisters (from one cause or other,) you alone know my feelings and respond to them.⌝

To Charles Robert Newman

Nuneham. Oct 10. 1828

My dear Charles,

Your former answer to my letter of February last was much more sensible than your present;—then you understood me, and now you have totally misrepresented me. Had I any misgivings I said in it any thing wrong or unkind, I should not hesitate one moment in confessing it—had I any hopes of undeceiving you in the very strange view you now take of it, I would try to do so—I have neither conscience of the one nor expectation of the other—*so I will not reply to you*. I will *not* get into any unprofitable correspondence with you.

Why is it you thus persecute me? for I can call it no other name. It is hard I may not be left alone. It was *you* first wrote to me in February requiring an immediate answer; now you write again and require an immediate answer. This is nothing new. Years past you have from time to time attacked and insulted me, forcing me into correspondence from which to *you* no good could ensue.

It would be useless in me to waste on you any expression of the kind feeling which I really bear towards you: you would reject it. So this letter will seem harsh—that I cannot help. I beg distinctly to be understood, that, should you reply to this, I shall not hold myself bound to answer your letter—

Yours affectly John H Newman.

To Mrs Newman

⌜March 1. 1829

[[To my Mother]]

We have achieved a glorious Victory.[1] It is the first public event I have been concerned in, and I thank God from my heart both for my cause and its success. We have proved the independence of the Church and of Oxford. So rarely is either of the two in opposition to Government, that not once in fifty years can independent principle be shown; yet in these times, when its existence has been generally doubted, the moral power we shall gain by it cannot be overestimated. We had the influence of government in unrelenting activity against us—the 'talent' so called of the University, the Town Lawyers, who care little for our credit, the distance off and the slender means of our voters; yet we have beaten them by a majority of 146 votes, 755 to 609. The 'rank and talent' of London came down superciliously to remove any impediment to the quiet passing of the Great Duke's bill, *confessing* at the same time that *of course* the University would lose credit by turning about, whatever the Government might gain by it. They would make use of their suffrage, as members of the University to degrade the University. No wonder that such as I, who have not, and others who have, definite opinions in favour of Catholic Emancipation, should feel we have a much nearer and holier interest than the pacification of Ireland, and should with all our might resist the attempt to put us under the feet of the Duke [of Wellington] and Mr Brougham.[2]

Their insolence has been intolerable; not that we have done more than laugh at it. They have every where styled themselves the 'talent' of the University—that they have rank and station on their side, I know; and that we have the inferior Colleges and the humbler style of men; but as to talent, Whately with perhaps Hawkins is the only man of talent among them—as to the rest, any one of us in the Oriel Common Room will fight a dozen of them apiece—and Keble is a host—Balliol too gives us a tough set—and we have all the *practical* talent, for they have shown they are mere sucking pigs in their canvass and their calculations. Their excessive confidence amounted to infatuation. Several days since their London chairman wrote to Mr Peel assuring him of complete and certain success. They strutted about (peacocks!) telling our men who passed through London that they should beat by eight to one, and they wondered we should bring the matter to a poll. We endured all this, scarcely hoping for success, but determining, as good Churchmen and true, to fight for the *principle*, not consenting to our own degradation. I am sure I would have opposed Mr Peel, had there been only just enough with me to take off the appearance of egotism and ostentation, and we seriously contemplated, about ten days since, when we seemed to have too slight hopes of victory to put men to the expense of coming up, we, the residents seventy, simply and solemnly to vote against Mr Peel, though the majority against us might be many hundreds. How much of the Church's credit depended on us residents! and how inexcusable we should have been, if by drawing back we had deprived our country friends of the opportunity of voting, and had thus in some sort betrayed them!

Well, the poor defenceless Church has borne the brunt of it—and I see in it the strength and unity of Churchmen—An hostile account in one of the Papers says, 'High and Low Church have joined, being set on ejecting Mr Peel.'

I am glad to say I have seen no illhumour any where. *We* have been merry all through it.]

---

[1] The defeat of Sir Robert Peel as the University's MP in the by-election when he offered himself for re-election after changing his position and deciding to support Catholic emancipation.

[2] A prominent Whig supporter of Catholic emancipation, whom Newman was later to call 'the very patriarch of . . . liberalism' in religion (*Campaign*, p. 333). cf. *Apo.*, p. 15: 'Also by this time I was under the influence of Keble and Froude; who . . . disliked the Duke's change of policy as dictated by liberalism.'

To Edward Hawkins

Oriel. April 29. 1830

My dear Provost

Many thanks for the kind things you said of me and others in your note to the Dean, the contents of which did not reach us;—but why cannot a Provost speak to his Fellows except through an organ?[1]

As I would have nothing undone on my part to explain to you my views, I suggest the following remarks, which I apprehend have a great deal of truth in them (certainly as far as my knowledge of the facts goes), in answer to your observation 'that the system you would uphold has *worked well.*'

1. Men who distinguished themselves in the Schools in the late Provost's time, had *private* Tutors.
2. Oriel men ceased to take high honors, when the Tutors ceased to take private pupils—This has ever been assigned as a reason.
3. Here then we see one *defect* of what was then practically a private-Tutor system—for the private-Tutor connexion, being *voluntary*, went out of fashion after 1823, when an idle set of [men] got admittance—i.e. just at the time when it was [most] wanted.
4. —Almost the only pupils who became permanently attached to their Tutors, were the private pupils—e g in the case of Tyler, Whately, and Keble, men of very different minds.
5. Men, who took honors under that System, *do* refer their success to the licence they managed to obtain of *acting against the System.*
6. Since few men can distinguish themselves in the Schools, i.e. prove their having fully availed themselves of their advantages here, without having private Tutors in one shape or other, the Provost's system is calculated to drive candidates for honors (and has in time past) to a *great* additional expence.—Nature (so to say) forces us into the private-tutor system—why not recognize it, control it, and make it economical?

Ever Yrs J H Newman

---

[1] The dispute between Provost Hawkins and Newman over the tutorial system was gathering momentum: 'by 1829 their relation towards each other had become very different from what it was in 1824, when the latter had been the unpretending and grateful disciple of the former. Newman had been eager in Hawkins's behalf for years, and had sung his praises loudly, wherever he went. He had expected great things from his promotion to the Provostship, and had taken great interest in it, when it was in agitation. And then on the other hand from the first he had been deeply disappointed in the results of it.' *A.W.*, p. 101.

From Edward Hawkins

O.C. [Oriel College] Thursday April 29. 1830

My dear Newman,

I abstain of course from making any remarks at present upon the notes on the Lecture-system which you have sent me, and merely return you my thanks for them, and for your kind present this morning.

But really you are not doing me justice in your question 'why cannot a Provost speak to his Fellows except thro' an organ?'

If you will refer to my extracts from my note to the Dean you will find no implication of the kind; but you will see that I intended to speak myself, if I saw occasion for it. But I did not, because I trusted there was happily no occasion of the kind. I asked the Dean only to assist me in doing away erroneous impressions if he found them existing; knowing that he was much more likely to find this out, and to have opportunities of remedying such an evil, than I could possibly have.

And I could not be desirous of renewing a painful subject, if I saw no necessity for it.

Ever yours affectately Edwd Hawkins.

To Edward Hawkins

Oriel College. ⌈June 8. 1830

My dear Provost,

Many thanks for the kind consideration which dictated the detailed account of your views, which I received yesterday.—I think I can answer you clearly and decidedly—and withal, chearfully and without embarrassment.—

Indeed I have been surprised and pained on finding you expressing your persuasion more than once that I am acting under the influence of personal mortification or other absurd uneasiness:—which, I am sure, could not be gathered from any avowal of mine (if correctly understood)—nor, as I think, from my conduct. But it is unnecessary to enter into an explanation of the real state of the case, if I am assured in my own mind, as I am, (however the case may unfortunately appear to you,) that, in matter of fact, the determination which I have before expressed to you on the subject of your letter and have now to express again, arises from no such unworthy feeling.

My chief private objection to the system you propose, is, that in my own case, as I know by experience, (whatever others may be able to effect) the mere lecturing required of me would be incompatible with due attention to that more useful private instruction, which has imparted to the office of Tutor the importance of a clerical occupation⌉. This is to me an *insuperable objection*, ⌈not that a few words can do justice to it—but, without needless discussion, pray believe me to be in earnest in saying once for all, I cannot act on the *principles* of your system.[1]

I am sorry to be obliged to abide by my letter of the 5th of May.—The University Statutes seem to me to require that each Pupil should on entrance be especially committed to the care of a particular Tutor. If my Pupils were not committed to me in this University sense, to whom were they committed? I understood you to say in answer to this question, that they were committed to the Senior Tutor for the time being. If this is in future recognized in the University Calendar in some such way as I proposed, *then* I shall feel assured I never had Pupils really committed to me—and so finding my office not to be an University one (as I supposed it was), shall feel myself bound in honor to retire at the end of this term from a situation, the duties of which I am unwilling to undertake.

But without such assurance that my office does not come under University jurisdiction, I feel no call upon me to retire *voluntarily*—and it is only this voluntary retirement,—or the alternative of altering my views (which of course is not in my own power)—to which your letters and conversation have hitherto directed my attention.

As the course I intend pursuing has been determined on mature consideration, you *will easily perceive* that suspense may already have been an inconvenience to me—while no one gains by it.

I feel much your kind intentions towards me expressed in your letter—and am truly sorry, should any expressions I have used appear to you inconsistent with the deference I owe to you both as a Provost and a friend—and I wish you fully to believe, as I think and trust I may promise, that, in the event of your exerting any power, which may be shown to belong to you, in displacing me from the situation I hold, you will not find me less faithfully attached to you than I ever have been—

I am, My dear Provost, Yours most respectfully and sincerely

John H Newman][2]

[1] '[W]hat irritated Newman most was [the Provost's] imputing Newman's conduct to irritation, and refusing or not being able to see that there was a grave principle in it earnestly held, and betraying a confident expectation that what was, he considered, mere temper in Newman, would soon pass away, and that he would eventually give in' *A.W.*, p. 103.

[2] For Hawkins's reply of 9 June 1830, see *L.D.* II, pp. 239–41.

To Mrs Newman

[June 18. 1830

[[To my Mother]]

It is at length settled that the Provost gives us no more pupils—us three (Wilberforce, Froude, and me) and we die off gradually with our existing pupils. This to me personally is a delightful arrangement—it will materially lessen my labours, and at length reduce them within bearable limits, without at once depriving me of resources which I could not but reckon upon, while they lasted. But for the College, I think it is a miserable determination.]

To Mrs Newman

⌈Bracknell. July 16. 1830

[[To my Mother]]

My horse, owing to my better management, was so fresh, that I came on to this place, five miles beyond Bagshot. The road from Guildford here is not a turnpike; which was my great gain. I have gone today 39 miles, of which I have walked nearly half. It is 13 miles to Henley, to which place I shall set out at five tomorrow morning. An Oxford coach passes Henley at nine.

I have so much daily to be grateful for, that I am sometimes overpowered with surprise. I quite reproach myself I have so many enjoyments, and this comes upon me especially when I am by myself. I seem so selfish. I believe my first wish on earth is for your happiness and comfort, my dear Mother, though I know I do not show it near so much as I ought and desire. It hurts me so that we should be so little together this vacation.⌉

To Hugh James Rose

Oriel College. August 24. 1831.

Dear Sir,

I hope you will not consider this letter an intrusion; but I think you may like to know my present thoughts on the work I have undertaken, and may wish to give me your advice as being Editor—Should however you think it better to leave me to my own judgment in these matters, I have no right to be dissatisfied.—[1]

Whether or not all the other Councils will go in one volume, certainly those on the Trinity and Incarnation, i.e. those of the *Greek* Church, (to speak generally of them), will take one volume by themselves—and with this first volume alone I am at present concerned. I will tell you my thoughts upon it. For the last six weeks I have given some time to the examination of my materials—and am of opinion that I shall best answer the object of making an useful work by giving a *connected* history of the Councils—i.e. not taking them as isolated, but introducing so much of Church History as will illustrate and account for them. Do not suppose that I mean in the least to evade the strict discussion of the subjects settled in the Councils—this is the main object of the whole work—but since only the conclusions come to, not the arguments and controversy, are given in the Acts (i.e. for the most part,) and since the Acts are often spurious, to analyze these would be doing nothing. What light would be thrown on the Nicene Confession *merely* by explaining it article by article? to understand it, it must be prefaced by a sketch of the rise of the Arian heresy, the words introduced by Arius, his perversions of the hitherto orthodox terms, the necessity of new and clearer tests etc.—I propose then to commence (after an introductory chapter) with the rise of Arianism, suggesting some of its probable sources and the reasons for its marvellous extension, trace the history of the controversy to the Council of Nice—then proceed to show how the Arians gained Imperial countenance and influence in the Church, their attempts to remove the ὁμοούσιον in their various Councils, their splitting into sects and how differing (for all this tends to illustrate the catholic doctrine,)—then proceed to the council at Alexandria where the questions about the word ὑπόστασις were settled; then attempt a view of the difference between the Greek and Latin Churches in their use of words expressing the doctrine—and so to the 2nd General Council against Macedonius. After this, I shall take up the history of heresies about the Incarnation from the beginning till I fall in again with the history of Nestorius and the 3rd Council—and so on.—I do not confine myself to the Œcumenical Councils, tho' I have mentioned them—but take those which will at all illustrate the phraseology or doctrines of our Articles.—(By the bye, might not the book be called 'Illustrations of the phraseology and doctrine of etc from the history of the Councils of the Church—' or by some such title?)—I have a difficulty in combining history and doctrinal discussion, which besides the irregularity which it might occasion in the work by causing frequent digressions, may render it heavy, load the text with notes at the foot of the page, and after all prevent the complete investigation and elucidation of various points of doctrine. I propose then to clear my text of argument as much as may be—and state my conclusions—and to enter so far into the subject matter of debate, as to explain it generally, connect the history, introduce the subjects, and excite curiosity—then to add a series of notes or discussions under various heads—'On Sabellianism—' 'On the tenets and character of Lucian—' 'on the word ὑσία' [sic] etc—In this way I think the book may be somewhat more attractive (if that is an object)—and beginners will be less clogged with difficulties and delays—while I shall feel more at liberty, should I any where have the means and capacity, to investigate points in my notes, which I shall of course try at the same time to condense as much as possible. In these notes I might give an account of Bull's arguments on certain points, or Waterland's or Petavius's etc. etc.

Another difficulty is the principle of arrangement in the order of the Councils—historically or according to their subject matter? at present I incline to the latter—and think 3 volumes might be written 1 on the Trinity and Incarnation; 2 on original Sin, grace, works etc; 3 on the Church System—If you approved of this, I would add to the first volume after the history of the Monothelite controversy, a sketch (for after the earlier full discussions more would not be required) of such controversies as that between Bernard and Abelard—between the Greek and Latin Churches on the Procession of the Holy Ghost—and Calvin's notions about the Trinity.

I fear I am promising a great deal. Let it be an earnest of my good will, for that I can profess without fear of overstatement

I am, Dear Sir Yours faithfully J H Newman

---

[1] Newman had begun work on the book that became The Arians of the Fourth Century.

To Mrs Newman

⌈July 16. 1832

[[To my Mother]]

Having come to this place with no anticipations, I am quite taken by surprise, and overcome with delight. This doubtless you will think premature in me, inasmuch as I have seen as yet scarcely any thing, and have been writing letters of business to Mr Rose and Rivingtons. But, really, when I saw at the distance of four miles, on an extended plain, wider than the Oxford, amid thicker and greener groves, the Alma Mater Cantabrigiensis lying before me, I thought I should not be able to contain myself, and, in spite of my regret at her present defects and past history, and all that is wrong about her, I seemed about to cry out, 'Floreat æternum!' Surely there is a genius loci here, as in my own dear home—and the nearer I came to it, the more I felt its power. I do really think the place finer than Oxford, though I suppose it isn't, for every one says so. I like the narrow streets—they have a character—and they make the University buildings look larger by the contrast. I cannot believe that King's College is not far grander than any thing with us—the stone too is richer, and the foliage more thick and encompassing. I found my way from the inn to Trinity College, like old Œdipus, without guide, by instinct; how I know not. I never studied the plan of Cambridge.

Mr Rose is away—he is very ill—which accounts for his silence. Should you see Froude, tell him, alas! he *is* married. This has quite troubled and grieved me,—still, if he manages to give his whole soul to the Church, it matters not—though it seems impossible.

Let me know about the cholera—I trust we should have no cases; but it would distress me deeply, should a case occur, while I am away.⌉

To George Ryder

Oriel. July 22/32

My dear Ryder,

I have been very busy, and now write with an effort—or you should not have been so long without an answer to your letter. It is quite absurd to suppose that you are not *at liberty* both to marry and to go into the Church—indeed I think that country parsons ought, as a general rule, to be married—and I am sure the generality of men ought, whether parsons or not. The celibate is a high state of life, to which the multitude of men cannot aspire—I do not say, that they who adopt it are necessarily better than others, though the noblest $\mathring{\eta}\theta o\varsigma$ is situated in that state. While I allow you full liberty to marry, yet, if you ask my opinion, I certainly think you too young to marry. Since I do not know who it is your heart is set upon, I may say without seeming to cut at individuals that I think most likely you will make a bad choice. What can you know of others at your age? how likely are you to be captivated by outside show, tho' not show in the common vulgar meaning of the word! Depend upon it, many a man would repent of his marriage, if he did not think it right (as it is) to repress the rising sigh. It is a fearful thing to tie yourself to one person for life. Again I am not at all satisfied at your want of self command. You *gave up* the notion of taking a degree, before you had this impulse—if *it* has been the cause of your changing your mind back, then you have been just swayed by two πάθη to and fro, indolence and love,—you yourself, the proper *you*, having no power or will of your own.—Do you know yourself enough? Have you not talked a good deal on politics even without feeling what you said? Are you sure you will not sink into a Conservative after all?—a character which may be right or wrong, but could not easily be G.D.R. if he had always really understood the words he used. Again, *supposing* a time of trial is to come, (for argument's sake) what a scrape a man has got into, who did not contemplate its possibility, when he married!—is it not worth while to ascertain whether your hoped-for partner is prepared to be a pilgrim? I think I have now said all that strikes me on the subject, and with best wishes for your coming to a right determination in your difficulties

I am Ever yrs affly John H Newman

To Richard Hurrell Froude

Oriel College. ⌈September 13. 1832⌉

My dear F

Your letter, which I received yesterday, was very welcome. I am sincerely glad of the good hopes you have on the subject which comes first in it—and glad too of your intention of going abroad, though annoyed, not surprised, at the necessity of your resolving on that measure. ⌈As to your proposition for me to accompany you, it is very tempting—It quite unsettled me and I have had a disturbed night with the thought of it—indeed it makes me quite sad to think what an evidence it has given me of the little real stability of mind I have as yet attained. I cannot make out, why I was so little, or rather not at all, excited by the coming of Cholera, and so much by this silly prospect which you have put before me—it is very inconsistent, except perhaps that the present novelty has come upon me suddenly. But enough of philosophizing.

I am much tempted by your proposal for several reasons—yet there is so much of impediment in the way of my accepting it,⌉ that I wish you to say nothing to any one yet, even about my entertaining the notion of it, as I do. ⌈I cannot quite divest myself of the feeling that I may be intruding upon your Father—but supposing this put away, I see much in favor of the scheme. Probably I never shall have such an opportunity again—I mean, that of going with a man I know so well as yourself; and going with a person older than myself, as your Father, is to me a great temptation. I am indolently distrustful of my own judgment in little matters, and like to be under orders.[1] Then what a name the mediterranean is! and the time of year, for I think summer would be too hot for me; and the opportunity of getting there without touching Gallic earth, (for I suppose you go by water) which is an abomination. And if I *ever* am to travel, is not this the time that I am most at liberty for it? my engagements being slighter now than they have been these many years, and than they are likely to be hereafter—and I feel the need of it;—I am suspicious of becoming narrowminded, and at least I wish to experience the feeling and the trial of expansiveness of views, if it were but to be able to *say* I had, and to know how to meet it in the case of others. And then I think I may fairly say my health requires it—not that I ever expect to be regularly well, as long as I live—it is a thing I do not think of—but still I may be set up enough for years of work for which at present I may be unequal.⌉

But before I can say any thing, ⌈you must tell me more. 1. as to *time*. I could not⌉ go before the end of November, nor could I ⌈allow myself to be absent from England beyond Easter, (say, the beginning of April)⌉—*you* doubtless will be away longer;— ⌈would it not be possible for me to part company with you?⌉ are there not steam vessels from Malta etc to England?—⌈2. as to *expence*; which I apprehend will be a serious subject.⌉ I would go as far as £100—but I fear this is a small sum. I ought not to go further—and could not go so far without some inconvenience; but that I think I might allow myself to bear. ⌈3. as to my *health*. It is quite enough that *you* should be an invalid—but it would be an ungracious πάρεργον² for me to fall sick also—Now I cannot *answer* for my health. I all of a sudden fall ill⌉—which is the way with persons who suffer what are called nervous complaints. Sometimes, if I could say what I mean, I am obliged to take great care of myself—a vessel is a bad place for taking physic. I can fancy a cabin such as in steamers being distressing to me. Now I do not *anticipate* this, nor is such wretched fastidiousness of long continuance or frequent; but still I [am] led to think of it before I determine. On the whole I want information about your plan. . . .

Ever Yrs affly J H Newman

P.S. I am amused on looking over my letter, to see how entirely I have dispensed with the impediment of my prospective Deanship.

⌈Do send Mr Rose one or two more architectural articles before you go.⌉

¹ [[N.B my leaving them in the event at Rome and going through Sicily by myself, is a curious comment on this.]]
² 'appendage'.

To Mrs Newman

On board the Hermes. Dec 11. 1832

My dear Mother

My Sisters will perhaps quarrel with me for writing three letters running to you— but I wish that you should receive the first letter I write home from foreign parts, and therefore they must wait the next time—though you will all receive from me letters at the same time. Today has been the most pleasurable day, as far as external causes go, I have ever had, that I can recollect, and now in the evening, I am sleepy and tired with the excitement. We are now off Cape Finisterre, but the moon is not yet risen, and we can see nothing of it, tho' some lights were just now visible from farm houses on shore, which is maybe 15 miles off. This morning early we saw the high mountains of Spain, (the first foreign land I ever saw,) having finished most prosperously our passage across the formidable Bay of Biscay. The land first discovered was Cape Ortegal and its neighbourhood—magnificent in its outline, and, as we neared it, marked with three lines of mountains, and in some places very precipitous and hoving over the sea. At first we were about 70 ⟨50⟩ miles off them— then 25 perhaps. At the same time the day cleared, all clouds vanished, and the sea, which had ever hitherto been very fine, now became of a rich indigo colour, and the wind freshening was tipped with the most striking white edges, which breaking in foam turned into momentary rainbows. The seagulls, quite at home, were sailing about, and the ship rocked to and fro with a motion, which unpleasant as it might have been in the bay or had the wind been from the southwest, yet was delightful as being from shore. I cannot describe the exquisite colour of the sea—which, tho' in no respects strange or novel, is yet unlike any thing I have seen, unless this be a bull. In the sense I should call it a most gentlemanlike colour—i.e. so subdued, so destitute of all display, so sober. And then so deep and solemn, so resistlessly strong, if a colour may be so called—and the contrast between the white and indigo so striking—and in the wake of the vessel, it changed into all colours, transparent green, white, white-green, etc.—As evening came on, we had every appearance of being in a warmer latitude—The sea brightened to a glowing purple inclined to lilac—the sun set in a car of gold and was succeeded by a sky first pale orange, then gradually hightening [sic] to a dusky red—while Venus came out as the evening star, with its peculiar intense whiteness. Now it is bright starlight. We passed Corunna in the afternoon, but too far off to see more than the mountains above. We are to pass through the English Squadron at Lisbon, if the wind permits—to land at Cadiz—to land at Gibraltar—thence to *Algiers*. We shall not make Malta by Christmas Day— and, as things now stand (there being quarantine there) we shall go on to Corfu, thence (still in the steam vessel) to the rest of the 7 islands, thence to Patras, near <on> the gulf of Corinth, and we do not know more. I think it very probable I shall not be home by Easter but do not you say so. And if I can from Malta, I shall send you a packet with a letter for the Bishop begging leave of absence till June. As to my work, I think even if I returned at Easter I ought to give several months of correction to it, which would any how delay it over the season—this correction I might now give in the Long Vacation: Please to write (in my name ⟨?⟩) (in the third person if you will) a letter to Rivington post paid, asking whether his reason for wishing to print directly after Easter was not that which I have given above (i.e. the season) and stating the probability of my not returning till June, and what had best be done in that case.[1] I have not been idle in the matter of verse making—I have written a copy a day since I have been on board, besides others at Falmouth and Whitchurch— Altogether since you saw the book, I have added 8, i.e. in about 10 days—I have in all 18 already—which will allow me to be idle, should other things come in the way. The Captain is a very pleasant man—and accomplished—he sings agreeably to the guitar, and paints—and is a relation of Lord Hill's—There are three midshipmen and one above them, who may or may not be called lieutenant—for steam-vessels are anomalies. (They are all of the Navy, as is the case with all packets now.)—There are besides a purser and a doctor. They are all of them young men from 20 to 25; have seen a great deal of all parts of the world—have much interesting information (Lights on the land are just visible again) and are very gentleman-like. It amuses me to scrutinize them—one is clever, the others hardly. They have (most of them) made very few inductions, and are not in the habit of investigating causes. The very reverse of philosophers. They have good spirits and are very goodhumoured. There is besides a Spanish merchant, an emigrant Constitutionalist, going home (I believe) under King Ferdinand's late amnesty. We are altogether about 60 on board. We started from Falmouth about one on Saturday the 8th, having been kept in uncomfortable suspense about the arrival of the Vessel till the night before—She had suffered much hard weather in the downs—and we embarked (readily enough) at a short notice. It was most amusing to see the stores arrive. Fowls, Ducks, Turkeys, all alive and squatted down under legs of beef, hampers, and vegetables. One unfortunate Duck got away, and a chase ensued—I should have liked to have let him off, but the poor fool did not know how to use his fortune—and instead of making for the shore, kept quacking with absurd vehemence close to us—he was not caught for a considerable time, as he ducked and fluttered away, whenever the men got near him.—Then the decks had to be cleaned—for the vessel had been ordered off from Woolwich in a great hurry, and coals had since been taken in. This is a curious scene, if you never saw it, what with the spouting of the pipes and the scrubbing brooms of a dozen men. Cape Lizard was by this time past—and we were bidding adieu to old England—I got hungry (it was between 3 and 4) and what at home would have been lassitude and craving began now to discover itself in qualmishness. When dinner came, I eat because I ought, but with such absurdly uncomfortable feelings, that I could not help laughing out. I will not here enter into the details of seasickness, but shall reserve the interesting subject for another letter, if I can by any reminiscences do justice to it. At present suffice it to say that my disordered feelings did not last much above 24 hours—and the greater part of this time shewed themselves merely in languor and apprehension. Do not I write well, considering the sea is rocking up and down, up and down? but this is nothing to shaving. At first this operation seemed so formidable, that I dared not attempt it; but, when I saw every [one] else tidy, I thought it better to cut my nose off than be singular; so the second morning I attempted, and am surprised at my own success. I am surprised too at the ease with which I walk the decks, i.e. how soon I have got my sea legs—and altogether I am surprised to find how easily I do many things which seem difficult—and I am disposed to think I have hitherto been working under a great pressure (as they say) and should it please God ever to remove it, I shall be like steam expanding itself.—Tomorrow morning we expect to be off the coast of Lisbon—and by Sunday at Gibraltar ...

---

[1] Mrs Newman wrote as directed about 5 January 1833 and Rivingtons replied that it would be advisable to defer printing till October, as summer and autumn were unfavourable seasons for publishing.

To Mrs Newman

Malta Dec 24.

My dear Mother,

. . . I am quite recruited now and proceed. I told you in the letters I sent to you from Gibraltar that I cared little for sea sickness and so I say now, but the attendants on it are miserable. I was very often and violently sick, but whenever it was over I was quite well, and my qualmishness was short; but the worst of seasickness is the sympathy which all things on board have with the illness, as if they were seasick too. First all the chairs, tables, much more the things on them are moving, moving, up and down, up and down—swing, swing—a tumbler turns over, knife and fork run down, wine is spilt—swing, swing. In this condition you go on talking and eating, as fast as you can, hiding your misery, which is provoking[ly] thrust upon you by every motion of the furniture which surrounds you. At length you are seized with sickness, up you get, swing, swing, you cannot move a step—you knock yourself against the table—run smack against the side of the cabin—you *cannot* make the door, the only point you want—you get into your berth at last, but the door will not shut—bang, bang, you slam your fingers. At last things go right with you and down you lie. You are much better, but now a new misery begins, the noise of the bulkheads (i.e. the wooden partitions thro' the vessel). This is not heard on deck—in the cabin it is considerable—but when you lie down, you are in a perfect millhouse. All sorts of noises tenfold increased by the gale; creaking, clattering, shivering, and dashing. And then your bed is seasick too—up and down—swinging without exaggeration as high and as fast (to your feelings) as a swing in a fair—and incessantly—you cannot say, 'Let me out, I have had enough now—you are in for it'—This neverending motion is the great evil, and requires strong nerves to bear . . . And last of all the bilge water has been a most unspeakable nuisance (the water which *will* drain from the vessel down to the bottom)—a gale puts it all in motion—our vessel was hastily sent off from Woolwich before it was properly cleaned—and in spite of all that can be done by means of pumps the smell is intolerable—it is like nothing I ever smelt and very suffocating. What would I have given to have been able to sleep on deck on Thursday night last! but the hail and sleet-showers made it impossible. Of course I had no rest, tho' I had no sickness. And there were other things <thoughts matters> made landsmen somewhat uncomfortable. You know perhaps that a leeshore is always formidable to sailors; now we were off a most fearful coast without a port in it, and the wind shifting about from NW to NE. This indeed is little to a steamvessel, which moves against the wind, so as hardly to have a leeshore; but on Wednesday the air-pump of one of our engines had broken and had taken a long time to mend—and it naturally suggested itself to us, that it might <not> be strong enough to go through the gale, which was severe. About 2 in the morning, the engines stopped—that we heard as we lay in our berths—and what anxiety we had arose from our *not* knowing how things were. So I got up and went on deck, and was instantly relieved at finding all was right, but it had been rough work. The next day (Friday) the sea was succeeded by the usual swell, which is sadly fatiguing. I have not had a night's sleep since I left England, except when we were quiet at Gibraltar, and it is wonderful how little I suffer from it—I either have no sleep, or broken, with bad dreams—and I am sore all over with the tossing, and very stiff, and (according to my feelings) strained and sprained—and so weak at times that I am hardly able to put out a hand. However my spirits have never given way an instant, and I laughed when I was most unwell—and now we are safe at Malta, and I hope (please God) to have a quiet night before Christmas Day—We start for Corfu on Wednesday, but it is only a passage of a day or two—and we remain there 6 days and so back. Then we shall indeed have rest enough, for miserable as it is to say it, our quarantine here will be 15 days! we shall be put into Lazaretto, under which we now lie, a miserable prison looking building, with nothing but whitewashed walls except what furniture you put in yourself, and the recollection that the plague and all other ailments have done quarantine there before you. However we shall make the best of it—Archdeacon Froude has most attentive friends here, and I shall try to write some verses. N.B. not a day has passed without my doing a copy since I embarked—some days I have done two. When I was most qualmish, I solaced myself with verse-making, and flatter myself that not my least praiseworthy were then done. . . .

Ever Yrs dutifully John H Newman

To Harriett Newman

On board the Hermes. Malta. Dec 25. 1832

My dear Harriet,

I hardly know how I shall have spirits to tell you what little I have to say about our arrival at Malta, for we are keeping the most wretched Christmas day I can conceive it to be my lot to suffer, and it seems a sad return to that good Providence who has conducted us hither so safely and so pleasantly. By a strange bad fortune we are again taking in coals on a holy day, and, as the Captain's orders are precise about his stay at the different places he makes, there seems to be no alternative. But what provokes me is that the coals will be got in by the afternoon, and when daylight is gone they are making preparations for a Christmas feast, which seems to me so incongruous that I mean, if I can do so with any decency, barely to taste of it. I do think, that deprived of the comfort and order of an Established Church, it is one's duty almost as Paul and Silas to sing praises in prison, so that others may hear. But all such cases, as befal one, are cases of degree—and St Paul was absolute and unlimited in his ministerial authority. This morning we saw a poor fellow in the lazaretto [*sic*] close to us, cut off from the ordinances of his Church, saying his prayers towards the house of God which lay in his sight over the water—and it is a confusion of face indeed that the humble Romanist testifies to his Savior in a way in which I, a minister, do not—yet I do what I can, and shall try to do more—for I am very spiteful. . . .

Ever Yrs affly, with love to all, John H Newman

To Jemima Newman

Naples. February 19. 1833

My dear Jemima,

. . . Oh that I could tell you one quarter of what I have to say about it [the temple of Egesta in Sicily]—but neither memory nor expression serve me! Wonderful place, piercing the heart with a strange painful pleasure! First the surrounding scenery in approaching it—a rich valley. Now do not fancy valleys and hills as in English—there is nothing lumpish or broken here—it is the great depth and height, the bold *flatness* of the slant, which characterize these—and even at this season of the year the richness of the colouring. We went through groves of olives and prickly ⟨⟨cactus⟩⟩ pears, and by orange orchards, till we came to a steep hill covered with ruins, on the other side of which the remains of antiquity lay. We wound up an ascent, once (doubtless) a regular road to the city gates—and on surmounting it we saw what we had seen at a distance, the temple. Here the scene of desolation was as striking as the richness of the contrasted valley which we had passed. Opposite the hill on which we stood, which was covered with ruins, (especially the ruins of a theatre) rose a precipitous rock, starting out of the ravine below—there were ruins on the hill beyond it, which we conjectured were the remains of the *Greek* town—but on this circular hill was nothing but a single temple.—Such was the genius of early Greek worship, grand in the midst of error; simple and unadorned in its architecture, it chose some elevated spot, and fixed its faith as a solitary witness on heights where it could not be hid. No words can describe the piercing effect of the sight of this temple. It is (I believe) the most perfect remaining—very plain—Doric—six gigantic pillars before and behind—twelve in length—no roof.—Its history is unknown—the temples of classical times, which came after it, have vanished—the whole place is a ruin—this alone remains in a waste solitude—A shepherd's hut is near, surrounded with the mud which accompanies a farmyard—a number of eager dogs—a few rude intrusive men, who would have robbed us, I fancy, had they dared—on the hill of the theatre (which we thought might be the Roman town) a savage looking bull prowling amid the ruins; mountains around us—and Eryx in the distance. The past and the present! What a contrast from the time when the two hills were full of life. I began to understand what Scripture means by speaking so much of cities set upon hills—what a noble but ungodly sight it must have been, like Satan himself, the mockery and imitation of true greatness, when this place was in its glory. And then its historical associations—to say nothing of Virgil's fictions, here it was that Nicias came—this was the ally of Athens. What a strange wild place! how did people ever take it into their heads to settle here!—At length we returned to get back to Calatafimi and dinner by 6 o'clock. And now I should tell you but have not room, about Calatafimi, which is necessary (as well as some account of the towns we passed through) to complete my picture—Yet I fear I shall not be able here to get beyond this simple announcement, which means far more than I tell you—'Truly is this place called Calatafimi.'

With love to H and my Mother...

Ever Yrs affectly John H Newman

To George Ryder

Rome. March 14. 1833

My dear Ryder,

By the time you receive this, I shall be getting out (unless any thing happens to recal or detain me) on a pilgrimage to Sicily, alone. The Froudes make for England after the Holy Week—and I am drawn back by an irresistible love of Sicily, of which I have seen just so much as to wish to see more. And it has so many associations connected with it, that, in seeing it, I seem to see the most interesting of all profane lands, Egypt excepted. And then it is so beautiful and so miserable that it is an emblem of its own past history, i.e. the history of heathen countries, being a most noble record stone over the grave of high hopes and aims, pride, sin, and disappointment. For one reason I am not sorry to be going alone, that I shall have my part in an especial way in the privation which I recommended to you last November. Were you here with us, most probably you would go with me, and with what pleasure should I have you as a companion! As it is, you see I suffer from my own advice. You may be sure that your absence will not cause you to be *less* thought of. It will be like the absence of the statue of Brutus from the procession which brought him to the minds of the people negatively.[1]

We are surprised to find Rome so intelligent and liberal a place—we get English publications here regularly, hearing the news about 12 or 14 days after it comes out in England. At Naples you are in a barbarous land—and their post office is so shamefully conducted that it is impossible to make use of it—We have not heard from England (I at least) since we left—we fully believe our letters are lodged at Naples but we cannot get them. Naples too is so noisy, crowded, and dirty—here there are few beggars, no importunate ciceronis, and no mobs in the streets. The great quiet of this city is a charm indeed—and it well becomes the place which has concentrated in it more recollections pleasant and painful than any city excepting Jerusalem. It is a mine of wonders and I do not know how we shall ever get through them....

Well, and what is your opinion of the accursed Whig spoliation bill? for I do not hesitate so to call their so-called Irish-Church-Reform.—For myself, I am perhaps not sorry, in a bad matter, to see things proceed so quickly to a crisis—since it is very annoying and disheartening to linger on in an ague, and to feel every one around you neither hot nor cold. The time is coming when every one must choose his side. On the other hand, I am much afraid we shall not know our own principles, if we are not allowed a little time to get them up. When you have taken your degree, you must get up the history of Church changes at the time of the Reformation, and set others to do the same. I feel more and more the blunders one makes from acting on one's own partial view of a subject, having neither that comprehensive knowledge nor precedents for acting which history gives us.—I am resolved, if I can help, not to move a step without some authority to back me, direct or by fair inference; and I look upon it as one good of travelling, (the same in mind as that of *reading*) that it takes one out of oneself, and reduces in one's eyes both the importance of one's own particular station and of one's own decisions in acting in it.—Not that I have gained a vast deal in this way myself, but doubtless I have gained more than I am aware of.—....

Ever Yrs affectionately John H Newman

[1] cf. Tacitus, *Annals*, 3, 76.

To Mrs Newman

Rome. March 25 1833

My dear Mother,

At length I am glad to be able to acknowledge the receipt of Numbers 2 and 3— they came the day my last to J went (the 21st) . . . I have just seen the ceremonies of this day—and, while they are fresh in my mind, I will say what occurs to me. The Service is performed in the Church of St Maria sopra Minerva—so called from its being built over the ruins of the temple to Minerva built by Pompey after his conquests in Asia.—The Pope attends and the Cardinals and he gives dowries to 12 (about, I counted but forget the number) young girls, in honour of the Virgin. At first entrance, it seems hopeless to approach the chancel end of the Church, where the Service (of course) is performed, the crowd was so dense. After wading about to and fro for a time, we saw the Pope brought in, in the fashion which is observed at Christmas and Easter Day in St Peter's, and perhaps at other times. In order to be seen by all the multitude, as well as for a mark of honor, he is carried in a chair on men's shoulders—it is very well managed so far, there seems no trouble about it— tho' the effect is not pleasant. I had seen the Pope before, who looks like other men, and tho' I think I know his face well, there is nothing to describe about it—yet it is a great thing to say that it is *negatively* good,—that it is not fat, or red, or ugly, or unpleasant—it becomes the Pope—it is grave. His robes, which are *very* long all round, are white satin with a broad facing of gold work—he had his triple crown on his head—which is much lower than I imagined it would be, a sugar loaf curved close to his head, white, with gold circles—at his breast a round or oval plate set with jewels, I suppose in allusion to the Aaronic breastplate. He is attended by two immense fans of white (peacock?) feathers—and as he moves, blesses the people. The mode of blessing is solemn, and is a contrast to the usual attitudinizing of the preachers etc. here, it is indeed the attitude you see prelates (e.g. Wolsey) drawn in, apparently one hand pointing thus but really, I believe, it is a union of 3 fingers (as I have heard years ago, from Dr Nicholas, to present the notion of the Trinity)—he scarcely moves his hand, and appears to be praying as he goes. By the time he had passed, I managed to stumble on a chair in the crowd—and getting on it, saw some people getting into the body of the Church thro' the guards on one of the sides—so making for that quarter, I found myself admitted without a question to my great surprise thro' rank after rank—till I got bold enough to *make* myself a way—and soon found myself near a crowd not above three deep of well dressed persons (for the former crowd was most offensive) which edged the portion of the Church set apart for Service. By this means, however, I was separated from the Fs, who, not crediting my information, had not followed me—so here I am now at home waiting for news of them—perhaps they got in another way. And now I had a sight full of deep interest. First it was curious, to speak as a man, to see the *court* of Rome assembled. It is the only court in Europe, perhaps in the world, which is a religious court—its levies, so to call them, are held in Church. The high altar was decked out sumptuously, incense swung to and fro; a crowd of priests were preparing for the service, salutations and genuflexions were making on every side, and a choir (behind the altar?) were chanting. On the right on the episcopal throne was the Sovereign Pontiff, his mitre on his head, with a train, partly of gentlemen ushers with their frills and bag wigs (?) partly of ecclesiastics with shaven heads. The dresses at the altar were very splendid white and gold—below on either side, down to where I was, were the cardinals in scarlet gowns with rich lace half-shirts over, and over this, immense scarlet robes with very long trains and fur tippets—at their feet their respective attendants, priests, with small red boxes (without tops) to receive their masters' red scull [*sic*] cap, when the service required them to be uncovered, and ready also to manage their trains for them when they moved. A vast number of ceremonies went on, little of which I could understand,—except to say that blessings were past round, and the osculum pacis, etc. Besides, Mass was celebrated.—At the close the young girls were introduced in white with fancy crowns on their heads; a curious contrast, for tho' muffled up over the mouth even, and scarcely more than the eyes visible, they were very nicely dressed, and had apparently silk stockings on, which one could see. They are introduced to the Pope, kiss his foot, and receive the present. Then the Pope retires as he came.—All this I say is a curious sight, considered merely as a citizen of the world would consider it—a court day of a sovereign priest.—Nor, viewing it as a Christian, should I condemn it, were the ceremonies other than they are, and were it not at Rome. But, not to speak of *doctrinal* errors, there is much unedifying dumbshow—I cannot doubt it—(tho' its *origin* of course is in the notion that the church is too large to make people hear, *tho'* they spoke)—nor can I endure the Pope's foot being kissed, considering how much is said in Scripture about the necessity of him that is greatest being as the least, nor do I even tolerate him being carried in on high.—Next it is in Rome—and Rome is a doomed city, it is one of the 4 monsters of Daniel's vision—and tho' a priest might have temporal power elsewhere, I begin to think that it was a sin, as such, in the Church's uniting itself with that enemy of God, who from the beginning sat on her 7 hills, with an enchantress's cup, as the representative and instrument of the Evil Principle. And yet as I looked on, and saw all Christian acts performing the Holy

Sacrament offered up, and the blessing given, and recollected I was in church, I could only say in very perplexity my own words, 'How shall I name thee, Light of the wide west, or heinous error-seat?'—and felt the force of the parable of the tares—who can separate the light from the darkness but the Creator Word who prophesied their union? And so I am forced to leave the matter, not at all seeing my way out of it.—How shall I name thee?...

Ever yours dutifully John H. Newman

To Mrs Newman

Rome. Good Friday. April 5. 1833

My dear Mother,

...As to the Roman C. system, I have ever detested it so much, as Christie e.g. can bear witness, that I cannot detest it more by seeing it, tho' I may be able to defend my opinion better and to feel it more vividly,—but to the *Catholic* system I am more attached than ever. I feel much for and quite love the little monks [[seminarists?]] of Rome—they look so innocent and bright, poor boys—and we have fallen in more or less with a number of interesting Irish and English priests, and quite regret that our limited stay hinders us from forming something like intimate acquaintance with them.—I fear there are very grave and farspreading scandals among the Italian priesthood, and there is mummery in abundance—yet there is a deep substratum of true Christianity, and I think they may be as near truth (at the least) as that Mr B.[1] whom I like less and less every day...

Ever yours dutifully J H Newman

[1] Perhaps Mr Bennett, the chaplain at Naples?

To John Frederic Christie

Rome. April 6. 1833

My dear Christie

This is the first day of the Oriel Examination, and, knowing the unpleasantness to each Elector which that process involves, I sympathize with you all and wish you well through it, and feel almost as if I were a runaway.[1] I am sure, when once back, I shall not of my free will leave England again.

You ought to have had a letter from me, but the post here seems not a little uncertain in its operation at least as regards letters imported. One curious case I heard from the Ws [Wilberforces]. They were here five weeks and to their surprise got no letters from England. At last they got at the cause of it. The Italians have no W; so the unhappy initial, like puss in the corner, shifts as best it can, being sometimes disposed of among the Hs, sometimes in the list of Ms, sometimes among Vs, according to the taste of the letter-sorter. Again there is a good deal of jealousy about political matters, particularly at Naples. Also, being afraid of the Cholera they wash all letters till they are quite dirty and illegible, as some letters that I have received.

Till I got here, I have had little leisure to write to any of my friends. I shall regret Rome very much; it is a delightful place, so calm and quiet, so dignified and beautiful, that I know nothing like it but Oxford; and, as being the place of martyrdom and burial of some of the most favoured instruments of God, it has an interest and a solemn charm which no other place can possess except Jerusalem. Before the remains of the Saints the grandeur of pagan Rome crumbles as utterly as have its material structures, and in the ruins which lie scattered on all sides we do but see the 'disjecta membra' of the fourth monster of Daniel's Vision. I confess, I cannot enter into, rather I protest against, the state of mind of those who affect a classical enthusiasm at the sight of Rome. How can we lay aside our Christianity? even as men, to whom 'nihil humanum alienum est,' we are bound to triumph over the fall of most hardhearted and crafty Empires, but, as Christians, if we do not raise the song of rejoicing over great Babylon, surely we do not follow those who sin[g] the song of Moses and of the Lamb. Nothing can make the queen of the seven hills any thing but evil, and it surprises me to find clergymen so inconsistent as to praise what God has cursed.

As to my view of the Romanist system, it remains, I believe, unchanged. A union with Rome, while it is what it is, is impossible; it is a dream. As to the individual members of the cruel church, who can but love and feel for them? I am sure I have seen persons in Rome, who thus move me, though they cast out our name as evil. There is so much amiableness and gentleness, so much Oxonianism, (so to say) such an amusing and interesting demureness, and such simplicity of look and speech, that I feel for those indeed who are bound with an iron chain, which cripples their energies, and (one would think,) makes their devotion languid. What a strange situation it is, to be with those who think one in a state of perdition, who speak calmly with one, while they have awful thoughts! what a mixture of grief and indignation, what a perplexity between frankness and reserve comes over one!

Next Tuesday, we go our separate ways; the Froudes homeward, I drawn by an irresistible attraction to the fair levels and richly verdured heights of Sicily. What a country it is! a shadow of Eden, so as at once to enrapture and to make one melancholy. It will be a vision for my whole life; and, though I should not choose, I am not sorry to go alone, in order, as Wordsworth would say, to commune with high nature. I hope to be home at all events not later than the beginning of June. I want to set-to again at my book [[the 'Arians']]. I trust I shall be conducted back safely, to be made use of. I do not mind saying this, for I do not think I am actuated by ambitious views, though power, when possessed or in prospect, is a snare. At present to me it is neither in possession or prospect; so let me enjoy my freedom from temptation, while I am sheltered from it; and, should it be ordained that I am never to have the temptation, so much the happier for me. At present I can truly say that I would take the lot of retirement, were the choice offered to me, provided I saw others maintaining instead of me those views which seem to me of supreme and exclusive importance. But I am talking great nonsense, and cannot think how I have come to say it, though I do not know why I should be ashamed of it either, for in matter of fact we of Oxford have a high place in trying times of the Church.

Well, my dear Christie, my thoughts are with you all this week, and I pray you may be guided to make a selection which may be for the advantage of Mater Ecclesia. How anxious I am! it will be all over before you get this. I cannot hear it at soonest for a month to come. It is a secret which the Sicilian mountains cannot reveal. I hear L. stands and M. as well as Marriott and W. Of these I would bet on Marriott.

JHN

J. F. Christie Esqr Oriel College

[1] Newman's friend, Frederic Rogers, became one of the new Fellows of Oriel at this election.

To Mrs Newman

Palermo, June 9. 1833

My dear Mother,

Here I am, waiting day after day, and week after week for a vessel—and very anxious lest you should be uneasy about me. Had I written to you via Naples when I first came here, tho' the letter would have been 3 weeks in going, you would have heard in good time—this I do now, tho' late, but I heartily hope I shall be at home before you read this. The Captain of a Sicilian vessel promises to sail for Marseilles tomorrow—Then again, I am told calms are common at this time of year—so I may be out at sea a long while. ⟨12 or 20! days. But I run the chance. The average is 6.⟩ I have two letters written for H. and J.—one of which I have destined for the Post at Marseilles—and as I have said so in the letter and sealed it, I shall not send it by Naples today. The second is a continuation of the first and unintelligible without it. My further adventures you shall hear, when we meet, (please God) by word of mouth—a more pleasant way. Excuse my scrawling—but the weather is very hot—which must be an excuse also for its brevity. I have enjoyed myself here much—been a good deal on the water—the breezes are most refreshing and there is a delightful public garden—and terraces. And I know one or two of the merchants, who are very kind. I saw by chance in Galignani Rogers' success the other day.[1] Mr Ingham, Froude's friend, is not here.—From Catania to Palermo I passed thro' a country, which baffles description. I never *saw* a country before—it was a new thing. And Taormini is perfectly wonderful. I was very idle in the versemaking way, till June, when I made a start, and have done one every day since the first inst—having done only 3 in April and May . . . .

Love to H and J. Yours dutifully in much longing, for I am literally homesick J H Newman

[1] Frederic Rogers' election as a Fellow of Oriel.

To Mrs Newman

Lyons: July 1. [1833]

I trust when you receive this I shall not be far from you. Really it seems as if some unseen power, good or bad, was resisting my return. The thought of home has brought tears in my eyes for the last two months. God is giving me a severe lesson of patience, and I trust I am not altogether wasting the opportunity of discipline. It is His will. I strive to think that, wherever I am, God is God and I am I. It is only forty-eight hours' journey from Marseilles here (200 miles), yet on arriving here last night I found my ankles so swollen and inflamed, that I have judged it prudent to remain here a day, though in a miserable, dirty inn, yet the best in Lyons. I have the prospect of confinement in my bedroom all day, with the doubt whether I shall be able to proceed tomorrow, for at present it is with difficulty and pain that I hobble across the room. Rest is the great remedy, I suppose. So it is a simple trial of my patience. I am quite desolate. I am tempted to say, 'Lord, heal me, for my bones are vexed.'[1] But really I am wonderfully calm, and I trust from right principles. Thwarting awaits me at every step. I have had much of this ever since I left Naples. I earnestly hope that tomorrow will end your doubts and anxieties about me by the receipt of my letter from Palermo on June 9.

I have said nothing about France, which is truly *La belle France* in all externals. I am enchanted with it.

[1] *Psalm* 6:2.

To Edward Hawkins

Oriel College. July 12. 1833

Dear Mr Provost,

At length I am returned—and am most happy to be again among places and persons I love, from whom I have been separated much longer than I wished.—It has been a great trial to me the last two months to feel that I ought to be at home, yet to be unable to get there.—When I was in the heart of Sicily, (the beginning of May) I was attacked with a fever which was (most unseasonably) epidemic in the island, and is supposed to have been occasioned by the excessive rains of the winter and spring. Indeed such a season has not be[en] known for years; the rain fell 34 inches, whereas commonly it falls not more than 7—and the weather was cold even in May. For a week the people about me gave me up; for mine seemed a bad case, and the sick were dying every day; but, through God's mercy, nature brought me through.—This delayed me three weeks—then I was delayed another 3 weeks at Palermo, waiting for a vessel—and by that time the calm weather had set in, so that, instead of being from 3 to 6 days, I was a fortnight getting to Marseilles. When I got to Lyons, I was again laid up—but only for 48 hours—I then started again, and arrived here in less than a week, having been up 6 nights out of the 7.—Yet the fatigue has not seemed great, and I am now recruiting.

Sicily is a most beautiful country—and all my anticipations are far more than answered about it.—Of course it was a drawback on my gratification that I was by myself—yet, since I was attacked with fever, I have been very thankful that no friend was near me—for it was very catching, and I had a very attentive servant to nurse me.—I have been unfortunate in respect to temporary indisposition during my whole tour—tho' my general health is certainly much benefited by it. At Malta I had a serious cough—and I owe it to your friend Dr Davy that I recovered of it—he volunteered a prescription which removed it, when a blister and other remedies had been resorted to in vain. Both he and Mrs D. were very kind in their attentions to me while there—and I only regretted my cough hindered me fully availing myself of them.

I hope soon to set about the work which has already been almost in the Press. Perhaps you know, it is not to form one of Rivington's Theological Library, but to appear as a separate publication—I suppose in October. Many thanks for the present of your Sermons, which it will give me much pleasure to read. I will attend to your wishes about the return I made to the Ecclesiastical Commission of the Income of St Mary's Vicarage.

Pray give my best compliments to Mrs Hawkins and Believe me, Dear

Mr Provost Yours most faithfully

John H. Newman[1]

[1] Hawkins wrote on 27 June: 'I am greatly disappointed at not having the pleasure of seeing you before I leave Oxford. Will you be so good as to fill up the other leaf with the sum you inserted in your return to the Commissioners of Ecclesiastical Revenues; not, as you will readily suppose, to gratify any idle curiosity of mine, but to enable me at the October Audit to present a statement of the incomes of our Vicarages, some of which it seems most probable the College will wish to augment, under succeeding incumbencies, in more permanent manner than theretofore.'

To Henry Wilberforce

Oriel College. ⌈July 16/33⌉

My dear Henry,

I have been so tired and languid since my return, that I have written no letter which I was not driven to write—else you were in my thoughts—and I hoped you would here [sic] of my return some how or other. ⌈I was tired from my journey, having been up 6 nights out of the last 7;⌉—which shows my strength. Indeed I must not call it strength, meaning by that any inherent thing, for my strength is as if the mercy of God externally holding me up day by day. ⌈All sorts of evils came upon me in Sicily—the fever, of which many were dying on all sides of me,⌉ and which in some places was so bad that they in their fright called it cholera, ⌈was but one though the greatest (*perhaps*) of the (before strange to me) complaints which suddenly fell upon me (in connexion with it). For a week and more my nurses etc thought I could not recover—no medicine was given me⌉ which could grapple with the disorder—they know nothing of calomel—⌈they bled me indeed, but took away so little blood that both Mr Babington and Dr Ogle say, it could be of no use to me—In fact the fever ran its course; and when the crisis came, I was spared⌉—and immediately after gained strength in a surprising way. ⌈I was so reduced, I could not lift my hand to my mouth to feed myself⌉—much less rise, or (again) sit up, in bed—in four or five days time I could (with help) walk about the room—⌈and in ten days I was able to travel to Palermo—performing one day a journey of 60 miles over a rough country. A determination of blood to my head came on, as I was getting well⌐—but it has gradually gone off, as I get strength. ⌈(August 4.—) the only remaining signs of my indisposition now are my hair falling off, and a slight cough,⌉ which is very slight.—⌈I was taken ill first at Catania, after spending two nights (unwillingly) in the open air,⌉ which I believe is a very dangerous thing in Sicily. However it could not be called more than weakness, and I was able to proceed on my journey. ⌈When I got to Leonforte in the very heart of the country, I broke down. For three days I lay without any medical assistance—on the morning of the fourth a notion seized me that my illness was all fancy, so I set out on my mule—After proceeding about 7 miles in great distress from a sort of suffocating feeling, I was forced to betake myself to a hut by the wayside, where I lay the greater part of the day. On a sudden I found fingers at my pulse—a medical man happened by chance to be in a neighbouring cottage and they called him in. His prescription enabled me to get on that evening to Castro Giovanni,⌉ the ancient Enna, ⌈where I was laid up for 3 weeks.⌉ Thence I travelled to Palermo; where the time I had to wait for a vessel was of material service to me in the way of recruiting. After another delay of 3 weeks I set out for Marseilles, and it being the season of calms, was a whole fortnight on the water. Thence I came to England with all speed; and ⌈not till I got home, could persuade myself I was not in a dream. So strange has every thing been to me.

I hope it was not presumptuous, but from the beginning of my illness I had so strong a feeling on my mind that I should recover, that, whatever I did in the way of preparation for death (I mean, of giving my servant directions about letters etc) was done as a mere matter of duty. I could not help saying, 'I must act as if I were to die, but I think God has work for me yet.'—Thus I cannot answer your question, never having realized eternity as about to break upon me. Yet I had many serious thoughts. It was a lonely situation, I found myself in, at Leonforte; at a miserable inn. I am not sure my mind was quite clear at all times, so as to be sensible of its desolateness—yet I had once, doubtless when I felt myself lonely, quite a revelation come upon me of God's love to His elect, and felt as if I were one—but of course I mention this, not as laying stress upon it, but as an instance of God's mercy to me:—not that I can describe the feeling in words.—Then again I was much relieved next day, by being able to discover, (as I thought) sins in my conduct, which led God thus to fight against me. This he had been doing ever since I left Rome, and I from time to time had been impatient under the obstacles he put in my way, and had (as it were) asked why He did so. But now I came to think that there was some wilfulness in my coming to Sicily, as I did—and, tho' no one had advised me against it, yet I fancied I ought to have discovered they thought it an over-venturous thing. And then I felt more than I had done the wilfulness of my character generally—and I reflected that I was lying there the very day on which three years before I had sent in my resignation of the Tutorship (or something like it)—and, tho' I could not (and do not) at all repent the doing so, yet I began to understand that the *manner* was hasty and impatient. And then I recollected that the very day before I left Oxford, I had preached a [[University]] Sermon against wilfulness, so that I seemed to have been predicting my own condemnation. And I went on to ask myself whether I had not cherished resentment against the Provost—and whether in me was not fulfilled the text 1 Cor XI, 29–32, (as I still think it has been).—But after all I was comforted by the thought that, in bringing myself into my present situation, I had not (as I just said) run counter to any advice given me—and I said 'I have not sinned against light—' and repeated this often. And then I thought I would try to obey God's will as far as I could, and, with a dreamy confused notion, which the fever (I suppose) occasioned, thought that in setting off the fourth day from Leonforte, I was *walking* as long as I could in the way of God's commandments, and putting myself in *the way* of His mercy, as if He would meet me. (Is. xxvi, 8) and surely so He did, as I lay in the hut—and though I have no distinct remembrance of the whole matter, yet it certainly seems like some instinct which He put within me and made me follow, to get me to Castro Giovanni, where I had a comfortable room, and was attended most hospitably and kindly.⌉—It is most strange, and shows what is the hardness and inconsistency of my mind, that since I have been in England I have had hardly one feeling of joy and gratitude, tho' the thought of home drew tears into my eyes abroad, as oft as I thought of it—especially in my dreary voyage from Palermo to Marseilles.

⌈Sept 3.⌉ Your letter this morning induces me to send you the above at once. I was afraid I might be teazing you with it, before I heard from you. I suppose you could not come here for this week, previously to your going to Scotland? or on your return?— I should so rejoice to see you. ⌈As to the queries of your letter, I would rather talk than write to you. Be assured I shall stick to the State as long as I can—but God forbid I should betray my trust, or diminish the privileges of Christ's Church committed to me. I do not fear a schism. The Clergy will wake—at least great numbers. I will not answer for the Bishop of Winchester, whose vote on the Sacrilege Bill has pained me much.[1] We have set up Societies here—for the defence of the Liturgy and the enforcement of the doctrine of the Apostolical Succession. They are already forming in Oxfordshire, Berkshire, Glocestershire, Devonshire, Kent and Essex and Suffolk. And we are sure (I believe) of the support of some Bishops. Let us behave like men, and we have nothing to fear. Of course we are lost, if we are cravens.—You will see the writings of many of your friends, if you ever see the British Magazine. We are publishing tracts in our Society, and *perhaps* may proceed to a Periodical Quarterly. We have already got subscribers for our general plan, The country clergy *must* rouse, *in order to* save themselves.⌉ They will keep possession of their places if they are brave—but ⌈woe to them if they knock under—væ victis! My work ⟨⟨the Arians⟩⟩ is passing thro' the Press⌉ and appears in October. If you have an opportunity, tell your brother W. I am quite well, with many thanks to him for his kindness

Ever Yrs affly John H Newman

As to books, why ask me? It would be a great thing to get up Hooker's Ecclesiastical Polity and the Epistles of St Paul. But really much as I should like to *talk*, I cannot write advice.

---

[1] The Irish Church Temporalities Bill, which became law on 14 August. After strong opposition by the Archbishop of Canterbury and Bishop Phillpotts, the English bishops were overawed by a letter of the King to the Archbishop.

The Oxford Movement
(1833–39)

Within days of Newman's return from his Mediterranean travels on 14 July John Keble preached the Assize Sermon at Oxford on 'National Apostasy'. He identified that apostasy as the suppression of Irish dioceses by Parliament, whereby the State usurped the responsibility of the bishops to govern the Church. Newman regarded that date as the start of the Oxford Movement.

The main doctrine of the Movement was the apostolic succession, the conviction that the Church, founded by Jesus, was to be recognized through its communion with the successors of the Apostles, who were the bishops. Apostolic succession was the bedrock of orthodoxy. Breaking with contemporary understanding of the nature of Establishment, Newman and his associates viewed Parliamentary suppression of dioceses as an utterly unacceptable assault on episcopal authority and to be resisted at all costs. How could that be done? Newman was impatient with committees. Instead he and some of his friends produced pamphlets which sought to popularize their views and rouse people. These pamphlets were called tracts, and so the Oxford Movement became known also as the Tractarian Movement.

At the start the Tracts were short, but before long they became more substantial, and Newman soon began to acquire a name for himself. But he met resistance. The insistence on episcopal power seemed too much like Popery to the Protestant English. Before long Newman was joking to his friend, Simeon Pope, 'tho' I am already called Papist and Pelagian—well, I am neither Puritan or Protestant at least—what I aim at is to be a-Postolical'.[1]

The letters of this period are full of his desire to champion the apostolical cause, but there was action as well. When Newman found himself requested to marry a young woman, Miss Jubber, at an hour and a half's notice, though the bride, a Baptist, had not yet been baptized, he refused. There was public outrage, but Newman explained to his bishop, 'I felt I could not on my own responsibility bestow the especial privilege of Christian matrimony on parties who had not taken on themselves even the public profession of Christianity'. This stand for 'apostolic' principle was widely perceived as Tractarian bigotry.

In spite of such a difficulty, Newman in general was in his pomp at this time and enjoying himself. In 1835 he was drawn into a correspondence with a French priest, the Abbé Jean-Nicholas Jager. Their published exchange petered out unsatisfactorily,

---

[1] 21 August 1834, *L.D.* IV, p. 325.

but it stimulated the ideas for Newman's first major theological work, his *Lectures on the Prophetical Office*, in which he sought to articulate his understanding of the Anglican Church as a *via media*, a middle way, between Protestant error and Roman excess. He followed up those lectures with another pioneering treatise, his *Lectures on Justification*, which sought to reconcile Protestant and Catholic teaching on one of the key reformation issues. Shortly before their publication, he described to his sister, Jemima, how he wrote over and over again, correcting: 'I cannot count how many times this process goes on.'

A further source of Tractarian teaching was Newman's sermons. They have become renowned, but initially amidst the praise there were those who felt their scope was too limited. Newman, however, argued, 'No one, who *habitually* hears me, ought to have any other than the whole Scripture impression', and declared, 'I lay it down as a fundamental Canon, that a Sermon to be effective must be imperfect.' He was not encouraging poor preaching, but recognizing that not everything can be said at once.

Against this backcloth controversies began to arise. The most spectacular was provoked by Newman's antipathy for the views advocated by Renn Dickson Hampden. Newman campaigned against his appointment as the Regius Professor of Divinity at Oxford. He sat up one night writing a pamphlet entitled *Elucidations of Dr Hampden's Theological Statements*. He treated Hampden roughly, some would say unjustly. It was robust, even by the pamphleteering standards of those days. He saw himself as confronting the spirit of liberalism in religion and defending religious dogma, combatting a relativism that would reduce divine truth to the uncertain conclusions of human speculation.

These fraught years were also marked by personal tensions. His younger friend and disciple, Henry Wilberforce, wanted to marry, but was too nervous to tell Newman himself, aware of Newman's high ideals and the value he placed on celibacy. Instead he asked Newman's sister, Harriett, to inform him. But she never did. When he did not hear from Newman, Wilberforce thought Newman had taken offence at his marrying. Newman was indeed offended, though not, he claimed, by the plan to marry. He told Wilberforce that he had never 'questioned the propriety of your marrying'; but he said that he was hurt at not being told straightforwardly. The breach with Wilberforce indicates how sensitive Newman could be, even in dealings with close friends. Their relationship was strained for a while, though they managed to communicate on other matters freely and with good humour.

During these years as well there were deaths. On 28 February 1836 after struggling with ill-health for years Hurrell Froude finally died. 'I can never have a greater loss, looking on for the whole of life,' Newman told the great friend of his Trinity days, John Bowden. Then in May his mother became ill quite suddenly and she too died. 'It is indeed', he wrote, again in a letter to Bowden, 'a most bitter affliction'. And two friends were widowed, Manning in July 1837 and Pusey two years later. Newman wrote letters to them both. Pusey indeed remained in Oxford for five weeks after his wife's death before taking a break and, according to

Newman's diary, Newman called on him or took a walk with him every day until he went, except for Wednesday 12 June, which was Encaenia when honorary degrees are awarded in Oxford, and Sunday 30 June, the day before Pusey left, when Newman had many pastoral duties. His support bears witness to the depth and strength of their friendship.

Throughout these first years of the Oxford Movement one shadow soon began to loom. In November 1834 Newman drafted a letter to Mary Wilberforce, the wife of Henry's eldest brother, William, warning her against the enticements of Roman Catholicism: 'there is that in Romanism which makes it a duty to keep aloof from it'. In 1838 he was sensitive to his bishop's critique of the Tracts and wondered whether he should bring them to an end. After all, the Movement rested on an episcopal foundation. His bishop, however, reassured him that there was no call for so drastic an action. Yet still there was a fear that the Tracts were opening too ready a path to Rome. In September the following year he was telling Manning, 'I am conscious that we are raising longings and tastes which we are not allowed to supply—and till our Bishops and others give scope to the development of Catholicism externally and visibly, we *do* tend to make impatient minds seek it where it has ever been, *in* Rome'.

All the same, Newman had complete confidence in his own position. That summer, however, during the long vacation he had gone back to reading the Fathers at more leisure, and told Frederic Rogers he was going to 'read through' the Monophysite controversy. A storm was brewing.[2]

---

[2] 12 July 1839, *L.D.* VII, p. 105.

2

The Oxford Movement (1833–39)

To Charles Portales Golightly[1]

Oriel College. Aug 11/33

My dear Golightly,

Froude missed seeing you by an unlucky accident. My letter to him about you miscarried, else he would have waited for you in Town or run down to you. I shall be truly glad of a meeting with you in September—write to Mozley and get him to come at the same time.—As to your proposition about Ireland, we have come to this determination;—that we have not strength to do any thing *at once*, that we must dissemble till we gain more on our side—protesting the while on every occasion. We have formed a society here for the purpose of rousing the clergy—on these principles etc. 1. to *assist* the Bishops by our voice. 2. and, for this purpose, each to engage to open a correspondence with all his clerical friends, and to get them to do the same in their turn—so that when the right moment comes, an address (e.g.) to the Archbishop might promptly be got up on any matter. In short to *prepare for [the] next* session of Parliament that we may not be taken by surprise. 3 we intend to keep our names secret, as far as may be, lest we seem to domineer—i.e. no one in writing to his friends will do more than say *there is* a society, without specifying the members—and this is all we want—I could write to many a man whom I hardly knew, if I could say I was *one of a many*—as in the case of an election etc. 4 Our main doctrine is the Apostolical Succession and the exclusive privilege of Bishops and Priests to consecrate the Bread and Wine. 5 We protest against doing any thing directly to separate Church and State, while we think it necessary steadily to contemplate the contingency of such an event. 6 We wish to make the Church more *popular* than it is—how, is of course a question—This is a rough sketch of our plan—if you wish to join us—we shall be rejoiced to secure your co-operation. Keble, Palmer, etc. are members—Let me hear from you at once. *Keep our names a secret*, but you may mention the fact of a society's being instituted. In time we may raise a rent, if God prospers us—but this is for future consideration. We are in hopes through our friends of forming branches in other parts of the Kingdom, and at length of circulating books, tracts etc.

Aug 13 Yesterday we have [*sic*] a consultation, and K. [Keble] came over. We have decided to keep most of our views in the background at present—and to unite on this simple principle—'with a view to stir up our brethren to consider the state of the

Church, and especially to the practical belief and preaching of the Apostolical Succession,'—and we mean (if possible) to get the opinion of some Bishop, and his allowance, if not his consent.—We shall probably begin printing tracts bearing on this subject—perhaps Ignatius's epistles first. If you can in the course of a fortnight write to friends and get men (not to *join* us) but to receive and distribute our tracts, do so—tho' to join us is best of all—but I fear people will be scared at the notion of a Society. I shall write to Trower, but you may as well drop him a letter. Dear is sadly out of the way, and (I suppose) without influence—yet should not you write to him in justice? if you do, remember me to him, and say that the only reason I do not write is the number of letters on the subject which lie before me to despatch. I shall write to Blencowe, and do you too.[2] Two letters are like two witnesses, they prove a point.—We must not be disappointed, if we do not get many names at first. You see I am assuming you will join us. I trust so—it does not do for the friends of the Church to split on trifles. Already we have been obliged to give way to each other. Another object we shall bring forward in time is that of doing all in our power to hinder heretical etc. appointments to Bishopricks. Excuse an apparently short letter—but I write so close, it is already twice as long as yours

Ever Yrs affly John H Newman

P.S. I should add that a defence of the Prayer Book from Socinian etc alterations is another of our objects.

[1] Golightly, who became a bitter opponent of the Tractarians, was friendly with Newman at this stage. This letter sets out the aims and hopes of the Oxford Movement in its early days and its way of working.

[2] Walter John Trower (1805–77) was a Fellow of Oriel from 1828 to 1830 and later Bishop of Glasgow and Galloway, and later still Bishop of Gibraltar. William Smith Dear (1804–78) had been at Ealing School with Newman and later was Rector of Aldbourne, Sussex. Edward Everard Blencowe was not the future Fellow of Oriel, but a member of St Alban Hall, Oxford.

To Richard Hurrell Froude

Oriel College. ⌈Nov 13. 1833⌉

My dear F,

⌈I am in the midst of troubles, with no one but such οὐτίδανοι[1] as Rogers to consult with. Palmer musters the zs[2] in great force against the Tracts, and some Evangelicals—He presses, and I am quite ready to admit, a disclaimer (in the shape of a circular) of the Tracts. But he goes further, and wishes us to stop them. In these cases success is the test of sagacity or rashness. The said Tracts give offence I know— but they also do good—and I maintain will *strengthen* his Association by enabling it to take high ground, yet seem in the mean [[μέσον]]. I suggested to him that we were only doing here, what Rose is doing elsewhere—who nevertheless is a member of the grand scheme. He said R. was *known* as the Editor of the Magazine—and so I replied that I supposed Keble would have no objection to give his name to the Tracts. What will be done, I know not—but I want advice sadly. I have no confidence in any one. If I could be sure of 5 or 6 vigorous co-operators in various parts, I would laugh at opposition—but I fear being beaten from the field. K. says we *must* be read, unless we grow stupid—but I am not over certain about our fertility even.⌉ We have had two splendid donations, as I think I told you. ⌈The Tracts are certainly liked in many places—among other persons, by the Bishop of Winchester.[3] O! that he would take us up—I would go to the length of my tether to meet him. H. W. [[Henry Wilberforce]] is now there—doubtless palavering him about us—as he is us about him. I wonder whether, if one knew him, one might exert any influence over him. Evangelicals, as I anticipated, are struck with the 'Law of Liberty;—' and 'the Sin of the Church—'⌉[4] the only one (by the bye) the Bishop did not like. ⌈The subject of Discipline too (I cannot doubt) will take them. Surely my game lies among them. I can make no hand of the zs.—I am half out of spirits—but how one outgrows tenderness! Several years back, to have known that ½ or all Oxford shook their heads at what I was doing, (e.g. about the Church Missionary Society) would have hurt me much—but somehow now I manage to exist. Do give me some advice and encouragement.⌉

The Duke of Newcastle has joined the Association with his heart and life—he bids us only be true to ourselves. He has seen the Tracts. ⌈I do think our Tracts, if we persist, will catch all the enthusiastic people among the Associated—which will be wretched for the zs.—Our proposition is, that we should cease the issue of the Tracts, till the Address is happily got over—but I say, 'P. [[Palmer]] you delayed us 5 weeks with your scruples, which you yourself got over at last—and now you are playing the same game again.' Yet I should shrink from spoiling the Address, and do not know what to do.[5]

Tyler at last has plucked me, and sent back the Sermons⌉ in the most ludicrously hypocritical way imaginable—⌈he is dying for love of the Church, and most seraphic.[6] I will give you the conclusion of his letter. I cannot find it. 'Salvam fac ecclesiam tuam Domine' is one of his suspiria. He gives *no reason* for not taking my Sermons.

My dear F.—I so fear I may be self willed in this matter of the Tracts—pray do advise me according to your light⌉

Ever Yrs affly John H Newman.

⌈P.S. I have written to P. [[Palmer]] to say, I will join his open association, if he wishes it, in spite of my dislike to it—but I will not cease my issue of Tracts. At Christmas I hope to make a Missionary Tour to Derby, Leicester, Huntingdonshire, Suffolk, Northamptonshire etc.⌉

What do you think of a certain x. x. (do not mistake) having proposed to his great niece?

They say the first act of the New Session is to appoint a *Commission* to visit Oxford. O that Daniel Whittle may roughride All Souls!

⌈Shuttleworth has, I believe, brought before the Hebdomadal board the expediency of removing the subscription of the Articles at entrance.[7]⌉

---

[1] 'men of naught' [[this is ironical]].

[2] [[establishment men]]. In the code the Tractarians used, the Xs held Apostolical views that were the heart of the Tractarian position, the Ys were the Evangelicals, and the Zs, as Newman noted here, were the establishment men. William Palmer of Worcester College represented the establishment party and favoured a formally organized association for the defence of the Church, rather than the Tracts.

[3] Charles Richard Sumner (1790–1874), who had been a favourite of King George IV, was himself an Evangelical, and his elder brother, John Bird Sumner (1780–1862), became Archbishop of Canterbury. Whatever early enthusiasm for the Tracts he may have had, was to fade.

[4] *Tract* 8 and appendix to *Tract* 6.

[5] In the event an Address in defence of the Church was drawn up and signed by seven thousand clergyman. It was presented to the Archbishop of Canterbury on 6 February 1834. Newman thought its terms were too mild, but approved of it in principle.

[6] J. E. Tyler (1789–1851), a Fellow of Oriel who was Dean when Newman was elected, was editing sermons for the SPCK. For Newman's proposed reply to him see letter of 12 December 1833 (*L.D.* IV, p. 139).

[7] Philip Nicholas Shuttleworth (1782–1852) was Warden of New College, Oxford.

To Anthony Grant

Oriel College. November 16. 1833

My dear Grant,

I thought at first of writing to Dr Arnold direct, in answer to his letter to you, which at his desire you have shown me; but perhaps I shall be able to express my meaning with less appearance of disrespect towards him by addressing you, if you will be kind enough to forward my letter to him.[1]

Dr Arnold remonstrates with me, because, in the Spring of the present year, being in company with four friends at Rome, on one of them observing in vindication of Niebuhr, that 'Dr A. considered him to be a Christian,' I remarked, 'but how are we to know that Dr A. is a Christian?'—or words to that effect.

I do not object to be called to account for any words of mine, however privately and casually spoken; though I cannot but think, that there are questions which it is as unbecoming to ask as it is unmanly not to answer.

I have no recollection of the words attributed to me; though, as they are stated on your authority, I most fully acknowledge them to be mine. It may be necessary to state this, lest in the meaning I now put on them, I should be understood to speak from memory, whereas I am only judging of them from my knowledge of my own habitual sentiments towards the class of opinions which Dr Arnold's writings put forth.

I have no hesitation in saying, that the words in question are not such as I should use in mixed society or before strangers;—nor again such as I should have used where nothing had led to them, my actual adoption of them arising from a previous remark of another person which seemed to me to involve the absurdity, that one who was suspected of unsound religious views should be vindicated by the authority of parties themselves implicated in a similar suspicion. Of course I am sorry, should Dr Arnold's character have been prejudiced through a misconception of any words of mine; but I do not feel I owe him any apology for them, because they were *not* used in public, but before friends who either fully assented to them, or at least understood my meaning.

That meaning was as follows;—and I trust I shall give no offence to Dr Arnold in the course of an explanation which is forced upon me. I conceive, that, although in order to be formally and outwardly a Christian, it is sufficient to be baptized and to assent to certain revealed doctrines, yet that the word is very commonly restricted to those whose temper and conduct evidence a Christian mind; that faith is the primary characteristic of a Christian; that faith includes reverence for God's word and ordinances, for His saints both under the Old and New Covenant, for the will and appointments of His Apostles, and for the declarations and usages of His Church;—that on the other hand, where this high spiritual principle is wanting, there may yet be piety of an irregular and uncertain kind, which of course has its praise, but must not be confused with the essential Christian character, formed by the especial influences given under the Gospel, which is no speculative and curious temper, not given to argument and debate, nor to an undue reliance on the intellect in the search of truth, but, in Scripture language, like a little child, speaking little and loving and obeying heartily.

That this really was the sense in which I used the words, is confirmed to my mind by its fitness for the occasion which gave rise to them; for, as Niebuhr is accused, not of denying Christianity, (as far as I know,) but of being sceptical in his views of the Old Testament history, it did seem very apposite to suggest that there were statements in one of Dr Arnold's works, which implied in the judgment of many men a most painful irreverence towards that Sacred Record, its Divine Author, and His servants revealed in it.

I believe my words had no direct reference to Dr Arnold's ecclesiastical principles; though I should not duly respond to the frankness of his letter, if I did not plainly declare, that, as far as I understand them, I think them unscriptural, unchristian, and open to ecclesiastical censure.

Having explained the words, in which I implied a doubt of Dr Arnold's Christianity, I do not feel myself called upon to defend my opinion thus acknowledged, or to allude to the other points on which Dr Arnold touches in his letter.

With much sorrow that I should have innocently been the cause of involving you in this unpleasant discussion

> Believe me, My dear Grant, Yours very truly John H Newman

[1] Anthony Grant was at this time a Fellow of New College, Oxford. Thomas Arnold of Rugby had heard through him about Newman's apparently disparaging reference to his opinions as a Christian and had written to Grant to protest. Grant, as Arnold wished, had shown Newman Arnold's letter. See *L.D.* IV, pp. 107–8.

From Anthony Grant

[16 November 1833]

My dear Newman,

I have no difficulty in saying that from my recollection of the occasion and the import of the words under consideration, they might naturally have been understood to convey such an opinion as you have expressed.—What interpretation I applied to them at the moment

I cannot *precisely* state, nor would it be of much consequence if I could, as that would depend on the colour which my own thoughts would give to them. This however I can unhesitatingly state that they were never understood by me to imply any imputation on Dr Arnold's belief in Christianity, but that, generally, his views on some Scripture, and perhaps I should have added, Ecclesiastical Points were not such as conveyed to your mind Evidence of a Christian temper. I hope you will observe that the construction I should have put on the words would certainly not have been *stronger* than what you have given.

I shall be very ready to forward your letter to Dr A whenever you may wish.

Believe me Yours very truly A. Grant

To Miss M. R. Giberne

⌈Oriel College. Dec 22. 1833⌉

Dear Miss Giberne,

⌈I was much pleased and encouraged by your letter, being in the midst of worry and fidget,⌉ if such uncomfortable words bear to be written down. It really is a great encouragement to know there are any persons who at all value what one tries to do in the cause of the Gospel. ⌈A person like myself hears of nothing but his failures or what others consider such—men do not flatter each other—and one's best friends act as one's best friends ought, tell one of all one's mistakes and absurdities. I know it is a good thing thus to be dealt with—nor do I wish it otherwise—All things one tries to do, *must* be mixed with great imperfection—and it is part of one's trial to be obliged to attempt things which involve incidental error, and give cause for blame. This is all very humbling, particularly when a person has foretold to himself his own difficulties and scrapes, and then is treated as if he was quite unconscious of them and thought himself a very fine fellow. But it is good discipline and I will gladly accept it. Nevertheless it is very pleasant to have accidentally such letters as yours to encourage one, though I know well that it goes far beyond the occasion, owing to your great kindness.⌉

As to the Lecture, I do not suppose any objection can arise to translating it, as you propose.[1] However, as I wish for some of my Sermons here which you have, I will request of you the favour of your sending them one and all down here at once including the Lecture. I am (I believe) on the point of publishing a volume of Sermons, and Rivington is anxious I should lose no time about it.—As to the Liturgy Course, really it is much too imperfect to publish. Many thanks for your extremely gratifying offer. It would require a good deal of reading and thought to make any thing decent of it—however, I will not forget your wish, (though I cannot quite *promise* to fulfil it,) for to have contributed at all to the satisfaction of a mind such as yours, must be a gratification to any Clergyman, and a cause of thankfulness.

My Sisters said they would rather delay writing a day or two—so this letter goes with a blank side. ⌈Mr Terrington called on me yesterday—he was very kind—and said he intended to sign the Address to the Archbishop, and did not call me a Papist to the face as some other persons have.—I really believe that if Ridley or Hooker could be published without their names, their works would be called papistical]

Yours very sincerely John H Newman

[1] Miss Giberne wrote on 19 December, 'Have you any objection to my translating into French the interesting Lecture which you have lent me on the Annunciation? I have a great desire to send it to my Roman Catholic friend in France. I do not know whether H. [[N.B. my sister]] told you how much I admired the beautiful cameo you brought me from Rome.'

To Henry Wilberforce

Oriel College. January 8/34

not sent

My poor dear foolish Henry,

Dear, for auld lang syne—foolish, for being suspicious of me—poor, because I suppose you have been pained at your own suspicions, why have you left it first to a casual word of yours, next to a letter of Christie's to acquaint me that the time is fixed for your changing your state and commencing to be a citizen of the world that now is? Was not this very gross μικροψυχία[1] on your part? for I will not fancy there was any more pugnacious feeling mixed in the procedure. Yet it shows almost a want of kindness towards me. What have I done, (state any grounds,) to justify it? I really believe that, when you search your heart, you will not find that your unwillingness proceeds from any thing I can have done or said, however easy it is by word of mouth to make vehement and voluble speeches. When have I ever questioned the propriety of your marrying, or dared to interfere with your Christian liberty? As exceptio probat regulam, it may be as well to remind you that the single thing I said was I thought you would do better to wait awhile—not that here I did more than state my opinion when asked. But you surely are inconsiderate—you ask me to give you my heart, when you give yours to another—and because I will not promise to do so, then you augur all sorts of illtreatment towards you from me.— Now I do not like to speak of myself, but in self defence I must say, it is a little hard for a friend to separate himself from familiarity with me (which he has a perfect right, and perhaps lies under a duty to do,) and then to say, 'Love me as closely, give me your familiar heart as you did, though I have parted with mine.' Be quite sure that I shall be free to love you, far more than you will me—but I cannot, as a prudent man, so forget what is due to my own comfort and independence as not to look to my own resources, make my own mind my wife, and anticipate and provide against that loss of friends which the fashion of the age makes inevitable. This is all I have done and said with respect to you—I have done it towards all my friends, as expecting they will part from me, except to one, who is at Barbadoes. I dare not even towards my sisters indulge affection without restraint. Now is it not hard, when I a poor individual see what the chance is of my being left alone, and prepare for it, that then I should be said to be the breaker of friendships? it is the story of the lamb and the wolf; unless indeed you think I have that confidence in myself that I could calmly contemplate putting the whole world into coventry. You know very little of me, if you think I do not feel at times much the despondence of solitariness—(if I had had no experience of it this last year,) and why may I not arm myself against what is inevitable? why must I give my heart to those who will not (naturally, it would be a bad bargain for them,) take charge of it? God grant all this discipline will make me give my heart more to Him—but it is hard to be accused of inflicting it on others.

You are ever in my prayers, and will not cease to be—and I trust you will never forget your present principles, nor the sentiment of Keble's in which you seemed fully to acquiesce, that 'celibacy and marriage were accidents, and did not alter by one jot or tittle a true Christian's mode of acting.'

My dear H.—you really have hurt me—You have *made* a *difficulty* in the very beginning of our separation. You should have reflected that to remove it, you would not only have to justify it to yourself but to explain it to me.

Ever Yrs affectionately John H Newman.

P.S. At first I intended not to write, lest I should say what would seem unkind. But that itself seemed unkind—so I changed my mind. This is not the first letter I have written; I plucked it. Now, if you write and explain, please do not expect another letter from me at once—[2]

[1] 'pusillanimity'.
[2] The misunderstanding continued with further letters until August 1835. Wilberforce married Mary Sargent on 24 July 1834.

Memorandum. Misunderstanding with Henry Wilberforce

August 27. 1860

NB. If I am asked, on looking back, what the origin of this misunderstanding with H W was, I say it was the feeling etc. of my poor sister H., now dead, about it.

She triumphed in her heart over me, that H W married, *as I knew she did*. He on the other hand fancied that she was the best person to communicate the news to me—He told her to do so—she never did it.

As I was never told by any one, I simply did not write to him on the subject. He, thinking I had been told by my sister, expected a letter, and kept fidgetting about my not writing. Then he said, 'Evidently you are cutting yourself off from me—else, you would write to me about my marriage; whereas you have not written to me *at all*.'

To Richard Bagot, Bishop of Oxford

July 9/34

My dear Lord,

I am sorry to be obliged to trouble your Lordship with the particulars of an occurrence which took place last week in St Mary's Parish, and which I find is noticed in the Oxford Papers of Saturday.

One of my Parishioners, by name Jubber, is (I believe) a Baptist. About a year and a quarter since, in my absence from England, Mrs Jubber sent to my Curate Mr Williams begging him to come and baptize her (adult) son—He in answer expressed his readiness to do so, and said he would baptize him and his sisters with as much privacy as she could wish, and did all he could to encourage the intention, but said he must first consult your Lordship on the subject and have some conversation with the parties. He afterwards saw the young man, but found that the only notion which he and his friends had [of] the Sacrament was as of a civil ceremony; and it was supposed that perhaps some secular motive, whether to facilitate apprenticeship or similar object was the occasion of the application. Mr W. fixed several times afterwards to see him, and then fell ill of the influenza. On recovering he called more than once on Mrs Jubber, but did not succeed in seeing her. The youth was then gone from home; the baptism of the daughter did not seem to be contemplated. On my return he told me what had happened, and I seconded his endeavours to persuade the daughter to be baptized.—I was glad to hear they sometimes attended my service at St Mary's; and I had some conversation with Mr Jubber about their baptism. Last Easter I made them a present of a volume of Sermons.—

Under these circumstances, it was extremely painful to my feelings on Tuesday morning July 1 to have ⟨receive⟩ intelligence at ½ past 7 A.M. that I was to be called on at 9 o'clock to marry one of the daughters. (I had heard between 4 and 5 PM. on the preceding day that there was to be a marriage, the parties not being mentioned— a letter containing the names was sent to my rooms the same evening, as I suppose—but, as I slept out of Oxford, I did not receive it till I came into Oxford at ½ past 7 next morning, as I have above stated.) Had time allowed, I should have consulted your Lordship what to do—situated as I was, I had to make up my mind for myself, and I thought it safer not to commit myself to an act, which I was not sure was right. Indeed my own judgment (as far as it is formed) is against performing the ceremony under such circumstances. I felt I could not on my own responsibility bestow the especial privilege of Christian matrimony on parties who had not taken on themselves even the public profession of Christianity (i.e. Miss Jubber. The other party is called I believe a churchman) It seemed as if an inconsistency in me to profess that unbaptized persons are 'children of wrath' and outcast from God's covenanted mercies in Christ, yet to treat them as Christians; moreover that to do so was throwing suspicion on the sincerity of my own professed belief;—and uncharitable towards those whom I had few opportunities of warning and who I believed were disobeying a solemn command of our Lord's, and making light of a condition of Christian salvation. Then when I looked to see, if the Church gave me any direction what to do, I saw that I was forbidden by the Rubric to *bury* unbaptized persons. This as far as it went seemed an indication of what was intended. I accounted for the absence of direction in the Marriage Service by considering that the Church was scarcely called upon to consider the case of unbaptized adults applying for matrimony whereas the death of unbaptized infants was a contingency plainly contemplated; and I argued that if even infants unbaptized were debarred the privilege of a mere service (the Burial,) much more should adults unbaptized be debarred the privilege of a divine ordinance, (Christian Matrimony.) And further the direction that the newly married persons should receive the Holy Communion would seem to imply that they had been already admitted to the first sacrament.— And lastly I believed that the Primitive Church was decidedly opposed both in its rule and practice to such marriages as that I was called to solemnize; and would take no part in promoting them.

How far I put all these arguments into form at the moment I read the note alluded to, I cannot tell—but I felt them more or less. And, accordingly I lost no time to calling on Mr Jubber to state to him that I must decline to marry his daughter under such circumstances; that I could not do so with my views of his daughter's state. At the same time I observed upon the suddenness of the notice, and begged him to convey to his daughter my extreme regret at having to act an apparently harsh and unkind part towards her, which it was very far from my wish to do.

I have understood since, that they betook themselves without delay to the clergyman of the parish (St Michael's) in which the other party lives—and were married by him without his knowing (of course) whether she was baptized or not, or that any thing extraordinary had happened.

I believe I have now put your Lordship in possession of all the facts of the case— and will only add in conclusion, (what however I trust I need scarcely profess) that, while I have the privilege of having a cure of souls in your Lordship's diocese, I shall ever think it my duty to obey whatever directions you may be pleased to lay upon me.

I am etc.[1]

[1] Archdeacon Clerke wrote to Newman on 16 July:

'I take blame to myself that I have not long before this time informed you that Mr Copley [the Baptist Minister at Oxford] has written to the Bishop of Oxford on the subject of Miss Jubber's marriage. His letter was very temperate, he wished to know whether there was any Statute or Ecclesiastical Canon prohibiting the marriage under such circumstances as those in which you have been so lately placed. The Bishop answered that no such Statute existed as far as he could ascertain. From the tone of his letter, I am persuaded that had there been time to have consulted him his advice would have been that you should solemnize the marriage.'

Mr Copley wrote to the *Oxford Herald* on 4 July asking the same question, and adding, 'If parties thus circumstanced are excluded from CHRISTIAN matrimony, how may they obtain *civil and legal* matrimony? Or are they excluded from this also?'

To Mr Jubber

[19 July 1834]

I am induced to write to you in consequence of your letter in this day's Journal,— without meaning that what I write should go out of your possession.—I write to you, because some where in your letter you 'appeal to me for the truth' of one of your statements—Again, at the end of your letter you speak of 'holding out the right hand of fellowship to me'—and as I have a great desire to be on good terms with every one, and I have not for a moment (I am conscious to myself) felt any anger, resentment, or other bad feeling towards you, I am prompted to avail myself of your invitation (if I may so call it) to put matters if possible right with you.

I wish you may be able to say, as truly as I have, that you have felt no resentment on your part—but the conduct *which it was my duty* to pursue, took you by surprise perhaps and put you off your guard. I assure you on my part I am sincerely sorry if in doing my duty I hurt your feelings. It is a very difficult thing to speak the truth without giving offence. If there was any thing faulty in my manner, I am sorry for it; I by no means grant there was fault, yet I hope you will believe that, if I gave you offence, I did so unintentionally.

If you knew more of a Churchman's views and principles, you would not accuse me of 'an after meaning' in the use of the word 'outcast.' Even the reference to the Catechism which I gave in my Memorandum would show you this. The one notion I have before me at the sight of an unbaptized person, is that such an one is (as far as Scripture tells us), still in the wrath of God as being a child of Adam. You may call this superstition if you will; but there is nothing of an after thought in it at least; it is a constant abiding thought with me from the beginning to the end of the year; it was the cause of my anxiety for your daughter's baptism. I repeat, if you knew more of a Churchman's feelings, you would not fancy my explanation made for the occasion. Nor would you fancy it, I think, if you knew me better than you do, for it is accusing me of something like dishonesty

I will notice a misapprehension in your letter for the sake of relieving your mind, if possible. You say that I said some of your statements were 'unfair' 'complained' of you in my Memorandum—etc. Now I complained of no one. I was misrepresented in the Herald and did but state plain facts in explanation. Much less, if you will credit me, did I think to complain of you—for, in truth, I *did not think* you were answerable for the account in the Herald. I thought you have told the occurrence to one and to another according to your own impressions of it, and it had so made its way to the paper. Read my Memorandum again, and judge calmly if there is any complaint or soreness in it. To give one instance of your misunderstanding me— you say I 'complain' ⟨in the Memorandum⟩ 'that I had not timely notice—' no such thing—I am *charged* with abruptness in telling you my intention, and I answer 'I could not help it—I spoke as soon as I was informed what was proposed—' but I never meant to blame you for not telling me sooner. I think you will see this on looking again at it.

You say I used the word 'lecture'—I positively deny it. Here again you state in *substance* what I said, but so express it, as to make me seem rude and harsh.

This was the fault I found with the Herald's report of my words—'I will not marry her for etc'—This manner of speaking to you would have been very harsh, but it was not mine. I here repeat what I said in my Memorandum, I did not use those very words, 'I will not marry her.'

Again I plainly deny what you confidently appeal to me to confirm, that I used the word 'outcast' *in leaving the room*. I used it immediately upon your speaking about *superstition*. You made your remark about superstition thrice, nearly in the same words—It was on your making it the *second* time that I said that I came not to be taught by you, but to tell you my intention—and, I think if I had not done so you would have gone on to say much more than you did. It was on your making the remark the first time, that I made the answer in which the word 'outcast' occurred; which I still say was incorrectly reported in the Herald, and made to appear *reproachful* which was not my way of using it.

I shall only say in conclusion that friendly inclined as I am towards you and those who agree with you in religious opinions, I think my greatest friendliness will be shown in speaking out what I think to be christian truth; with God's help I will ever do so, and I doubt not that, tho' I may be misunderstood and thought harsh for a while, yet in the end I shall get honor for my honesty even from those who differ from me.

Yrs etc

P.S. Should you want any further explanation, I will be here in my rooms any time you choose to call.

To Mrs Newman

⌈Sept 20. 1834. Alton[1]

I left Stevens this morning, and got here about two o'clock. As I got near the place, I many times wished I have not come, I found it so very trying. So many strong feelings, distinct from each other, were awakened. The very length of time since I was here was a serious thought, almost half my life; and I so different from what a boy, as I then was, could be;—not indeed in my having any strong stimulus of worldly hope then, which I have not now—for, strange though it may seem, never even as a boy had I any vision of success, fortune, or worldly comfort to bound my prospect of the future, but because, after fifteen years, I felt after all that I was hardly the same person as to all external relations, and as regards the particular tempering and colouring of my mind.

And then the number of painful events, and pleasant too, which have gone between my past and my present self. And further, the particular season at which we lived here, when I was just entered at Oxford, so that this place is, as it were, the record, as it was the scene, of my Undergraduate studies and opinions. The Oxford reminiscences of that time have been effaced by my constant residence there since, but here I am thrown back upon those years, which never can come again.

There are many little incidents, stored in my memory, which now waken into life. Especially I remember that first evening of my return from Oxford in 1818, after gaining the scholarship at Trinity, and my Father saying, 'What a happy meeting this!' Often and often such sayings of his come into my mind, and almost overpower me; for I consider he did so very much for me at a painful sacrifice to himself—and was so generous and kind; so that whatever I am enabled to do for you and my sisters I feel to be merely and entirely a debt on my part, a debt which he calls me to fulfil.

81

All these various thoughts so troubled me, as I came along and the prospect opened clearer and clearer, that I felt quite sick at heart. There was something so mysterious too in seeing old sights, half recollecting them, and doubting. It is like seeing the ghosts of friends. Perhaps it is the impression it makes upon one of God's *upholding* power, which is so awful—but it seemed to me so very strange, that every thing was in its place after so long a time. As we came near, and I saw Monk's Wood, the Church, and the hollow on the other side of the town, it was as fearful as if I was standing on the grave of some one I knew, and saw him gradually recover life and rise again. Quite a lifetime seems to divide me from the time I was here. I wished myself away from the pain of it. And then the excitement caused a re-action, and I got quite insensible and callous—and then again got disgusted with myself, and thought I had made a great fool of myself in coming here at all, and wondered what I should do with myself, now that I was here. Meanwhile the coach went on, and I found myself at the Swan.

I took possession of a bed room and ordered dinner etc etc.]

---

[1] The Newman family had moved to Alton in 1817 after the bank of which Newman's father was a partner had to suspend payment in the financial crisis after the Napoleonic Wars. Its creditors were soon paid in full.

To Mrs William Wilberforce

Oriel College. Nov. 17. 1834

[[not sent]]

My dear Mrs Wilberforce,

Harriet has just had a letter from you, which gives me your direction. Had I written indeed in answer to your very kind letter at once, I should have had no difficulty—but I delayed, and then doubted whether you had not left Sorrento. I delayed writing—yet it was from the great satisfaction, as well as the pleasure, your most acceptable letter gave me—I found my anxiety, as it were, rested—and as being thus at rest, I kept silent, when perhaps I ought to have acknowledged to you how pleased I was. Really, you must not suppose that I do not feel the force and influence of those parts of the Roman Catholic system, which have struck you. To express vividly what I mean, I would say, 'I would be a Romanist, if I could. I wish I could be a Romanist.' But I cannot—there is that mixture of error in it, which (though unseen of course by many many pious Christians who have been brought up in it,) effectually cuts off the chance of my acquiescing in it. I admire the lofty character, the beauty, the sweetness and tenderness of its services and discipline— I acknowledge them divine in a certain sense, i.e. remnants of that old system which the Apostles founded. On the other hand I grieve to think of our own neglect in realizing the Church system among us, which our Reformers *intended* to be ours, though we have degenerated from their notions; but after all there is that in Romanism which makes it a duty to keep aloof from it, there is a mixture of corruption, which, when seen, it is a duty to protest against—and *we* have been so circumstanced *as to* see it; and instead of shutting our eyes to it, we must feel that we are called upon to protest against it. On the other hand, instead of deserting our own Church, because its members are rebellious, rather let us rally in its defence and try to strengthen its hands. Consider the fallen state of the Jews when our Savior came, how mixed they were with the world, how political, Herod their king a man of Edom, and the Romans their great friends, yet after all did not such as Zechariah, Anna and the rest gain a blessing by quietly going on with *their own* worship as the Saints of old, in spite of the degeneracy around them? and at last they gained by their perseverance the blessing of seeing the Lord's Christ. And so we, though we are thought unfashionable and born centuries too late, may go on in our own Church as our forefathers, secure through Christ's mercy of a blessing from Him, and sure, even though He does not come in our day to make the glory of the second House greater than that of the first, yet that at least we shall be preparing the way for Him, and may be the means of bringing the blessing on our children's children, though it may be delayed.

The more I examine into the R.C. system, the less sound it appears to me to be; and the less safely could I in conscience profess to receive it. I hardly know whether to say any thing on the subject, not knowing whether I shall speak to the point; yet perhaps I ought not to be silent on the nature of my objections to it. E.g. it seems so very irreverent and profane a thing to say that our Savior's own body is carnally present on the Altar. That He is in some mysterious incomprehensible way present I fully believe; but I do not know what way—and since the way is not told us in Scripture or the ancient Fathers I dare pronounce nothing. Much less dare I be so irreverent as to determine that His flesh and blood are there as they were on Calvary. Surely He who came into the apartment the doors being shut, has ways of being there innumerable, such as we know not—We believe that now He has a 'spiritual body'—and a spiritual body may be present, the bread and wine still remaining. Therefore it seems safe and according to Scripture to say He is present *in* the bread and wine—but unnecessary and irreverent to insist on our saying that the bread and wine are *changed* into that same flesh and blood which were on the Cross.

Again the honor paid to the Saints surely is practically a dishonor to the One God. Is it not practically a polytheism? Are not the Saints the Gods of the multitude in R. C. countries? is there not a natural *tendency* in the human mind to idolatry, and shall the Church, the pillar of the Truth, cherish it instead of repressing it?

Again, after all excuses, is there not something against one's sense of right in praying to images? is there not a still small voice telling us not to do so?

Again, consider what a frightful doctrine purgatory is—not the holiest man who lived but must expect to find himself there on dying, since Christ does not remit all punishment of sin. Now, *if* Christ has promised to wipe away all guilt and all suffering upon death, what a great affront it must be to Him, thus to obscure His mercy, to deprive His people of the full comfort of His work for them!

I feel very much the weakness and poorness of these remarks—but hope you will take them as they are meant in kindness. It requires many words to do justice to them, and conversation rather than writing. I feel the R. C. system to be irreverent towards Christ, degrading Him, robbing Him *practically* of His sole honor, hiding His bounty;—i.e. so far forth as it *is* R. C.—*so far as* it differs from ours. Its high points are our points too, if it would but keep them, and not give up our jewels. But, while what is good in it is reverent, solemn, and impressive, its corruptions *practically* undo all this excellence. Surely we shall be judged according to our conscience, and if we have a clear sight of what is wrong in Rome, we must not follow our inclinations, because Rome has what is attractive in some part of her devotions. Pray excuse what I feel to be most imperfect. I wish I spoke by mouth, not by letter. Best love to the two Williams. The Revolutionary Ministry is just out—and the Duke of Wellington sent for to the King.

Ever Yrs most sincerely John H Newman

To Renn Dickson Hampden

⌈Nov 28/34⌉[1]

Dear Mr Principal,

⌈The kindness which has led to your presenting me with your late pamphlet, encourages me to hope that you will forgive me if I take the opportunity it affords to express to you my very sincere and deep regret that it has been published.[2] Such an opportunity I could not let slip without being unfaithful to my own serious thoughts on the subject.

While I respect the tone of piety which the pamphlet displays, I dare not trust myself to put on paper my feelings about[3] the principles contained in it, tending as they do in my opinion altogether to make shipwreck of Christian faith.[4] I also lament that by its appearance the first step has been taken towards interrupting that peace and mutual good understanding which has prevailed so long in this place, and which if once seriously disturbed will be succeeded by dissentions the more intractable because justified in the minds of those who resist innovation by a feeling of imperative duty⌉[5]

I am Dear Mr Principal Yours faithfully J H Newman

---

[1] [[This letter was the beginning of hostilities in the University]] and the date is underlined.

[2] *Observations on Religious Dissent* (Oxford, 1834; 2nd edn, rev. 'with particular reference to the use of religious tests in the university', 1834). Newman is commenting on the latter (a *Postscript* to which appeared in 1835). Pages 3–4 of the second edition contain the words:

'In pursuing such an inquiry, we are naturally led to consider the principle on which Christian doctrine takes its rise; that is, whether there is foundation for the common prejudice, which identifies systems of doctrine—or theological propositions methodically deduced and stated—with Christianity itself—with the simple religion of Jesus Christ, as received into the heart and influencing conduct. This point does not appear to have been attended to at all in any discussions of the subject of Christian dissent. Yet the principle here referred to, clearly involves in it the whole question of our separation into parties or distinct communions; and according to the determination of it,. our treatment of communions differing from ourselves, must essentially depend.'

[3] [[I feel an utter aversion to]]

84

[4] [[as (in my opinion) legitimately leading to formal Socinianism.]]

[5] [[The Pamphlet was H's application of his Bampton Lectures [1832] to the question of Subscription in Oxford]]

To Samuel Wilberforce

Oriel College. March 10. 1835

My dear Wilberforce,[1]

I think [a] good part of our difference in the *idea* of a Sermon, lies in this—that you think of it as much more of a totum and rotundum than I do. It seems to me abundant, to bring out one point—and to speak my mind I think that other subjects introduced have a tendency to defeat this. You will say, 'What? are we to leave a different *impression* from that of Scripture?' no—not on the *whole*. No one, who *habitually* hears me, ought to have any other than the whole Scripture impression—but any one who reads only certain 26, and much more only one or other of them, *must*. I lay it down as a fundamental Canon, that a Sermon to be effective must be imperfect. A second sermon will correct it. If indeed any passage can be pointed out, the *spirit* of which is against Scripture, that is a fair and sound objection, and thus your objection against my first is quite fair—you say, not that it is an *imperfect* view, but a view *beside*, out of, unlike Scripture—Here I join issue with you on the fact, not on the principle. But when you refer to Phil. ii, 12, 13 as the type of Scripture Exhortation, I agree with you—but it is Exhortation *as a whole*, not of every particular exhortation. Else how do you account for the Addresses to the Seven Churches? which contain not a word (I believe) of 'the doctrine of the Holy Spirit's help as a quickening and encouraging thought;' unless indeed you give over those Churches has [sic] having no 'desire of striving after holiness' and therefore reprobate. Do seriously (please) think of this instance, and see whether in singling out my viith Sermon (*which I do NOT give up to your criticism*, but wait a while) you are acting as we none of us dare act towards our Lord's address to Sardis (vid especially iii, 4) or towards St Paul's address to the Elders of Ephesus, or a thousand passages of the New Testament. I feel this as a vital principle—viz till we consent to follow Scripture in abandoning *completeness* in our Sermons, we do nothing *accurately*.

Next let me take your sentence as it stands. 'I think the entire omission of the doctrine of the Holy Spirit's help as a quickening and encouraging thought to those who are desirous of striving after holiness another instance of it' etc.

'The *entire omission*' . . . 'as a *quickening* etc. thought.' Now observe in my view the whole force of the statement lies in the word 'entire'—I mean I have already said it is my *principle*, not to bring in every doctrine every where—To that point you have not had occasion to direct your remarks—and I shall be truly obliged to you at any spare half hour to do so. But I now am finding out *where* we differ. If I have *entirely* omitted the doctrine, I have apparently transgressed my own principle (I say *apparently*, for 26 Sermons are not a Body of Divinity) and may be blamed; if not, I am within it—and our difference is, (as I am maintaining) *upon* this principle. Now then as to the matter of fact.

(1) Vid. Sermon i, (the very Sermon which most disapproves itself to you) Sermon i, p 14, 15. from 'Lastly'—vid too the text quoted, and the word 'comfort.' Serm. v. p 80 bottom. Sermon xiii, p 200 first part, here 'comfort' again—Sermon xiii, p 170.

(2) Again wherever the Holy Eucharist is mentioned there *the Spirit* is mentioned. This is what I meant, which you have not fully apprehended, when I spoke of the Sacraments being the means of persuasion. They are the embodied forms of the Spirit of Christ. And our fault at this day is, that the very *name* of them does not kindle us. And I remark that it is not very much the way of Scripture to tell us to seek the Spirit for strength, but God, or Christ, or the means of grace. I mean this is the form into which the doctrine is thrown. Take the Hebrews e.g. Now is not my book as a whole, not unlike the Epistle to the Hebrews? Suppose that Epistle was the whole of the Bible could you blame me? (As to the Priesthood and the Jewish Law that is another point) and it *is the whole of the* Bible to a preacher reproving a backsliding, cowardly generation.

Vid Sermon iii, p 41.–44. Sermon xxiv, p 372. xxvi, p 399,–401.

—But after all (in spite of particular passages about the Spirit etc) you may say that the *impression of the whole* volume is not quickening and encouraging—that it on the whole induces fear, and depression. *I grant it.* It was meant to do so. *We require the 'Law's stern* fires.' We need a continual Ashwednesday. I have already referred to the Epistle [to the] Hebrews. Take again the Exhortation in the Ashwednesday Service—see whether it does not go further than me. See if there is any thing 'quickening in *it*'—any thing free—any thing except under an 'if'. I think I could bear to be tried by it. (Vid our Tracts Number 41. Via Media ii)

Pray believe all this said mainly as explaining myself. I own indeed it would be a high gratification to me to find I could do so *satisfactorily* to you,—but my main reason is somewhat short of this—so to explain as to receive your clear and definite objections; for I am sure whether I coincide ultimately or not, I cannot but gain good from the objections of any one like yourself. I have confined myself to one point, for letter writing is endless—else I have felt quite an impatience, to say something on other things in your letters—especially your theory to account for my shrinking from the peculiars. Rightly or wrongly, *I think they tend as a body to Socinianism.* 'Is there not a cause ⟨for my earnestness⟩?'

Ever Yrs most sincerely John H Newman

P.S. I am very sorry to hear how ill you have been, and hope by this time you are recruited.

---

[1] In a long letter of 23 February Wilberforce wrote that we should trust Scripture rather than reason; and Scripture did not support Newman's tone about repentance and the length of time necessary for it. God could give repentance in an instant; the only fear would be that death-bed repentance was not real. Newman's reply explains much about his approach to preaching.

From Renn Dickson Hampden

⌈St Mary Hall June 23. 1835⌉

To the ⌈Revd Mr Newman⌉

⌈Sir,

I have ascertained to my great disgust that you are the Editor of a Collection of Pamphlets professing to be on the Matriculation-Question just put forth, and the Author of some remarks prefixed to them. I say, I have heard it with disgust: for no other feeling I am sure, is so due to the conduct of a person who can act with the dissimulation, and falsehood and dark malignity, of which you have been guilty. I charge you with dissimulation, because you have concealed your name in the background, and have only put it forward, when it was extorted through your publisher. You have been among 'the crafty firsts who have sent their silly seconds' to fight their mean and cowardly battles by their trumpery publications: you have worked the machine, but hid yourself behind it.—I charge you with falsehood, because you have sent out to the public what you know to be untrue. You have insidiously repeated the calumnies originally advanced by Mr Henry Wilberforce, both by placing his Pamphlet in the Collection, and by your own remarks prefixed to the whole—notwithstanding my indignant denial of the imputations conveyed in it. You have acted falsely again, in including Mr Sewell's Pamphlet (the only one which has any real merit) in the Collection,—when it had been expressly stipulated by Mr Sewell that Mr H. Wilberforce's disgraceful Pamphlet and any others which might be personally offensive, should be excluded. Mr Sewell, greatly to his honour (and I sincerely respect him for it) has distinctly disclaimed being a party to such a proceeding; and yet his name and authority have been shamefully applied to support the iniquitous cause. Further, the very title to your publication is false: four of the pamphlets being almost exclusively attacks on me, and the rest, little to the purpose, nothing to the defence of matriculation-subscription. I charge you with malignity, because you have no other ground of your assault on me but a fanatical persecuting spirit. I have done no wrong or unkindness to you, but on the contrary have always treated you with civility and respect. Have you (to take the lowest ground) acted towards me in the manner due from one gentleman to another? Would you have dared to act in such a way, had you not taken the advantage of the sacred profession? I should be sorry, Sir, to bear in my heart such a practical refutation of my religious views as you have evidenced by your conduct. I would readily submit to the heaviest charge of erroneous doctrine which your proud orthodoxy could bring against me, rather than exchange for your state of mind my conscious satisfaction at having neither willed, nor thought, nor done, any thing to hurt the feelings of a single person, by what I have written, or by any part that I have taken in the late question. I have been roused to resent injurious treatment, and to call improper behaviour by its right name; but I have not provoked resentment, nor have I shewn my own resentment in any other way than becomes a man, and, I trust, a Christian.

I require that your name should be put to the collection of pamphlets, as the responsible author of the several anonymous attacks,—or I may be induced to take further steps to expose to the public the shameful party-spirit which has been brought into play on this occasion. Why did you employ coadjutors, if you are ashamed of them: and why should they be ashamed to own themselves the followers of such a master?

I am your humble Servant R. D. Hampden]¹

¹ See letter of 7 August 1871 to H. Wilberforce in which Newman calls this an 'atrocious' letter (*L.D.* XXV, p. 374).

To Renn Dickson Hampden

⌈Oriel College. June 24. 1835⌉
(Copy)

⌈Mr Newman observes, in answer to the Principal of St Mary Hall's letter received yesterday, that he cannot enter at length into the details of it without doing violence to his own feelings of self respect.

He makes the following remarks by way of protesting against some of the points contained in it.

He seriously and gravely protests, first of all, against the idea implied in the following sentence; 'would you have dared to act in such a way, had you not taken the advantage of the sacred profession?' words, which he considers to convey an unjust reflection on Dr Hampden's own principles and consistency as well as his own.

He altogether disallows Dr Hampden's imputation, that he has been 'guilty' of 'dissimulation, and falsehood, and dark malignity.'

As to the charge of 'dissimulation', he observes, with reference to his having not announced himself in print as the Editor of the Collection of Pamphlets on the question of Subscription to the xxxix Articles at Matriculation now published by Mr Parker, that, although this is true, he cannot conceive that the fact of his being Editor has been 'extorted' from him, as Dr Hampden asserts, considering Dr Hampden learned it without any difficulty immediately on his inquiring.

As to the charge of his having 'concealed' his 'name in the background', he refers Dr Hampden, as far as Dr Hampden himself is concerned, to the following extract from a note on the subject of Dr Hampden's Observations on Religious Dissent, frankly addressed to Dr Hampden in November last. 'While I respect the tone of piety which the pamphlet displays, I dare not trust myself to put on paper my feelings about the principles contained in it, tending (as they do in my opinion) altogether to make shipwreck of Christian faith. I also lament that by its appearance the first step has been taken towards interrupting that peace and mutual good understanding which has prevailed so long in this place, and which, if once seriously disturbed, will be succeeded by dissentions the more intractable, because justified in the minds of those who resist innovation by a feeling of imperative duty.'

He observes also, that, while announcing himself now as the responsible Editor of the Collection of Pamphlets, he nevertheless does not mean to own, (as Dr

Hampden supposes,) nor does he feel himself called upon to own, the authorship of 'some remarks prefixed to them.'

As to the charge of 'falsehood,' as far as grounded upon his 'including Mr Sewell's pamphlet, ('the only one', as Dr Hampden proceeds to say, 'which has any real merit,') in the Collection, 'when it had been expressly stipulated by Mr Sewell that Mr H. Wilberforce's disgraceful pamphlet and any others which might be personally offensive should be excluded,' in consequence of which, 'his' (Mr Sewell's) 'name and authority have been,' as Dr Hampden continues, 'shamefully applied to support the iniquitous cause', Mr Newman acquaints Dr Hampden that Mr Sewell had the remarks on Dr Hampden's Bampton Lectures, prefixed to the volume, left in his hands *in proof*.[1]

As to the charge of 'dark malignity,' which Dr Hampden asserts to be founded in Mr Newman's case on a 'fanatical spirit,' and Dr Hampden's remark that he has 'done no wrong or unkindness to' Dr Newman, 'but on the contrary always treated' him 'with civility and respect,' he observes that he should rejoice at nothing more than a return to that state of good understanding with Dr Hampden which he has before now enjoyed, and that he shall be ever watchful and eager to discern any approach to a removal of the differences which separate him from Dr Hampden. At the same time he certainly does recognize as conceivable the existence of motives for approving or disapproving the conduct of another, distinct from those of a personal nature.

Mr Newman protests against the 'conscious satisfaction', which Dr Hampden professes himself to feel, at not having 'done any thing to hurt the feelings of a single person by what' Dr Hampden has 'written;' believing as Mr Newman does, that Dr Hampden's published statements of doctrine, running counter to received opinions, have much distressed a number of religious persons.]

[[I almost think I should have added two other protests, one against his imputing *motives* to me—the other against his calling any of the pamphlets *trumpery* etc. But perhaps this would have been too absurd.]]

---

[1] William Sewell (1804–74) was a Fellow of Exeter College. Newman sent him Hampden's letter and he acknowledged the same day that the fault was his own for not reading carefully what had been put before him.

To Richard Hurrell Froude

Oriel College. [July 20. 1835]

Ricarde Frater,

You must not be impatient that you do not see improvement in you week by week. A complaint of such long standing as yours of course will not yield in an instant. Think how great a thing it is to know, as we trust, that your lungs are all right; and how much it tells for the strength of your constitution that the ailment, whatever it is, has been stationary so long. [I should like of all things to come and see you but can say nothing to the proposal at present—being very busy here, and (to my great anxiety) being in point of finances in a very unsatisfactory state.]

But as to the Abbé.[1] I have not yet read your dialogue, as you conjecture, wishing first to set down my own sense, and then to consider it. Now this is what I mean. *N.* Scripture forbids admission into the Church to those who disbelieve its doctrines, Tradition does not. *Abbé* What? does Scripture forbid it to those who do not receive (e.g.) that David reigned 7 years in Hebron? *N.* No. I mean there are *certain doctrines* in Scripture to which it attaches this sanction, i.e. fundamental doctrines. *Abbé.* True but Tradition also has such, e.g. the Apostles' Creed. *N.* You are using Tradition in two senses. *Abbé.* I do not see it. *N.* Still so it is. The popular sense of Tradition is the voice of the body of the Church, the received system in the Church, the spirit circulating through it and poured out through the channels of its doctors and writers. Is it not so? *Abbé.* Granted. *N.* Which I may call *prophetical Tradition*, or the system taught, interpretative, supplementary, illustrative ⟨applicative⟩, of the Scripture doctrine. Now I maintain that Tradition in this sense, and this is the sense in which I contrasted it to Scripture, does not carry with it any witness of its reception being necessary for Church Communion. Its reception is the privilege of the Christian when admitted, not a condition of his admission. ⟨(Disciplina Arcani comes in here.)⟩ Even were the Tradition semper, ubique, et ab omnibus, nothing short of his public disavowal of it and teaching openly contrary to it, would justify his rejection or exclusion from the Church. All I have said then [is] that at the first blush of the matter, if any fundamentals are to be found any where *over and above the Apostles' Creed* (which both of us agree in holding fundamental for communion and about which there is no question) Scripture *is likely* to be the depositary, not tradition—Scripture being an authoritative depositary, i.e. speaking by inspiration. Tradition not. I did not use the argument for more than a primâ facie one and hastened on to others stronger. *Abbé.* But you seem to forget that the Apostles' Creed, to which you have alluded, i.e. the very series of articles which you consider to *be* the fundamentals, is received on Tradition not on Scripture. *N.* To this I answer, first it is in Scripture too, so that it is not a case in point. And if you wish me to consider the hypothetical case, I will freely confess that were the Apostles' Creed not in Scripture, and only conveyed to us by the prophetical Tradition just described, I do not see there *would* be any reason for considering its articles *the* foundation of Church communion. But here we come to the other sense of Tradition, viz that strict Traditio from one hand to another, from definite person to definite person, official and exact, which I may call *Apostolical* or *Episcopal*. I will allow to you that such a Tradition does carry its sanction with it as fully ⟨?⟩ as Scripture does—I will receive as necessary for Church Communion all the articles conveyed by it. *But I do already.* They are the Apostles' Creed, which are the fundamentals even if the Scripture said nothing about them. And if the Scripture mentioned others, there would be two sets of fundamentals; but this is impossible, else the Scripture and Church would be at variance. Therefore *no wonder* Scripture *agrees* with this Apostolical Tradition. *Abbé.* But in your letter to me, you were speaking not of the *terms of communion*, but of doctrines necessary to salvation. [*N.*] True—but it was you who began speaking of fundamentals, which to me mean *nothing else* than terms of communion. Drop the word fundamental and take the latter, and then see what I have said. I quote my words 'Perhaps you will ask, Why do you Anglicans make such a difference between the written and the unwritten word? If the belief in the one is necessary to salvation so is belief in the other.' We answer, first of all, that on the very first face of the matter, it is clear that Scripture does absolutely declare belief in its doctrines necessary to salvation, but Tradition (i.e. Prophetical) does not say so of its own ... Scripture and Tradition, taken per se, come to us in a different aspect; the one with a demand upon our faith, the other not.

Froude. But hark back. You said just now that the articles necessary for *Church communion* could not be conveyed by Prophetical Tradition; *need they be contained in Scripture?* N. Why certainly our articles say nothing on the subject; they only speak of necessary to salvation. *F.* Then why not at once maintain that Scripture warrant is not necessary for an article being in your sense (i.e. Laud's etc) fundamental?

I am reading your dialogue. First I observe that I *start with* this definition of Tradition (i.e. Prophetical) 'that which comes without sanction of its necessary importance'—and fairly, *for it is a matter of fact*; therefore for the Abbé to put the question '*Supposing* I could show that the early Christians regarded the doctrine of the Eucharist as fundamental?' is quite out of place. My answer would be, not 'No—in that case I should admit that it was fundamental, but you cannot show it—' but 'If so, Tradition would not be what *by nature* it is.' I deny that 'after I have made good my assertion that the doctrine cannot be proved from Scripture, I should *also* have to make good that the Fathers did not think it fundamental—' rather, '*since* all tradition is in matter of fact of an unauthoritative nature, an *instruction* not a *command*, I am *driven* to Scripture as a denier resource, to find there, *if anywhere*, fundamentals.'

Please to keep this letter—that I may think over it; and help me out of any puzzle, I may have got into. I cannot help thinking you have perverted my meaning in turning a primâ facie argument into a (supposed) conclusive one.

Let me hear from you soon—Thank your Father for his kindness in wishing me to come down. ⌈I am at present at the Abbé and Dionysius whom oh that I could despatch this vacation. Acland has sent a *fifth* Cambridgian to me,⌉ but he has not yet called. ⌈I am somewhat anxious lest I have gone too far in *confessing* Monastic doctrines.⌉

Ever Yrs amantissime J H N.

[1] Jean-Nicholas Jager with whom Newman had been corresponding. The correspondence led to his *Lectures on the Prophetical Office.*

To Jemima Newman

Nov. 19 1835

My dear Jemima

I called instead of answering your note, first—and since I have waited, not knowing how matters stood. My Mother has told me by a note last night.[1]

It is impossible of course I can say what I would in a few hurried words. All I know is, that, if, as the guiding of God's Providence probably will be found to lie, you resolve on what you consider in your note as possible, brother never had a greater loss, nor another a greater gain. I have been thinking, praying, dreaming of you ever since—You must be a blessing wherever you are—not the least, (if it should so be) when you are the bond of union between those who already, as friends, love each other, without tie of relationship

Ever Yrs most affectionately John H Newman

[1] Jemima Newman had become engaged to John Mozley. They were married on 28 April 1836.

To Renn Dickson Hampden

Oriel College. Febr 14. 1836

(copy)

Sir,

I am much obliged to you for your note, and the charitable spirit which it breathes. I trust that nothing but a sense of duty would have led me to publish the remarks which I left at your door this morning. It would greatly rejoice me to find that I had mistaken the language of your published works; and, should you bring this home to my conviction, I will retract the whole or any part of my pamphlet. Or again, if you will join with me in submitting the whole matter to fair and competent judges, I am willing that they should decide between us, how far you have justly incurred my remarks.

The first duty of all of us seems to be the defence of divine Truth. If without betraying its interests, I can in any way show my deference or consideration for yourself, I am desirous of being allowed to do so. Believe me, I feel much for the arduous and trying circumstances under which you have at present to act, and earnestly pray that, whatever is to follow, you may be guided to act as God would have you.

As to your particular claim on me, to alter a statement in my pamphlet, on which your eye has rested, I do not yet see grounds for admitting it. I hope I am duly impressed by your serious protestation of your belief in the Trinity and Incarnation, and beg to remind you, I have no where expressed a doubt of it. I have spoken of you only as an author, and, *as such*, you seem to lie open to my remark, for since you state in your pamphlet that an Unitarian holds 'the *whole* revelation' *as holding* 'the basis of divine facts' (vid Observ. pp 13. 19) you surely do deny that 'the truths of the Trinity and Incarnation' are 'revealed'[1]

I am, Sir Your faithful Servt J H N

[1] When it was rumoured that Hampden was to be appointed Regius Professor of Divinity in 1836, Newman wrote a pamphlet attacking his views, entitled *Elucidations of Dr Hampden's Theological Statements*. He left a copy for Hampden that Hampden acknowledged courteously, while expressing shock that he had been declared not to hold the truths of the incarnation and the Trinity as revealed (*L.D.* v, p. 235). In spite of the controversy, Hampden's appointment was confirmed.

To John William Bowden

[Oriel College. Ash Wednesday. Feb. 17/36]

My dear Bowden,

⌈I had hoped by this post to have sent you some definite intelligence about our affairs here—but after all nothing is yet decided though the Archbishop expected it would be—and the most discordant rumours prevail. Rose seems to fear we shall be unsuccessful—and if so on the ground that Hampden was made Moral Philosophy Professor after his Bampton Lectures. Now I am malicious enough to feel some amusement at this—for Gaisford and the Vice Chancellor were afraid of me as being ultra, and thought Hampden a safer man. By the bye Wood perhaps has told you— else you will be amused to hear of the following speech of Lord Melbourne's to his (W's) brother—it must not be told about of course—'Wood, how is it that in your sluggish University a College should be found, and that not a large one, which has produced so many men of unusual views. There was Whately, and Arnold—now again this Dr. H. and then again theologians too, though in a different way, Keble and Newman'.—The Archbishop fears to present our Petition as being on the verge of constitutional precedent—and, I believe, it is certain that if H. is not appointed, some moderate man, such as Denison will be Professor. Our friends have no chance. Another friend in London tells us that we are pretty safe from Hampden—and that then the affair will lie over for some time.

I do not know what to wish—we gain and lose on both alterations. If he is not appointed, we have gained a victory—and besides we are safe from the extreme annoyance and mischief which must attend the appointment. And whoever suc- ceeds, will be virtually curbed in any liberalistic propensities by our present pro- ceedings and their success. On the other hand, if H. is appointed, a headship of a Hall and a Professorship will both, I suppose be let loose—and that Keble might have a chance of the former! Again the Ministry will be at open war with the Church—the Archbishop will be roused, and a large number of waverers in this place will be thrown into our hands. Our Theological Society will increase in consequence at once. What a lucky thing it is just set up! my final scope in devising it was to restrain the vagaries of H. and such as he—but I little thought it would be so soon needed. Moreover, were H. appointed, we should be enabled to push a formal investigation into his opinions before the Vice Chancellor—and nothing would do us more good in these times than the precedent of a judicial investigation and sentence. It is said that Arnold had the offer of the Professorship before Hampden, and declined it.

When the Heads of Houses met, H. appeared too—when all stood awkward enough, the Dean of ChCh [Christ Church] broke silence by saying 'Do you mean to stop here Dr. H? we are going to talk about you?' On his answering in the affirmative, Shuttleworth asked him, if he meant to vote? he said he should be guided by circumstances—Gilbert and Symons conducted the attack. H. turned to the Vice Chancellor 'as head of the present inquisition' and told him he would find as bad things as his in the Sermons of Mr. Pusey, Newman, or Hook. He ended by voting for himself and just turning the scale thereby. He threatens to indict all 78 subscribers under the University Statute of writing famosi libelli against any one. I suppose I shall soon hear of something from him in answer to my pamphlet though that must be in other words an answer to himself, since I do but quote *him*.

I am glad to hear so good an account of your article. I luckily wrote mine (which refers to Hampden) before his appointment.] By the bye that Tract in which 'the home of Athanasius and Cyprian' occurs is mine.

I believe I have now told you all I had to say, which has not been much so I will conclude.

Ever yrs most sincerely. John H. Newman.

To Richard Hurrell Froude

Oriel College. Febr 20. 1836

My dear Hurrell,

I will only say that you are ever in my thoughts and prayers, and (by God's blessing) ever shall be—may I ever be in yours—Though you are at distance, I feel you are now with me in Oxford.

Ever Yrs most affectionately John H Newman

To Jemima Newman

Oriel College. Febr 21. 1836

My dear Jemima,

Many thanks for the news contained in your letter. It is a subject about which I have been very anxious—and I knew you would tell me if there was any thing to be told—so I waited patiently.

Thanks too, and thank also my Mother and Harriet for their congratulations upon this day. They will be deserved, if God gives me the grace to fulfil the purposes for which He has led me on hitherto in a wonderful way. I think I am conscious to myself that, whatever are my faults, I wish to live and die to His glory—to surrender wholly to Him as His instrument to whatever work and at whatever personal sacrifice—though I cannot duly realize my own words when I say so.

He is teaching me, it would seem, to depend on Him only—for, as perhaps Rogers told you, I am soon to lose dear Froude—which, looking forward to the next 25 years of my life, and its probable occupations, is the greatest loss I could have. I shall be truly widowed, yet I hope to bear it lightly.

As to Hampden's appointment, I think we might have had much greater calamities, unless it affects Pusey's health.

Should my face allow me, I shall call at Rose Hill tomorrow—which I have been hindered doing, the few times I have walked out lately.

Ever Yrs most affectionately John H Newman

To John William Bowden

⌜Oriel College. March 2. 1836⌝

My dear Bowden,

I write in a very great hurry, being just at present quite laden with business. ⌜Yesterday morning brought me the news of dear Froude's death—and if I could collect my thoughts at this moment, I would say something to you about him—but I scarcely can.[1] He has been so very dear to me, that it is an effort to me to reflect on my own thoughts about him. I can never have a greater loss, looking on for the whole of life—for he was to me, and he was likely to be ever, in the same degree of continual familiarity which I enjoyed with yourself in our Undergraduate days; so much so that I was from time to time confusing him with you and only calling him by his right name and recollecting what belonged to him, what to you, by an act of memory. It would have been a great satisfaction to me, had you known him—you once saw him indeed, but it was when his health was gone, and when you could have no idea of him. It is very mysterious that anyone so remarkably and variously gifted, and with talents so fitted for these times, should be removed. I never on the whole fell in with so gifted a person—in variety and perfection of gifts I think he far exceeded even Keble—for myself, I cannot describe what I owe to him as regards the intellectual principles [[i.e. philosophy. J H N]] of religion and morals. It is useless to go on to speak of him—yet it has pleased God to take him, in mercy to him, but by a very heavy visitation to all who were intimate with him. Yet every thing was so bright and beautiful about him, that to think of him must always be a comfort. The sad feeling I have is, that one cannot retain on one's memory, all one wishes to keep there—and that as year passes after year, the image of him will be fainter and fainter.

I trust you are all recovering your late very great affliction—particularly your Brother. I fear, when I saw you in Town, I behaved with very little sympathy—but really, when you and Mrs. Bowden spoke to me as you did, why, I felt I had no right to hear such things, said about me—and knowing how very unworthy I am, I could only be quite ashamed, and desirous to disclaim every thing you said—And this, I fear, might seem like not meeting and answering your kindness—and it distressed me very much afterwards.

We are full of our painful controversy here—nothing decisive is done—but the feeling of indignation and apprehension is, I think, growing.⌝

With kindest remembrances to Mrs. Bowden.

Ever yrs affly. John H. Newman.

---

[1] Hurrell Froude died on 28 February 1836.

To Simeon Lloyd Pope

Oriel College. March 3. 1836

My dear Pope,

I hope you will take care of yourself and get quite strong after your late unpleasant disorder—for I believe it leaves a person for a time weak and liable to sickness. It would give me great pleasure, should any thing throw us together. I am so full of business always, that I have no time to write. As to Dr Hampden, your imagination, I am sure, cannot picture any thing a quarter so bad as he really is—I do think him worse than a Socinian—In the British Magazine of this month, you will see a Pamphlet called 'Elucidations etc' stitched in, which gives you some but a very faint notion of his opinions. There is no doctrine, however sacred, which he does not scoff at—and in his Moral Philosophy he adopts the lowest and most grovelling utilitarianism as the basis of Morals—he considers it is a sacred duty to live to this world—and that religion by itself injuriously absorbs the mind. Whately, whatever his errors, is openhearted, generous, and careless of money—Blanco White is the same, though he has turned Socinian—Arnold is amiable and winning—but this man, *judging by his writings*, is the most lucre loving, earthly minded, unlovely person one ever set eyes on.

I have just had one of the greatest losses I can have in this world the loss of my dear friend Froude—I forget whether you saw him here ever.

The present state of things is miserable indeed. The Clergy are in various places getting up petitions in favor of the Archbishop and the Minister having the appointment of Bishops etc. Of course we cannot go on as we are for any long time. The Heads of Houses are betraying us in Oxford, and we mean to go any lengths in opposing them. Considering Oxford is the only strong hold of Truth in the Country, the guilt of these men, though they know not what they do, is great indeed. Shuttleworth has commenced bullying the weaker of them, and hitherto with success.

I am writing you a very stupid letter, but my heart is sad, and I cannot find what to say. By the bye one of my sisters (the younger) is going to be married to a brother of a friend of mine, of this College, whom you may have met, named Mozley.

If you wish to read an instructive and cheap work, send up for Dr Pusey's work on Baptism, which Rivington sells. I think it will interest you much—it costs about 3 shillings—and contains as much in letter press, and ten times as much in matter, as many an octavo volume.

I saw Wood lately in Town—and he talked of you. A nice fellow he is—I forget whether you have kept up your acquaintance with him.

Ever Yrs most sincerely John H Newman

To Elizabeth Newman

Iffley. May 17. 1836

My dear Aunt,

I tell you with very great pain, for I know how your affectionate heart will feel both on your own account, and for us, that my dearest Mother is taken from us.[1] If you knew how dreadfully she has suffered in mind, and how little her wanderings left her like herself, you would feel, as we do, that it really is a release. Who would have thought it! Every thing is strange in this world—every thing mysterious. Nothing but sure faith can bring us through. My dear Mother was not herself even before the end—she sank into a slumber and so died. She seemed so strong and well, it is most surprising. Little did I think, when she laid the first stone at the new Church, she would not live to see it finished.

My dear Aunt, may God Almighty preserve and keep you, and soothe and comfort you in all trouble through the grace of His dear Son our Saviour

Ever Yrs affly John H Newman

Harriet bears it very well

[1] Mrs Newman died on 17 May 1836.

To Hugh James Rose

Iffley. May 23/36

My dear Rose,

The size of my paper threatens you—I do not know how it will turn out.

Your last letter was at once very interesting in itself, and very satisfactory as tending to bring things so much to an issue. I think we very much understand each other; and, should it turn out that, on the comparison of views between us which is now practical, I have exaggerated or spoken vaguely without corresponding ideas, which I by no means deny in part, for it is very difficult to keep realities before the mind, I shall have an opportunity of speaking and thinking more guardedly in future in such respects.

You have spoken the truth, not that I would go and tell everyone at Charing Cross, I do *not* love the 'Church of England—' The Anglican Church, the old Church of 1200 or 1600 years, the Church of the builders of our Cathedrals, the Church again of Andrewes, Laud, Hammond, Ken, and Butler, (so far forth as they agree together, and are lights shining in a dark place) the Church discriminated by imposition of hands, not a tyrant's jurisdiction, I love indeed, and the later not a whit less fervently than the earlier—On Ken or on Hammond, or on King Charles, I dwell far more affectionately than on any thing before them. But I do not like that adventitious encrusted system in which they found themselves. I do not like the Church of the Reformation more than the King of the Barricades. I love the Church too as embodying the good characteristics of the English $\tilde{\eta}\theta o\varsigma$—I love it for its *human* traits as sanctified and assimilated into the substance of the Church Apostolical; but I cannot endure, except by patience and resignation, the insults of the world which she has worn now three hundred years.

In like manner I love our Church as a portion and a realizing of the Church Catholic among us—but this leads me to mourn over our separation from the Latins and Greeks, not to exult in a 'Law Church,' ⟨(of course I hold it to be the *duty* of a Christian government to uphold the Church)⟩ the creature of Henries and Williams. I cannot love the 'Church of England' commonly so designated—its very title is an offence (though it were absurd to insist on this) for it implies that it holds, not of the Church Catholic but of the State. And this is why I insisted on speaking against King William, Wake, etc. for this is *the* system under which we find ourselves, *actually* not indeed the system of the Prayer Book, but de facto; and, one shall be sure to seem to innovate, whether one does so or not, if one rises a little above it.

Now suppose one had been born 30 years sooner, I think one should have kept quite quiet. But the times will not allow of this. They force us to speak our opinion— and I cannot so economize as not to speak in *substance* what I think. Again, outward circumstances are changing, the State is deserting us—we have a *reason* for being bolder.—In saying this, I seem to myself to be tracing the principle of conduct of men like Hooker, Andrewes, and Laud—they acted *in the system* they found themselves. The single difference between their views and those I seem to follow is this—they had a divine right King—we in matter of fact have not. To this perhaps may be added a matter of expedience which does not come in at this day. The Christians of Germany and Geneva were still hopeful—and, being orthodox, it seemed hard to condemn them—this brought the 17th century into difficulties on the subject of Episcopacy. Take away these differences, and I cannot but think that Laud in this day would have approved of such advance in apostolical principles as we should advocate.

Surely it is matter of fact, the 'Church of England' has never been one reality, except *as* an Establishment. Viewed *internally*, it is the battle field of two opposite principles; Socinianism and Catholicism—Socinianism fighting for the most part by Puritanism its unconscious ally. What is *meant* when I am asked whether I love the 'Church of England?' Even granting there *was* a deliverance at the Reformation, I cannot be more than thankful for it, I cannot rejoice and exult, when it is coupled with the introduction of doctrinal licentiousness, ⟨in my opinion as bad and more like 'a brothel'⟩ Lord Chatham said we had—Popish Liturgy, Calvinist Articles and Arminian Clergy; is not this *in substance* the witness of every external impartial spectator? Is not the highest *praise* given to the Establishment, that it admits a variety of opinions? a praise which runs just in the same line. As to the Articles, luckily they are none of them positively Calvinistic, luckily what is wanting in one is supplied in another—but taking separate articles there are grave omissions, which it is a mercy have been elsewhere set right. What an account of Baptism is the 27th! and of the Church the 19th! I must say then it is 'a *happy* thing, the articles are what they are—' they are a 'port' in distress—a $\kappa\alpha\tau\grave{\alpha}\ \tau\grave{o}\nu\ \delta\epsilon\acute{u}\tau\epsilon\rho o\nu\ \pi\lambda o\hat{u}\nu$.[1] How can I love them for their own sake, or their framers!

On the other hand why may I not in my own heart deplore the hard heartedness and coarsemindedness of those, whoever they were, who gave up (practically) to the Church of Rome what we *might have* kept—so much that was high, elevating, majestic, affecting, captivating—so depriving us of our birthright that the Latins now claim it as if theirs solely. My heart *is* with Rome, *but not* as Rome, but as, and so far as, she is the faithful retainer of what we have practically thrown aside.

Now here comes your difficulty, which I have *long* dwelt on (I think) in my own mind, 'is it not dangerous to interest persons' feelings in what their judgments are against?'—I thought it might be met in two ways.

1. by strongly pointing out the impassible barriers which lie between us and Rome. This is the *intention* of our series of Tracts on Romanism. e.g. the worship of the Virgin, etc. etc.—
2. By showing that what captivates in Rome *might be ours* the minute we chose— ⟨⟨a distinct reason for insisting on this is, the advantage the Romanists take of confusing primitive customs with their corruptions—as Prayers for the dead with Purgatory⟩⟩ for there is nothing in our articles against it—and much in our great writers for it. Now comes the question *what* are these things in particular?

I do really think I agree in the main with you; and so I suppose I have spoken vaguely if you have been led to think I go much beyond you. All through Tract on Romanism Number 1 we speak of 'the English system as *at present worked*'—our additions are in the main *restorations*, recoveries of the faith of the 17th century. Do not you and I quite agree here? The Sacraments—the Holy Church Catholic etc. *are* the *substance* of these practical additions of which I have spoken. Do tell me, where I have implied any thing different from this and if it is in any thing which comes to a second edition it shall be altered.

(Next we do not know *how* things may go—and if any revolution or quasi revolution is coming on, it is well to be ready. I could just *fancy* a state of things in which a *novelty* in the Reformation Church, such as the rise of Monastic bodies, would be expedient—and if so, it is no harm to talk of it—Again the talking suggests a new ἦθος to people's minds.)

To go back—I will *mention* as instance of restoration, which we have just been enabled to begin—and which I know you have some time wished. Has the condemnation of Dr Hampden been nothing?[2] Now this tends to the very sort of *practical reform* which I would desire.

Again—a Church Council—I should be decidedly against a *Convocation* at present—but I am not so against the rudiments of a Council. E.g. were the Bishops, as a body, formally to give their sanction to any measure of the Church Commission.

Again—there are a hundred family prayer books about the land, few good. I should desire much a selection from the Breviary; were it only to show people *how much is in the book of Psalms*, of which the bulk of people have no knowledge. Why not claim the Breviary as ours, *showing historically* that the addresses to the Virgin are in matter of fact modern interpolations? This instance answers your question—'what is it precisely and distinctly which you aim to do now?' I aim at getting up a feeling towards Antiquity among the members of the Church, leaving it to work in time *on* the Church itself as Providence shall order.

Again the use of *crossing* I should think another *practical* improvement—though not expedient at this moment.

Formal Communion with the American Church would be another *most important one*—and ought to exist now.

There are two things I must say, lest you have mistaken me.

1. *Where* have I bid people search into Antiquity without guide? Where have I not told them to *build on what we have*? Where have I said that all that once was de facto Catholic is therefore binding now? Where has Pusey advocated Exorcism except on the ground of *expedience*? certainly, unless my memory fails me, his chief ground is that we have by giving it up lost a practical witness concerning the reality of the devil's power.

2. You speak of the necessity of trying to love in order to love. My dear R. if you had been years with Keble, dear Froude, and me, I think you would recollect a time when we were all bigotted (as others would say) to the Church of England. Let the Christian Year speak for K.—I will not now commit *him* by what I say—but when you read his preface to Hooker, I think you will see his *tone* is changed—not as if he loved the Mother of Saints less, but that exact measure of doctrine and rite inflicted on us by the Reformers. As to dear F.,— he was a furious Church and King Man—I do believe reading mainly opened his eyes—as to myself, it has (I may say) been my failing and got me into scrapes, my looking up to those who happened to be just over me. Thus for a while Whately and Hawkins beguiled me. Really, I boast, and with some truth, tho' one speaks broadly for an antithesis, that I was never taken in by an equal, continually by a superior. And so again with the Church of England. I have by my lectures on the Liturgy, on the peculiar doctrines of the Articles etc. and my Sermons teem with the spirit of high Establishmentism. I do not for an instant mean I had not, or K. and F., *other* principles which have occasioned our change since—only that I cannot accuse myself of not beginning, as all ought to begin, with reverence and enthusiasm towards the system I found myself in. But no more on this.

One word in conclusion—I have one and but one point of conscience, or almost of conscience. Our alterations in the Eucharistic Service seem to me *a sin*—not in us but in our forefathers. It is our *misfortune*—and I bear it resignedly, as I should the loss of a limb. Nor would I therefore, if I could, impose a Restoration of the ancient rite on our Church—for it being a sin of the Church still, in the sense of national sins etc, till the Church feels its want, repents, confesses etc, it is unworthy of the privilege. I say this as to the *practical* question. But in itself I so regard it that I never perform the Service without praying after Hezekiah's manner 'The good Lord pardon etc.' The evanescent state of the $\pi\rho\sigma\sigma\phi\sigma\rho\acute{\alpha}$,[3] the omission of the Prayer to the Holy Ghost, and of the commemoration of the dead, are defects in doctrine, looking at the matter by *Antiquity* ⟨(I fully agree with you—and Pusey—that it should not be 'the *dead*' but 'the dead in Christ')⟩—or looking at it by *Tradition* the alteration of the old form which probably came from St Peter seems so great a sin in the perpetrators, (do pardon me) that I will but keep silent and bless God we of this day are pure from it personally. To speak in confidence I even do, what others before me have done, silently make an offering and pray for the dead in Christ. Now you see on this point I am off the ground of expediency—therefore do not wonder at my pressing the doctrine of prayer for the dead in Christ; though not *on our Church*, which is not yet worthy of it, but on such among us as acknowledge and intercede for her sin. I have thought it best to be quite open towards you—Not above one or two of my friends, not even Pusey (till now) has ever heard me say this

Ever Yrs J H N

[1] 'second best'.

[2] Hampden, though appointed Regius Professor of Divinity, had had his powers limited slightly by a vote in Convocation on 5 May.

[3] Consecration in the eucharist.

To Jemima Newman, Mrs John Mozley

Oriel. June 2. 1836

My dear Jemima[1]

I must write you a hurried letter. Harriet has been somewhat in low spirits these two days—and I *think* is fussed in having to choose *where* to go first. It would be better, I see now, were she coming to you at once—but she is so unwilling to disappoint my Aunt at Richmond. The Rogers etc have asked her to come to them, and though she has declined, I think it teazed her. Write, as if from yourself, to insist on her coming to you by a certain day. Or do what you think best. Frank has written her a kind letter—I wrote to him to give up his interest at present from his share in the trust money—he will do that or what is equivalent I doubt not.

I have nothing to say except that Charles has sent an interesting letter, yet with this kind of sentence which makes me anxious 'I doubt not I shall become religious, though not perhaps in the way you would like.' I want him to come here, but am so uncertain about my own movements, I do not know how to fix a time. He is inclined to leave Chippenham.

I wish I could devise aught for Harriett—do not suppose she is unwell—she is only naturally dejected and I am anxious in consequence.

God bless you, My dear Jemima with best love to J M and remembrances to all your party

Ever Yrs affly J H N

[1] Jemima wrote on 1 June: 'I am afraid you will feel lonely when Harriett leaves, to find us all gone, as it were at once. Pray do always consider this a home, whenever you choose to make use of it. I can always keep a room for you.' Harriett was to marry Tom Mozley, John Mozley's brother, on 27 September.

To Elizabeth Newman

Derby. Oct 10. 1836

My dear Aunt,

I wished to have written you an account of the Consecration of Littlemore Chapel at the time, but I could not recollect your new Landlady—and suspended my intention till I came here and got your direction. It was in all respects a most gratifying and pleasant ceremony. It took place on the 22nd of September. The day was fine; and, it so happened, I had a party of friends from various parts; Tom Mozley and his sister, who were on their way through from Cholderton to Derby;—Henry Wilberforce and his wife—Rogers whom you may or may not have seen when you were at Oxford; and R. Williams (the son of Mr W. the Banker) who came from Dorsetshire for the purpose. Besides there was Williams of Trinity, who is Curate of Littlemore. The Bishop read the Consecration portion of the service—the Archdeacon the Gospel—I the Epistle—Williams the morning prayers—I preached. The Chapel was as full as it could hold—we had two Baptisms afterwards. The Chapel is 60 feet long by 25 broad, and 40 high.—The font is on the right side of the entrance—being the old font of St Mary's—once very beautiful with sculpture, which has been all hacked off by the Reformation or Rebellion mobs. It is very large. The pulpit is on the same side, at the upper end, close to the Altar rail. There is no reading desk, but a stand for reading the lessons from. A fourth of the area is set aside for the Altar end, or Chancel—a step rises—and then there is a broad pavement, on which is the Pulpit and reading stand as above mentioned—after another step or two, comes the Altar rail—all across the Church. The Windows in the East end are three, lancet shape, with light columns running on each side of them. Under these are seven arches with a good deal of carving, all in stone—under four of them, in the recesses, are the 10 Commandments, Creed, and Lord's Prayer. In the centre recess is a simple Cross in Alto relievo [*sic*]. The Altar is of stone with some very handsome carved work. It has a ruby coloured velvet cover at top. There are two oak chairs on each side—and an oak table for the Elements before consecration. The Walls of the Church are 3 feet thick, which gives a great depth to the windows. The Church yard was also consecrated. The Sunday after, Williams and I both officiated, and celebrated the Holy Communion. Williams has got a very nice lodging in the village close by. I quite envy him—and were it not that St Mary's Oxford is an important post, should be tempted to become Curate myself instead of him. The Chapel is dedicated to St Mary and St Nicholas—to whom the old Monastery at Littlemore belonged.—You may have heard we found skeletons, when we began to dig—to the number of 22, laid east and west—well, Dr Ingram of Trinity has now discovered that in all probability there was actually a *Church* on about the same spot on which we have built. Considering the site was taken quite at random, this is a remarkable coincidence.

You have heard, doubtless, all particulars of the marriage. Tom and Harriet are now at Oxford at Golightly's; and we suppose attended Service at Littlemore yesterday. They have been at Leamington, where H con[sulted] Dr Jephson, whom many people think a great deal of. She was much pleased with him. I go back to Oxford on Thursday, I suppose.

I hope you have been quite well, My dear Aunt, and as happy as those ought to be who are looking forward to the next world, with no hopes or fears about this, except considered as a preparation for the next

Yrs ever affectionately John H Newman

To Mr Miller

Oriel College Nov 9. 1836

My dear Miller

I fear you must have been annoyed at the delay of hearing from me; but something has occurred to interfere with the arrangement you so kindly offered about the De Sacerdotio. We have understood that Bishop Jebb translated it, or at least good part of it, and that the translation is still in the possession of Mr Jebb, the Bishop's nephew. If we find we can get his M S, considering how important it is to connect the name of so popular a writer with our undertaking, it will be no absence of gratitude towards you, to take his translation.[1] This is how the matter stands; I write to Mr Jebb tonight.

There is no news in this place except that the Irvingites have come in force—and are going round introducing themselves to the Parochial Clergy. I heard the following good story the other day. Mr Fox is keeper of the Lunatic Asylum at Bristol—another Mr Fox is Priest or 'Angel' of the Church at Bristol (Irvingite.) Two Irvingites came down to see the latter and asked for Mr Fox. They were sent to the Lunatic Keeper. On asking for him, he made his appearance. They asked if his name was Fox—he said it was. They said, 'then you are the Angel of the Church at Bristol.' Mr Fox thought a minute, looked hard at them, and answered. 'Yes I *am Angel of the Church of Bristol*—and pray walk in.' On getting them safe within he put straight ⟨strait⟩ waistcoats on them—He took them for Lunatics. Now if you have heard this story before, I shall have made a fool of myself.

With many thanks, I am, My dear Miller, Very truly Yrs

John H Newman

[1] Of Chrysostom. In the event the work was not included in the Library of the Fathers. It is not clear whether Newman's correspondent was Charles Miller of Magdalen or John Miller of Worcester.

To Frederic Rogers

Oriel: January 7, 1837.

...I am very anxious about this book.[1] I cannot conceal from myself that it is neither more nor less than hitting Protestantism a hard blow in the face. I do not say whether the argument is good or not. I need not have the better of it, and yet may hit a blow. Pusey has seen one lecture, and he said, without my speaking, that it would put people out of breath, so that they would not be able to retort; and that before they recover their wind, we must fetch them a second blow. It is curious Froude compared my letter to Arnold to a blow in the stomach; and the Bishop of Winton, the tracts, to shaking the fist in the face. I speak seriously when I say I think I shall be considered an infidel. I have not room to say why. . . .

What an egotistical letter this is!—as all mine are.

[1] His *Lectures on the Prophetical Office of the Church.*

To Mrs John Mozley

⌜St Mark's [[April 25]] 1837

What you say about my book is very gratifying [[Prophetical Office]] I hear the same in various other quarters—and it is selling very well. It only shows how deep the absurd notion was in men's minds that I was a Papist; and now they are agreeably surprised. Thus I gain, as commonly happens in the long run, by being misrepresented—thanks to Record and Co. I shall take it out in an attack on popular Protestantism. I call the notion of my being a Papist absurd, for it argues on utter ignorance of theology. We have all fallen back from the Reformation in a wonderful way. Any one who knew any thing of theology would not have confounded me with the Papists; and, if he gave me any credit for knowledge of theology or for clearheadedness, he would not have thought me in danger of becoming one. True it is, any one who by *his own wit* had gone as far as I *from* popular Protestantism, or who had been taught from *without*, not being up to the differences of things, and trained to discrimination, might have been in danger of going further; but no one who either had learned his doctrine *historically*, or had tolerable clearness of mind, could be in more danger than of confusing the Sun and the Moon.

However, I frankly own that in some important points our Anglican ἦθος differs from Popery, in others it is like it—and on the whole far more like it than like Protestantism. So one must expect a revival of the slander or misapprehension in some shape or other—and we shall never be free of it, of course.⌝

To H. E. Manning

Oriel College, July 23 / 1837

My dear Manning,[1]

I thank you for your welcome tho' sad letter—when I read it, it quite affected me, yet I cannot say why, and it seems almost taking a liberty to say that it did. We must take these things as they are sent; only be sure that you will never pass happier days in your whole life, than this awful and still time, before you lose what is so dear to you. You will feel it to be so in memory, so make much of it, and thank God. We do not feel His Hand while it is upon us, but afterwards. Have you not felt this is the case in the Church Services? These days will make your future life only happier, that is in real happiness, tho' it is so difficult to understand at the time. Everything is good and acceptable, which tends to bring us into the calm expectant state of indifference to the world, which is the perfection of earthly comfort. The thought of the dead is more to us than the sight of the living, tho' it seems a paradox to say so. I mean it has a happiness peculiar to itself, unlike and higher than any other. Do you not recollect the touching words 'Heu quanto minus est cum cæteris versari quam tui meminisse'[2]

I am writing what I know would be quite unworthy your reading were it not that I may thereby shew that I really feel for you—that I trust you do believe. I put up prayers in the Church as you desired, and will continue. Marriott who is here desires his kindest thoughts.

God bless and keep you, my dear Manning.

Yours affectionately, John H. Newman.

[1] Manning had written that his wife was dying and wrote again on 25 July, the day after her death: 'Many and heartfelt thanks for your kind letter of this morning. I hardly know what has drawn me so closely, and in one way suddenly to your sympathy, but I feel something in the way you deal with my sorrows, particularly soothing and strengthening.'

[2] 'Alas, how much less precious is it to converse with others than to remember thee!' Epitaph by William Shenstone (1714–63).

To John Keble

[Oriel. Aug 27 / 37]

My dear Keble,

[I do wish *you* would seriously think of the objection which will be made to dear Hurrell's papers,] which the Journal I shall send on Tuesday will confirm.[1] [I will put it as an opponent might.

'In these papers there is much to interest and improve the reader—but the most instructive point of view is the light it casts on a certain school of theology now rising. Here we see ten years since the workings of the minds which have there developed themselves. They are accused of Popery, they deny it; what do we see here? Here is a young man, deeply oppressed by the feelings of his imperfections etc. etc. coming to God for forgiveness, yet not a hint in his most intimate thoughts that he recollected he had a Saviour. His name is not once mentioned. On the contrary what do we hear of? "the holy and great people"—"the Saints" "the righteous men whom he would imitate;" he expresses his belief in the presence of spirits, of the departed, and Angels—etc. What is his mode of approaching God? by fasting and austerities etc—We do not hesitate [[to say]], here is Dr Pusey's system complete; and what we notice it for is to point out to the [[reader]] that it really does arise from [[is founded on a]] *practical neglect* of our Saviour. We most fully believe the deceased writer to be entirely orthodox—firmly to believe the great doctrine of the Atonement etc. but here is no real *apprehension* of this great truth, no practical adherence to Christ etc etc.—What wonder that in his later papers he actually expresses his leaning to Popery, nay his bitter hatred of our Reformers etc etc. Both then by what he omits and by what he maintains,⌉ by his blindness towards the doctrine of Xt's merits and his attachment to Popery, ⌈he shows us *what is in the mind* of such as Dr Pusey,⌉ much as *they* may disclaim against Popery, much as they may profess to receive the doctrine of justification by faith and Xt's merits.' etc etc

Now, should one in a certain sense admit all this, and say that dear H *felt* (what he did not till afterwards *intellectually know*) that there was but one Baptism for the remission of sins—that our Lord's merits were then *fully* applied—and that, after sin, he *was bound* to go to other subordinate sources for recovering lost ground? I do really think this was in his mind. When he first read the lines in the Lyra called Bondage (vii) there was that in his manner, which showed he felt them more than the writer who ought to have felt them rather.[2] But you know what passed in his mind so much more than I, that I should like your opinion on the subject. *Some* explanation I think required. I think it was his profound awe and remorse. Is mine too Roman?[3]

Tell Williams there is no occasion for him to come up.

Your brother is with you or you with him—whichever it is, my kindest thoughts to him, and all the Bisley party, if you are at Bisley. ⌈Thank you for wishing me at the Consecration, I should have much liked it. I think I am very cold and reserved to people; but I cannot ever realize to myself that any one loves me. I believe that is partly the reason—or I dare not realize it⌉

Ever Yrs affly J H N

[1] Newman and Keble were preparing to publish in four volumes Froude's *Remains*, his papers, journals, and letters, which were to prove highly controversial and divisive.

[2] Newman's poem, addressing a 'prophet', ends:

'Then plead for me, thou blessed saint,
    While I in haste begin
All man e'er guessed of work or plaint
    To wash away my sin.'

[3] Replying on 31 August, Keble wrote, 'I have read over all that you have sent, and find little or nothing to wish altered . . . If any person when they read the journal gives it the sort of construction which you have imaged out, as to the point of not making more express mention of our LORD and His Mediation, I can only say that I firmly believe it would be a most untrue surmise.'

To John Edward Bowden

Oriel College. (In my rooms, sitting opposite
the windows looking into the Quadrangle)
Jan. 17. 1838[1]

My dear John

This is not so large a letter as yours, but by writing smaller perhaps I may make it as long. Did you write the Greek word in your letter? I dare say you find Greek harder to pronounce than Latin, and the words are often longer. I shall so like to hear how you get on—but I fear you will find the irregular verbs difficult.

Love to your sisters and brother,

Yrs affly John H Newman

¹ John Edward Bowden was at this time aged eight. His father wrote on 21 December 1837, 'John insists on sending you a line—which I enclose—but you need not trouble yourself to read it, much less to acknowledge it—'.

To Mrs John Mozley

O. C. ⌈Jan 29/38⌉

My dear Jemima

I have very little to say except to thank you for your letters. Mrs Small is so much better that for weeks she has not been prayed for, and I suppose is counted well. ⌈The glass in my inner room has stood at 10° — 22° below the freezing point. I have never had it so cold for a continuance, or at all, since I have been in them⌉

As to M R G.'s [Giberne] MS, since this engagement with the British Critic has destroyed the possibility of my undertaking any thing else, I have not (being busy) looked into it.

⌈I am quite sick at the thoughts of having the British Critic but there was no one else, and I did not like so important a work to get into hands I could not trust. I do not begin with it till the July Number.¹

My book on Justification has taken incredible time. I am quite worn out with correcting. I do really think that every correction I make is for the better, and that I am not wasting time in an overfastidious way, or making it worse than it was,—but I can only say the means [[openings]] of correcting are inexhaustible. I write—I write again—I write a third time, in the course of six months—then I take the third—I literally fill the paper with corrections so that another person could not read it—I then write it out fair for the printer—I put it by—I take it up—I begin to correct again—it will not do—alterations multiply—pages are re-written—little lines sneak in and crawl about—the whole page is disfigured—I write again. I cannot count how many times this process goes on.⌉—I can but compare the whole business to a very homely undertaking—perhaps you never had it—washing a sponge of the sea gravel and sea smell. Well—as many fresh *waters* have I taken to my book. I heartily wish it were done. Seven Lectures out of 15 (say) are in the Printer's hands—Two more nearly finished. I have to write at the end a sort of Essay as an Appendix on the Formal Cause of Justification which will cost me some thought and reading.

Thank John for his letter. I suppose the *first* sheet of Lyra² has passed the Press.

Ever Yrs affly J H N

Love to Aunt

¹ The *British Critic* was a well established journal which had come to be seen as an organ of Tractarian views. However, when tensions arose between Newman and the editor, J. S. Boone, who eventually

resigned, it proved difficult to find a new editor. Newman in due course had to take the position himself and remained editor till 1841.

[2] The third edition of *Lyra Apostolica* was being printed by Henry Mozley and Sons at Derby.

To Mrs E. B. Pusey

Good Friday April 13/38

My dear Mrs Pusey

I feel much obliged indeed by your wish to entrust me with the disposal of the £50—and will gladly take charge of it.[1] Your letter is altogether most kind, far more so than I deserve. Pray believe you have been constantly in my prayers night and morning, and particularly this week again and again. Let me in turn beg you, as I do most sincerely, to forgive me if I have at any time been rude or cold to you.

Ever Yrs affectionately My dear Mrs Pusey John H Newman

[1] The £50 was a legacy which Mrs Pusey had received at the time that she first heard about the possibility of a conditional baptism. Her relief was so great that she set it aside for a while. She wrote to Newman, 'I venture to ask you to employ it, in any way you prefer, that may be to the glory of God.'

To John Keble (I)

Oriel. ⌈Aug 14/38⌉

My dear Keble,

I write to you partly for instruction, and partly as a relief—⌈I am just come away from hearing the Bishop's charge—and certainly I am disappointed in the part in which he alluded to us. He said he must allude to a remarkable development both in matters of discipline and doctrine in one part of his Diocese—that he had had many anonymous letters, charging us with Romanism—that he had made inquiries;—that as far as discipline went,⌉ (by which he meant *acts* as opposed to *writings*) ⌈he found nothing to find fault with—one addition of a clerical vestment there had been, but that had been discontinued—(alluding to Seager;⌉[1] though many persons, I doubt not, thought it meant me,) ⌈but this he would say that in the *choice* of alternatives, he had rather go back to what was obsolete in order to enforce the Rubric, than break it in order to follow the motley fashions now prevailing. Next as to doctrine (i.e. writings) he had found many most excellent things in the Tracts for the Times (this was the only book he referred to) and most opportune and serviceable—but for other words and expressions he was sorry, as likely to lead *others* into error—he feared more for the disciples than the Masters, and he conjured those who were concerned in them to beware lest etc etc.

Now does it not seem rather hard that he should publickly attack things in the Tracts without speaking to me about them privately⌉ and hearing what had to be said for them? I suppose it is such expressions as 'making the Bread etc.'[2]—else, I know not what it *can* be—⌈What good then does it do to fling an indefinite suspicion over them, when the things alluded to may be orthodox?⌉ Perhaps

I may recollect in time, but I literally do not know what he alludes to. ⌐Then again, it seems hard that those who work and who *therefore*, as men, *must* mistake, should not have those mistakes put to the score of their workings, and be thanked for that work which others do not. It is very comfortable to do nothing and criticize.⌐ It is easy to sit as many a clergyman does and shake his head and find fault—and I suppose it is wise. However, one has nothing to do with this.

What I write to you about is for advice—The Bishop means every thing that is kind, and I dare say I am making too much of it—And this is the point I am coming to.

My first impression was to take it seriously, and to write to the Archdeacon if he would wish the Tracts stopped—for if so, they should be. Then I thought, that I should be writing something else; so that that would do no good; and I did not see my way to promise to write nothing, at a time when the Faith is in jeopardy; though I confess nothing would be more pleasant to my feelings if it was right to do it, than to retire into myself and to set about reading without writing. I have long wished it. Then I thought whether I should ask him what the things were he objected to in the Tracts—but my difficulty there was, what if it was the phrase I have above alluded to—*could* I, salvâ integritate fidei, withdraw it—and if I could not, should I not have made matters worse? then again supposing it was Pusey's remarks about exorcism, or penance etc? or supposing he were to turn round and say, 'Well then, discontinue turning to the East' etc etc?—or 'do not publish more of the remains'? and moreover might I not oblige him against his will to say more and command more than he intended, *in order* to give his words a definite and consistent meaning?

I am led then secondly to treat the matter *not* seriously—to consider that the Bishop having several times done Pusey marked favours, ordaining James Mozley etc and letting me dedicate my book to him, has been *forced* to say something, conniving at us all the while—and that it is unkind and unwise to make him commit himself to a meaning—that all I have to do therefore is to go on just as usual—and to take it as one of those rebukes one reads of in history, which are like a smack in the face and nothing more. Other persons probably would be disappointed the other way. If Cornish thought it for us, how much more open enemies? (At the same time, I saw by their faces our men were disappointed.) The Bishop having given us a hit, now the debt is on his side—and on the strength of it he may be kind to us again.

These are the thoughts which have passed through my mind—I dare say I shall be well tomorrow—but it is disheartening to be snubbed, while persons who do nothing, may look wise and say 'Yes, that's it—you go *too far*—the Bishop has just hit the thing—we approve of a great deal etc—' without being able to point out what they *mean*, or knowing more how to go *any* 'far,' 'too' or not, than to command a squadron of horse.

Ever Yrs affly John H Newman

P.S. A stranger has made me a present of an autograph letter of Butler to Clarke dated Oriel

---

[1] Charles Seager, a pupil of Pusey's and an ardent Tractarian, had worn a cross on his stole for a time.

² The first edition of Newman's *Tract* 10 contained the words, 'as intrusted with the awful and mysterious gift of making the bread and wine Christ's Body and Blood', which some had read as equivalent to transubstantiation. In later editions the words were softened to 'the awful and mysterious privilege of dispensing Christ's Body and Blood.'

To John Keble (II)

⌈Aug 14/38⌉

My dear Keble

⌈You will perhaps think me fidgetty not to wait for your answer to my letter of today, but as despatch will be requisite if I adopt the following plan, I write at once by coach.

It seems to me that my course is to send the Archdeacon [[Clerke]] a short note to the following effect—that I was glad to find he approved of some things in the Tracts [;] I am sorry to hear for the first time that the Bishop thinks some parts of the Tracts for the Times of unsafe tendency—that I do not ask which parts he means, because in his Charge he pointedly declined any thing like controversy to which such a question might lead—that he gave his opinion as a judgment and as such I take it—that under such circumstances it would be very inconsistent in me to continue the publication of these Volumes with this general suspicion thrown over them by my Bishop—accordingly I now wrote to say that if he would specify any Tracts which he wished withdrawn from publication, nay if he said all of them, I would do so forthwith—that I should not like to suppress *parts* of Tracts, that might be unfair to the writers—however, that I must except numbers 67 and following and number 82 [81] (they are Pusey's) over which I had no control. Also, that there were a few others which⌉ were published in another shape, and so far ⌈were not my property—but which should not be published in the Tracts,⌉ if they were in the number of those objected to.'

⌈By doing this I think I set myself right [[with him]]. I really cannot go on publishing with this censure against them.⌉ I do not think the pecuniary loss will be great, ⟨⟨could we not ship them off to America?⟩⟩ except in the Tract on the Breviary which I fear would be one of those selected. ⌈And if he ordered some to be suppressed, the *example and precedent* I am sure would be worth ten times the value of the Tracts [[suppressed.]]⌉ likely to be selected. ⌈Unless you think this quixotic, I am disposed very much to do it⌉

Ever Yrs affly John H Newman

⌈P.S. Since writing this the idea so grows on me of the absolute impossibility of going on with the Tracts with the Bishop saying parts are dangerous⌉ as received by others, ⌈that if I do *not* write thus to the Bishop, I certainly *must* cease them.⌉

P.S. I suspect it is a general impression that it is a snub.

To Archdeacon Clerke

Oriel College, August 16. 1838

My dear Archdeacon,

If there was any one else I could write to, I would do so; as I am unwilling that this letter should have at all a formal air, or be a call for a formal answer. I would not have written it to one like yourself officially attached to the Bishop; but I know no one else near enough to him to be of service to me; and therefore I must trouble you against my will.

In his Charge the other day he said, that there were things in the Tracts for the Times, of which I am Editor, which might do harm to certain minds. He did not specify what things; in consequence, as you will easily perceive, a general suspicion is made to attach to them as containing something dangerous in one part or another. There is no part of the work from beginning to end which escapes such suspicion.

I do not write this on the spur of the moment, but have thought over what I am going to say. As far then as I can at present judge, I say with great sorrow that it is quite impossible for me to continue the Tracts with this indefinite censure upon them from my own Bishop. It is repugnant to my feelings, as well as to my principles, to do so. Considering what the subjects discussed in the Tracts are, I feel it to be clearly my duty to withdraw from the position in which I now find myself,—that of being the author of works which have attracted the public notice of the Bishop. As matters stand at present, I think it my duty, much against my will, to discontinue the Tracts and to withdraw, as soon as may be, the existing volumes from circulation.

I do not think that in so acting I am influenced by any undue sensitiveness; I do not rely on my own view of the case only. A Bishop's lightest word ex cathedrâ is heavy. His judgment on a book cannot be light. It is a rare occurrence.

It has struck me, (and this causes me to write to you) that there is one way in which I may escape what is very disagreeable to me. I do not ask to know any particular passage which the Bishop disapproves; because he said he did not wish to be supposed entering into the controversy, which I take to be an intimation that he wishes to avoid discussion. But if I could learn from you, as a friend, not as Archdeacon, which are the Tracts which he disapproves, (which I most honestly say that I do not know) I will at once withdraw them without a word, and shall be saved the necessity of suppressing the rest;—that is, I will withdraw any of them, except two over which I have no control, the Tract on Baptism and No. 81.

With the best expressions of my gratitude to the Bishop for the kindness he has so often shown me, not without some feeling of pain also, now expressed for the first and last time, that the first notice I should have of his dissatisfaction with any part of my writings, should be on so solemn and public an occasion,

I am, etc. J.H.N.[1]

---

[1] Archdeacon Clerke replied on 18 August that he did not know what details of the *Tracts* the Bishop had in mind.

To Richard Bagot, Bishop of Oxford

Oriel College. Aug 21/38

My dear Lord,

I am very much obliged by your Lordship's kind letter, and will most certainly take the course you recommend, of waiting till the Charge is printed.[1]

It has ever been my wish to approve my words and acts to your Lordship's judgment. I know indeed that, among any persons whatever there must always be differences of view in minor matters, whether relating to points of expedience, or of opinion, or to modes of speech; and I have interpreted your Lordship's ordinary silence, as regards the Clergy generally, as an intimation that you allowed that difference, and that, whether in such details your judgment lay this way or that, you did not think them of importance enough to prescribe to us any particular course respecting them. But I have ever considered also, that you had at any moment the power of setting bounds to this liberty; and that the formal expression of your feelings in any matter ought to be my rule. As to the Tracts, in so large a work, there must be, I am quite sure, very much of human infirmity, much incorrectness both of thought and expression. This must be the case any how, whatever was the nature of such imperfections but your Lordship's alluding to them in your charge has of course pronounced upon their importance,—and for that reason, and because it is my duty to obey you, and from a reluctance to appear to others, particularly to those who differ from me, to be transgressing the bounds of speech which you prescribe, and from a feeling of the inconsistency there would be between such conduct and the professions of the very Tracts which would give rise to it, I felt it impossible to entertain the idea of allowing them to continue the object of your Lordship's remarks if I could hinder it. A withdrawal of them in whole or part seemed both to observe my duty to you and to avoid discussion. And I hope you will believe what I trust I may say quite sincerely, that I shall feel a more lively pleasure in knowing that I am submitting myself to your Lordship's expressed judgment, in a matter of this kind, than I could have even in the widest circulation of the volumes in question.

I will not but answer your Lordship's question. The impression that I carried off from the Charge was this:—'that as to the Tracts for the Times, fully believing the sincerity of the writers, your Lordship still thought they contained expressions which in the case of minds peculiarly constituted might produce injurious effects; that you were apprehensive of the scholars more than of the masters; but that the chance of the effects alluded to led you seriously to warn the latter to weigh their words and to consider what might come of them.'—

Let me express once more my sense of the kind anxiety which your Lordship shows in your letter to consult my feelings and let me assure you that I am, with great sincerity

Your Lordship's faithful and obliged Servt J H N

---

[1] In the Charge as printed, p. 21, the Bishop added this footnote to his remarks about the *Tracts*:
'As I have been led to suppose that the above passage has been misunderstood, I take this opportunity of stating, that it never was my intention therein to pass any *general censure* on the Tracts for the Times.

There must always be allowable points of difference in the opinions of good men, and it is only where such opinions are carried into extremes, or are mooted in a spirit which tends to schism, that the interference of those in authority in the Church is called for. The authors of the Tracts in question have laid no such painful necessity on me, nor have I to fear that they will ever do so. I have the best reasons for knowing, that they will be the first to submit themselves to that authority, which it has been their constant exertion to uphold and defend. And I feel sure, that they will receive my friendly suggestions in the spirit in which I have here offered them.'

To E. B. Pusey

In fest SS. Trin. [26 May] 1839

My dear Pusey

This, you will see, requires no answer. I have nothing to say—only I wish you to remember that many persons are thinking of you and making mention of you, where you wish to be mentioned. Do not fear you will not be strengthened according to your day. He is nearest, when He seems furthest away. I heard from Keble a day or two since, and he wished me to tell you they were thinking of you at Hursley. This is a day especially sacred to peace—the day of the Eternal Trinity, who were all blessed from eternity in themselves, and in the thought of whom the mind sees the end of its labours, the end of its birth, temptations, struggles, and sacrifices, its daily dyings and resurrections[1]

Ever Yrs most affly John H Newman.

[1] Pusey's wife, Maria, died this day and Newman preached his sermon, 'Peace in Believing' for the first time on this day (cf. *P.S.* VI, pp. 369–70).

To Mrs J. W. Bowden

Oriel College May 27. 1839

My dear Mrs Bowden,

Manuel will tell you the particulars of Mrs Pusey's release.[1] It is a great relief. Pusey was being worn out. Now he may and must take care of himself. She died without any pain, and was sensible almost to the last. His Mother is here.

The little girls came up for some days the week before last—they sent them away again, for fear of the health of Lucy, the eldest, who took to heart her Mother's illness very much.

It is now 21 years since Pusey became attached to his late wife; when he was a boy. For 10 years after he was kept in suspence; and 11 years ago he married her. Thus she has been the one object on earth in which his thoughts have centered for the greater part of his life. I trust and earnestly hope he will be supported under this heavy blow. He has not realized till lately, that he was to lose her.

We are to have a gathering here on June 5, on a very unpleasant matter. Manuel will tell you particulars.[2]

I hope today is bringing a change of weather, which will be favorable to John. Give him my love. I should rejoice indeed in the prospect of coming to Roehampton, but do not know my plans yet.

I grieve to hear they have some anxiety about Charles Thornton's lungs. What a world of change this is.

My love to the children. I take Emily's wish as a particular compliment, considering how select she is in her friendships.

Yours most sincerely John H Newman

[1] Manuel Johnson was John Bowden's cousin, who was appointed Radcliffe Observer in 1839 and developed the Observatory during the next twenty years. He and Newman remained always good friends.
[2] There was to be a vote on the Readership in Logic (cf. *L.D.* VII, pp. 85, 89–91).

To H. E. Manning

Oriel College. Sept 1. 1839

My dear Manning,

I feel very anxious about such a case as you mention; from the consciousness that our Church has not the provisions and methods by which Catholic feelings are to be detained, secured, sobered, and trained heavenwards. Our blanket is too small for our bed. I say this, being quite in the dark as to the particular state of mind of your friend—and how she has come into it. For ourselves, I am conscious that we are raising longings and tastes which we are not allowed to supply—and till our Bishops and others give scope to the development of Catholicism externally and visibly, we *do* tend to make impatient minds seek it where it has ever been, *in* Rome. I think that, whenever the time comes that secessions to Rome take place, for which we must not be unprepared, we must boldly say to the Protestant section of our Church—'*You* are the cause of this. You must *concede*—you must conciliate—you must meet the age. You must make the Church more efficient—more suitable to the needs of the heart, more equal to the external pressures. Give us more services—more vestments and decorations in worship—give us monasteries—give us the "signs of an Apostle—" the pledges that the Spouse of Christ is among us. Till then, you will have continual defections to Rome.'

This is, I confess, my view. I think nothing but *patience* and *dutifulness* can keep us in the Church of England—and remaining in it is a test whether we have these graces.—If then your friend is attracted to Rome by the exercise of devotion etc which it provides, I should press on her the duty of remaining in the calling in which God has found her, and enlarge upon the doctrine of 1 Cor vii. Also I think you must press on her the prospect of *benefiting* the poor Church, through which she has her baptism, by stopping in it. Does she not care for the souls all around her steeped and stifled in Protestantism? How will she best care for them, by indulging her own feelings in the Communion of Rome, or in denying herself and staying in sackcloth and ashes to do them good? Will she persuade more of her brethren by leaving them or by continuing with them? Is she unmarried? is there any chance of making her a 'Mother Superior'?

If, however, she takes the grounds of *distrusting* the English Church, doubting its Catholicity, and the like, then I suppose you must retort with the denial of the Cup—the doctrine of Purgatory as *practically* held—the (non-) *evidence* of the Church's Infallibility—the anathema etc. with the additional reflection that she is *taking a step*, and therefore should have some abundant evidence on the side of that step. (And ought one not seriously to consider whether accidental circumstances have not determined her—disgust at some particular thing, faith in some particular person etc?) That step is either a clear imperative duty or it is a sin. On the other hand can she deny that the hand of God is with our Church, even granting *for argument's sake* Rome has some things which we have not. Is it dead? has it the signs of death? has it more than the signs of disease? has it not lasted through very troublous times? has it not from time to time marvellously revived when it seemed to be losing all faith and holiness? is it to be *given up*—for her step would be giving it up—would be saying 'I wish it swept away and the Roman developed in its territory—' not 'I wish it reformed—I wish it corrected—I wish Rome and it to be one.'

I have written you a most pompous letter on general τόποι[1]—but since I do not know any thing in particular, I can but preach to you.

As to young Christie, he is just beginning to work hard at Theology for me—very unwilling should I be to give him up—yet if it be for his interest, as it would seem, I must do so.[2] I must ask you some questions which I should like you to answer. 1. *when* would he have to come. He is not 22 yet. would it do when he took orders? ⟨(is he not too young for you?)⟩ 2. would all his time be taken up—for he is a very apt reader, which is a rare commodity. His talents would be wasted on a Secretary-ship. 3. Would it lead to any thing—for, you see, he gives up standing for a fellowship etc. 4. has he any lodgings, parsonage house etc.

Ever Yrs affly J H N

P. S. Pray give my best thanks to Mr Anderdon for his kind letter—As it crossed mine, I did not answer it.

---

[1] 'considerations'.

[2] Manning had suggested Albany James Christie for the post of Secretary of the recently founded Chichester Theological College. Christie (1817–91) had entered Oriel in 1835 and was to be elected a Fellow in 1840. He was a more extreme Tractarian, joined Newman at Littlemore in 1845, and was received into the Catholic Church in October the same year. He became a Jesuit.

Under Siege
(1839–43)

Confident in the cause he was championing, Newman returned to reading the Fathers at his leisure during the Long Vacation in 1839. That September he was shown an article written by Nicholas Wiseman on the Anglican claims, but he paid it little attention at first until one friend, Robert Williams, pointed out to him some words of St Augustine's, quoted by Wiseman, 'Securus judicat orbis terrarum'—the judgement of the universal Church is certainly true. By those words, Newman remarked later, 'the theory of the Via Media was pulverized'.[1] At the time he told Frederic Rogers the article gave him 'stomach-ache'. He felt the force of Wiseman's argument: those who separate from Rome are in schism. As the pressure grew, he seemed to be under siege. His correspondence during these years was taken up largely with the events that gradually were overwhelming him. He was receiving letters from all quarters.

In 1841 he attempted to shore up his position by writing *Tract 90* which proved to be the last of the *Tracts for the Times*. There he examined some of the more obviously anti-Catholic of the Thirty-Nine Articles, arguing that they were nevertheless patient of a Catholic interpretation: as the Articles had been drawn up before the Council of Trent had finally ended, they could not be regarded as simply opposed to the Council; and as, moreover, they were drawn up to include Catholics, 'Catholics now will not be excluded'.[2] He did not expect the Tract to receive much attention, but it did. The Heads of Houses at Oxford censured it as evasive and inadmissible. Although kindly, Bishop Richard Bagot of Oxford also expressed his regret at the Tract's publication and asked Newman not to discuss the Articles further and to discontinue the series. Newman agreed. But when soon afterwards the Bishop went further and requested that the Tract be withdrawn and not reprinted, Newman refused because to do so would seem to concur with the censuring of his view. On both those fronts, University and bishop, Newman found himself defending the position he had set out.

Then from a different viewpoint there was correspondence with those who were drawn to Rome and asking Newman's advice. Time and again he sought to dissuade them. He wrote typically to W. C. A. Maclaurin, 'I really do think that God does not require any one of us, however moved to do so, to go over to Rome by himself.' And then there was correspondence with Wiseman himself, now back in England as

---

[1] *Apo.*, p. 117.   [2] *V.M.* II, p. 348.

a bishop, who took Newman to task for using expressions that might be painful to Roman Catholics. Newman expressed his regret at causing pain, but answered robustly that he too was pained when Catholics held Anglicans 'to be heretics and schismatics'. He also wrote Wiseman a letter which he did not send in fact, about scandal and corruption in the Roman Church, asking why the Church of Rome did not confess these failings. 'It is little men who are jealous about themselves', he observed, 'and defend their conduct at every point; but a Church with such claims surely need not be loth to be candid when speaking of its private or individual members.'

With the pressure on him becoming more intense, Newman was forced to consider his own position as Vicar of St Mary's more closely. He discussed the matter particularly with Keble. He hoped to be able to resign St Mary's, but remain as Vicar in the village of Littlemore on the outskirts of Oxford. It was a part of the University parish that he had taken time to develop. But his hope was denied.

Soon afterwards to his surprise and consternation, the bishops, one by one, attacked *Tract 90*. Newman had understood that, as it was to be allowed to go out of print, it would be ignored. But now his position was being repudiated by the very people whose ministry was fundamental to the case he was supporting. And then came a further blow when a plan was put forward to consecrate a Bishop for Jerusalem, an Anglo-Prussian post, to be held alternately by an Anglican and a Lutheran or Calvinist. Newman recoiled from the scheme. While he was arguing that the Church of England was a branch of the Catholic Church, this plan identified Anglicanism as another Protestant denomination.

Although there are warm family letters in this period and a reconciliation with his brother, Francis, other relationships were becoming strained, notably his friendship with Frederic Rogers, which would not be resumed for another twenty years. Then his sister Harriett came to believe that Newman had been trying to persuade her husband, Tom Mozley, to be received as a Roman Catholic. Although she was entirely mistaken, this conviction led to a break between them that still had not been healed when Harriett died in 1852. And he was made more anxious as the health of the closest friend of his Trinity days, John Bowden, deteriorated rapidly.

In September Newman resigned as Vicar of St Mary's and preached his last Anglican sermon, 'The Parting of Friends', at Littlemore. He then retired to live in the cottages that he had acquired there, to ponder his future. A letter from Manning, intended to persuade him to stand fast in the Church of England, had, if anything, the opposite effect: 'It makes me realize my views to myself, it makes me see their consistency'.

3

Under Siege (1839–43)

To Frederic Rogers

Oriel College: September 22, 1839

Since I wrote to you, I have had the first real hit from Romanism which has happened to me. R. W. [Robert Williams], who has been passing through, directed my attention to Dr Wiseman's article in the new Dublin.[1] I must confess it has given me a stomach-ache. You see the whole history of the Monophysites has been a sort of alterative,[2] and now comes this dose at the end of it. It does certainly come upon one that we are not at the bottom of things. At this moment we have sprung a leak, and the worst of it is that those sharp fellows Ward[,] Stanley and Co will not let one go to sleep upon it. Curavimus Babylonem et non est sanata[3] was an awkward omen. I have not said so much to any one but C. who came in the other day, seems quite prepared to leap, only he says he is not to be the first. As to B.[4] I tried him the other day. Someone was talking of some disorders or inconsistencies in Rome. I said. 'You see, B. there is not perfection in Rome'[.] He answered in his gravest way shaking his head. 'No.' I pushed my advantage. 'Not *even* in Rome.' 'No, No, indeed' still shaking his head. I seriously think this is a most uncomfortable article on every account, though of course it is ex parte. How are we to keep hot heads from going over? Let alone ourselves. I think I shall get Keble to answer it—as to Pusey I am curious to see how it works with him.

And now Carissime, good bye. It is no laughing matter. I will not blink the question, so be it; but you don't suppose I am a madcap to take up notions suddenly. Only there is an uncomfortable vista opened which was closed before. I am writing upon *first* feelings.—

---

[1] 'Tracts for the Times: Anglican Claim of Apostolical Succession', *Dublin Review*, VII, 1839 (August), 139–80. Robert Williams (1811–90) had been a pupil of Newman's and became a friend. He was for a while an ardent Tractarian, but later became more Evangelical.

[2] 'medicine, treatment, that alters process of nutrition', *OED*.

[3] *Jeremiah* 51:9: 'We tried to heal Babylon, but she could not be healed.'

[4] These abbreviations may refer to Robert Williams and Arthur Acland who had visited Newman on 19 September.

To John William Bowden

⌈Oriel College. Nov. 4. 1839⌉

My dear Bowden,

I have written you a letter, and find it is too heavy for the Marseilles post—so I begin again. We have heard with great pleasure of your safe arrival at your destination; and I congratulate you on your progress towards health and strength, and Mrs Bowden on the miseries of the voyage being over.

⌈The chief thing I have to tell you concerns Morris of Exeter, whom perhaps you know, perhaps not.[1] He is a most simple minded conscientious fellow—but as little possesst of tact or common sense as he is great in other departments. He had to take my Church in my absence; I had not been one Sunday from Oxford till lately since October 1838. I had cautioned him against extravagances in St Mary's Pulpit, as he had given some specimens in that line once before. What does he do on St Michael's day but preach a Sermon, not simply on Angels, but on his one subject, for which he has a monomania—of fasting, nay and say it was a good thing, whereas Angels feasted on festivals, to make the brute creation fast on fast days. So I am told—May he (salvis ossibus suis) have a fasting horse the next time he goes steeple chasing. Well this was not all. You may conceive how the Heads of Houses, Cardwell, Gilbert etc. fretted under this—but next Sunday he gave them a more extended exhibition quid posset. He preached to them totidem verbis the Roman doctrine of the Mass, and, not content with that, added in energetic terms that every one was an unbeliever, carnal, and so forth, who did not hold it. To this he added other speculations of his own, still more objectionable. This was too much for any Vice Chancellor—In consequence he was had up before him—his sermon officially examined—and he formally admonished—and the Bishop written to. Thus the matter stands at present—The Bishop is to read his sermon—and I have been obliged to give my judgment on it to him—which is not favorable, nor can be. I don't suppose much more will be done but it is very unpleasant. The worst part is that the V. C. has not said a single word to me, good or bad, and has taken away his family from St Mary's. I cannot but hope he will have the good sense to see that this is a mistake. I wish all this kept secret, please, for it is not known even here.

...⌈The authorities of this place are said to have returned very much frightened about the spread of Apostolicity—but they cannot stop matters here. The only fear is of persons going too far. You should read the late article in the Dublin—it is the best thing Dr Wiseman has put out. It is paralleling the English Church to the Donatists; and certainly the parallel is very curious—the only question is whether Augustine's notions are Catholic on this point—he certainly does seem to make for Dr W.—The papers say that the question of mixed marriages is coming on in Russia—and that the Emperor has sent off the Catholic Clergy to Siberia. Other accounts (improbable) are that 4.000.000 Catholics have gone over to the Greek Church. There was a curious document in the papers the other day in the shape of a firman of the Porte[2]—I was struck by observing that it called the Romans and not the Greeks Catholics.

... We have fixed on the patterns for the painted glass at Littlemore, and I think they will be very beautiful.

My sister Harriet has just got a little girl.[3] She was born on All Saints day. I heard of it yesterday morning, and all was going on very well. ⌈Sewell is to give me the Plato article for next number of the British Critic and I expect it will be a very good one. The last number is reckoned one of our best.⌉

This is a most dull stupid letter, not worth the postage—still you may like to hear, even if it is to know that Oxford stands, where it did.

With kindest remembrances to Mrs Bowden and the children.

Ever Yrs affectionately John H Newman.

P.S. I thought to have sent you a letter by one of Rogers' brothers—but he is not going. ⌈P.S. In the Christmas B.C.⌉ we shall have a review of Keble's Psalms ⟨⟨Williams'⟩⟩—a paper on the Greek Church ⟨⟨T. Mozley⟩⟩, and ⌈I have thought of writing an indirect answer to Dr Wiseman's article.⌉

[1] John Brande Morris (1812–80) was a rather eccentric Fellow of Exeter College who became a Catholic in 1846 and was ordained a priest in 1849.

[2] i.e. an edict of the Sultan of Turkey.

[3] Grace Mozley, his niece, who was to visit him on 9 August 1890, two days before he died.

To Francis William Newman

Littlemore April 11 [1840]

My dear F

I write to you with much pleasure in consequence of a letter which Aunt N has sent me by this morning's post

What I have lately heard of you, which I regret to say has been of late years but little, has led me to ask whether the cause which had occasioned my separating myself from your society some years since were not removed. That cause was, as I think you know well, my feeling that you were heading a separation from the Church, presiding or preaching at Meetings, and the like.[1] And I need scarcely add that I have never considered such cause as a reason for interrupting any but *friendly and familiar* intercourse with you; though, since you were displeased with my letter to your wife in January 37 or 38,[2] all intercourse whatever has ceased to my great sorrow;—so much so, that a letter I wrote to you about a year since, not indeed requiring but admitting an answer, did not receive one from you.

Do not suppose that in saying this I am complaining of you; I am only unwilling you should not do me that justice, which I wished to do you. The conduct of mine at which you took offence had nothing in it for which I can reproach myself. I had been most anxious to be delicate and considerate throughout, as my conscience bears me witness. I meant nothing at all of what you imputed to me. I had no notion of offending you. But to return.

In consequence of what I lately heard I wrote to my Aunt N. and have just received her answer. She says in answer to my asking whether you preached or conducted service, 'In regard to F. I believe I may venture to say that he does nothing of the kind. I generally knew his movements every day, and I never heard of any thing of the kind. Indeed from my observation and from the conversation we frequently had, I do not think he accords in opinion with any of the Sectarians around him, although he attends Broadmead meeting'[3]

From what she adds I suppose this '*has* been the case some time'; but, when you consider the little I hear of you, and that Dean Moberly,[4] and others with whom I have talked, know nothing of you, you will not be surprised that I did not know it before. I do not deny that I might have taken more pains about it—but my mind has been occupied with many subjects.

It is plain however from this account that all reason for my separating myself from your company is at an end; which is to me a most exceedingly great relief. Should any thing ever bring you this way I shall at all times be glad to see you—and should I come to Bristol, I certainly would make trial whether or not you would receive me.

And now, before concluding let me express to you, my dear F. what is no great thing to say, my own consciousness of much infirmity in the *details* of my conduct towards you. In saying this, you must ⟨do⟩ not suppose that I have changed my mind at all in regard to *principles*; or as to the *mode* in which persons should be dealt with who are what you were. I think as I did; and have acted quite lately towards a Roman Catholic clergyman, as I did to you, though not precisely on the same grounds.[5] But I am very sure that in my manner and my tone there was what there should not have been; and, to go back to earlier times, I quite confess that especially in the years 1821–1822 and later, I did not behave to you with that habitual meekness which was likely to inspire confidence in you towards me.[6] I was very sorry for this at the time, but still that does not alter facts.

Be sure that you are ever in my prayers and believe me
Yrs affly J H N[7]

---

[1] See letter of 23 November 1835 (*L.D.* v, pp. 166–7). Francis Newman later wrote: 'My brother was taking a position, in which he was bound to show that he could sacrifice private love to ecclesiastical dogma; and upon learning that I had spoken at some small meetings of religious people, (which he interpreted, I believe, to be an assuming of the Priest's office,) he separated himself entirely from my private friendship and acquaintance . . . In my brother's conduct there was not a shade of unkindness, and I have not a thought of complaining of it . . . I had, however, myself slighted relationship in comparison with Christian brotherhood;—*sectarian* brotherhood, some may call it', F. W. Newman, *Phases of Faith: or, Passages from the History of my Creed* (6th edn, London, 1860; repr. with an introduction by U. C. Knoepflmacher, Leicester, 1970), pp. 34–5.

[2] See *L.D.* VI, pp. 15–16.

[3] The 'historic Baptist chapel' in Bristol.

[4] George Moberly and Francis Newman had both been elected Fellows of Balliol in 1826 and had become friends.

[5] In January Newman had refused an invitation to have dinner with Fr George Spencer (1799–1864), who became a Passionist in 1847 and took the name Ignatius (see the letter of 8 January 1840 to Frederic Rogers, *L.D.* VII, pp. 205–6).

[6] See *A.W.*, pp. 174–89, for Newman's confessions of ill temper towards Francis.

[7] Francis Newman's reply on 15 April 1840 was warm and friendly, as was Newman's the following day (*L.D.* VII, pp. 307–10).

To Mrs John Mozley

Oriel ⌈Ascension Day May 28/40⌉

My dear Jemima

I am rejoiced to see your handwriting, just now received—Nothing could be more pleasant, than to come and see you, while Tom and H. are at Derby; but I cannot promise for myself. ⌈What a beautiful spring this has been after the last four bad years! We have bought nine or ten acres of ground at Littlemore, the field between the Chapel and Barnes's—and, so be it, in due time shall erect a Monastic House upon it—but I do not wish this mentioned. This may lead *ultimately* to my resigning my fellowship—but these are visions as yet. The painted glass is up, and most beautiful it is.⌉ And the Altar cloth is visited by all sorts of persons—I think it will set a fashion (or something better)—Some persons asked me yesterday, if it was to be removed today, as some ladies wished to inspect it who happen to be here. Rogers' sisters, I hope, will be here for a few days soon, and I am going to get them to set on Eliza Barnes, her sister etc to some work of the kind not so laborious. A Kirk Minister is here, a very pleasing man, sent by H. W. [Wilberforce] he is lodging at J. M.'s [Mozley]—and we shall try to indoctrinate him.

I hope Aunt is tolerable.

⌈The Children at Littlemore are improving in their singing. We hope soon to be able to chant the whole service with them.⌉

I will inclose the quinine prescription, and am very sorry A. M. [Anne Mozley] needs it. I suppose you know that quinine should not be taken without (separately, not mixed with it) rhubarb pills. And it should never be so taken, as to make the head ache.

You cannot tell what hopes and fears we have had about the 9 acres.

I am in a lot of controversies—from Ward of T. [Trinity] who was set on me for the Article in the B. C.[1] and from Mr Hornby for the attack on Knox in Froude's third volume.[2] Also the egregious Goly [Golightly] has written 100 pages, but this requires no answer. Besides there are little ones with other persons for little reasons.

⌈My Library is in most applepie order. I suppose I shall soon make it over to the parties who hold the 9 acres.⌉

Ever Yrs affly J H N.

P.S. ⌈The Tracts are most flourishing—We have cleared by them this year, between £300 and £400.—*Perhaps* in the Autumn, I may have to sell out some portion of my money in the Funds.⌉

---

[1] George R. M. Ward, an undergraduate contemporary of Newman's at Trinity, who became a Fellow, but later resigned. He had a high opinion of Newman and was friendly when they met in London soon after Newman had become a Catholic. He died in 1846.

[2] James Hornby, a High Churchman, was the editor of Alexander Knox's *Remains*. The reference is to Froude's *Remains*.

To Mrs Thomas Mozley

[July 8. 1840

While I was sitting in my surplice at the altar in Margaret Chapel on Sunday, during the first lesson a large cat fell from the ceiling, down close at my feet, narrowly missing my head. If I am not mistaken, it fell on its back. Where it came from, no one I have met can tell. It got [up] in no time, and was at the end of the Chapel and back again, before any one knew what the matter was. Then it lay down thoroughly frightened. I had heard a mewing since the beginning of the service, Mrs Bowden, who observed a large cat at S. Mary Maggiore at Rome, suggests that the Record may note it as an additional proof, that, in the Clerk's words, the Chapel in Margaret Street 'goes as near as ever it can to Roman Catholics.']

To W. C. A. Maclaurin

Oriel College. July 26/40

My dear Sir

I am truly relieved to find matters have not gone so far with you as I was afraid[1]— let me then candidly put before you some thoughts, without looking at the question controversially,—though afterwards I am ready to do so.

You have in fact given me a warrant for doing this—for in asking what I myself and persons I look up to are likely to do, you have made it a personal question, and have made it not irrelevant in me to direct your attention to them and to ask you to guide yourselves in some measure by them.

Now is it not highly desirable in the case of any one, that he should not change his religion merely on his *private judgment*? are you not, as all of us, *very* likely to be perplexed and deceived by argument? does Almighty God *commonly* require a man to go by private judgment? I think not. *Three thousand* souls were converted on the day of Pentecost; whereas when he asks of us *singly* to follow Him, He then usually gives overpowering evidence, as to St Paul. Just consider whether this is not true— and if so, whether you can be called upon, *being in perplexity*, to change your present state. I am far from denying that a truth may be brought home to a man's mind so strongly that it is his duty to act upon it against the whole world—but is this the case with your convictions about the Roman Church?—they amount at utmost only to grave and uncomfortable doubts.

Consider too that it is a vastly less responsibility to *remain* in error than to *change into* error. Only think what a fearful account will be against us at the last day, if the Roman Communion be corrupt, to have of our own act joined it and taken upon us a corrupt creed—We ought to be *very* sure we are right in doing so, considering this risk. We are born in a certain state—we have *many* signs of God's favour upon us—as *I* think, we have quite enough to make it dangerous to *undertake* a change.—Our Church must become much less like a church than it is, must have less signs of life and truth, before I can bring myself to think that it is God's will that I should change to the Church of Rome.

I am not entering into the question, whether our *actual* state of belief is not very corrupt—for argument's sake I would admit it—I would in the same way admit also, if it must be, that our state is inferior in point of privilege to Rome, but we did not bring ourselves into that state, we *find* ourselves in it—the simple question is, *What is God's will concerning me?* 'Lord what wouldest Thou have me to do?' I do not ask 'What is best?' 'What is most Catholic?' but 'What is *my duty?*'—I admit all this, for the sake of argument only—but the admission does not affect my conclusion.

I really do think that God does not require any one of us, however moved to do so, to go over to Rome by himself—If I felt reasons for conforming, *and* saw a number of other persons in various circumstances feeling reasons also, then I should *not* go by private judgment—I should be following an external *note*. But I will not trust myself. I do not think that it is God's will that I should trust myself.

Now just take the state of Oxford and the English Clergy at the present moment, and consider whether God *is* not, as ever, so now, *superseding* the necessity of private judgment. A great experiment is going on, whether Anglocatholicism *has* a root, a foundation, a consistency, as well as Roman Catholicism, or whether (in the language of the day) it be 'a sham.' I hold it to be quite impossible, unless it be *real*, that it can maintain its ground—it must fall to pieces—This is a day in which mere theories will not pass current. If *it* be a mere theory, it will not *work*. If you knew Oxford, you would know that a vast number of jealous, and of keen, though friendly eyes, are upon the Anglican theory—It is being sifted, and its system drawn out, or pushed out in every direction. Nothing is allowed to remain undeveloped—but inferences are drawn, or must be refuted—questions are asked and must be satisfactorily answered—the internal consistence of the whole is being severely tested. I securely leave it to this issue—I will not defend it if it will not stand it.

And again it really is being taken up with the utmost seriousness. I do not know about the country generally, but of this place I will say that almost without any one exception, the persons who have embraced Apostolical doctrines here, have taken them up in a deeply religious, practical, earnest and (what is sometimes called) spiritual way. Again, you have among their supporters some of the most highly gifted, holy and heavenly persons in the Church, if one may so speak. To mention names were improper, but I see persons who are as unlike the common run of men as light is unlike darkness. Now is it likely that God would leave these men in error? can such a body be abandoned to a lie? are they not seeking God in the way of His commandments? will they not find?

If then you are in doubt, (which *I* do not profess to be) but if so, then, is it too much to say Watch the steps of this body of earnest inquirers and see whither God is leading them. *They are the Church to you*—If Rome be true, they are her Messengers guiding you to her. If England be true, they again are hers. Excuse this very free note which I should like to send you first and

believe me Yours very faithfully
John H Newman

[1] His thought of becoming a Roman Catholic. For Maclaurin's letter of 18 July, see *L.D.* VII, pp. 357–8.

To John Keble

Oriel. Oct. 26 1840

My dear Keble,[1]

I am sorry to trouble you with this annoying letter—but whose advice will be more useful to me in a difficult matter than yours?

For a year past a feeling has been growing on me that I ought to give up St Mary's, and I am no fit judge in the matter. I cannot ascertain accurately my own impressions and convictions which are the basis of the difficulty—and though you cannot of course do this for me, yet you may help me generally and perhaps supersede the necessity of my going by them at all.

First, it is certain that I do not know my Oxford Parishioners; I am not conscious of influencing them; and certainly I have no insight into their spiritual state. I have no personal, no pastoral acquaintance with them. To very few have I any opportunity of saying a religious word. Whatever influence I exert on them is precisely that which I may be exerting on persons out of my parish. In my excuse I am accustomed to say to myself, that I am not adapted to get on with them, while others are. On the other hand, I am conscious that by means of my position at St Mary's I do exert a considerable influence on the University, whether on Undergraduates or Graduates. It seems then, on the whole, that I am using St Mary's, to the neglect of its direct duties, for objects not belonging to it; I am converting a parochial charge into a sort of University office.

I think I may say truly that I have begun scarcely any plan but for the sake of my parish; but every one has turned, independently of me, into the direction of the University. I began Saints' Days services, daily services, and Lectures in Adam de Brome's Chapel for my parishioners; but they have not come to them. In consequence I dropped the last mentioned, having, while it lasted, been naturally led to direct it to the instruction of those who did come, instead of those who did not. The weekly Communions, I believe, I did begin for the sake of the University.

Added to this, the authorities of the University, the appointed guardians of those who form great part of the attendants on my Sermons, have shown a dislike to my preaching. One dissuades men from coming; the late Vice Chancellor threatens to take away his own children from the Church; and the present [P. Wynter], having an opportunity last spring of preaching in my (parish) pulpit, gets up and preaches against doctrine with which I am in good measure identified. No plainer proof can be given of the *feeling* in these quarters, than the absurd myth, now a second time put forward, that Vice Chancellors cannot be got to take the office on account of Puseyism.

But, further than this, I cannot disguise from myself that my preaching is not calculated to defend that system of religion which has been received for 300 years, and of which the Heads of Houses are the legitimate maintainers in this place. They exclude me, as far as may be, from the University Pulpit; and though I never have preached strong doctrine in it, they do so rightly so far as this, that they understand that my sermons are calculated to undermine things established. I cannot disguise from myself that they are. No one will deny that most of my Sermons are on moral subjects, not doctrinal; still I am leading my hearers, to the Primitive Church if you will, but not to the Church of England. Now ought one to be disgusting the minds of young men with the received religion, in the exercise of a sacred office, yet without a commission, and against the wish of their guides and governors?

But this is not all; I fear I must allow that, whether I will or no, I am disposing them towards Rome. First, because Rome is the only representative of the Primitive Church besides ourselves; in proportion then as they are loosened from the one they will go to the other. Next because many doctrines which I hold have far greater, or their only scope, in the Roman system—e.g. the principle of reserve, or the consequences of post-baptismal sin. And moreover, if, as is not unlikely, we have in process of time heretical Bishops or teachers among us, an evil which ipso facto infects the *whole* community to which they belong, and if again, what there are at this moment symptoms of, there be a movement in the English Roman Catholics to break the alliance of O'Connell and of Exeter Hall,[2] strong temptations will be placed in the way of individuals, already imbued with a tone of thought congenial to Rome, to join her communion.

People tell me on the other hand that I am, whether by sermons or otherwise, exerting at St Mary's a beneficial influence on our prospective clergy; but what if I take to myself the credit of seeing further than they, and having in the course of the last year discovered that what they approve so much is very likely indeed to end in Romanism?

The *arguments* which I have published against Romanism seem to myself as cogent as ever; but men go by their sympathies, not by argument; and if I feel the force of this influence myself who bow to the argument, why may not others still more who never have in the same degree admitted the argument?

Nor can I counteract the danger by preaching or writing against Rome. I seem to myself almost to have shot my last arrow in the article on English Catholicity;[3] and I am troubled by doubts, whether, as it is, I have not in what I have published spoken too strongly against Rome; though I think I did it in a kind of faith, being determined to put myself into the English system, and say *all that* our Divines said whether I had fully weighed it or not.

It must be added that this very circumstance that I have committed myself against Rome, has the effect of setting to sleep men's suspicions about me, which is painful now that I begin to have suspicions about myself

I mentioned my general difficulty to Rogers a year since, than whom I know no one of a more fine and accurate conscience. It was his spontaneous idea that I should give up St Mary's, if my feelings continued. I mentioned it again to him lately, and he did not reverse his opinion, only expressed great reluctance to believe it must be so.

I have not mentioned the subject to Pusey. He is so apt from affection to adopt ideas put before him, that I know not how to proceed with him

Ever Yrs affly J H N[4]

---

[1] Newman noted: '(*This* was to prepare him. (J H N September 17. 1850))'.

[2] i.e. the alliance between Irish Catholic MPs and Dissenters in Parliament.

[3] 'Catholicity of the English Church', *British Critic*, 27, 1840 (Jan.); *Ess.* II, pp. 1–73.

[4] Keble replied on 3 November 1840, encouraging Newman to stay (see *L.D.* VII, pp. 431–3).

To John William Bowden

⌈Oriel March 15/41⌉

My dear Bowden

⌈The Heads, I believe, have just done a violent act—they have said that my interpretation of the articles is an *evasion*.[1] Do not think that this will pain me;—you see no *doctrine* is censured, and my shoulders shall manage to bear the *charge*.

If you knew all, or when you know, you will see that I have asserted a great principle, and I ought to suffer for it—that the Articles are to be interpreted, not according to the meaning of the writers, but (as far as the wording will admit) according to the sense of the Catholic Church⌉

Ever Yrs affly J H N

[1] The Vice-Chancellor, Heads of House, and the Proctors had censured *Tract 90*.

To Philip Wynter, Vice Chancellor

Oriel College March 16. 1841

Mr Vice Chancellor,

I write this respectfully to inform you, that I am the author, and have the sole responsibility, of the Tract on which the Hebdomadal Board has just now expressed an opinion, and that I have not given my name hitherto, under the belief that it was desired that I should not. I hope it will not surprise you if I say, that my opinion remains unchanged of the truth and honesty of the principle maintained in the Tract, and of the necessity of putting it forth. At the same time I am prompted by my feelings to add my deep consciousness that every thing I attempt might be done in a better spirit and in a better way; and, while I am sincerely sorry for the trouble and anxiety I have given to the members of the Board, I beg to return my thanks to them for an act, which, even though founded on misapprehension, may be made as profitable to myself as it is religiously and charitably intended.

I say all this with great sincerity and am

Mr Vice Chancellor, Your obedient Servant
John Henry Newman

To Richard Bagot, Bishop of Oxford

Oriel College, March 18, 1841

My dear Lord,

I am very much pained at your Lordship's letter, from the expression of opinion which it contains, but not at all at what it desires of me.[1]

There shall be no more discussions upon the Articles in the 'Tracts for the Times,' according to your Lordship's wish; nor indeed was it at all my intention that there should be. I need not enter upon the circumstances with your Lordship which led to my writing the Tract which has led to your letter. I will only say that it was not done wantonly, and the kind tone of your letter makes me sure that your Lordship does not think so, however you may disapprove of the Tract itself.

> I am, my dear Lord, Your Lordship's faithful servant,
> John H. Newman.

[1] Bagot had written in a kindly way, but expressing his judgement that *Tract 90* contained views that would disunite and endanger the Church and that such views should be discontinued.

To E. B. Pusey

In Vigil Annunc. [24 March] 1841[1]

My dear Pusey,

After writing the passage in my projected letter about the Bishop's wish that my Tract should be suppressed, and my submission to it, I have on second thoughts come to the conclusion that I cannot do this, without surrendering *interests* with which I am providentially charged at this moment, and which I have no right to surrender.

However the passage is worded, it will be looked on by the world as the Bishop's concurrence in the act of the Hebdomadal Board, which declares such a mode of interpreting the articles as I adopt, to be evasive and inadmissable. At this moment I am representing not a few, but a vast number all through the country, who more or less agree with me.

I offered the Bishop to withdraw the Tract; but I did not offer to concur, by any act of mine, in his *virtual censure* of it, which is involved in its being suppressed at his bidding.

And I am pained to see that authorities in London have increased their demands according to my submissiveness. When they thought me obstinate, they spoke only of not writing more in the Tracts about the Articles. When they find me obedient, they add the stopping of the Tracts and the suppression of No. 90.

And they use me against myself. They cannot deliver charges of a sudden, but they use me to convey to the world a prompt and popular condemnation of my own principles.

What too is to be our warrant, that, in addition to this, the Bishops of Chester, Chichester, Winchester etc will not charge against the Tract though suppressed? And what is to stop pamphlets against it? Will Price of Rugby be stopped? and one of the Four? and the Strictures? and the Record and Standard? All this is painful; they exert power over the dutiful; they yield to others.

I feel this so strongly, that I have almost come to the resolution, if the Bishop publicly intimates that I must suppress it, or speaks strongly in his charge against it, to suppress it indeed, but to resign my living also. I could not in conscience act otherwise.

You may show this in any quarter you please

Ever Yrs affly J H N

P.S. You will observe *I draw back* no offer, but I do something additional, resign my living, to meet something extreme which they do, publish a censure.

P.S. In fest. Annunc.

I add as follows this morning: merely to clear my meaning. I am sorry you should have so much trouble.

1. The Bishops limited their wishes to my discontinuing any discussions about the Articles in the Tracts.
2. Now they wish me besides, to suppress No. 90, which I offered; and to say I suppress it *at their bidding*, which I did not offer.
3. Considering the act of the Hebdomadal Board, it will be taken, however explained by them, as equivalent to a condemnation like that of the Heads.
4. This would compromise principles held by vast numbers in the Church.
5. And it puts me in a most painful situation at St Mary's, with both the Heads and the Bishop against me.
6. Under these circumstances I cannot co-operate with such an act. And if the Bishop were to publish in any way his wish that I should suppress the Tract, I should do it, but I think I should resign my living too.
7. Whether I should resign it if the Tract were merely suppressed without the Bishop's wish being published, depends upon what I shall see of the effects consequent on suppressing it.

[1] Pusey had visited Bagot at the Bishop's invitation on the morning of 24 March. He wanted Pusey to inform Newman that he wished *Tract 90* to be suppressed and the series of Tracts to cease. Pusey saw Newman that afternoon and later Newman wrote him this letter.

To Nicholas Wiseman

Oriel College April 6/41

My dear Lord,

I thank you for your Lordship's note[1] just received and the kindness it expresses. It gives me very great sorrow to pain members of your Lordship's communion in what I write; but is not this the state of Christendom, that we are all paining each other? If the terms I have used pain Roman Catholics, must not I be pained, though I am not so unreasonable as to complain of it, at their holding us to be heretics and schismatics, as they do?—is it not painful to be told that our Sacraments have imparted no grace to us, that we are still in the flesh, that we worship Christ in His Sacrament but that He is not there? Yet to hold this, is part of their religious system—they cannot help it; it is one of the necessities of their position. And it is part of our religious system and we cannot help it to think that they admit doctrines and practices of an idolatrous character into their communion. Such a belief is an essential element in our religious profession; else why are we separate from so great a portion of the Catholic world? have we placed ourselves in this miserable isolation for nothing?

I trust I never make accusations against Rome in the way of railing or insult. I have never meant to say, as you seem to think, that your Lordship's authoritative teaching is 'blasphemous'; I have not used the word except to disclaim the application of it by the English Church to the Mass. I have expressly said that the authoritative teaching was not such as to hinder other senses of the Decrees of Trent short of it, being 'now in point of fact held' in the Roman Communion, as considering that what is objectionable in the teaching in great measure lies in its tone, the relative prominence of doctrines, and the practical impression conveyed. And after all the phrase 'authoritative teaching' is not mine,—but having it urged upon me by others, I say in my letter to Dr. Jelf, that in *my own* sense of it, which I explain, I can accept it. On the contrary I have quoted at the same time a passage from a work of mine in which I apply the word to the *formal* and *recognised* doctrine of the Church. I say, speaking of the Church of Rome, 'Viewed in its formal principles and *authoritative* statements, it professes to be the champion of past times.'[2]

And as to the charge of 'idolatrous' usages, I expressly say that I use the word in such a sense as not to interfere with their advocates belonging to that Church from which it is said that 'the idols shall be utterly abolished.'[3] And, without professing to be able to compare one error with another, I am ready to allow that we too have our own idolatries, though of a different kind. Covetousness is called idolatry in Scripture, and I have hinted at other kinds of possible idolatry in a letter I have just published to the Bishop of Oxford.

I feel as much as any one the lamentable state of Christendom, and heartily wish that the Communions of Rome and England could be one—but the best way of tending to this great end seems to me to be, in charity and meekness, to state our convictions, not to stifle them

Yr Lordship's faithful Servt J. H Newman.

[1] Wiseman had written on 4 April, expressing the pain he felt that Newman should have spoken of authoritative teaching as 'blasphemous and idolatrous' (*L.D.* VIII, p. 154).

[2] From the 'Letter to Jelf', *V.M.* II, p. 377, quoting *Lectures on the Prophetical Office*, (*V.M.* I).

[3] *V.M.* II, p. 371.

To Miss Mary Holmes

Oriel College April 8. 1841

Dear Madam,

Of course your letter could not fail of being most gratifying to me. I am not surprised at any one being drawn to the Roman Church under your feelings, wrong as I think it—And I lament as much as one can, our present state in the English, in which high aspirations have so little means of exercise. If you will allow me to add it,

I think you were *hasty* in your resolve—so great a matter as a change of religion ought not to be thought of without years (I may say) of prayer and preparation. Nor do I think it God's way, generally speaking, for *individuals* to leave one religion for another—it is so much like an exercise of private judgment. Three thousand *at once* were converted on the day of Pentecost. When *miracles* are brought before an individual, the case is different.

However, it is of course most satisfactory news to me that your purpose was arrested, and a cause of much thankfulness that any work of mine was a means of it.

Your interest in the disturbance which has been raised against me in this place is very kind indeed. I have no misgivings about my own past proceedings, and I wait securely (under God's blessing) for all to go right. I think it will. Every thing seems in a good train. The cause of Catholic truth, I trust, will not suffer—and if not, then it matters little if some slight inconvenience or trouble falls to my share.

It is good for all of us to have reverses, and to have our patience tried. Patience and forbearance are great virtues—perhaps they are more difficult in the case of attacks made on persons we feel an interest in, than in our own case. But we must one and all *resign* ourselves, except where duty comes in, to the disorders with which our Church labours at this day

> I am, My dear Madam, Yours very faithfully
> John H Newman

To Charles Russell

> Cholderton, April 26. 1841

My dear Sir

I write a few lines to acknowledge and thank you for your most kind letter, received by me here, where I have come for a few days.

I do not look so despairingly at our Church as you do.[1] While I think (of course) that she is a branch of the Church Catholic, I also have lately had my hopes increased as to the prospect of her improvement in doctrinal exactness, by the very events which seem to you to show that Catholic truth is but barely tolerated within her pale. I have every reason to be made sanguine by the disturbance which has followed Tract 90, which I never have been before. When I began the Tracts 7 or 8 years since, I did so in a sort of despair—and felt surprised to find persons influenced by them. I had intended them mainly as a protest. I have never courted, or anticipated success—yet success came. I may be as mistaken now when I have become more sanguine—yet in matter of fact not only myself, but others too, have had their spirits raised by what has happened. My only anxiety is lest your branch of the Church should not meet us by those reforms which surely are *necessary*—It never could be, that so large a portion of Christendom should have split off from the communion of Rome, and kept up a protest for 300 years for nothing. I think I never shall believe that so much piety and earnestness would be found among Protestants, if there were not some very grave errors on the side of Rome. To suppose the contrary is most unreal, and violates all one's notions of moral probabilities. All aberrations are founded on, and have their life in, some truth or other—and Protestantism, so widely spread and so long enduring, must have in it, and must be witness for, a great truth or much truth. That I am an advocate for Protestantism, you cannot suppose—but I am forced into a Via Media, short of Rome, as it is at present.

Let both communions pray for an increase of grace and illumination, and then, though no steps be made in our day towards a reconciliation, yet it may be effected after we have left the world by the generations which follow us.

I am, My dear Sir, Most truly Yours John H Newman[2]

---

[1] Charles Russell, President of Maynooth, had written sympathetically, but critically, of the Church of England (see *L.D.* VIII, pp. 180–2).

[2] For Russell's reply *L.D.* VIII, pp. 186–7.

To Charles Russell

To Revd C Russell Maynooth

Oriel College May 5. 1841

My dear Sir

I have to acknowledge your kind letter, received during my absence from this place. I have only to observe upon it that, while I most sincerely hold that there is in the Roman Church a traditionary system which is not necessarily connected with her essential formularies, yet, were I ever so much to change my mind on this point, this would not tend to bring me from my present position, providentially appointed in the English Church. That your communion was unassailable, would not prove that mine was indefensible. Nor would it at all affect the sense in which I receive our Articles— they would still speak against certain definite errors, though you had reformed them.

I say this lest any lurking suspicion should be left in the mind of your friends that persons who think with me are likely by the growth of their present views to find it imperative on them to pass over to your communion. Allow me to state strongly, that if you have any such thoughts and proceed to act upon them, your friends will be committing a fatal mistake. We have (I trust) the principle and temper of obedience too intimately wrought into us, to allow of our separating ourselves from our ecclesiastical superiors because in many points we may sympathise with others. We have too great a horror of the principle of private judgment, to trust it in so immense a matter as that of changing from one communion to another. We may be cast out of our communion, or it may decree heresy to be truth—you shall say whether such contingences are likely; but I do not see other conceivable causes of our leaving the Church in which we were baptized

For myself, persons must be well acquainted with what I have written before they venture to say whether I have much changed my main opinions and cardinal views in the course of the last eight years. That my *sympathies* have grown towards the religion of Rome I do not deny; that my *reasons* for *shunning* her communion have lessened or altered, it will be difficult perhaps to prove. And I wish to go by reason not by feeling.

Pray excuse a note hastily written, though it expresses what are no hasty opinions, and believe me

My dear Sir, Yrs faithfully John H Newman

P.S. Will you allow me to beg your acceptance of a volume of my sermons? I shall take your silence for consent.

To Miss Mary Holmes

Oriel College. Aug. 8. 1841

Dear Madam,

I thank you for your painfully interesting letter. Of course your determination cannot surprise me, considering what you have at former times told me of your feelings and opinions.

That the Church of Rome is possessed of much which your mind naturally looks for and asks, and which the English Church cannot supply, is undeniable—and will be the cause of your conversion, if that takes place.

And I suppose it will. I suppose that the feelings and reasonings of a few months will lead you to decide on an irremediable step—to leap whence you cannot return. Once a member of the Church of Rome, you will not leave it, except to experience a state of mind so miserable, that I do not know how I could wish a return from Rome at such a price. You are then taking a last step, which must give a character to your whole life, which must, for good or for bad, have a momentous influence on your last account—and this you are doing on the thoughts of a few months.

Some holy man, I think St Bonaventure, speaking about inward suggestions to a Monastic Life, observes to this effect:—'Never trust a first suggestion—You cannot tell whether the voice is from above or from below—Your rule is, not to attend to it but to go on as usual—At first shrink from it. If it is from God, it will in due time return'.[1] And hence to all great changes, a season of thought and preparation is a necessary introduction, if we would know what God's will is.

Apply this to the case of a change of religion. I have known various persons who have felt inclined to join the Church of Rome, but they have given themselves time for thought, and as yet I do not know of one who has actually joined it. Grievous as are the defects of the English system, painful as is the position of Catholicly minded persons in it, still these persons do *remain* in it. They have waited, they do not recognise that clear voice of God directing them to change, which they desiderate. They do not find that England is out of the Covenant; or they cannot overcome their repugnance to much that is Roman.

To any friend who asked me what to do, I should prescribe three years, during which his thoughts and prayers should be directed this one way, to learn God's will.

It is a comfort in a matter of religion to follow not to originate. If persons patiently wait some time, they may see the English Church get better or worse and in either case will be more able to discern God's will concerning them. I would say of the present movement in the English Church what Gamaliel said of the work of the Apostles—'If this counsel and work be of men etc.'[2] Wait and see. 'Stand still'[3] as Scripture says—Do not rush forward—follow.

Again it is better to go with a number than by oneself, if one must go. Do you think that what *you* feel is not felt by others? Why cannot you strengthen or correct your own impressions by theirs? If yours are right, they will, please God, have them too. If they still do not have them, perhaps yours are wrong.

As to the question of danger to your soul from delaying, you know that the belief in the early Church concerning catechumens who died without Baptism was, that on death they were for their intention-sake, received into that grace which they were seeking. Can you suppose that, if you are really seeking, God will cut short life that you may not find? either He will not cut it short, or He will grant the grace while shortening it.

Mr Palmer, whose tone I do not like, answered Dr Wiseman's second pamphlet immediately. He showed that most of Dr W.'s passages were *spurious*, by confession of all the great Roman Catholic critics themselves. It formed his fifth letter to Dr W.

I am, My dear Madam,

---

[1] The ascription seems unlikely. Newman refers to a similar rule in an 1844 Memorandum: 'I did not dare to trust my impression—and I resisted it. I trust I did so on principle; certainly I have long thought it a duty to resist such impressions—If true they will return', and gives the source as St Teresa, which seems more feasible.

[2] *Acts* 5:38.

[3] Cf. *Exodus* 14:13; *2 Chronicles* 20:17.

To Nicholas Wiseman

Oriel College. Oct 4. 1841

[[not sent nor any instead]]

My dear Lord,

I thank you for the present I received from your Lordship the other day of your very interesting Letter on Catholic Unity;[1] and wish I had time or recollection to put together some thoughts which came in to my mind on reading it. However, I shall take the liberty of troubling you with one or two, though I fear I shall not do my own meaning justice.

Of course it was very satisfactory to find that you could say what occurs in pp. 30 and 31 on the subject of corruption and scandal in the Church of Rome. I really do not know why so great a Communion should not feel itself at liberty to confess many things of itself. It is little men who are jealous about themselves, and defend their conduct at every point; but a Church with such claims surely need not be loth to be candid when speaking of its private or individual members. I do really think that the more candid the Apologists of the Church of Rome are, the more they will weigh with Englishmen, and gain their favor. If there ever were a case, when honesty is the best policy, it is this. I cannot suppose you will mistake me as attributing anything *but* honesty to controversialists on your side—but we all naturally are *tender* of our own friends. Who does not feel this? I think we all *ought* to feel it. We are afraid of hurting persons—we are bound to members of our own communion by ten thousand ties—When we say ever so little about them in the way of confession, we strike against ever so many hidden rocks—and learn (what we consider) the wisdom of being silent in future. I am saying what I see continually among ourselves—and I refer to the same feeling, a feeling right and commendable except when indulged too far, that great reluctance of Roman Catholics to confess things against themselves, which does them incalculable mischief with us. Let me earnestly beg, then, all persons who desire a good understanding between yourselves and us, to let their minds dwell upon this point. They are naturally ever looking to the effect of what they write on their own people—they are disputing with *us*, but *their own* friends are the moderators. They understand, they are instantly apprized of the effect of their words on *them*—they do not see their effect upon us. They are fighting in the dark.

Allow me to say frankly that, whoever is the writer, I desiderated a bold and (what I may call) *English* tone in the article in the last Dublin, in which Dr Pusey was answered.[2] You will not suppose I am going to defend what I am saying in detail— but I hope you will kindly take it as my *impression*. My impression is a fact—what I feel, others feel, still more. Where many feel alike, there is some truth at bottom. People feel as if the answers made by Roman disputants were often shuffles—I am not of course now speaking of the Dublin Review—but I wish to give you the impressions of persons, about your writers generally.

Pray let me be taken to have this object on some other occasions in which I may seem to have spoken rudely, (I mean in private letters,) of Roman Catholics. Really it would be a great thing if they would enter into and study our impressions. They are worth attending to.

It has struck me that a very useful paper might be written of this sort, and your writers alone can do it;—a statement of the efforts of your Bishops and others to repress what we consider the extravagances of your members. A friend tells me that he was lately shown, I think at Treves, a circular from the Bishop against dressing up Images, or the like—(I hope the Bishop was not an Hermesian)[3]—now if such a document were translated for English readers it would be of great service. It would be an instance of the Roman Church, without the pressure of controversy, and not in words merely but by a pastoral act, repressing what we consider a great evil. Could not a number of such be brought together? The present Pope is said to have suppressed many books of devotion to St Mary as extreme.—Facts of this kind, frankly submitted to the scrutiny of our jealous eyes, and you may be sure your enemies would do their utmost to find a flaw in them, would have great effect in conciliating our minds towards the Church of Rome.

Before I quit these pages of your pamphlet, I will notice by the way, if I may do so without disrespect, that it pained some persons to find that you spoke of our interpretation of the 39 Articles so severely. It was not necessary for your argument, and is merely giving a triumph to our opponents. For myself I really am too callous to care about it—but I suppose we must expect to see it quoted in the Record and similar publications as 'Dr Wiseman's opinion of Tract 90.'

But now to come to a more important subject, in which I fear I shall disappoint you. As far as I see, it really appears to me my plain duty, instead of directly advocating the re-union of the Churches, to remain quite silent and quiet—and this I intend to do, unless something very unexpected occurs. I feel as if I were taking a liberty with you in speaking about myself and my own feelings, but I do not like to speak as one of a *party*, I cannot speak as a specimen of our Church itself—and on the other hand it seems but fair to you that you should know what the feelings of such as myself are.

First I say, some of us have been active for eight years in making our members more Catholic. We have brought opinions some way towards the question of union. It is our turn to rest. When you have done with your own members or with public opinion as much as we have done, then there will be a call upon us. At present there is none in *justice*.

And on the other hand there are many reasons the other way. The foremost is that my own Bishop has indirectly checked what I was doing. I profess in my letter to him to give over the course of action I was pursuing; there was no call on me to enter upon it, except as thinking it would benefit our Church—when she expresses dissatisfaction, there is a call to cease. I am now returning to the studies to which from the first I have wished to give myself and from which I was called away eight years since—those connected with the sacred doctrines of the Trinity and the Incarnation. Unless something unexpected occurs, this is the only line of controversy on which I shall enter.

And I am sure it is expedient so to act. Divine grace can effect any thing, but, humanly speaking, nothing is well done, which is done hastily. We cannot mend inveterate evils, or unite broken ties, in a day. Enough has been written on Church subjects by us to last a long while—it has not yet spread among our members, it has not done its work. I trust it will in time—but we must have patience. On the other hand nothing would be so likely to throw inquirers back as others going very much ahead of them. To consider the terms of re-union, the concessions and explanations to be made on either side, would be the way to produce a reaction. St James tells us that 'the husbandman waiteth for the precious fruit of the earth and hath long patience for it—' I wish to leave it entirely to a Divine disposal to assign 'the times and the seasons.' I cannot hasten His time; He will 'hasten it in its time.'[4] If a true seed has been sown by the books which have proceeded from this place, it will in time bear fruit. If it has life, it is worth any thing, it will do its own work. If it has not life, if it be not a true seed, what is the use of additional efforts of the same kind, why go on with formal outward acts, and hollow pleas of union when the heart is wanting? It is but washing the blackamore[5] in that case. This is a very fruitful subject—and I feel it very deeply, though I am unable to bring out my meaning.

You will see what my opinion is on the whole;—that at the present moment, it is a duty and a matter of expedience in us to remain quiet—and to occupy ourselves in attempts to teach and improve our own body. If we can make our members more apprehensive of the high theological truths defined in the first 6 Councils, and more holy in their lives and aspirations, it will be a gain so great that I do not know why I should desire any thing beyond it, though of course more would and must follow. And on the other hand if influential persons among yourselves raised and purified your own tone, reformed abuses, and conciliated us in word and deed, the happiest results would follow. Such conduct on both sides must tend eventually to unity, *in God's time*, though, it may be, not in our day.

I do not write this with the idea of having any answer from you, but that you may know my sentiments.

I am, My dear Lord, Yours faithfully John H Newman

[1] *A Letter on Catholic Unity, addressed to the Right Honourable, the Earl of Shrewsbury* (London, 1841).

[2] In his article 'The Catholic and Anglican Churches', *Dublin Review*, 11, 1841 (Aug.), pp. 240–63, Wiseman reviewed *Tract 90* and six of the pamphlets which had appeared in its wake, the greatest space being given to Pusey's *The Articles treated on in Tract 90 reconsidered and their Interpretation vindicated in a Letter to the Rev. R. W. Jelf...* (Oxford, 1841).

[3] i.e. a follower of Georg Hermes (1775–1831), who sought to reconcile Catholic theological teaching with the philosophy of Kant. After a period of popularity in the Rhineland, his doctrines were condemned by Pope Gregory XVI in 1835, and a number of his works put on the Index.

[4] *James* 5:7; *Acts* 1:7; *Isaiah* 60:20.

[5] Taken from the title of one of Aesop's *Fables*, 'wash the blackamoor white' means to take up a hopeless and useless task.

To Richard Bagot, Bishop of Oxford

[13 November 1841]

It seems as if I were never to write to your Lordship, without giving you pain, and I know that my present subject does not specially concern your Lordship; yet, after a great deal of anxious thought, I lay before you the enclosed Protest.

Your Lordship will observe that I am not asking for any notice of it, unless you think that I ought to receive one. I do this very serious act in obedience to my sense of duty.

If the English Church is to enter on a new course, and assume a new aspect, it will be more pleasant to me hereafter to think, that I did not suffer so grievous an event to happen, without bearing witness against it.

May I be allowed to say, that I augur nothing but evil, if we in any respect prejudice our title to be a branch of the Apostolic Church? That Article of the Creed, I need hardly observe to your Lordship, is of such constraining power, that, if *we* will not claim it, and use it for ourselves, *others* will use it in their own behalf against us. Men who learn whether by means of documents or measures, whether from the statements or the acts of persons in authority, that our communion is not a branch of the One Church, I foresee with much grief, will be tempted to look out for that Church elsewhere.

It is to me a subject of great dismay, that, as far as the Church has lately spoken out, on the subject of the opinions which I and others hold, those opinions are, not merely not *sanctioned* (for that I do not ask), but not even *suffered*.

I earnestly hope that your Lordship will excuse my freedom in thus speaking to you of some members of your Most Rev. and Right Rev. Body. With every feeling of reverent attachment to your Lordship,

I am, etc.

Protest against the Jerusalem Bishopric[1]

Whereas the Church of England has a claim on the allegiance of Catholic believers only on the ground of her own claim to be considered a branch of the Catholic Church:

And whereas the recognition of heresy, indirect as well as direct, goes far to destroy such claim in the case of any religious body:

And whereas to admit maintainers of heresy to communion, without formal renunciation of their errors goes far towards recognizing the same:

And whereas Lutheranism and Calvinism are heresies, repugnant to Scripture, springing up three centuries since, and anathematized by East as well as West:

And whereas it is reported that the Most Reverend Primate and other Right Reverend Rulers of our Church have consecrated a Bishop with a view to exercising spiritual jurisdiction over Protestant, that is, Lutheran and Calvinistic congregations in the East (under the provisions of an Act made in the last session of Parliament to amend an Act made in the 26th year of the reign of his Majesty King George the Third, intituled, 'An Act to empower the Archbishop of Canterbury, or the Archbishop of York for the time being, to consecrate to the office of Bishop persons being subjects or citizens of countries out of His Majesty's dominions'), dispensing at the same time, not in particular cases and accidentally, but as if on principle and universally, with any abjuration of error on the part of such congregations, and with any reconciliation to the Church on the part of the presiding Bishop; thereby giving some sort of formal recognition to the doctrines which such congregations maintain:

And whereas the dioceses in England are connected together by so close an intercommunion, that what is done by authority in one, immediately affects the rest:

On these grounds, I in my place, being a priest of the English Church and Vicar of St Mary the Virgin's, Oxford, by way of relieving my conscience, do hereby solemnly protest against the measure aforesaid, and disown it, as removing the English Church from her present ground and tending to her disorganization.

November 11, 1841.   John Henry Newman

[1] The text is taken from *Apo.*, pp. 145–6. Contemporary copies kept by Newman show some small variants.

To Mrs J. Mozley

⌜Nov 16 [1841]⌝

My dearest Jemima

I have just got your note and not yet read it through, and scribble a few lines. ⌜Sibthorp has to my mind acted most hastily, but if he had acted ever so well, he would have been abused certainly.[1]

This Jerusalem matter is miserable—and has given me *great* uneasiness. At length (what no one yet knows of) I have delivered in a formal protest to my Bishop— which when it comes to be known will make a stir. It is to the effect that I consider the measure (if carried out) as 'removing the Church of her present position and tending to her disorganization.'

I do not believe I can be touched for it, and I have not any intention of doing any thing more—but future events are quite beyond us. I assure you I fully purpose having done this to sit quite still.

Do not believe any absurd reports. They talk in the papers of secessions from among *us* to Rome.[2] Do not believe it. Not one will go.

At the same time I cannot answer years hence if the present state of things is persevered in. The Heads are refusing testimonials for orders. The effect will be in time to throw a number of young men on the world, *if* it is persevered in.

Again if the whole Church speaks against us [[me]]—if Bishops one by one, etc etc of course the effect ultimately will be very fearful—but I assure you, my dearest Jemima, that every one I know tells me every thing about themselves, and there is nothing done, said, or written, but what in some way or other I see (though I do not mean to make myself responsible for every thing), and unless some strange change comes over men, there is *no fear* at present.⌝

The post does not allow me to read this over

J H N

P.S. Kindest remembrances to M R G I had a very [?] note from H. the other day

---

[1] Richard Sibthorp (1792–1879) was an Anglican priest who was received into the Catholic Church in 1841 and ordained as a Catholic priest the following year. He returned to the Church of England in 1843 and was reinstated as a clergyman in 1857, before resuming work as a Catholic priest in 1865.

[2] His sister had written the previous day, ⌜it would be a great pleasure to have a few lines from you just to hear what you say of passing events. This Jerusalem Bishoprick is indeed deplorable . . . Also Mr Sibthorp's business. He is most shamefully abused by some of the Papers, but I was glad to see others properly gave him the credit of disinterestedness etc. Do you know it is reported in London that you have thrown off your gown, and are expected to follow Mr Sibthorp's example? M R G. [Giberne] had a letter full of alarm from her Mother on this subject. Some of the Papers have been so charitable as to *wish* that many others would follow Mr S's example.⌝

To Robert Isaac Wilberforce

[26 January 1842]

My dear Wilberforce

I fear I cannot answer your letter candidly without paining you—yet I do not wish to conceal any thing from you. I assure you I am much put to it when others ask me about my views, not thinking it right to speak out, yet feeling the difficulty and pain of shuffling.[1]

The simple case then, much as I grieve to say it, is this:—about two years and a half ago I began reading the Monophysite controversy, and with great concern and dismay found how much we were in the position of the Monophysites. I am not saying there is any thing *peculiar* in their history, but merely that it put me into a new train of thought. After that I turned my mind to the Donatists, and there the same truth, or a parallel one, came out in the strongest colours. In the Monophysite history it is that the Church of Rome, in the Donatist that that body which spreads through the world, is always ipso facto right. I am not measuring my words as if I were arguing, but giving you my line of thought. Since then whatever line of early history I look into, I see as in a glass reflected our own Church in the heretical party, and the Roman Church in the Catholic. This is an appalling fact—which, do what I will, I cannot shake off.[2]

One special test of the heretical party is absence of *stay* or *consistence*, ever crumbling ever shifting, ever new forming—ever self consumed by internal strife. Our present state, half year by half year, the opposition of Bishop to Bishop, is a most miserable and continual fulfilment of this Note of error. ⟨This *fact* is not new to me. I have discussed it in my last Lecture on Romanism.[3] What *is* new, is, that the Fathers consider that in this point the Christian *excels* the Jewish Church, which had not the Spirit.⟩

Another is a constant effort to make alliance with other heresies and schisms, though differing itself from them. Thus the Semiarians attempted the Donatists, and the Arians the Meletians, and the Nestorians (I think) the Pelagians, etc—Now, I confess, miserable as this Prussian business is to my mind in itself, it is rendered still more startling and unsettling by its apparent fulfilment in this Note of error. Other notes of the same kind might be mentioned.

Nor is it the mere *coincidence* between the state of things now and formerly which harasses me, but it seems something *prophetic*—it scares me.

This has led me anxiously to look out for *grounds* of remaining where Providence has placed me—and the most remarkable historical evidence is the case of St Meletius which I have drawn out in an article in the B. C. [*British Critic*] two years ago.[4] It has also forced me back upon the *internal or personal Notes* of the Church; and with thankfulness I say that I have received great comfort there. But, alas, in seeking to draw out this comfort for the benefit of others, who (without knowing my state) have been similarly distressed, eager inquisitive sensitive minds have taken the alarm, and (though I acted with the greatest anxiety and tried to do what I could to avoid the suspicion) they are beginning to guess that I have not an implicit faith in the validity of the *external* Notes of our Church.

My present purpose is from sheer despondency lest I should be doing harm, to give over, at least for the present, preaching at St Mary's. Nothing I can say, though I preach Sermons 17 years old, but is made to have a meaning—much more when I write fresh ones. And I think it may be of use in itself, in the present excited state of Oxford and the country. My going to be at Littlemore, which has long been in contemplation and progress, will be an excuse, to save appearances.

One obvious consequence is to be mentioned besides—a growing dread lest in speaking against the Church of Rome I may be speaking against the Holy Ghost. This is quite consistent with a full conviction of the degraded state of that Church whether here or elsewhere.

And now, My dearest W, I know what pain this will give you. But understand— *I have stated my feelings at the outside*, lest I should not be open—but do not suppose I mean more than I say.

Two persons,[5] beside you, know my unsettled state of mind, or rather my misgivings—(for of course, as you will understand, at different times I feel very differently—and think I said quite sincerely all I said in my letters to Jelf and the Bishop of Oxford, for my fears slept for very many months, and have only lately been re-animated by our dreadful divisions, the Bishops' charges, and this Prussian affair, though I have been very eager for more than a year ⟨two years⟩ to back out of St Mary's, could that be done) but those two only know it generally. You are the first person to whom I have drawn it out.

Excuse the pain I give you and believe me

Ever Yrs affly J H N

P.S. You will understand that I hold *quite as fully as ever* I did the views of tradition and doctrine etc which (from our Divines) I have expressed in my Lectures on Romanism. I think them unanswerable. Any one with my view of them who conformed to the Church of Rome could but do it *on faith*; or believing that those arguments were directed against a school in the Church of Rome, not against Rome itself. And it is certain as I notice in my Lectures, that Rome has not formally committed herself to the doctrine of infallibility.[6]

Of course this painful thought comes into my mind—whether, if Rome be the true Church, the divinely appointed method of raising her from her present degradation be not to *join her*. Whether either she or we *can* correct our mutual errors while separated from each other. This is contrary to what I have said in my Letter to the Bishop of Oxford viz that each must be holier *before* separation[7]—but the question arises whether *unity* would not bring a sacramental grace with it. Excuse all this.[8]

---

[1] Wilberforce had written, alarmed by remarks of Newman's that suggested he might be drawn towards Rome.

[2] Cf. *Apo.*, pp. 114–18.

[3] See *V.M.* I, pp. 336–45.

[4] 'Catholicity of the English Church', *Ess.* II, pp. 1–73.

[5] Frederic Rogers and Henry Wilberforce.

[6] See *V.M.* I, Lectures III and IV, 'Doctrine of Infallibility Morally considered', and 'Doctrine of Infallibility politically considered', especially pp. 122–7.

[7] A slip for 'reunion'. See *V.M.* II, p. 421.

[8] Wilberforce wrote on 29 January, 'I don't think that I ever was so shocked by any communication, which was ever made to me, as by your letter of this morning. It has quite unnerved me.'

To Henry Wilberforce

⌜Littlemore. Sabbat. post Cineres [12 February] 1842⌝

Carissime,

⌜Your kind note came to me last night;—kind but inconsistent, for don't you know you once wished me dead rather than otherwise disposed of. I have sometimes thought that if I were seriously prompted to join the Church of Rome, I should beg my friends' prayers that I might die rather than do it, if it were wrong.[1] ⌝

That poor fellow who has conformed called on me here yesterday. He had only met me once (at dinner at Trinity)—so his call out here was very kind. He said he did not know how to look me in the face for the trouble he should cause me—however, he is a relation of Mr Biden of Bruges, who (I understand) has had a good deal to do in his conversion.[2]

⌜And now as to my own matters. I will tell you what I will do. I am going in to Oxford this afternoon. I will call on Dr Wootten and let him see my throat, and if he forbids me to do as I am doing, I will obey. And I will offer to show myself to him once a week or a fortnight—but I will not tell him *what* I am going [[doing]]—for Doctors always go à priori.

As to your question about yourself, though I know perfectly well that leaving off the *least* things are [[is]] at first a greater trial to strength, or at least to vigor, than could be supposed, yet I think a person might any how leave off in Lent butter, milk, sugar, pastry, fruit etc—and rather take medicine (e.g. quinine) than wine, if it answer the same purpose. Or look at the Lent Indult[3] and you will see what is possible for average constitutions. I think it allows meat on Sunday, Tuesday, and Thursday

Valeas Carissime, et sis memor nostri [[mei]]

Qui sum tuus J H N.⌝

[1] Wilberforce replied on 15 February: 'I do feel that it would give me less pain to hear of your death than of your leaving the Church of your Baptism (a thing which I hardly like to write even hypothetically).'

[2] The visitor was Johnson Grant who had recently been received into the Catholic Church. He became a Jesuit.

[3] In relaxation of the strict fasting customs of earlier centuries, the Holy See granted successive Indults, allowing meat at the principal meal, first on Sunday, and then on two and more weekdays, throughout nearly the whole of Lent.

To Richard Bagot, Bishop of Oxford

Oriel College. April 14. 1842

(Copy)

My dear Lord

I am very much obliged by your Lordship's kindness in allowing me to write to you on the subject of my house at Littlemore; at the same time I feel it hard both on your Lordship and myself that the restlessness of the public mind should oblige you to require an explanation of me.[1]

It is now a whole year that I have been the subject of incessant misrepresentation. A year since I submitted entirely to your Lordship's authority; and with the intention of following out the particular act enjoined upon me, I not only stopped the series of Tracts, on which I was engaged, but I withdrew from all public discussion of Church matters of the day, or what may be called ecclesiastical politics. I turned myself at once to the preparation for the Press of the translation of St Athanasius to which I had long wished to devote myself, and I intended and intend to employ myself in the like theological studies, and in the concerns of my own parish and in practical works.

With the same view of personal improvement I was led more seriously to a design, which had been long on my mind. For many years, at least thirteen, I have wished to give myself to a life of greater religious regularity than I have hitherto led; but it is very unpleasant to confess such a wish even to my Bishop, because it seems arrogant, and because it is committing me to a profession which may come to nothing. What have I done, that I am to be called to account by the world for my private actions, in a way in which no one else is called? Why may I not have that liberty which all others are allowed? I am often accused of being underhand and uncandid in respect to the intentions to which I have been alluding: but no one likes his own good resolutions noised about, both from mere common delicacy, and from fear lest he should not be able to fulfil them. I feel it very cruel, though the parties in fault do not know what they are doing, that very sacred matters between me and my conscience are made a public talk. May I take a case parallel though different? suppose a person in prospect of marriage; would he like the subject discussed in newspapers, and parties, circumstances etc etc publicly demanded of him, at the penalty of being accused of craft and duplicity?

The resolution I speak of has been taken with reference to myself alone, and has been contemplated quite independent of the co-operation of any other human being, and without any reference to success or failure other than personal, and without regard to the blame or approbation of man. And being a resolution of years, and one to which I feel God has called me, and in which I am violating no rule of the Church any more than if I married, I should have to answer for it, if I did not pursue it, as a good Providence made openings for it. In pursuing it then I am thinking of myself alone, not aiming at any ecclesiastical or external effects. At the same time of course it would be a great comfort to me to know that God had put it into the hearts of others to pursue their personal edification in the same way, and unnatural not to wish to have the benefit of their presence and encouragement, or not to think it a great infringement on the rights of conscience if such personal and private resolutions were interfered with. Your Lordship will allow me to add my firm conviction that such religious resolutions are most necessary for keeping a certain class of minds firm in their allegiance to our Church; but still I can as truly say that my own reason for any thing I have done has been a personal one, without which I should not have entered upon it, and which I hope to pursue whether with or without the sympathies of others pursuing a similar course.

I should consider an apology due to your Lordship for this detail of my private feelings, as well as that which is to follow of a household and domestic nature, except that the sort of rumours which are afloat have compelled your Lordship to be general and me to be particular. I can only say that I will at once, as I am bound, answer to any point to which your Lordship will proceed to direct my attention; meanwhile I will state, as I proposed, the circumstances of my house at Littlemore, which has occasioned your letter.

Last spring a person holding property at Littlemore turned a long low stone granary into a number of cottages with the intention of letting them to poor people. I made an offer of renting the lot, with no definite intention. I considered whether I could not underlet them myself, or make them an almshouse. Difficulties rose as to either plan, and then I reverted to that personal object which was also prominently in my mind when I first thought of them. I considered it best to take them for my own use. There was however this objection, which had interfered with former plans at Littlemore, the want of a room for a Library. The parties offered to turn an adjacent stable into such a room. This change is the only one which has been made in the buildings at my instance; every other part of them stands just as it did before I made my offer. The doors were all inside, as now; opening in to what was intended to be an alley. All I have done has been to add *inside* (which cannot be seen from without, if this is worth while mentioning) a shed connecting one cottage door with another, so that an inmate can now pass from one to another without exposure to the weather. And I have planted with shrubs and flowers the inclosed space at the back. I have taken up my books there.

As to my intentions, I purpose to live there myself a good deal, as I have a resident Curate in Oxford, Mr Lewis of Jesus College. In doing this, I believe I am consulting for the good of my Parish, as my population at Littlemore is at least equal to that of St Mary's in Oxford, and the *whole* of Littlemore is double of it. It has been very much neglected; and in providing a parsonage house for Littlemore, as this will be, and will be called, I conceive I am doing a very great benefit to my people. At the same time it has appeared to me that a partial or temporary retirement from St Mary's Church might be expedient under the prevailing excitement.

Mr Copeland, my Curate at Littlemore has at present lodgings in the place; perhaps he will remove into the Parsonage, that is, take possession of one of the cottages. We are going to change our schoolmaster—we propose, if possible, to get a young unmarried man, and to place him in another cottage. I need not enlarge to your Lordship on the great benefit which would accrue to the schoolmaster of a parish to be thus under the superintendence and influence of the Clergyman. Perhaps I may need a youth as a secretary or librarian and half servant—him I should place in a third Cottage. Any promising boys in the Parish School, I might be led to take in there for a year or two, till they were apprenticed, making them halfscholars, half-servants. Perhaps I might take one or two pupils who were reading for orders. Perhaps friends in orders might wish to come there for a while. Or I might have friends staying with me, as other clergymen receive their friends at their Parsonages. Sometimes there would be friends from Oxford.

Your Lordship will think the building a very large one to admit of such prospective arrangements, but I am setting before you all my views, as far as I have any; and not knowing how or whether they will be fulfilled. There are six cottages of two rooms apiece, making from 6 to 12 beds—and one additional room over the Library.

I propose to occupy myself and persons who are there in study and in joint devotion.

As to the quotation from the John Bull Newspaper, which I have not seen, your Lordship will perceive from what I have said, that no 'monastery is in process of erection;' there is no 'chapel;' no 'refectory,' hardly a dining room or parlour. The 'cloisters' are my shed connecting the cottages. I do not understand what 'cells of dormitories' means. Of course I can repeat your Lordship's words that 'I am not attempting a revival of the Monastic orders, in any thing approaching to the Romanist sense of the term,' or 'taking on myself to originate any measure of importance without authority from the Heads of the Church.' I am attempting nothing ecclesiastical, but something personal and private, and which can only be made public, not private, by Newspapers and letter writers, in which sense the most sacred and conscientious resolves and acts may certainly be made the objects of an unmannerly and unfeeling curiosity[2]

I am, My dear Lord etc etc J H N.

[1] Rumours that Newman was establishing an Anglo-Catholic monastery at Littlemore had prompted Bagot to ask him for an explanation.

[2] On 18 April Bagot replied, 'Your answer is just what I anticipated, proving the assertions respecting the buildings at Littlemore to be totally untrue.'

To William Prescott Sparkes

[25 October 1842]

Sir

I am not at all surprised that you should have made up your mind to join the Church of Rome, considering you call our attention to the question of less than two years 'long and deep consideration, much research, and patient counting of the cost.' Allow me to say, that those who take more pains than you profess to have done are accustomed to come to a very different view of their duty

I am etc J H N

To Miss Mary Holmes

Oriel College. Nov 20. 1842

My dear Miss Holmes

I thank you for your kind letter. It pained me a good deal, as you would suppose, to find that I had spoken so unseasonably the other day—and then I fear I made matters worse by being rude, when I wished to show my sympathy. As for myself, you are not the first person who have been disappointed in me.[1] Romantic people always will be. I am, in all my ways of going on, a very ordinary person. However, ordinary or not, I shall not cease, if you will suffer me, to speak from time to time when I think a word may be useful—for though I am not an old man, as you expected, I suppose I am about double your age, and have a right to advise.

You must expect the first days at a place like your present home to be awkward and uncomfortable—but from your last note, I suppose the dreariness has in a measure past away already.[2] Do not suppose I meant that you will not like your hosts for a continuance—I only meant to guard you against looking at things in too bright a light at first—which would perhaps be followed by a re-action.

I have sent your MS to Rivington. There was a passage in which you say more good of our Reformers than I think you have any right to do—and accordingly I have taken the great liberty of putting a pencil across it; but you can easily restore it, if you wish to do so. It was one of the passages I wished to speak to you about when I saw you.

With every kind wish, and serious wish, that every year as it goes may enlighten you in the knowledge of God's law, and conform you to the image of the Saints which have gone before us

I am, My dear Miss Holmes, Yours very truly John H Newman

[1] Mary Holmes had met Newman for the first time on 9 November.
[2] Mary Holmes was intelligent, but restless. She found it hard to settle and used to seek Newman's advice.

To Charles Russell

Littlemore. Nov. 22. 1842

My dear Sir,

I have read quite enough of the Volume of Sermons you were kind enough to send me, to feel a great respect for their author, if his name itself did not create a deeper feeling than respect, before opening them. I only wish that your Church were known among us by such writings. You will not interest us in her, till we see her, not in politics, but in her true functions of exhorting, teaching and guiding. I wish there were a chance of making the leading men among you understand, what I believe is no novel thought to yourself. It is not by learned discussions, or acute arguments, or reports of miracles, that the heart of England can be gained. It is by men 'approving themselves,' like the Apostle, 'ministers of Christ.'[1]

As to your question, whether the Volume you have sent is not calculated to remove my apprehensions that another gospel is substituted for the true one in your practical instructions, before I can answer it in any way, I ought to know how far the Sermons which it comprises are *selected* from a number, or whether they are the whole, or such as the whole, which have been published of the author's. I assure you, or at least I trust, that, if it is ever clearly brought home to me that I have been wrong in what I have said on this subject, my public avowal of that conviction will only be a question of time with me.[2]

If however you saw our Church as we see it, you would easily understand that such a change of feeling, did it take place, would have no necessary tendency, which you seem to expect, to draw a person from the Church of England to that of Rome. There is a divine life among us, clearly manifested, in spite of all our disorders, which is as great a note of the Church, as any can be. Why should we seek our Lord's presence elsewhere, when He vouchsafes it to us where we are? What *call* have we to change our communion?

Roman Catholics will find this to be the state of things in time to come, whatever promise they may fancy there is of a large secession to their Church. This man or that may leave us, but there will be no general movement. There is indeed an incipient movement of our *Church* towards yours, and this your leading men are doing all they can to frustrate by their unwearied efforts at all risks to carry off individuals. When will they know their position, and embrace a larger and wiser policy?

I must conclude with thanking you, which I do very sincerely, for your letter and present, and begging you to excuse the freedom of these remarks. Should you at any time pass through Oxford, I hope you will give me the opportunity of making your personal acquaintance. I could at any time come to my rooms in College, if I know of your arrival beforehand.[3]

I am, My dear Sir, Very faithfully yours John H Newman

[1] See 2 *Corinthians* 6:4.

[2] Three weeks later, Newman sent off a 'Retractation of anti-Catholic statements' to the editor of the *Oxford Conservative Journal* who, for some unknown reason, delayed publication until 28 January 1843. (See V.M. II, pp. 425–33.)

[3] Russell called on Newman in Oxford on 1 August 1843.

To E. B. Pusey

Littlemore. The Martyrdom [[30 January]] 1843

My dear Pusey

I very much fear you will think it necessary that I should ask your pardon for something I have been doing, as if it were rash—but my conscience would not stand out. You have before now said that *I* have said far severer things against Rome than yourself—and I am so sure of it that I have thought I ought to unsay them. This I did about six weeks or two months ago—and I believe what I have said is in the Periodicals—but I have not seen it yet. I have said *nothing* of course on *doctrinal* points, but only as to *abuse*. *You* stand on very different grounds, and have had to unsay nothing—I would not take advice of any one, because I wished to have the sole responsibility.

Is there any chance of the Arnold Testimonial passing the Hebdomadal Board? I do trust not—would there not be an opposition in Convocation, and would it be wise in them to agitate the University again?

If any one values his Luncheon on Thursday, he must not go to hear me at St Mary's, for my sermon[1] is of portentous length—and my only satisfaction is that, if any persons go out of curiosity, they will be punished.

I have not wished you a happy New Year.

Ever Yrs affly J H N

---

[1] 'The Theory of Developments in Religious Doctrine', *U.S.*, pp. 312-51.

To John Keble

Littlemore. March 14. 1843

My dear Keble,

I am sorry to trouble you with my concerns, yet I want to write to you on a subject, which has before led me to apply to you, and which I hardly know how to bring out properly. It seems to me as if Lent were a fitting time, when one has more hope than at ordinary seasons of being guided amid perplexity.

I wrote to you on the subject of St Mary's two and a half years since[1]—and my difficulty has not diminished in the interval. The question is, as you know, about my resigning the Living, but I am so bewildered that I do not know right from wrong, and have no confidence of being real in any thing I think or say.

My abiding difficulty in holding S Mary's is the circumstance that the persons whom I am influencing are not my Parishioners, but the Undergraduates with whom I have no concern. It distresses me to think how little I am fitted for the charge of such a Parish, and how little I do—I dread to think the number of years I have been there, yet how unprofitably. On the other hand persons, who are not given me in charge, attend my Services and Sermons, and that certainly without, perhaps against the wish of their proper guardians. If I felt this, as you know I did, before the No 90 affair, how much I feel it since!

Another circumstance, which pressed on me painfully when I wrote to you before, was, that what influence I exert is simply and exactly, be it more or less, in the direction of the Church of Rome—and that whether I will or no—What men learn from me, who learn any thing, is to lean towards doctrine and practices which our Church does not sanction. There was a time when I tried to balance this by strong statements against Rome, which I suppose to a certain extent effected my object. But now, when I feel I can do this no more, how greatly is the embarassment [*sic*] of my position increased! I am in danger of acting as a traitor to that system, to which I must profess attachment or I should not have the opportunity of acting at all.

149

What increases my difficulty most heavily is the gradual advance, which is making to a unanimous condemnation of No 90 on the part of the Bishops. Here I stand on a different footing from all who agree to that Tract on the whole, even from you. No one but myself can be answerable for every word of it. The Bishops condemn it, without specifying *what* they condemn in it. This gives an opening to every reader who agrees with it on the whole, to escape the force of their censure. I alone cannot escape it. Two years have passed, and one Bishop after another has pronounced an unmitigated sentence against it. By October next the probability is, that hardly a single Bishop but will have given his voice against it; that is, given his voice against that comment on the Articles on which alone I can hold my Living. How can I with any comfort, with any sense of propriety, retain it? There is nothing said by them in mitigation of this sentence. My own bishop says that by such expedients as the Tract exhibits I may make the Articles mean any thing or nothing.

The Bishop of Exeter I am told is quite violent in his language about me. The Bishop of St David's, the most candid of all, says that the explanations which others have offered of the Tracts just suffice to show that I need not be dishonest. And so on with the rest. I declare I wonder at myself that I have remained so long without moving. Now there *are* cases where a consciousness of being in the right suffices to outweigh the censure even of authority; but in this instance I cannot deny, first, that my interpretation has never been drawn out, to say the least, before—and I suspect our Catholic-minded Divines have rather had recourse to the expedient of looking on the Articles as Articles of Peace—and next I am conscious too, as I have said above, that I am not advocating, that I am not promoting, the Anglican system of doctrine, but one very much more resembling in matter of fact, the doctrine of the Roman Church. I have nothing to fall *back upon*.

Another reason may be added which, though of very inferior importance, at least tells as far as this,—to diminish the dread that, in retiring, I should be recklessly tossing away influence which Providence has put into my hands—occupation is growing on me of a different kind, and which is likely to interfere with my duties at St Mary's—I mean, that of directing (as I best may) the consciences of persons. I very much doubt, whether I should not by relinquishing St Mary's, have a great deal more work than at present of a pastoral kind—and moreover of a directly *practical* nature, not strictly speaking theological.

The great objection to any such plan, (which I am not proposing even as an hypothesis before the Autumn) is lest it should seem to imply a great dissatisfaction with the Church of England; though really any sensible person ought to see that my situation fully justifies, if not calls for it. Pusey suggested, and I had thought myself, if it were determined on, that I might manage to retain Littlemore, which, I suppose, would be a sufficient answer to the suspicion. The College indeed, as you may recollect, refused to separate Littlemore from St Mary's for such a purpose last October 2 years[2]—but I think some arrangement of the kind might be managed. And then I might keep Littlemore on according to circumstances. I think my coming to live here, my occasional periods of absence from St Mary's, which have now gone on for three years, and the continual rumours of my resigning it, have prepared people for such an event, over and above the Heads of Houses and the Bishops.

I am very sorry so to trouble you—but will you kindly bear my anxiety in mind? and the more that really I cannot say whether I feel a word of what I have written and whether it is not all pretence—Of course there is no hurry for your answer; indeed from the nature of the case I do not wish a speedy one.

Ever Yours affectionately John H Newman

[1] Letter to Keble, 26 October 1840.
[2] See letter to Edward Hawkins dated 20 October 1840, *L.D.* VII, p. 409.

To Frederic Rogers

Easter Eve, April 15. Littlemore

My dear Rogers

If I understand the following sentence in your letter aright, 'I have been of use to you as habitually showing you in my own person what ordinary men would think of this or that course of conduct, and enabling you to adapt your course to their notions,' my conscience altogether repudiates the idea contained in it; and I am writing in a holy season. But really I hardly know to what extent you may think me deceiving whether myself or you.

Will you let me add without offence that it has been growing on me for some time, that there is a trait of suspiciousness (the nearest word I can find) in your character, and that, not as regards myself, which it has not till lately come into my head to think, but persons and things generally, or at least certain classes of persons and things. Another person once remarked to me what I think meant the same thing.

May you find others as *reverential* in their feelings towards you as I have been

Yrs affly J H Newman[1]

⟨April 15. N B. He is wrong in saying I USED him as a *specimen* of others. I have gone *by his advice*. I have not done, or have modified, by his *judgment* what I should have done by my own. No one has so much restrained me as he. But it is not worth while to write to him to explain. J H N

Yes I think I must write a line to repudiate such an idea. I did *not* write'.⟩

[1] After this episode, the two men met from time to time in Oxford as mere acquaintances. After Newman left the Church of England in 1845, they did not meet again till 1863.

To John Keble (I)

Littlemore. Thursday May 4 1843

My dear Keble,

On this very day, on which I have received your kind letter, giving me conditional leave of retiring from St Mary's, I have been disappointed in my last expedient for keeping Littlemore by itself. This circumstance, combined with the most kind tone of your letter, has strongly urged me to tell you something which has at last been forced upon my full consciousness.

There is something about myself, which is no longer a secret to me—and if not to me, surely it ought not to be so to someone else; and I think that other person should be you whose advice I have always wished to follow.

I have enough consciousness in me of insincerity and double dealing, which I know you abhor, to doubt about the correctness of what I shall tell you of myself. I really cannot say whether I am stating my existing feelings, motives, and views fairly, and whether my memory will not play me false. I cannot hope but I shall seem inconsistent to you—and whether I am or have been I cannot say. I will but observe that it is very difficult to realize one's own views in certain cases, *at the time* of acting, which is implied in culpable inconsistency; and difficult again, when conscious of them, to discriminate between passing thoughts and permanent impressions, particularly when they are unwelcome. Some thoughts are like hideous dreams, and we wake from them, and think they will never return; and though they do return, we cannot be sure they are more than vague fancies; and till one is so sure they are not, as to be afraid of concealing within what is at variance with one's professions, one does not like, or rather it is wrong, to mention them to another.

I do trust that I am not trifling with myself now, nor am about to say to you what is beyond my own settled impressions. If I am, it is most cruel to you in many ways. Any how, you will be undergoing a most dreadful suffering at my hands, if you read the other paper.[1]

I do not feel distress at putting on you the *necessity of advising*; because, so that you give your best judgment, it is all you can give, all that Divine Mercy expects from you or me; and by acting honestly upon it, I shall, so be it, be pleasing Him, whatever comes of it; but what shall I say for the *pain* I shall be causing you?

Ever Yrs affly John H Newman

[1] That is, the following letter, being part two of the same letter.

To John Keble (II)

Littlemore. May 4. 1843

O forgive me, my dear Keble, and be merciful to me in a matter, in which, if I have not your compassion, my faith is so weak and I have so little sense of my own uprightness, that I shall have no refuge in the testimony of my conscience, such as St Paul felt, and shall be unable to appeal from you to a higher judgment seat. But if you do on deliberation accuse me of insincerity, still tell me, for I shall deserve to bear it, and your reproof will be profitable.

In June and July 1839, near four years ago, I read the Monophysite Controversy, and it made a deep impression on me, which I was not able to shake off, that the Pope had a certain gift of infallibility, and that communion with the see of Rome was the divinely intended means of grace and illumination. I do not know how far I fully recognized this at the moment,—but towards the end of the same Long Vacation I considered attentively the Donatist history, and became quite excited. It broke upon me that we were in a state of schism. Since that [then], all history, particularly that of Arianism, has appeared to me in a new light, confirmatory of the same doctrine.

In order to conquer this feeling, I wrote my article on the Catholicity of the English Church,[1] as I have written other things since. For a while my mind was quieted; but from that time to this the impression, though fading and reviving, has been on the whole becoming stronger and deeper.

At present, I fear, as far as I can realize my own convictions, I consider the Roman Catholic Communion the Church of the Apostles, and that what grace is among us (which, through God's mercy, is not little,) is extraordinary, and from the over-flowings of His Dispensation.

I am very far *more* sure that England is in schism, than that the Roman additions to the Primitive Creed may not be developments, arising out of a keen and vivid realizing of the Divine Depositum of faith.

All this is so shocking to say, that I do not know whether to wish that I am exaggerating to you my feelings or not.

You will now understand what gives edge to the Bishops' charges, without any undue sensitiveness on my part. They distress me in two ways; 1. as being in some sense protests and witnesses to my conscience against my secret unfaithfulness to the English Church; and 2. next, as being average samples of her teaching and tokens how very far she is from even aspiring to Catholicity.

I must add that Rogers, who has known, perhaps better than any one, my opinions and their history, has for two years past peremptorily refused to give me any advice on Church matters, one way or the other; and has *within the last month* told me his reason; viz that it would be treachery in him to the English Church, to assist one who is conducting a movement, tending to carry over her members to Rome.

Of course the being unfaithful to a trust is my great subject of dread, as it has long been, as you know. Still there is another alternative, besides that of carrying members of our church to Rome, viz. disposing *herself* that way, and so healing a schism instead of making one. Yet, all this being considered, it does seem to me *safer* to retire from a post, in which, whether I will or no, I may be employing a sacred authority committed to me against the giver.

However, this is the point which I am submitting to your judgment. What ought I to *do*?

Whatever pain I may have on many accounts in giving up Littlemore, and that to a person like Eden,[2] and great as the loss of Copeland would be to the Parish, I hope that on the whole things would go on pretty much as usual—And I cannot wish to be without personal pain or inconvenience in taking a step of this kind

Ever Yours affectionately John H Newman[3]

---

[1] 'Catholicity of the English Church', *Ess.* II, pp. 1–111.

[2] Charles Page Eden (1807–85), six years Newman's junior, had the reputation for being aggressive, for being rude to strangers, and for slanging college servants in public for trivial matters.

[3] A year later, Keble recalled reading the two letters in a 'deserted old chalk pit'.

To John Keble

[Littlemore. May 18. 1843]

My dear Keble,

Thank you for your speedy as well as compassionate letter.[1] I feel it to be almost ungenerous to entangle you in my troubles; at least it would be so, were it not a rule of the Gospel that Christians should not stand alone or depend on themselves. And, if so, to whom can I go, (for surely I may so speak without irreverence), but to you who have been an instrument of good to so many, myself inclusive? To whom is it natural for me to go but to you whom I have tried to follow so long and on so many occasions? to whom would Hurrell go, or wish me to go but to you? And doubt not that, if such is the will of Providence, you will in the main be able to do what is put on you.

I feel no doubt that in consulting you I am doing God's will; for, since I lay claim to no such infallible perception of His leadings, as may be granted to some, and as would oblige me to follow it, the alternative lies between selfwill and consulting you.

Yet, after saying this, still I know that some questions in detail to which I am coming, are so very intricate, that it will not at all surprise me to find you decline them. Only then answer as much as you like; and I will take your answers as far as they go.

But first, in answer to some suggestions you make, I will briefly say; 1. that by a 'hideous dream' I meant, what surely is hideous, to begin to suspect oneself external to the Catholic Church, having publicly, earnestly, frequently, insisted on the ordinary necessity of being within it. 2. I do not think I have ever been sanguine of success *in my day* or at all. The Lyra,[2] and the beginning of my Letter to Faussett[3] will, I think show that. It is true, however, that I have spoken very confidently about our being in no danger from Rome; and I doubt not with much presumption and recklessness. But I had a full conviction, (and have still) of the independence of the Anglican view compared with the Roman, and the formidableness of the former to the latter, and I had great faith in our Divines, so as to take (I suppose) for granted, what I had not duly examined, the irrelevancy of the charge of schism as urged against us. If I have been very bold in nearing the Roman system, this has risen mainly from over-secure reliance on our position, and from a keen impression of our great need of what the Roman system contains. I have spoken strongly against that system itself, that I might use it without peril. 3. Re-actions are, I suppose, sudden; strong opposite impulses occurring in immediate succession; but my present feelings have arisen naturally and gradually, and have been resisted. It is true, that I have now laid down my arms rather suddenly. This was caused, I believe, by Rogers' note, which I opened a few hours after writing to you on Easter Eve, and by Eden's avowal to me the other day, that, were he Vicar of St Mary's, he would not engage even to let me read daily prayers at Littlemore, though he did not provide any one else. But though I have been thrown upon telling you, I hardly know how, yet I do not think I have said any thing to you beyond the fact; and surely when a misery is of so long standing, any how you should know it.

And now I come to the main subject of my letter.

I would ask, whether I should not be sufficiently kept in order, as you desire, by retaining a Fellowship, and the Editorship of the Library of the Fathers, though I had not a living.

On the other hand contemplate the great irritation of mind to which St Mary's exposes me continually.

I do not think I could take the Oath of Supremacy again, though I quite know that there are fair and almost authorized modes of understanding it in a Catholic sense; but, considering my opinions and the opinions of the mass of Churchmen *on the whole*, I do not think it safe to do so. Now then, am I not exposing myself to a constant risk of detection, considering too the number of eyes, friendly and hostile, which are upon me? (I take this oath as a mere illustration of many things, which in fact would press more heavily upon a beneficed Clergyman than a Fellow.) A detection would be far more calamitous, than a quiet withdrawal while things were so tranquil. Might I not fairly assign the Bishops' Charges as the reason of it? for surely I should feel no anxiety at all about treachery to the Church, if they, as organs of prevailing opinion as well as Bishops, had one and all *approved* and *recommended* No 90, instead of censuring it.

My office or charge at St Mary's is not a mere *state* (though that would be painful enough) but a continual energy. People assume, and exact, certain things of me in consequence.

With what sort of sincerity can I obey the Bishop? how am I to act in the frequent cases in which in one way or other the Church of Rome comes into consideration? I have, to the utmost of my power and with some success, tried to keep persons from Rome, but even a year and a half since my arguments were of that nature, as, though efficacious with the men aimed at and they only, to infuse suspicions of me in the minds of lookers-on.

By retaining St Mary's, I am an offence and stumbling block. Persons are keen sighted enough to make out what I think on certain points, and then they infer that such opinions are compatible with holding situations of trust in the Church. This is a very great evil in matter of fact. A number of younger men take the validity of their interpretation of the Articles etc from me *on faith*. Is not my present position a cruelty to them, as well as a treachery towards the Church?

I do not see how I can either preach or publish again, while I hold St Mary's, but consider the following difficulty in such a resolution, which I must state at some length.

Last Long Vacation the idea suggested itself to me of publishing the Lives of the Saints, and I had a conversation with Rivington about it. I thought it would be useful, as employing the minds of persons who were in danger of running wild, and bringing them from doctrine to history, from speculation to fact; again, as giving them an interest in the English soil and English Church, and keeping them from seeking sympathy in Rome as she is; and further, as tending to promote the spread of right views.

But within the last month it has come upon me, that, if the scheme go[goes] on, it will be a practical carrying out of No 90, from the character of the usages and opinions of Ante-Reformation times.

It is easy to say 'Why *will* you be doing *any* thing? (a note has suddenly come to me from Pusey which I will transcribe, though it will give you additional pain) why *won't* you keep quiet and let things alone? What business had you to think of any such plan at all?' But I *cannot* leave a number of poor fellows in the lurch; I am bound to do the best for a great number of people both in Oxford and elsewhere. If *I* do not act, others would find means to do so. Again is Mr Taylor[4] etc to abuse the Saints, and no one to defend them? but this is off the subject.

Well, the plan has been taken up with great eagerness and interest. Many men are setting to work. I set down the names of men, who are most of them engaged, the rest half engaged or probable; some writing. ⌈Bowden, Johnson (observatory)[,] Church, Haddan, Oakeley, Tickell (Univ.)[,] Lewis, J. Mozley, Stanley (perhaps)[,] Lake, Macmullen, [F. W.] Faber (Univ.)[,] Brewer, Coffin, Dalgairns, Ashworth, T. Ryder, Pattison, A. Christie, Pritchard [Prichard] (Balliol)[,] Ormsby [Ornsby] (Lincoln)[,] Bridges (Oriel)[,] Lockhart (Exeter)[,] Harris (Magdalen)[,] Barrow (Queen's)[,] Meyrick (C C C)[,] Chretien (Oriel)[,] Murray (Christ Church)[,] Collings [[Collins]] [Collyns] (Christ Church)[,] etc.⌉

The plan has gone so far that it would create much surprise and talk, were it now suddenly given over. Church, whom I asked, agrees in this. Yet how is it compatible with my holding St Mary's, being what I am? On the other hand, is not such an engagement in itself a sort of guarantee, in addition to the Editorship of the Library of the Fathers and my Fellowship, of remaining quiet, though I did not retain St Mary's for that purpose.

I have another plan of a series of Devotional works, but of this I will speak at another time

Ever Yrs affectly J H N

[1] Keble had replied on 14 May.

[2] *Lyra Apostolica*, a collection of 179 poems by six Tractarians published in 1836.

[3] Reference to Newman's 'Letter Addressed to the Rev. The Margaret Professor of Divinity, on Mr. R. Hurrell Froude's Statements Concerning the Holy Eucharist, and Other Matters Theological and Ecclesiastical', first published in June 1838, and republished in *V.M.* II, pp. 195–257.

[4] Isaac Taylor (1787–1865), artist, inventor, and controversialist who, in his two-volume *Ancient Christianity, and the Doctrines of the Oxford Tracts for the Times*, claimed that the Church of the fourth century was already riddled with doctrinal error and superstitious practices.

To J. R. Bloxam

Tuesday June 27 [1843]

My dear Bloxam,

They tell me that you are at present performing the character of mope—and that the due maintenance of that character forbids your coming so far as Littlemore. If you have nothing better to do, I would come and mope with you at your rooms at dinner on St Peter's day (Thursday) at any hour you please.

I am, My dear Bloxam, Your sympathetic mope John H Newman

To Mrs William Froude

Littlemore. July 28, 1843

My dear Mrs Froude[1]

I wish I could write you such an answer to your letter as it deserves—I mean a real open letter, saying just what I think—but I feel it so difficult to bring out what I would say, that when I attempt it, I become unreal. One difficulty is the analysing and knowing one's feelings—but another is to be able to exhibit them on occasion. I do not carry them in my hand, and, much as I wish it, I cannot put you in possession of them on the mere asking.

There is no doubt at all that I am approximating towards Rome; nor any doubt that those who are very much about me see this, little as I wish it. These two facts, coupled with the very significant and corresponding fact of the Bishops, Heads of religious parties, and organs of religious opinion having disowned me, have determined me on resigning St Mary's, though as yet I have not made this known, nor shall I till the time comes. I feel I am no longer able to fulfil such a *trust*, as a pastoral charge in our Church implies; and, as on the whole I have hitherto ever been aiming at obeying and supporting her rulers, to the best of my ability, so, when I can no longer do this, and especially when they refuse my assistance, it seems a call upon me to release myself from the obligation. As time has gone on, *I* have become more dissatisfied with the established system, and *its conductors* have become more dissatisfied with me; I do not see what good can come of continuing a relation, which each party wishes brought to an end.

If I were ever so sure of continuing just in my present state of mind, these considerations would tell—but it is obvious that, taking circumstances as they are, I may get into serious difficulties if I continue to hesitate about a step which has already employed my mind for three years.

Speaking candidly with you I will say that I do not see beyond this point. I shall retire from St Mary's, if nothing happens, as quietly as I can, and then shall remain here, with pretty much the same occupations as I have at present. Alas! There is something very awful in putting an end to duties which have lain upon me now for 16 years nearly, and, as it were, making up a book which will not be opened till another world. And if you had any idea how miserably those duties have been fulfilled by me, you would partly enter into my feelings on losing all opportunity of retrieving them.

As to the future, I think that of one thing every one may be quite certain, as far as I may dare promise any thing of myself, that I should do nothing sudden, or without people in general being prepared for it. It may be the will of Providence to leave me just where I am—or to lead me on further. His guidance is commonly slow. Quick movements offend people, as for other reasons, so because they are unlike the effects of a heavenly guidance. And they shock, unsettle, and distress them besides.

Now, my dear Mrs Froude, this will seem to you a very cool letter, but you asked me a very cool question—and as you are about the only person who have so asked, you are the only person who has been so answered.

Let us not take thought for the morrow, but be content with what is put before us for the day present. *You* feel this quite, as your letter shows. I am very sorry my talk with William was interrupted. I had long wished for one, yet dreaded it; dreaded it, because it is not pleasant to be running the risk of unsettling a person. And though I know well he is of far too manly a mind to be swayed by another in such a matter, yet I might be suggesting objections to him in the course of our conversation which would afterwards hang about him and trouble him. I have had no hesitation of writing freely to you, because you have anticipated me.

Ever yours affectionately John H Newman

P.S. I cannot answer for what Ward may have said—but I don't at all think that he would remain in our Church merely on the grounds of expediency. I do not believe he said what you have heard—at the same time it is quite true (as *I* think) this [that] his occupation would be almost gone,[2] *did* he join the Church of Rome. I mean his powers of argument *tell* now very much, and would not tell then, for he would have no one for them to tell upon. I suppose we are all liable to be biased by such circumstances, but I believe that he seriously feels that he has no call to join the Church of Rome—and that if he *did* feel he had a call, he would not stay with us. He considers it a sacred duty to remain where Providence has placed him, believing as he does that God's presence is in it.

I have not read the article in the Critic you mention[3]—but I wish to read all of them.

I have kept this letter a post or two—but can write nothing better, though dissatisfied with it.

J. H. N.

---

[1] The present state of Newman's mind was the subject of much speculation by friends—and enemies— and it was commonly thought that he would secede to the Church of Rome at any moment. None of his friends, however, dared to ask him whether or not he was thinking of making such a move—not so Mrs William Froude. This is Newman's reply to her enquiry.

[2] In addition to be being a Fellow of Balliol College, W. G. Ward was also Mathematical Tutor.

[3] W.G. Ward, 'The Synagogue and the Church', *British Critic*, 34, 1843 (July), pp. 1–63.

To Mrs John Mozley

Oriel College. ⌈August 31 / 43⌉

My dearest Jemima

⌈I am very sorry to put you to such pain.[1] Your letter, and Anne's to you, would have brought me to many tears, unless I had so hard a heart. You must take what I do on faith—at least, if not, I cannot find a better way of consoling you.

I wonder my late letters have not prepared you for this. Have you realized that three years since I wished to do it? and that I have printed, that then a friend[2] only prevented me?

It has been determined on since Lent—All through Lent I and another kept it in mind—and then for safety I said I would not act till October, though we both came to one view. October is coming.

No time is 'the' time. You may have thought as you read on—'Three years ago would not have mattered—' will three years hence be easier? The question is, Ought it to be done?

I mention a great secret, because I do not wish others to share in the responsibility; but I will say this,—that I have always said 'I cannot go wrong when A. [[Keble]] and B. [[Rogers]] agree that I should do a thing.' These two men agree in *this*. I have not persuaded them.

I wrote to one of them the other day, whether I should assign some reason—he answered to this effect—'No one who knows the history of Number 90 can be surprised at it—any one but you would have taken the step before.'

My dearest Jemima, my circumstances are not of my making. One's duty is to act *under* circumstances.

Is it a light thing to give up Littlemore? am I not providing dreariness for myself? if others, whom I am pierced to think about, because I cannot help them, suffer, shall I not suffer in my own way?

Every thing that one does honestly, sincerely, with prayer, with advice, must turn to good. In what am not I likely to be as good a judge as another? in the consequences? true—but is not this what I have been ever protesting against, going by expedience, not by principle?] Most religious, most natural, is it to take into account such considerations as A. M. [Anne Mozley] mentions, nay most cruel and wicked not to do so, when principle does not come into question—but if this be a case of duty, and if I be able to judge whether or no it is, I must leave the consequences to Him who makes it a duty.

[My sweetest Jemima, of whom I am quite unworthy, rather pray that I may be directed aright, rather pray that something may occur to hinder me if I am wrong, than take the matter into your hands.]

Ever Yrs very affectionately John H Newman

[1] Jemima's distress at Newman's resigning St Mary's.
[2] John Keble.

To Richard Bagot, Bishop of Oxford

Oriel College. Sept 7. 1843

My dear Lord,

I shall give your Lordship much pain, by the request which it is necessary for me to make of your Lordship, before I proceed to act upon a resolution on which I have made my mind up for a considerable time. It is to ask your Lordship's permission to resign the living of St Mary's.

If I intended such a step three years since, and was only prevented by the advice of a friend, as I have said to your Lordship in print, it is not surprising that I should be determined on it now, when so many Bishops have said such things of me, and no one has taken my part in respect to that interpretation of the articles under which alone I can subscribe them.

I will not ask your Lordship to put yourself to the pain of replying to this request, but shall interpret your silence as an assent.

Were I writing to any one but your Lordship, it might be presumption to suppose I should be asked to reconsider the request which I have been making; but kindness like yours may lead you to suspend your permission. If so, I may be allowed perhaps to say, in a matter in which I am able to speak, that I should much deplore such an impediment as probably leading to results which would more than disappoint your Lordship's intentions in interposing it. My resolution is already no secret to my friends and others.

Let me heartily thank your Lordship for all your past acts of friendship and favor to one who has been quite unworthy of them, and believe me My Lord, to be keenly alive to your anxieties about the state of the Church, and to feel great sorrow as far as I am the occasion of them. On the other hand I will say on my own behalf, that I have ever felt great love and devotion towards your Lordship, I have ever wished to please you, that I have honestly tried to bear in mind that I was in a place of high trust in the Church, and have laboured hard to uphold and strengthen her and to retain her members. I am not relaxing my zeal, till it has been disowned by her rulers; I have not retired from her service till I have lost or forfeited her confidence.

That your Lordship's many good words and works for her welfare may receive a blessing in this life and a full reward in the next, is the prayer of

Your Lordship's affectionate Servant John H Newman

To Mrs Thomas Mozley

Littlemore. In fest. S. Mich ⌈[[Septr 29]] 1843⌉

My dear Harriett

⌈Your distressing letter just received has equally surprised and perplexed me. I really do not think that any answer can sooth[e] you at present, yet no answer seems worse still.

I am much pained at Tom's great indiscretion⌉ [two indecipherable words] which is most irritating, were it right to be irritated;—⌈but I am as sure that he meant every thing that was kind; and he thought (most erroneously) that he gave the least pain by being frank and open. I think his abruptness arose from awkwardness how to tell you what he felt must be told.

Only see what a position we are in, and how difficult to please you. Tom ⟨A B⟩ you blame for telling you a thing—me for not telling. Tom ⟨A B⟩ is cruel, and I am disingenuous.

However, I am only concerned with myself. First, I will say that Tom ⟨A B⟩ had no right to tell what he told you about me,⌉ and I shall write to him to beg him not to do the like to others. ⌈Next, Jemima has not understood me, certainly has not quoted my words.

I do so despair of the Church of England, I am so evidently cast off by her, and, on the other hand[,] I am so drawn to the Church of Rome, that I think it *safer*, as a matter of honesty, not to keep my living.

This is a very different thing from having any *intention* of joining the Church of Rome. However, to avow generally as much as I have now said would be wrong for ten thousand reasons,⌉ which I have not time to enter upon here, and I hardly think you will consider necessary. ⌈People cannot understand a state of doubt, of misgiving, of being unequal to responsibilities etc—but they *will* conclude either that you have a clear view one way or the other. All I know is, that I could not without hypocrisy profess myself any longer a teacher in and a champion of our Church.

Very few persons know this—hardly one person, (only one I think) in Oxford, [[viz James Mozley.]]⌉—not any one in Oxford at present. ⌈I think it would be most cruel, most unkind, most unsettling to tell them. I could not help telling Tom the other day at Cholderton.

As to Tom he surprised me by writing me word that he thought he must go over at once to the Church of Rome.[1] I never had a dream that he was unsettled. I set off for Cholderton the next hour; and though I could not get any promise from him, I succeeded in restraining him from any immediate step. 2nd from giving up Cholderton at once—but 3rd I acquiesced readily in his relinquishment of the British Critic. It is a step I had twice formally recommended to him in the last two years. As to his state of excitement it is very great, but if you knew what the feeling is for it to break upon a man that he is out of the Church,—that in the Church only is salvation, you would excuse any thing in him.

My dear H you must learn patience—so must we all—and resignation to the will of God.⌉

[1] The beginning of Harriett's estrangement from her brother.

To H. E. Manning

Derby. Oct 25. 1843

My dear Manning

Your letter is a most kind one, but you have engaged in a dangerous correspondence. I am deeply sorry for the pain I must give you.

I must tell you then frankly, lest I combat arguments which to me, alas, are shadows, that it is from no disappointment, irritation, or impatience, that I have, whether rightly or wrongly, resigned St Mary's—but because I think the Church of Rome the Catholic Church, and ours not a part of the Catholic Church, because not in communion with Rome, and feel that I could not honestly be a teacher in it any longer.

This conviction came upon me last summer four years. I mentioned it to two friends in the autumn of that year, 1839. And for a while I was in a state of excitement.

It arose in the first instance from reading the Monophysite and Donatist controversies; in the former of which I was engaged in that course of theological study to which I had given myself.

This was a time, when no Bishop, I believe, had declared against us, and when all was progress and hope. I do not think I have ever felt, certainly not then, disappointment or impatience, or the like; for I have never looked forward to the future, nor do I realize it now.

My first effort was to write that Article on the Catholicity of the English Church in the British Critic, and for two years it quieted me. But since the summer of 1839 I have written little or nothing on modern controversy. My Lectures on Romanism and Justification were in 1836–38. My writings in the Tracts for the Times end with 1838, except Bishop Andrewes's Devotions, and Tract 90, which was forced on me. You know how unwillingly I wrote my Letter to the Bishop of Oxford, in which (as the safest course under circumstances) I committed myself again. My University Sermons were a course begun; I did not finish them. The Sermon on Development was a subject intended for years. And I think its view *quite* necessary in justification of the Athanasian Creed.

The Article I speak of quieted me till the end of 1841, *over* the affair of Number 90, when that wretched Jerusalem Bishoprick affair, *no personal matter*, revived all my alarms. They have increased up to this moment.

You see then, that the various ecclesiastical and quasi-ecclesiastical acts, which have taken place in the course of the last two years and a half, are not the cause of my state of opinion; but are keen stimulants and weighty confirmations of a conviction forced upon me, while engaged *in the course* of duty, viz the theological reading to which I have given myself. And this last mentioned circumstance is a fact which has never, I think, come before me till now that I write to you.

It is three years since, on account of my state of opinion, I urged the Provost (in vain) to let St Mary's be separated from Littlemore, thinking I might with a safe conscience serve the latter, though I could not comfortably continue in so public a place as a University. This was before Number 90.

Finally I have acted under advice and that not of my own choosing, but which came on me in the way of duty, nor of those only who agree with me, but of new friends who differ from me.

I have nothing to reproach myself with, as far as I see in the matter of impatience, i.e. practically—or in conduct. And I trust that He who has kept me in the slow course of change hitherto, may keep me still from hasty acts or resolves with a doubtful conscience.

This I am sure of, that such interposition as yours *kind as it is, only does what you* would consider harm. It makes me realize my views to myself, it makes me see their consistency, it assures me of my own deliberateness—it suggests to me the traces of a Providential Hand. It takes away the pain of disclosures, it relieves me of a heavy secret.

You may make what use of my letters you think right.

I am, My dear Manning, Yours affectionately John H Newman

From Oxford to Rome
(1843–46)

Newman's retirement to Littlemore inaugurated a period of personal calm. In January 1844 he remarked to Keble, 'I am in no distress of mind at present...I do not feel called to do anything but to go on where I am.' His calm survived even the attempt by the Heads of Houses in February 1845 to have *Tract 90* condemned, a proposal which in a dramatic scene was vetoed by the Proctors. Newman at Littlemore was unmoved by the controversy in Oxford and claimed to be without curiosity as to the outcome. Throughout this time, however, his confidence in the Church of England was waning. He told Keble that he had 'uncomfortable feelings as if I should not like to die in the English Church'. In general he tried to keep his closest friends abreast of his thoughts and feelings, although Pusey in particular found it difficult to accept what Newman was telling him.

During 1844 he also wrote a series of long letters to Catherine Froude, the sister-in-law of his close friend, Hurrell, who had died eight years earlier. They began as letters to her husband, William, but were intended for her as well. They are invaluable because they supply a narrative of Newman's state of mind as he moved towards the Catholic Church, and he was to use them when he came to write his *Apologia* in 1864; but here the account is more straightforwardly descriptive than apologetic.

None the less, in spite of that outward calm, pressure was mounting within as he became more and more convinced, as he observed to Manning, that the Church of England was in schism. Once he was clear about that, then his own salvation depended on his joining the Church of Rome. That would not be true for those who did not share this conviction, but for him there could be no alternative. And he was aware that such a move would involve sacrifice. 'I have no existing sympathies with Roman Catholics', he went on in this letter to Manning. 'I hardly ever, even abroad, was at one of their services—I know none of them. I do not like what I hear of them.' He was agonizing over a decision that seemed to be inevitable, even though some days later he was still telling his sister, Jemima, 'I have no intention of an early step even now'. That was in November 1844. Before Christmas, however, in a further and prescient letter to her, listing the kind of motives that would be attributed to him for moving, he stated that his actual motive 'simply is that I believe the Roman Church to be true'.

The following year he began writing his *Essay on the Development of Christian Doctrine* to clarify his position. It was, he declared, a hypothesis to account for a difficulty: as Protestantism was in error and the Church of England in schism, could it be that what had hitherto appeared as Roman excess, additions to the deposit of faith, were in fact authentic developments of living doctrine? On 11 July he told Richard Westmacott, with whom he had been at school in Ealing, 'it is morally certain I shall join the R. C. Church'.

There were then letters to members of his family, preparing them for what was going to happen, and in October Newman resigned as a Fellow of Oriel, welcomed the Passionist priest, Dominic Barberi, to Littlemore, and was received into the Catholic Church on 9 October. Letters to family and many friends, written in anticipation of the event, were then posted.

Further letters in the months following tried to comfort those who were distressed by what he had done, but he was immediately testy with Jemima when she wrote, advising him to leave Littlemore: 'if I said I *ought in duty* to go away, I should be confessing I ought not to join the Church of Rome at all'. He was writing this letter at 5.30 in the morning of 9 October. After so long a time, pondering and preparing himself, his mind was clear and he was not going to be deflected in any way. He felt wounded by his family's behaviour. Jemima tended to be their mouthpiece, so she bore the brunt of his sharp reactions.

Newman left Littlemore the following February and moved to Maryvale near Oscott. He was deeply sad to go. 'Very happy times have I had here,' he told Henry Wilberforce, '(though in such doubt)—and I am loth to leave it.'

Plans for the future began to unfold. During the summer, it was decided that he would go to Rome to prepare for ordination as a Catholic priest. He and Ambrose St John, who remained so steadfast a friend from his Littlemore days on, set off in September and the letters that describe the journey are sometimes reminiscent of those written when he had visited the Mediterranean with the Froudes. As well as news, there were shafts of humour. Writing to Dalgairns who had been part of the community at Littlemore, he commented, 'I have asked St John what else I have to say, and he says "Tell him, you bully me!" This is true, but he deserves it.'

4

From Oxford to Rome (1843–46)

To Mrs William Froude

Littlemore. Dec. 9. 1843

My dear Mrs Froude

I seem to myself to have behaved quite cruelly to you, yet what could I do?[1] Really I feel very much about it, though that will not mend matters. I keep saying to myself continually 'I did not make my circumstances'. Not that I can doubt that much that is wrong and earthly mixes up in every thing I do, or that my present state of perplexity is a punishment on me for sins committed; yet after all surely, on the supposition that people are born under a defective religious system (and that there are such we all grant) what can their course be, if they act religiously but first to defend it, and, as time goes on, to mistrust it? Surely I cannot blame myself, whatever my present opinion may be, in having done all I could first to maintain myself and others where we are providentially placed,—yet this is the circumstance which, I suppose, has given you the most distress, though for what I know it is in a measure past—viz the very unsettling effect which it must produce, to have given yourself to a view of theology such as is drawn out in my Lectures on Romanism, and then to begin to suspect, or at least to be told by the person who wrote them, that it is not trustworthy. For the feeling occurs: 'if my reason has taken me in once, why may it not again? if I thought the Anglican argument sound and it is not, why should the Roman be sound to which I am drawn now?' One begins to be sceptical about all arguments, and to question whether truth can be found, or is any where.

Yet, I repeat, I do not know how to blame myself for writing that book, though selfwill and self confidence doubtless were mingled with the work. If Catholic doctrines were to be inculcated, it was an act of treachery to our church, not to accompany the teaching with such safeguards against Romanizing which would be their infallible effect on the mind, if they were left to work freely. One could not give our church the benefit of Catholicism, without opening upon it the danger of Romanism. To throw up bulwarks then against the Church of Rome was necessary for our position. We could not remain the Church of England, unless we did so.

And again I was struck and impressed with the theological theory of Laud and his school, and I attempted to develop and define it, for the benefit of others.

And moreover, this I will say for my own consolation and that of others, that a vast deal of that book remains to me where it was. The two great principles remain, first of Scripture having an authoritative interpretation, next of Scripture being the sole document of faith. At least the Church of Rome has never denied the latter; the Council of Trent leaves it an open question.

Again many of the *issues* to which I reduce questions, remain as before—as facts, though the R.C. takes the one side, and the Anglo Catholic the other. E.g. I have drawn out the history or the argument of the doctrine of Purgatory—a person reading it, when the book came out, said that it was almost a proof of it. Again, it is true any how, that in various doctrines the R.C.s have proceeded by scripture only, without or in spite of tradition; and that in others they have gone by abstract arguments.

Moreover a great part of the book is an attack upon Protestantism, and *that* stands any how. When it was published, a friend said in conversation 'Oh he did not consider the Anti-Roman part of it—it was the Anti-Protestant part alone which gave character to it'—This was no extreme man—it was T. Acland.[2]

And still further it is plain from beginning to end, that I was under the great apprehension lest the view should prove a mere paper view, a fine theory, which would not work, which would not move. I felt strongly the objection that it has never been carried into effect, and in the opening sentences of the last Lecture I speak in the language of despondency.

But enough of this—or rather far too much, except that I feel I owe you some amends, such as it is, for having led you to take up what now you find I question myself.

So far at least results from what has passed—that it is a duty to be very slow in taking up and acting upon any new belief. Granting that there is this great distinction in the two judgments, that the former was biassed (properly so) by a deference to a system in which one found oneself, and the latter is unwillingly forced upon the mind, still there is the greatest reason for dreading lest one should be the sport of mere argumentative demonstrations.

Time alone can show whether a view will hold—but then there is this consolation, that, if time has shown the untenableness of one, it will do the like service to another, if it be untenable.

Time alone can turn a view into a conviction—It is most unsatisfactory to be acting on a syllogism, or a solitary, naked, external, logical process. But surely it is possible in process of time to have a proposition so wrought into the mind, both ethically and by numberless fine conspiring and ever-recurring considerations as to become part of our mind, to be inseparable from us, and to command our obedience. And then the greater the sacrifice, the more cogent the testimony shall we have to its authority, for to overcome impediments is a token of power.

And time alone can show whether what forces itself upon us, influences others also. It seems impossible, humanly speaking, that we should be moved, and others not moved. If others were not moved, and their impassibleness could not be referred to definite causes, I confess it would be a very strong argument against us. And it seems so much the merciful rule of Divine Providence thus to rescue us from dependence on our private judgment.

Alas! I know all this is far more satisfactory to such as myself than to you who have been put in trust with souls whom you are to train from infancy in the fear of God—and this is the topic you chiefly dwell on in your note—but I trust it will not prove a practical difficulty to you—and sufficient for the day is the evil thereof.

It quite put me out, when William was here, to think how little I could explain myself to him. In truth, it is hardly possible to do so in a little while. Every thing I said seemed to be shot out like bullets, round and hard and sudden—Arguments grow out of the mind, but when you see friends but seldom, there is a necessary abuse of a certain medium of communication which is the very life of conversation and discussion—I could only lament it; and wish, what at present seems out of the question, that we are thrown together more.

Pray thank him for his very kind present, which doubtless by its very presence will frighten away cold, cough and face-ache from our premises. I have told them in London to send you my new volume of Sermons at once—so I am almost in hopes you have it by now[.]

I am very much concerned indeed to hear your news of Miss Froude[.]

Do you know I am in the greatest anxiety about my oldest and most dear friend Bowden? He is [at] St. Leonard's[3] for the winter. Four years ago he was given over on account of an abscess on his lungs—and now the complaint has returned.

Long as this letter is, I know still you will take it as proceeding from a wish at least to be of use to you[.]

> Yours, My dear Mrs Froude, very affectionately John H Newman

[1] Mrs Froude had written to Newman on 1 November 1843: 'Mr. Rogers' suspicions that you might be approximating towards Rome, were the first hint that I had had,—and I will own it was a great blow and shake altogether—.'

[2] Thomas Dyke Acland (1809–98), who had just become Conservative MP for West Somerset and would remain MP until his retirement in 1857.

[3] St Leonard's-on-Sea, near Hastings, Sussex.

To H. E. Manning

Dec 24/43

My dear Manning

How can I thank you enough for your most kind letter received last night?—and what can have led you to entertain the thought I could ever be crossed by the idea which you consider may have been suggested to me by the name of Orpah?[1] Really, unless it were so sad a matter, I should smile; the thought is as far from me as the Antipodes. Rather I am the person who to myself always seem, and reasonably, the criminal; I cannot afford to have hard thoughts which can more plausibly be exercised against myself. And yet to speak of myself, how could I have done otherwise than I have done or better? I own indeed to great presumption and recklessness in my mode of writing on ecclesiastical subjects, on various occasions, yet still I have honestly trusted our Church and wished to defend her as she wishes to be defended. I was not surely wrong in defending her on that basis which our Divines have ever built and on which alone they can pretend to build. And how could I foresee that when I examined that basis I should feel it to require a system different from hers and that the Fathers to which she led me would lead me from her? I do not see then that I have been to blame; yet it would be strange if I had heart to blame others who are honest in maintaining what I am abandoning.

It is no pleasure to me to differ from friends—no comfort to be estranged from them—no satisfaction or boast to have said things which I must unsay. Surely I will remain where I am as long as ever I can. I think it right to do so. If my misgivings are from above, I shall be carried on in spite of my resistance. I cannot regret in time to come having struggled to remain where I found myself placed. And believe me, the circumstance of such men as yourself being contented to remain is the strongest argument in favor of my own remaining. It is my constant prayer, that if others are right I may be drawn back—that nothing may part us.

Thank you for your charge and the passage you point out. I was pleased to see the coincidence between us.

I am, my dear Manning, Ever yours affectionately, John H. Newman.

[1] After reading Newman's sermon, 'The Parting of Friends' (S.D., pp. 395–409), Manning was anxious that he might be identified in Newman's thoughts with Orpah in the Book of Ruth, someone who caused disappointment (p. 402).

To Mrs John Mozley

Littlemore [January 21. 1844]

My dear Jemima

I am kept at home all day with a bad cold, which (I am thankful to say) has not happened to me on a Sunday for years. Perhaps it is that I am not bound any how to go out on a Sunday, but still I think that it *is* more than an ordinary cold, and, that going out would increase it much. I expect it will be gone tomorrow or next day, for my colds last so little a time now. [I would write you a long letter, were it not for my stupid fingers or wrist—I cannot tell where the ache and stiffness are. As to rubbing, as my Aunt [Elizabeth] recommends, I might as well rub my nose as my wrist, or, as some one says, it is like cutting one's nails for the toothache.]

You didn't see the point of H's [Harriett's] two letters. I cut off half the first (which was all but two words, the beginning of the sentence I sent you, about other matters) because it was so queer—your bad looks was one of the queernesses. Poor H. is full of perversions and cannot really help it—and I only wish to do what is kindest. The point was (to return) that in the first she quarrelled with me about a matter of *fact*— then when she found that she was wrong in what she thought I said and that I agreed with *her*, still she would not let me off, but attacked the *spirit and tone* of this opposite statement. You see it was not *old* matters; she is determined to begin and keep up some thing new and present. Now I say this to you, sincerely because I wish to do what is best. [She may of course, she has full right, to differ from me in opinion. She remains (I fully grant) just where she was. She has not changed. I have read what she has not read, and have changed. I read first (as I was bound to do) with other people's eyes, and since I have read with my own, not being able to help it—but still I do not force my views upon *her*, I have not obtruded them in any way—I have felt nothing but pain—but she is resolved to get into argument with me—and I am resolved⌉ (so be it) ⌈not⌉ to do so. I wish to have an argument with no one; by which I mean any thing between person and person. And it is very bad tact in her, for it is just the way to drive one in one's *feelings* further from her opinions. She is doing what our rulers are doing on a large scale—trying to show us we are in a false position—that we are not in our place. So, when she was abroad, her letters insisted much on the essential distinction and contrariety between the Church of Rome and ourselves. She said it was absurd to say we could be one and the same system—there are temptations enough for persons to think so, without adding to them.

I was glad of your and John's opinion about St Stephen Harding.[1] I am far from denying that it might startle some people—nay many—nor did it annoy me that Rivingtons should reject it, but that they should cast all the expense on me *so cavalierly*. They might just as well have sent in the bills to me of an edition of my Sermons instead of paying me sundry pounds they had promised. ⌈The terms were that they should have the copy right, and pay the writers, and I expressly excepted myself as Editor from payment, as I said I did not want any thing. The real history of the abandonment of the plan is this. ⟨⟨All this is in strict confidence⟩⟩ Pusey happened to see some sheets of St Stephen H. in my room, and told Hope that he expected it would create a fresh storm. I then said I would stop the plan; that I had never wished to get into rows, that I had all but stopped the Tracts, and should have done so but for Froude—that I had set about this plan for other reasons which were not so cogent as that of peace etc etc Pusey begged me not to stop them on his opinion—on which I said that, as Rivingtons had been writing to me rather anxiously, I would be decided by what they thought—and that I would recommend them to read St Stephen. R [Rivington] (as you know) spoke in the strongest terms against it and another. I still doubted what to do when it came to the point—I was pledged so far. So I got Gladstone to look over it—He was frightened too—then I resolved to give up the plan.⌉ However, it was natural that the Lives which were done or doing, should be published, for various reasons—and this will happen. This *may* lead to a continuance of the work—that must be left to the chance of things—of course whatever one does leads to other things—if one were *silent* quite, *it* might lead to a despair and abandonment of Anglo-Catholicism on the part of some. Nor should I be sorry, rather I should be very glad, if these Lives could be all done, could it be without a storm—and ⌈my *name* and the profession and process of a series are what at the *moment* seem to be the cause of P's and G's fear⌉ As to Rivington, he wishes to shake himself loose; that is the beginning and end of it—and this is a pretext.

And now, my dear J, I have written you so cross a letter that you will think my cold has affected my temper—but that is not the case—and I rejoice to say that (whether from being in better health or other cause) I am not so moody, as when you, dearest, knew me better

With love to all, Ever Yrs affly J H N

P.S. Emma falls off the last half. I have been reading Sintrim [Sintram] again, and it has made me cry.[2]

[1] This Life of St Stephen Harding, written by John Dalgairns, was the first in a series of *Lives of English Saints* that Newman was planning in order to rein in the growing enthusiasm of some of the younger Tractarians for Rome (see *Apo.*, pp. 210–11).

[2] *Emma*, by Jane Austen (1775–1817). *Sintram and His Companions*, by Friedrich de la Motte Fouqué (1777–1843).

To John Keble

Littlemore. January 23. 1844

My dear Keble

It is not for want of thinking of you and meaning to write to you that I keep silent, but I have so great a reluctance to take up my pen, though I have long owed you a letter—and I do not know how to talk about myself, even for fear of saying not [what] is not exact about my feelings, of saying what is unreal and the like. Yet I do owe you a letter and mean some time to pay it.

More thanks to you than I can give, for your present most kind letter, which is just like you. Thanks for what you tell me about yourself, and thanks for your kind anxiety about me.

I am in no distress of mind at present—that is, whatever is truth, and whatever is not, I do not feel called to do any thing but to go on where I am, and this must be peace and quietness—and whatever is before us, in this one may rejoice, and not take thought for tomorrow. I fear I must say I have a steadily growing conviction about the English Church—you will understand what I mean—And this I think without any effort of mine. The early Church has all along been my line of study— and I am still occupied upon it. For some time, I suppose, I shall be upon the 'the Arians'[1] and the second part of the volume of St Athanasius.[2] It is this line of reading, and no other, which has lead me Romeward. Not that I read it with that view.

I wish to resist, as I always have—and think it a duty. I am sure, *if* it be right to go forward, I shall be forced on in spite of myself. Somehow I cannot feel the question of dutifulness so strongly as it is sometimes put. Was it undutifulness to the Mosaic Law, to be led on to the Gospel? was not the Law from God? How could a Jew, formerly or now, ever become a Christian, if he must at all hazards resist convictions and for ever? How could a Nestorian or Monophysite join the Catholic Church but by a similar undutifulness?

What I wish is, not to go by my own judgment, but by something external, like the pillar of the cloud in the desert. Such is the united movement of *many*. The publishing those Sermons is like Gideon's fleece.[3] If it were permanently to stop people, this would have a great influence on me. I should think there was something *real* in the view. What I fear is, that they are only ingenious; but the event alone can show this, and it seemed to me right to make the experiment, that is, rather burying what might be a talent *not* to publish them [*sic*]. A simplehearted and clever young woman,[4] who had been perplexed with doubts about Rome, on reading my *University* Sermons, suddenly rose from her chair and said 'This what I wanted, this satisfies me—' *How* they satisfied her I have no notion, or whether they will eventually. But still, if this kind of effect did follow from what I have written, (or from what any one else wrote) it would tend greatly to convince me that my duty was where I am. On the other hand I must not conceal, that letters, which I receive continually from persons whom I know and whom I know not, show me that a movement is going on in cases which are little suspected and in minds which are struggling against it.

Every thing is hid from us as to the effect of things. People are unsettled as it is. As years go on, they either will become settled, or they will be gradually more and more unsettled. If *my* thoughts have been led through the early Church to Rome why should not others? We know nothing of the effects of one's own hypothetical acts. There have been events ten thousand times more unsettling than the change of individuals now. St Paul must have unsettled all the good and conscientious people in the Jewish Church. Unsettling may be a blessing, even where minds are *not* already unsettled.

I hope I am not wrong,—but I have lately been praying that 'if I am right, Pusey, Manning etc may be brought forward; but if Pusey, Manning etc are right, I may be brought back—that nothing, if it be possible may separate us.'

One thing I will add—I sometimes have uncomfortable feelings as if I should not like to die in the English Church. It seems to me that, while Providence gives one time, it is even a call upon one to make use of it *in* deliberateness and waiting—but that did He cut short one's hour of grace, this would be a call to make up one's mind on what seemed most probable.

I have written all this, as it occurred to me only that you might see my state of mind—not in the way of argument.

I wish I could sufficiently thank you for, or duly feel the kindness of your letter. May God bless you for it.

What you told me about Wilson was a great relief—Bowden, thank God, is certainly better. It *looks* as if a crisis were past, but we must be cautious in speaking. I wish my sister were really better, but her recovery will be very slow.

Ever Yours most affecty John H Newman

---

[1] Newman was engaged in a new edition of *Arians of the Fourth Century*. It never materialized.

[2] At the time, Newman was also at work translating Part II of *Select Treatises of S. Athanasius, Archbishop of Alexandria, in Controversy with the Arians*, for the Library of the Fathers.

[3] *Judges* 6: 36–40.

[4] See Elizabeth Crawford Lockhart (1812–70), letter to Newman, 7 October 1843 (*L.D.* IX, pp. 556–8).

To Miss Mary Holmes

Littlemore. Febr 17/44

My dear Miss Holmes

How little you know yourself. Of course it now appears I ought not to have let you go to Prior Park—but you were confident as to your stability, and it would have seemed harsh to have refused. As to your being called to join the Church of Rome, this fickleness seems to me to prove the reverse—conversion should be the result of deliberate intention—but you are influenced by an impulse. There is nothing to show that, if you committed yourself, you would not next day get disgusted and wish yourself back. If you ever joined it, your conversion should be an act founded on a deliberate resolution made and written down six months before and not repented of in the interval. Our Saviour bids us count the cost.

I wish you had said whether you wished to go to Church here or in Oxford—In the balance which to choose for you, I have decided on Oxford, by the circumstance of the labour it will cause man and horse to come here. This is sufficient to turn the scale. As you are in St Mary Magdalen Parish, I think you had better go to Church there. I will send some one there for you. The Church has lately been put to right, and has a stained window by Wailes.[1]

Yours very sincerely John H Newman

P.S. I will come to you after morning service, that is, one o'clock.

Sunday morning. Littlemore. I have written to my old friend Dr Ogle, a physician in this place, to give you a seat in his pew at St Mary Magd. He will send to you. Him and his daughters I have known all *their* lives. I have said you did not want any other civility.

[1] William Wailes (1808–81), stained-glass artist from Newcastle.

To E. B. Pusey

Littlemore. Febr 19/44

My dear Pusey

A note from you has been picked up on the road and brought to me. It relates to the present you have made me today, and is most kind as all you do is.

It is, however, written under a false impression from which I can relieve you. I am in no perplexity or anxiety at present. I fear that I must say that for four years and a half I have had a conviction, weaker or stronger, but on the whole constantly growing, and at present very strong, that we are not part of the Church. I am too much accustomed to this idea to feel pain at it. I could only feel pain, if I found it led me to action. At present I do not feel any such call. Such feelings are not hastily to be called convictions, though this seems to me to be such. Did I ever arrive at a full persuasion that it was such, then I should be anxious and much perplexed. My case is described in the note at p 414 of my New Volume of Sermons.[1]

Alas—I fear I have removed pain from your mind in one way, only to give a greater pain in another. Yet is it possible you can be quite unprepared for this avowal? It was the Monophysite and Donatist controversies which in 1839 led me to this clear and distinct judgment.

May all good attend you and all comfort, My dear Pusey, is the prayer of

Yrs affectly John H Newman

[1] 'Nothing that is here said about uncovenanted mercies must be taken to imply that individuals ought to be satisfied in remaining external to the Catholic Church, when they are once *convinced* of the fact; but mere impressions, impulses, fancies, frames of mind, logical deductions, or the blindness which follows on religious carelessness, may easily be mistaken for convictions. It is a duty, then, to doubt about them, nay to resist them, and often for a very long time; and under this painful and weary trial, though not under other circumstances, surely the mind may religiously dwell on the thought of God's extraordinary dispensations of grace, as a relief of its apprehensions.' *S.D.*, p. 366.

To E. B. Pusey

Littlemore. In Vigil. S. Matt. [Matthias 23 February] 1844

My dear P

Thanks for your note, which I know gave you pain to write. I do not doubt that there must be some fault in me which has led you to such impressions; but think you mistake in attributing my manner etc to sensitiveness, or sharp feeling. Suppose it has been in part a latent wish to convey to you in *detail* my view of things which I dared not say plainly, and a sort of fidget that you did not know? And I think you do not put yourself enough into my position, and consider how a person would view things, and at the end of near five years. I suppose it is possible for a Church to have some profound wound, which, till healed, infallibly impeded the exercise of its powers and made attempts to act futile. How should we feel, e.g. if we saw a man with a broken leg attempting to walk?—But if such a state be possible, what would a person's feelings be who saw it but those which we entertain towards such a disabled man? Would he be wrong in having them? However, I repeat, I have no doubt there is fault in me, which has made you so write

Ever Yrs affly J H N

To Mrs William Froude

⌈Littlemore. April 3/44.

My dear Mrs Froude,[1]

Pray take my writing as a proof of my anxiety to act rightly towards persons I love so much as William and you—and please continue to do what I am sure you do already, remember at sacred times and places me and my difficulties.

What I was going to remark upon yesterday was what seemed W's chief distress—viz that my changing my opinion seemed to unsettle one's confidence in truth and falsehood as external things, and led [lead] one to be as suspicious of the new opinion as one became distrustful of the old. Now in what I shall say, I am not going to speak in favour of my second thoughts in comparison of my first, but against such scepticism and unsettlement about truth and falsehood generally—the idea of which is very painful—at least, this will be my main subject.[2]

The case with me, then, was this, and not surely an unnatural one:—as a matter of feeling and of duty I threw myself into a system which I found myself in. I saw that the English Church had a theological idea or theory as such, and I took it up. I read Laud on Tradition, and thought it (as I still think it) very masterly. The Anglican Theory was very distinctive. I admired it, and took it on faith. It did not (I think) occur to me to doubt it, and I saw that it was *able*, and supported by learning, and I felt it was a *duty* to maintain it. Further on looking into Antiquity and reading the Fathers, I saw such portions of it as I examined fully confirmed (e.g. the Supremacy of Scripture.) There was only one question about which I had a doubt, viz whether it would *work*, for it has never been more than a paper system.

Of course it is a difficulty to speak from memory of feelings and thoughts, which belong to eight and nine years ago, and moreover, to an exciting and busy time—yet I trust I have represented my former self correctly, though such a representation needs as much caution as I can give it.

One thing of course I saw clearly—that there was a great risk of Anglican principles running into Roman. They, i.e. primitive had done so once—as I notice in the Advertisement to my third volume of Sermons[3]—they might do so again. And I felt both admiration and love of Rome, as far as I dare. This is plain from one of the notes in smaller type on the Translation of Vincentius in Records of the Church (in the Tracts) No xxiv, in which I say, 'Considering the high gifts and the strong claims of the Church of Rome etc, on our admiration, reverence and love, and gratitude, how could we withstand it, as we do; how could we refrain from being melted into tenderness and rushing into communion with it, but for the words of Truth itself etc. "He that loveth father and mother more than Me etc." '? Other of the early Tracts show the same thing—and some of the Lyras. 'O Mother Church of Rome" and "O that thy creed were sound.'[4]

Nothing then but a strong positive difficulty or repulsion has kept me from surrendering my heart to the authority of the Church of Rome; a repulsive principle, not growing out of Catholic, Anglican, or Primitive doctrine, in the way in which I viewed that doctrine, but something antagonistic, arising from *particular doctrines* of the Church of Rome, particular historical views, etc etc.

And this very circumstance led me to be violent enough against the Church of Rome—because it was the only way of resisting it. A bulwark or breakwater was necessary to the position of the English Church and theory. And in being violent, I was not acting on private judgment against so great a Communion, but I had the authority or rather the command of all our Divines, who, doubtless from the same constraining necessity have ever been violent against her also. To be violent against Rome was to be dutiful to England, as well as a measure of necessity for the English theory.

Now on all these respects I was contrasted, as you may easily see, with Hurrell Froude. He went by no theory, he was bent on defending no system, he was no advocate, laughed at economies, merely investigated—and in consequence, and just in the same proportion, did not attack the Church of Rome, and disliked attacks upon it.

But to be brief—such were my feelings and views from 1833 to 1839. It was my great aim to build up the English system into something like consistency, to develop its idea, to get rid of anomalies, and to harmonize precedents and documents. I thought, and still think, its theory a great one. What then was my dismay or excitement, call you which [sic] you will, when in 1839 it flashed upon me in the course of reading the Fathers, which I had hitherto read with the eyes of our own Divines, that (not only was it a theory never realized) but a theory unproved or rather disproved by Antiquity? but I must stop.

Yr affte friend J H N⌉

[1] At the time, Froude was working as an engineer on the Exeter–Barnstaple railway with Brunel and was frequently away from home. Hence Newman's reason for addressing the rest of the correspondence to Mrs Froude, on the understanding that the correspondence was a three-sided one. A section of the line from Exeter to Beambridge was due to open on Wednesday 1 May 1844.

[2] Newman incorporated this paragraph and the following one, with minor variations, in *Apo.*, p. 205.

[3] This Advertisement was omitted from the uniform edition of Newman's sermons.

[4] *Lyra Apostolica*, clxxiii 'The Cruel Church', clxxiv, 'The Good Samaritan'.

To Mrs William Froude

⌈Littlemore April 4/44. In Cœnâ Domini.⌉
(all good gifts to you at this season)

⌈My dear Mrs Froude

Without waiting for any answer from you, here I go on, making up pretty considerably for my delay and silence; and all about myself.

So far from my change of opinion having any fair tendency to unsettle persons as to truth and falsehood as objective realities, it should be considered whether such change is not necessary, *should* truth be a real objective thing, and made to confront a person who has been brought up in a system *short of* truth. Surely the *continuance* of a person who wishes to go right in a wrong system, and not his giving it up, would be that which militated against the objectiveness of Truth—leading to the suspicion that one thing and another were equally pleasing to our Maker, where men were sincere.[1]

Nor surely is it a thing that I need to be sorry for that I defended the system in which I found myself, and have had to unsay my words. For is it not one's duty, instead of beginning with criticism, to throw oneself generously into that form of religion which is providentially put before one? Is it right, is it not wrong, to begin with private judgment? May we not on the other hand look for a blessing *through* obedience even to an erroneous system, and a guidance by means of it out of it? Were those who were strict and conscientious in their Judaism, or those who were lukewarm and sceptical, more likely to be led into Christianity, when Christ came? Yet in proportion to their previous zeal, would be their appearance of inconsistency. Certainly, I have always contended that obedience even to an erring conscience was the way to gain light, and that it mattered not where a man began, so that he began on what came to hand and in faith—that any thing might become a divine method of Truth, that to the pure all things are pure, and have a self-correcting virtue and a power of germinating. And though I have no right at all to assume that this mercy is granted to me, yet the fact that a person in my situation *may* have it granted seems to me to remove the perplexity which my change of opinion may occasion.

I am writing in a most miserable prosy way, which I cannot just now get out of. Perhaps it will go of itself presently. Well—but it may be said,—I have said it to myself,[2]—'Why, however, did you *publish*? had you waited quietly, you would have changed your opinion without any of the misery, which now is involved in the change, of disappointing and distressing people.' I answer, that things are bound up together as to form a whole, and one cannot tell what is not a condition of what. I do not see how possibly I could have published the Tracts or other works professing to defend our Church without accompanying them with a strong protest or argument against Rome—The one obvious objection against the whole Anglican line is, that it is Roman; and I really think there is no alternative between silence altogether, and forming a theory and attacking the Roman system. In my Lectures on the Prophetical Office, I apologize for doing the latter from 'the circumstances of the moment,' both because 'till they (persons who teach the "Holy Catholic Church") do *more than they have hitherto done*,' 'they hazard a deviation into Romanism etc' and next because in teaching that doctrine, 'the plan of attacking Romanism' is 'the most convenient way of showing what our own views are.'[3] As far as I recollect I give the same *defensive* reason in the first of the Tracts against Romanism, Number 71,[4] I think. Either then I was obliged to commit myself to a theory of the Church and against Rome publicly and argumentatively, or not a Tract could be written. And where I should now be in opinion as well as many others, if no Tract had appeared, is a speculation quite beyond me.

Nothing indeed all through this course of things strikes me as more strange than the intertwining of things good and bad. E.g. one is tempted to say, knowing what misery has resulted and does result from Dr Hawkins being Provost of Oriel. 'O, that Hurrell's wish had been accomplished of placing Keble in his place!' But if Keble had been Provost, I for one should probably be Tutor of Oriel to this day. What great things K. might have done there, of course is quite hid from us—they would have been great—but we should never have been dismissed from the Tuition, we (K, H. R. F. [Richard Hurrell Froude] and I) should never have turned our minds so keenly to other subjects, not a Tract would have been written—I should have gone on with Mathematics (which I was bent on doing and did, till Jenkyns[5] *on the ground* of my *leaving* the Tutorship introduced me to Rose and so to the History of Arianism) I should have gone on with Neibuhr and Aristotle.

You must not suppose I am arguing against my having committed all sorts of faults in my *mode* of doing things—so much so, that all the comfort I might have had is taken away, of feeling an *assurance* that I might have been brought on by a divine guidance to my present point. Alas! though I do not think there is any thing in the mere fact of my change to show that I am wrong or to unsettle people, yet I have so bad a conscience in details, as to have *very little* claim to feel confidence that I am right. This of course is what keeps me back.

And now this insufferable prose has exhausted my paper. O my dear Mrs Froude, I am very much disgusted at it.

Ever Yrs affly J H N⌉

¹ This paragraph and the following one appear in *Apo.*, pp. 205–6.

² The next four sentences appear in *Apo.*, pp. 206–7.

³ See *V.M.* I, p. 6.

⁴ Later republished with minor alterations as 'On the Mode of Conducting the Controversy with Rome' in *V.M.* II, pp. 95–141; see pp. 139–40.

⁵ Richard Jenkyns (1782–1854), Master of Balliol College from 1814 until his death.

To Mrs William Froude

⌈Littlemore. Good Friday Evening. April 5 1844

My dear Mrs Froude,

I write with some apprehension lest I should be making a great fuss about nothing and to no good—and yet I think too that what I have said and shall say may tend to make you less uncomfortable.

My confidence against the Church of Rome lay in two things; first, my feeling that we had the Apostolical Succession—next my conviction that her peculiar doctrines were not held by the Fathers.

As to the first of these, I acknowledged great irregularity in the transmission, and vast and various disorders and faults in our Church—but I got over all by the parallel of the Jewish Church, which was a Church when Christ came, in spite of anomalies as great as ours. My view is drawn out in my last Lecture on the Prophetical Office.

As to the second it was to me as clear as day (as it is now) that the honors paid in the Church of Rome to St Mary were not primitive. On this I rested our case mainly—for those honors are at once the farthest removed from primitive usage and especially characteristic of the Roman Church. I have drawn out the general argument in Lecture ii on 'Romanism as neglectful of Antiquity.'

My defence of the English Church against Rome was conducted under the shelter of these two convictions, with the expression of which my Lectures begin and end. They were written in 1834–1837; and during 1836 and 7 the Tracts against Rome.

In the summer of 1839 I was led in the course of my *regular reading* (which is a point on which some stress might be laid) to the Monophysite controversy, and to the Council of Chalcedon and St Leo's works inclusively. I found what surprised me very much. It struck me at once, but when it began to assume an unsettling character I do not recollect—but I found more matter for serious thought in that history than in anything I had read. The Council of Chalcedon is the fourth

⟨A.D. 452⟩ [*sic*] Ecumenical Council, which it is generally considered the English Church receives. Our Divines consider its opponents heretics, as denying that 'Jesus Christ has come in the flesh.' Eutyches[1] was condemned then, who said there was but one nature in our Lord. Now I cannot bring together all the strange things I found in its history. I found the Eastern Church under the superintendence (as I may call it) of Pope Leo. I found that *he* had made the Fathers of the Council unsay their decree and pass another, so that (humanly speaking) we owe it to Pope Leo at this day that the Catholic Church holds the true doctrine. I found that Pope Leo based his authority upon St Peter. I found the Fathers of the Council crying out 'Peter hath spoken by the mouth of Leo', when they altered their decree. I found a portentously large body of Christians thrown into schism by the Council—at this day the Churches of Egypt, Syria (in part) and Armenia; and the Schismatics, not like the Arians of a rationalist, but with a theology of a warm and elevating character. I found that they appealed, as with much plausibility to certain of the Fathers, as St Athanasius and St Cyril of Alexandria—that they professed to be maintainers of Antiquity—that they called their opponents (the Catholics) *Chalcedonians*, as we call RCs Tridentines, that their cause was taken up by the civil power, and created a contention between Emperors and the Church. Further I found there was a large middle party as well as an extreme. There was a distinct Via media, which indeed the Emperor took up—and there was a large body who went on for centuries without Bishops. I am writing from memory, but I am sure I am right in all points of consequence—and in a word I found a complete and wonderful parallel, as if a prophecy, of the state of the Reformation Controversy, and that we were on the Anti-Catholic side.

I will go on with part of the subject at the expense of the order of time. I add then that from that time to this, the view thus brought before me has grown upon me. I had hitherto read ecclesiastical history with the eyes of our Divines, and taken what they said on faith, but now I got *a key*, which interpreted large passages of history which had been locked up from me. I found every where one and the same picture, prophetic of our present state, the Church in communion with Rome decreeing, and heretics resisting. Especially as regards the Arian controversy, how could I be so blind before! except that I looked at things bit by bit, instead of putting them together. There was Pope Julius[2] resisting the whole East in defence of St Athanasius, the Eusebians at the Great Council of Antioch[3] resisting him, and he appealing to his own authority (in which the historians support him) and declaring that he filled the see of St Peter. The lapse of Pope Liberius,[4] carefully as it needs considering, does not interfere with the general view. There were two parties, a Via Media, and an extreme, both heretical—but the Via Media containing pious men, whom St Athanasius and others sympathise in—there were the kings of the earth taking up heresy against the Church—there was precisely the same appeal to Scripture, which now obtains, and that grounded on a liberal interpretation of its text, to which St Athanasius always opposes the 'ecclesiastical sense'—There was the same complaint of introducing novel and unscriptural terms into the Creed of the Church, 'Consubstantial' 'Transubstantiation' being both of philosophical origin, and if Trent has opposed some previous Councils (which I do not recollect) at least the Nicene Council adopted the very term 'Consubstantial' which a celebrated Council of Antioch 60 or 70 years before condemned or discountanenced.

When shall I come to an end?

Ever yrs affectionately J H N⌉

[1] Eutyches (c.378–454) was archimandrite of a large, flourishing monastery in Constantinople and wielded considerable influence in imperial circles.

[2] Julius I, pope 337–52 who supported the orthodox decrees of the Council of Nicaea (325) and its champions, Athanasius of Alexandria (d.373) and Marcellus of Ancyra (d.376), whom the Arian party, under the leadership of Eusebius of Nicomedia (d. c.342) and now a majority party in the East, had expelled from their sees.

[3] The Council of Antioch met in the summer of 341, reaffirmed the excommunication of Athanasius, attacked the theology of Marcellus, and adopted the First Creed of Sirmium, which omitted that key phrase from the Nicene Creed, 'consubstantial with the Father'.

[4] Liberius, pope 352–66, was elected to the see of St Peter at a time when the Arian party was in the ascendancy and the pro-Arian Constantius II—now sole emperor—was pressuring the western bishops to toe the imperial line and join the eastern bloc in anathematizing Athanasius. For a time, because Liberius refused to cooperate, the emperor banished him to Borea, Thrace, on the Black Sea. After several months in exile, Liberius caved in to imperial pressure, acquiescing in Athanasius's excommunication and accepting the First Creed of Sirmium.

To Mrs William Froude

⌈Littlemore. Easter Tuesday. April 9/44

My dear Mrs Froude

I have received your kind letter this morning, and at present cannot make up my mind whether I ought to send you any more of these harassing letters. Not that I meant them either to be many or harassing;⌉I set about overcoming what seemed to be a difficulty pressing on William—and I suspect I both exaggerated it, and have been led into a great error in my way of meeting it. However I write on, whether you see it or not, wishing, (since I have begun to do, what I had no notion of doing in my first letter to you,) to complete what otherwise probably I may never get myself to do.

What I described in my last was the view that burst upon me, that separation from the body of Christendom, and again, or especially, from the see of Rome, is, (to those who would go by primitive views of Christianity,) a *presumption* of error. I cannot recollect by what degrees or at what time it became an unsettling principle in my mind, though I perfectly recollect the lively feelings produced in me by the Monophysite history. These I mentioned to H. Wilberforce among others at the end of July when we met at the consecration of the new Church at Otterbourne. But I cannot make out that I realized on them practically till the end of the Long Vacation, when something else occurred to give them very serious force.

I know how very coolly, that is, historically, I must seem to you to be writing on these most serious matters, but it does no good to be roundabout. If I am to write, I must write plainly—yet I can hardly get myself to say what now comes, though it is difficult to say why. At the end of the Long Vac. (1839) a number of the Dublin Review appeared containing an article by Dr Wiseman which made some talk in Oxford. I looked at it, and treated it very lightly. Persons who (I suppose) half took up our views, said we were bound to answer it, meaning it was a great difficulty in the way of the Anglican theory. I recollect saying it was 'all the old story'—and would not think about it. I do not know what made me take up the Number again, but I found it on careful attention to contain so powerful an argument, that I became (I may say) excited about it. I was leaving Oxford for a few weeks, in the course of which I paid visits to Rogers and to H. Wilberforce, and to both I mentioned that I was shaken in my confidence in the Anglican theory;—but to no one else.

The argument in the Article in question was drawn from the History of the Donatists, and was directed to show that the English Church was in Schism. The fact to which the Monophysite controversy had opened my eyes, that antagonists of Rome, and Churches in isolation, were always wrong in primitive times, and which I had felt to be a *presumption* against ourselves, this article went on to maintain as a recognised *principle and rule* in those same ages. It professed that the *fact* of isolation and opposition was *always taken* as a *sufficient* condemnation of bodies so circumstanced, and to that extent that the question was not asked *how did the quarrel arise?* which was right, and which wrong? who made the separation? but the *fact* of separation was reckoned anciently as decisive against the body separated. This was argued chiefly from the language of St Augustine, as elicited in the Donatist controversy, and the same sort of *minute* parallel was drawn between the state of the Donatists and our own, which I had felt on reading the history of the Monophysites.

On my return to Oxford, my immediate business was to set about answering the argument. It is my sincere belief and principle that it is right to resist doubts and to put aside objections to the form of doctrine and the religious system in which we find ourselves. I think such resistance pleasing to God. If it is His will to lead us from them, if the doubt comes from Him, He will repeat the suggestion. He will call us again as He called Samuel;[1] He will make our way clear to us. Fancies, excitements, feelings go and never return—truth comes again and is importunate. The system in which we have been placed is God's voice to us, till He supersede it—and those means by which He supersedes it must be more distinct than the impression produced on us by that system itself. Accordingly I then set about, as I have since, to keep myself in my own place. What I wrote [w]as an article in the British Critic in January (I think) 1840, under the title of 'Catholicity of the English Church',[2] and, though important practical effects followed from the shock I had received, the view of the subject which it contains kept me quiet for nearly two years, that is, till the Autumn of 1841.

The practical effects of which I speak of, were such as these:—1. to attempt to give up St Mary's. I brought this before the College in 1840, wishing to retain Littlemore; but the Provost would not hear of the separation of the Living. In 1841 I took the Cottages I now inhabit, and from the beginning of 1841 I had a Curate at St Mary's and gradually took less and less share in the duty there. Last year, as you know, I resigned it. 2. I gave up society etc in Oxford as far as might be. The affair of

Number 90 was an excuse for this. In consequence, i.e. in 1841, our theological meetings at Pusey's came to an end,[3] and my weekly evening parties also. 3. I gave up the British Critic in the Spring of 1841, this was settled before the affair of Number 90. 4. As far as possible I left off writing on any subjects of the Day (except in Sermons, when I felt it my duty while I held St Mary's). My contributions to the Tracts, as a *course*, came to an end in 1838. In 1840 I added the Devotions of Bishop Andrewes,[4] and nothing else, except indeed Number 90, which shall be mentioned presently. As to my University Sermons, I went on with them as finishing a course; the last, which has made some talk, I wrote quite lately, but I will speak of this elsewhere,[5] if I ever write so much. Except Number 90, I have not (as far as I remember) written any thing on subjects of the Day since 1838, six years—I have always excepted Sermons. (I suppose you will say certain Letters in the Times in the beginning of 1841[6] are exceptions. I was *pressed* to write them). 5. Of course I became very careful of saying things against Rome. In the new Edition of the Volumes[,] I corrected many passages, and at the end of 1842 I took measures for the publication of a retractation of certain passages which called for it. I published an Article on Antichrist in the B.C. [*British Critic*] in 1840 I think.[7] (By the bye several B.C. articles form an important exception since 1838). 6. I was very desirous of an adjustment, or at least of the contemplation of an adjustment between ourselves and the Church of Rome, and without feeling I knew enough about the matter to dare to pronounce that it might be upon the basis of the Council of Trent, I hoped it might be so. And feeling very strongly the corruptions in the Church, I felt more and more inclined to regard them, as had very frequently been done by our writers, as *in* the Church, not *of* the Church. 7. Number 90 originated in various causes. The desire just mentioned of drawing towards Rome; a feeling of the need which various persons had to know *how* Catholicly to interpret certain articles; a feeling as if our opponents had a right to ask and ought to be told, and as if it were disingenuous, and would clearly seem so, not to state plainly how we reconciled our subscriptions with our opinions; and moreover a hope that to state the Catholic interpretation was to *make* it; for what was allowed, became de facto an interpretation. I did not foresee the great opposition made to it and such condemnation from authority. I had taken up my notes here for writing it in Lent 1840, but I did not write it till the beginning of 1841.

At the time of the publication of Number 90, I was 1. desirous of union with Rome, i.e. Church with Church. 2. I was strongly opposed to the idea of *individual* moves. 3. I thought the *practical* system of Rome very corrupt—and thought those corruptions balanced our quasi-schism (I have drawn out my view in the B. C. of July 1841, article on Private Judgment)[8] 4. I thought my occupation quite gone in the Anglican Church. My feeling is shown in a Preface I wrote to Nelson's Life of Bull (I think), in 1840.

You will clearly see, if you see this letter at all, that it is written with a minuteness consistent with what I have stated in the first lines of it, rather than in a way which will interest you.

Your affectionate Friend John H. Newman.

[1] *1 Samuel* 3.

[2] 'The Catholicity of the Anglican Church', in *Ess.* II, pp. 1–111.

[3] A Theological Society established by Pusey in 1835.

[4] *Tract* 88, 'The Greek Devotions of Bishop Andrews, Translated and Arranged', published 25 March 1840.

[5] Later republished in the uniform edition as *Fifteen Sermons preached before the University of Oxford between A.D. 1826 and 1843*; the last was 'The Theory of Developments in Religion Doctrine', preached 2 February 1843. See below Newman's letter dated 19 May 1844.

[6] 'The Tamworth Reading Room', *D.A.*, pp. 254–305, published in seven instalments between 5 and 26 February 1841.

[7] Republished as 'The Protestant Idea of Antichrist' in *Ess.* II, pp. 112–85.

[8] *Ess.* II, pp. 336–74.

To Mrs William Froude

Littlemore. May 19. 1844

My dear Mrs Froude,

I said in my last that difficulties presented themselves to me in the Anglican theory of the Church from which the Roman is free. On both theories the Church is considered, as the Creed declares it, *one*—now the meaning of 'one' is simple, if 'one Church' means one *kingdom*, one body politic, but in what sense do Anglicans consider it one? They consider it a *succession*, propagated through different countries, independent in each country and claiming the adherence of Christians in this or that country to itself as it exists in this or that country. Each bishop is isolated from every other and supreme in his own diocese, and if he unites with others, it is only as the civil power or his own choice happens to unite him. He claims *obedience*, yet without claiming to be a depository and transmitter of true *doctrine*, the succession being a point of order, not a condition and witness of Christian faith. And all other bishops or religious bodies acting in his diocese without his leave are schismatical. Now if this be so, the question occurs in what sense do Anglicans consider the Church *one?* in what sense are Rome and England one?

If Rome and England *are* one, what is meant by the common phrase of 'the church of our baptism'? Baptism is 'one' and admits into the 'one body'; not into any local society. A child baptized by a clergyman of Oxford is not admitted into that diocese or Church, but into the Catholic Body, which is diffused throughout the world, and which is the real Church 'of his baptism'. It puzzled me to make out, in what sense, on the hypothesis that Rome and England formed one Church, a man changed his Church who went from the English to the Roman branch, any more than he changed it, if he communicated here with the Church of Oxford, there with the Church of London. He changed his *faith* indeed; that is another matter; but how was he guilty of schism, how could he *change* his Church, when there was no *other* Church to change to?

To meet this difficulty Anglicans are forced into the following argument—that is, I believe so; certainly I was, and have expressed it, among other places, in the article on the Catholicity of the English Church, and in a note at p.150 of the Oxford translation of St Cyprian's Treatises. (No—I have explained the *general theory* in these places). They say, that since there is but one Bishop and Church in each place, and our succession, not the Roman, has possession in England, therefore the Roman succession and Church are intruders *here*. But surely this is very technical and unreal; for who can deny that the true difference between us and Rome is one of *doctrine and practice?* yet such an explanation sinks that difference altogether, and reduces our quarrel with Rome to one of ecclesiastical arrangement. Its irrelevance is shown as soon as you put the question of members of our Church on going abroad; are they to communicate with the Roman Church in places where that Church has possession? If we are one Church with Rome, only locally distinct, they ought,—yet few would feel it right to do so; and if they do not, we are *not* one Church with Rome. The Anglican theory then cannot be acted upon—it is a mere set of words—facts confute it.

It was, I think, in the beginning of 1840, that a lawyer,[1] with whom I was slightly acquainted wrote me several letters on this subject, in opposition to Palmer, which had the effect of convincing me that it was absurd to call Roman Catholics Schismatics in England. As I recollect, his plain argument was, how preposterous that a man who across the Channel believes in purgatory, the Mass, the Pope's supremacy etc must all of a sudden, if he comes to England, change his creed and worship, and become [a] member of a local community which denies all that he has hitherto received? This led me to investigate the Anglican theory of local Episcopacy itself, from which these absurdities follow, and I found it as untenable as its consequences; as a few words will show.

May 29, I think it is Hooker who tells us the distinction between 'Bishops by restraint' and 'Bishops at large'. Bishops by restraint are Bishops with a certain definite jurisdiction. Bishops at large are Bishops over the *whole* Church. Now I believe it is generally granted that this 'restraint' is the consequence of a bye law of the Church, and that local jurisdiction, which it implies, is not of the essence of the Episcopate. In the theory of the Episcopate there is never more than *one* Bishop in the whole Church—for every Bishop is but the shadow and repetition of every other. Every Bishop has the full Episcopate in his person, as in a firm every partner has all the responsibilities of the whole house. They are, to use a law phrase, 'joint tenants' in power, or (as St Cyprian expresses it) they have the Episcopate 'in solidum'. There is then one and one only Bishop in the Church, with a universal jurisdiction, the Vicar of Christ, and the Pastor of souls. *Each* Bishop is *all this* in his *essential* character;—such is the theory which I think you will find in Bingham,[2] and among ancient writers in St Cyprian's Treatise De Unitate (published in the Library of the Fathers) and in St Ignatius's Epistles. But now it is obvious how inconvenient, or rather how impossible such a theory is in practice, while men are men. If a thousand absolute and independent monarchs rule over the whole heritage of Christ, what is to secure their agreement? Who is to decide their differences? This being so, by a series of bye laws and usages (similar to that by which three Bishops at least are necessary for a consecration, though, in the theory and really, one is enough) the intrinsic power of individual Bishops is curtailed, and one is put under another. The great majority of Bishops deprive themselves of their intrinsic universal jurisdiction and take a subordinate place under others, and all limit their *immediate* jurisdiction to some particular spot, or what is called a Diocese. They are then called what they all are in fact, ('Bishops by restraint'), and thence results the great Patriarchal system. They divide between them, for the sake of order, their own power—one is a suffragan, another a metropolitan, another a primate. And again, since such an arrangement depends on bye laws or canons, when matters arise of greater consequence than canons, e.g. matters of faith, then all parties return to first principles and rights. Thus, as you will read in Bingham, during the Arian troubles each Catholic Bishop considered himself quite free to consecrate and order things anywhere, where Arianism prevailed. They thus became Bishops at large again, or had a universal jurisdiction.

But if this be so, how absurd is it, I was going to say hypocritical, when we have actually broken from Rome in matters of faith and order, when we have asserted an independence which can only be defended by an abolition of all usages and canons, then again to affect a delicacy and profess an etiquette on the point of local jurisdiction. This is straining out a gnat and swallowing a camel. We have a greater right to place a Bishop at Malta, than we had to disobey the Pope; local episcopacy and the Popedom—stand on the same basis, viz. that of canons. And the R. Cs have as great a right to create a Church in England, or we to create a Church out of the Roman communion—if their congregations are disobedient to the Bishop of London or Winchester, yet so are the Diocese of London and Winchester to the Pope. At the Reformation the Patriarchal system was broken up as in Arian times, Bishops at large succeed to Bishops by restraint, and though we may have rules among ourselves, as Roman Catholics have, yet England and Rome, viewed as Churches, each claims its inherent original jurisdiction over the whole Church. If at the Reformation there was, division indeed, but not a schism, much less are the particular acts growing out of that division deserving that serious name. The presence of Rome in England and of England in Rome is the legitimate and necessary consequence of that great event.

However, this being the case, we see how preposterous it is to talk of the Pope's 'usurped power'. As to his exercising power over the *whole Church*, he only does what all Bishops have a right to do, except they are restrained by definite provisions. As to his claiming power over other Bishops, he only does it by usage, by Prescription, by the canons, as the Archbishop of Canterbury. If he goes beyond these warrants he acts unjustifiably—while he can appeal to them, he is blameless. What he possesses, is either what he retains or what he has received. And in saying this, I am not going to question whether his power is by divine right or not. Even though it has been brought about by natural and human means, it may be the fulfilment of the prophetic promise to St Peter as recorded in xvi of St Matthew.

A further conclusion seemed to follow from what has been said. If the ecumenical authority of the Pope has been created, not by his exaltation but by the canonical depression of other Bishops, and is no assumption, but the result of a voluntary arrangement, it follows that while it is lawful as being in their own power, it must necessarily be gradual as being the consequence of their positive acts. Canons are not framed, nor do usages obtain, in a day—nor do dispositions and ordinances which are the subject of them. The Papacy then could not but be of slow growth, and if it were the subject of prophecy in Matthew xvi, there is still greater reason for saying so. All then that we look for in antiquity, is tendencies and beginnings of its greatness, and these are found abundantly. This is the further conclusion which I meant, and with reference to it I will bring this long letter to an end.

I write from memory, and therefore may make some mistakes in detail, though I am correct on the whole. St Clement of Rome, vid. Library of the Fathers vol. 8, p. 44, note f who is mentioned by St Paul, wrote a pastoral letter which is extant to the Church of Corinth. St Ignatius addresses the Church of Rome as the Church 'which presides' or 'is the first see in the country of the Romans'. Dionysius of Corinth in the second century speaks of its alms and benevolences as extending all over the Church. St Irenaeus in the same century calls it the Church with which all others must concur. Pope Victor at the same time threatened the Churches with excommunication. Tertullian, Origen, and St Cyprian use language in the third [century] like Irenaeus's. Pope Stephen repeats towards St Cyprian the threat of Pope Victor. Pope Dionysius is appealed to against Dionysius Bishop of Alexandria in a matter of doctrine by the Alexandrians, entertains the appeal, requires an explanation of him, and receives it, and the Roman civil government submits the deprivation of Paul, Bishop of Antioch, to the decision of the see of Rome. In the fourth century St Athanasius and his friends appeal to Rome, and St Jerome professes in a matter of doctrine and in the choice of a patriarch of Antioch, to rule himself by its decision. Moreover in every case the view whether of doctrine or discipline taken by the see of Rome, ultimately prevailed, and, if success is the token of truth, is the true one. It is the Pope who has determined the rule for observing Easter, and for treating the baptism of heretics, who has confirmed or pronounced the condemnation of Arianism, Apollinarianism, Pelagianism, and the other numerous heresies which distracted the early Church. He appears to exercise an infallibility which in after ages he has more distinctly claimed.

All these things being considered, I was forced to admit that the doctrine of the papacy was a primitive one—for

1. If we do not allow of developments, especially in a matter which from the nature of the case *requires* time for its due exhibition, hardly any doctrine can be proved by antiquity.
2. Nor is it any thing to the purpose that the Pope's power was withstood in early times, e.g. by St Cyprian—for when a doctrine or ordinance has to be developed, collision or disturbance seem previous conditions of its final adjustment.
3. Nor is it to the purpose that certain passages such as those which I have referred to above from writers of the first centuries *may* otherwise be explained—for the question is which of the two interpretations is the more likely—and the event seems to suggest the true interpretation, as in the case of a prophecy.

But I am getting hard and dry, if I have not been so all along

Ever yr affectionate friend John H Newman

P.S. Your letter of this morning has led to my finishing this. Since my object in writing has ceased to be that with which I began, (viz that of removing a painful feeling which William seemed to have) I have become both somewhat indolent about writing—and also very anxious about the *effect* of my letters to you. Both these feelings will account for my long silence. The same change of purpose makes me indifferent as to hearing what you think about my letters, so that I am made certain they do not unsettle you, for I am not writing with a purpose so much as finishing a subject I may not otherwise get myself to work out.

[1] George Bowyer who had become a Catholic in August.

[2] J. Bingham, *Origines Ecclesiasticæ: or, The Antiquities of the Christian Church. In twenty three Books* (London, 1726), Book ii, Chapter III, Section 1, 25–6. *The Works of the learned Joseph Bingham, M.A. Late rector of Hawant, and sometime Fellow of University-College in Oxford.*

To John Keble

Littlemore. June 8/44

My dear Keble,

Pattison wishes me to tell you that friends of his, a lady and daughter, are going into your Parish. So far you must know—at least you know *them*, and have been civil to them already—but what you do not know, and he wishes you to know, is, that they have come to Hursley to be 'under your superintendence.' I do not know what the phrase means, but when he and I had repeated it several times, and no light seemed thrown upon it, I dropped the subject. Perhaps he does not know either. If you wish, I can inquire.

I ought to take this opportunity of writing to you a long letter, to which I have a great repugnance because it is about myself—not to say that writing intelligibly makes my hand ache. But you should know my state of mind—and though the disgust of writing, and the thought of the worry and worse that my letters give you, almost deter me, and I don't know how I shall get on, I will attempt to do it.

I have thought much lately of the words in Bishop Andrewes's Morning Prayer— 'Despise not the work of Thine own hands'—he repeats it in various forms, as addressed to Each of the Persons of the Most Holy Trinity. May I not take comfort in the plea which they contain? 'Thine Hands have made me and fashioned me.' I look back to past years, or rather to all my years since I was a boy, and I say, 'Is it come to this? had God forgotten to be gracious? would He have led me on so far to cast me off? what have I done to be given over, if it be such, to a spirit of delusion? where is my fault? which has been the false step, if such there be?'

I know He taketh up and setteth down[1]—and of course I know that I have done enough to provoke Him to give me over and to deserve all that is evil. But still such is not His way, and I cannot get myself to believe that He means evil towards me, yet month by month my convictions grow in one direction.

When I was a boy of fifteen, and living a life of sin, with a very dark conscience and a very profane spirit, He mercifully touched my heart; and, with innumerable sins, yet I have not forsaken Him from that time, nor He me. He has upheld me to this hour, and I have called myself His servant. When I came up to reside at Trinity, the verse of the Psalms, which was most in my heart and on my lips, and it has brought tears into my eyes to think of it, was 'Thou shalt guide me with Thy counsel,' etc.[2] He has brought me through numberless trials safely and happily on the whole—and why should He now leave me to a blinded mind? I know I have done enough to provoke Him;—but will He?

He led me by a series of Providences from the age of 19 till 27. I *was* 'the work of His hands,'[3] for He repeatedly and variously chastised me and at last to wean me from the world, He took from me a dear sister[4]—and just at the same time He gave me kind friends to teach me His ways more perfectly.

Time went on, and various things happened by which He went on training me—but what most impresses itself upon me, is the strange feelings and convictions about His will towards me which came on me, when I was abroad. When I went down to Sicily by myself, I had a strong idea that He was going to effect some purpose by me. And from Rome I wrote someone, I think Christie, saying, I thought I was to be made some thing of in His hands, 'though if not, the happier for me.'[5] And when I was in Sicily by myself, it seemed as if some one was battling against me, and the idea has long been in my mind, though I cannot say when it came on, that my enemy was then attempting to destroy me. A number of sins were committed ⟨involved⟩ in the very act of my going down by *myself*—to say nothing else, I was wilful, and neglected warnings—from that time every thing went wrong. As I lay at Leonforte, before I got to Castro Giovanni, while I was laid up, I felt this strongly—My servant thought I was dying—but I expected to recover, and kept saying, as giving the reason, 'I have not sinned against light.' I had the fullest persuasion I should recover, that some work was in store for me. But any how when I was getting up again, after it was over, this feeling was strong upon me. I recollect, when travelling down the country from Castro G. to Palermo, (the ecclesiastical year was on the same days as this year, as the year of my getting in to Oriel, so that Rogers and I were both elected on the 12th of April) it must have been Whit Sunday or Monday morning, sitting on my bed as I was dressing, and crying profusely. My servant, who was obliged to help me from my great weakness (for I could not walk by myself) of course could not think the meaning of it—and I could but say to him, what was quite as unintelligible as my tears, that I thought God had some work for me. And then when I got to England, the very first Sunday after my arrival (July 14) you preached your Sermon on National Apostasy, which was the beginning of the movement.

And now at the end of eleven years from that time, was [what] is my own state? Why, that for the last five years (almost) of it, I have had a strong feeling, often rising to an habitual conviction, though in the early portion of it after a while dormant, but very active now for two years and a half, and growing more urgent and imperative continually, that the Roman Communion is the only true Church—And this conviction came upon me while I was reading the Fathers and from the Fathers—and when I was reading them theologically, not ecclesiastically, in that particular line of study, that of the ancient heresies, to which circumstances, external to myself, had led me fourteen years ago, before the movement began.

And when this trial came upon me, I told only two persons[6] with whom I happened to be at the time—and set myself to resist the impression. As you know, I wrote against it, and I am not aware in what respect I have indulged it. And I have attempted to live a stricter life. Every Lent since it first came upon me, I have spent up here, except such necessary returns to Oxford in the course of the week as Oxford duties made necessary—and for the last two years I have been here almost entirely. And I have made great efforts to keep others from moving in the direction of Rome also.

Of course there is no fear of your supposing me not to be conscious of innumerable weaknesses and errors in my heart and conduct—but I cannot help trusting they need not come into account here. Or, even though there has been at times sin more than ordinary, I trust it is not being laid to my charge.

Moreover I certainly think I may say, that in many respects my heart and conduct have improved in the course of this five years, and that, in respects in which I have prayed for improvement. Then the question comes upon me, why should Providence have granted my prayers in these respects, and not when I have prayed for light and guidance?

And then, as far as I see, all inducements and temptations are for remaining quiet, and against moving. The loss of friends what a great evil is this! the loss of position, of name, of esteem—such a stultification of myself—such a triumph to others. It is no proud thing to unsay what I have said, to pull down what I have attempted to build up. And again, what quite pierces me, the disturbance of mind which a change on my part would cause to so many—the casting adrift, to the loss both of religious stability and comfort—the temptation to which many would be exposed of scepticism, indifference, and even infidelity.

These last considerations are so serious, in the standard of reason as well as in the way of inducement, that, if it were not for antagonist difficulties, I don't see how I could ever overcome them. But it does strike me on the other side 'What if you are the cause of souls dying out of the communion of Rome, who have had a *call* to join it, which you have repressed? What, if this has happened already?' Surely time enough has been allowed me for wavering and preparation—I have fought against these feelings in myself and others long enough. And then another terrible thought strikes me. We hear of physicians, thinking they have cured a complaint, when they have but thrown their patient into a contrary one—and enough has happened to make me fear greatly, lest a sort of latitudinarianism and liberalism *may* be the end of those (though forbid it!) whom I am keeping from Rome. I am quite sure there is this *danger*. I dread it in particular persons. The time may even come, when I shall beg them to join the Church of Rome and they will refuse. Indeed I sometimes feel uncomfortable about myself—a sceptical, unrealizing temper is far from unnatural to me—and I may be suffered to relapse into it as a judgment.

What then is the will of Providence about me? The time for argument is passed. I have been in one settled conviction for so long a time, which every new thought seems to strengthen. When I fall in with friends who think differently, the temptation to remain quiet becomes stronger, very strong—but I really do not think my conviction is a bit shaken. So then I end as I began—Am I in delusion, given over to believe a lie? am I deceiving myself convinced when I am not? Does any subtle meaning or temptation, which I cannot detect, govern me, and bias my judgment?—But is it possible that Divine Mercy should not wish me, if so, to discover and escape it? Has He led me thus far to destroy me in the wilderness?

Really I dread what would be the consequence if any intimate friend of mine joined the Church of Rome. Might I not feel it impossible to disobey what seemed a warning to me, whatever trial and pain of mind it involved?

How this letter will distress you! I am ever thinking of you, My dear Keble,

Yrs affly J H N

[1] *Psalm 75:7.*
[2] *Psalm 73:24.*
[3] *Job 34:19.*
[4] Mary who died suddenly and unexpectedly from peritonitis on 5 January 1828 aged nineteen.
[5] See letter to John Frederic Christie, 6 April 1833.
[6] Frederic Rogers and Henry Wilberforce.

To Mrs William Froude

[Littlemore June 9/44

My dear Mrs Froude

At the end of my last[1] I touched on a subject of great importance, which introduces me to the second of the two considerations, mentioned some letters back[2] as having kept me satisfied and secure in the English position, as it may be called. I said there were two considerations which kept me from having any fear of Rome—the one that we had the Apostolical succession. I have hitherto been employed in showing how I have been forced from this ground, considered as an argument—viz by the question of Schism, which suspends the grace of that succession, even where the succession is found. The second point was my conviction that certain definite doctrines of Rome were not to be found in Antiquity—and this objection has been removed from my mind by a consideration of the principle of *development*, which I implied without (I think) mentioning in what I said in my last about the growth of the Papal power.]

I really do not quite know why I am going on prosing to you at this rate, and all about myself. I hope it will not look very absurd some little time hence—and I fear it really must be very dull for you. I am sure my last letter must have been a regular quietus—and by its sedative effects must have tended to undo all the excitement I have caused you (as Punch says that a pun of the Duke of W's [Wellington's] this day week made the Emperor of Russia go home and sleep sound for two hours) but to proceed, if it must be so.

[It is quite plain that the early Christians had no images in worship—there is very little trace of invocation among them, no special honors to St Mary, purgatory in its

Roman form was not acknowledged except in places—transubstantiation was not professed or taught, the Holy Communion was commonly administered in two kinds, and the like. In this they differ from Rome, as it is at present—Is not this a *corruption* of Christianity, as originally given? No, I answer, I think it a development of it.

Now before going on to say my reasons for thinking so, I will say what I used to hold.

I have always held a development of doctrine, at least in some great points in theology. E.g. I have thought that the doctrine of the Holy Trinity and Incarnation are intellectual developments of the inspired declarations of Scripture—but I used to think either that this development was made in the Apostles' life time and given by them traditionally to the Church, or at least that it was made by the Church in the *first* ages.

1. Thus in the 'Arians' I say, 'As the intellect is cultivated and expanded, it cannot refrain from the attempt to analyse the vision which influences the heart, and the Object in which it centres, nor does it stop, till it has, in some sort, succeeded in expressing in words, what has all along been a principle both of the affections and of practical obedience . . . The systematic doctrine of the Trinity may be considered as the shadow, projected for the contemplation of the intellect, of the Object of scripturally informed piety . . . given to the Church contemporaneously with those Apostolic writings which are addressed more directly to the heart' etc pp. 159, 160.[3]

2. In an article on Apostolic Succession in the British Critic for July/36 I say 'We confidently affirm, that there is not an article in the Athanasian Creed concerning the Incarnation, which is not anticipated in the controversy with the Gnostics. There is no question which the Apollinarian or the Nestorian heresy raised, which may not be decided in the words of Irenaeus and Tertullian.' p. 193.[4] There is a parallel passage in my article on Ignatius in the British Critic January/39 p. 64.[5] And another connected with a passage of St Gregory Nazianzen in Arians p. 169.[6]

3. In sermons vol 2 (as in University Sermons and Arians) I allow of a development to meet the objections of heretics. 'When the light of His advent faded, and love waxed cold, then there was an opening for objection and discussion, and a difficulty in answering. Then misconceptions had to be explained, doubt allayed, questions set at rest, innovations silenced. Christians were forced to speak against their will, lest heretics should speak instead of them.' Sermon 3.[7] There is a parallel passage in Vol. 3 Sermon 12.[8] Here no *limit of time* is fixed.

4. I go much further in Romanism Lecture 10, not confining any developments to any fixed period, but rather allowing them at any time. I speak of 'Prophetical Tradition, existing primarily in the *bosom of the Church itself*, and recorded in such measure as providence [h]as determined in the writings of eminent men'; of its being 'the thought and principle which breathed in the Church, her accustomed and *unconscious* mode of viewing things, and the body of her received notions, rather than any definite and systematic collection of dogmas elaborated by the intellect. *Partially*, indeed, it was fixed and perpetrated in the shape of formal articles or doctrines, as the rise of errors or other causes gave

occasion; and it is preserved *to a considerable extent* in the writings of the Fathers.'[9] And in the foregoing Lecture, I say that 'an explanation of the original wording (of the Creed) might be made, I conceive, even now, if the whole of Christendom agreed together in the explanation, and in such explanation conveying the uniform sense of the Church Catholic, and its expediency. At the same time' I add 'the Church necessarily has less power over the Creed, now than anciently; for at first it was but a form of sound words, subjected to a Faith vividly and accurately engraven on the heart of every Christian, and so of secondary importance; but now that the living power of truth has declined, it is a witness of the primitive instead of being a mere summary of an existing faith.'[10]

My present view of development is contained in my last University Sermon;[11] and differs from this, not in principle, but in two respects.

1. In considering that developments may be made at any time, for the Church is always under the guidance of Divine Grace. (though I have in fact granted this in some of the foregoing passages)
2. that developments are not only *explanations* of the sense of the Creed, but further doctrines involved in and arising from its articles.⌉ The direct contrary is maintained in the paragraph following the last extract—but I shall have more to say about this.

⌈Your affte friend J H Newman⌉

June 12 P.S. I received your letter yesterday . . .

[1] See letter dated 19 May 1844.
[2] See letter dated 5 April 1844.
[3] *Ari.*, pp. 144–5.
[4] 'Apostolical Tradition', republished in *Ess.* I, p. 130.
[5] See 'The Theology of St Ignatius' in *Ess.* I, p. 242.
[6] *Ari.*, p. 154.
[7] *P.S.* II, pp. 27–8.
[8] *P.S.* III, pp. 159–60.
[9] *V.M.* I, pp. 250–1.
[10] *V.M.* I, p. 232.
[11] *U.S.*, pp. 312–51.

To Mrs William Froude

⌈Littlemore. July 14. 1844⌉

My dear Mrs Froude

⌈I find the subject I have now got into is endless, and I must cut it short. I meant to have drawn out the mode in which I have got reconciled to the (apparently) modern portions of the Roman system. It has been by applying to them that *principle* which, as my last letter showed, had long been in my mind, the principle of developments. From the time I wrote the Arians, or at least from 1836, I have had in my thoughts, though I could not bring it out, that argument or theory, which at last appeared in my closing University Sermon. It was delayed as long as I could in the *series* of Sermons, from inability, or fear of not doing justice to it—as it ought, in the due order, to have preceded the one before it.

Yet I must confess that the Sermon does not, as Palmer has observed in his Pamphlet,[1] go the whole length of theory which is necessary for the Roman system, and that something is still necessary to the discussion of the *theory*, though I have no difficulties about receiving the system in matter of fact. The kind of considerations, which do weigh with me, are such as the following:—[2]

1. I am far more certain (according to the Fathers) that we *are* in a state of culpable separation *than* that developments do *not* exist under the gospel, and that the Roman developments are *not* true ones.
2. I am far more certain that *our* (modern) doctrines are wrong, *than* that the *Roman* (modern) doctrines are wrong.
3. Granting that the Roman (special) doctrines are not found drawn out in the early Church, yet I think there is sufficient trace of them in it, to recommend and prove them, *on the hypothesis* of the Church having a divine guidance, though not sufficient to prove them by itself. So that the question simply turns on the nature of the promise of the Spirit made to the Church.
4. The proof of the *Roman* (modern) ⟨special⟩ doctrines is as strong ⟨(or stronger)⟩ in Antiquity, as that of certain doctrines which *both we and the Romans hold*. E.g. There is more evidence in Antiquity for the necessity of Unity than for that of the Apostolical Succession—for the supremacy of the See of Rome than for the Presence in the Eucharist—for the practice of Invocation than for certain books in the present Canon of Scripture etc etc
5. The Analogy of the Old Testament and the New leads to acknowledgment of doctrinal developments. E.g. the prophetical notices concerning our Lord before His coming. Again the gradual revelation of the calling of the Gentiles through St Peter and St Paul. Again, the distinct theological announcements of St John's gospel compared with those which preceded it. Again it is undeniable that the doctrine of the Holy Trinity, as we now hold it, is historically the result of a great deal of discussion and controversy, of much heresy and much antagonist development. Again the rule for baptizing heretics, or of infant baptism etc., etc. was unsettled and contested in early times, but at last universally obtained as it is at present.]

And now I have said enough on the whole subject—and I cannot get over the feeling that I have intruded it upon you.

⌈Your affectionate friend John H. Newman⌉

---

[1] 'I am not quite prepared to concur in the statement, that "the controversy between our own Church and the Church of Rome lies, it is presumed, *in the matter of fact*, whether such and such developments are true (e.g. Purgatory a true development of the doctrine of sin after baptism), not in the *principle* of development itself" (*US*, p. 320 n). It seems to me, that it is a question of *principle*, whether developments,

in the sense of *inferences made by human reason*, are, or are not always to be considered as articles of Catholic Faith. If the modern theory of development be true, these developments are as Divine, and as much parts of Christianity as the great articles of the Creed. The doctrine of Purgatory, as a *development*, must be as binding as that of the Trinity; the worship of the Virgin, or of the Sacred Heart of Jesus, as necessary as the worship of God. Processions, Pilgrimages, Monastic Vows, perpetual adoration of the Sacrament, Indulgences, &c., must be as sacred and as necessary as the sacraments of Baptism and the Eucharist.' William Palmer, *A Narrative of Events connected with the publication of the Tracts for the Times* (Oxford, 1843), p. 60 n. 7.

[2] The following statements appear in an abbreviated form in *Apo.*, pp. 197–8.

To Elizabeth Newman

Roehampton. St James's day [25 July] 1844

My dear Aunt,

Having a quarter of an hour before I am summoned to administer the Holy Communion to dear Bowden (for this is the reason of my frequent journeys here—I come in the evening and go away next morning) I will begin to tell you what in fact there is nothing, (as it turns out,) to tell about—but it is this.

You know Roehampton is a bad place for coaches, and yesterday was not the first time I have felt the want. I had to walk the whole way with my luggage, which, considering the glass had been 80 or 84 in the shade (I believe 86) and that it was a vigil,[1] and that I had walked from Littlemore to the Oxford station with my luggage, had walked and rode for 2 hours and a half about town, was a good day's work.

When I got to Fulham, I thought I would make an excuse of taking a dose of quinine, to have a peep at my Grandmother's house which I recollected forty years before, or at least 39–for I think you left in 1806. (I recollect your leaving, or at least mine, quite well. I went in one of those long coaches which were like the modern omnibuses.) You know I told you some time ago that part of the front of the house is turned into a chemist's shop.

I wanted to have a peep at the house, but the good chemist, civil as he was, did not take my hints—so I saw nothing, except the hall through the door. I saw too the staircase which I had forgotten. But I described to him the lie of the house, which he confirmed. I told him where the kitchen was, where I recollect you going to superintend the making of apple puffs. And the room opening on the garden where were the two card-racks with a lion (I think) on them; and the pictures of the prodigal son, and giving alms to the poor, and the unjust steward, or some one or other paying a number of people. There you used to breakfast—at least I recollect coming down in the morning and seeing the breakfast things looking bright and still—and I have some vague reminiscence of dry toast. And I have a sort of dream of my father and mother coming one day to call, and the room being crowded.

I told the worthy man where the drawing room was—and I spoke of a sort of loft above, in which I have a dim vision of apples on the floor and a mangle. And of the garden—the summerhouse, he said was gone ⟨(Littlemore July 28)⟩ but the drying ground behind it remained;—By this time my quinine was compounded and swallowed, and so I came away.

How strange it is, I wish I could describe it, to stand in a house which was so much to me, as that house was, and it so different, and I so different! Whatever good there is in me, I owe, under grace, to the time I spent in that house, and to you and my dear Grandmother, its inhabitants. I do not forget her Bible and the prints in it. Alas, my dear Aunt, I am but a sorry bargain, and perhaps if you knew all about me, you would hardly think me now worth claiming; still I cannot help—I am what I am—and I have grown into what I am from that time at Fulham.

What a strange change forty years makes. How little did the little child whom you used to fondle, think of what *he* thinks now! He had no thoughts. There is a poem in the Lyra, ('Did we but see, When life first opened, how our journey lay' etc)[2] which applies to one at any two periods—but how strangely does it apply to me then and now! I know not now of course what is before me, before my end comes—still more strange may be the contrast—but it is very touching and subduing as it is.

I think I had more to say on the subject, but it has gone from me.

May we all meet again in peace, when this troublesome world and its many contentions are over. I really do think I love peace, yet I am destined to be a 'man of strife'.[3] I am talking a great deal of myself, but, if anyone will pardon it, you will, My dear Aunt, from

Your affectionate Nephew, John H Newman

P.S. Love to Harriett, Jemima, their husbands, and the children—and kind thoughts to every one else who will receive them from my worthless self. Only think of my likeness having been taken by Richmond for Henry Wilberforce!

---

[1] Vigil of St James.　　[2] *V.V.*, p. 133.　　[3] *Jeremiah* 15:10.

To E. B. Pusey

Oriel College. Aug 28

My dear Pusey

I have great anxiety about answering you.[1] For myself I like to know and prepare for the worst of things—it distresses me not to look at things full in the face, and in my case it is on the whole a saving of pain—but I cannot tell whether it is so to others. I would not for the world give you pain I could avoid. It would be most unworthy and shocking in me. Yet in so painful a subject, it does seem better to me to have all out once for all (which I had hoped Manning had done last year) than to keep hacking and hacking bit by bit.

Surely great part of our pain is from suspense, anxiety, suspicion, anticipation—surely if I could but make you feel the worst, it must be a relief to you.

You very greatly over rate my consequence, and the surprise which any step on my part would cause. I believe a great number of people are prepared for it—more and more are coming to expect it daily. I cannot realize it myself—any more than that today I may be in Oxford and tomorrow in York. You cannot realize it. But I believe we, who are close to the act, are the persons most difficult to be impressed with an anticipation of it. The shock and unsettlement attending it I have felt acutely for years—but every month is reconciling the minds of persons to it.

What am I to say but that I am one who, even five years ago, had a strong conviction, from reading the history of the early ages, that we are not part of the Church?

that I am one whose conviction of it now is about as strong as of any thing else he believes—so strong that the struggle against is doing injury to his faith in general, and is spreading a film of scepticism over his mind—who is frightened, and cannot tell what it may end in, if he dares to turn a deaf ear to a voice which has so long spoken to him—

that I am one who is at this time in disquiet when he travels, lest he should be suddenly taken off, before he has done what *to him* seems necessary.

For a long time my constant question has been 'Is it a dream? is it a delusion?' and the wish to have decisive proof on this point has made me satisfied—it makes me satisfied to wait still—but, should such as I be suddenly brought down to the brink of life, then, when God allows no longer time for deliberation, I suppose he would feel he must act, as is on the whole safest, under circumstances.

And now, my dear P. do take in the whole of the case, nor shut your eyes, as you so kindly do continually, and God bless all things to you, as I am sure He will and does

Ever Yrs affectly John Henry Newman

(I only had your letter this morning)

[1] Pusey was finding it impossible to accept that Newman might cease to be an Anglican.

To Mrs John Mozley

[17 Grosvenor Place Sept 16/44]

My dear Jemima,

[What long and many recollections this house has to me; so many, so far back, they make me feel like an old man—and now my early and most dear J W B. [John William Bowden] lies in it, or rather what is mortal of him.]

I was summoned midday yesterday to Mrs B. He died in the morning most peacefully.

[When I saw him on Wednesday he was very much altered. He then talked of moving to St Leonard's in a fortnight, having a dislike of remaining in a strange place as Clifton was to him. On Thursday morning, having had a bad night, and, I suppose, feeling himself weaker, he had curtailed the delay to a week] and talked of my coming in consequence *early* in the week to Clifton, as today, before he went. But Henry B. [Bowden][1] was going to him Thursday or Friday, and was to see the physician who attended him. On Friday he limited his hopes to getting to Grosvenor Place. [On Saturday morning Dr Bernard said that] his strong wish to die at home ought not to be resisted, that the journey might even prolong his life a day or two, but any how [his time was short, and that there must be no delay. It distresses me to

think I was so little aware of this on Thursday—I did not know he was so near his
end. He had made me read Sext with him, and we were encroaching upon the
Railroad hour. So I rose and said 'Well I must go, goodbye, you will see me next
week'⌐—or the like. Somehow he had taken it into his head I was going to stay,
though I had always gone the second day, and had said I was going as usual. ⌈He was
taken by surprise and the perspiration, under which he suffered, came suddenly
upon him.⌉ I went to Mrs Bowden and told her what had happened, and ⌈she assured
me, after going to him, that it was nothing. So I went at once, though I had had no
time for breakfast, and missed the omnibus, as it was.⌉ Now I wish I had stayed. It
almost seemed as if his wish was a presentiment. Well ⌈but to return to Dr B. He
added 'No time is to be lost—why not go by the next train?' This was⌉ Saturday
morning (the day before yesterday) ⌈at 11. They were off by 12. When they got to
the station, they were just too late for the train—and had to wait, he in his carriage,
for more than two hours. What a trial for her! But he was most peaceful and
cheerful—showed no disappointment⌉—sat all the time in the carriage—⌈and when
she was out of the carriage, put his head out, and whispered to her 'Wish not, dear
friends, my pain away' etc.[2] He was quite happy all through the journey, and was
ever smiling and alluded to some things which amused him some days before.
When he got to Grosvenor Place, they put him to bed at once. At 4 o'clock Sunday
morning, he had a little coughing, his throat was full and he could not get rid of it. In
a moment she saw what was to happen, and it did happen at once.⌉

Henry B. at once came off to Oxford, where his family were, and I returned with
him at 5. Mrs H B. and Johnson came at one today. Mrs Ward, Mrs B.'s sister, is here.

Ever Yrs affly J H N

⌈I suppose I shall stop here till after the funeral.⌉

[[John William Bowden died September 15. 1844.

I sobbed bitterly over his coffin, to think that he left me still dark as to what the
way of truth was, and what I ought to do in order to please God and fulfil His Will.

J H N

May 20. 1862]].

[1] John Bowden's younger brother.
[2] Opening lines of a poem in Keble's *Christian Year* for the sixteenth Sunday after Trinity, entitled
'Hope is better than Ease'.

To Elizabeth Bowden

Littlemore. Sept 26. 1844

My dear Mrs Bowden,

...I do not know how to touch upon the subject nearest my heart now, in a
letter—yet before I began I intended to have said several things, which it is so
abrupt, when it comes to the point, to set in writing. It is impossible you should

know the feeling which John raised in the minds of persons who knew him ever so little towards himself and towards all of you, or the sorrow which his loss now causes. I know of one person years ago whom the sight of him in his family hindered being able to say that celibacy was more excellent in its nature than married life—it was just the thing which touched and moved him—and the other day some one was saying that to see him with those who were dear to him around him just realized the idea of a holy family. And these are but the expression of a very widespread feeling—which I mention for the very reason that it is so seldom expressed in words, and cannot be put into words on the moment, and because I was so little able the other day to show you anything such as you wished in letters I had received.

We are commemorating him at Lauds and Vespers through the thirty days...

With love to all the children, I am, Ever Your most sincerely

John H Newman

To Mrs John Mozley

Littlemore ⌈Oct 31/44⌉

My dear Jemima,

I don't suppose I shall finish this tonight ⟨⟨yes, I have⟩⟩—⌈I begin it, not for a very complimentary reason, but, having a very unusual visitor, a headache, which hinders me from working,⌉ I think I may pleasure myself with writing a few lines to you.

⌈You ask me about my meeting Arnold—and though there is nothing but what is commonplace to tell, I cannot tell it without introducing myself more than is pleasant. Indeed, the less I have to say, the more I must bring in myself, if I am so [to] say any thing—but even then I have little enough.

The second of February,[1] as you know, is our Great Gaudy of the year—The Provost dines in hall at the top of the Table; and in the Common Room, to which the party adjourns, sits at the right hand of the Dean, as the guest of the Fellows. Eden was Dean, and was taken ill, I think—when the news came that Arnold[2] was coming with the Provost, and I, being Senior Fellow, must take the Dean's place. My first feeling was to shirk—'It is not my place,' I said, 'to take this office upon me—It is nothing to me—I am not bound to entertain Arnold.' etc etc. However, I thought it would be cowardly; so after all I went, knowing that both in Hall and Common Room, the trio at the top would be Provost, Arnold, and I, and that in the Common Room I should sit at the top between them as their entertainer.

The Provost came into hall with Arnold and B. [Baden] Powell, (who made the fourth) I being already in my place at table, waiting for them. Provost came up in a quick brisk way, as if to cut through an awkward beginning—and said quickly and smartly 'Arnold, I don't think you know Newman—' on which A. and I bowed, and I spoke. I was most absolutely cool, or rather calm and unconcerned all through the meeting from beginning to end—but I don't know whether you have seen me enough in such situations, to know (what I verily believe is not any affectation at all on my part, I am not at all conscious of any such thing, though people would think it,) that I seem, if you will let me say it, to put on a very simple, innocent, and modest manner. I sometimes laugh at myself, and other absurdities which result from it, but really I cannot help it, and I really do believe it to be genuine. On one occasion in the course of conversation, I actually blushed high at some mistake I made,—and yet on the whole I am quite collected and calm. Now, are you not amused at all this? and ought not I to blush now? I never said a word of all this about myself to any one in my life before—though perhaps that does not mend the matter that I should say it now. However, to proceed.

So, when the Provost said, 'I don't think, Arnold, you know Newman—' I was sly enough to say very gently and clearly, that I had before then had the pleasure of knowing Dr Arnold, for I had disputed with him in the Divinity School [[before]] his B. D. degree, when he was appointed to Rugby,[3] at which B. Powell laughed out, and Arnold seemed a little awkward, and said, 'Oh, I thought it had been Pusey.' You must know that in the said disputation I was doing him a favour, for he could get no one to go in with him when I volunteered—though in the event it turned to my advantage, for I had not to dispute before Hampden, when I actually took my degree [[in 1836]]

We then sat down at table, and I thought of all the matters possible which it was safe to talk on. I recollected he had travelled with W. [William] Churton, and that made one topic. Others equally felicitous, I forget. But I recollect the productions of North Africa was a fruitful subject, and I have some dream of having talked of a great tree, the name of which I now forget, as big as a hill, and which they bring as an argument for the indefinite duration of the present earth à parte ante. In the Common Room I had to take a still more prominent part, and the contrast was very marked between Arnold and the Provost,—the Provost so dry and unbending and seeming to shrink from whatever I said, and Arnold who was natural and easy, at least to all appearance. I was told afterwards that on one occasion B. Powell made some irreverent remark, and people were amused to see both Arnold and myself in different ways, as far as manner was concerned, retired from it. At last, the Provost and Arnold rose up to go, and I held out my hand, which he took, and we parted.

I never saw him again; he died the June [[July?]] after.[4] He is a man whom I have always separated from the people he was with, always respected, often defended—though from accident he got a notion, I believe, that I was a firebrand, and particularly hostile to him. There is no doubt he was surprised and thrown out on finding that I did not seem to be what he had fancied. He told Stanley that it would not do to meet me often. When Stanley tried to clench the remark, he drew back and said he meant that it was not desirable to meet often persons one disagreed with, or something of that sort. This is what I heard to the best of my recollection;—after his death. For myself, I don't think I was desirous of pleasing him or not—but was secretly amused from the idea that he certainly would be taken aback by coming across me in propriâ persona. At least so I think.]

I have no more room

Ever Yrs affly J H N

To H. E. Manning

Littlemore. Nov 16/44

My dear Manning

I am going through what must be gone through—and my trust only is that every day of pain is so much from the necessary draught which must be exhausted. There is no fear (humanly speaking) of my moving for a long time yet. This has got out without my intending it, but it is all well.

As far as I know myself my one great distress is the perplexity, unsettlement, alarm, scepticism which I am causing to so many—and the loss of kind feeling and good opinion on the part of so many, known and unknown, who have wished well to me. And of these two sources of pain it is the former is the constant, urgent, unmitigated one. I had for days a literal ache all about my heart, and from time to time all the complaints of the Psalmist seemed to belong to me.

And, as far as I know myself, my one paramount reason for contemplating a change is my deep unvarying conviction that our Church is in schism and that my salvation depends on my joining the Church of Rome. I may use argument ad hominem to this person or that—but I am not conscious of resentment, or disgust, at any thing that has happened to me. I have no visions whatever of hope, no schemes of action, in any other sphere, more suited to me. I have no existing sympathies with Roman Catholics. I hardly ever, even abroad, was at one of their services—I know none of them. I do not like what I hear of them.

And then how much I am giving up in so many ways—and to me sacrifices irreparable, not only from my age, when people hate changing, but from my especial love of old associations and the pleasures of memory.

Nor am I conscious of any feeling, enthusiastic or heroic, of pleasure in the sacrifice—I have nothing to support me here.

What keeps me yet, is what has kept me long—a fear that I am under a delusion—but the conviction remains firm under all circumstances, in all frames of mind.

And this most serious feeling is growing on me, viz that the reasons for which I believe *as much* as our system teaches, *must* lead me to believe more—and not to believe more, is to fall back into scepticism.

A Thousand thanks for your most kind and consoling letter, though I have not yet spoken of it. It was a great gift.

Ever Yrs affectly John H Newman

To Mrs John Mozley

Littlemore. ⌈Dec. 22. 1844⌉

My dear Jemima,

I do not wonder at any one's first impression being, ⌈when he hears of the change of religion of another,⌉ that he is influenced by some wrong motive. It is the necessary consequence of his thinking himself right, and I fully allow that the onus probandi that he is not so influenced lies with the person influenced. While then I think you are rather hard on the various persons who have joined the Church of Rome, I think you are justified in being so, for they have to prove that they do not deserve a hard opinion. I say the same of myself. ⌈A person's feeling naturally is, that there must be some thing wrong at bottom—that I must be disappointed, or restless, or set on a theory, or carried on by a party, or coaxed into it by admirers, or influenced by any of the ten thousand persuasives, which are as foreign from my mind as from my heart, but which it is easy for others to assign as an hypothesis. I do not quarrel with persons so thinking.

But still I think as time goes on and persons have the opportunity of knowing me better, they will see that all these suppositions do not hold; and they will be led to see that my motive simply is that I believe the Roman Church to be true—and that I have come to this belief without any assignable fault on my part. Far indeed am I from saying 'without fault' absolutely—but I say without fault that can be detected and assigned. Were I sure that it was without fault absolutely, I should not hesitate to move tomorrow—it is the fear that there is some secret, undetected fault which is the cause of my belief, which keeps me where I am, waiting. But I really can say that nothing occurs to me indicative of any such fault, and the longer time without such discovery, the more I hope I have there is none such. I cannot detect such—Some time ago I wrote down for Keble every thing of every sort I could detect as passing in my mind, in any respect wrong or leading to wrong, day by day, for a certain period—and he could detect nothing bearing on this particular belief of mine. I have been as open with him as possible. Now I am far from saying I can find in myself good motives⌉—I have not any confidence whatever that I am acting from faith or love—⌈but what I say is that I cannot detect any bad motives—and I seem to realize to myself most completely St Paul's words, 'I am conscious of nothing to myself, yet am I not hereby justified—but He that judgeth me is the Lord.'[1] Of course I know that I am continually doing what is wrong—but what have I done, what has been my sin, which has brought this judgment upon me, to take so awfully wrong a step as to change my Church, if it be wrong [?]

In saying this, I am not saying another is wrong who does not do the same. I am only looking at myself. If God gives me certain light, supposing it to be such, this is a reason for *me* to act—yet in so doing I am not condemning those who do not so act. There *is* one truth, yet it may not please Almighty God, to show every one in the same degree or way what and where it is. I believe our Church to be separated from Catholic communion; but still I know very well that all divines, ancient and modern,

Roman as well as our own, grant even to a Church in schism, which has the Apostolical Succession and the right form of consecrating the sacraments, very large privileges.⌉ They allow that Baptism has the gift of the Holy Spirit, and the Eucharist the Real Presence—What they deny to such a Church is the power of *imparting* these gifts. They say that the grace is locked up, though present, and is not fruitful to the souls of individuals. However, they grant that unavoidable ignorance and love are efficacious in removing the bar or obex.[2] They consider all children regenerated who die in infancy, and they allow that the Divine mercy may overflow its own prescribed limits. ⌈I am then, how can I be otherwise? far from denying that great grace has been, and is, given to our members—but the question is, whether it will be given to one, who is *not* in ignorance? whether it is not his duty, if he would be saved, to act upon knowledge vouchsafed to him concerning the state of his Church, which acting is not required for salvation in those who have not that knowledge?⌉ Our Church may be a place of grace and security to another, yet not to me.

Now, my dear J, ⌈I am sure you will feel that I am not arguing, but I wish you to understand where I stand, and what I feel—for my own comfort. I have never wished there should be any reserve between us—it is most repugnant to my nature to conceal things. Long indeed I had this sad secret, when I thought it would be wrong to mention it. By degrees, often without my intention, it has come out—and growing conviction has justified me in mentioning it. And since now it is out, it will be a great comfort if you let me be open with you, and to tell you what the state of my mind is. Indeed, there can be no exercise of love between persons without this openness.⌉ In saying this, however, I am not contemplating any particular disclosure—indeed, I forgot almost, what I have told you, and what I have not—but I mean, generally.

I went to Town on Wednesday and returned on Friday, having not quite recovered from a severe influenza or something of the sort. And now I have a kind of cold, which kept me from Church yesterday and partly today, under fear lest else I should be knocked up on Christmas Day. But I must conclude

Ever Yrs affly J H N

[1] 1 *Corinthians* 4:4.
[2] 'bolt, bar, barrier, wall'.

To Mrs John Mozley

Littlemore. Febr 10/45

My dear Jemima

I knew without your writing how kind and affectionate your thoughts of me would be. Also I feel very much and value very much the sympathy of Mrs and Anne Mozley. It is just a case where others feel for one, more than one does for oneself. It is no exaggeration to say literally that I have no interest, no curiosity, at least as yet, about next Thursday's proceedings, as far as they relate to Number 90.[1] The Heads of Houses can do me neither good nor harm—I have distresses which they cannot increase or cure. Never was a truer image, than that in the English Churchman, that their act was like scattering the ashes of the dead. I had been likening myself to a dead man, as far as the University is concerned, before I saw it.

I dare say things may come out of the move, which may make me anxious. Its effect hitherto, I believe, has been to create a sympathy for me: this is a satisfaction and a pain. It is a satisfaction, as covering, so to say, my retreat—preparing people for it as a thing not unnatural under my circumstances (though in me it would not arise from those circumstances at all) and again as creating a kindly feeling and a compassion which may blunt the edge of resentment and censure. It is a pain, because, my great distress arising from the pain to which I am putting others, an increase of good-will towards me of course increases my trial, as if I were treating friends ungratefully, and disappointing them.

O that in the course I am pursuing, I might see more clearly than [that] I am following God's Hand, and am not judicially deluded for past sins!

This day is memorable to me—since ten years ago it was the day on which I had one of the most formidable attacks of illness which I ever had—though you at Rose Hill knew so little about it.

Ever Yours affectionately John H Newman

P.S. I left Mrs Bowden and her sister in the measles. The former had them very badly.

[1] The Hebdomadal Board was proposing to censure *Tract 90*, but, when the moment came, the motion was vetoed by the Proctors.

To Mrs John Mozley

Littlemore. Saturday March 15/45

My dear Jemima,

I have just received your very painful letter, and wish I saw any way of making things easier to you or to myself.

If I went by what I wished, I should complete my seven years of waiting. Surely more than this, or as much, cannot be expected of me, cannot be right in me to give, at my age. How life is going! I see men dying who were boys, almost children, when I was born. Pass a very few years, and I am an old man. What means of judging can I have more than I have? What maturity of mind am I to expect? If I am right to move at all, surely it is high time not to delay about it longer. Let me give my strength to the work, not my weakness—years in which I can profit His cause who calls me, not the dregs of life. Is it not like a deathbed repentance to put off what one feels one ought to do?

As to my convictions, I can but say what I have told you already, that I cannot at all make out *why* I should determine on moving except as thinking I should offend God by not doing so. I cannot make out what I am *at*, except on this supposition. At my time of life men love ease—I love ease myself. I am giving up a maintenance, involving no duties, and adequate to all my wants; what in the world am I doing this for, (I ask *myself* this) except that I think I am called to do so? I am making a large income by my Sermons, I am, *to say the very least*, risking this—the chance is that my Sermons will have no further sale at all. I have a good name with many—I am deliberately sacrificing it. I have a bad name with more—I am fulfilling all their worst wishes and giving them their most coveted triumph—I am distressing all I love, unsettling all I have instructed or aided—I am going to those whom I do not know and of whom I expect very little—I am making myself an outcast, and that at my age—Oh what can it be but a stern necessity which causes this.

Pity me, my dear Jemima—what have I done thus to be deserted, thus to be left to take a wrong course, if it be wrong. I began by defending my own Church with all my might when others would not defend her. I went through obloquy in defending her. I in a fair measure succeed—at the very time of this success, before any reverse, in the course of my reading, it breaks upon me that I am in a schismatical Church. I oppose myself to the notion—I write against it—Year after year I write against it—and I do my utmost to keep others in the Church—From the time my doubts come upon me, I begin to live more strictly—and really from that time to this, I have done more towards my inward improvement, as far as I can judge, than in any time of my life. Of course, I have all through had many imperfections, and might have done every single thing I have done, much better than I have done it—Make all deductions on this score—still after all, may I not humbly trust that I have not so acted as to forfeit God's gracious guidance? And how is it that I have improved in other points, if in respect of this most momentous matter I am so fearfully blinded?

Suppose I were suddenly dying—one may deceive oneself as to what one should do—but I think I should directly send for a Priest—Is not this a test of one's state of mind? Ought I to live where I could not bear to die? Again, I assure you it makes me quite uncomfortable travelling, lest some accident should cut me off in my present state. Is this a right frame of mind to be in? Have I lived so many years, have I made such high professions, have I preached to others so peremptorily, to be myself now in fear of death? What is the difference between me and a poor profligate? we both feel we have a work to do which is undone?

Why should I distress your kind heart with my miseries? yet you must know them to avoid the greater misery of looking at me externally, and wondering and grieving over what seems incomprehensible. Shall I add, that, distressing as is my state, it has not once come upon me to say. 'O that I had never begun to read theology!' 'O that I had never meddled in ecclesiastical matters!' 'O that I had never written the Tracts! etc' I lay no stress on this—but state it.

My wish has been, as I have said above, to wait seven years, that is, till the summer of 1846—but I cannot determine to do so. I cannot promise myself beyond next Christmas—My resolution to move has grown so much stronger lately, I cannot answer for my state of mind. Meanwhile may I not, may not you and all of us, humbly take comfort in the thought that so many persons are considerately praying for me? Of course the human heart is most mysterious. I may have some deep evil in me which I cannot fathom—I may have done some irreparable thing which demands punishment—but may not one humbly trust that the earnest prayers of many good people will be heard for me? May not one *resign* oneself to the event, whatever it turn out to be? may not one hope and believe, though one does not see it, that God's hand is in the deed, if a deed there is to be, that He has a purpose, and will bring it to good, and will show us that it is good in His own time? Let us not doubt, may we never have cause to doubt, that He is with us. Continually do I pray that He would discover to me, if I am under a delusion—what can I do more? what hope have I but in Him? to whom should I go? who can do me any good? who can speak a word of comfort but He? who is there but looks on me with sorrowful face? but He can lift up the light of His countenance upon me. All is against me—may He not add Himself as an adversary!—may He tell me, may I listen to Him, if His will is other than I think it to be!

Palm Sunday. And then on the other hand it comes on me, Have not there after all been persons in my case before now, and were they not right? Were persons never yet in a schismatical or heretical Church, and would not their trial, when they came to see their state, be exactly what mine is? Have Jews never had to turn Christians, and been cursed by their friends for doing so? Can I shock people so much as they did? Is the Church of Rome, can it be, regarded more fearfully than Jews regard Christianity, than Jews regarded St Paul?—was he not the prince of apostates? Has Nestorian, or Donatist, or Monophysite, never discovered that he was out of the Church, and had to break through all ties to get into it? Nay is not this the peculiar trial which happens in Scripture to be set upon a Christian (I don't say of course which is necessary to a Christian, or which is his badge, but what happens to be insisted in Scripture) the quitting of friends and relations and houses and goods for Christ's sake? Surely all the distress and unsettlement I shall give, however great a warning to me not to act hastily, cannot be a *real reason* against moving, for it is, so it happens, the very condition under which a follower of Christ is drawn in Scripture—But I need not proceed.

So, my dear Jemima, if you can suggest any warning to me which I am not considering, well, and thank you—else do take comfort, and think that perhaps you have a right to have faith in me—perhaps you have a right to believe that He who has led me hitherto, will not suffer me to go wrong. I am some how in better spirits this morning, and I say what it occurs to me to say at the time.

Have I not a right to ask you not to say, as you have said in your letter, that I shall do *wrong*? What right have you to judge me? have the multitude, who will judge me, any right to judge me? who of my equals, who of the many who will talk flippantly about me, has a right? who has a right to judge me but my Judge? who has taken such pains to know *my* duty (poor as they have been) as I myself? who is more likely than I to know what I ought to do? I may be wrong, but He that judgeth me is the Lord,[1] and judge nothing before the time.

His ways are not our ways, nor His thoughts as our thoughts.[2] He may have purposes as merciful, as they are beyond us. Let us do our best and leave the event to Him. He will give us strength to bear all that is to come upon [us]—whatever others have to bear, surely I have to bear most; and if I do not shrink from bearing it, others must not shrink. May I do my best—am I not trying to do my best? may we not trust it will turn to the best?

What you tell me about Aunt disappoints as well as pains me. I had been doing all I could through last summer to prepare her, and I thought the report in November most happy in that point of view. On the whole I am disposed to think that nothing need be told her yet; but I think it quite necessary to throw as much cold water as you can upon any *expressions* of confidence of hers. In October or November at latest, I suppose I shall give up my fellowship, and this must startle her. It will be time then to think of what is best to be done. *Supposing* I do not move till next spring, it may be time enough to tell her at Christmas—and *I* will do it, if you think best. Any how I think nothing need be done at once

Ever Yrs affly J H N

[1] *1 Corinthians* 4:4.   [2] *Isaiah* 55:8.

To Miss Mary Holmes

Littlemore. May 31 1845

(Copy)

My dear Miss Holmes,

I have received your letter of the 29th written under changed feelings.

You know I have wished to break off our correspondence, except on matters in which I thought (with your director's leave) I could serve you, from the time you joined the Church of Rome.

After your recent letters, I have come to the resolution of breaking it off altogether.

I have many reasons for this. It is enough to say to you that you have no claim whatever on me to continue it.

I have already given up much time and thought to you, to the loss of others who have a real claim on me.

I have borne the burden long enough, and think the time is come at length when I may be relieved of it.

It is useless to attempt to alter my resolution.

I pray that you may ever find advisers as patient and thoughtful as I have been to you. I do not doubt you will. Their duty *lies* in their being patient with you—I have been patient *beyond* my duty

Yours very truly (signed) J H N.

To Richard Westmacott

Littlemore. July 11. 1845

My dear Westmacott,

It was very kind in you at the present time going into my matters. I suppose I may now tell you, that it is morally certain I shall join the R C. Church, though I don't wish this *told* from me. It has been the conviction of six years—from which I have never receded. It was gained while outward circumstances were promising all around us, and every thing spoke of hope. I told my feeling to one or two persons who were about me in the autumn of 1839. I have waited patiently a long time.

My conviction has nothing whatever to do with events of the day. It is founded on my study of early Church history. I think the Church of Rome in every respect the continuation of the early Church. I think she is the early Church *in* these times, and the early Church is she *in* these times. They differ in doctrine and discipline as child and grown man differ, not otherwise. I do not see any medium between disowning Christianity, and taking the Church of Rome.

This being the ground of my conviction, I have at various times been reluctant to tell it to you—and I dare say seemed to you either reserved or afraid to argue. It was the latter—I was afraid. I will be frank with you, and tell you why. It was because I had got a notion that you had been inclined to scepticism—and it seemed a most serious thing to tell a person so inclined that one's own conviction was that he must believe every thing or nothing. You have been so kindly persevering, from the interest you take in me, that I am forced to tell you my ground of conviction; and besides, I think you are stronger now than to be put out by such an avowal on my part. But for myself I say fairly, that I cannot believe only just as much as our Reformers out of their own heads have chosen we should believe—I must believe less or more. If Christianity is one and the same at all times, then I must believe, not what the Reformers have carved out of it, but what the Catholic Church holds.

I do not agree with Ward and Oakeley in their ground, but think you are hard on them. You call them disingenuous in trying to *stretch* the articles of our Church. Well then, do you wish them to *leave* our Church? that I suppose would not please you better. You abuse them for staying—you remonstrate with me for going. What middle course is there? I suppose, going into 'lay communion,' giving up preferment etc and remaining quiet. This might be very well for a middleaged, indolent person like myself—but do you really mean that a number of active, able men between 23 and 40, can think it their duty to waste their prime in doing nothing? Is it not a more fantastic idea than turning Mormonite or Jumper?

I am amused at your calling me 'cloistered'—it is true—but I am a sharper fellow than you think

Ever Yrs affectly J H Newman

To Edward Hawkins, Provost of Oriel College

Littlemore. Oct. 3. 1845

Mr Provost,

I hope you will find the inclosed form correct.

I shall be obliged to you if you will remove my name from the books of the College and the University

I am, Mr Provost, Yours truly John H Newman

To Henry Wilberforce

Littlemore. Oct. 7. 1845

⌈My dearest H W

Father Dominic the Passionist is passing this way, on his way from Aston in Staffordshire to Belgium, where a chapter of his Order (if it is an Order) is to be held at this time. He is to come to Littlemore for a night as a guest of one of us whom he has admitted at Aston. He does not know of my intentions, but I shall ask of him admission into the one true Fold of the Redeemer. I shall keep this back till after it is all over.

I could have wished to delay till my book was actually out,[1] but having all along gone so simply and entirely by my own reason, I was not sorry to [[in]] this matter [[of time]], at an inconvenience, to submit myself to what seemed an external call. Also I suppose the departure of others has had something to do with it, for when they went, it was as if I were losing my own bowels.⌋[2]

Father Dominic has had his thoughts turned to England from a youth, in a distinct and remarkable way. For thirty years he has expected to be sent to England, and about three years since was sent without any act of his own by his superiors. He has had little or nothing to do with conversions, but goes on missions and retreats among his own people. I saw him once here for a few minutes on St John the Baptist's day last year, when he came to see the Chapel. He is a simple quaint man, an Italian; but a very sharp clever man too in his way. It is an accident his coming here, and I had no thoughts of applying to him till quite lately, nor should, I suppose, but for this accident.

With all affectionate thoughts to your wife and children and to yourself I am My dear H W

Tuus usque ad cineres J H N

[1] An Essay on the Development of Christian Doctrine.

[2] John Dalgairns had left on 27 September, and had become a Catholic two days later. Three others of those at Littlemore had also recently left. Richard Stanton went away for a month, on 24 September, after intimating to Newman his strong desire to become a Catholic. On 2 October he was writing to say that he saw no sufficient reason for waiting, and proposing that, since he was staying at Chorley in Lancashire, he might be received at Stonyhurst. Newman replied on the 4th, suggesting that they might both be received at Littlemore. Ambrose St John left on 30 September, for the Catholic College at Prior Park, where he was received on 2 October. Albany J. Christie also left on 30 September, for London, whence he wrote to say that he would call on Dr Doyle, the priest at St George's, Southwark, on 8 October, unless Newman forbad him. He was received on 18 October.

To Mrs John Mozley

Littlemore. Oct. 8. 1845

My dear Jemima,

I must tell you, what will pain you greatly, but I will make it as short as you would wish me to do.

This night Father Dominic the Passionist, sleeps here. He does not know of my intention, but I shall ask him to receive me into what I believe to be the One Fold of the Redeemer.

This will not go, till all is over.

Ever Yours affectly John H Newman

To Mrs John Mozley

Littlemore. 5½ a.m. Oct 9/45

My dear Jemima,

Before your letter came last evening,[1] I had written an important line to you, which will go, I suppose, tomorrow.

It is very natural that persons should have the feeling you express about my leaving Littlemore—but in having it, they do not put themselves in *my* position, but view me from their own. Few people can put themselves into another's position.

The Apostles, when converted, were told to begin with Jerusalem, not to quit it— and the reproach urged against them is that they had filled Jerusalem with their doctrine. St Paul preached first to them of Damascus, Jerusalem, and Judaea. St James the Just died Bishop of Jerusalem. Could they indeed without the greatest cruelty, not have set the gospel before their own countrymen?

Why should I go, if I think I am right, as one of a large body which is poured over the earth, and of which the whole earth is the inheritance according to the prophecies? Of course I must think any other body a usurper, and as having no place, according to the Divine Scheme, in any part of the earth. If I thought any other body but that which I recognise to be the Catholic to be recognised by the Saviour of the world, I would not have left that body.

All this is quite consistent with believing, as I firmly do, that individuals in the English Church are invisibly knit into that True Body of which they are not outwardly members—and consistent too with thinking it highly injudicious, indiscreet, wanton, to interfere with them in particular cases—only it is a matter of judgment *in* the particular case. It might be indiscreet in me to remain here, it might not. Persons have quite a right to blame my judgment if they will— though even here they should recollect that I may be in the position to be the better judge. But it must be put on the ground of discretion—if I said I *ought* in *duty* to go away, I should be confessing I ought not to join the Church of Rome at all.

I think I have found that those who fear me and wish me away, think I ought to go—and those who really wish me to stay, have no such thoughts. All depends on their own view of the general question. Also I doubt not there are persons who want some tangible ground on which to blame me (which I am sure is on the whole difficult) and they will fasten on this, if they can.

As to 'sacrifice,' which do you think would be *pleasanter* to me to leave this place or to stay?

One person I met the other day, (who showed no intention of doing as I did) who was much relieved on being told by me that I was not going away, of which there had been a report.

If I am right, all persons who wish to know the Truth, should wish me to stay,— and in proportion as they have any misgiving that I am right, ought they to wish it.

I inclose a note to Aunt—I will say nothing about my feelings all along to one so good and sweet as you are. There is One who knows how much it has lain upon my heart to pain you. But I am not going to make apology, or to seem to try to recommend myself to you

Ever Yours affectionately J H N

[1] In this letter dated 6 October Newman's sister, after excusing herself for not writing sooner, and after thanking him for telling her of the resignation of his Fellowship and imminent conversion, continued: 'One thing has been on my mind ever since I saw you, and the more I think of it, the more it seems to be the case—it is that you purpose remaining at Littlemore under your altered circumstances. I certainly had not expected it, and shall be very sorry if it should be so.'

To James Hope

Oscott. November 2/45

My dear Hope,

[You will be glad to know that I had a very satisfactory talk with Dr W. [Wiseman] yesterday. He absolutely declined to see my book.[1] He said that, as it professed to be the course of reasoning which I *had* had, it was *a fact*, which all his seeing could not alter. There might be error in it, if it so happened—but still so that I professed it to be historical, and professed (as of course I do) in all things to submit [[it]] to the Church, he had nothing to say to it. I have no reason whatever to suppose there is anything at all in it, which I should now disclaim—but still he has *not* seen it, and of course speaks *on the chance* of its containing any thing [[such]].

Also he professed quite to agree with Döllinger (and Father Dominic) in his view of letting the controversy take its course, not hastening people, but letting principles work.

All this, please, is for yourself alone.

Ever, my dear Hope, Yours affectionately

John H Newman

P.S. I was confirmed yesterday.]

[1] *The Development of Christian Doctrine.* Wiseman changed his mind a few days later, but eventually left the book uncensored.

To John Keble

Littlemore. November 14. 1845

May the Holy Trinity,

Father, Son, and Spirit,

return to you sevenfold, My dear Keble, all the good, of which you have been the instrument towards me, since I first knew you. To you I owe it, humanly speaking, that I am what and where I am. Others have helped me in various ways, but no one can I name but you, among those I ever knew, except one who is gone,[1] who has had any part in setting my face in that special direction which has led me to my present inestimable gain.

Do not let me pain you, My dear Keble, by saying this. Let me not seem rude. Let it be your comfort, when you are troubled, to think that there is one who feels that he owes all to you, and who, though, alas, now cut off from you, is a faithful assiduous friend unseen.

Ever Yours very affectionately John H Newman[2]

[1] Richard Hurrell Froude.

[2] This was Newman's reply to Keble's letters of 3 and 11 October, *K.C.*, pp. 384–6. Keble wrote again on Easter Tuesday 1846, a letter to which Newman did not reply for reasons he could not recall thirty years later. The friendship was renewed in August 1863, *Ward*, II, p. 590.

To Miss M. R. Giberne

Littlemore. Dec 21/45

My dear Miss Giberne

This morning's news from you was indeed a joyful surprise. You have not told me the history of your anticipating your happiness—but the event is enough. How glad I should be to have heard of your friend's reception also—For I suppose your silence means that it is yet to come.[1]

And now, My dear Miss G. that you have the power, pray begin your intercessions very earnestly (though I need not say it) for those dear friends of mine, or ours, who are still held back, or rather imprisoned in their old error, and that by their own good feelings and amiable affections. You have all the Saints of heaven to add [aid] you now, and especially that first and most glorious of Saints whose name you bear. First of all pray for dear Isaac Williams who is to appearance on his death bed. He has an abscess on his back, from which they augur the worst. Mr Demainbray too is dying, if not dead. Circumstances led me to write a line, not knowing what his state of mind might be, and not wishing to neglect the chance of an opening. But he answered (most kindly) saying that he hoped I should repent and return. And next do not forget the two Kebles, to one of whom we owe so much. And lastly let me name Pusey, whose conversion (of which there are no signs) would be followed by so many.

And now I have time for nothing but to sign myself Your affectionate Friend

John H. Newman

P.S. Of course you need not wait for Confirmation in order to communicate. So I understand Mr B. [Brownbill] told you. If however he left it *quite at your option* (which I hardly suppose he did) and you have a strong feeling against it, I suppose you had better wait.

[1] Miss Giberne was received into the Catholic Church on 19 December. Her friend, Selina Bacchus, who was to be married on 8 January, did not become a Catholic until 1848.

To The Abbé Jager[1]

[1845 or 1846]

I thank you very much for your kind letter, which circumstances hindered me from answering at the time I received it. Since it was written, you will see I have published a work, giving some of my reasons for my change of opinion. I have no wish at all that it should be kept secret that I was your opponent 11 or 12 years ago in the correspondence you inserted in the *Univers* newspaper, and afterwards published separately. Many thanks, indeed, for your kind wish to know me, if I went to Paris. I should rejoice in such an opportunity.

[1] Jean-Nicholas Jager (1790–1868), French church historian, whose correspondence with Newman between 1834 and 1836 in *L'Univers* and *Moniteur de la Religion*, he published in book form as *Le Protestantisme aux prises avec la doctrine catholique*. In a note dated 20 February 1868 Newman wrote, 'in 1845 or 1846 he [Abbé Jager] wrote to me to ask whether I did not owe my conversion to him, or some such question. I was obliged to answer, No.'

To Henry Wilberforce

Littlemore. In fest. Sti Joan. Chrysost. [27 January] 1846

Charissime,

⌈While it occurs to me, I send you a word or two by way of protest against an article in the last Chr. Rem. [Christian Remembrancer] about me, and will mention two or three facts which I may forget, if I delay. [[NB. with reason or not, I thought the article James Mozley's]]

The writer says that I never simply believed in the Anglican Church, or received it as divine. This I suppose is his meaning.

Now first I suppose it will not be denied that I have in many instances and habitually submitted myself *in fact* to the Church in which I was, and have practised an implicit obedience towards its living authorities. My conscience at least so witnesses.

Next I have freely expended large sums on the Anglican Church, which seems a proof of my never contemplating a change. At least it is to myself, for of course, I expended those sums, which now would be an assistance to me, under some feeling, with some view, or other—and I should recollect, I am sure, if I had doubts on my mind at the time I spent them.

But in truth the writer confuses faith in the English Church, with faith in the particular theory on which it is to be supported and the particular body of evidence which forms its credentials. This theory is familiarly called the Via Media. Now in the year 1834 or 35 my belief even in this theory was so strong, that I recollect feeling an anxiety about the Abbé Jager, with whom I was controverting, lest my arguments were unsettling him and making him miserable. Those arguments were not mine, but the evolution of Laud's theory, Stillingfleet's etc which seemed to me clear, complete, and unanswerable. I do not think I had that unhesitating belief in it in 1836-7 when I published my Prophetical Office, or rather I should say that *zeal* for it—for I believed it fully or at least was not conscious I did not. It is difficult to say whether or not a flagging zeal involves an incipient doubt. The feelings under which I wrote the volume will be seen in the commencement of the last Lecture. I thought the theory true, but that all theories were doubtful and difficult, and all reasoning a weariness to the flesh.

As time went on and I read the Fathers more attentively, I found the Via Media less and less satisfactory. It broke down with me in 1839.

So much on the *theory* of the Anglican Church—but as to the Church itself I implicitly believed in her divinity till a late date. I cannot tell when—I suppose till I gave up St Mary's.[1] But much later than that did I give private absolution in the form contained in the Visitation Service—a fact which the Reviewer seems not to know. And when I was at the early Eucharistic Service at St Mary's (I thus specify it, because I am appealing to my memory distinctly) I had an absolute and overpowering sense of the Real Presence.

For my feeling towards the English Church *before* I knew the theory of the Via Media vid. many of the poems in the Lyra Apostolica. [[1832-3—the year before the Abbé Jager.]]

In this connexion my four Advent [[1841]] Sermons (which made a noise) on the *Internal Notes* of the Church, are remarkable.[2] When I was driven back from the Theory of the Via Media, I retreated upon the Church herself, with which I had set out and wished to make out that the proofs lay in herself—I did not at once give her up. There cannot be a more cogent proof of my confidence in the Church, in some way or other, any how; whatever might turn out to be her real evidence, evidence there was I was sure. [[Yes, but in those Sermons it was implied that faith in the Anglican Church was a Difficulty.]]

I believe *I* was the *first* writer who made *life the* mark of a true Church, yet this writer speaks as if I went to books in the first instance not to life. But my *Sermons* are a wholesale refutation of his theory.]

Ever Yrs affly J H N.

[[I considered James Mozley the writer of the Article in question; and felt myself much aggrieved, for I considered that he had availed himself in it, however illogically and unfairly, of the very confidential talks we had had on the subject, talks, which he had pressed upon me, and in which I had opened to him all my mind. Febr. 16. 1876.]]

[1] 19 September 1843.
[2] *S.D.*, pp. 308–80. Cf. *Apo.*, pp. 152 ff.

To Miss M. R. Giberne

Littlemore. January 28. 1846

My dear Miss Giberne,

Your feelings at present must indeed be very much tried, and I sincerely thank you for letting me share them. Take your present trial,[1] as you do, as a gracious means of bringing you under the more intimate protection of your true friends, those Saints and Angels unseen, who can do so much more for you with God, and in the course of life, than any mere child of man, however dear and excellent. You speak as if I were not in your case, for, though I left Littlemore, I carried my friends with me, but alas! can you point to any one who has lost more in the way of friendship, whether by death or alienation, than I have? but even as regards friends of this world I have found that Divine Mercy wonderfully makes up my losses, as if 'instead of thy fathers thou shalt have children' were fulfilled in individuals as well as to the Church. I am now engaged in looking over, sorting, burning my papers and letters, and have had pangs and uttered deep sighs, such as I have not at all yet, (though I used before) since my reception into the Church. So many dead, so many separated. My mother gone; my sisters nothing to me, or rather foreign to me; of my greatest friends Froude, Wood, Bowden taken away, all of whom would now be, or be coming, on my side. Other dear friends who *are* preserved in life *not* moving with me; Pusey strongly bent on an opposite course, Williams protesting against my conduct as rationalistic, and, dying—Rogers and J. Mozley viewing it with utter repugnance. Of my friends of a dozen years ago whom have I now? and what did I know of my present friends a dozen years ago? why, they were at School, or they were freshmen looking up to me, if they knew my name, as some immense and unapproachable don; and now they know nothing, can know nothing of my earlier life; things which to me are as yesterday are to them as dreams of the past; they do not know the names, the state of things, the occurrences, they have not the associations, which are part of my own world, in which I live. And yet I am very happy with them, and can truly say with St Paul 'I have all and abound—' and moreover, I have with them, what I never can have had with others, Catholic hopes and beliefs—Catholic objects. And so in your own case, depend on it, God's Mercy will make up to you all you lose, and you will be blessed, not indeed in the same way, but in a higher.

I am sorry I did not tell you any thing about the impressions I formed of things and persons in my wanderings. If any thing takes me to Cheltenham, I will give you an account of all I have seen. Every thing has been as I could wish it to be. I have received most abundant cordial simple-hearted kindness—and have found a great deal to admire—and every where the signs of an awful and real system. I was especially pleased with Ushaw College, near Durham, with the professors and above all the President, Dr Newsham. The Bishops have been especially kind to me, and I think I have made the friendship of some of them, as far as it can be done in a day or two. But, as time goes on, I shall have more to tell you of course—and will wait patiently till I see you

Ever Your affectte friend John H Newman

P.S. Tell me, *as far as is right*, all about Mr Brownbill.

[1] Her loneliness.

To Henry Wilberforce

⌜Mary Vale Febr 26/46

Charissime

I write my first letter from my new home to you. Pusey is my oldest friend since dear J W B. [Bowden] was taken away—you come next. I am going to write to him, and had got out my paper, but somehow my fingers have slipt away with my purpose, and I write to you, who have been so faithful to me. No one can be truer or more faithful to me than Pusey himself—but Aristotle says something about our hearts going more with those younger than ourselves than with others; and of those who in any sense have been providentially placed under me you alone have been affectionate to me. And that is the reason perhaps I love St John so much because he comes from you and from your teaching.[1] Oh that he might be a pledge to me that you are yourself to repair that breach which you sorrow over, by your doing what he has done—but I say the above whatever you resolve upon, Carissime, great indeed as must be my distress, as well as yours, while we are divided.

I am writing next room to the Chapel—It is such an incomprehensible blessing to have Christ in bodily presence in one's house, within one's walls, as swallows up all other privileges and destroys, or should destroy, every pain.⌝ To know that He is close by – to be able again and again through the day to go in to Him; ⌜and be sure, My dearest W, when I am thus in His Presence you are not forgotten. It is *the* place for intercession surely, where the Blessed Sacrament is. Thus Abraham, our father, pleaded before his hidden Lord and God in the[2] . . .

My last morning at Littlemore, when I was by myself, the call of Abraham, as you know in the English Service, was the subject of the lessons—and when I got here the first office was that of St Matthias, who took his place in the Apostolate later than his brethren.

I have brought here your little reading desk which was [Samuel] Wood's—I had not the heart to let it remain behind. (You should not have lost it, if it had) It formed part of the altar on which Father Dominic offered mass, and from which I received my first communion, last 11th of October.⌝[3]

Please come and fetch it—I can't help saying so—excuse this importunate letter, and believe me, ever Yrs most affectionately J H N

P.S. ⌈Don't think in any thing I have said above I mean to reflect on [[include]] such dear fellows as C. M. [Marriott] and Church, but they were never exactly under me.⌉

[1] Ambrose St John had been Henry Wilberforce's curate from 1841 until he came to Littlemore in 1843.
[2] The sentence is unfinished.
[3] A mistake for the 10th.

To W. J. Copeland

Mary Vale. Oscott March 10. 1846

My dear Copeland,

As you suppose, it was of course a very trying thing to me to quit Littlemore[1]— I quite tore myself away—and could not help kissing my bed, and mantlepiece, and other parts of the house. I have been most happy there, though in a state of suspence. And there it has been, that I have both been taught my way and received an answer to my prayers. Without having any plan or shadow of a view on the subject, I cannot help thinking I shall one day see Littlemore again, and see its dear inhabitants, including yourself, once again one with us in the bosom of the true fold of Christ. Crawley has been in trying circumstances with me, and has been most kind—Yet it pained me to see in him an involuntary wish to get us away. Forbid it, that any of us should find at the last day, that we have been of those who 'when they saw Him, besought Him to depart out of their coasts.' To many doubtless my going is a present relief, who do not anticipate the chance of this.

We are busy in getting our books up—the bookshelves are a long business; the carpenters have been at them this fortnight, and have not near done. One bookcase, with the Fathers all in it, is up—the modern divines are up too. History is in preparation—Exegetics have a place—Classics are a difficulty. Hagiology and Liturgies have their place too. But the Library is only a part of our labour—it will be long before we are to rights. I have always anticipated leaving the country for a while, and shall be hardly settled, when, I suppose, I shall have to move. It is well to be a pilgrim—and with the Blessed Sacrament ever upon one's footsteps, as it now dwells under our very roof, one cannot be much of an exile any where.

Please thank Chase[2] for the account he sent me. And tell Master Barnes, whom I did not take leave of, that we sadly miss him here, where we are at some distance from any manufactory of rods, hobs, bars and the like. As to Mr. Walsh's question[3] I don't see that I can destroy the conveyance to certain trustees in joint tenancy without the leave of those trustees, which must be asked. Also will you get him to give his reason why this conveyance had better not pass out of his hands? I don't understand *what* papers he thinks had better be destroyed, if not the conveyance.

Love to C. M. [Marriott] and thank him for his letter. Tell him that so far from his needing to be surprised at my leaving the knives, etc. my very principle was to leave the house as nearly as possible furnished. I have taken away some of the chief bookcases, as much because I thought it a shame to leave so many as for my own convenience, though it is convenient for me too. Love to Pusey, Church, and Johnson—to Lewis and Bloxam—to any one else?

Ever Yrs affectly J H N

[1] Encouraged by Wiseman, Newman had left Littlemore on 22 February and moved to Old Oscott, known as Maryvale. Copeland wrote from Littlemore on 7 March: 'The poor old place seems indeed a strange place without you . . . and deeply did I think when I was with you on Sunday week what it must have cost you to have left it'.
[2] D. P. Chase, Fellow of Oriel and Junior Treasurer.
[3] The question of Mr Walsh, the Oxford lawyer, concerned Newman's property at Littlemore.

To Henry Wilberforce

17 Grosvenor Place, London. July 4. 1846

My dear Henry

I have not got your letter with me,[1] but I doubt whether I should answer it, if I had. When two persons differ in their view of a fact, the point must be left. Such seemed the case between your and my last letters. If on returning home, it seems not to be so, then I will write again.

You do not seem to have apprehended, or rather I to have expressed, why I introduced what I said about 'the Church.' ⌈What I mean is this:—If we can get a tolerable notion *which* is the Church [[out of existing religious bodies]], and know (as we do) that it may be trusted [[in its words and deeds]] because it is the Church, then comes the question *why* should not the Pope's Supremacy [[as being one of those words and deeds]] be one of the points on which it may [[is to]] be trusted?— For myself I have had so great experience of the correctness of the Roman [[*Catholic*]] view where once I thought otherwise [[it incorrect]], that I should be a beast if I were unwilling to take the rest on faith, from a confidence that what is still obscure to me (if there be any thing such, [[obscure]], I am not alluding to any thing [[in particular]]) is explainable. And it seems to me extravagant or unreasonable in you to demand proof of one certain particular tenet which it so naturally comes to the Church to decide. If the Roman [[*Catholic*]] Church be the Church, I take it [[and submit to it]] whatever it is [[monarchical, aristocratic or democratic]]—and if I find that Papal Supremacy is a point of faith in it, this point of faith [[though not capable of proof on its own merits]] is not to my imagination so strange, to my reason so incredible, to my historical knowledge so utterly without evidence, as to warrant me in saying, 'I *cannot* take it on faith.'⌉

[[This, I consider an important passage—I have interpolated words, to bring out my meaning fully—The *argument* is that on which my Essay on Doctrinal Development is founded—but I would lay the greater stress here on its application, as made in this letter, to the Papal Supremacy. There are men, as I suppose T. W. Allies, who have been converted to the Catholic Church by their belief in the divine Mission of St Peter and his successors; I on the contrary, (though thinking that much might be said positively for that divine mission from Scripture, Tradition, History and reason, and that that doctrine was much more than 'not strange,' 'not incredible,' not 'without evidence') mainly received it on the word of the Universal Church, that is, on faith. I believed that our Lord had instituted a Teaching, Sacramental, organized Body called the Church, and that the Roman communion was as an historical fact its present representative and continuation—and therefore, since that communion received the Successor of St Peter as the Vicar of Christ and the Visible Head of the Church, such he was. I have at various times since my reception had to insist on this, once, say 20 years ago or more, in correspondence with a stranger who was perplexed by, I think, the Filioque, (though I forget his middle term)—once, I think, with W. G. Ward. I do not recollect at this minute what comes of this aspect of Catholic motiva credibilitatis, and of my adherence to it, but I know there are reasons for noting it down. Febr 17. 1876]] [[Also it illustrates the passage in my letter to Pusey pp 370 etc—as does what I say about Loreto below in letter of Jany 19, 1848[2]—J H N Febr 19/76.]]

I have not, I say, your letter here, but I know you say something about sanctity as the test of the Church.[3] I should still, as far as I see, take it as such. Day by day, am I more and more struck with this note in the Roman Church as contrasted with the Anglican. The series of evidences depending on the inward work of the Spirit, from miracle to personal graces, has been most wonderfully unfolded to me since my conversion, in the natural intercourse and conversation I have had with Catholics. As to personal graces, as far as I have had experience, I have been extremely struck with their rigid purity. Evidence of this has come before me in a way not to be mistaken. How low the Anglican Church is here. Of course, I am speaking of religious [[i.e. pious]] persons in both communions. Again, I have a passage in my first volume of Sermons, about the inconsistencies of good men.[4] And I have ever made consistency the mark of a Saint. Now I think the Anglican History presents very few patterns of this virtue. You have, as a parallel, in the Roman Church great Popes, great divines—why are these not Saints? I have asked myself. Why I see, on looking closer, they perhaps had some one failing—wanted a certain elevation of mind—or were peevish or petulant—or had something or other about them which an 'Advocatus Diaboli' would discover, which deprives them of the title. Now the Anglican worthies very seldom indeed rise above this sort of excellence—Moreover, I have been exceedingly struck with the abiding φαντασία[5] of religion which Catholics have. The articles of faith are external facts taken for granted—worship is an offering really made to a real Presence—etc etc. [but I have] not time to go on. My best love to you my dear H W

from Yrs affly J H N

---

[1] Dated 27 June, and referring to infant baptism.
[2] Newman refers to 3rd and 4th edn of *Diff.* In the later edn, *Diff.* II, pp. 18 ff.; and letter to Henry Wilberforce, 19 January 1848, *L.D.* XII, p. 16.

[3] Wilberforce had argued that the note of sanctity had been at times obscured in the Church, and that the same could be the case with the note of unity.

[4] *P.S.* I., pp. 136–8.

[5] 'The power by which an object is made apparent to the mind.'

To Ambrose St John

17 Grosvenor Place. July 8/46

My dear St John,

This afternoon I had a long talk with Dr Fergusson about Propaganda, and you will all laugh at his information.[1] I don't mind your knowing it—but I should not like it to get beyond our own brotherhood. Above all, don't tell Faber.

He gave me a minute description of the day there. Every quarter of an hour has its work, and is measured out by rule. It is a Jesuit retreat continued through the year. You get up at ½ past 5, having slept (by compulsion) 7½ hours at ¼ to six you run into the passage and kneel down for the Angelus. Then you finish your dressing. At 6 you begin to meditate—the prefect going up and down and seeing you are at your work. Three minutes off the ½ hour a bell rings for the colloquium. At the ½ hour (6½) mass—which everyone attends in surplice—7 breakfast, some bread and some milk and (I think) coffee—Then follow schools—at ½ past eleven dinner and so on. A compulsory walk for an hour and a half in the course of the day. Recreation an hour after dinner and supper—but all recreate together—no private confabs.—In like manner no one must enter any other person's room. (Corollary. It is no good two *friends* going to Propaganda.) This corollary is thus further confirmed—viz. the whole body of students is divided into 8 classes or portions—⟨camaratas?⟩—who are never allowed to speak to each other. If you and Christie and Penny went, they would of course put you into three separate camaratas.

Further, your letters are all opened, and you put the letters you write into the Rector's hand.

To continue—You must not have any pocket money. You must give up your purse to the Rector. If you want to buy any thing, you must ask him for money. Every thing necessary is found for you. 'Then there is no good' I asked 'in taking money'—No, said Dr F. none at all.

Next, you may not have *clothes* of your own—the Rector takes away coat, trowsers, shirts, stockings etc etc. and gives you some of the Propaganda's. 'Then it is no use' I asked 'taking a portmanteau.' No, said Dr. F. it is no use. They give you two cassocks, an *old* one and a new one. It is a great object to use up the old clothes. Mr Eyre (who was present) even said, though I suppose it was fun, that they gave you old shoes. Why, one might catch the plague, for depend on it, there are Egyptians and Turks there.

Yes, they are from all nations—except English. Dr F. said there was not a single Englishman all the time he was there.

To complete it, he said that I shall be kept there three years, and that I should have to read Perrone.

Meanwhile Talbot assures me that my going there gives the greatest satisfaction in London, and you know we heard that at Rome they are much pleased also and that 'apartments' have been got ready at Propaganda for Dr Wiseman and me.

The only allowance I extracted from Dr F. was that you might have private papers in your writing desk.

Ever Yours affly J H N

July 9. Dr F. said that the moths destroyed all woollen things instanter—things out of *use* I suppose. He said that the Lectures got on very slowly, and seemed to admit that I could get up in one year what the course travelled over in two. After talking and thinking he recommended in preference, and strongly, the Collegio Nobile with Lectures at the Roman College. He said it was hard to get in—so is the Propaganda—I put down things as they occur, for after recollection. I wonder whether they would let me have my own physician. Dr. F. said one thing was provided gratis, snuff ad libitum, and I should be allowed to take a snuffbox.

I have just returned from Mass with Mrs B. [Bowden] and find Bowles' and your letter. I sent you word yesterday that I should not return till Monday. You well rebuke me for not being more grateful. For some time I had taken[2] and just now it seemed so wonderful to be taking herself.

---

[1] Thomas Tierney Ferguson, a relative of Elizabeth Bowden, who became a Catholic in 1838 and studied for the priesthood at Propaganda. He was ordained in 1844.

[2] A line has been scored out here. Elizabeth Bowden had been received into the Catholic Church the day before.

To Ambrose St John

⌈Tenby. Aug 11[12]/46

My dear St J

Though this will precede me, I trust, but a few hours, I write. Pusey is as I expected—very feeble and in bed—but decidedly improving. This is the first day he *could* have seen me! he only sees me, as it is, for three hours at different parts of the day. I had a bad passage, 12 or 13 hours—thick drizzle perhaps half the time—cabins full of people prostrate—myself on deck, never so sick in my life; chairs tumbling about. I go 130 miles tomorrow in 20 hours! a long halt at Carmarthen is the cause—price inside being £3 odd,—I mount. Have bought a *shawl* to cover my legs⌉ on the strength of the difference between inside and out.[†] My fault was in *taking* my wrapper—I should not have *thought* of a choice between wrapper and cloke. It was my false shame caused it. Also, ⌈had I thought of writing to *Wootten*,[1] I need not have come at all. Nevertheless since I acted for the best I cannot repent⌉ or be sorry for it.[‡]

Ever Yrs affly J H N

[†] [[N.B. It rained all day on my return. I got *very* wet. The shawl I still have in use, but it was too scanty to be of any real use atop of a coach. Two gentlemen on the coach took pity on me. They turned out to be the two Mr Eystons.[2] Decr. 2. 1875.]]

[‡] [[N.B. The news came to me at Maryvale, that Pusey was dying. He too wrote, begging (I think) to see me. So Dr Wiseman bade me go to him. There was no opening whatever for religion.]]

[1] Pusey's doctor at Oxford.

[2] John Ferdinand Eyston and his nephew, of the old Catholic family at East Hendred, Berks.

To Mrs John Mozley

St. Mary's Vale, Perry Bar, August 16, '46

My Very Dear Jemima,

I have ever been very ready to give you a full account of myself and my doings, but you have behaved towards me in a way which has been a virtual rejection of my offers.

It is now going on for three years since you knew of my extreme want of confidence in the English Church; and nearly from that time, or soon after, I said to you something like this: 'I do not want to discuss religious points with you—I wish simply, letting you have your opinion and keeping my own, to put you in possession of what I feel, and what I am doing, and to write easily to you, as if (as far as might be) there were no differences between us.' One time I recollect, in 1844, thinking you cold, I remonstrated about it to John, saying I really could not tell you more about myself, if you responded so little. You replied by saying it was a mere accident.[1] This I refer to as showing the footing on which I all along wished to stand towards you.

But now after this what have you done? First of all, John, in spite of the above remonstrance, in answer to my question about his publishing my book, wrote me a letter, not merely declining it, but with such unnecessary harshness that, laden as I was with anxiety and with the effort to that work, so struck down my spirits on receiving it, that I could have gone to bed from very despair and grief. I walked out, instead of working, sick at heart, with hands hanging down and feeble knees. Job's comforter, he grounded his refusal mainly on a rumour(!) that my book was to be severe on the English Church, to which in matter of fact I had been tender even to the prejudice of my argument. It was conscientious in him, doubtless, but it was quitting that neutral ground which I had hoped to preserve between us, and taking a side and putting me on the other. I send that letter back to you, and never wish to see it again.

Then, when my great trial came, my own relations, and they only, were those who could find the heart, or the want of reverence, to write censoriously to me. Others, agreeing with me or not, thought that something was due to my long suffering; it was otherwise with those on whom I had nearer claims. You were their organ; for I will not believe of so gentle and kind a heart that all you said was your own. I will not believe that it was you, though it was your hand, in answer to my own affectionate and confidential letters of many months, that wrote to me in so cruel a way—that wrote, for instance, so prematurely about my remaining at Littlemore, as if it were modest or seemly in you to advise in a matter of detail one from whom you differed so widely in the greatest matters, or as if the World, which had parted company with me, had any claim to know my mind at once on a point of expedience.[2]

Such letters as these completely swept away that footing which for a year or two past I had been wishing to preserve with you. I could not press you further to what, perhaps, on a feeling of conscience, you rejected. Next, as if to show in a marked way your feeling against that footing, you kept silence about yourself and those about you. You went to the Isle of Wight; for five weeks I knew nothing of your movements. Dear Johnnie was burnt; I heard it first from the people at Littlemore. Then after Frank's birth you kept silence for above two months. Again, at Christmas I mentioned my intention of having called on my aunt in passing through Derby; your answer contained nothing which sounded like an encouragement to do so.

Now, had my letters been full of controversial matter, there might have been an excuse for this; had I called on you to become a Catholic, you might fairly have retorted on me your protestation. But when I wanted simply to go on with you without controversy, and you on your part volunteered so high a tone towards me, and then on the back of it kept silence about yourself—of course, you had a right to do so, you might feel it a duty to do what no one else did, but—you cannot, my dear Jemima, be surprised that I should feel I could not, as I had forewarned you in 1844, go on telling you in an easy and familiar manner what concerned myself, as I could have wished to have done.

And now, my dearest Jemima, before answering me, do me the kindness to read over my letters to you from August, 1844, to Christmas last. It will not satisfy me that you verily wish to make matters up with me. I want you to feel that you have not been so kind and considerate as I have been. Better feel pain now than by and by.

Ever yours affectionately, John H. Newman.

P. S. Your letter came this morning.

[1] See letter of Mrs John Mozley, 20 November 1844, *L.D.* X, p. 424.
[2] See letter of 9 October 1845 to Mrs John Mozley and of 14 October (*L.D.* XI, pp. 16–17).

To J. D. Dalgairns

Milan. Oct 18/46.

My dear Dalgairns

Of course it is so great an honor to have my name put down with so many great persons that I can do nothing but put it absolutely in the Bishop of Langres's hands through you—yet I cannot possibly make out any other good that can result from it except doing me honor, so I really suppose that is the reason. I hope you will say all that is proper for me to the Bishop, to assure him that I entertain a grateful sense of his condescension when I was at Langres; and do not forget to say how much we feel indebted to M. Lorain, and how affectionately minded we feel to him and to all the good priests and others to whom he was so kind as to introduce us. I don't expect we can anywhere find such a warm open-hearted reception as we did there.

Nor will we forget to remember you at St Ambrose's; as we have not, either you or any other of our Maryvale party. You are always in my thoughts when I am at St Carlo's shrine, who was a most wonderful saint, and died just at the age at which I have begun to live. But this is altogether a wonderful city—this city of St Ambrose, St Monica, St Augustine, St Athanasius to say no more . . .

We expect to set off for Genoa on Friday, with the intention of going by the steamer first to Leghorn then to Civita Vecchia. The steamer proceeds by night, I believe, and rests during the day—setting off Sunday afternoon—thus we shall have near two days at Genoa, and part of a day (from Leghorn) at Pisa—But the wind began to blow last night, and I fear we shall have rough weather at sea to spoil our pleasure. The weather here has been cativissimo, as people say here—quite out of the common, and the recompense for the hot summer. By the bye, you may like to know how St John gets on with Italian—the other day he expressed a wish to meet a person in the *winter*, pronouncing f for v.[1]

We have missed Manzoni—but been lionized almost daily by his chaplain, Ghianda, whom we like very much indeed. He speaks Latin like a *native*, though he has given it up in his late conversations with us. Rosmini passed through Milan, sending me a civil message, with an explanation that he did not call since he could not speak Latin nor I Italian. This is not enough to explain his not calling. Ghianda has a great admiration for him, and Manzoni has also. I wish we had more to tell of him—but I cannot get at the bottom of his philosophy. I wish to believe it is all right, yet one has one's suspicions. I don't think we have got a bit further than this in our reflections and conclusions, to think that Dr Wiseman was right in saying that we ought to be Oratorians. What we saw at Paris rather blunted our zeal in favour of the Vincentians, the Jesuits seem out of place everywhere—we hear no good whatever of the Dominicans; and altogether it seems rather the age for external secularism with a gentle inward bond of ascetism—and this is just Oratorianism. We have been asking Ghianda about the Dominicans, and whether they had preserved their traditions any where. He said he thought they had at Florence, and some where else. We asked him what he meant—why that they were still Thomists etc. However, on further inquiry we found that the said Dominicans of Florence were manufacturers of scented water, etc and had very choice wines in their cellar. He considered La Cordaire quite a new beginning, a sort of knight errant, and not a monk. However, as to our prospects, I repeat, nothing can be known till we get to Rome.

I have asked St John what else I have to say, and he says 'Tell him, you bully me?' This is true, but he deserves it—I am glad to tell you he is decidedly stronger. I have been making him take some quinine. The journey along the Valley before we came to the Simplon was very trying; and the weather now is not good. We have been so happy here for a month or 5 weeks, I quite dread the moving again—and if it is wet, so much the worse—but it does not do to anticipate evils. Bellasis is here—he came

the day before yesterday—we saw him yesterday and breakfast with him to-morrow—he is kind and pleasant as ever, but rather shy.

I have little news to tell you from Maryvale. Christie has not got a cat yet, and
Bowles has found the rain come in upon the Processes of Canonizations. One very
bad piece of news, however, is that Lloyd is *very* ill, and I fear beyond hope. There
has been a break up at Prior Park. We don't know the particulars, but Capes and
Northcote have gone to Oscott, and Neve to Rome, and the Bishop is with our
friends—Meanwhile Mr Woodmason has just taken a house at Bath in order to send
poor Charles there.

I have not time to read this over—St John's love

Ever Yrs affectly John H Newman

---

[1] i.e. 'Inferno' (hell) instead of 'inverno' (winter).

Early Catholic Years
(1846–51)

When Newman arrived in Rome to prepare for priestly ordination in 1846, he needed still to decide what type of priest he would be. Might he join a religious order, Dominican, Redemptorist, or Jesuit? Or should he become a diocesan priest? Very soon, however, he felt drawn by the figure of St Philip Neri and the idea of becoming an Oratorian. Before the year ended, he observed, 'If I wished to follow my bent, I should join them.' They were secular priests, but living in community: 'It is like a College with hardly any rule.' It was also what Wiseman preferred for them. This possibility began to take shape and by February it was settled.

If Newman's Anglican life since 1833 had been spent championing the Catholic tradition within the Church of England, his life after his conversion in 1845 had moved on. He was to describe it as 'like coming into port after a rough sea'.[1] But his life remained stormy. His mind might be at rest, but he would find himself caught up constantly in situations that he would then be required to unravel. The first of these emerged almost at once. It was his relationship with Frederick Faber.

Soon after Faber heard the news that Newman was to become an Oratorian, he announced that he and the group that had formed around him, known as Wilfridians, might wish to join Newman. Newman, while welcoming him generously, also challenged him by asking whether he had fully 'mastered *what* Oratorianism is', pointing out that it was not as ascetic, poetical, or devotional as Faber's preferred style. Hindsight reveals that the seeds of the difficulties between them were there from the beginning. Faber's profession of devoted commitment to Newman was qualified in fact by a previous commitment that he had undertaken to care for a mission at Cotton in Staffordshire. Newman was left to resolve the difficulty. Faber was also anxious for the Oratorians to be based in London, although their brief from Rome obliged them to begin in Birmingham. In the event their numbers made a division of the community necessary, so some remained with Newman in Birmingham, while Faber became the Superior in London. Nevertheless there were tensions. Further difficulties would follow.

And Newman was already dealing with rumours of his dissatisfaction with the Church of Rome. In 1848 he explained to Henry Bourne, the father of the future Cardinal Archbishop of Westminster, that 'from the moment I became a Catholic, I never have had, through God's grace, a single doubt or misgiving on my mind that I did wrong in becoming one'. Such denials would be a common theme of his Catholic years.

---

[1] *Apo.*, p. 238.

Then there was his dealing with other converts. He was delighted in 1850 when William Monsell, who had been an undergraduate at Oriel and became one of his closest friends, was received into the Catholic Church, but in a way that was typical of him he discouraged Monsell's wife, Anna Maria, from following him, 'till her way is clearer to her than it seemed to me the other day'. This wisdom was sometimes held against him. He was said by those who were hostile to him to discourage people from becoming Catholics.

But there was humour as well. He wryly discouraged the hero-worship of an enthusiastic lady, assuring her, 'I have no tendency to be a saint—it is a sad thing to say. Saints . . . do not write Tales'. And he answered deadpan in a letter to the Editor of *The Morning Chronicle* absurd claims taken up in the House of Commons that had referred to 'the underground cells' of a large convent in Birmingham. He acknowledged that he was the Superior of that House and explained what the cells were for: a larder, a coal-hole, a cellar for beer, or perhaps wine. 'Where is this inquisition into the private matters of Catholics to end?' he asked.

Then in 1850, when Pius IX restored the Catholic Hierarchy of Bishops in England and Wales, anti-Catholic prejudices were aroused amid denunciations of papal aggression. Newman wrote anxiously to the influential English priest in Rome, Monsignor George Talbot, concerned about the timing of Cardinal Wiseman's return to England. Although he was confident of the outcome, he was cautious in case a wrong move might make matters worse. Not long after, in February 1851, there occurred the first of three occasions when there were rumours that Newman himself might be made a bishop. Again he wrote to Talbot, 'to arrest proceedings, if there be such'.

Later that year he received a letter from Archbishop Cullen of Armagh about the establishing of a Catholic University in Ireland, asking for advice about who might be its superior. Soon afterwards he was invited to take up the position of rector himself. The prospect was attractive, but would also prove frustrating. A sequence of events was beginning that would sap Newman's energies for the next seven years.

As 1851 ended, however, he faced a more specific crisis. He found himself charged with libelling the former Dominican friar, Giacinto Achilli, who had been brought over to England by the Evangelical Alliance to lecture and feed anti-Catholic prejudice in the country. In lectures of his own, Newman had taken the opportunity to denounce Achilli's immorality and hypocrisy. He took advice from legal friends and believed that Wiseman had to hand the decisive evidence he needed to establish his case, but Wiseman had mislaid the papers and matters began to spin out of control.

5

Early Catholic Years (1846–51)

Mrs J. W. Bowden

Collegio di Propaganda. Febr 21. 1847

My dear Mrs Bowden,

My first business this morning is to write to you—and you will be glad to be told, that, not only the day leads me to do so,[1] but that, as it happens, this very evening Mgr Brunelli (the Secretary of Propaganda) is to go to the Pope to gain his approbation to what I suppose is to be henceforth our calling. So many things succeed, one the other, in a place like this, that all this cannot but be abrupt to you— and I cannot in a few words explain all about it. I suppose we shall be *Oratorians*, that is, of the Congregation of St Philip Neri—we shall try to pass some time as Novices here in Italy; and if we can, we shall bring back a Father with us. Certain it is, we shall do our best to import a tradition, not to set up something for ourselves, which to me is very unpleasant. I still hope to be back at the time originally proposed—Dr Wiseman is very anxious for it—but I must leave all this in the hands of others. I shall keep this letter to tell you of Mgr's interview with the Pope. He proposes to get a Brief from him with such alterations of the Rule as will be necessary for England. I do not doubt we shall be backed up with all the Holy See can possibly do for us—and that (what is most anxious to say) all will depend on ourselves. In the Rule of St Philip this is especially the case—for as there are no vows, there is nothing to fall back on, but the personal religiousness and mutual love of the members, for the well-being of the body. I wish (but perhaps it is not right to wish) I had more confidence in myself—but I seem to have none. I cannot realize to myself that my time is not past—I may be of use by past recollections of me and by personal influence, to bring and keep others together—but that I shall be able to *do* any thing by myself, beyond being this bond of union, I do not feel. Indeed I do need the prayers of all friends, and you must all of you bear me in mind.

You will be disappointed, I fear, to be told what our duty will be—It will be to plant ourselves in a large town, say Birmingham, and attempt to get hold of those classes which at present are any thing or nothing, members of clubs, mechanics-institutes etc etc. Not that this is not a great object, but perhaps you would not wish it for me. But it has great recommendations for me personally—It gives me what I want, active work, yet as much or as little as I wish—time for reading and writing— and a rule without being a very severe one. It will associate also together persons of very different tastes—as we want to argue, to preach, to sing and play, and to train young people. I trust we are doing what is intended for us. I have so many letters to write, that I shall make this a short one. Our mind has been made up ourselves sometime, but we have waited for letters from England. They came last Tuesday— since then; Mgr B. has wished to push the matter on. Love to the children

Ever Yrs affly John H Newman

No, perhaps you had better not say it, beyond the children.

Feb. 23. The Pope has taken us up most warmly—offered us a house here for a noviciate, proposed others joining us here—and our going back together to England. I trust this plan would not keep us beyond the Autumn. It is *no* secret we are to be Oratorians—but matters of detail I don't wish mentioned. Will you kindly send the inclosed to the Post.[2]

[1] Newman was born on 21 February 1801.
[2] Other letters that were posted in England.

To Father Dominic Barberi

Collegio di Propaganda. March 14/47

My dear Father Domenico

I have thought of writing to you many times since I have been here, but am not sorry to have waited till I can tell you something about ourselves. We are to be Oratorians. The Pope has been very kind to us—suggested that others of us had better come here and pass their novitiate with us all together under an Oratorian Father. How long we shall remain here I do not know—when we return, we shall set up, I suppose, in some large town, and try to convert that numerous class of youths who at present have a little education and no religion.

We dined at St John and Paul's this day three weeks[1]—The Father General was very well. What people remark of the Passionists here is that they all have a look of[2] about them which other orders have not. To me the Passionists look peaceful, and the Capucins cheerful—yet these are the two severest orders. Ours will not be very severe—yet we must manage to be cheerful in order to convert young persons, and peaceful in order to bear disappointment. Say every thing that is kind and respectful from me to Brother Ignatius a Sancto Paulo, (if I am right in his name in religion)[3] and to the rest of your community. I regret *we* shall not, according to the Oratorian Rule, have such sacred names—they might do something towards making one good—As you know well, they are written up under the pictures of the departed, in your house on the Celian. Some of them were pointed out to us as your own novices—The Oratorians and Jesuits are only Father this and Father that, instead of being Ambrosius ab Assumptione, or Athanasius ab Incarnatâ Sapientiâ—but only those who do severe penance deserve such names. And now I have nothing to add but to beg your charitable prayers for us and our undertaking, and to subscribe myself, My dear Father Domenic,

Respectfully & affectionately Yours, John H Newman[4]

[1] SS Giovanni e Paolo, the Passionist House in Rome.

[2] Letter torn here, and word missing.

[3] Father George Spencer, who became a Passionist novice on 5 January 1847. See Newman's letter to his brother, Francis, on 11 April 1840.

[4] Father Dominic replied warmly on 6 April, speaking of the great need of priests in large towns.

To F. W. Faber

March 31/47

My dear Faber

Your very kind letter came yesterday, about the time (I suppose) you have received mine of the 16th. Thank you much for your congratulations. Do not for an instant fancy our plans will clash; there is not a chance of it.[1] You have your own ways and powers, which no one can rival, of working out your object, even if our object were precisely the same, which is not the case. At the same time I am surprised to find that our general plans are more the same than I thought at first. I know how great a devotion you have to St Philip and that he is one of your patrons; but I had fancied that both in devotional exercises upon which you fell back and in the great prominence given to your lay brothers, you differed from him essentially. Besides, the very fact that you had not become an Oratorian when you might, was quite enough to put me off the idea that in our becoming Oratorians we should interfere with you. This was our feeling when, after a good deal of beating about, we finally determined to offer ourselves to St Philip. But I repeat, there is not a chance of your and our interfering with each other. England is large enough—we have no preference for any town—Birmingham is nearest to us, that is all—and you have no particular connexion with Birmingham—but depend on it, we shall not be such fools if we can help it as to come near you, who will suck away all our young men from us—and again we do not [know] what precise form we shall take or whom address.

Love to brothers Austin [Mills] and Anthony [Hutchinson] and to all your community and believe me &c.[2]

[1] Faber wrote on 18 March, 'The news of your becoming an Oratorian of course raised a fresh little assault on us, as we ought to follow your example and merge in an old order etc etc, and it was rather curious that I had proposed to Dr Wiseman to make an oratory, but he discountenanced it, and we gave it up a little bit grumpily. But we have now received letters from some old catholics . . . suggesting that we . . . were bound to consider ourselves "*supplanted.*" In short—it seems that people think we are now in opposition to you. All this is very ludicrous . . . when you return we could have a conference, and if it still seemed advisable . . . that we should not be merged in another institute . . . then let us cede everything which might interfere with you or the spread of your houses. . . . We have now quite given up our notion of returning to Birmingham'.

[2] Faber replied on 5 April, 'Already one can see one mark of your vocation in the uneasiness of the evil one. Some say that you craftily got the bishop to remove us from Birmingham that we might not stand in your way. . . . Then the priests at Birmingham are exceedingly irate and fierce with us; I *think* because they are more afraid of you than of us, and fancy that if we had stayed, you would have gone elsewhere . . . Of course I heard a good deal during the ennuyante fortnight I spent at distracting, gossiping Oscott, and people seemed inclined to doubt and criticize. What strikes me as oddest is the way people have mixed you and our piccola famiglia together'.

To Mrs J. W. Bowden

10 a.m. Trinity Sunday. May 30/47

My dear Mrs Bowden,

You will be pleased to hear I was ordained Priest about two hours ago; surprised perhaps, for things have progressed so rapidly that I do not know what I said in my last letter. St John and I received the subdiaconate last Wednesday, the 26th, St Philip's day—in Cardinal Fransoni's private Chapel—the Diaconate yesterday in St John Lateran—the Priesthood today in the Propaganda Church from Cardinal Fransoni. We expect to say our first Mass on Corpus Christi Day. My three first Masses are of a formal character, and have indulgences attached to them, Thursday, Friday, and Saturday; on Sunday June 6 I shall say mass expressly for you and yours, and especially for John, who I suppose is at Oxford. My first seven Sundays shall be given to this sa[me] special intention to the exclusion of others—unless (which I am not aware can be the case) any direct obligation interferes to prevent me. May 31. This is the day the Bowdens lost Maryanne in 1819, whom, I believe you never saw.[1] I have just been at a Solemn Mass for O Connell.[2] We are on the point of starting to see Stâ Croce—and I do hope shall get into it in a few days. The weather is VERY hot, but not oppressive—the nights worse than the days—some air always in the days. What we have to guard against is variations of temperature. They say that after a thunderstorm the glass sometimes falls 20 degrees. There is a report in Rome that Dr Pusey is converted—which would simply be a miracle—but I do not know why miracles should not take place; all human probabilities and laws are against his changing. Nothing can exceed the kindness of people here and our ordination has excited great interest.

We have just returned from seeing Sta Croce. It is a most beautiful site—the rooms are large and airy, and the corridors long. If a place can be cool in hot weather, it is such as this—and the air is said to be good—but I know we must be very careful. I shall set about getting furniture etc to-morrow. I believe Propaganda will do all for us. The Abbot[3] told us that he heard we were to be there six or eight months, which would bring our return to December or February. The Malta scheme seems to fade away; but we know nothing definitely. We are expecting Dr Wiseman. Wednesday June 2. A great change of weather—a deal of rain, which has refreshed everything—but evidently very catch cold. I fear we shall not get into Sta Croce for these 10 days—not that St John and I like the thoughts of leaving Propaganda—but our friends are not very comfortable at the Passionist Convent—tho' the poor monks are as kind to them as they can be—and the sooner we get to Sta Croce, the sooner we shall get back to England. I suppose my first Mass (tomorrow) will be in the Jesuit private Chapel here—my second the community Mass in the Propaganda Church—the third at St Thos' [Thomas's] Altar in the English College

Love to all the children Ever Yrs affly J H N.

[1] Marianne Bowden (1800–19) sister of J. W. Bowden.

[2] Daniel O'Connell died at Genoa on 15 May 1847.

[3] Of Sante Croce, Don Nivardo Tassini.

To F. W. Faber

London Dec 31. [1847]

My dear Faber

Dr Wiseman has told me of your most welcome offer,[1] and I wished to have written you by the first post, but in London this was impossible. I now write before day-light this morning, to secure doing so at all. To-day I go down to Mary vale—so write to me there. (Mary vale, *Perry Bar*)

You may fancy the joy with which St John and I heard the news that you proposed we should be one—I should say 'gratitude,' except that the confidence of course is not shown to us singly, but to St Philip.

I cannot say more now till I know your precise wishes and intentions—I will but say that, from the very wish I have that we may come to an understanding, I am anxious you should [try] if you have fully mastered *what* Oratorianism is. In many important respects it differs from what you are at present. It is not near so ascetic—indeed it is *not* ascetic. It is not poetical—it is not very devotional. Now it is a question what your youths will say to this. Again, as you know, it has but few lay brothers compared to your present society. And (though this could be obviated) the lay brothers have *secular* offices, e.g. gardener, cook, maniciple etc etc. An Oratorian ought, like a Roman Legionary, to stand in his place and fight by himself, though in company—instead of being a mere instrument of another, or a member of a phalanx—Or he is an Athenian, as described in Pericles's Oration, as contrasted with a Spartan. I am so desirous of our coming together, that I wince while I put down these objections, but no good will come of it, if we don't consider the matter first in all its bearings

Ever Yrs affectly John H Newman

Love to your party and a happy new year

[1] Wiseman had told Newman of Faber's offer to join the Oratory with his Brothers of the Will of God, Wilfridians, in Staffordshire (Diary, 25 December 1847, *L.D.* XII, p. 137).

To Charles Russell

Mary Vale, Perry Bar, Birmingham Febr. 20 1848

My dear Dr Russell,

Your very kind letter has been forwarded to me from Rome. I value your criticism on my book very much.[1] You have said nothing, I should not say myself, except that you have praised it more highly. I have been accustomed to say the same things in other words—It does not pretend to be a *dogmatic* work. It is an external philosophical view. As in Paley's Evidences, our Lord is spoken of as 'a young Jewish peasant—' so the *way* in which the book approaches the Catholic Church is by *phenomena*, which phenomena, when we get inside the Church, do not turn out always to be the full measure of the truth. I say in the book that the phenomena of the Catholic history, the visible growth of doctrine, may be accounted for by a certain theory—If, on further and truer examination, it be discovered that there is not *so much* growth, then that theory is *so far* not needed—The question of *more or less* does not affect the pretensions of the theory. Only two objections can be made to the theory—that it is a dangerous one, or that it is perfectly superfluous or inadmissible, there being no growth of doctrine at all. I never met with any one who had read the Fathers, who maintained there was no growth of doctrine, though they may account for it on other theories—The only question then is, Is the theory *dangerous*? Mr Brownson says that it is—and that is a very fair objection. But to say, as is sometimes said, that I have *mis-stated* this or that particular doctrine, or *overlooked* this or that passage of the Fathers, though very necessary to notice, *lest* a dogma should be compromised, yet to my book *itself*, as a philosophical argument, *not* a dogmatic treatise, is, in my opinion, no objection at all. Again, I think it very possible that my theory may require some modification, though I don't mean that I am aware of it. It is an attempt to give the *laws* under which implicit faith becomes explicit—this is the very subject of the book—now is it wonderful that, in so arduous an undertaking, it should not be any thing more than it professes to be, 'an Essay'?

I assure you, it would be a great delight to me to see you in Ireland, as you propose—and, though I don't see how just at present, yet I hope the day will come, I can't tell when, when I shall be able to pay my homage to the Church of St Patrick.

I am, my dear Dr Russell, Very sincerely Yours,

John H. Newman

[1] Russell had written about Newman's *Essay on the Development of Christian Doctrine*.

To the Earl of Shrewsbury

Maryvale. Perry Bar. Febr 25. 1848

My dear Lord,

I feel much obliged by your Lordship's candid statement, received this morning, of your views of the duty of our Congregation towards St Wilfrid's; and am happy to have an opportunity of laying before you our own.[1]

Your Lordship will feel, I am sure, for our difficulties in the matter, while, I assure you, I most entirely enter into your own anxiety respecting it.

The case stands thus, as we view it:—We come to England Oratorians; the Oratorians are notoriously, even more than the Jesuits, inhabitants of cities; the community of St Wilfrid's proposes to join us, and, at the very time I receive their application, I am expressly told that it has your Lordship's sanction. How can we avoid coming to the conclusion that your Lordship contemplates and acquiesces in the ultimate departure of Mr Faber's community from their present home?

So much as regards your Lordship:—but the case is stronger still as regards ourselves, Our Brief expressly destines us for 'urbes ampliores,' and for the 'nobilior splendidior, doctior' class of society. We had a difficulty in gaining leave to retain Maryvale; and on one of our last interviews with Cardinal Fransoni, when he heard we were going there for the present, he said, 'What Oratorians in the country? impossible!'

We could not, I really feel, as our Brief now runs, without disobedience to the Holy See, settle at St Wilfrid's. Why go to the Pope, if we go our own way to work afterwards? Our Indulgences are attached to the observance of our Rule: how could we observe our Rule in the country?

This is our difficulty, which none but the Pope can get us out of; I entreat your Lordship carefully to consider it;—if you are in anxiety, so are we;—your Lordship is responsible, as well as we, for the St Wilfrid's community have joined us. You knew Mr Faber's purpose before I did; you entertained it before me; you recommended it to me by your sanction.

There is an additional difficulty though of a different kind;—we cannot sustain the expence of St Wilfrid's; Your Lordship will see at once the seriousness of this fact. Who can ask us to be responsible for a second establishment at Cotton, when we are barely equal, if equal to the expence of Maryvale?

Should your Lordship be able to suggest any thing which would relieve us of this double perplexity, it would *rejoice* us to take it into our consideration

I am, my dear Lord, Very truly Yours John H Newman

[1] Lord Shrewsbury maintained that what he had done for St Wilfrid's had all been done for a *community*, and it would be a breach of contract to abandon it as a monastery.

To F. W. Faber

March 28/48

My dear F. Wilfrid,

Your letter, which I answered immediately yesterday, has of course dwelt much on my mind, and I have brought the subject before Congregatio Deputata.[1] And now I am going to send you a business-like letter in few words, and you must not take it ill, if it is a dry one.

It seems to us that we misunderstood the kind of offer which in January last you made of St Wilfrid's to us. We thought it was absolute You 'surrendered yourselves, house etc to us'[2] but, as time goes on, we see more clearly than we did, that there are anxious conditions attached to it, under which, in our own *meaning*, we have not accepted it—and cannot accept it. As yet, it is legally *yours*.

The conditions practically result in the following alternative, which you urge on us, and which we do not see our way to accept. You urge us either to give up St Wilfrid's at once, or to promise at once to keep it for good.

We, on the other hand, cannot *promise* to keep it, considering the nature of our Brief; we cannot give it up at once, considering the responsibility of our inflicting such loss on you. Therefore, we ask for *delay* before we come to a resolution.

We have taken two steps; neither has approved itself to you;—the first is that of *delaying* our decision, the second that of *asking Lord S.* to co-operate with us in keeping up St Wilfrid's, on your conveying to us that it could not be kept up, without expenditure of capital, for above three or four months more.

Now then, we think it will be best for you to make in turn *your* proposition of a settlement, and not as novices, but frankly and fully, and see if we can assent to it, since you cannot without effort assent to ours.

Let me hear then from you what you think ought to be done in our difficulty.

Ever Yours affectly John H Newman

P.S. All the laybrothers shall go to St Wilfrid's on Easter Tuesday,[3] and besides Fs *Ambrose, Bernard and William*, and Brs Austin and Alban. Perhaps two or three other novices.

[1] i.e. the governing council in an Oratory, four 'deputies' and the Superior.

[2] Faber wrote on 1 January 1848, 'Now as to our wishes, they are simply these,—that you should consider us as giving ourselves over to you in the spirit of surrender', and again on 2 January, 'So we have no *terms* to come to, but the great thing is whether we shall suit you, or have the grace to carry out the spirit of surrender in detail, as it may be wanted. So please bear this in mind:—we do not come to you as a community asking filiation, asking to be constituted into an Oratorian House at Cotton, in other words, asking to get under the shelter of an approved institute with the least amount of selfwill sacrificed; this would make us much less useful, and possibly endanger or thwart you:—but we offer ourselves to you as 18 postulants for the Oratory (together with our house and Church), to be removed and distributed just as meets your views, and desirous to undress ourselves of any habits or traditions we may have as quickly as we can do so with safety. This is what I particularly begged Dr Wiseman to make clear to you'.

[3] For the opening of the church on 25 April.

To Henry Bourne[1]

Maryvale, Perry Bar June 13. 1848

Dear Sir,

I return an immediate, though necessarily hasty, answer to your inquiry, which made me more than smile.

It is wonderful that people can satisfy themselves with rumours, which the slightest examination, or even attention, would disprove; but I have had experience of it long before I was a Catholic. At present the very persons, who saw through and reprobated the Evangelical misrepresentations concerning me, when I was in the Church of England, believe of me things quite as extravagant and as unfounded. Their experience of past years has taught them nothing.

I can only say, if it is necessary to say it, that from the moment I became a Catholic, I never have had, through God's grace, a single doubt or misgiving on my mind that I did wrong in becoming one. I have not had any feeling whatever but one of joy and gratitude that God called me out of an insecure state into one which is sure and safe, out of the war of tongues into a realm of peace and assurance. I shrink to contemplate the guilt I should have incurred, and the account which at the last day would have lain against me, had I not become a Catholic—and it pierces me to the heart to think that so many excellent persons should still be kept in bondage in the Church of England, or should, among the many good points they have, want the great grace of *faith*, to trust God and follow His leadings.

This is my state of mind, and I would it could be brought home to all and every one, who, in default of real arguments for remaining Anglicans, amuse themselves with dreams and fancies

I am, Dear Sir, Truly Yours John H Newman

---

[1] Henry Bourne (1826–70), whose son, Cardinal Francis Bourne, was Archbishop of Westminster from 1903 to 1935, was worried by rumours that Newman was dissatisfied as a Catholic.

To A. Lisle Phillipps

Maryvale. Perry Bar June 15/48

My dear Mr Phillipps

I am very much concerned that even in a small matter there should be a difference of opinion between one I esteem and admire so much as yourself, and me. But I really will not let you make it greater than it is. I really will not let you say, without protesting against it, that we are 'preaching a Crusade' against you, or are throwing in what 'weight,' as you kindly say, we have, against Mr Pugin.[1]

It really is no such thing; but the case stands thus. Mr Pugin is a man of genius; I have the greatest admiration of his talents, and willingly acknowledge that Catholics owe him a great debt for what he has done in the revival of Gothic architecture among us. His zeal, his minute diligence, his resources, his invention, his imagination, his sagacity in research, are all of the highest order. It is impossible that any one, not scientifically qualified to judge of his merits, can feel a profounder reverence than I do, for the gift with which it has pleased the Author of all Truth and Beauty to endow him. But he has the great fault of a man of genius, as well as the merit. He is intolerant, and, if I might use a stronger word, a bigot. He sees nothing good in any school of Christian art except that of which he is himself so great an ornament. The Canons of Gothic architecture are to him points of faith, and everyone is a heretic who would venture to question them.

Now something might be said in defence of this extreme view of the subject, had Gothic Architecture prevailed over the *whole* face of the Church, so that never had a rite been introduced, never a doctrine promulgated, but it came out in Gothic shape, and had been perpetuated under Gothic emblems. But this is notoriously not so— Nevertheless Mr Pugin, with only half Christendom on his side, to say nothing of the Greek and Oriental bodies, rules, that the other half is, what he calls reproachfully, *pagan*. But more than this, this pagan half happens to include in it the see of St Peter, which nevertheless does not escape that appellation. The see of St Peter itself, (for if the Apostle had a seat, it is there where his body lies and where the awful dome rises above it,) that earthly home of the Apostle, that treasure house of his merits, a building, be it grand or be it mean, which is the creation of a succession of Pontiffs, this central monument of Christianity, is pronounced by him to be *pagan*, pronounced not historically, but contumeliously—or, to use the best word dogmatically, as if though infallibility in doctrine is found at Rome, a parallel authority in architecture was to be found in this century in England.

Nor is this even all—Something more might be said for his view of the subject, had there been an *uninterrupted tradition* of Gothic architecture from the time it was introduced till the present day; but this even is not the case. Mr Pugin is notoriously engaged in a revival—he is disentombing what has been hidden for centuries amid corruptions; and, as, first one thing, then another is brought to light, he, like a true lover of the art, modifies his first views, yet he speaks as confidently and dogmatically about what is right and what is wrong, as if he had gained the truth from the purest and stillest founts of continuous tradition. But there is even more than this and what is very important;—we know that the Church, while one and the same in doctrine ever, is ever modifying, adapting, varying her discipline and ritual, according to the times. In these respects the Middle age was not what the First Centuries were, nor is the Age Present the Middle age. In order that any style of Architecture should exactly suit the living ritual of the 19th century, it should be the living architecture of the 19th century—it should never have died—else, while the ritual has changed, the architecture has not kept pace with it. This defect is actually found in the case of Gothic. Gothic is now like an old dress, which fitted a man well twenty years back but must be altered to fit him now. It was once the perfect expression of the Church's ritual in those places in which it was in use; it is not the perfect expression now. *It must be altered in detail* to become that expression. That is, it must be treated with a freedom which Mr Pugin will not allow. I wish to wear it, but I wish to alter it, or rather I wish *him* to alter it; not that we do not feel the greatest admiration of the Gothic style, but that we will not allow details which were proper in England in the middle ages, to be points of faith now. Now for Oratorians, the birth of the 16th century, to assume the architecture simply and unconditionally of the 13th, would be as absurd as their putting on them the cowl of the Dominicans or adopting the tonsure of the Carthusians. We do not want a cloister or a chapter room but an Oratory. I, for one, believe that Gothic can be adapted, developed into the requisitions of an Oratory. Mr Pugin does not; he implied, in conversation with me at Rome, that he would as soon build a mechanic's institute as an Oratory. I begged him to see the Oratory of the Chiesa Nuova, he gave me no hope he would do so. Now is it wonderful that I prefer St Philip to Mr Pugin? and is it not wonderful that he should so relentlessly and indissolubly unite the *principles* of his great art with the *details*?—

But I have not put this last remark of mine on its highest grounds. The Church, in accordance with that view at once of change and of advancement which has marked her discipline from the first, has consolidated her Rubrics since the death of Gothic Architecture. Our Padre Ceremoniere tells me that the rigid observance of Gothic details is inconsistent with the Rubrics—that he must break the Rubrics if he would not break with Mr Pugin; which is he to give up, Mr Pugin or the Rubrics?

Now you must not be surprised, My dear Mr Phillipps, at my taking the views above expressed, for it is in my nature, as you must have had other opportunities of seeing, and till I am convinced it is a bad nature, will, I think remain in me.

It is no new thing with me to feel little sympathy with parties, or extreme opinions, of any kind, I ever felt it in the English Church—I advocated what are called High Church principles, while I believed them to be the teaching of the English Church; I first gave up my living, then left that Church as it broke upon me that they were not. I never joined the Camden movement. I never committed myself to the Rubric movement, nor allowed of innovations, though for the better, in St Mary's—much less gave in to such extravagancies as they at present practice in Margaret Street Chapel. I did not even join in Dr Pusey's movement for the London Churches, and (think) I did not subscribe to it *anything*; there seemed to me something excessive and unreal in it.[2]

I will not take up your time longer, except to thank you for all your kind thoughts of me and others, now and in the past. Do not cease to entertain them, give us the benefit of your prayers, do not be hard with us.

and believe me, My dear Mr Phillips Ever Yours most sincerely in Christ

John H Newman. Priest of the Oratory.[3]

P.S. I grieve indeed at your feelings towards Fr Wilfrid but hope time will change them.[4]

---

[1] Phillipps had written on 9 June, attacking Faber and accusing Newman and the Oratorians of preaching a crusade against the views shared by Pugin and himself.

[2] The Camden Society was founded in 1838 by Cambridge High Churchmen, for the publication of antiquarian church records. It had much influence on the restoration of mediaeval churches.

[3] Phillipps replied on 19 June at great length, beginning, 'I cannot easily express how I value and how deeply I shall treasure the beautiful and most kind, (may I not say affectionate and parental) Letter, I have just received from you.'

[4] They did before the year's end.

To Catherine Ward

Maryvale Perry Bar Oct 12. 1848

My dear Madam

The Catholic doctrine concerning Faith and Reason is this—that Reason proves that Catholicism *ought to* be believed, and that in that form it comes before the Will, which accepts it or rejects it, as moved by grace or not. Reason does not prove that Catholicism is *true*, as it proves mathematical propositions are true; but it proves that there is a *case* for it so strong that we see we ought to accept it. There may be many difficulties, which we cannot answer, but still we see on the whole that the grounds are sufficient for conviction. This is not the same thing *as* conviction. If conviction were unavoidable, we might be said to be *forced* to believe, as we are forced to confess that two sides of a triangle are greater than the third; but, while there is enough evidence for conviction, whether we *will* be convinced or not, rests with ourselves. This is what the Priest means, when, on being asked 'If a man has not evidence enough to *subdue* his reason, what is to make him believe?', he answers, 'His will.' And this is just our trial; and one man rejects what another accepts. On the contrary, were we *forced* to believe, as we are forced to believe mathematical conclusions, there would be no trial of our affections, nothing morally right in believing, or wrong in not believing.

The simple question then with you is, How [Have] you *sufficient grounds* for being convinced that the Catholic Church is from God? If you have, it is nothing to the purpose that you find it difficult to believe. Of course you do; for belief is a supernatural act; you must pray to God for the *will* to believe, and the will has the power to command the mind. *You can believe what you will*; the only question is whether your reason tells you you *ought* to believe, and I think it does.

I think it does; for consider, by way of contrast, whether you have any *comparable* grounds in behalf of any other religion. I am not arguing that *therefore* Catholicism is true; but merely I wish to illustrate to you what is *meant* by conviction. You seem to me to have a feeling towards Catholicism *different in kind* from any you entertain towards other religions. And I do not think you can be happy or have an easy conscience till you confess this in *act*, by becoming a Catholic. You *cannot* be a latitudinarian; I will not argue the matter with you, till I have cause to suppose it possible.

Nor is it any thing to you what God will do with others; to his own master he standeth or falleth. No one is a real heretic who is not *wilfully* so. I am ready to enlarge on this subject, if you wish me.

As to yourself, you are in a very critical state; your Lord is making trial of you, as when He was on earth. He calls and goes forward. He does not stay. I do not forget you at Mass, and I trust and am sure you will be led on with whatever trial and distress to do this great and necessary work, to lay hold of salvation now for the first and perhaps for the last time offered you. God has led you forward wonderfully; He has been so gracious with you that, instead of your starting forward in the first instance to follow your own will, He gave you grace to submit yourself to another, to submit to the direction of the holiest man you could find.[1] He is now rewarding you for your corresponding so faithfully to His grace; He is showing you, that, useful as that honored and loved superior has been to you, he cannot be more to you than he is in himself, he cannot be your teacher in *the* faith, unless he were inspired, because he has never learned it. You are being led on from self discipline to knowledge; he has done his part, and hands you on; unwillingly indeed, but still he has but his measure, as we all have our own. Use him for what he was given for. If his teaching *is* correct, he is like St Paul, for from man he has not been taught it; nor do I think that he, or any other Anglo-Catholic, would submit to put down his entire creed in writing, and lay it before the world.

If, as I have said, those who believe have incidental difficulties in reason, in spite of their believing, and their merit arises out of this, you see what view I take of all you urge about what Catholics believe of the Blessed Virgin;—accept all this as the specific trial of your faith, and be sure that, when you are a Catholic, that very doctrine, which is now your burden, will become your reward. I never can think it right, any more than you, to separate the dry letter of the decrees of the Church from the existing belief of Catholics. The existing belief is the true comment upon the decree. You must hold *substantially* what St Alfonso holds; his words are *not* mere figures of rhetoric, though of course the expression of doctrine always does take a colour from nation, language, speaker etc. When we say that our Lady has the care of the goats, it cannot indeed be literally true, if by goats is meant the finally reprobate; but he means that, to those who are *all but* reprobate, or rather who *feel themselves* all but reprobates ⟨or who feel themselves reprobates⟩, Christ gives a last chance in the intercession of his Mother. As to her being the sole hope of sinners, this, I conceive, *is* literally true, *that is*, in the sense in which such words are commonly used. Thus the sole cause of our salvation is God, is Christ, is a certain illness or other providence, is baptism, is faith, is the Blessed Virgin, *in that sense in which she IS a cause.* In like manner our Lady has a delegated omnipotence *in her own sphere*, i.e. of *intercession*, as when Solomon said to his mother, 'Ask on, my mother, for I will not say thee nay.'[2] On the other hand, Esther was promised any thing from Ahasuerus, up to the *half* of his kingdom; i.e. she had, what may be called, a semi-omnipotence.[3] I will write more on this subject if necessary.

May God guide you forward is, My dear Madam, the fervent prayer of

Yours very sincerely John H Newman

[1] Catherine Ward had taken counsel from Pusey.

[2] *1 Kings* 2:20.

[3] *Esther* 5:3.

To Henry Wilberforce

St Wilfrid's Cheadle. Nov 30/48

⌈Charissime,

What mean you by talking of my 'honouring you with intimacy'? Come near me, and I will revenge myself by kissing your feet. What have I done to be so treated?

But to your question. No. I shall lower myself in the eyes of dear friends still Anglican, but duty to truth, duty to the sacred cause of Catholicism, which *needs no miracles* to those who hear Moses and the Prophets, obliges me to say that I had nothing at all like a supernatural call. The contrary—it was a mere conviction, however flickered with doubts, *which were no parts* of it, any more than motes are part of the sunbeam, but a simple conviction growing through years, the more I read and thought, that the Roman Church was the Catholic Church, and that the Anglican Church was no Church. It came to me first in reading the Monophysite controversy, and then the Donatist. When the affair of No 90 happened, Manning said 'Shut up your controversy, and go to the *Fathers*, which is your *line*.' Well *they* had been the beginning of my doubts, but I did so. I began to translate St Athanasius. The truth kept pouring in upon me. I saw in the Semi-arians the Viamedians, I saw in the Catholic Church of the day the identical [[image the]] self of the Catholic Church now;—as you know a friend by his words and deeds, or see an author in his works.[1] Well then I fled back to one's inward experiences—and said that after all I felt the Anglican Church had done me so much good, that, in spite of all outward forebodings, it must be God's minister. But in time this would not stand, it was no sure footing—and would lead to the veriest liberalism. Curious enough I have lately read some words of Pusey's (I tell you in confidence) in argument, which parallel with some late words in a letter to me of my poor dear Brother, (who thinks that it is a moral fault to say a man may not be as religious who denies the *existence* of Christ as one who confesses it), in the most marvellous way. Pusey says that to deny the Catholicity of the English Church, Frank that to deny the acceptableness of such an unbeliever, is (the ipsissima verba of *each*) 'blasphemy against the Holy Ghost.' To return:—then I fled to the notion that perhaps I was in a dream—I had muddled and heated myself with reading, and was no fair judge—so I waited. All along I trust I acted as in God's sight, but neither expecting nor experiencing any thing supernatural. At length I felt I dared not wait longer—and I acted—and from that day to this I bless God for it—for here is truth, and all else is shadow, and I have had (what might, had God so pleased, been otherwise, though I *know of no such* case,) not even the *temptation* to doubt. Yes, I believe that God's grace so accompanies that great act, whereby we unite ourselves to His visible dwelling place, that the devil does not touch us.

2. You will find that Roman doctrine on Justification stated in the best and clearest way in the Decrees of the Council of Trent ⌐—which, if you have not, I suppose you could get at Burns's for a few shillings. But as to the *definition* of faith, I hardly know what you want—the common definition is, 'Virtus theologica, à Deo infusa, inclinans nos ad firmiter assentiendum ob divinam veracitatem omnibus quae revelavit Deus, proponente Ecclesiâ.' ⌐I consider that Bull's doctrine and that of my book are substantially the same as that of the Catholic Church. F Passaglia at Rome spoke extremely highly of Bull's work. At the same time Bull's *language* is, I suspect, rather used with us polemically than admitted in teaching. E.g. Bellarmine speaks (if I recollect) of fides formata, as Bull does, but his language is not heard ⟨found⟩ in didactic writing.⌐

It delighted us to hear what you say about George's [Ryder] wife. ⌐We are in great trouble just now. The Palma, the Pope's Secretary, who was shot, is (unless there is some gross mistake in the paper) our own confidential friend and benefactor. We had 6 masses for him yesterday, 2 to-day. Rest his soul! He quite loved F. Ambrose. It is a blow for the Oratory, (still, the Pope loves us personally)⌐ but *don't repeat this*

Ever Yrs affly J H N

[1] [[(This account is important for it agrees so exactly with what I have said in my Anglican Diff. xii [*Diff.* 1, pp. 372 ff.] and my Apologia [e.g. *Apo.*, pp. 114 ff.]. I had not seen this letter when I wrote them; only *now*. Febr. 10. 1876)]]

To William Philip Gordon

40 Alcester Street. Febr 7. 1849

My Dearest Br Philip,

It is strange to write to you a note about nothing; but such is my fate just now and for some time, that, since I have nothing to say to you, I must either be silent or unseasonable.

Many is the time I have stood over the fire at breakfast or looked at you at Recreation, hunting for something to talk about. The song says that 'Love cannot live on flowers;' not so; yet it requires material, if not for sustenance, at least for display. And I have fancied too that younger and lighter minds perhaps could not, if they would, care much for one who has had so much to wear him down.

All blessing come on you, My dear Brother Philip, in proportion to my waning

Ever Yrs affly John H Newman[1]

[1] Philip Gordon replied the following day 'It was very kind of you to write to me. I have never doubted that you loved me as one of your children although the most unworthy of all. I have ever had the greatest difficulty in manifesting my affections and this in proportion to their depth, it almost pains me to have to profess my love'.

To F. W. Faber

Oratory Alcester Str Febr 16/49

My dear F Wilfrid,

I wish you quite to understand what I am doing in writing to you. First, I am writing under a very anxious sense of *what our duty is*. Secondly I am not *ruling* what it is, the matter is too serious for that, but wishing to discuss. If in the whole argument any one treats me as superior, and does not argue the matter out, he is unfair to me, as preventing me from knowing all that has to be said to and fro.

I say then that our coming to Birmingham does *not* depend on the accident of Dr Wiseman having been Vicar Apostolic when we were at Rome.[1] In my letter to Cardinal Fransoni taken by Mgr Brunelli to the Pope, I rest the matter on this, that Birmingham and the like provincial towns are the main holds of political power at this day among us, and I seriously doubt whether I ever should have felt it my duty to submit myself to St Philip, had I considered that the ordo honestior, etc was to be our scope—considering that the Oratory did not address itself specially to it.

When the Pope *added* 'ordo honestior etc,' of course one wishes to obey him *literally*, i.e. to see that his purpose is fulfilled; but I am persuaded that he meant merely to *fulfil* what *I* had set down. What can the Pope know of the constitution of English political society? to him ordo doctior, honestior, was in *great measure* synonymous with the classes I had specified—so that *if there* be a class in Birming-ham of sharp intellects, who are the recipients of political power, and who can be made Catholics, I think we are fulfilling the Brief, not only in letter as to Birmingham, but in spirit as to the ordo honestior.

On the other hand, considering he actually does *name* Birmingham, every one agrees that we could not *give up* Birmingham without going to him for leave. If we had any doubt of this before, Dr Acquerone has made it plain to us; and considering our relations with Bishop Ullathorne, it is quite certain he would avail himself of the letter of our Brief to complain of us at Propaganda. It is also certain that, when we intended last August to suspend our settlement here and go first to London, as getting no money here, he said distinctly that Propaganda had sent him to us,[2] and Propaganda fully expected us to settle at Birmingham; and I have the gravest doubts whether, if at this minute we tried to get the Brief altered, we could. I really think Propaganda would not *allow* your argument, but would tie us down to Birmingham. If so, *it is not in our power*.

Moreover we had engaged ourselves to Birmingham, and to the Bishop, and taken a house, when the question came on and was voted upon in January; I don't see how we could have receded.

Next, I say that, if there is to be a House in Birmingham, I am by the Brief Superior of it, and, except by a change in the Brief, must be. Moreover at least I am charged with its execution, now *tell me, how* can there be a House in Birmingham *except* I am here? who will stay here, if I do not? *make* a House if you can.

I do not see how the conclusion can be avoided, that I must be here—with the future we have nothing to do—we cannot make plans, we cannot make *promises* for the future, certainly not at my time of life.

The question which follows is, shall all come and remain here, or some go off to form another House, and if so, where?—

The objections to their all coming here are such as these:—

1. There will not be for an indefinite time, perhaps for ever, work for all—
2. Many of us are evidently better suited to London.
3. Many of us have an aversion to Birmingham.
4. The Pope evidently contemplates our extending ourselves through the urbes ampliores.
5. It is most desirable, if not necessary, *literally* to fulfil the words about the ordo honestior;—i.e. to go to London.
6. The ordo honestior in London earnestly calls for and invites us.
7. Many of us wish to go to London.
8. There is another most cogent reason for our not all coming here, but some parting off for London. Birmingham will not support us all. Nor can we sustain ourselves at St Wilfrid's. London *will* support us. To go to London is a way of getting out of an increasing debt. Is there any other way?
9. But you will say 'we are all one—it is hard to separate.' The pain to some of us will be very acute, if so it must be. *I* would try to avoid a distinct separation—but I suppose my methods will not satisfy. So I do not mention them here. Taking then the objection by the horns, I answer, so far from being hard to separate, separation of a certain kind is the only thing which will preserve us.

Recollect, my dear F Wilfrid, what I have already urged on you—your own words, that *I* am the bond of union among those who otherwise would not have come together. F. William says the same this morning 'You know it is not to be Oratorians, but to be with Newman that we are met together—we came not seeking the Oratory but you.'

Now, Carissime, look at the fact—what is to happen when I am taken away? does not history, does not your knowledge of human nature tell you that for certain animosities, or at least differences of temper and view, will then come to light which at present may be smothered?—and in so large a body as we shall be can we possibly hope to get on without dissensions? Is it not better, if you can find in our whole body the elements of two distinct concordant communities, like in temper and view, to divide us into two, and found two Oratories, while I am with you to be of use to you?

Moreover, if there be acute pain in the division in some instances, is not that pain a warrant and safeguard that the two bodies though separate, have many mutual ties? for that pain argues affection.

Moreover, is not this to be considered—that perhaps differences between various members of our whole body will *not* be smothered now—so that we may be forced in the event to separate, and then there will be irritation, bitterness, and the memory of quarrels, whereas it is hard indeed if we do not separate with many a tender regret and much yearning of affection even between those who are not specially congenial.

Moreover, if all cannot for an indefinite time be accommodated here, some must in the meanwhile be running to seed at St Wilfrid's, and may leave us.

I do not want more than these considerations looked in the face. Meet then, and propose something better than separation. Or make such a separation as will not be painful in the case of individuals. I proposed a plan,—let others be proposed. Moreover I have proposed alleviations, one seems unpopular, the other you have not taken notice of. The first was that here and at London we should for a time be one Oratory, with the members moving to and fro—the other a certain number of our members should be *fixed* in London, with the prospect of being formed into an Oratory at the end of a given time—in both cases my being their Superior till the separate Oratory is established.[3] Make other proposals, but do not confine yourself to mere disapproval. Grapple with things as you find them.

And observe I am not arguing, *the contrary*, any immediate decision. As I have said, such a measure should have three 'readings—' moreover as we have told Dr Wiseman, we must fairly set up the Birmingham Oratory before we think of London. But even the prospect of London, now set before them, may quiet restless spirits

Ever Yrs affly J H N.

P.S. To reply in one word to your letter I should say that 1. *till* Dr Ullathorne came we did not know for certain that Dr Wiseman was not to be in Birmingham (there was a report that Dr *U.* was Archbishop.) 2 *When* he came, he by countenance of Propaganda, nailed us to Birmingham. If Palma had lived, he might have done something.

P.S. *Please to keep this.*

[1] Faber argued that the fixing of Newman and the first English Oratory in Birmingham was accidental, and that the clause which Pius IX inserted in the foundation Brief, telling the English Oratorians to care for the 'doctior et honestior ordo' was incompatible with it, and could only be fulfilled if Newman and the Oratorians moved to London. 'You sacrifice', said Faber, 'what the Pope suggested to you for what you suggested to the Pope.' The letter to Cardinal Fransoni is that of 14 February 1847 (see *L.D.* XII, pp. 36–40).

[2] i.e. Ullathorne was transferred to the Central District as Vicar Apostolic, because the Oratorians were there.

[3] This plan of Newman's, which allowed for the fact that the English Oratory depended entirely on him, was not devised on the spur of the moment. He had worked it out during his novitiate in Rome, thanks to a minute study of the origins of the Oratory. In his first chapter address, written at Maryvale on 17 January 1848, he compared the state of the English Oratorians to that of the Oratory in St Philip's day. They would be 'for a time a floating mass or collection of Oratorians without definite and final location', but had the sanction and consolation of seeing, from the example of the first Oratorians, 'that such an unsettled [in]determinate state arises from the nature of things'.

To F. W. Faber

Oratory March 29/49

My dear F Wilfrid,

I think you have viewed in too *prominent* a light what I said of F. Ambrose; it related to his going to *St Wilfrid's at once.*[1] Had I seriously thought it best for him to go there, or to London, nay or to separate from me for the sake of the Congregation, I doubt not he would have done so. Excuse me if I did not write accurately; but I thought *your reason* (about the boys) insufficient for his leaving, and I thought *his* reason for staying just as good.

Now as to the state of the case. You have all of you, through kindness to me, made it turn on *what is my place*, much more than I like or judge right. We must decide for the *long run*, and for *all*.

However, I will speak of myself—I say then:—

1. that one of two incompatible courses is open to me, for the rest of my life, between which I have to choose, viz *either* a life which admits of leisure for reading and writing, or a life of unmixed missionary or quasi-missionary work. Which I do, is to me indifferent, if I could know God's will; but, as far as I can see His will, it is to take the former.
2. To take the former is to be in Birmingham; to take the latter is to be in London.
3. In saying that London is more suited to me than Birmingham, I mean more suited to me as a missioner; *therefore* it would absorb my time in mission etc work, while Birmingham does not.
4. Did I go to London, I should have various work for which I am wellfitted; to preach, lecture, converse etc. Also much semi-religious work, far less suited to me, measures for the good of Catholicism, projects for bills in Parliament etc. And much merely routine business,—Golden Square soirees,[2] Committees, preaching for public objects, speeches at meetings. These engagements, with my correspondence, would absorb my time.

In Birmingham, on the other hand, my day is mainly free; I am busy two or three hours in the evening, and confessions etc drop in through the day. It is just the life I have ever coveted, time for study, yet missionary work of the most intimate kind, confessing, preaching, or catechising. It is most suitable to my years, especially as they increase, and to my turn of mind etc. I might be laying the foundation of a school, for which a London life is too busy. If I have certain talents which I must use in the best way, I ought to *find* that way, and this seems it.

5. It follows that my Library would be wasted on *me*, (for I am speaking of myself,) in London; whereas, next to my own claim on it, is Birmingham's. Accordingly my Library stays here, whether I go to London or not. Here I am with it; there I am without it. This is irrevocable.

Thus then I bring my own case to an issue, and I wish to decide on it *first of all*, and thereby to simplify the arrangements which follow. Therefore I ask you all your opinion on the above alternative of disposing of myself; which course shall I take of the two, or have you nothing to say? *Shall I go to London without my Library, or remain here with it?* Do not do me the injustice to suppose, that I am putting out a reductio ad absurdum, or driving you into a corner. I could make up my mind readily to leave my books here, and go to London. It would be a relief to me, though in some respects a pain. The only real misery to me, would be to go to London with them; I will not do so, for I should then have *conflicting* duties. I have had too much of this misery in past times to incur it again. A man cannot do everything, even that he is fitted for. He must make a choice out of his capabilities, and cultivate one or the other to the neglect of the rest.

Now, my dear F Wilfrid, we have arrived at the first step forward; the caravan is in motion; give me the general opinion (if there be any) on the above question, and after settling that I will proceed to step the second.

Ever Yrs affly J H N

P.S. Thank F. Rector for his letter. Make my apologies to Mr Bramah on my not writing to him about his coming here.

---

[1] Faber wrote on 28 March to complain that St John was claiming the right not to leave Birmingham until Newman did, and that Stanton also said he would not be parted from Newman. Faber added, 'WILL IT COME TO THOSE BEING SACRIFICED WHO ARE WILLING TO BE SO, AND THOSE HAVING THEIR OWN WILL WHO WANT IT?'

[2] 35 Golden Square was the house of the London Vicars Apostolic.

To Miss Munro

Oy Bm Feb 11/50

My dear Miss Munro,

If I understand a passage in your letter, it simply shocks me. It is to the effect that you have been allowed by a director to take a vow of obedience to him! I doubt its legality, and, without of course compromising you at all, shall inquire generally.

We think it best to introduce a religious body, if we can get one—and then get you to join it. So we shall not expect you in Lent—but we shall think of you.

I return you Miss Moore's letter. You must undeceive her about me, though I suppose she uses words in a general sense.[1] I have nothing of a Saint about me as every one knows, and it is a severe (and salutary) mortification to be thought next door to one. I may have a high view of many things, but it is the consequence of education and of a peculiar cast of intellect—but this is very different from *being* what I admire. I have no tendency to be a saint—it is a sad thing to say. Saints are not literary men, they do not love the classics, they do not write Tales. I may be well enough in my way, but it is not the 'high line.' People ought to feel this, most people do. But those who are at a distance have fee-fa-fum notions about one. It is enough for me to black the saints' shoes—if St Philip uses blacking, in heaven.

Ever Yours affecty John H Newman Cong. Orat.

[1] She called Newman a saint.

To A Recent Convert

Oratory Birmingham June 25/50

My dear[1]

I have thought often of your letter and you, though I wrote you so few lines. Now too I shall write few lines also, still I trust you will not refuse from me what comes from the true interest I feel in you, and my anxiety to hear about you. The first months of a convert's life are often trying amid their sweetness—for, as I have heard them say, they have both joys and sorrows they never had before. For me, so old a person cannot be supposed to have either—but so much I bear witness to, the trouble arising from the strangeness of a new position, and from a want of ascertaining what my own position exactly was. At first I was not clear that it was my duty to be a priest—and this trial, while the lot of only a few, was made heavier to me by various circumstances. And then when it was clear I was to be, it was very difficult to bring stiff old branches into a new form—and every successive step which was necessary for the end, was not a physical, but a parallel *mental* pain, though my will and desire was with the path chosen for me. And it was a trial to me going abroad, though I wished to go—indeed there was nothing which was not a burden. In a word, for this is the sum total of the whole—I was called into the Catholic Church, not for enjoyment simply, but for work also. And so, whom God calls, He calls in some way or other for service, for His glory;—and in time He makes His will clear to every one.

May you ever have the light and the comfort of His Grace, and the Sweetness of His Presence, and the protection of His Saints—and let me sometimes have the pleasure of knowing you have it.

Ever Yours very sincerely in Xt
John H Newman Congr. Orat.

[1] The name has been cut out.

To George Talbot

Oratory Birmingham Oct 23/50

My dear Talbot,

This is to say how I had hoped soon to write to you and to thank you for your interesting letter—but I am led to take up my pen at once, and to put before you some anxious matters connected with the coming of the Cardinal. The whole public is up against him, and the press, I believe, without the exception of any Paper.[1] The first question that arises is, Should his Eminence wait awhile at Florence, till the first ferment is over? I have asked a friend to write to him, and put him in possession of the whole state of the case,[2] yet still I think it best to write to you also. Next, ought he not to have about him, not only good Canonists, but some good *English Constitutional* lawyers? a false step would be most damaging and disastrous—We might find ourselves in a Praemunire[3] and I don't know what. Then, ought he not to have some persons who know the English world well? It seems most impertinent in me thus to write to you about the Cardinal, treating him as a third person—but I do it to save time, and to put you au courant. I dare say all I have said or have to say, has occurred to him, and that he has provided against it, but, depend upon it, we shall have a hard game to play, and it does not do to leave it to chance. As you know well, besides the Cardinal himself, there is no one, I may say, in England, who knows how to deal with the world, no one has lived in society so as to be a match for politicians and lawyers. Our enemies would like nothing so much as to get his Eminence into some technical difficulties, and then to ridicule us. The *status* of the Cardinal is perfectly [new] every thing has to be determined—and so of the Hierarchy. It seems very presumptuous in me to say all this, but, if you can extract any one good suggestion from it, it may be worth the saying—and you must pardon what is absurd, and put my letter behind the fire.[4]

One great advantage of the erection of the Hierarchy and the coming of the Cardinal is that it *will force us* to have Canonists, theologians, men of business, and men of savoir faire; but at present every thing has to be organized. My only fear is, that in the process of gaining experience and the necessary defences of our new position, we shall have reverses and mishaps.

I shall have a talk with Dr Ullathorne, or, as I ought to say, the Bishop of Birmingham on this matter tomorrow, and perhaps I shall have something to add to this before closing it.

I have spoken above of the Cardinal delaying his coming—at the same time I cannot help thinking the whole matter of the hierarchy should be settled before Parliament meets, i.e. before the end of January next.

Don't interpret me to be an advocate of *fears*. Fear is the worst of counsellors. We must not retreat a foot. The Holy See has decided—but we must be very cautious.

I want you to get me a good opinion on another question. I have lately had good advice from Rome that one may act as if the rule about prohibited books had not been promulgated in England. Now about my own parochial sermons. They do

247

good and advance people to Catholicism, I do not doubt. I have *personally* no difficulty on the *moral* question. Now, I have attempted a new edition *corrected*, i.e. leaving out whatever sounds uncatholic—, *and people won't buy it*. Might I publish it, (leaving out indeed any *distinctly* heterodox sermon, but) leaving uncorrected what is incidentally heterodox, and *putting a notice at the beginning* that I submit it to the Church and wish unsaid whatever is inconsistent with faith and morals?[5]

Ever Yours most sincerely in Xt John H Newman

P.S. Will you thank Case very much for his letter which I hope to answer soon.[6]

Oct 24. I have seen Dr Ullathorne today, and he advises some of the Cardinal's immediate friends meeting together and some one going out to him. I have written to Dr Whitty on the subject—but *he* says he does not know where he is. I hope all will go well, still we can't be too cautious

[1] The reconstitution of the Catholic hierarchy was viewed as papal aggression. The first leading article in *The Times* of 14 October was a violent attack on 'the newfangled Archbishop of Westminster', and was followed by another on 19 October. On Sunday 20 October Wiseman's florid pastoral 'from out the Flaminian Gate' was read in the Catholic churches. Robert Whitty, who was acting as his Vicar General, considered he had no mandate to withhold it, although he realised how it would fan the flames of the agitation that was beginning. On 22 October *The Times* returned to the attack, and the rest of the newspapers followed its lead.

[2] This was George Bowyer, who had become a Catholic in August. Badeley, Bellasis, and Hope being still Anglicans, Bowyer, an authority on the Constitutional Law of England, was the Catholic lawyer most qualified to advise. Whitty asked him to consult Newman about the situation, and he wrote on 22 October about its seriousness, and Wiseman's need of worldly-wise advisers.

[3] i.e. the statutory offence, dating from the fourteenth century, of promoting papal encroachments on rights claimed by the Crown.

[4] Newman is reproducing advice received from Bowyer in his confidential letter of 22 October.

[5] Talbot took advice and then replied that Newman could not publish the sermons in his own name, but he could allow any bookseller to sell them who chooses.

[6] George Case (1823–78) entered Brasenose College in 1841, and after being a curate at All Saints, Margaret Street, became a Catholic in 1850. He then went out to Rome and was ordained. In 1857 he entered the Jesuit novitiate, but left to work as a priest in the Clifton diocese, where he was made a canon.

To F. W. Faber

Oratory Bm Nov 4. 1850

My dear F Wilfrid

I have wished to write to you since your letter came on Saturday, but have been both engaged and knocked up with writing for publication my Hierarchy Sermon. I expect it will be out on Thursday next. Get a number of copies from Burns for your Fathers.

I said Mass for you all this morning in consideration of Times and Punch persecution to which you are exposed.[1] Caswall's brother[2] was followed by the rabble the other day in London, having on a long cloke which they took for an Oratorian. He faced round, pulled aside the cloke, and showed his trousers—When they saw him all sound below, they gave him a cheer and left him.

Let me hear how you go on—How have you managed about your Series of sermons, and of Lectures? I suppose it will be hardly safe now to undertake persecution; also our Protestant brother will give us a touch of it. All is very quiet here, tho' some apostate Polish priests are going about describing horrors, and saying they doubt not our hands are red with blood. There is a talk of burning the Pope and Bishop in effigy for Guys tomorrow.

My best love to F Richard [Stanton]—I would write a letter, half-rowing, half-comforting to him, were I not so pulled down myself.

We are beginning a Novena for the success of these Hierarchical arrangements.

Let me know all about you, chiefly about F Richard

Ever Yours affectly John H Newman Congr. Orat.

[1] The campaign against 'Papal Aggression' was gathering momentum.
[2] Henry Caswall (1810–70), Vicar of Figheldean, Wiltshire.

To William Monsell

[13 December 1850]

My dear Monsell,

I congratulate you on your reception, which I suppose has taken place—and pray and am sure that you will be ever kept safely and happily under the shadow and in the arms of that communion of Saints to which you now belong.

Don't let Lady Anna Maria be received till her way is clearer to her than it seemed to me the other day. She had not a *view* of any thing, did not know many simple truths, and had to think over them, understand them, and familiarize her mind with them. To do this well takes time—and it is not time lost. Let her count the cost. She must learn, and thro' God's grace she will learn, to accept the Church as God's oracle—When she does this, all is done—before it, nothing is done. We cannot precede God—we can but follow, and pray to follow.[1]

Be sure I shall be very anxious to hear tidings of you and her. On Thursday next the 19th I shall say a Mass of Thanksgiving for you, Anderdon, Bastard and some others.[2]

Yours very sincerely in Xt John H Newman Congr. Orat.

[1] Monsell's wife never became a Catholic.
[2] William Henry Anderdon was received at Paris on 23 November, and Edmund Bastard by Newman on 30 November.

To George Talbot

Oratory Birmingham February 3. 1851

My dear Talbot,

There has been a report some time that my name has been sent to Rome for one of the new Sees. We thought nothing of it till yesterday, when it appears in a leading article of the Tablet. I earnestly trust that nothing will be determined on till *our representations* are heard.

We are all of us in the greatest fright about it. Depend on it, the Oratory is not consolidated enough to do without me. The Holy Father has put me to this work, and I feel that, with St Philip's blessing, this work I could do—I have no confidence that I could do any other work, though God's grace is all in all.

I will not enter into particulars here, for my only object in writing is to arrest proceedings, if there be such. Surely we ought to be heard. Of course *when a thing is done*, I shall bow to it as the act of the Vicar of Christ. But *till then*, I will boldly say, that it would be very inadvisable. My *line* is different—it is to oppose the infidels of the day. They are *just* beginning to attend to me—Every thing shows this. My appointment to a See would take me off this opening field. *My writings would be at an end*, were I a Bishop. I might publish a sermon or two, but the work of a *life* would be lost. For twenty years I have been working on towards a philosophical polemic, suited to these times. I want to meet the objections of infidels against the Church. I saw a letter of Montalembert's lately, in which he expressed pleasure at two of my late Lectures, which were on that tack. A fearful battle is coming on and my place seems to lie in it. Make me a bishop, and I am involved in canon law, rubrics, and the working of a diocese, about which I know nothing. It is a very hazardous thing to put a man of 50 on an *entirely new line*. Do think of this. You cannot think how strongly I feel this. Surely my opinion on the subject is of weight.

Will you let my feeling be known at Propaganda? Pray for me

Ever Yours most sincerely in Xt

John H Newman Congr. Orat.

To Archbishop Cullen

Oratory Birmingham April 16. 1851

My dear Lord,

I feel exceedingly the honor you have done me by asking me the questions contained in your letter[1]

I write at once to acknowledge it—but I cannot of course say any thing to your Grace's purpose, without some thought.

One difficulty is this—that the leading men and authorities in the University would necessarily be priests—and England as your Grace knows, has none to spare. I do not know how far the Professors would fall under the same rule—perhaps those who filled the chairs of Classics, History, Mathematics etc, need not be. Of course my own acquaintance chiefly lies with married converts, who have been clergymen in the Protestant Church, such as Mr Allies.

I hope soon to write a second letter on the subject and meanwhile

Begging your Grace's blessing, I am, My dear Lord, Your faithful Servant

John H Newman Congr. Orat.

P.S. I ought to have noticed your Grace's very flattering invitation of me to Ireland. There is nothing at all which I can feel more interest in than the subject of Irish Education—yet I do not know how I can possibly promise myself the pleasure of the visit in question.[2]

---

[1] Cullen wrote on 15 April to Newman that the collecting of funds 'for the purpose of establishing a catholic university in Ireland' had been 'very successful.' Cullen added, 'we must now proceed a step farther. I suppose the first thing to be done is to select a fit and proper superior. In this matter your advice would be of the greatest importance. Would you be able to recommend us any one that would give a character to the undertaking. We shall also have to appoint a vice president and professors Would you be so kind as to give us any suggestions you may think useful in this business ... It is now time to make some effort to have at least one college for the higher branches of science and litterature [sic] ... Should you have any intention of coming to Ireland this season, your presence at the meeting of our committee in Dublin would be most useful. Indeed if you could spare time to give us a few lectures on education, you would be rendering good service to religion in Ireland.' Newman replied fully on 28 April (see L.D. XIV, pp. 267–70).

[2] It was Robert Whitty, writing to Cullen on 12 April, who suggested that Newman should be consulted about the proposed university, and should be invited to lecture on education.

To The Editor of the Morning Chronicle

Oratory, Birmingham, May 15. [1851]

Sir,

The *Times* newspaper has just been brought me, and I see in it a report of Mr. Spooner's speech on the Religious Houses Bill. A passage in it runs as follows:—

'It was not usual for a coroner to *hold an inquest*, unless when a rumour had got abroad that there was a necessity for one, and how was a rumour to come from the *underground cells* of the convents. Yes, he repeated, *underground cells*; and he would tell honourable members something about such places. At this moment, in the parish of Edgebaston, within the borough of Birmingham, there was a large convent of some kind or other being erected, and the whole of the *underground* was fitted up with *cells*; *and what were those cells for?* (hear, hear).'

The house alluded to in this extract is one which I am building for the Congregation of the Oratory of St. Philip Neri, of which I am Superior. I myself am under no other Superior elsewhere.

The underground cells, to which Mr. Spooner refers, have been devised in order to economize space for offices commonly attached to a large house. I think they are five in number, but cannot be certain. They run under the kitchen and its neighbourhood. One is to be a larder, another is to be a coal-hole; beer, perhaps wine, may occupy a third. As to the rest, Mr. Spooner ought to know that we have had ideas of baking and brewing; but I cannot pledge myself to him, that such will be their ultimate destination.

Larger subterraneans commonly run under gentlemen's houses in London; but I have never, in thought or word, connected them with practices of cruelty and with inquests, and never asked their owners what use they made of them.

Where is this inquisition into the private matters of Catholics to end?

Your obedient servant, John Henry Newman.[1]

[1] The speech of Richard Spooner, MP for North Warwickshire, and uncle of Henry Wilberforce, was made during the second reading of the Religious Houses Bill, and reported in *The Times* of 15 May.

To James Hope

⌈Oratory Bm July 16/51

My dear Hope,

I wish I could write to you about the University; I wish I had not to bore you with my present matters. But at present I am a man of one idea. The Printers are upon me; by the morning after next I must have copy finished and transcribed to the amount of 40 pages close type; and it is not near ready.

Could you off hand answer me a question? Can I be had up for a libel, in criminal court or civil, for saying against Dr Achilli the contents of the article in the Dublin, since published as a pamphlet?[1] I can't make out he has answered it. It contains the gravest charges, about his seducing women etc *with many of the legal documents proving them.*[2]

I am too dull and stupid to say more⌉

Ever Yrs affly in Xt John H Newman

[1] Giacinto Achilli, an ex-Dominican, who had been condemned by the Inquisition in Rome for immorality and for preaching against the Catholic religion, had been lecturing in England to enthusiastic Protestant audiences since the early part of 1850. Wiseman wrote an article in *Dublin Review*, XXVIII (June 1850), pp. 469–511, exposing in great detail Achilli's offences against morality. The article was revised and issued as a pamphlet, entitled *Authentic 'Brief Sketch of the Life of Dr. Giacinto Achilli,' containing a Confutation of the Mis-statements of Former Narratives. Extracted from the Dublin Review No. LVI, with additions and corrections* (London, [n.d.]).

[2] Hope replied on 17 July, 'If you publish libellous matter, although it has been published before, you are open to an action. But as in this case the Challenge has been fairly made by others and no notice taken I do not think you would be in much danger. I have also been assured that abundant proof is forthcoming of the allegations against Achilli, and if you are satisfied on this point it is an additional security.'

To Archbishop Cullen

Oratory Bm July 23./51

My dear Lord,

I am going to say something to you which will make you smile.

Our Fathers here feel reluctant that I should be any thing but Rector of the New University, as your Grace kindly proposed to me; under the notion that since I am *their* Superior, I ought not to have a subordinate place elsewhere.

I do not feel this *at all* myself—and I hope you will over rule it by showing them what the way of doing things is at Rome. But since they urge me, I write to you on the subject.

What I should desire is, to do as much work for the University as possible with *as little absence as possible* from this place. This problem being satisfied, I do not care what you are pleased to make of me

Begging your Grace's blessing I am, My dear Lord, Your faithful Servt

John H Newman Congr. Orat

To George Talbot

Oratory Birmingham Sept 1. 1851

My dear Talbot,

I am entering on a most anxious matter, in which I shall have to act, I may say, for the whole Catholic body. You know the Cardinal accused in the Dublin, and then in a pamphlet, Dr Achilli of certain crimes. I have repeated what he, ⟨the Cardinal⟩ said—and he ⟨Dr A⟩ is going to bring an action against me; not willingly I believe, but his friends, the Evangelical Alliance, force him.[1] They wish to bring the matter to a point. In a little while I shall write again—at present I write to prepare you. It is a most important crisis. I have a *most difficult* thing to do, yet a great thing, if I do it. First you must get me the Holy Father's blessing. Next I must have all the assistance you can give me, from documents etc. Achilli is charged of three (at least) sins with women at Viterbo about 1831–33—a sadly long time ago. Witnesses may be dead now, but there must be documents, police and other. However, I am now speaking generally, I shall write again to tell you *what* to do; now I write merely to *prepare* you. The evidence must be primary, *not secondary*—this is the great difficulty. I must produce evidence as good as if *I* were bringing a charge of crime against an innocent man, instead of being on my defence. I have written to the Cardinal, who is in the north, and has not yet answered me. Badeley tells me I have a work of *extreme difficulty*; but I rely on our Blessed Lady and St Philip to carry me through. Indeed it is not my cause, but the cause of the Catholic church. Achilli is going about like a false spirit, telling lies, and since it is forced upon us, we must put him down, and not suffer him to triumph.

Thank you for your very consoling letter about [?] my helping the new University. It was more pleasant than I can say, as you may imagine, my hearing the Holy Father was pleased at the idea.

Say a Hail Mary for me sometimes at some holy place, and believe me,

Ever Yours most sincerely in Xt

John H Newman Congr. Orat.

[1] The Evangelical Alliance was founded in 1846 as a non-denominational body, to work for religious liberty, and to 'associate and concentrate the strength of an enlightened Protestantism against the encroachments of Popery and Puseyism, and to promote the interests of a Scriptural Christianity'. It made arrangements to bring Achilli to England (*Evangelical Alliance. British Organization. Abstract of the Proceedings of the Fourth Annual Conference, held in Liverpool, October* 1850...(London, 1850)). It is now known as the World Evangelical Alliance.

To Archbishop Cullen

Oratory Birmingham Oct 11 1851

Private

My dear Lord Primate,

I want to put down two or three thoughts I have on paper, that I may state them more distinctly than I could in conversation, unless they have gone out of my head.

It strikes me that the only right way of beginning the University is that which your Grace proposes, experimentally—The Rector, (with a constant subordination of course to a board,) (say of the Archbishops,) should be autocrat. Two authorities will ruin the attempt. And he ought, with the same subordination, to have the choice of his associates, and the power of choosing, especially, *lecturers* and *tutors*. I think it is more necessary that he should choose lecturers and tutors even than Professors—by lecturers and tutors I mean a sort of informal (or, so to speak, Propaganda) system, as contrasted to a normal state of things, (or, to continue the illustration, a Diocesan Episcopacy or Hierarchy). Whether he should have the choice of Professors is a further question, and scarcely an initial one—but I think he ought to have 1 the *decision* whether there *should* be (as yet) Professors in this or that department—2. the *choice* of Lecturers and Tutors.

A Rector, with a number of Professors at once assigned him by others, nay with the necessity of choosing them himself, could do little. I say 'even did he choose them himself,' because he *must* choose eminent men, i.e. men who would have a right to exert a distinct and personal influence on the management of things. E.g. were I Rector, and had to choose a Professor of History, I might think it a point of duty to make an attempt to get so distinguished a man, as Dr Dollinger—yet not knowing his views etc. how can I tell if I should work well with him? (and so again Dr Jerrard in Classics)[1] When a University is *once set up*, and a system established, different influences are beneficial; they are fatal in its commencement. I think then I must stipulate for an autocracy of this kind—and say for 2 or 3 years.

I inclose a sort of plan of what I should propose.

There are two difficulties to this arrangement

1. We want to be doing something at once to meet the Queen's Colleges in the way of *demonstration*, to show we are not a mere school etc.—To meet the difficulty, would it not be possible (1) to name a definite time, e.g. October 1853, by which the University would be constituted in form. (2) to purchase ground at once. (3) to set about building at once. (4) to publish a code of *elementary* statutes etc. (no matter tho' they *are* eventually modified) (5) actually to appoint some Professors, though of course (since they would not come into their office for 2 or 3 years) they might draw back when the time came. (Would this last be impracticable? I wish it may not be) etc etc.

2. If I had the provisional appointment (i.e. for the first two years) I should naturally take my own friends—i.e. I should bring in *too much* of an English and convert element into the commencement of the Institution. This, I feel, to be a great difficulty, yet I do not know how to dispose of it. The Deans of discipline would be Irish, and some of the Lecturers—but I fear I might create remark by the number of those who were not.

Hoping your Grace will excuse the freedom with which I have written, I am, begging your blessing, Yours faithfully & affectly in Xt

John H Newman Congr. Orat.

P.S. I may seem inconsistent in *first* agreeing to the joint report we made at Thurles, and now writing this—but it is not so—I write this *because* your Grace seemed dissatisfied with that Report.[2]

I shall send this first to Mr Hope to see if he has any thing to remark on it.

---

[1] Joseph Henry Jerrard (1801–53), Scholar and then Fellow of Caius College, Cambridge, 1824–44, first Principal of Bristol College 1831–8, and Examiner in Classics at London University from 1838 to death, had become a Catholic in April 1851. He was one of the educationalists from whom the Sub-committee sought suggestions for the organization of the Catholic University.

[2] Since Cullen and Newman agreed that at first there should be no staff of professors, the Thurles Report was amended on this point, before it was brought before the University Committee on 12 November 1851. See *A.W.*, pp. 282–3.

To Bishop Ullathorne

24 King Wm Street Nov 5. 1851

My dear Lord,

I am afraid this Achilli matter will prove a serious one. So it has seemed to me from the first, the more so, because I knew how serious it was before I involved myself in it, though of course I thought the risk so small as not to be regarded. I did not do it without a good deal of thought and anxious prayer. However he has denied on oath every one of the charges; and if I cannot prove some of them against him I shall be liable to fine and imprisonment.

I have written to the Cardinal and the Primate of Ireland about the expences, as well as to Mr Hardman. The matter will be put off till January—and then again, if necessary, till after Easter—but I suppose, if it proceeds, it will be all over by the Long Vacation. I expect to return to Birmingham tomorrow.

Please get some prayers for me, and give me your blessing, and believe me, My dear Lord, Your faithful Servt

John H Newman[1]

---

[1] Ullathorne replied on 6 November, 'My faith is not at all shaken in the success of your, and our cause. It will be an anxious thing, and expensive, but that is all—. . . . I will set all my convents to pray, and neglect no means in my power to help you.'

To Ambrose St John

⌈London Nov 6/51

Charissime

I now know the worst, and it is very bad—but I am not so troubled as I was, and hope the calm will continue.

I have just returned from the Attorney General [[Cockburn]]—he is the first *impartial* person who has given an opinion,⌉ for Badeley and Lewin are friends—⌈next, he is so near the judges, that he speaks *their feeling*, (so Lewin said)

1. Observe, that Lord Campbell showed a bias, by calling it ribaldry.[1] And Lord C. is very likely to have the decision [[the trial]].
2. The Attorney General evidently was indignant [[with me]]. He called it a bitter libel etc—(it imputed a pretence of religion as a cloke for bad practices etc) Asked whether I had thought of knocking under etc. if so, the quicker the better.
3. He said we *must prove the* [[our]] *points*: i.e. bring primary evidence; secondary, without primary, would do more harm than good.
4. He said the Judges would send on the matter to trial, if they could.
5. That there would be no chance at all with a jury.
6. that they would come down more heavily upon me than upon Burns.

The alleviation was this—first, that they think they can get the matter postponed till Easter Term: yet what a time for suspence! next, that IF Achilli's confession is made good, it will go a very great way indeed⌉

The Attorney General was evidently hostile. If I go to Ireland to the new University *doubtless* I shall be doing myself an injury—but it must be.

⌈And now, Charissime, you know the whole—things can't be worse—they may be better. I said this morning I never would be sad again; I will try not to be. May He⌉ who was on the Cross, ⌈enable me to bear whatever He gives me, in love, of His sufferings⌉[2]

Ever Yrs affly J H N

⌈P.S. Brodie pronounces very well of me.⌉

Thanks for F Joseph's letter. I propose to come down tomorrow (Friday) and may have to come up here next week.

[1] When the passage concerning Achilli in Newman's lecture was read in court on 4 November, Lord Campbell said: 'The ribaldry with which the passage commences would not be a sufficient ground for the Court to interfere; but it certainly imputes specific and gross breaches of morality, which justify our interposition.' *The Times*, 5 November 1851, p. 6.

[2] [[May He support me, who in love gives me to suffer.]]

To W. G. Ward

Oratory Bm Nov 26/51

My dear Ward

The marvellous mistakes which have been made show most strikingly that God's hand is in the whole matter. As to its hurting my influence, it is absurd, but it will be a most severe cross.

I have anticipated it since August last and said with St Andrew O bona crux, diu desiderata—Nothing has been wanting on my part in point of vigilance and promptitude.

Lewin had *nothing to do* with the Affidavit.[1] I will tell *you in confidence* the origines mali.

1. The Cardinal, who *did not look* for his documents till the *hour* when the Rule was made absolute and it was too late.[2] In that hour he looked and he found. F Hutchison brought them me. I took up my hat and went to Lewin. He had just returned from Westminster. It was all over.

2. The Cardinal ditto; who sent our dear Fathers to Naples with introductions not *strong enough* to open the Police books. They were told there that every thing would have been done, had the Cardinal been more alive.

3. The Attorney General, who said confidently that we should gain till Easter—who took it for granted, and threw us off our guard completely. *Consequently* the Affidavit was drawn up as a form, and the Attorney General had it with him several days, before he brought it into Court. When it was unsuccessful, Badeley drew up other and stronger affidavits, but the Attorney General would have nothing to do with them.

4. Lord Campbell, who from the first has been against me.

I brought the point of the Dublin Review before my lawyers, but they said that it would only tell in mitigation of punishment—as indeed Hope had told me *before* I published the passage.

I cannot help thinking matters will go on to conviction and imprisonment; but for three months I have been saying 'nothing but prayer will save me'—and I have been a Cassandra—my words have fallen idle—, men have but laughed

Ever Yrs affly J H N

[1] Ward forwarded to Newman a letter he had received on 24 November from Frederick Oakeley, who wrote in great distress, having heard that Newman's case was being 'messed', and that Lewin was inexperienced. Oakeley added, 'Altogether I am grieved beyond description at the idea of N's sufferings and of his influence being weakened.' The affidavit was that in which Newman affirmed that he could prove the truth of the charges, if given time to collect the evidence.

[2] Wilfrid Ward, in *Life and Times of Cardinal Wiseman*, II (London, 1897), pp. 39–40, claims that Wiseman did look for the papers, but cites no documentary evidence. His account of an interview between Philip Gordon of the London Oratory and Wiseman differs completely from the only interview for which evidence exists. See note to letter of 8 September to Badeley (*L.D.* XIV, p. 352 n. 1). Even on the hypothesis of another interview, for which there is no evidence, Ward's account is highly suspect, for he claims that Wiseman, in the greatest distress of mind, said: 'I dare not write to him [Newman].' All the evidence indicates that it was only after Badeley's interview with him (see letters of 11 and 13 November to Badeley, *L.D.* XIV, pp. 420–2, 423–4) that Wiseman became alarmed, and, by that time, he had already written to Newman, on 31 October, saying he did not know where the documents were.

To F. W. Faber

Oy Bm Dec 30/51

My dear F Wilfrid

I am going to write you a very ungracious letter, that is, to express my *sorrow* at your return.

The truth is, I have been fuming ever since you went, at the way you have been going on. I wrote to Malta to protest against your preaching—the letter missed you, and next I heard of you as lecturing an Orat. Parv. in Italian.[1] The tone of your letter from Palermo pleased me not at all—I had no confidence in your sudden restoration, and I thought your letter excited. Then suddenly you were making for Rome, which was *forbidden* you—and before [a] letter could hit you, you are, against all medical orders, in England.

St Philip used to obey his physician. Have you taken one of the few opportunities a Father Superior has for obedience? I saw his letter—he prescribed six months for you.

You are *not* recovered—the very impatience with which you have come back shows it. As far as I can see, you are still bound to obey your medical adviser, and explere numerum. Your life is precious

This, I know, is very ungracious but I am bound to say it.

Ever Yrs affly J H N

P.S. As *I* am like to have to submit to Ἀνάγκη[?][2] so must you.

---

[1] *Oratorium Parvum*, Little Oratory, the confraternity for men.
[2] 'Restraint'.

The Pressure of Crises
(1852–58)

Newman faced a series of very different crises during the 1850s. Those years were punctuated by the drama of the Achilli trial and the clash with the London Oratorians, and all the while he was trying to establish the Catholic University in Ireland, a task that elicited one of his most celebrated works, *The Idea of a University*, but which proved otherwise to be deeply frustrating. The Achilli affair dragged him down just as he was preparing to launch his efforts in Dublin.

At the start Achilli's advisers had wanted to hold the trial as soon as possible, but when they discovered Newman was bringing witnesses from Italy they sought instead to delay the proceedings, adding to his expenses, while hoping that the witnesses would tire and return home. His friend Maria Giberne had worked wonders to find them, and Newman's amused relief is evident when he wrote to her that she wasn't allowing the husband of one of them enough cigars. 'Let him have an unlimited supply', he told her. 'Let him have anything else he takes to . . . is there no equestrial exhibition? no harmless play? no giant or dwarf? no panorama, cosmorama, diorama, dissolving views, steam incubations of chickens, or *menagerie* . . . which he would like to see?'

In the event, the trial was held in June and Newman was found guilty of libel. There was outrage at the verdict, and when Newman was brought back to court in November for sentencing, his counsel, Sir Alexander Cockburn, astonished the judges by requesting a retrial, attacking ferociously the way the trial had been conducted. His request was denied, but when sentence was passed the following February, Newman was fined a mere £100, a moral victory despite the technical legal defeat.

The other significant crisis of this period was the increasingly bitter clash between Newman and Frederick Faber, and the resulting break between the London and Birmingham Oratories. The London Fathers wished to be able to undertake the spiritual care and direction of nuns, which was not considered a usual part of their mission. Without informing Newman, they wrote to Rome, requesting for themselves an interpretation of the Rule to permit the practice. When the news leaked out, Newman wrote to the London House expressing his concern: a formal interpretation from Rome of the Oratorian Rule would affect Birmingham as well as London. That was the essential issue. But there was also in fact a clash of styles of Catholicism, and even more of personalities, Newman living inconspicuously and contentedly in Birmingham, while Faber, flamboyant and excitable, monopolized the limelight and wealthy Catholic patronage in fashionable London. In their increasingly fraught correspondence, expressions of personal affection by the London Oratorians did nothing to mollify Newman who was well aware of their lobbying against him in Rome. Though he had right on his side, the quarrel does not show Newman at his best: his outraged stance on principle could make him seem prickly and implacable. Cardinal Wiseman made matters worse by showing Faber Newman's letters and by gossip. Newman's suspicion of Faber grew, and would never be overcome. As he commented to Ambrose St John, Faber 'now finds himself as he was before he sought the Oratory—independent, with all the additional advantages, which St Philip, extended reputation, and years give him'. In 1856 he felt forced to go to Rome to set the record straight.

Throughout these years, Newman was seeking steadily to establish the new university in Dublin. He wanted to move the project on quickly, but was hampered by delays, and here too there were other difficulties. The Irish bishops in general mistrusted Archbishop Cullen; and Newman, having come at Cullen's invitation, was tarred with their mistrust. He was caught in the crossfire between the two parties. Nor could he get decisions out of Cullen when he needed them, and then he would find that decisions had been taken without consulting him. For a time it seemed that he would be made a bishop, and this was the one occasion on which he would have welcomed it, because he felt it would give him the status he needed to deal effectively with the Irish bishops. However, the idea eventually dissolved, never to be heard of again. Frustration overwhelmed him and, with it, disillusion with Cullen: 'He has treated me from the first like a scrub.'[1] And so, although he stayed on in Dublin longer than he had originally intended in order to support what had been accomplished, finally he left, pleading the need of his community in Birmingham.

These years contain comic letters, describing his early experiences in Dublin, and sad letters, notably when his sister, Harriett, whom he had not seen for nine years, died in 1852 and when Father Joseph Gordon died the following year. But there are also some extremely harsh letters to the Fathers at Birmingham, often to his closest friend, Ambrose St John: 'Does it not come to this, that I am unnecessary to you?'; 'Don't send me Fr Faber's letters . . . I know they would make me angry.' He seems angry enough already. This anger bears witness to the strain that Newman was feeling, separated from his home, but under pressure at first during the Achilli trial and then from the dispute with the London Oratory.

[1] Letter to Robert Ornsby, 17 October 1858, *L.D.* XVII, p. 487.

6

The Pressure of Crises (1852–58)

To Miss M. R. Giberne

Oy Bm Jany 23/52

My dear Miss Giberne,

A letter, which I have opened, has just come for you, forwarded from Rome, from Mr Harting under date of Naples January 7, to the effect that he had two, perhaps four, more women for you. It amuses me that you should be thought capable of such a tail. They must come as they can. FF Joseph and Vincent must bring them. You have done quite right in setting off. To secure *one*, and that from Viterbo, is the great thing. There is all the difference between one and none—far more than between 4 or 5 and one. To get 5 is but to increase in *quantity*—but by securing at least one, you altered the *quality* of the evidence. And then again, *supposing* you *had* brought Naples and Capua, *they* may come as it is—whereas you might have lost Viterbo altogether. So that I think you and Mgr Talbot judged right.

We think you don't allow Gippina's husband cigars enough—let him have an unlimited supply. Let him have any thing else he takes to—perhaps he would get tired if he rode in legno [in a carriage] every day—but is there nothing else? is there no equestrial exhibition? no harmless play? no giant or dwarf? no panorama, cosmorama, diorama, dissolving views, steam incubation of chickens, or *menagerie* (the jardin des plants!) which he would like to see. Surely beasts are just the thing for him. I wonder he has no taste for a review. I should not *ask* him, but I should *take* him to the jardin des plants, as if I wished to see them myself.

I shall send, if all is well, F Ambrose to see you soon. Did I tell you we are in an anxious crisis! Achilli is trying to find a flaw in our pleas—so that, as he got rid of the process of affidavit by finding fault with my affidavit, so by finding fault with the Pleas, he is attempting to get rid of our witnesses, now we have been at the trouble to get them, and wishes to get me condemned without coming into court!

Lady Olivia is rather better.[1] We talk of beginning our church directly.

Ever Yrs affly J H N

---

[1] Lady Olivia Acheson, daughter of the second Earl of Gosford, had become a Catholic in 1845 and had come to Birmingham to support the Oratorians. She was to die on 28 March 1852.

To Sister Mary Imelda Poole

Oratory Bm March 7/52

My dear Sister

I wish I could give you good news. It is sad to think how many prayers, how much money I am exacting—but the prayers do good in some way or other, while the money apparently makes to itself wings, and vanishes.

When our opponents found that we had good witnesses, they, who had been in such breathless haste up to that moment, and had refused me a moment, so precious was Achilli's character, took just the opposite course. They put off the trial—we find they can do so for 8 months—meanwhile our witnesses are costing £40 a week and *wish to go*.

What makes all this more marvellous is, that the *whole* proceeding is founded upon a false (perjured) affidavit of Achilli, which the judges would not give me time to meet by counter affidavits. Had this been done, no money would have been necessary, for written documents are no expense to get or to keep. They must by this time, I do think, see their gross mistake. My counsel Mr Badeley warned them of this very thing, but in vain.

Of course we must succumb if this goes on; there is to be a meeting of my friends in London the day after tomorrow.

What I think myself is, that my opponents *cannot* play this game much longer than next term—i.e. the end of April. The only thing they care for is public opinion, and I think their own friends will be too much for them. The great Independent preacher here Mr Abyell Jones,[1] assures the young men of Achilli's innocence. He would not assure them unless they *needed* assurance. I hear questions asked among Protestants 'Why does not the trial come on?' Hitherto my opponents have had the face to say that *I* am delaying it—with the fact of the expense of my witnesses before them. Yet Achilli's sollicitors *who do all this* are highly respectable men. Is it not wonderful?

Well, it is my private opinion, not, I am sorry to say, that of others, that they cannot in shame let April pass without trial. And what looks like making up their minds to it, they have the second face (as if their face were not all gone by this time,—their front I should say) they have the front to ask me to consent to try before a common, not a special jury—i.e. not by my peers who have characters to lose, but by a set of pot-house fellows, such as those who acquitted the poor perjured girl at Hammersmith.[2] I will not repeat Is it not wonderful? for nothing is wonderful:—be sure of that. I thought I knew it—I have said for years 'nothing is wonderful against the Truth'—So much have I had in the way of personal experience of this for 20 years, that I have always said 'Anything may happen; men are up to anything—,' but still there seems a lower depth. It is *intellectually* wonderful—this is what I mean; it is *no* wonder there are bad men in the world. I muse over the analysis of such ways of acting, as over a problem. To explain and account for such face, front, or whatever you call it, is as difficult as squaring the circle.

Well, what is the upshot, leaving the squaring the circle to itself?—that depends on what my friends determine on Tuesday. For myself I should decide thus—to keep the witnesses till the end of April—and then peremptorily discharge them—and if the trial comes on to state the circumstances. The Law, the Judges would suffer, not I.

I don't know what to ask you to pray for;—except it be generally a speedy and happy issue.

Yrs affectly in Christ John H. Newman of the Oratory

P.S. Don't suppose I do not feel very grateful for all your continual prayers.

---

[1] This is the copyist's misreading of 'Angell James'. John Angell James (1785–1859) was the Independent Minister at Carr's Lane Chapel, Birmingham, from 1805, and one of the chief promoters of the Evangelical Alliance.

[2] Mary Anne Burke, an orphan, assuming the alias Angelina Adams, claimed that she had been forcibly detained in the Convent of the Good Shepherd, at Hammersmith. In court she perjured herself, and although the nuns wished the case simply dismissed, she was tried for perjury. The jury, after a few moments of deliberation, acquitted her.

To Ambrose St John

⌈22 Lower Dorset Street Dublin May 11./52⌉

My dear Ambrose

⌈You are all expecting news, and I have no one to be my trumpeter.⌉ Stanislas passed thro' on Sunday.

⌈The Lecture, I suppose,⌉ thanks to our dear Lady, ⌈has been a hit; [1] and now I am beginning to be anxious lest the others should not⌉ duly ⌈follow up the blow. The word 'hit' is Dr Cooper's word.

The room is [[was]] very good for my purpose, being very small.[2] It is [[was]] just the room I like, barring want of light; [[I cannot make myself heard, when I speak to many, nor do the many care to hear me]]; paucorum hominum sum. The room holds, say, 400—and was nearly full. Mr Duffy[3] whom I met in the train to Kingstown after it, said he had never seen so literary an assemblage—all the intellect, almost, of Dublin was there. There were 13 Trinity fellows etc. Eight Jesuits; a great many clergy—and most intense attention. When I say that Dean Meyler was much pleased, I mean to express that I [[it]] did not offend Dr Murray's friends. Surgeon O Reilly, who is the representative perhaps of a class of laity, though too good a Catholic perhaps for my purpose, and who on Saturday had been half arguing with me against the University, said, when the Lecture was ended, that 'the days of mixed Education were numbered.' Don't you suppose I am fool enough to think I have done any great things yet—it is only good as far as it goes. I trust it could not be better, as far as it goes—but it goes a very little way.

The Lectures are to be in extenso in the Tablet—and I am going to publish them at /6 a piece—and then I think I shall have a library edition afterwards.[4] Dr Moriarty, whom I made censor beforehand, was the first who gave me encouragement, for he seemed much pleased with the Lecture—and spoke of its prudence, and said it went with the Queen's College party just as far as it was possible.[5]

I was heard most distinctly, or rather my voice so filled the room and I had such perfect command of it, that people *would not believe* I could not be heard in a great Church—but I know myself better. It was just the room I have ever coveted, and never had.⌉ The room will be fuller next week. There were a number of ladies, and I *fancied* a slight sensation in the room, when I said, not Ladies and Gentlemen, but Gentlemen. ⌈My one object here is that of hastening on these University matters. *Three new and stronger Rescripts about them have* JUST *come from Rome.*⌉

J H N.

[1] On 10 May Newman had delivered the first of five lectures on university education.

[2] This was the Exhibition Room in the Rotunda.

[3] Evidently Charles Gavan Duffy (1816–93), the leader of the Young Irelanders, who soon became one of Newman's friends in Dublin.

[4] Only the first lecture appeared in full in the *Tablet*, XIII (5 May 1852), pp. 307–9.

[5] David Moriarty was the President of All Hallows College in Dublin and became Bishop of Kerry in 1856. He and Newman became good friends.

To Nicholas Darnell

22 Lower Dorset Str. Dublin. May 16/52

My dear Nicholas,

I wish you would oblige 'the Dean'[1] to keep to his rooms till he is well. Nothing is done without nursing;—impatience and imprudence are bad doctors—he will lose twice, four times, as much time in the event. The wind having changed, he has no excuse—and I do insist on his getting well at once, under obedience. On the principle of 'who drives fat oxen, must himself be fat,' I commit him to your prudence and patience.

F. Joseph's letter is just come. Never a truer word than the Protestant's that I have too many ideas in Lecture 1. But if they were all to be developed, they would make the whole volume.

I am amused at the great cleverness of the Irish, which far surpasses any thing I ever saw elsewhere. The very ticket takers in the room followed my arguments, and gave an analysis of the Discourse afterwards. The printer makes most judicious remarks and alterations in the proof—always clever and well meant, though generally wrong. As to the poor servant girl here, she is supernaturally sharp-sighted and subnaturally dirty; but her eyes seem every where, she anticipates every want, and how she discovers some things I really find a deep mystery. She closed up both windows in my bedroom with the shutters the first night—when I went to bed I opened the right, *after* putting out my candle; the first thing in the morning, I opened the left also. How she found it out I cannot conceive—but next night and ever since the left was closed up, and the right open. She has taken to sort my papers and put away books, and fill my drawers—but here she is beyond her province, and

I have been obliged to snub her just now. As I generally seem very cross or very stupid, sometimes both, she puts me down doubtless as a specimen of an English Priest.

I wish you would let William know that *I really wish to* see or talk with H. Coleridge. Press it on him with my love.

Wilberforce is going to furnish my new room for me with East Farleigh leavings.[2] I bought an iron bed *here*.

Ever Yrs affly J H N

[1] i.e. Ambrose St John.
[2] Wilberforce was Vicar of East Farleigh, Kent, until he became a Catholic in September 1850.

To Miss M. R. Giberne

Edgbaston Bm May 26/52

My dear Miss Giberne

I should have written to you from Ireland, where you have been continually in my thoughts, had I not been quite worn down with anxiety and over work. Any how, I should have sent you a Tablet with my first Lecture, had I known your direction.

I trust I am doing good in Ireland, but really it is like drawing my blood—so much am I pulled down.

It grieves me indeed to think that you have so long a trial—for it bears upon you most heavily. It can't help coming on in June—i.e. they cannot now put it off—I am getting all the prayers I can—for prayer alone can do it. Yet I cannot think it intended that the wicked should prosper

The letter boy is come—so I must hurry a conclusion
Ever Yrs affly in Xt

John H Newman of the Oratory

P.S. I go back on Saturday to 16 Harcourt Street, Dublin.

To Austin Mills

16. Harcourt Street Dublin June 3. 1852

My dear F Austin

I fear this won't get to you in time. It struck me that, tho' I only spoke to the Bishop about the tonsure for our two novices, he might mean minor orders. If so, they must go up Friday night to Oscott. But it is useless writing now, when I have missed the post.

Tell F Nicholas I have made a great mistake about the size of my room. It is not more than 30 feet long at most—but it is certainly 17 or 18 feet high—and a fair width. It is, bating the wind which may come in at the window, the warmest room I could desire. The size precludes draughts, and the doors are all double with an interval between them.

When I got here, I found that the house-keeper, who would not let any other of the servants do it, had arranged, not only my clothes, but all my papers for me. I had put my letters in various compartments according to my relations towards them—and my Discourse papers, according as I had done with them or not. She had mixed every thing, laying them most neatly according to their *size*. To this moment I have not had courage to attempt to set them right—and one bit, which was to have come in, I have from despair not even looked for. And so of my linen; I had put the linen in wear separate from the linen in reserve. All was revolutionized. I could find nothing of any kind. Pencils, pens, pen knife, tooth brush, boots, 'twas a new world—the only thing left, I suppose from a certain awe, was, (woe's me,) my discipline. Mind, every thing was closed up, as far as they could be without lock and key, which I had not. She then came in to make an apology, but was so much amused at her own mischief, as to show she had no deep sense of its enormity.

I have found all sorts of useful books in the Bookcase—two copies of Shakespeare, Mitford's Greece, Aristotle's Ethics, Crabbe, Scott, Dryden, Wordsworth, Swift, Berkeley, Waverley Novels, Blackstone, Blair, Ovid, and Gibbon

Ever Yrs affly J H N

To Sir Alexander Cockburn

Edgbaston, Birmingham June 25. 1852

Sir,

I may be taking an unusual or informal step in addressing these lines to you; if so, I must trust you will excuse it in consideration of the feeling which leads me to it.

This is the first of many letters which I am writing on the subject of the late proceedings against me in the Court of Queen's Bench, and its object is to express my sense, however unworthy in itself of your notice, of the power and effect with which you have conducted my defence in the presence of a Judge and Jury, neither of whom could be considered friendly to me.[1]

It is few persons who would be willing to throw themselves with the zeal and heartiness which you have manifested, into the cause of a person of another religion, and of habits of thought and place in society altogether different from their own. This real earnestness has as strong claims on my lasting remembrance as the splendid intellectual efforts with which it was accompanied had upon the respect and admiration of all who were witnesses of them. You are in a sphere so removed from mine, that I am perplexed to know how to frame a form of thanks which may be at once acceptable to you and natural in me; but perhaps you will not be displeased if I express the warmest wish of my heart, that, for every benefit you do to others, you may gain a tenfold reward to yourself from the Source of all good.

This is not written with a view of putting you to the trouble of an answer[2]

I am Sir With much respect Yr obedient Servt

John H Newman

¹ The jury found that Newman had failed to prove his charges against Achilli. However, *The Times* of 25 June, p. 7, reported the profound effect of Cockburn's speech: 'Sir A. Cockburn addressed the jury for the defendant during a period of four hours, and in a speech which was listened to throughout with breathless attention. We . . . cannot hope to convey . . . more than a faint idea of the nervous eloquence by which it was characterized. It is very rarely indeed now-a-days that our courts of justice are so thoroughly roused from their habitual state of dull repose, and some difficulty was experienced in suppressing the spontaneous bursts of applause with which the highest efforts of the advocate's forensic powers were received.'

² There is no trace of a reply from Cockburn.

To F. W. Faber

Edgbaston. Birmingham June 25/52

My dear Father Supr

I almost stole away like a thief last night—but since I must go to Ireland, I wished to be some little time here first. I intend to go tomorrow—

It strikes me to say, *you must none of you be doleful*. We are floored, if we think ourselves floored. Of course we *are* floored, whether we think ourselves so or not, *in a worldly standard*—but we must steadily recollect that we are above the world, above human law, above the feelings of society—and therefore must cultivate a lightness of heart and elasticity of feeling, which, while deeply based on faith, looks at first sight to others as mere good spirits. Mere good spirits are not enough—but bad spirits will be a positive hallucination. We are done if we feel beaten. We must have no indignation against Judge and Jury, or any thing else—they act according to their nature—and accomplish according to God's will. Poor shadows, what are they to us! You must make your Brothers meditate on the nothingness of the world unless the subject be too intellectual . . .

Ever Yrs affly in Mary & Philip

JHN

P.S. You must bear this in mind, viz that we *always* thought the verdict would be unfavorable—and relied on the *moral effect* of the evidence—now the article in today's Times is sufficient to prove that we have attained the *moral effect*.¹

¹ This postscript must have been added on 26 June, after the leading article of that day in *The Times*, p. 5, which strongly criticized the conduct of the trial and the verdict. It stated, 'Roman Catholics will have henceforth only too good reason for asserting, that there is no justice for them in cases tending to arouse the Protestant feelings of judges and juries.'

To Archbishop Cullen

Edgbaston Birmingham July 4. 1852

My dear Lord,

⌈I wish to put you in possession of my feelings about the appointment of a Vice-Principal,⌉ [[Vice-President]] which I can do better on paper than in conversation.

⌐As to the Professors,⌐ since our state is to be at first provisional and *they* will not have any thing to do with the government, ⌐I have no personal interest in their appointment,⌐ and do not care who they are, so that they are good ones and creditable to the University.

⌐But it is different with those immediately about me,⌐ who are to help me and share my responsibilities. ⌐I must have perfect confidence in them,⌐ and power over them. I mean the Vice President, the Deans, the Tutors, and perhaps the Lecturers. These are the *working body* who will be, at least at first, and for a time, the real life of the Institution.

⌐Of these the Vice President is the most intimately near me,⌐ and most involved in my doings and responsibilities. He takes my place when absent—I depend on him simply. It is not enough even that I have full confidence in his zeal and desire to act with me—he must see things from the same point of view as I do.

⌐If there is one office, of which I ought to have the absolute appointment, it is this. But I do *not* wish to have it, for this simple reason, that, knowing so few persons, I have not the *power* of choosing,⌐ though I had leave to do so. I am obliged to depend on the choice of others.

Yet the difficulty is *how can* others choose for me? how can they prophesy who will get on with me, and who will not?

This difficulty, of getting a person who would pull well with me, is all in *addition* to the difficulty of finding a person possessing the requisite qualities for the *office*— which is very great. We want a person of method, of resource, of business like habit, of firmness yet gentleness, and of largeness of mind.

⌐The conclusion I come to from all this, is, that it is *inexpedient* to appoint a Vice President at once.⌐ It may be ruining every thing.

Would it be possible to appoint a 'Prefect of Studies?' *an office which might die a natural death at any moment*, its holder being translated to a professorship, lectureship, or the like?[1]

> Begging your Grace's blessing, I am, Yr affte Servt in Xt
>
> John H Newman[2]

[1] 'Dr. Cullen never wrote a word to me in answer to this letter.' ('Memorandum about my connection with the Catholic University,' *A.W.*, p. 291.) Twenty years later Newman noted: '(N.B. When I wanted to do without a Vice Rector, Dr Cullen, without any reply to me, suddenly gave me one; and afterwards when I really wanted one, and asked for one, he, without answering my application, persisted in not giving me one.)' Cf. letter of 13 October to Cullen (*L.D.* xv, pp. 179–80).

[2] 'Since the need, and the choice of a Vice Rector runs through nearly all my correspondence with Dr. Cullen, and gave colour and shape to the termination of my Rectorship, it is worth while to note that it was my first as well as my last difficulty.' (*A.W.*, p. 290).

To Mrs J. W. Bowden

> Oratory Birmingham July 19/52

My dear Mrs Bowden,

It took me quite by surprise to hear from dear Emily. You must indeed be very much tried just now—Yet still, how joyful it is, and what an honor to you, that you should be allowed thus to give up to your Lord those He has given you![1]—And what a wonderful contrast to the uncertainties, risks, and darkness of the future, to which a mother generally surrenders her children, and thinks herself happy in the surrender, what a contrast to this will be your parting with these dear girls, whom I cannot look at without wishing to weep, as a relief to me.

You may think how tried I am at this moment with my sister's death (Harriett's) which I wrote to you about last night—I have not seen her for nine years.[2] I have had a second letter this morning, but throwing no light upon it—I suppose she died worn out with years of mental fidget—*but it is simply my supposition*, for *nothing* is told me. All I know is, that they did not think her in any great danger, that she had been ill since she was with the Ogles after Easter (where she was taken ill) that the medical man saw her about 11 PM on Friday night, that her maid sat up with her, and at 5 A.M. finding her asleep, went to sleep too, and was found later in the morning by another servant asleep still, and Harriett by her dead.

Where I feel most *practically* the pain, is, that my Lectures in Dublin require, at my age, all the steam I can put on—and this affliction, coming upon the Achilli affair, pulls me down so much, that nothing but God's grace can keep me up. You must indeed pray for me, as I for you.

Alas! I have to preach at Limerick on August 1; and, I suppose, must leave this place a day or two before it.

Ever Yours affectly in Xt

John H Newman of the Oratory

---

[1] Her daughter, Marianne, had decided to become a nun. See the following letter.

[2] Harriett Mozley died on 16 July 1852.

To Marianne Bowden

Oratory Edgbaston. July 19. 1852

My dear Marianne,

I am, and always have been, so cut off from people, that I have no means of showing how I love them—and I love you, my dear Child, very dearly—and when God gives you the wish of your heart and brings you to the home of peace and the sanctuary of His intimate Presence, you must not forget that I have said so to you—and to pray for one who is getting older and older every day, and needs strength above himself to carry him on.

What you tell me of Westbury is very pleasant[1]—and the corroboration you have received from the Bristol Good Shepherd seems to me quite to settle the matter. I have no fear now in recommending you to go there. Since I began writing this, I have been talking to the Bishop of Southwark, who is stopping here, on the subject. He tells me one of the Miss Buckles is there, and delighted with the place. The family live at Bristol—I wish I had known it before—for you might have heard something from them. But however, I think you have heard enough, and I do not see why you may not look steadily forward to Westbury, as the place to which our Lord and His dear Mother are leading you.

Ever Yours, My dear Child, Most affectionately in Xt on earth, till we meet, so be it, in heaven

John H Newman of the Oratory

[1] Marianne Bowden was entering the Convent of the Visitation at Westbury, near Bristol.

To H. E. Manning

Edgbaston Bm Oct 14/52

My dear Manning

I inclose the two papers the Cardinal gave me. The Latin I never had. I shall be rejoiced to see your Sermon in print.

It is a shame I did not answer your kind letter—but you must not measure my pleasure at it by my silence.[1]

A happy journey to you, and a peaceful sojourn in the Eternal City. I have nothing to send by you, but, what I wish you *very much* to convey emphatically and to spread about, my exceeding gratitude for the interest and pains which have been manifested in my behalf in the Achilli affair. I do not know how it will turn out, but nothing but good can come of it, whatever happens to me.

I wrote to Talbot the other day, and I forgot to say any thing to him about the Synod. You may tell him, though he knows it already, how satisfactorily every thing went off.

Pray for me at St Philip's shrine and believe me

Ever Yrs affly in Xt

J H N

[1] Manning wrote on 14 August about Newman's sermon 'The Second Spring,' 'Long years have passed since I have heard anything which touched me more. And I had a delight which no one else there present could know—for no one there could look back over two or three and twenty years of kindness, from you and of memories such as we have.'

To Mrs John Mozley

Edgbaston, Bm Nov 26/52

My dear Jemima,

Thank you for your affectionate sympathy. I was very glad to have it, and to know that only an accident prevented me having it before.

What has happened seems an illustration of the proverb, Man's extremity is God's opportunity—though through the whole office there has been such frequent vicissitudes that one cannot be sure what will be the event yet.[1]

I did not publish the passage in my Lectures without the greatest deliberation.[2] I took the advice of friends, one a lawyer—and kept saying 'Nothing [Nobody] says no—'and if any one had said no, I should not have done it—and up to this moment I never have had a wish, however transient, that I had not published it. And, though all that has happened is as yet mysterious, yet I doubt not Providence will be seen at last to have a great end in allowing it.

Directly I heard Achilli was moving (in August 1851) I at once foresaw all that would take place—for I knew 1. that his friends simply hated me. 2 that he would stoop to any thing. My confidence before and since, [was grounded in the fact] that he had not attacked Cardinal Wiseman,[3] though challenged to do it, when, if there was any one who seemed a but [sic] for the whole nation, it was the Cardinal.

However, directly he moved, I anticipated any thing, even prison—sent off two friends[4] to get evidence. By a series of accidents, so strange as to be providential, nothing was done by November—and by another accident between Sir A. Cockburn (then Atty General) and my other lawyers, my affidavits (about the *form* of which I knew no more than the *lawyers* would know about the Council of Sardica or the Type of Constans) was carelessly drawn [up]—and in spite of Badeley's[5] solemn warning to the judges (who act in this matter [with] the force of a grand jury) not to act till my counter affidavits came from abroad, lest they made themselves the tools of a perjury, they accepted Achilli's affidavit as sufficient, without any regard to 'audi alteram partem',[6] and sent me to trial.

This was the origin of all the evil—and they have not got over it now—for, even if I am able to annul the past proceedings, Achilli, under the sanction of this act of the Judges, can recommence them at any moment. If they had but given me a month, if they had given me to the first day of the following Term, I could have met Achilli's affidavit with affidavits counter to his so many and so strong, that the case would never have gone to trial.

In this the Judges did me a great injury, which they never can make up. Badeley had assured me beforehand that it was impossible that such a thing could be done. He said that a criminal information was so very serious a thing, that the judges were very slow to grant it and that they were particularly careful to see that the accused came into Court with clean hands. I consider that the Judges[7] did me a far greater injury than the Jury, for *they* made me incur the expense, and the long proceedings. I believe they are now much annoyed at the Verdict—but I cannot help saying that educated men and judges have more to answer for when they do wrong, than a vulgar prejudiced Jury.

Then to complete the injustice, they put it about that my affidavit was DISHONEST; as if I knew more about what ought to have been said in it than I know of Sanscrit. And other people took it up from Coleridge, and went about shaking their heads (I am not exaggerating) and saying that it was a proof that my character had 'deteriorated' since I was a Catholic. It was not Campbell alone who bore in mind that I was a Catholic—I count against Coleridge or Whitman [Wightman] and I have felt all along as St Paul, when he said 'Yea, let *them* take me out' of a difficulty into which they have thrust me.

I believe now, though of course I have nothing but circumstantial proof of it, that they think me hardly treated, and wish to set right what really has been their own act. I came up to London a week ago, prepared and willing to suffer any thing, with my speech too ready which I hoped to be allowed to deliver. I was disgusted to find that, at a consultation on the Thursday evening, my counsel had determined to advise me to move for a new trial. I was present at a consultation (two days after), last Saturday—and then I took strongly the negative side. I said 1. I could not ask for a new trial without intending to *use* it. 2. I could not express any such intention, for I had no means whatever to carry it on—that whatever I had done hitherto had been by the spontaneous offerings of friends and others—that I had asked no one for pecuniary support and I could not; and that *then* was an end of the matter. They said that they could not in such a matter act against me, and so we parted, I thinking the question quite decided. All Sunday Badeley was kindly importuning me to consent to a new trial, but I would not hear of it. On Monday I went down to Court with Lord Arundel, in whose house I was staying. Monsell, Bellasis, Bowyer, Mr Monteith, Mr Valentine Brown,[8] and various other persons, who sat above me. I was under [with] my Counsel, and Cockburne [*sic*] leant over and asked 'Well, what about the new Trial?'—'*No* new trial,' I answered, 'I have decided.' He said, 'I have been looking through the evidence, and I tell you plainly, we can get one.' I repeated, 'No, I can't consent. I have never taken an aggressive step throughout. I have been obliged to litigate as being defendant. I have no money—I cannot change my course;' and I sat down. Then Sergeant Wilkins began.[9] He had been up half the night getting up the evidence, and he said 'Money shall not be an object. I will go round begging from Protestant friends for you—I will take no fees myself, if you let it go on. I repeated, No. After a time the Judges came in, and Cockburn lent over and said 'You have a last chance, will you have a new Trial? Yes or no—' I answered 'No.' He began grumbling and complaining with an other Counsel, and left the Court, I thought in annoyance. I said to Bellasis, 'I suppose it is all over'. He answered 'Yes.'

It seems Cockburn went to Badeley and said '*I* can make nothing of Dr Newman—you must attempt it—' Badeley had a talk with Bellasis who was sitting next me. He told him my five counsel[s] were all of one mind, and I must give in. Bellasis then spoke to me. *He* had agreed with *me* all along, in being against a new trial—and he now changed, and said 'You must not stand out against your Counsel [any] longer.' I said 'Why, it is all over'. He said 'It *isn't*'. 'Well then,' I said, 'let them have their way'.

Accordingly, when the time came for me to put in my affidavit in mitigation of judgment, Cockburn rose. Campbell interrupted to set him right, with a studied appearance of consideration for the man he was going to punish. 'Sir Alexander' he said, 'there is doubtless Dr Newman's affidavit,' Cockburn replied, 'My Lord, I am going to propose to your Lordship to consider whether there is not ground for me to move for a new Trial'. I did not look at the poor old man—but my friends on either side tell me the effect on him was most striking. One of them, a military man, said it was as if he had been shot through the ear. His face changed colour, he trembled, and could hardly make a reply. And all that followed was a pitiable assault upon him, which lasted at least two hours. Had I any [of] the slightest resentment upon me, which (thank God) I trust I have not, I should have had my fill of revenge—and I believe it is but the beginning of what he will have to endure—for my other lawyers will be upon him, before the Judges decide upon the point finally, which will be in January. Meanwhile every one congratulates me, and the lawyers think there never will be a new trial—but all this is in the hands of God.

Since writing the above, it has struck me you might like to see a specimen of the feeling and the sympathy which Catholics at present are showing me. I take it as being the last which has come to me, not as selecting it out of others. It is this feeling which has raised for me from £10,000 to £12,000 for my expenses. Some people prophesised I never should get on with Catholics, in that they would never value me. I can but thank them in the words of Scripture, which are their *reward*, 'I was a stranger, and ye took Me in.'[10]

Three medical men, Mr Babington, Sir Benjamin Brodie, and Dr Evans of Birmingham speak most seriously of my health.[11] They gave in affidavits to prevent, if possible, my going to prison. I asked Ogle for one, and *offered to come round* by Oxford for him to see me.[12] The only answer I got from him was, that he had not seen me for 7 years, and could only testify up to that date. He accordingly put down something or other in London which the Lawyers told me was worth nothing.

My friends are sending me from home. I am to do nothing till Easter—They wish me to go abroad, but in the first instance I am going to Hope at Abbotsford.[13] I am quite well at present, but distressingly weak. I had symptoms of stone a year ago, but they have gone off. Wonderful to say, though the year has been the most trying to me in my life, I have steadily gained health all through it. However, they tell me my vital forms are very feeble, and that, unless I do nothing, I cannot live long. The debility will fall on my liver, or lungs, or some organ or other. I have been thinking and writing for 20 years, and at last it begins to tell on me. However, I shall see how I am at Easter.

I am very much distressed at what you tell me about Jemima Marsh—If you have an opportunity, tell her I do not forget her in my prayers

Yrs affly John H Newman

---

[1] Sentencing was scheduled for Monday, 31 January 1853.

[2] The attack on Achilli that caused Newman to be tried for libel.

[3] Wiseman's article, setting out in detail Achilli's exploits on the Continent, was entitled 'Dr. Achilli', *Dublin Review*, XXVIII, 1850 (June), pp. 469–511.

[4] Two fellow Oratorians, John Joseph Gordon and Nicholas Darnell.

[5] Edward Lowth Badeley, Barrister-at-law at the Inner Temple who was a close friend of Newman's.

[6] 'without hearing the other side'.

[7] The case was argued before a jury and four judges: Lord Chief Justice John Campbell, Sir John Taylor Coleridge, Sir John Patteson, and Sir William Wightman.

[8] William Monsell, Liberal MP for Limerick from 1847 until 1874; Edward Bellasis, Seargeant-at-law since 1844, and a friend of Newman's who had become a Catholic in 1850; George Bowyer, the barrister and Liberal MP for Dundalk from 1852 until 1868; Robert Monteith, benefactor and son of a rich Glasgow cotton merchant who had become a Catholic in 1846; and Valentine Brown, MP for Kerry from 1851.

[9] Charles Wilkins, Sergeant-at-law since 1845.

[10] 'Hospes eram, et collegistis Me', *Matthew* 25:35.

[11] George Gisborne Babington, Newman's London physician, Sir Benjamin Collins Brodie, Sergeant-Surgeon to Queen Victoria, and George Fabian Evans, Newman's personal physician in Birmingham.

[12] James Adey Ogle, Newman's former physician at Oxford.

[13] Abbotsford was the former home of Sir Walter Scott, Melrose, in the Scottish borders, on the bank of the River Tweed. Hope had married Charlotte Harriet Jane Lockhart, Sir Walter Scott's granddaughter, in the parish church of Marylebone on 19 August 1847. In 1848, Hope had rented Abbotsford from his brother-in-law, Walter Lockhart Scott, and moved in with Charlotte in August of that year. Following Walter's death at Versailles on 10 January 1853, Hope became its possessor-in-right, changed his name to Hope-Scott, and resided there for the rest of his life. At Hope's invitation, Newman spent more than five weeks at Abbotsford, recuperating from the ordeal of the trial from 17 December 1852 to 25 January 1853.

To John Joseph Gordon

January 7/53

My dearest F Joseph
(Private)

Badeley, who has been here since Christmas Eve, goes tomorrow—and it came upon me with such a thrill of horror that I might have cried out before every one when I heard it, 'O that I were going with you.'

Every one is as kind and considerate as possible, and I have quite my own way. Hope is most vigilant in seeing I am quite at ease; he is ever eager to get me out, ever careful to guard me from wind and wet. The consequence is that various expeditions have been projected, but the upshot has been one walk to Galashiels, and one to Thomas the Rhymer's glen, which is in the Abbotsford domain. Sometimes there is a fair morning, and we all take advantage of it—or an hour or two after lunch. Under such favorable circumstances, we go out two and two, Hope and his wife and Lord and Lady A. [Arundel] first with outriders in the form of Lady Victoria or little Henry,[1] and I and Badeley to bring up the rear. We are able to go down the Terraces to the walk by the Tweed; or we attempt the Terrace through the plantation, which is always tolerably dry. Sudden storms come on, however, and make the neighbourhood of the house an advantage.

The House itself is dark and the rooms low. The first floor passage is not so broad ⟨(not above half)⟩ as the 'Newman Alley' leading to my room from our corridor. Very dark withal, and winding. I could shake hands with the nursery maids in the rooms opposite me, without leaving my own room—and sometimes of a morning or evening in going down stairs, seeing nothing, I hear a step approaching, and am obliged to stand still where I am, for fear of consequences, and then a little light figure shoots past me on the right or left, she having better eyes than I. Once there was an awful moral stoppage, neither daring to move. Every other day is stormy, and I have found the Tablet of great use in acting as a blower to my grate—where a portion of it has remained steadily for hours till it was fairly crumbled into tinder. The rooms are small; I am surprised there is not more draught than there is; but as for light, it was not much after ½ past 3 one day that I left off attempting to employ the sun's light. The House is lighted with gas, even in the bedrooms it is very good gas, but I burn a candle a good deal.

From 10 till 2, and from 3 till 7, I sit in my room—except what time I am in chapel. The post goes at a little past noon, and you get a letter then posted in the evening of the next day—It comes in at 7, and brings me your letters of the evening before.

I dare say, when you see me, you will see that the change of air has freshened my face. Otherwise I have no reason to think I am better—I have the anxiety of being from home—and now this Achilli business, like a bad tooth which for a while has ceased to ache, is making itself felt again. It will come on *some time or other* between next Tuesday and the end of the month.

Hope anticipates every want of mine—gives me the easiest seat, and has not listened to the notion of my preaching, since he heard the Fathers were against it. Never was a party which got on so well together, yet even here there is considerable cause for anxiety, and I am not at ease. It is from no over fidget, that I am led to recollect the proverb, 'Familiarity breeds contempt.' The very absoluteness with which I feel at home is certainly dangerous—and I have ever to be on my guard lest I go too far. I am in danger of arguing too much, or of laughing too much—and, though I ought not *personally* to care that persons should go away with a lower and truer notion of me, the thought of giving scandal comes before me, and annoys me. I very much doubt whether it is good, i.e. expedient, for a person like me to be in a house like this with others, however kind and friendly.

Certainly very inexpedient, were they any persons but the Hopes and Arundels, but really the As (to say nothing of the Hopes) are quite Saints. I do not know which of them is in the Chapel most. I suppose they are ordinarily there at four stated times of the day (including Mass) and for a good long space each time. Indeed it is impossible to be in a more simply religious house, which was not a convent. Some of the servants, I see, come in to visit the Blessed Sacrament and the communions have been very good during the Christmas season.

I have not noticed this great compensation of my banishment, which I could hardly have expected any where, an altar, nay the Blessed Sacrament in the House. I had no hope of the Blessed Sacrament and was taken quite by surprise, when I heard it—and every thing is as it should be for the service of the Altar. And, when I once get on the staircase, (there are two capes to pass first) it is straight down stairs without any trouble to get at. There is a fire in the chapel all day. I have been able to go to confession four times, and might have gone a fifth.

Is it not mysterious, that, considering I have so soon to go to Ireland, I should thus be kept from home apparently for nothing at all, except St Philip's wish to mortify me? I do not allow myself to think of any thing—but go on at a jog trot through the day, seeming very merry and cheerful to every one, but with an aching heart.

Every one here is so truly kind and good, that I should be pierced at what I have said to you getting known *even to our Fathers*—but you may show this to F. Ambrose

Ever Yrs affly in Mary & Philip

J H N

[1] Lady Victoria Howard, born in 1840, was Lord Arundel's eldest daughter, and Henry, born in 1847, his eldest son, who succeeded him as fifteenth Duke of Norfolk.

To Ambrose St John

[[Abbotsford]] ⌈Monday Jany 10/53

Charissime

I know this letter will pain you, but I must write it.

You wish to act *with me*. Yet

1. *Without* me you recommend a Brother of the Congregation to become a Trappist, i.e. to leave the Congregation—or at least you contemplate doing so.
2. *Without me*, you send a Brother of the Congregation to Father Lans!!
3. *Without me* you allow, or contemplate allowing, F. Lans to see *your* letters to that Brother—i.e. give F. Lans (an extern, nay a person, with whose dealings towards us on former occasions I was not satisfied, as you know,) the opportunity of a direct interference between the Congregation and its subject.

In a word you have all but settled the question of Br B's [Bernard] return, by putting *external* obstacles, almost insurmountable, to it.

Meanwhile, you all profess you are not acting without me.

Can you bring against poor Br B. himself a more direct instance of *self-action* than this? Should you not therefore feel a little mercy for him?

What makes this more painful *to me* is that I am conscious that my one thought, since I left you, has been to keep myself before you all. Hardly a day has gone but I have written one or other of you letters. I bought 5/ worth of stamps—all are gone but 8. I have hardly written to any one but to the Fathers—often two letters in one cover. I have sent you addresses for the Chapters⌉ (which, by the bye, have never been acknowledged.) ⌈And my one occupation [[here]] has been making a book for the use of the Refectory.⌉

Does it not come to this, that I am unnecessary to you? I thought of taking a *year* ticket for the Rail, when I went to Ireland, so that, any night I pleased, I might come home, if needed—but what is the good of it?

In bringing in F Lans, you have touched me in one of my tenderest points, and you know it.

Ever Yrs affly J H N.

P.S. I assure you I have not forgotten your request about yourself.

And now I drop the subject till I return. You will observe ⌈I have waited 60 hours before writing this—three nights.⌉ Your letter came Friday evening

To Sister Mary Imelda Poole

London Jany 31 [1853]

My dear Sister Imelda

I have been fined £100, and imprisoned *till* the fine was paid—which of course meant no imprisonment at all. I have not heard opinions, but my friends present think it a triumph.

I had a most horrible jobation from Coleridge, of which the theme was 'deterioration of converts.' I had been everything good when I was a Protestant—but I had fallen since I was a Catholic.

They would not let me speak.

Thank you for all I have gained by your prayers. Every kind thought of Revd Mother and your whole Community.

Thank Sister M. Gabriel [Du Boulay] for her welcome letter just received.

Ever yrs affectly in Xt John H. Newman

To Ambrose St John

⌈Bath. Febr 7 / 53⌉

My dear A

⌈No one wrote for me, no one expected me, and I took every one by surprise.[1] They were looking out for Philip [Gordon], and I made my appearance instead. Philip came soon after—I fear I turned him out of his bed. The Doctor says this⌉ now; viz⌈'had you not come, I should not have wished you to come—now you are here, you had better stop.'⌉ I have wished to send you a Telegraph all the morning, but he has not let me.

⌈He says that J. [[Joseph]] is slowly going with ebbs and flows—yet at first he would not let us propose anointing. Now he desires it, but he has so impressed dear J. with the notion that perfect absence of excitement is the *one* thing for him, and that he will die, if he does not watch his own recovery as the one thing, that J. on principle will not even think of God. I suppose his mind is his own—but he is like a child—the least thing makes him cry, and brings on a spasm in his throat. I have not yet seen him.⌉

St Philip perhaps has ordered the mistake—for I shall have greater authority than Philip can have. ⌈I said I should leave by the 2 o'clock train, as having nothing to do, which I think has softened the Doctor's resolve a bit. Now Philip is frightened, and, with his sister, [[is]] on my side, and I should not wonder if they determined that at all risks I should see him—when I should simply recommend anointing, the Priest being at hand—⌉ and it would be over in five minutes.

⌈When I got here, he was better than when the despatch came off [[to us]]—they came to me at 2 A M and said he was much better. This morning he has fallen off again. The Doctor is indefatigable in his attentions, but is somewhat⌉ like a ⌈Protestant in his ways,⌉ [[being a Catholic]] and has infected Mrs Gordon. ⌈He let one or more persons die without anointing lately from the same fear of their nerves.⌉

(I cannot help thinking that poor B's [Bernard] business has killed him—His present profound prostration is the re-action from that excitement.) I am very thankful I sent for Mr McDermot to bring him down here—in spite of all—and ⌈if we [[can]] manage to get him anointed and to dare to think⌉ a little ⌈of religion, all will be well. Philip he naturally does not care for. Mr McDermot protests he will not die without some hours notice.

I am to send you a despatch [[(telegram)]] in an hour or so—Whether or not I return tonight is quite uncertain.⌉ I shall keep this open for the last news—the post goes at 6.

⌜I send a paper for Plater to copy⌝—two copies. 2 PM.

Ever ⌜Yrs affly⌝ in Xt ⌜J H N⌝

⌜5 PM.⌝ You must not be surprised if I do not inclose the paper for Plater, tho' it is done. ⌜The Priest has just given him extreme unction. The Doctor was strong against *my* introducing the Priest, or his knowing I was here. Ph. [Philip] and I strong for it. I had my way—When he [[Joseph]] saw me he broke into a cry of joy. I said 'Hush'—He said, 'No, I can talk to you as to my mother.' I then brought in the Priest—He was anointed, and then said I am so happy. I said 'Go to sleep,' and he is now trying to do so. I ought to be most thankful. Remember me, O God, for the bitter things Thou bringest on me. The Doctor says he is sinking. A true loyal son of Philip—he has got a relic of him round his neck.⌝

(Write to me directly, tho' alas it will be too late, *in Latin*, every thing I have to do circa lavandum corpus et vestiendum)

⌜8 o'clock.⌝ Alas! I just find you will not have this till evening. ⌜The anointing has had almost a miraculous effect on him. All nervousness and anxiety is gone—he is cheerful, smiling—and happy and the Doctor says he will probably so continue to the last, which he thinks not 12 hours off.⌝ [[J H N (He lasted nearly a week)]]

[1] Newman visited Fr John Joseph Gordon in Bath who died on 13 February.

To William Philip Gordon

June 14/53

My dear Philip

I have stupidly left my *shaving* brush—*tooth* brush—and *nail* brush on my washing table in F Richard's room. Will you kindly ask Br Andrew to dry them and make a small paper parcel of them. Messrs Meyer and Mortimer, the Tailors in Conduit St, are about to send me a coat—and these articles may come with it, if some one will compassionately take them to Conduit Street.

Tell F. Bernard that Berkeley[1] was at the Station—came up and was very friendly, but awfully solemn—in his best style, and I dare say pained at me, as he used (reverently) to be, at Pembroke. He wanted to know if it was true that Faber had got fat—and was Jack [Morris] in Birmingham. By that time I think he was exhausted, and had not heart to ask after any one else. When I said that 'St John was fat too,' he made no response. He was very affectionate

Ever Yrs, J H N

[1] George Berkeley (1812–90), Vicar of Southminster, Essex.

To F. W. Faber

16 Harcourt Street. Dublin April 26/54

My dear Fr Wilfrid,

I am only too happy to have any such memorial as you offer me from your Fathers and youths of the London House.[1] At the same time I hope the very fact of their offer is a proof that I shall be securing as *cheap* mitres as possible. I mean, not only, as they will know well, that as much love goes with the gift of a cheap mitre as a grand one, but really for my own comfort let me not have about me more precious things than I absolutely *need*. 'The abundance of the rich, says Ecclesiastes (at least in the Protestant version) does not suffer him to sleep.'[2] At present I sleep in a rail-carriage or a steam boat tolerably well—but, if I know that in the van behind I have a lot of precious things to lug about with me, which I must be seeing after, with no 'Newman' (such as the Cardinal's) to be my cad,[3] why all I can say is, it is next door to travelling with nursery maids, and their paraphernalia, and a worse penance than St Philip's cat, or 'cruel scourge of human minds.'[4]

Your letter has come to me from Birmingham, or I would have replied sooner—but I am sorry to say, that, even as it is, I have delayed a post

Ever Yrs most affectly J H N

[1] Faber wrote on 21 April asking if the London Oratorians might present Newman with the three mitres he would require as a bishop.

[2] *Ecclesiastes* 5:12.

[3] Newman was the name of Wiseman's (and later Manning's) manservant.

[4] St Philip used to mortify his disciples by making them look after his cat.

To Archbishop Cullen

[May 11/54]

My dear Lord

I send the corrected statement, and am pleased that the substance of it has met your approval.[1]

[It occurs to me that I ought as a matter of duty to represent to your Grace the absolute necessity of your bringing one point before the [[Synodal]] Meeting[2] which I know has long been on your own mind.

I cannot, I ought not at this very critical time to forget the way in which I have been received by two of the Irish Prelates. The one was most courteous to me *personally*, when I went into his Diocese, but pointedly directed his courtesy to my person not my office[3]—the other [Archbishop John MacHale of Tuam] was condescending enough to second my appointment in Committee two years ago—but he has since expressed much distrust of me personally.

With facts such as these before me, I find it imperative to ask that their Lordships should do me the kindness of taking the distinct step of constituting me, after the precedent (I believe) of Louvain, their Vicar General (say for 3 years) for the establishment of the University—if they do not, it is very plain I shall not know where I stand. When the meeting separates, I may find to my perplexity that majority of votes does not bind the minority; and that the decision of the Episcopal body is considered no rule for the acts of its members, taken individually.

Such things have occurred before now, but would be precluded by an arrangement such as I now propose which alone can give me courage to engage in a work, most arduous, undertaken by me from a simple sense of duty, and already hanging over me and keeping me from other employments without result for two years past.

Should your Grace see your way to suggest any other expedient to the Vicar Generalship in gaining me the sanction of the Bishops severally and personally, of course I shall be content]⁴

I am &c J H N

[1] This was the Memorandum of 29 April on the objects of the University and the means for attaining them, which Newman sent to Cullen on 1 May, and which was to be read at the Synod on 20 May.

[2] [[This was the formal meeting, convoked by Brief of the Holy See and held in May 1854, at which the Fundamental Constitution of the University was settled]]

[3] This was the Bishop of Cork, William Delany who was 'cold and courteous—stiff and donnish . . . the only Irish Bishop I have met unlike an Irishman; I think I had rather be pawed by a lion', letter of 23 February 1854 to the Oratorians at Birmingham (*L.D.* XVI, p. 54).

[4] [[Of course nothing came of this appeal!]] At the end of April it had become clear to Newman that he was not to become a bishop after all. He wanted to be made Vicar General at least so as to gain the support of the bishops as a whole and of the individual bishops.

To Robert Isaac Wilberforce

The Oratory Hagley Road, Birmingham. Sept 1/54

My dear Robert Wilberforce,

I have been saying Mass for you this morning, and have just received your letter, which you may be sure I read with great interest.[1] Of course I can enter into your special pain, better than anyone else except Manning. In my own case, the separation from friends was the one thing which weighed on me for two years before I became a Catholic—and it affected my health most seriously. It is the price we pay for a great good. Every one has to give his best—there are few things, besides, which either you or I had to give; for I don't suppose that either of us cared much for any thing else.

As to the books, we shall prize them very much, and be very grateful. Your name, I dare say is in them, but please, add in your handwriting that you give them to the Irish Catholic University. I expect to leave this place for Dublin on Monday.

Bear your agony, which is but a little while. The last death bed I attended some time ago, the poor sufferer kept saying 'will it soon be over?' It is a terrible stream to pass—but you will be soon through it. We have been praying for you here some time—So has Miss Ryder at the Good Shepherd—and my dear child, Mary-Anne Bowden at the Visitation—and Fr Burder and his Trappists at St Bernard's.

Ever Yours affly John H Newman of the Oratory

P.S. We shall be very grateful for the books.

[1] On 30 August Wilberforce wrote to the Archbishop of York that he could no longer accept the Royal Supremacy, and that in consequence he resigned his preferments, and put himself in the condition of a lay member of the Church. His resignation was accepted by return of post. Wilberforce became a Catholic at Paris on 1 November. Wilberforce also offered Newman some of his books for the University library.

To Edward Caswall

Mount Salus Dalkey Oct 4. 1854

My dearest Edward

I have to tell you *in strict confidence* that Frederic is going to leave the Oratory.

The reason he gives is, that you have treated him like a servant.

You said to him something like this; that the Brothers were like Servants waiting on Gentlemen.

I do not write to you, however, about him but merely to say, that I think you will find it your wisdom, as I have found it mine, *not to interfere with the brothers.* Leave them to the Father Minister.[1] *I* do not interfere with the Brothers' work at all—If I did, they would have *two* masters, the Minister and me.

Therefore I should recommend you to have nothing whatever to do with the Brothers, as such, except as *a private Father*—nothing as Rector.

I have already heard you had some words with John who is gone—who, though not a brother, was in loco fratris. I have serious anxiety lest you should hurt *Laurence's* vocation on his return.

All this makes me say, Leave the brothers to the Fr Minister.

I am somewhat pained, my dear Edward, to hear you speak of us as 'Gentlemen—' We are not Gentlemen in contradistinction to the Brothers—they are Gentlemen too, by which I mean, not only a Catholic, but a polished refined Catholic. The Brothers are our equals in the same sense in which a Priest is a Bishop's equal. The Bishop is above the Priest ecclesiastically—but they are both sacred ministers. The Father is above the Brother sacerdotically—but in the Oratory they are equal.[2]

Excuse this hint, my dearest Edward, and forgive me, and believe me Ever Yours affly in St Philip

J H N

---

[1] The lay brothers were under the care of the Minister, St John. Frederic (Thomas Godwin) complained to St John about the way he was treated by Caswall, who was Rector or Superior in Newman's absence.

[2] Caswall's defence was that he had on one occasion described a dirty lamp as 'not fit for gentlemen', meaning it as a proverbial phrase.

To John MacHale, Archbishop of Tuam

Mount Salus, Dalkey, ⌈Oct. 8, 1854.⌉

My Dear Lord,

⌈I hope this letter will find you still in this country, for I should be very sorry not to have the opportunity of submitting to you a few words in explanation of my letters of August 17 and October 3, which I am concerned to find have not met with your approbation.

It would be a serious trouble to me to have it brought home to me that I had misconceived the powers which your Grace and the other Irish prelates have, in so flattering a way, bestowed upon me as rector of the new University; and, if I have really overstepped them in consequence, I beg to offer you my sincere and humble apology.

It is very plain that, whatever powers I have, come from the Irish episcopate; and that, as it gave them, so it may at any moment withdraw them. But it seems to be equally plain, that the confidence their Lordships have placed in me is very full, and the powers in consequence intrusted to me are very ample; and you will have, I am sure, no difficulty in entering into my feeling when I say that, unless I have that full confidence and those ample powers, it would have been the height of presumption and folly in me to aspire to such very anxious responsibilities as I have accepted.

The purchase of the Medical School was one of those measures which I certainly did think came upon me by virtue of my situation. I never should have ventured to trouble the bishops with a matter of business which was nothing else than a part of the work which they had imposed upon me; nor should I have been able to form any clear idea of my duties, had I been told that this was not included in them. Accordingly I acted on my own responsibility. When, however, the negotiation was brought to a satisfactory issue, the feeling, never absent from me, that I am acting for the bishops, prompted me, on the other hand, at once to acquaint you with my success, by way of offering you an evidence that I was not idling at my post. Writing under these circumstances, I wrote without form, and did not keep a copy of my letter; I cannot, however, but be surprised and deeply pained to find that I so expressed myself as to admit of the interpretation, foreign from my real meaning, which you have been led to put upon my words.

As to the *ad interim* appointments of professors and lecturers, still more distinctly do I bear in mind that they rest with a power more authoritative than my own. At the same time, I thought I was required to suggest them to your Grace and the other archbishops; and, if we are to open our schools without delay, it is surely undeniable that, had I not moved in the matter, the schools would be opened without lecturers to lecture in them. The meeting of the bishops to which your Grace postpones the *ad interim* decision will take place, by the very force of the terms, at a time when the *ad interim* season has expired. [[for my appointments are 'ad interim *donec* coeant Episcopi.']]

I do not like to keep anything back from your Grace; and, since you have opened the subject, you will, I know, suffer me to speak, with the generous condescension which is so much your characteristic. From the bishops, then, I hold whatever power I possess in the University; they have the appointment of professors, and they can exert their Veto at their pleasure upon the names which I present to them. But I am deliberately of opinion, that, if they exercise it except on definite grounds, sufficient in the judgment of each other, they will be making the commencement of the University an impossible problem to any one who is not better fitted for the work than I am. Having so many instances of their consideration for me, I do not fear any such misfortune.]

I am, my dear Lord, with profound respect, your Grace's obedient servant in Christ,

John H. Newman, of the Oratory.

The Most Rev'd The Archb'p of Tuam.

To Isy Froude

6 Harcourt Street Dublin July 9. 1855

My dearest Isy

I am very glad to have your present. A pen wiper is always useful. It lies on the table, and one can't help looking at it. I have one in use, made for me by a dear Aunt, now dead, whom I knew from a little child, as I was once. When I take it up, I always think of her, and I assure you I shall think of you, when I use yours. I have another at Birmingham, given me by Mrs Phillipps of Torquay, in the shape of a bell.

This day is the anniversary of one of the few times I have seen a dear brother of mine for 22 years. He returned from Persia, I from Sicily, where I nearly died, the same day.[1] I saw him once 15 years ago, and now I have not seen him for 9 years.

My dear Isy when I think of your brother, I will think of you. I heard a report he was to go and fight the Russians.[2] I have another godson, called Edward Bouverie Pusey, who is a sailor already, fighting the Russians either in the Baltic or at Sebastopol[3]

Ever Yours affectionately John H Newman of the Oratory.

P.S. You will have a hard matter to read this letter

[1] Newman returned from his Mediterranean tour, and his brother Francis from his missionary journey, to their mother's house at Iffley on 9 July 1833.

[2] Isy Froude was fifteen and her brother Richard Hurrell, Newman's godson, thirteen.

[3] Edward Bouverie Pusey (1838–1921), Captain RN, was the second son of William Pusey, Rector of Langley, Kent, the younger brother of E. B. Pusey.

To Mrs J. W. Bowden

The Oratory Hagley Road Bm. August 31/55

My dear Mrs Bowden,

I have just felt like you—wishing to write, and having nothing to say. We must remember each other at holy times and seasons the more. What I heard from Henry [Bowden], that you were troubled with rheumatism, annoyed me, because I really feel you do not take care of yourself, as you should.

We are getting on with the University as well as we possibly can. It is swimming against the stream, to move at all—still we are in motion. The great point is *to set up* things—That we are doing. The medical schools will begin in October—the Church is building—and an Institution for Physical Science in course of formation. It will be years before the system takes root, but my work will be ended when I have made a beginning. Four years are now gone since I have been engaged upon it—the Holy

Father has given me leave for two years more—and, as you may think, I shall be heartily glad when they are at an end. A Rector ought to be a more showy, bustling man than I am, in order to impress the world that we are great people. This is one of our great wants. I feel it vividly—but it is difficult to find the man who is this with other qualifications too. Do you recollect how we used to laugh at poor Goldsmith's 'My Lord Archbishop' uttered from one extremity of a long room, crowded and in hubbub, to the other?—that voice is the symbol of what we want in Dublin. I ought to dine out every day, and of course I don't dine out at all. I ought to mix in literary society and talk about new gasses and the price of labour—whereas I can't recollect what I once knew, much less get up a whole lot of new subjects—I ought to behave condescendingly to others, whereas they are condescending to me—And I ought above all to be 20 years younger, and take it up as the work of my life. But since my qualifications are not those, all I can do is to attempt to get together a number of clever men, and set them to do what is not in my own line. I think of St Gregory of Nazianzus at Constantinople, and see, that at least I resemble him in his deficiencies[1]

My best love to dear Emily Ever Yours affectly in Xt

John H Newman of the Oratory

Mrs Bowden

[1] Cf. *H.S.* II, 'The Church of the Fathers', Chapter IV and *Apo.*, p.59: 'Thou couldst a people raise, but couldst not rule.'

To William Monsell

Bm Sept 4/55

My dear Monsell

I send you the inclosed as a specimen of Dr Cullen's way.

I wrote to him six weeks ago to know whether we had got from the Pope *the power of granting degrees*, which they exercise independently of the State in Belgium, which the Irish Bishops put into my hands, and which the Holy See has said should be given to the Bishops, *provided they asked for it.*

The question was, *had* the Supplica been presented, and accorded.

Dr Cullen has to this day sent me no answer. About a week ago, I asked Ornsby to *call* on him to get me a categorical answer; he went *from me* and for me

You will see his answer opposite.[1] Independently of the want of businesslike carefulness as regards the University (for we are pledged to give the Scholar's Degree in November, and ought to have the Supplica presented and granted before then) is there not something of rudeness as regards myself? Might he not at least have said, 'I will write to Dr Newman?'

Ever Yrs affly J H N

The Rt Hon Wm Monsell M P

Let me have this back please, Ornsby had called on him once before and could not find him.

¹ Newman wrote this letter to Monsell on the unused second sheet of Ornsby's morning letter of 3 September, in which the latter said, 'I called this morning on the Archbishop, and asked him, from you, the question whether we had the power of granting Degrees in arts? He replied he could not say at present,—he would look into the papers and see whether we had or not. I then referred to the question of the supplication to the Holy See, but his Grace only repeated his previous answer. He was just going out, and the interview lasted scarcely a minute.'

To Cardinal Wiseman

6 Harcourt Street Dublin Oct 19. 1855

My dear Lord Cardinal,

I am sure your Eminence will allow me to avail myself of the kindness and interest, with which you have ever regarded the Congregation of the Oratory, which you yourself have placed at Birmingham, to express to you the great pain with which both our Fathers and myself have suddenly found, within the last day or two, that, without our petitioning, without our knowing what was going on, and without our, as we trust, deserving it, the Sacred Congregation of Propaganda has been holding communications about us, which have terminated in its judging it right to suspend or to alter that portion of our Rule which forbids us to undertake the care of Nuns.

I speak in behalf of the Fathers alone in Birmingham, as I have already spoken to the Bishop, than whom no one can be kinder to us. And I write to your Eminence besides, as being the highest ecclesiastical authority in England, and having had so much to do with the introduction of the Oratory into it.

Even if any portion of our Rule required explanation, the Rule itself gives us the privilege of furnishing that explanation for ourselves; but in this case I consider that it requires no explanation at all.

I speak with the more confidence on this point, because the Decree in question, as it stands in the English Rule, was altered from the letter of the Rule of the Chiesa Nuova at my suggestion by Mgr Palma, who took the alteration to the Holy Father for his sanction.[1]

And I speak with the more pain, because I consider the suspension or modification of the Decree, now determined on by the Sacred Congregation, makes that the ordinary rule of the Congregation, which, as the Decree stands, is only permitted in an exceptionable and extreme case, and thus touches a great principle of the Oratory, which is a home institution, bringing work into its homestead, and not seeking it at a distance.

But a far wider principle is compromised even than this, and with still greater pain I remark upon it. If our Rule may be relaxed in one point without our having cognisance of it, before the event, the same misfortune may happen in any other; and what is to hinder its being swept away altogether without our knowing it? Where are we, without a special vocation? and where is our special vocation without our Rule?

The suspension may indeed be technically called a privilege; but if I may say so without want of reverence to the Sacred Congregation, of which I trust I am not guilty, it is really no privilege bestowed on us, but a penalty inflicted, if our Rule is touched in a vital point, against precedents, to the danger of vocations, without our being asked, without our asking, without our knowing, without fault alleged against us, and when that Rule is expressly committed to our own keeping.

As these are my feelings on the subject, your Eminence will, I am sure pardon my expression of them; nor wonder that I have taken the resolution of expressing them also in the name of our Fathers here, to the Sacred Congregation.

I am, My dear Lord, Kissing the sacred Purple, Your Eminence's affectionate Servt in Xt

John H Newman of the Oratory[2]

His Eminence the Cardinal Wiseman

[1] The London Oratorians had only intended to ask about a dispensation or suspension of Decree LXX for themselves so that they could hear nuns' confessions, but the Roman authorities assumed that Faber would not have made the application without Newman's agreement. So the Rescript, when it was issued on 24 November 1855, although sent to London, seems to have been meant to apply to Birmingham as well. It was in fact permissive and so did not oblige the Birmingham Oratorians to make use of it. Newman's concern was less about the particular issue of nuns' confessions, but rather about a change without consultation in the Oratorian Rule.

[2] This letter was sent to Wiseman after being approved by the four Birmingham deputies, St John, Caswall, Darnell, and Flanagan. St John wrote to Newman on 21 October, 'We all think it puts matters admirably, and is quite unmistakeable.' Wiseman did not reply to it. Newman wrote to him again on 15 November. On 14 November Wiseman saw Faber and discussed with him this letter of 19 October.

To F. W. Faber

6 Harcourt Street Dublin November 8. 1855

My dear Father Faber,

I write this letter to your Congregation.

I transmit it through you, and hope you will read it to them.

We have learned at Edgbaston within this last several weeks, that an application of your Congregation to Propaganda for a relaxation or suspension of one portion of the Rule of the Oratory, has been, unintentionally on your part, misunderstood by the Sacred Congregation to come from us as well as from you.

In consequence, to our surprise, we learn from accidental information, confirmed by our Bishop, that he has received, or is to receive, in our behalf a relaxation or suspension, which we neither desire in itself, nor desire should come to us without our asking for it.

It is desirable for your sake, as well as for ours, that such misconceptions should not recur; for, as your House has unintentionally involved us, so we unintentionally might involve you.

Suppose we were to petition Propaganda, (to take a parallel case) that the Birmingham Oratory might claim the private property of each of its subjects, and your Bishop received a letter empowering the Oratory at Brompton to exercise a similar power over its own subjects, and you were suddenly informed of this by an accidental channel, after the transaction had been going on for months over and around you, I think you would consider our act at Edgbaston a great inconvenience to you.

Therefore, for your sake as well as ours, writing as Father Superior of the Edgbaston Oratory, I think it fitting to ask your Congregation to draw up a formal petition to Propaganda to beg the Sacred Congregation to recognise, in some such way as is suitable to its forms, that fundamental principle of the Oratory of St Philip, whereby its Houses are entirely independent of each other, and what one does is not the act of the other.

And, as being the person who brought the English Rule of the Oratory to England, and has given it to your Congregation, and set the Congregation up in the Archdiocese, I think it right to ask that your application to Propaganda should be put into my hands to transmit to Rome.

Moreover, I think that your Congregation will see that it is fitting to draw up the Supplication at once.

And I shall feel the kindness of your writing me word almost by return of post that your Congregation intends doing it.[1]

Yours affectionately in Christ, John H. Newman of the Oratory[2]

The Very Revd Fr Faber

[1] Thus was formulated the request which Newman thought 'so reasonable', and which he and the Oratorians in Birmingham were sure those in London would grant. It was 'sent with the simple conviction that it would immediately succeed in its object', with those to whom Newman stood in a relation 'peculiar to himself' (letter of 14 June 1856, *L.D.* XVII, pp. 266–70).

[2] Subsequent letters from Richard Stanton, 21 February 1856, Antony Hutchison, 2 March 1856, and Faber, 8 and 10 May 1856, show how offended the London Oratorians were by Newman's tone. As he wrote to Henry Bittleston on 16 June 1856, 'I think that most of them, knowing nothing of the circumstances and meaning of their act in applying to Rome, were angry at my original letter to Fr Faber, and thought it domineering and unjust; nor should I have written it in the very words I did certainly, had I dreamed of what was to be their course.' Thus Newman's three arguments for his one request, from expedience, from justice, and from gratitude were insufficiently grasped.

To Richard Stanton

6 Harcourt Street Novr 19. 1855

My dear Fr Secretary

Assure the Fathers of your Congregation, that I really do not think I have, after the receipt of your letter, any but the warmest, tenderest, most affectionate, and most grateful feelings for them.

I pray for every blessing upon them—long years of service, many graces, abundant good works, and much merit to carry with them out of the world.

May they increase, as I decrease.

Tell them, I never loved them so much as now, when they have so exceedingly wounded me.

But, if you please, you will oblige me by not answering this.

Yours affly in St Philip John H Newman of the Oratory

The Fr Secretary

To Cardinal Wiseman

6 Harcourt Street Dec 10. 1855

My dear Lord,

This letter requires no answer. I write it, hoping you will let me take your Eminence's opinion on it, when next I see you.

Looking at the *future* of the Oratory in England, it seems to me that we must provide against the following difficulty, viz that its separate Houses have no *natural* safeguard of mutual independence, as they have in Italy. Naples and Rome are only 150 [miles] apart; Brompton and Edgbaston nearly 120; yet no one would fear that measures carried out as regards Naples would be extended as a matter of course to Rome, since the difficulty of travelling and the political separation of the places enforce practically the theoretical independence laid down in the Rule. London, however, and Birmingham, are practically next door neighbours, though the circumstances of the two places may be more different from each other, than those of Rome from those of Naples.

I do not know the forms of Propaganda, or in what way it can best meet our difficulty; but it will express my meaning, if I say that I should like to petition it to determine as follows:

1. that no measure, adopted by Propaganda towards one House of the Oratory in England, should be considered, as such, to have any force at all, direct or indirect, in any other House.

   There is one case, which this provision does not meet, viz that of Propaganda being asked by one particular House to *interpret* the Rule of the Oratory. Such interpretation *cannot but* indirectly affect other Houses. It is evidently unfair, then, that one House should do this of itself; and the more so, because, since the Rule itself gives the general power of interpreting itself to the Fathers, such a course is virtually a depriving the other Houses of a privilege. Accordingly I should supplicate.

2. that no interpretation of the English Rule of the Oratory should be made by Propaganda on the exparte supplication of one House, and without the cognisance of all the Houses, in order that they too may have the opportunity of submitting their own views upon it to the Sacred Congregation.

I dare say, however, that your Eminence will be able to suggest something more apposite and comprehensive than these two provisions, which accordingly I do but offer as matter for consideration.

Kissing the Sacred Purple, I am, My dear Lord Cardinal, Your Eminence's Affte friend & servt in Xt

John H Newman of the Oratory[1]

His Eminence the Cardinal Wiseman

[1] As he had done with Newman's earlier letters, Wiseman sent this one to Faber, on 13 December, with a note 'Private Dear F. Faber Read the enclosed, and say what you think had best be done.'

Faber replied on 15 December, begging Wiseman to have nothing to do with Newman's letter, 'I do not think he would have sent his letter to Mgr Barnabò, unless he had got a sanction for it from your Eminence; and as all this is simple hostility to ourselves, it is in fact using our Ecclesiastical Superior against us . . .

Anyhow the manner in which, as far as we can fathom the business, he *seems* to have treated us, has produced a more complete alienation from him in our minds, than I should like to describe to you. He appears resolved that no reconciliation shall take place. Deeply as he has wronged us, it seems as if he were becoming actually hostile to us. However, the one thing *I* want to avoid now, is an open appeal to Rome against him, as attempting to alter the Institute and bring in a generalate' (London Oratory Archives).

To Edward Caswall

St Paul's Conversion [25 January] 1856 47 Piazza di Spagna
7th letter on Oratory matters.

My dear Edward

We have just had a long and most satisfactory interview with the Pope—and I can only say that it is well we have come here. He knew all about *us*, down to Fr Dalgairns, and wished evidently to *hear our side*, having heard the other. I suppose he got part of his information from the Bishop,[1] but the greater part came from the London House. Mr Doane who has happened just now to drop in, having come from Paris, stopping at Genoa, heard that *I* was expected at the Oratory there, the London House having written to say so. I doubt not they have written to all the Houses they thought I should go to. We fancied the Fathers knew about us at Florence. The direction of a letter in the writing of Fr Stanton was on the Pope's table, addressed to Mgr Barnabo, with the word 'Palazzo' on the cover. It was a copy of the same paper that was on Fr Conca's [sic] table.[2]

The Pope appointed us in the kindest way to see us by ourselves; we were with him from three quarters of an hour to an hour. He began by saying I was thin and had done much penance—and that Fr Ambrose had got older. We began by thanking him for his many favors, which pleased him. He said 'Ah you are come about a question;' and we both say that he went on to say something hurriedly (tho' not disapprovingly) about the English Congregation being *one*—Fr Ambrose, if left to himself, would say without hesitation that the Pope said or implied that I had come to make myself head of the whole Congregation. He has no doubt of it, and was almost going to interrupt—and said to me, some time after, when the Pope went into the next room (as I shall tell you presently) 'he has not got to the bottom of it.' I only wish my knowledge of Italian was sufficient to have followed him as minutely. We both agree that he went on to say 'We must think of it—' or 'a thing of deep consideration,' or 'for a Congregation.' He rather mumbled.

Then he went on to speak in extenso of various things, as if to put us on our ease, as we afterwards found—but we both thought at the time (of course independently of each other) that he really was going to avoid the whole subject, for some reason or other. He talked of Santa Croce, his own troubles, Talbot '*my* friend' and the Antilles[,] Dr Cullen, Dr McHale, the Irish wrongs, Lucas, the Cardinal (Wiseman) his lectures on the Concordat—my Conferences—Dr Briggs—the Immaculate Conception etc etc

He then spoke of the Cardinal's trial—and said *I* got better off, for I had a large sum over, and said he was pleased that I had given it to the University.[3] Fr Ambrose said I was building a Church there, which seemed much to please him. Some how or other he came abruptly to the subject of our matters, so much so that he was in medias res before I knew he had begun. Fr Ambrose recollects the *order* of things better than I do. The Pope now said that he had an image of St Philip, given him by an old priest, no great thing, but dear from memory—he had had it over his bed for 18 years. He said he would give it me, and went to fetch it. (I should have said that, in answer to his words on beginning our matters, Fr Ambrose had said that we had come to see various Oratories and especially Chiesa Nuova, and to learn most exactly the traditions of the Oratory. I fancied he did not quite like the 'most exactly' and said to Ambrose, 'with adaptation to present circumstances,' which Ambrose *said*, and the Pope seemed gladly to catch up. I saw how the land lay, and saw that he conceived that we were sticklers for old forms. He asked if we had been to Turin and seemed pleased, and mentioned the Blessed Sebastian—and he was pleased about our being at Florence.)

He returned, not only with the image, but with the letter of the London House, which I have spoken of above. He began reading it to himself till he got to some words about me—and he said they speak of you as their Founder and most kind Preposto—' (startled, I put in 'di Birmingham.') He then went on to ask in a kind and confidential and feeling way 'Is there not some quarrel "briga" (difference) between you—' I assured him not—and Ambrose took this opportunity to make an oration. 'If your holiness will allow me,' he began, 'I will explain the whole matter—' and then most clearly narrated how the London House had asked to hear the confessions of nuns, (which was useful doubtless in their case,) and that Mgr Barnabò had written to our Bishop to consult him about giving the faculty to *us*, without our wishing it—which would make the Oratory seem one order. The Pope nodded his head and said 'Adesso capisco tutto,' or very much that. He went on to allude to what he had done to the London House, and said in a serious confidential tone 'I will tell you my mind about Nuns. It's not my wish you should have them—Nuns should be in this day rather active then contemplative. As to contemplative, I do not wish you to have to do with Scaramelli and other writers of mystical theology. It takes you too far. You might waste a good deal of time,' or some such words. We asserted that we had many works and nuns would take up our time. We said that the nuns in our case were 'lontano'—that in London they were round about them. We said that at Florence there was a Father lost his vocation even by extraordinary confessorship, and that the Fathers actually passed a rule that even extraordinary confessorship should not be undertaken. He listened with the most serious interest. Then we said that in England extraordinary confessorship was an uffizio fisso—3 times a year. He made a noise with his tongue and teeth, and said 'that will never do.' He then said 'Have you not a Father who is well adapted to hear the Confessions of nuns'—we answered that we had one who was most learned and pious, but we feared it would hurt the regularity of the House, if he *was* much away as extraordinary confessor.

Ambrose went on to recount what we did at Birmingham—a large parish—a poor house with hospital (he said, 'Good, Good—') a jail—schools etc. (He said 'Tutto eccelente [*sic*].') and that nuns did not suit us—and that what suited one Oratory need not suit another—and that all we wanted was that each Oratory should do its own work. He said 'Ne penserò io.' '*I* will see to that.' Upon this, I drew out the Supplicas which I had prepared. He looked serious as if something was coming. The first was a petition for the formation of a female Oratory—Ambrose prefaced it by speaking of the Sisters of Charity, Hospitals etc. The Pope he read it aloud with interest and then said 'Trovo buono—this can be granted—' and went on to tell us that in this age women did more than men and quoted St Paul to show that the weak do more than the mighty. Then I offered a Supplica for an indulgence on writing books, keeping boys (gentlemen's sons) and cultivating music and painting, and he read it to himself and said 'Trovo anche questo buono—' Then I brought out the Supplica for the Office for St Philip's heart saying 'Questo forse è più difficile—' he repeated the words 'What, più difficile?' looking sly (*we* both think as if some cat was coming out of the bag—) When he had read it, he said 'But the Fathers at Rome have not this—' Ambrose added that I had composed an office—He said 'All that's a matter to be examined and approved—' and added 'We will think of that too—' and put it with the other Supplicas. He said he would consult with Mgr Barnabò, and would see me another time. On this Ambrose said that I wished to get off, for Mgr Cullen had written for me—and he answered 'You mean to say that you want us to be quick it's not a great time to Sunday.'

Then we moved; kissed his ring, received his blessing, and then asked his blessing on the Congregation—which he gave solemnly—blessing patres et fratres totius congregationis.—

Ever Yrs affly J H N

Jan 29. Yesterday (Monday) morning, when Ambrose called, he found Barnabò *most* gracious. It was plain that the Pope had spoken well of us. He took him by the button, and tenderly hinted at his omission in putting Supplicas before the Pope, which he (the said B.) had not seen. He said that the Pope had simply put aside the Supplica for the heart of St Philip, from the danger, if he went beyond the Sacred Heart and the Immaculate Heart, he should have other orders and congregations petitioning, and it would be endless; however, the other two were granted, only he wanted explanations to be able to draw up the Rescripts. He saw me, with Ambrose, today (Tuesday) and we then presented a Supplica for the Blessed Sacrament in our House, which we take for granted we shall obtain. And then, which is so important and extraordinary that I have not got over my surprise, on my presenting a Supplica for the Pope to have, asking that nothing done by the Holy See by one Oratory might affect another, he said that he would present it, if I wished, but he advised *not*, because the grant of it would *diminish* my power, inasmuch as I was *Deputato Apostolico* for setting up the Oratory in any part of England (He said that our Brief was to be extended by Rescript to Ireland, where I suppose I should have the same Office.) This information is in itself unexpected and puzzling. He repeated it several times. It agrees indeed precisely with what Mgr Palma said originally—but it disagrees with the Oratories we have consulted, with Fr Concha especially, and with our Canonico of S. Maria in Trastevere, who saw our Brief. I can only explain it by supposing that Propaganda overrides Canon Law.[4] Another remarkable view it opens is this—that, in setting up a House, I may make *conditions*, if not inconsistent with the Brief and Rule. And this seems to be Barnabò's meaning, in saying that, for the Pope to rule any thing about the independent *action* of Oratories, is to limit my existing power. A question too arises, whether the London House is legitimately set up, *till* I express it in some formal act or document, tho' this is for *them* to determine, and is no look out of mine. We ought to be very thankful—for every day clears up our case and position more and more. I have had a good deal of talk too from Barnabò, (evidently from the Pope) about the University—but about this I shall only say that I see my position much better than I did. Every thing is turning out well— and I can never feel any thing but thankfulness and satisfaction that I have come here. Ambrose is beginning to suffer from diarrhoea, sore throat etc. The changes of climate, and *in themselves* first the scirocco and then the tramontane are most trying.

Jan 31. We have just been again to the Vatican. We *cannot* get the Monsignori to fix a time of taking our departure. This alone keeps us. Mgr Borromeo said this morning, that perhaps we should have it on Sunday. We propose to come by the Tuesday ⟨February 5⟩ Neapolitan boat, which goes straight to Marseilles.

I add obiter. (1) The reason which made me give up the notion of sending in *doubts* to Propaganda in addition to those which I gave, was that we heard that Propaganda might keep them 4 months! and we might have been kept here for the answers!

(2) Fr Concha says that he held the office of preacher to the Galley slaves for 26 years—at one time, against the will of Father Superior and Congregation, being supported by the Cardinal Vicar.

Write at once to Penny to say I expect to start by the boat of the 5th which comes direct for Marseilles (tell him to tell the Archbishop and Dr Leahy)

... I delivered [the third Supplica] to Mgr Barnabò about a quarter of an hour ago, and withdrew it on his saying from the Pope, in the presence of Father Ambrose, that I was in virtue of the Brief Deputato Apostolico (he mentioned the terms several times) for the foundation of Houses in England, as St Philip was appointed by the Holy See to do so. If, therefore this Supplica was granted, I should, in his opinion, lose power, not gain it. He said of course strongly that, when the House was once founded, it was out of my hands.

January 29, 1856.   J H Newman

P.S. (Jan 29) He said also, that one of the three Bishops[5] referred to by himself, on Fr Faber's application to Propaganda, had been adverse to the dispensation and that the Pope had agreed with this Bishop and had said to Mgr Barnabò let us steer a middle course, and give a dispensation ad interim for three years. Barnabò also said that he himself had wished that the Oratory of England should keep to the Rule, as it had already been adapted to England.

Birmingham Febr. 12 1856. I should add that the Pope in his first conversation with us said that he had not granted to the London House the *temporal* care of nuns at all.

J H N. A. St. J.

[1] Bishop Ullathorne, when consulted, had supported the London application, as he was anxious to use Dalgairns to hear nuns' confessions in the Birmingham Diocese.

[2] This was the 'Relazione dei Padri della Congregazione dell' Oratorio di Londra' to Propaganda. The word 'Palazzo' on the envelope meant that it was to go to Pius IX. The harm done to Newman by the London Oratory letter to Propaganda was lasting. When Bishop Brown delated Newman's *Rambler* article on the Laity in the autumn of 1859, the reply came back on 17 November that Barnabò was not surprised, in view of the delation a few years earlier (Archives of Propaganda, *Lettere e Decreti, 1859*, Vol. 350, f. 764).

[3] Wiseman had been sued for libel by one of his priests, Richard Boyle.

[4] Thus Newman withdrew the tentative proposal in his letter of 10 December 1855 to Wiseman, because it would have limited his power as founder of the Oratory in England. It was this proposal that had provided the basis for the suggestion that he aimed at a Generalate.

[5] Bishop Thomas Grant of Southwark argued that the dispensation was unnecessary as the Rule already gave the Oratorians discretionary powers.

To Mrs John Mozley

6 Harcourt Street Dublin Febr 22/56

My dear Jemima,

Thank you for your affectionate letter. I came from Rome in less than four days to London, and was down and slept at Birmingham the same night. I left at 7½ PM on the Monday, and was at Birmingham by midnight on the Friday. We came from Cività Vecchia to Marseilles in a beautiful Naples boat, and the sea and sky were both superb. We were only 27 hours in the voyage. Another 23 hours took us to Paris. In going I made a long circuit, viz by Lyons, Turin, Milan, Verona, Venice, Bologna, Florence, and Rome, with much fear of streams full, waters out, roads broken, and robbers abroad, but, I am thankful to say, with no impediment. One time we had to be dragged through a stream, another to get into a boat in the dark and wet, another time to be dragged out of the mud by 8 horses and 4 oxen, at another to be eased (our wheels) over a deep ravine by men's arms and shoulders, the terrace having disappeared under the fall of the rocks above, and at another to be brought straight when our wheel in the dark had got over a parapet—with a rising of the mob here a fortnight before, and the murder of a Frenchman there within a month or two, and shooting of 500 brigands within the last few years by the Austrians, and so on, but most happily with no trouble or inconvenience at all. We crossed Mont Cenis in glorious weather, were at Venice in a thick fog, but saw

San Marco, the most wonderful church I ever saw, knelt at St Athanasius's tomb at Venice, and at St Ambrose's at Milan, was mistaken, I suspect, for Frank by the Austrian police at Milan, and ate, I am sure, cat cutlets at Bologna, but got to Rome quite safe and well, where I remained above three weeks. While there I had two telegraphic despatches from Birmingham, which took from six to eight hours coming.

I don't like to boast, but I seem getting better and better every year. I am much relieved to say that there is not a chance of my being made a Bishop, which seemed settled a year or two ago. I have got most beautiful presents, chains, crosses etc, made to me by various friends on the prospect of it.

I found scarlatina here in my house on my return—but I trust it is gone. Harry Ryder and Aubrey de Vere had it here in the summer.

I have heard nothing from Frank about his experiment on Charles, and therefore have not sent any money.[1] I inclose a cheque for £20, if you will be at the trouble of keeping it till wanted. By which I mean, I don't want money wasted on him, or in experiments about him. But since I am able to give it just now, I put it out of my hands while I can.

Ever Yrs affly J H Newman

Mrs John Mozley

[1] See letter of 10 May 1855 (*L.D.* XVI, pp. 464–5). Jemima, Frank, and he were trying to work out how best to support Charles who was, by 1858, to settle in Tenby for the rest of his life.

To Thomas Grant, Bishop of Southwark

6 Harcourt St Dublin March 7/56.

Private

My dear Lord

If the report is true, which I hear, that Francis Blunt is intended by his Guardian for Oxford, I am sure your Lordship is in considerable anxiety—and with the hope that you will not be displeased by my setting before you some suggestions, supposing your mind not to be made up on the subject, I have, after several days of uncertainty and fidget to myself, taken up my pen to write to you.[1]

Speaking according to my knowledge of Oxford, I should say that it was a place very dangerous to a young man's faith—and, though he might be preserved from defection, he might be indelibly stamped with indifferentism, which would be his character thro' life.

He would be saved from this, if there were a Catholic *Hall* or *College* there, but this leads me to another aspect of the subject, which is my real reason for writing to you.

Every one looks at things from his own point of view, so your Lordship must make allowances for me, if I am personally alarmed at the notion of the Bishops of England allowing (should they allow) young Catholics to go to the English Protestant Universities. What is Ireland to me, except the University here is a University for England, as well as for Ireland? I wish to do good, of course, to all Catholics if I can, but to *English* Catholics, as is my duty. I have left England for a while, for what I conceive to be a great *English* interest. But, if I went by my own wishes or tendencies, of course I would far rather do good to English Catholics in Oxford than in Dublin.

However, the Holy See decided that Dublin was to be the place for Catholic education of the upper classes in these Islands, and, under this decision, I acquiesced in the wish of the Irish Bishops to have me here. But, if there is a College for Catholics in Oxford, or anything approaching to it, I am at once loosened from this place. And I should give as my reason, that I have a call nearer home. Oxford is close to Birmingham.

Nor only as regards myself would the allowance of Catholic youths to go to Oxford unsettle this nascent University. You may easily fancy that Catholic youths here look up with admiration and curiosity to Oxford. The Irish, as well as English youths, would wish to go there and this University would have to seek not only Rectors and Professors, but students altogether. As it is, I am very much alarmed, and have been for this year past, lest our youths, having spent a year or two here, should transfer themselves to Oxford, and make us merely tutors or providers of a Protestant Institution—but, if it is known here that a Catholic youth actually is in Oxford with the leave of a Catholic Bishop, the consequences may be serious.

For myself, I have only to look, and I hope I do look at what the Holy See wishes. It has fixed on Dublin as the seat of Catholic Education—and, till it undoes its work, it is of course my duty to do all I can to advance it.

Whatever judgment you form of this letter, I am sure you will kindly give it the attention suitable to the sincerity with which I trust it is written.

I am, My dear Lord, begging your Lordship's blessing Ever Yours affectly in Xt

John H Newman of the Ory

[1] Religious tests for entry to Oxford were abolished in 1854. In fact, Francis Blunt did not go there.

To Archbishop Cullen

6 Harcourt Street ⌈April 12/56⌉

My dear Lord,

⌈I thank your Grace for your letter just received.[1]

I am very glad to have elicited your Grace's questions. I should have been still more gratified to have elicited them some time ago; but your Grace is the judge whether they could have been asked at an earlier date.

I will wait on your Grace whenever you will appoint.⌉

Your faithful Servant in Xt John H Newman of the Oratory

His Grace The Archbishop of Dublin

[1] [[containing questions about my church which had been building for the past year and thus was just ready for opening.]] Cullen had written about the length of the lease as an obstacle to consecration, about which priests would officiate there, about whose Church it would be, were Newman to leave, and about those who would preach there.

To Richard Stanton

Oratory Edgbaston. May 27. 1856

My dear Fr Secretary

In replying to the Letter of your Congregation of May 22, I wish first to renew the words of affection towards your Fathers, contained in my last letter to them.[1] These will serve as a response by anticipation to the expressions of love and respect which they now unanimously offer to me.

They cannot wish me to use language more emphatic than I used in the letter in question. I said that, even after the receipt of their letter, I had not any but the tenderest and most grateful feelings towards them. I added that their very act, which had so much affected me, did but make me love them the more.

That act remains in force; and, unintentional at first, now embodies a deliberate principle. I will explain what I think of it.

Our Rule is our vocation, as far as any thing external can be so called. Were our rule other than it is, without less devotion to St Philip, perhaps we should never have been his children. To touch a Rule, is to unsettle vocations; to create suspicions about its stability, is to weaken the hope, which those who have embraced it humbly entertain of their own perseverance. We find in the Life of St Alfonso, how deeply a religious body is stirred, when some of its members, unknown to the rest, meddle with its Rule. 'A report became current among us,' says the writer, 'that innovations were to be made in the Rule, and general alarm ensued.' When these innovations had taken place, St Alfonso said, 'I deserve to be dragged at a horse's tail, for I ought to read every thing myself, as I am Superior.'[2]

What professes to be an interpretation, may really be an alteration. The Rule of the Oratory gives the Fathers of any House the power of interpreting it, when they can do so, for themselves. Houses may differ in their view of the clearness or obscurity of particular portions. When then a House appeals to Rome for an authoritative interpretation of a portion which it considers doubtful, adding its own comment, and not allowing to other Houses an opportunity of sending in their own views of it also, it is running the risk of the confusion and unsettlement of those other Houses, by what is relatively to them an unexpected, uncalled for alteration of the terms on which they gave themselves to St Philip. And if that House does so once, perhaps it will do so twice, perhaps it will do so many times.

Your Fathers have asked at Rome an interpretation of a Decree which belongs to us at Edgbaston as well as to them; an interpretation consequently, which, if obtained, would have affected us, as well as them; nay with which, in matter of fact, we were threatened for some time. This they did, without telling us what they were doing; and that, though they know that others knew it, and were consulted upon it.

I expostulated; and with what effect? Si pater ego sum, ubi est honor meus?[3] First, they gave me no notice what they were doing; then, they put aside my expostulation; now they ask my blessing. Do they ask a blessing on their unanimous, their persevering refusal to co-operate with me, in any way whatever, in providing against the recurrence of what they know I feel to be a great danger?

One thing more they did: they conveyed their unanimous, deliberate refusal in official notes, compositions, with balanced periods, and nothing besides them.

I am sure on reflection they will see that there is much in all this to affect me with the most lively surprise and the deepest pain.

To the mode, indeed, in which they conveyed their refusal, I am resigned. I withdraw my complaint so far, and wish them to take no notice of it. Certainly, I had hoped that, till the end of my life, they would have ever acted towards me familiarly, as towards a father. It cannot be. I forget the lapse of time. Forms, I own, are necessary. I was wrong in wishing them dispensed with.

Your Fathers, however, will see, that the substance of my complaint remains. Up to this time, they have done nothing, they have suggested nothing, to remove a difficulty, which as I reminded them, may one day be theirs as well as ours.[4] I have secured indeed my own House, while I live, at the trouble and expense of a journey to Rome; but I look to the future.

I should not be true to St Philip, if I acquiesced, as long as I lived, in a danger, which I could not under the circumstances have conjectured, when I set them up; which has so significantly manifested itself; and which exposes the English Houses, such close neighbours as they ever must be, to an external arbitrary action upon each other, the ultimate result of which it is not difficult to prophesy.

> I am, Dear Father Secretary, Yours in St Philip
> John H Newman of the Oratory

The Revd Father Secretary &c

[1] See the letter to the London Congregation of 19 November 1855.

[2] A. M. Tannoia, *The Life of S. Alphonso Maria de Liguori*, v (London, 1849), pp. 3, 12.

[3] *Malachi* 1:6. Besides acknowledging their obligations to Newman, the London Oratorians were in the habit of calling him 'The Father'.

[4] Letter of 8 November 1855 to Faber.

To Cardinal Wiseman

6 Harcourt Street Dublin June 7. 1856

My dear Lord Cardinal,

I rejoice to hear that we are to have your Eminence's panegyric. Thank you very much for the honor you do me in proposing to give me a place in your Dedication.[1] I hope you will not think I presume upon your kindness, if I accept it with a *condition*. That condition is, that, if I am not to stand by myself in the Dedication, you will be kind enough to include the Birmingham Fathers in it. You will not think it wonderful, that, separated as I am from them just now, I should jealously desire their protection. Your Eminence knows that ours is an Institution of a very domestic character. The Father Superior is hardly a son of St Philip, when he is from home;

nor should I view myself with any satisfaction, when transplanted from my own Oratory[2]

I may have to send you a letter soon; but it will require no answer.

Thank you for what you say of Callista. I am very glad Propaganda has been in correspondence with your Eminence about the Universities,[3] and am, kissing the sacred purple,

Your affte friend and servt in Xt

John H Newman of the Oratory

His Eminence Cardinal Wiseman

[1] Wiseman wrote from London on 6 June, 'The London Oratory have wished to have my poor panegyric of St Philip published. I have consented, as it was taken down; but on condition of dedicating it to you and F. Faber jointly. I am sure you will not refuse me this favour. Indeed I will not trouble you to write your acceptance. I must not lose this first opportunity of thanking you for the great treat you have given me in Callista, which I have read with great delight, as so many others have.'

[2] In spite of this request, Wiseman published his joint dedication and also sent Newman's letter of 7 June to the London Oratory.

[3] This Roman correspondence concerned Newman's anxiety at this time that access for Catholics to Oxford would undermine his efforts in Dublin. See letter to Thomas Grant, 7 March 1856.

To Henry Bittleston

Dublin June 16. 1856

My dear Henry

Thank you very much for your affectionate letter just received. I am very glad to have it. I, like you, consider the conduct of the London Fathers simply *mysterious*.[1] No hypothesis solves it. I *cannot* consider them guilty of deliberate humbug. I think that most of them, knowing nothing of the circumstances and meaning of their act in applying to Rome, were angry at my original letter to Fr Faber, and thought it domineering and unjust; nor should I have written it in the very words I did certainly, had I dreamed of what was to be their course. Then I think Fr Faber and Fr Stanton were carried off their legs by this general feeling, and concurred in conduct which did not quite please them, as *the price of their all keeping together*. Then, I think they are ashamed to undo their own act as formally as they have done it—and they wished to soothe me with private letters from *individuals*. These I resisted—I said 'Undo your *public* act—do not put on *record* one line of action, and reconcile me to it with *private* explanations.' I know the great mischief of this, from long experience. Accordingly when Fr Antony in March last sent me a private explanation, I wrote him word, as I had written to Fr Stanton before, and to Fr Faber since, that I would not read it; that I could not, and would not; that, if any thing was to be retracted, the *body* must do it. This they all know perfectly well. I should think they *had* something to say, but were too proud to say it, *except* that they say that my last letter is 'a new view'—which seems to mean they have nothing to say against it. And Fr Faber says to me 'It is a new view—Oh that you had said it last November!'[2]

which implies that they would *not* have acted as they did, *had* they apprehended it; (tho' their *public* letter says they would have acted just the same.) ⟨This is an instance of what I mean about the difference between public and private explanations.⟩ I think with you that it is *no* new view, but then perhaps they were angry last November, and did not trouble themselves to consider what I said. Then I think there may be something rankling in consequence of my taking away F. Bernard,[3] and they may have said 'When will this end? we must stop him.' And then they may have thought 'He is in two positions—head of the Bm [Birmingham] House and our founder—and he unfairly comes over us in favor of the Bm House with his authority over us.' And then Fr Faber has persuaded himself that I told Fr Joseph that I was sorry I had had any thing to do with the St Wilfrid's *people*—If I *did* say any thing, I suppose I said '*St Wilfrid's*' meaning the house and establishment, which sadly plagued us, which we long doubted whether to take, and then whether to keep— and about which Fr Faber went to and fro. And he may have said to his Fathers now, 'This is all an excuse of Fr Newman's—he wishes to break with us any how—and has long wished it.'

But any how it is most mysterious—and for this reason—1. they did not accompany their official letters last November with any private one. 2. they never any where (unless it be in Fr Antony's letter which I would not receive) have given any one *reason why* they did not comply with my demand or request.

As to your wish to write to one of the Fathers, I neither say Yes or No *ultimately*— but certainly not at present. I have sent a letter to the Congregatio Deputata which ultimately will come before you—But *this* might be considered:—viz: even if you pass what the Congregatio Deputata is preparing, the *execution* of it, might be left to me—so that the Congregatio Generalis should not commit itself in *act* to the London House, though it pass the measure—till the propriety of your correspondence is considered. But any how, I don't think any correspondence will touch the advisableness of the measure I am going to recommend to the Congregatio Generalis which is, that the two Houses should be on the same terms mutually as two Oratorian Houses on the continent. *They* keep *very shy of each* other—*they* have found what we are finding. Where there is no common superior, communities must ignore each other, or they fall foul of each other. We shall be best friends, depend on it, (put aside the particular case) when we keep at a distance from each other, and now we have an *opportunity* of doing what must come sooner or later—and St Philip may mean it

Ever Yrs J H N

P.S. As to Nicholas. I don't like certainly his taking the children's confessions yet, unless it would worry him, not, and so be injurious to him.[4]

---

[1] Bittleston wrote on 14 June, bewildered by the behaviour, as he saw it, of the London Oratorians.

[2] This must have been in a letter, now lost, to which Newman had replied on 31 May.

[3] Dalgairns who had gone to London, but then returned to Birmingham, before going back to London.

[4] Darnell was still convalescent.

To Ambrose St John

July 7. 1856

My dear Ambrose

Nicholas and Robert are just gone—I told them the *substance* of the inclosed Draft[1]—and now am sending it to them at Post office, Killarney, bidding Nicholas send it back to you with his and (to save time) Robert's remarks as soon as possible.

The Congregatio Deputata will bring it before the General.

In the General Fr Bernard will be present—but the word 'unanimous' is not wanted, tho' he oppose it and vote against it.[2]

I think you should now lay on the table of the Generalis, the two propositions 1. about all Oratories and all religious communities—and 2. about not going to them without express leave. I am sorry they have not been voted on. However, they will realize to Fr Bernard his position. Let them be laid before the Congregatio Generalis by the Deputata, to be voted on, when we all come together. (I fear some time will elapse first.)

I think on the whole that the state of the London House is this—

1. *They* did not know what was going on with Fr Faber, Fr Dalgairns etc etc. or the *bearing* of going to Propaganda.
2. My letter to Fr Faber for them, made the whole body very angry, coming on them by surprise.
3. They thought *me* angry and unreasonable. Did not apprehend my case; thought my rushing off to London, rushing to Rome etc etc. impotent anger;—ditto my sending back the mitres—ditto my refusing any explanations except through the Congregation. All this is what they mean by unkindness and disrespect.
4. Fr Faber has a deep conviction, as he told me, that what I complained of, is but an excuse, that the roots of the matter lie deeper. He has pumped Fr Bernard, as well as Fr Joseph, and found out the impression of the former, that the breach cannot be made up, that I think him ambitious etc etc.
5. Accordingly they say, what is the good of our doing any thing for Fr Newman? We are only making ourselves inconsistent—and recurring to an unconstitutional authority, (viz that of a Founder,) which henceforth will be exerted *against* us, for he will never trust us or love us again.
6. As to Fr Faber himself, he now finds himself as he was before he sought the Oratory—independent, with all the additional advantages, which St Philip, extended reputation, and years give him. When he first heard in 1847 that I was joining the Oratory, his first feeling was as if I were incroaching on his province. Such was the tone of his letters to me at Rome. On my return he came to me, joined the Oratory, seized some of our more valuable subjects, went off, and now simply sets up for himself. I don't mean to say that all this has been of set purpose, but it is what has been the fact. (This is only for the Congregatio Deputata)
7. On the whole, I am relieved by their last letter. It shows there is nothing in the back ground. They have *no case*, except to say that I have been disrespectful. For a time I thought of saying (as Stanislas wished) some thing like this:—'Should

any of our subjects from the Father downwards, have shown any disrespect to your Father Superior or to your Congregation, he is most ready to apologize for it. This we earnestly wish to express to you—but after all, when it is done, the main question between the two Congregations lies as before, and is one of right and wrong, of justice, fairness and charity in acting. Such a question is not materially altered, though there has been warmth of manner, or rudeness, or exaggerated claims, or unreasonable acts, whether on the one side or the other. If there has been any thing of that kind on our part, this is a reason for your expostulating with us and asking its withdrawal; not for refusing what stands on merits of its own, independent of the mode in which it has been urged.'—But on consideration I thought it spoke for itself, to posterity—and did but make a long letter, which, like a long book, is a great evil—and perhaps would *provoke an answer*, and then we should have to write a rejoinder. I don't think they *can* have excuse to reply to the draft of the letter I inclose.

8. I repeat I do not see my way out of the Fr B. [Bernard] difficulty—how he can bear us, or we him[3]

Ever Yrs affly J H N

P.S. I infer from Stanislas's letter that he *has* lodged Burns's two cheques—or at least that he has received them, which is the point. Give him back William's letter inclosed.

[1] i.e. the draft of the letter of 10 July to the Fathers of the London Oratory, signed by St John and Edward Caswall. It declared: 'We are sorry to hear from you that our Father has treated you throughout the affair in an unkind and disrespectful way, both in the person of your Superior, and as a Congregation. We think it right to refer you to his letter of November 19th of last year, in proof that such was not his intention. We remain Yr affectionate Brothers in St Philip.'

[2] Dalgairns had returned from France and the letter was sent to London without alteration. The votes were unanimous.

[3] Dalgairns left the Birmingham Oratory and returned to London the following month.

To Ambrose St John

[6 Harcourt Street Octr 30/56]

My dear A

1. Do take care of Ryder's and my letters which I gave you on the morning I went to Liverpool.

2. Whatever H W [Wilberforce] has said of *himself* in that letter is secret.

3. ⌈You have more physical courage than I have—but somehow you lack moral courage (1) when you bid me fear Dr C's [[Cullen's]] writing to Rome—(2) when you bid me thank the Cardinal for the extreme rudeness of joining Fr Faber's name to mine against my leave.⌉ Certainly, if I say any thing it will be to fire off—so μὴ κίνει Καμάριναν.[1]

4. ⌈One hears tales of men who cannot speak and are bound, and taken to and fro at the will of others. Obmutui et non aperui os meum.[2] I go to Rome to be snubbed. I come to Dublin to be repelled by Dr McHale and worn away by Dr

Cullen. The Cardinal taunts me with his Dedications, and Fr Faber insults me with his letters. I would be let alone, but I have no means of defending myself more than if my hands and tongue were tied. I cannot explain any thing to friend or foe intelligibly. Ryder strikes me, for I can call it nothing else. When I drop a word to H W he talks of 'sensitiveness, which is the penalty of great ability,'⌐ I can only think of my own lines, tho' Christians are worse to bear than heathens, 'Sit in the gate and be the heathen's jest—silent and self possessed.'³ ⌐What enormous irritation Job must have felt, when his friends came and prosed to him. And then there is old Talbot with his platitudes, and Fr Dalgairns⌐ scouting my distinct request, and ⌐going on corresponding with our Fathers.⌐ What is to be the end of it? ⌐Dr Whitty talks of my being sent to Rome to advise them about the University. Catch me going except under a sacratissimum praeceptum.⌐ Cardinal Bo [Barnabò] would like all the gossip I could give him—for every word of mine *would* be gossip, not advice or counsel.

5. *Don't let Dr Whitty pump you.*

Ever Yrs affly J H N

¹ 'Do not disturb Camarina', the reply of the Delphic Oracle concerning the stagnant marsh outside the walls of Camarina in Sicily.

² *Psalm* 38:10.

³ 'The Patient Church,' *V.V.*, p. 92. There and in all earlier editions, Newman wrote 'Smiling and self-possess'.

To J. M. Capes

The Oratory, Bm Febry 1. 1857

My dear Capes

I have been reading the Rambler article on the University—and feel how sensible and important are the general views and principles which it puts forward.¹

...And now I will add a second thing, which apparently your Reviewer does not smell out—I say it in confidence—the narrowness and party-spirit of Dr Cullen. It must not be told, for it *would damage* us. Further, I will add that, if I have any personal annoyance, it is in his treatment of me. I will tell you his *rule* of acting—not once, or twice, but his rule and principle—to let me ask a question in June, to call about it again and again, to let me write to him about it in July, to let me write to his intimate friend to get an answer for me in August, to give up the chance of one in September, and in January accidentally to find he all along has been telling others that he *has* decided it in the way I asked him *not* to decide in, though even now in February he has not, directly or indirectly, answered me. I say, this is his way of doing business—and the sort of confidence he puts in *me*.

I entreat you not to breathe this—and having said it, I repeat, that it does not hinder at all our progress—nor my confidence of success—though that collisions are ahead, perhaps between clergy and laity, I do not deny. The breach between them in Ireland is fearful—the University may bring it out.

Ever Yrs J H N

[1] 'The Catholic University: its Difficulties and Prospects', The *Rambler* (Feb. 1857), pp. 83–98. Capes was the writer of the article. In the course of a long letter Newman made various comments that were appreciative, but also critical, before adding a further point.

To Henry Wilberforce

The Oratory Bm ⌈Febry 11/57⌉

My dear Henry

⌈Every one thinks his own blow worst—else, I should say I suffered as much as any one at the news I heard at Mrs Roberts's yesterday,⌉ just after you had been there.

⌈How was it no telegraph had come?[1] [[William Wilberforce said it was owing to the direct purpose of a certain person who did not wish him, W.W. to come over to Robert.]] I was saying Mass for him yesterday morning. Now I shall say Mass for his dear soul for seven days following. I began this morning.⌉

I am overwhelmed at the mystery of it—you as a brother. ⌈I parted from him [[at Rome]] on the 4th of February last year—he gave us dinner, etc. and we went from his rooms to the Diligence.

Alas. Alas. I never found it so difficult to say—God's will be done—. But I say it— only, we are superexceedingly blind—we know nothing—⌉

Love to your wife,

Ever, Yrs most affectionately, J H N

[1] Robert Wilberforce, who had been ill for several weeks, died on 3 February, and shortly beforehand, Manning, in Rome, had sent a telegraphic message that he was in extreme danger, but none to announce his death.

To Archbishop Cullen

Dublin April 2/57

My dear Lord,

⌈The time is now approaching for the resignation of the high office which the Bishops of Ireland have so condescendingly committed to me. I named the subject to your Grace just a year ago this month, and now I beg leave to name the day.

I will name next St Laurence's day, November 14th; when the six years will be more than completed since I began to devote my thoughts and exertions to the service of the University, and when the term of absence from my Congregation will have arrived for which I have asked permission.

My most urgent reasons for this step are, the fatigue which I experience from my frequent passages between Dublin and Birmingham, the duty of the Rector to show himself in public more than my strength will allow, for the good of the University, and the need to [my Congregation] of my services, which have been [so long] intermitted.⌉

I am, My dear Lord, Your Grace's faithful Servant in Xt

John H Newman of the Oratory

His Grace The Archbp of Dublin

To Sir John Simeon

The Oratory, Hagley Road Birmingham April 17/57

Private

My dear Sir John

I am going to take the liberty of writing to you on a subject, about which I have already been talking with John Pollen.[1]

I believe, (though I do not wish it known just now) that I certainly shall get away from Dublin at the end of this year, having set the University off, which is all I proposed to do. If, having done this, I could be instrumental also, in setting off another great Catholic desideratum, a public school, I should have cause of great thankfulness to Him who gives strength and opportunity for useful undertakings.

Of course the idea of a large school implies the existence of boys to fill it, and I suppose that in fact there are plenty, if their parents would send them.

However, it cannot be supposed that any great number would be got together at once. The school then would necessarily have a very modest beginning. And moreover, it would meet with great difficulties, as involving an opposition to existing Catholic schools, *if* it started with any great pretension.

It is this circumstance that leads me to think, that the Oratory could help in it. Ultimately a school must be in the country, but, while it is small and the members of it children, this neighbourhood, which is airy, high, and covered with trees and gardens, would not, I conceive, be inappropriate.

It would not be difficult to find a convenient house with a paddock close to us. And I should propose to start, if possible, with children about nine years old, under the care of some lady, Father Darnell, who is a Wykehamist, being the Paedagogue. In the course of four or five years, when the boys became old enough for a public school, some change in the plan might take place, and the Oratory would retire from the charge or not, according to circumstances.

However I am going too far, considering I know so little at present, whether others will think such a project possible. You will be more able than I am to decide both on the idea itself and on the mode of carrying it out. All I have to add is, that the Oratory would not like to be concerned in the financial part of it, or to receive any remuneration.

Believe me, My dear Sir John, with much esteem Yours most sincerely

John H Newman of the Oratory

Sir John Simeon Bart.

[1] See the letter of 28 January 1857 to Pollen (*L.D.* XVII, pp. 510–11).

To Ambrose St John

6 Harcourt St May 7/57

My dear A [[Ambrose]]

I read the Rambler for May last night, and am pained, and almost frightened, at the first article.[1] It is the second or third successive stroke, each louder than the one before. Capes is too good a fellow, for one to have any fears of *him*—but his articles both register, and will blow up and spread, bad feeling, very bad feeling. I look at them in connection with a letter I sent you a few days ago—and the more anxiously, because the two complaints are so entirely independent of each other.[2]

It seems to me that a time of great reaction and of great trial is before us. I earnestly trust I may be wrong. I will do my best to prove myself wrong. But it seems to me that really I may be *wanted* in England, and that there may be a providential reason, over and above the compulsion of the Fathers at Bm [Birmingham], for me to return. I have too little perhaps made myself felt—and, while some like Fr Faber are going ahead without fear, others are in consequence, even if not inclined of themselves already, backing and making confusion.

The Bishops are necessarily engaged in the great and momentous ecclesiastical routine. They are approving themselves good stewards in the sense in which St Carlo or St Francis were such—meanwhile, the party of the aristocracy and the party of talent are left to themselves without leaders and without guides.

It makes me wish I were to live twenty years in full possession of my mind—for breakers are ahead. Yet the battle is not given to the strong, and divine purposes are wrought out by the weak and unarmed—so that I am making myself of more importance than past history justifies. Still here I am, as yet alive and well—and I assure you my thoughts have turned among other things to the subject which Ward wishes me to pursue, more than they did.[3] Do pray for me that I may find out what use God wishes to put me to, and may pursue it with great obedience

Ever Yrs affly J H N

[1] 'The Political Future', *The Rambler* (May 1857), pp. 323–37, drew attention to the divisions among Catholics and claimed that they were lacking in political sense and prone to intemperate criticism. It decried the Independent Irish Party, spoke slightingly of Cardinal Wiseman, and remarked 'that the clergy and laity of Ireland happen to exercise their privilege of disagreeing in what is not of faith to a most wonderful extent'.

[2] This was a letter from Sir John Simeon, critical of the way some converts in particular were giving up English attitudes in favour of continental extravagance.

[3] i.e. the subject of faith and certainty.

To *Ambrose St John*

[2½ oclock PM May 12/57]

My dear A

⌈The poor Archbishop [Cullen] is just gone—I say 'poor,' because he was evidently so nervous and distressed, as to melt me internally, though I was very stiff or very much moved, both at once perhaps, during the short interview.

First he begged me to stop, for everyone said I must—for three years more, so as to make six from the opening of the University.

I reminded him how I had urged him to begin sooner, for I had lost my first years in waiting. Also, that I told him a year ago what was to be.

Next he said Propaganda would give a dispensation, he was sure, of non-residence [[at Birmingham]].

I said I was sure that the whole Oratory would go off to Rome to present in person an expostulation, rather than let such dispensation pass sub silentio.

Then he said some arrangement perhaps might be made, by which I should be more time at Birmingham—and a Vice Rector who might reside always [[in Dublin]].

I said I was sure the Fathers, as I myself, would do every thing possible to serve an undertaking which they expected so much from.

Lastly he said that perhaps some of the Bishops, perhaps an Archbishop, might write to the Birmingham Congregation.

I said that I knew well how grateful the Bm Fathers would be for such condescension—for myself, I felt extreme gratitude to the Bishops, some of whom had sent me most touching letters in answer to my announcement.

All this took place with pauses of silence on my part and his—and when I spoke, I spoke with great momentum [[?]]. I say all this to bring the scene before you.

Then he rose, and I rang the bell—and there must have been something unusual in our faces, for when Frederic came in, he [[F.]] looked frightened.

He then said that he had spoken to some Bishops about my Church—delay had been unavoidable—but he thought they would buy it for the University—and they would settle it when they met in a few weeks.

I think your answer should be most courteous, warm, and grateful. Apologetic, on the ground of the *real* need of a Superior at Bm—expressive of your desire to do all you could—and saying that you answered without delay out of reverence and gratitude, but you wished to be allowed maturely to think over the proposition]

Ever Yrs affly J H N

To Mrs John Mozley

The Oratory Birmingham August 31. 1857

My dear Jemima

Will you kindly tell me Frank's direction? He always expresses it in initials, which I fear the Post Office would not recognise.

I should not wonder, from what she says, that Miss Giberne will be paying you a call. If she should ask for any thing early of mine, handwriting, letters to me, letters from me, pictures etc, pray do not give her any thing. I can't help having the suspicion that she means, if she lives longer than I, to write some account of me—which I should not know indeed then, but the prospect of which I cannot endure.

I hope you are well and am My dear Jemima Ever affectly Yours

John H Newman

Mrs J Mozley

To Cardinal Wiseman

The Oratory, Birmingham September 14. 1857

(Copy)

My dear Lord

I have received the copy of the Decrees of the Second Provincial Synod of Westminster, which your Eminence has had the kindness to send me—and, having read the particular Decree to which you have called my attention, in your letter of the 26th of last month, I now proceed to reply to the communication with which you have honored me in the name both of your Eminence and of the Bishops of England.

A greater honor, I feel, could not possibly have been done me than that which your Eminence in that communication has conferred, in selecting me for the office of preparing an annotated English version of the Bible; and I beg your Eminence and through you the Episcopal Body, to receive the heartfelt and most humble acknowledgments, which so high and singular a mark of approbation and confidence demands at my hands.

If I accept the work put upon me without hesitation or reluctance, it is not as if I did not feel its arduousness to be as great as its honor, but because nothing seems left to me but to obey the expression of a wish which comes to me from your Eminence with the concurrence of a Provincial Council.

As soon as ever I am free from some great engagements which at the moment are pressing, I will without delay address myself to the work.

Meanwhile, I should very much wish to know, whether any general directions will be given me for its execution, beyond those which its object involves; and also, whether your Eminence wishes me to meet the initial and incidental expenses, which are involved in its preparation, and which I foresee will be considerable, by means of the copyright, or whether any other mode of covering them has suggested itself to your mind.

Kissing the sacred purple, and begging your Eminence's blessing, I am, My dear Lord, Your affte Servt in Xt

John H Newman of the Oratory

His Eminence The Cardl Wiseman

To Cardinal Wiseman

(rough copy)   6 Harcourt Street Novr 7 1857

My dear Lord Cardinal,

My silence, since the receipt of your Eminence's last letter,[1] wishing me to estimate the probable expense of the projected Translation of Holy Scripture, has arisen partly from my anxiety to obtain the necessary information, and partly from my dissatisfaction with any answer I could make, even when I had got it.

What I propose to do, is as follows:—to engage three of our Fathers in the work:—Fr St John, who has in past times made Hebrew his study, and in some measure Syriac,—Fr Darnell, who, beside his classical attainments, has been giving himself to German,—and Fr Caswall, whose taste in translations sacred and ecclesiastical is well known. And I thought of employing as assistant translators, Mr Wingfield, Mr Ward's brother in law, who has already employed himself in collating the Hebrew and Greek texts of the Old Testament, and Mr Scott, late Fellow of Brasenose, Oxford, who is not only a good scholar, but has made the sacred text his particular study. I am fitting up a room in our Oratory as a Scriptorium, and propose working there with the friends whom I have named.

I intend, however, first of all, to print some preliminary queries and remarks, and to send them round to the most competent judges in the English Catholic body.

According as the translation is ready, I should print it in four portions, of which the N.T. [New Testament] would be the first; submitting each portion in succession to the Revisors whom your Eminence may appoint, receiving it back, making the corrections, and either striking off editions or taking off the stereotype plates; as the case may be, and then going on to another portion, till all four were through the press. Thus the quantity of type required will be a fourth of the whole type of the Bible, or, as the required number of letter types may run unequally in different letters of the alphabet, say a third.

As to the size of type and the general getting up of the Edition, it may be either a Library book, with a large type and on good paper, to be sold at a high price as a Princeps Editio, or it may be a popular stereotyped low-priced edition of (say) 10.000 or 20.000 copies.

What then I have to calculate, is the *additional* expense of the translation, over and above that of merely bringing out an Edition of Holy Scripture, which of course can be made to pay itself by the sale of the copies printed.

The additional expenses are 1 the preliminary matter or prolegomena. 2. the books. 3 the desks, racks, tables the fittings of the work room. 4. the translators and transcribers. 5. the cost of type kept standing during the revision. 6. the press men for copies for Revisors, and the extra composition after correction. 7 sundries, (e.g. parcels) etc.

I attempt to calculate them thus:—

	£ s.d
1. Prolegomena	100.0.0
2. Books, (I have already laid out towards £40, in editions of the Bible etc)	200.0.0
3. Desks and other fittings up	50.0.0
4. Transcribers 0.0.0. Translators (Mr Wingfield £100 for two years)	200.0.0
5. Purchase of type kept standing of one third of the Bible (cost of type of *whole* Bible £1000—sale of type after 3 years £250, resulting expenses £750 Therefore, for one third of the Bible = 750/3 or	250.0.0
6. Press men 0.0.0. compositors for whole Bible are £220—say half as much again for corrections	100.0.0
7. Sundries	50.0.0
Total	£950.0.0

⟨N.B. I shall add £50 for Scott—and to make the whole £1000.⟩

Of this £950, a good part would be ultimately recovered by the profits of the sale of 20.000 stereotyped copies.

The loan of the type, (the purchase and sale of which entered into the above calculation,) for the purpose of the selling edition should be deducted from the £950, and thrown on the edition. I do not know what charge printers make in printing a book for a customer, for the use of their type, but whatever it is, it should be put against the £250 for type which forms part of the £1000.

I have not thought of renting type (instead of purchasing it) because it is impossible to find enough available at any printer's, at least in Birmingham, where the printing must be.

I have not thought it necessary to take any account of the expense of notes, headings etc., because the calculations which I have used have been made from the copies of the Douay.

The large type (Bourgeois) which I inclose would be not only handsomer, but easier to read for the Revisors. As I have mentioned the Revisors, is it asking your Eminence too much, to express a wish, at the commencement of my anxious work, that you would inform me, who the Revisors are to be.[2]

I am &c J H N

His Eminence Cardinal Wiseman

[1] Wiseman had written on 6 October, retaining the copyright for the whole English-speaking Catholic body, but also inquiring about expenses.

[2] Wiseman replied in a letter of 13 February 1858 that he and Bishops Grant of Southwark and Ullathorne of Birmingham had been appointed as revisers.

To Ambrose St John

⌈6 Harcourt Street Nov 17/57⌉

My dear A

I think it cruel that no one has sent me one line about Stanislas, after telling me he was ill. I have been watching every post. You and Henry both said there were lumps in his throat—I asked inside or out—no answer.[1]

The truth is you are bound up in the Raccolta with an attachment which is quite worldly. ⌈I *thought* that article came from the Brompton Oratory and it turns out it did. I said to myself 'the impertinence of praising us⌉ and limiting the praise to *publications*, as if that was our ἔργον.[2] I mean the Review implied that we were worth nothing unless we wrote religious books for the public. The word 'sanctification' when alluding to the Dublin youths was of the same kind. ⌈Don't send me Fr Faber's letters.⌉ I have read *neither* of them. I know they would make me angry. ⌈I think it very impertinent his reviewing you—certainly, his speaking of us and of me.⌉ *Of course* he is getting over you; and you like a goose have let out to someone or other that I am the author of the translation of the Anima.

I don't like your answer to him at all. If you thank him, you are preferring yourself to the whole Oratory—for he is *not* to be thanked for speaking of *us*. What I said to myself was 'Why cannot the reviewer let us alone?' Nor should I say as you do 'more than I deserve;' it is not more than you deserve—but I wish you would not be set on human praise. This I was going to write to you quite independent of hearing from you that the article is Fr Faber's. He is the fox, complimenting you on your beauty, and hoping to get hold of the cheese, which is myself.

⌈I think you should say no more than 'Thank you for the kindness which dictated your review—I hope you have got rid of your attack.'[3]

I was fuming at the impertinence of the writer praising 'the Birmingham Oratory' and now I find it is Fr Faber! He wishes to sooth us like children who are teething. 'Pretty Dear.'⌉

Ever Yrs affly J H N

I hope to be with you Friday morning.

Depend upon it, you have put your foot into [it] by your letters to F F Faber, and Dalgairns—and they are laughing at you.

[1] Flanagan himself wrote on 18 November that 'it was a misuse of the word to say I was *ill*. I was nothing more than seedy and off my oats. I had, it is true, lumps in my throat, *inside*, but they quickly disappeared'.

[2] 'Employment'.

[3] St John used these phrases in his reply. Faber was suffering from what he feared was 'calculus in the kidney'.

To John Hungerford Pollen

The Oratory Bm Octr. 8. 1858

My dear Pollen,

Thank you for the novel. What a shame you should buy it for me—I thought it was a 3 volume work. I have not yet had time to read it—but I looked at the beginning, and one thing touched my fancy so much, that, after I was in bed last night, I am ashamed to say, I burst out laughing, and, when I woke in the middle of the night I began laughing again.[1]

As to your coming down next week I find that Miss Farrant stops here till next month for certain—therefore take your choice of coming down as you propose, or when the Altars are ready.

Ever yrs affly John H. Newman of the Oratory

J. H. Pollen Esq

[1] What was the novel? Can the novelist have been Trollope whose popularity was only beginning? *Barchester Towers* was first published in 1857 and the one volume copy still in Newman's room at Birmingham was published in 1858. Several things could have amused him in Chapter I, 'Who will be the new bishop?'

To P. N. Lynch, Bishop of Charleston

Oy Bm Dec 7. 1858

My dear Lord

I have to thank your Lordship for your obliging letter and the Document which accompanies it.[1] I cannot at the moment make a more suitable answer to it than by explaining to you and the other Prelates of the Province of Baltimore the relation in which I stand to the great work which the 2nd Synod of Westminster proposes, and the circumstances which have brought me into that relation.

I esteem it a great honor to hold it, and a great honor also to be made the subject of your Lordship's letter and of the Resolutions of your Rt Revd Brothers, and for my name to be associated in such a matter with your Archbishops

Soon after the 2nd Synod of Westminster, held at Oscott in July 1855, while I was in Dublin in my then duties in the new University, on my return here for the Vacation, my Diocesan, Dr Ullathorne, said in the course of confidential conversation 'we have put into your hands the duty of preparing a new translation of Scripture,' or words to that effect. The information simply took me by surprise, as I had not turned my thoughts that way, and I supposed I should have heard of it officially in a little while. This anticipation was not fulfilled for a reason to be stated presently and in consequence the subject passed from my mind, nor did I take any one step towards it.

So matters rested for above two years—when (under date of August 26. 1857) I received the following most gracious communication from our Cardinal Archbishop—'I beg to call your attention to the ninth Decree of the 2nd Provincial Synod of Westr [Westminster] p 30, "De Versione canonicarum scripturarum." You will easily understand, how it would have been inconvenient, not to say unfair, to have inserted the names of any persons in a Decree subject to approval or disapproval, in substance and in details, by a higher authority. And therefore no persons were named in the Decree itself. But the Bishops in reality had agreed, at the time they drew up the decree, that to you was to be committed the grave and most important work proposed in it, and that you had to select and name the persons whom you would wish to have for assistants in the undertaking.... But further, in the Letter, explanatory of the Decrees, which I forwarded to the Sacred Congregation of P.F. [Propaganda Fide] with the Acts of the Synod, I explained who were the "viri docti" contemplated in this decree, that is, yourself and your Colleagues. So that the approbation of this Decree has been granted by the Holy See with the cognisance and approbation of this circumstance ... I now therefore, in behalf of myself, and my episcopal brethren, request you to accept this expression of the confidence reposed in you by the English Episcopate, and to undertake etc.'

On receiving this letter, I requested a copy of the Acts and Decrees of the Synod, and found, at p 30, the following Decree:—

'Ut versio accurata Sacrae Scripturae ex vulgatâ Latinâ quam primùm habeatur, Patres censuerunt committendam esse viris doctis ab Eminentissimo Archiepiscopo eligendis ejus confectionem, servatis tamen regulis Indicis etc (quoad operis revisionem, notas apponendas ex SS Patribus et piis scriptoribus desumptas, et permissionem et approbationem lectionis ejusdem.)'[2]

Considering the great confidence and the great honor shown to me in this act of the united Episcopate of England, the authority of a Synod, and my duty as a priest to concur in its decisions, (to say nothing of the concurrence of the Holy See) and on the other hand the extreme ungraciousness and ingratitude of declining so high a mark of its consideration, I wrote a letter to the Cardinal, on the September 14th following, in acceptance of his Eminence's proposal. At the same time I asked among other questions, the very difficult one, how the expenses of the work were to be met.

To this question I did not receive any answer, owing to the great perplexities attending it, till a few weeks ago, when Dr Clifford, Bishop of Clifton, sent me the following official notice of 'resolutions passed at the Bishops meeting relating to the translation of the Bible March 10. 1858. "Dr N. [Newman] having proposed two alternatives respecting the expense of publishing a translation of the Holy Scripture, it was agreed to allow the copyright to be reserved to Dr Newman, etc"' Dr Clifford's letter is dated October 11 last.

And now, my Lord, I have told you every thing that has passed on the matter. Were I called on to relinquish the work at this moment, the only personal inconvenience I should sustain, would be the loss of a sum, considerable to me, though not great in itself which I have laid out in books etc etc for the prosecution of it.

As to considerations, which are not simply personal, but which have a just claim to decide my course of acting, on the one hand I feel the most extreme reluctance and pain in seeming to come into competition in such a matter with the Archbishop of Baltimore, a man so immeasurably superior to me, in station, in services to the Church, in theological knowledge, in reputation, in qualifications for the work, and in careful preparation for it, (who moreover has actually given to the world complete and ready for the use of the faithful, so great a portion of it); but on the other hand I am pledged to the Bishops of England by duty, by gratitude, and by my word.

May I then beg of your Lordship to present my humble respects to the Bishops of your Province, and, in answer to their condescending message, to assure them that I am quite ready to concur in any measure on which the bishops of England shall determine[3]

---

[1] The Bishop of Charleston sent Newman a printed copy of Resolutions passed at the Ninth Provincial Council of Baltimore on 8 May 1858. Archbishop Kenrick of Baltimore had already published a translation from the Vulgate of the New Testament, the Psalms and Sapiential Books, while his translation of the rest of the Old Testament was prepared for publication. The Council proposed that Newman should be asked to cooperate with Kenrick in producing a joint version that could be used in all English speaking countries. The Bishop of Charleston in his covering letter of 11 November explained that the rest of the American Bishops concurred with those of the Province of Baltimore.

He hoped Newman would not find 'any serious difficulty' in the proposal. Wiseman and Barnabò had also been asked to approve.

[2] 'In order that an accurate version of Sacred Scripture from the Latin vulgate should be available as soon as possible, the Fathers decided that the work should be committed to learned men chosen by the most Eminent Archbishop, observing however, the rules of the Index, etc. (regarding the revision of the work, the notes supplied from the Holy Fathers and selected by holy writers, and both its permitted and approved reading.)'

[3] Wiseman, Grant, and Ullathorne, who had been appointed, on 10 March by the English Bishops, 'to arrange with Dr Newman the conditions and duration of the copyright' never did so; nor did Wiseman and the English Bishops reply to the proposal made to them by the Council of Baltimore, with the concurrence of the rest of the American hierarchy.

Dark Days
(1859–63)

The years immediately following Newman's return from Ireland in 1858 were probably the most difficult of his life. Challenges and controversies, personal and private, arose around him. Nothing seemed to be going well. In the circumstances it comes as no surprise to find him remarking in his Journal in January 1863 that, since he had been a Catholic, 'I seem to myself to have had nothing but failure, personally'.[1]

In the first place, soon after his final return from Dublin Newman found himself entangled in the affairs of the *Rambler*. His direct involvement was brief; he was in charge for only two issues; but the consequences were to haunt him for years.

The *Rambler* was a highly respected literary periodical, but it had provoked anger among the bishops for the independent and critical attitude taken by its lay editor, Richard Simpson, on ecclesiastical issues. Some bishops wanted to censure it in their pastoral letters, while others feared the scandal that censure would cause. The crisis was resolved by asking Newman, as a friend of Simpson, to persuade him to resign. That he did. But who then was to become editor in his place? It was soon obvious that Newman himself was the one person acceptable to both the bishops and the *Rambler*'s proprietors. His own bishop, Ullathorne, anxious to salvage the situation, invited him, therefore, to accept the position. Although reluctant, he accepted. Almost at once, however, matters began to get out of hand. In his first issue he expressed the *Rambler*'s loyalty to the Church, while he explained the contribution that could be made by educated laity, referring to the way their view had been consulted prior to the recent defining of the dogma of the Immaculate Conception. This reference to consultation stirred Dr John Gillow, a priest and professor at Ushaw College, the seminary near Durham, to declare such teaching virtually heretical. Newman was able at first to pacify Gillow, but the dispute led Ullathorne to suggest that Newman should give up the editorship. Newman was in a way relieved, although surprised by Ullathorne's sudden change of view. However, he had one other issue to prepare. He decided to use the opportunity to highlight the importance of the laity in the life and teaching of the Church. And so he came to write an article 'On Consulting the Faithful in Matters of Doctrine'. Gillow was roused once more and Bishop Brown of Newport formally denounced Newman to Rome.

At this point the waters become muddier. Newman, when he learnt what had happened, wrote to Cardinal Wiseman who was in Rome at that time, asking for clarification and wishing to explain any disputed points, while marvelling, but not

---

[1] *A.W.*, p. 255.

complaining, as he observed, 'that, after many years of patient and self-denying labour in the cause of Catholicity, the one appropriate acknowledgement in my old age should be considered to consist in taking advantage against me of what is at worst a slip of the pen in an anonymous un-theological paper'. Wiseman, whether through overwork, indisposition, or neglect, never brought this letter properly to the attention of the Roman authorities. Manning wrote to Newman to say that all would be resolved. And there matters remained, Newman doing nothing further because he assumed that all was well, while Rome interpreted his silence as recalcitrance. It would take another seven years for the issue to be brought to a close.

Reports would appear regularly at this time that Newman was about to return to the Church of England. Eventually in June 1862 he wrote a fierce letter to the editor of the *Globe*, declaring that 'the thought of the Anglican service makes me shiver, and the thought of the Thirty-nine Articles makes me shudder'. The extreme language, he explained to his Anglican friends, was not directed at them, but was an attempt to stem these reports.

A further initiative of these years was the founding of the Oratory School. Newman wanted to establish a school that would offer the academic excellence of England's renowned public schools, combined with the pastoral care and religious devotion of their Catholic counterparts. He had appointed Nicholas Darnell as its first headmaster, but here too there was a crisis. Darnell came to want complete control of the school and sought to exclude and undermine Newman more and more. He threatened to resign with the entire staff. But his bluff was called. While eventually he and two other teachers left in December 1861, Newman, with the help of friends, re-assembled the staff in time for the following term. The school was saved.

A more personal matter was the death of Faber. Newman had long since lost trust in Faber whose health was now declining. Wiseman wrote to tell Newman this news, but Newman already knew and had, as he remarked, the 'sad satisfaction' of visiting Faber for the last time in July 1863. There are letters in these years, rare but full of feeling, expressing that mistrust: '[Faber] was a person of great natural gifts, and of high aspirations, and of an impulsive affectionateness. His great fault was that he was not the same man two days running—you never could be sure of him.'

Towards the end of these years, however, a particular ray of light begins to penetrate the gloom, as friends from long ago, Isaac Williams, William Copeland, and Frederic Rogers, made contact with Newman again. And then, after a silence of seventeen years, Newman heard once more from John Keble. He answered: 'You are always with me a thought of reverence and love—and there is nothing I love better than you, and Isaac, and Copeland and many others I could name, except Him whom I ought to love best of all and supremely.'

Newman's trials were not over, but the intense darkness of these years was beginning to recede.

7

Dark Days (1859–63)

To Richard Simpson

The Oratory, Birmingham Febry 16. 1859

My dear Simpson,

Since Fr Darnell wrote the letter, which you will receive by the same post as brings this, I have had a second communication from our Bishop.

I am concerned to say that the Bishops who have met together on the subject of the Rambler, are determined to act very promptly and severely. My own notion is that they have instructions from Rome to do so.

I know it is asking you a great deal to beg you to come here, and at once. If you cannot, I will write to you—but I am under orders to use such haste in what I do, that I fear I must give you the trouble of telegraphing to me, if you cannot come; so that I may write to you by to-morrow's post.

It pains me exceedingly to entertain the very idea of the Rambler, which has done so much for us, and which is so influential, being censured from authority. And the scandal would be considerable. I don't know what the Bishops could do, if they exerted their power to the utmost—but I suppose they could forbid their clergy to read it. That they will not be satisfied without doing a great deal, and that at once, is quite clear.[1]

Ever Yours very sincerely, John H Newman of the Oratory

R Simpson Esqr

[1] Simpson replied in a letter dated Thursday, 4 p.m., on which Newman wrote in pencil 'Febr 17. 59,' that he could not reach Birmingham until Friday. He had already had to sit up for two nights with his brother Robert, who was deranged. Robert Simpson, a priest of the Southwark diocese, had been sent to him by Bishop Grant, on Monday 14 February, in order to be nursed. Richard Simpson complained, 'I wonder that Dr Grant, when he sent me my brother, did not also write to Dr Ullathorne to postpone the Rambler business. I hinted to him today that it was a little unfair.'

To Bishop Ullathorne

The Oratory Bm ⌈Febry 19. 1859

My dear Lord,

Mr Simpson most frankly put the whole question of the Rambler into my hands, and expressed his wish to abide by my decision.

I did not hesitate to recommend at once the course to which your letters directed me, viz his ceasing to be Editor. This I did, encouraged by your kind and condescending assurance, or at least persuasion, that, in the event of his retiring from the Editorship without delay, the Bishops would omit allusion to the Rambler in their Pastorals.

Should his withdrawal be followed by the cessation of the Rambler, he will consider himself at liberty to publish his account of the whole transaction, but this he will not and cannot do, as Editor of the Rambler, which will by the hypothesis have ceased to exist, but, as it stands to reason, in his own person. Such a course I did not feel myself called upon to speak about and interfere with, by the duties which your Lordship had put upon me, which related solely to the existing Magazine and its Editor.

I ought not to conceal from your Lordship that Mr Simpson feels very severely some of the accompaniments of the Bishops' message to him. He is much pained that, at a moment, when, as his own Bishop knew, he had a sick brother on his hands, or rather, as medical men directed, under his watchful eye, he should be suddenly hurried to make up his mind on a difficult question; and that too, at the end of the month, when the March Number of the Magazine was already in type, and an expense incurred which he thinks he ought not to be the person to sustain—and all this without learning from any of your Lordships the definite charges, which lie against him, as he might in equity demand.

And now, my dear Lord, having brought, as I trust, this anxious matter to a satisfactory solution, I have but to beg your blessing, and to subscribe myself,

> Your faithful & affte Servt in Xt

> John H Newman of the Oratory⌉[1]

The Rt Revd The Bp of Birmingham

[1] While he was in Birmingham Simpson called on Ullathorne, who wrote to Newman on 21 February, 'I thank you in my own name and that of the other Bishops who have moved in the affair of the Rambler, for having brought the matter of Mr Simpson's editorship to a satisfactory conclusion'.

To Henry Wilberforce

> Rednall ⌈March 31 / 59⌉

My dear Henry

⌈I have the extreme mortification of being Editor of the Rambler. I have never had in my life (in its time) so great a one. It is like a bad dream, and oppresses me at times inconceivably.

Our Bishop wished me to get the Editor to give up—I said I would if the R. was not noticed in the Pastorals. He said he considered he could pledge the Cardinal to this. When [[i.e. Though]] the advertisement had appeared in the Papers announcing the stoppage of the R. [[then]] he brought me a letter from the Cardinal not confirming the arrangement and saying the R. *must* be mentioned in the Pastorals, for I might let ⟨(i.e. it might *happen* that I let)⟩ some one else take the R. who would be as obnoxious as the late Editor. From that moment I saw plainly I could get no one, in whom both parties would perforce agree, but myself.[1] I take it in an extremely ill humour, except so far as I have done my best to find out God's will, and have the consolation of thinking I have found it. But you may be sure I don't feel indebted to any one for the complication.

All my plans are upset—and for the moment I am a vessel without rudder or compass.]

Ever Yrs affly J H N

H W Wilberforce Esqr

[1] [[N. B. My own object was to save Simpson etc. and to cover up differences. Simpson had given up the Magazine to me absolutely, with the reserve that, if I *ended* it, he should be at liberty to publish an account of the matter as against the Cardinal. *Therefore*, to hinder this, I determined to continue it, taking of course another Editor. But the Cardinal had the greatest suspicion of any such editor, thinking it would be a shuffle, ending in the appointment, e.g. of Sir John Acton. The only step which kept both parties quiet, was my becoming Editor.]]

To Robert Monteith

The Oratory Birmingham April 5. 1859

My dear Mr Monteith,

As I find that you, as well as some others of my friends, are making inquiries of our Fathers, on the subject of my having requested Cardinal Wiseman some three years ago, not to dedicate a publication of his to Fr Faber and to me conjointly, I think it necessary, though with real pain and reluctance, to write to you as follows:—

1. I admit the fact.
2. I took the step in question, not under the influence of any personal feeling, but on motives of grave duty and with a definite object.
3. I made no talk of it. I told no one, except our Fathers. I only answered the Cardinal's letter on the subject. No one need have known it. I guarded against scandal.
4. If the matter came over again, I should consider myself plainly bound in duty to make just the same request, and with the same object:—that is, if I felt I had any chance of succeeding in it.
5. I add this condition, because, in spite of me, the Cardinal immediately proceeded, without a word of explanation to me, to publish the Dedication to Fr Faber and myself.
6. And further, after doing so, he proceeded, through Fr Faber, freely to show my private letter to various persons, without my leave or knowledge, and to comment on it through Fr Faber behind my back in most disrespectful terms. I have reason to know that this has been going on quite lately.

You are the first person to whom I have yet brought out these circumstances. I have not stated them even to my own Fathers here, till now that I am writing to you.

They are one out of various instances, in which those about Fr Faber have taken advantage of their position in London to say things about me to my disadvantage, which, were they true, (as they are false, either simply, or in the colour given them,) for that very reason, out of mere charity and respect for me, ought not to have been said.

Differences may arise with any one. It is a scandal to manifest or reveal them. Our Fathers here have been profoundly silent. Others have not been so.

It is obvious, how the publication of ex parte statements must tend, not only to perpetuate existing differences, but to create new ones.

You may use this letter according to your discretion. It requires no answer. I hope you will give me leave to use a copy of it, if I see fit, for the satisfaction of others.

I am, My dear Mr Monteith, Sincerely Yours in Xt

John H Newman of the Oratory

R J Monteith Esqr

To Miss Mary Holmes

The Oy Bm April 19/59

My dear Miss Holmes,

Thank you for your kind anxiety—but it was unnecessary. I did not misunderstand you.

There is no difference at all between the Cardinal and me. I think of him as *you* do. He has ten thousand good points—but, as an individual, you cannot *trust* him; not from any moral fault, but from his character.

Nor have we, nor I, any difference really, or which needs any showing, with the London Oratory. It often happens that one finds one cannot *trust* people. *We* cannot trust *them, as* one cannot trust the *Cardinal.* Nothing need have been known—but they have *wilfully* made the appearance, and, by the appearance, made in a certain sense the *reality* of a quarrel, by 1st saying that there *was* one, 2. (as necessarily followed) putting out their own view of it, and giving what *must* be ex parte views of it, because they were *their* views, without ours. The sole difference has been created by, or exists in, their talking. If they ceased to talk, there would cease to be any difference—But they *won't*; and now perhaps they *can't.*

We have continually been to see them, when any of us has been in London. I asked Fr Faber to preach for me in the University Church at Dublin (he said in answer, he was not well enough.)[1] Were I ever in London, I should go down to them myself. I never am, except for an hour or two, and don't go to my dearest friends. I made one attempt, and failed. I wanted to go up from this place on *purpose*—but our Fathers would not let me—they knew well, that it would not mend matters—that Fr Faber would give some other turn to it, and turn it against me perhaps—and I agreed with them.

You see I have not said a word about what has made us feel so little trust in them—but you must recollect *this*: viz: I never have been so intimate with Fr Faber from any *personal* tie, as to make it strange that I have no personal trust in him now. He was never one of my intimate friends—not at Littlemore—not at Rome. On my return from Rome the Cardinal made him and his people Oratorians. I took them as a duty, and made them my friends. In process of time they swarmed. In the interval I found that there was that in Fr Faber, with all his good qualities and talents, which made it impossible to trust him. I did not even tell my own people here of this.

Well, they swarm. The Houses are separate. Oratorian Houses are never intimate with each other. Even had nothing then happened, we should gradually have drifted from each other. Even the accession of new members in each would have brought about this in time.

Under these circumstances suddenly something was done to us, which, not I, but *we all* felt to be intolerable. It made it necessary I should go to Rome for *our own* safety *here*. The London Fathers *told* me to go to Rome! I went, but said not one single word about them; it was not necessary. To my surprise I found people at Rome, even the Pope, talking of our '*quarrel.*' I will not say what else had been said against me, and remains unsaid [*sic*] (to *our* great annoyance) to this day. You may fancy our extreme surprise when this second stroke came upon the original one.

Thus they began to *talk*, three years and a half ago—and they have talked ever since. *We can* be silent, as to what they have done—we *can* simply forgive what we consider they have misused us in—but how can we possibly hinder the *look* of a difference, when they go on talking, talking?

The Cardinal has given Fr Faber my *private* letter to him (the C.) about the joint Dedication, for Fr Faber to *show* to people—and he *does* show it. (I am not ashamed of it—there is nothing violent in it.) *In delicacy* the Cardinal ought never to have proposed that Dedication, which was an *injury* to us—however, it is his way—Fr Faber brings out this letter to people who call on him; I have heard of it from many quarters—with the names of persons to whom he has shown it. He showed it to a person who *told* me it had been shown to him. He gives the Cardinal's comments, which for the Cardinal's sake I will not mention.[2]

If they would cease talking, the whole matter would die away, else, it is *impossible*. E.g. what has been their *comment*, when our Fathers have called on them? 'that it was mere outside lip-kindness.' What *can* we do which they would not call external? They have only [to] cease to talk, and all will die away.

To my bitter mortification I have the Editorship of the *Rambler*, beginning with May. I have nothing to do with the Dublin

Ever Yrs affly J H N

[1] See letter of 9 June 1856 (*L.D.* XVII, p. 257).

[2] Acton was Newman's informant.

To Isy Froude

The Oratory Birmingham May 4. 1859

My dear Child,

Your most welcome letter came to me this morning, just after I had been saying Mass for you. You took me by surprise, for I expected the joyful event a few days later.[1]

Don't you wonder, though your feelings go up and down, and though the long suspense which has excited your mind, should be followed by a re-action. Your heart and soul are fixed on the Rock of Truth—which remains fixed, though the waters round it rise and fall.

Ever Yours affly in Xt John H Newman of the Oratory.

Miss Froude

[1] Isy Froude had just become a Catholic.

To Edward Healy Thompson

The Oratory Birmingham ⌈May 29. 1859

Confidential

My dear Thompson

I must not convey a wrong impression. Our Bishop expressed his *wish*; it was not an act of *authority*.[1] I have no intention of publishing to the world that it is his act. My only concern is, that those whom it concerns should receive from me that explanation which I am bound to give them. As to Ward, I have the greatest respect for his opinion—but he is a prodigious *blab*—and therefore, since I need not tell him, I have no intention of doing so. Certainly not at present. Consequently, I cannot give you leave to write to him, or talk to him about it.

Your letter leads me to state the circumstances under which the catastrophe took place—and, since I have no time to write it twice, I wish you would let Simpson see this if he cares. What I mean is, that, if I were he, I should fear my being annoyed too much. This has been the reason why I have not told him particulars—but, now that I take up my pen to tell them to you, there seems an impropriety in my keeping him in ignorance of them.

Dr Gillow of Ushaw wrote to me to say that there were 'statements and principles' in the May Rambler, 'which appeared to him very objectionable—' he instanced one. A correspondence ensued, in which he wrote with great friendliness and frankness—I on the other hand don't think I got the worst of it. I thought it a duty to show it to our Bishop. And at the same time, I asked him, since he had distinctly told me before, that all theological writings ought to have the Bishop's imprimatur, to appoint revisors for the theology of the Rambler. I felt strongly, (and I feel) that I should have been in a false position, if, after his expressed wish and Dr Gillow's letter, I had not done so.

He answered that he would come and talk with me on the subject, adding that he found there was a general impression that the old spirit was not clean gone out of the Rambler.

On Sunday last he came. He said first of all, that he would not undertake the revision. 1. I ought to go to the Ordinary of Westminster, in which Diocese the Rambler was published. 2. that *all* the Rambler, or no part, should be revised—for the theological difficulties cropped up in half sentences. I did not quarrel with the justice of either remark. But he put me thereby, as I felt, in a most awkward dilemma—committed to the principle of revision, over and above his express wish—[[by my request of him]] and bound, in a periodical, which comes out every other month on a fixed day, and which must be written in part currente calamo and at the last moment, to the slow machinery of a theological revision.

He then went on to ask whether I had seen the criticism on the R. [[Rambler]] in the Tablet of the day previous. He said it mainly expressed his sentiments. The Catholics of England were a peaceable people, the Church was peace. Catholics never had a doubt—it pained them to know that things could be considered doubtful, which they had ever implicitly believed. The R. [[Rambler]] was irritating. I stated my own view strongly. I said I thought I saw a side of things which the Bishops and Clergy did not see. It must be considered that England and Ireland were one country. The Irish laity must be considered as well as the English. The Holy Father had made them one by setting up the University. Looking at the educated laity as a whole, and in prospect, I could not say that I thought their state satisfactory. Why did I go to Ireland, except with the hope of doing something towards the various objects, for which I had consented to undertake the R. [[Rambler]]?

He did not allow the weight of anything I said. I then said that for no object of my own had I undertaken it. He said he knew it, and that every one knew it, but he had conversed with various persons, and they all agreed with him. It was the fault he found in Lucas, in spite of his excellences: and he implied that an old Catholic was different.[2]

I said that it had been an extreme annoyance to me to undertake it, and it would be an enormous relief to me, if I did not. And this, as he recollected, I had said to him already.

He answered that he had been surprised that I had taken it. Then he abruptly said, Why not give it up? I said, how could I do so without giving it back to the Proprietors? I said this, thinking he would feel it a great objection to let it revert to them—but he answered quickly, No difficulty at all, if you give them fair notice; if you give it up in July, you will give them fair notice. I then spoke of expense—I said I feared I should be out of pocket by having had it. He went off (not with any intention of evasion) to speak of the Translation of Scripture, hoped I would take care not to involve myself etc etc.

I then promised him I would give up the Rambler after the July Number. (There was no sort of unpleasantness of any kind in our conversation from beginning to end)

It is impossible, with the principles and feelings on which I have acted all through life, that I could have acted otherwise. I never have resisted, nor can resist, the voice of a lawful Superior, speaking in his own province. I should have been in an utterly false position, if I had continued, without a revision, which my Bishop thought necessary, and which was impossible, a work, of the very object and principle of which my Bishop disapproved.

Since then he has written kindly saying that he sees 'with pain and regret that I am overworking myself, and straining the machine. No man can be ten men. Are you not consuming the fuel of years in months? etc etc' Kind as this is, it means, 'I don't at all repent of what I have done, for "divergent occupations," as he calls them, "mixed" together, have or will have sad "results."'

You may show this, also to Mr Burns; but to no one but to him and Simpson.

Ever Yours most sincerely John H. Newman⌉ of the Oratory

N B. Additional notes, *not sent*.[3]

I do not like it to be known, for the reason that the Bishop came as a friend to advise or request me to give up the Editorship. I should be unfair to throw on him the responsibility.

My only concern is to see that the persons interested, as Simpson, know that I am not shuffling or backing out, but was directly and really asked or advised to give it up.

I don't suppose Simpson will make any exposé. I have not a dream *whom* you allude to as the writer of the Tablet Article. I should have thought the *matter* of it Ward's.

[[(N.B. Novr 28. 1862.[4]

It is rather strange the Bishop let me off my engagement so easily, or rather pressed a release on me, when I had gained his side of the bargain, and had not paid my own. Though I had rescued Simpson etc. from the Pastorals, I was allowed, or rather urged, to give him back the Magazine. Perhaps it was that the Cardinal etc. were seized with a panic, lest they had got out of the frying pan into the fire. But so it was, that, by my own brief Editorship, I had secured to Acton and Simpson a trial of three more years, i.e. up to 1862.

All would have been well, but for the unlucky paragraph in my July Number on the Arianizing Hierarchy.

On the other hand, though the Bishops released me *absolutely*, I did carry out the original engagement to the best of my power, and on the whole successfully—viz. *I hindered Simpson returning to the Editorship.*)]]

[1] Thompson wrote on 26 May from Taunton, about Newman giving up the *Rambler*, 'I am petrified. This exercise of individual authority is something I cannot understand, and I am simply mute and passive.'

[2] Frederick Lucas (1812–55), a Quaker who supported Catholic Emancipation and became a Catholic in 1839. He founded the *Tablet* in 1840, and moved it to Dublin in 1849 where he clashed with Archbishop Cullen. He was M.P. for Meath from 1852.

[3] This heading and the notes are in Newman's hand, on the back of a fair copy of this letter.

[4] This memorandum in Newman's hand is inserted after his copy of the letter of 29 May to Thompson, in the file 'In the Rambler 1858–1862 —'.

To John Gillow

Rednall Septr 2/59

Dear Dr Gillow

I beg to acknowledge your letter of August 28.

We certainly differ in our construction of the Article in the Rambler.

You consider 'suspense' in the Article to mean 'failure'. I think it has a meaning far lighter even than 'suspension.'

You consider that the 'body of the Bishops' in the Article means the Ecclesia docens. I think it merely means the actual mass at the particular time spoken of.

You consider that in the last sentence the writer denies the truism that belief in the Holy Catholic Church involves 'fides implicita' in her teaching. I think that he merely speaks of the possibility of our inculcating on the faithful a sort of fides implicita which would terminate in the evils which he specifies.

But these differences of opinion in matters of interpretation are bearable. What I really am surprised to read in your letter is, an assertion that we differ from each other 'materially in an important point of *principle.*'

I do not think you can be aware of the force of your own words. Surely to use such terms to another on a point de fide, is a matter of grave offence

Yours truly in Jesus Christ John H Newman of the Oratory

The Revd Dr Gillow

To Cardinal Wiseman

The Oratory Birmingham January 19. 1860

(Copy)[1]

My dear Lord Cardinal

Our Bishop tells me, that my name has been mentioned at Rome in connexion with an Article in the Rambler, which has by an English Bishop been formally brought before Propaganda, as containing unsound doctrine. And our Bishop says that your Eminence has spoken so kindly about me, as to encourage me to write to you on the subject.

I have not yet been asked from Propaganda whether I am the author of the Article, or otherwise responsible for it; and, though I am ready to answer the question when it is put to me, I do not consider it a duty to volunteer the information, till your Eminence advises it.

However, I am ready, without the question being asked of me, to explain the Article as if it were mine.

I will request then of your Eminence's kindness three things:—

1. The passages of the Article, on which the Cardinal Prefect of Propaganda desires an explanation.
2. A copy of the translations, in which His Eminence has read them.

3. The dogmatic propositions, which they have been represented as infringing or otherwise impairing.

If your Eminence does this for me, I will engage, with the blessing of God, in the course of a month from the receipt of the information,

1. to accept and profess ex animo in their fulness and integrity the dogmatic propositions implicated.
2. to explain the animus and argument of the writer of the Article in strict accordance with those propositions.
3. to show that the English text and context of the Article itself are absolutely consistent with them.

I marvel, but I do not complain, that, after many years of patient and self denying labour in the cause of Catholicity, the one appropriate acknowledgment in my old age should be considered to consist in taking advantage against me of what is at worst a slip of the pen in an anonymous un-theological paper. But I suppose it is a law of the world, that those who toil much and say little, are little thought of.

One great favour I ask your Eminence to obtain for me, viz that I may not be sent to Rome. A journey would seriously impair my health and strength, and would create great confusion.

Kissing the sacred purple, I am, My dear Lord Cardinal, Yr faithful & affte Servt in Xt

(signed) John H Newman of the Oratory[2]

The Cardinal Archbishop of Westminster

---

[1] i.e. Newman's fair copy. The actual letter sent was perhaps the one found among Wiseman's papers by his secretary, John Morris. See the *Month* (March 1896), p. 421; cf. H. I. D. Ryder, *Essays* (London, 1911), p. 284.

[2] On a copy of this letter, made for St John in May 1867, Newman wrote, '(I sent this to Cardinal Wiseman *at Rome*, at the Bishop's wish, *since he was on the spot*.)'

Newman's letter—or at least the requests it contained— must have reached Propaganda, because a minute is preserved in the Archives there. The schedule of the statements in the *Rambler* article to which objection was taken was sent to Wiseman on 30 January by Bedini, the Secretary of Propaganda, and is in the archives of the Westminster Archdiocese.

Barnabò in 1867 declared that he had never seen Newman's letter of 19 January to Wiseman. Bittleston wrote to Newman on 12 May 1867, from Rome, 'Your letter to the late Cardinal Wiseman quite thunderstruck him [Barnabò]. "Why," he said, "Cardinal Wiseman was at Propaganda, and we never heard of this."' *Ward*, II, p.173.

At all events, the schedule of statements in the *Rambler* article requiring explanation, for which Newman had asked, and which reached Wiseman, never reached *him*. In a letter of 29 April from Rome, Manning wrote to Newman that Wiseman would bring the matter to an acceptable termination on his return to England. See letter of 7 May 1860 to Ullathorne. That was the last Newman heard, and he concluded that no more was required. Meanwhile at Propaganda the affair was not forgotten and he was considered to be disobedient. Wiseman, who was preoccupied and ill, seems to have thought all was settled.

To Bishop Ullathorne

The Oratory. May 7/60

My dear Lord

I have just heard from Dr Manning. His letter contains the following sentence, which I lost no time in transcribing and sending to you.

'The Cardinal desires his kind regards to you, and tells me to say that he has thought it better to wait till his return, when he hopes to bring the matter of your letter to a termination which will be acceptable to you.'[1]

I think you will wish, from your kind interest in me, to know how the matter proceeds[2]

Begging your Lordship's blessing, I am, My dear Lord,

Your faithful & affte Servt in Xt John H Newman of the Oratory

The Rt Revd The Bp of Birmingham

[1] This was the last Newman heard of his offer to explain any questionable passages in his article 'On Consulting the Faithful in Matters of Doctrine'.

[2] Newman heard no more on the subject from Wiseman or Manning, and naturally thought the difficulty had been met.

To E. E. Estcourt

(Sent with the large omissions marked in brackets.)[1]

The Oratory ⌈June (2) 1860

My dear E⌉stcourt,

I have carefully thought over what you said to me ⟨when you called,⟩ (on Thursday), and send you, as I promised, the result. It agrees pretty much with my first impression; and I (am going to ask you to allow me to state some of the considerations which have led me to it.) ⟨will note briefly how the matter presents itself to me.⟩

⌈You seemed to think with me that the Catholics of Oxford do not require a new Church; if then a subscription is commenced for a new one, it will be with a view to making converts from the University.⌉ Indeed, I (need not prove this;) ⟨think if you will allow this to be the view;⟩ for it was on this very ground that you wished me, and the only ground on which you could wish me, to take part in it. You said that my name would draw aid from converts—and you were kind enough to wish that the Church thus built should be in a certain sense a memorial to my former position in Oxford. ⌈Now a [[the]] controversial character thus given to [[the]] new ecclesiastical establishments there, whatever be its expedience in itself, would be the very circumstance which would determine [[weigh with]] me personally against taking that part in promoting [[aiding]] them, which you assign to me. It would do more harm than good.⌉ go on to p.43 A[2]

(While ⌈I do not see my way to take steps to weaken the Church of England, being what it is, least of all should I be disposed to do so in Oxford, which has hitherto been the seat of those traditions which constitute whatever there is of Catholic doctrine and principle in the Anglican Church.⌉ Oxford deserves least, of any part of the Anglican territory, to be interfered with. ⌈That there are also false traditions there, I know well; I know too that there is a late ⟨recent⟩ importation of scepticism and infidelity; but till things are very much changed there, in weakening Oxford, we are weakening our friends,⌉ weakening our own de facto παιδαγωγὸς into the Church. Catholics did not make us Catholics; Oxford made us Catholics. At present Oxford surely does more good than harm. There has been a rage for shooting sparrows of late years under the notion that they are the farmer's enemies. Now, it is discovered that they do more good by destroying insects than harm by picking up the seed. In Australia, I believe, they are actually importing them. Is there not something of a parallel here?

⌈I go further than a mere tolerance of Oxford; as I have said, I wish to suffer the Church of England. The Establishment has ever been a breakwater against Unitarianism, fanaticism, and infidelity.⌉ It has ever loved us better than Puritans or Independents have loved us. And it receives all that abuse and odium of dogmatism, or at least a good deal of it, which otherwise would be directed against us. I should have the greatest repugnance to introducing controversy into those quiet circles and sober schools of thought, which are the strength of the Church of England. It is another thing altogether to introduce controversy to individual minds which are already unsettled, or have a drawing towards Catholicism. Altogether another thing in a place like Birmingham, where nearly everyone is a nothingarian, an infidel, a sceptic or an inquirer. Here Catholic efforts are not only good in themselves, and do good, but cannot possibly do any even incidental harm—here, whatever is done is so much gain. In Oxford you would unsettle many, and gain a few, if you did your most.

If a Catholic Church were in a position there suitable for acting upon Undergraduates, first it would involve on their part a conscious breach of University and College regulations; then, it would attract just those who were likely to be unstable, and who perhaps in a year or two would lapse back to Protestantism; and then, it would create great bitterness of feeling and indignation against Catholics, prejudice fair minds against the truth, and diminish the chances of our being treated with equity at Oxford or elsewhere.)

A To take part in this would be surely inconsistent with the sentiments which I have (I have never concealed—) ever acted upon, since I have been a Catholic. My first act was to leave the neighbourhood of Oxford, where I found myself, at considerable inconvenience. When I heard the question of a new Oxford Church mooted at Stonyhurst soon after, I spoke against it. In all that I have written, I have spoken of Oxford and the Oxford system with affection and admiration. I have put its system forward, as an instance of that union of dogmatic teaching and liberal education which command my assent. ⌈I have never acted in direct hostility to the Church of England.⌉ I have, in my Lectures on Anglicanism, professed no more than

328

to carry on the 'children of the movement of 1833' to their legitimate conclusions. In my Lectures on Catholicism in England, I oppose, not the Anglican Church, but National Protestantism, and Anglicans only so far as they belong to it.

⌈In taking part then in building a new Church at Oxford, I should be commencing a line of conduct,⌉ which would require explanation.

And I cannot help thinking that, in so saying, I shall have the Bishop with me. I know he is against a convert having the Mission of Oxford; much more inexpedient would it be for a convert to take part in the erection of a new Church there.

I am, my dear Estcourt, Yours very sincerely in Xt
John H Newman of the Oratory

[1] The omissions from the letter that was eventually sent are enclosed in round brackets. The parts of the letter included among 'Documents for Fr A St John's use at Rome,' in 1867, are marked by angle and double brackets. The letter as it finally went to Estcourt will be found at 10 June 1860 in *L.D.* XIX, pp. 359–60.

[2] This is Newman's note in his draft, showing that the long passage that follows was omitted in the letter as sent, until 'A' below.

To Francis Kenrick, Archbishop of Baltimore

The Oratory, Birmingham July 8. 1860

My dear Lord Archbishop,

I have received from Mr Shea a copy of the letter, which your Grace has been so good as to address to me through him on the subject of your translation of Scripture.

I beg to congratulate you on the progress you are making towards the completion of your work; which is not the least of the benefits, of which the good Providence of God has made your Grace the instrument towards us. I earnestly trust and pray you may have leisure and health to bring it to a termination.

I did not know, what I find by your letter, that your Grace had been in some suspense as to the intention of the English Bishops with respect to it. For myself, as you seem to wish me to speak on the subject, I can only say, that I have been in the same suspense myself, and know nothing beyond the fact of the Bishop of Charlestown's letter.[1] The Cardinal's many anxieties and engagements, and his late and present severe indisposition, doubtless are the cause of a silence which I am sorry you have felt to be an inconvenience.

Begging your Grace's blessing I am, My dear Lord Archbishop,
with great respect, Your faithful Servant in Xt.
John H Newman of the Oratory

His Grace The Most Revd The Archbp of Baltimore &c &c.

[1] See letter of 7 December 1858 to P. N. Lynch, Bishop of Charleston. Wiseman never replied to the proposal, sent on 8 October 1858, that Kenrick and Newman should produce a joint translation, and Newman relinquished an expensive undertaking which was abandoned by those who had commissioned it.

To James Hope Scott

[28 November 1860]

Thank you for your most acceptable account of the dear Duke of Norfolk's death.

Our Sacristan tells me you have sent us £20 for Masses, and, as I am writing to you, to acknowledge it for him. This I do, assuring you [we] will say the Masses with all speed.

As to what you say of Lady Victoria, assure her that if I have not sent her my affectionate thoughts and good wishes it was because I hardly knew if she recollected me—I certainly recollect her, since the time when the Duchess told me that Victoria had been saying her rosary for my success in the Achilli matter. I wish all blessings on her future with all my heart, and she has them already in being united to you.[1]

I quite understand the meaning of your sending me those lines you mention and it never came into my head to think them inconsistent with the letter you sent me soon afterwards. Say every thing right from me at the proper time to the Duchess; and give my affectionate regards to Father Faber.[2]

Ever &c J H N

P.S. Novr 28. 1860
Confidential.

As you love me, do not get me into a fresh correspondence about Fr Faber. I wish he would consent to let us alone.

To you I will speak frankly, and as I have done *to no one else*. I have had long experience of him, and have in consequence a profound and intense *distrust*. What I feel, is the feeling of all of us here. Some of course feel more strongly than others, but it is not I who feel the strongest and keenest.

We have suffered much from him; we cannot help suffering still; but the less we have to do with him, the less we shall suffer. He has a thousand attractive points, but he has a restless spirit of intrigue which nothing can quench. I have been sixty years in the world, and (excepting in a degree another who is with him,) I never met any one 'simile aut secundum.'[3] It is not a common English failing, at least among men; and, considering (as the Lives of the Saints show,) how religious communities abroad have suffered from it, I praise God that things are not worse. I should be a simple fool, to associate my name with his again.

Either he has been in fault, or I am in fault. This is common-sense. He is doing so much good in his important position, it would be so great a scandal if his name were touched, that (I say it from my heart) I gladly take the reproach upon myself. He has neither the power nor the temptation to deal with others whom he comes across, as he has dealt with us. There is One who will judge between us; you cannot.

Nothing would have been observed of the alienation, scandal there would have been none at all, had he not *talked*. But he would not sit down under the necessary result of his own acts; the confidence, which he had forfeited, could not in the nature of things be restored; so he talked. Then, *his* talked. *We* kept a religious silence. When he and his cease to talk, the scandal will gradually die away.

It is now years since the separation, 1855. To attempt to make things better, would be to rip up old wounds, and to make new ones. Things would be left worse than they were found. Crede mihi, let well alone. We quite desire to be at peace; more is impossible; but the first step towards a thorough peace, is for them to *say* that the two Oratories have ever been at peace (not to speak of a *reconciliation*, which would be making matters worse, but that the Oratories) have ever been friends, and *to cease to talk*.

P.S. To explain what I mean by 'talk', I inclose a copy of the only letter I have sent to any friend about Fr Faber before the present.[4] Let me have it back. I do not ask for any answer from you.

---

[1] Hope-Scott had written on 12 November from Arundel Castle, to tell Newman of his engagement to Lady Victoria Howard (1840–70), eldest daughter of the Duke of Norfolk. They were married on 7 January 1861.

[2] Hope-Scott wrote appreciatively on 26 November of Faber's visit to him.

[3] Horace, *Odes* I, xii, 18. Evidently Dalgairns is meant.

[4] This was the letter of 5 April 1859 to Monteith.

To Charles Crawley

The Oratory. Bm March 17. 1861

My dear Crawley,

I did not in my last allude to your remark upon my probable sentiments about the Church of England, because I felt it would only lead to unprofitable controversy. If I thought I had a chance of convincing you, most gladly would I discuss—but I had no reason to hope this, and knew too well my own sentiments, and therefore I felt that to keep silence was the only way in which I could avoid hurting your feelings.[1]

As to the Volume in question,[2] I deplore it extremely, but especially for a reason which bears on the difference of the two Creeds. The religion of England is 'the Bible, the whole Bible, and nothing but the Bible'—the consequence is that to strike a blow at its inspiration, veracity or canonicity, is directly to aim at whatever there is of Christianity in the country. It is frightful to think where England would be, as regards Revelation, if it once got to disbelieve or to doubt the authority of Scripture. This is what makes the Volume so grave a matter—and the responsibility of those who have had to do with it so great. This is the reason of the consternation of serious members of the Church of England at its appearance.

This then is one illustration of what I meant by saying that I never could hope to defend Christianity on the Anglican basis. Of course a Catholic holds the inspiration of Scripture—but the Church has defined very little upon the subject—much more freedom of opinion is allowed than with you—and we should have a sufficient ground of faith and teacher of doctrine, though, by some dispensation of God, the whole Bible were miraculously to vanish out of the world. I know that it would be the withdrawal of an immense privilege, but the Catholic believes in the word of God thro' His Church; et 'verbum tuum permanet in aeternum,' tho' Scripture were not. Moreover, in matter of fact, there is nothing which binds the Catholic to belief in various portions of Genesis etc as popularly interpreted, to doubt which would simply shock, unsettle, break, the faith of most Protestants in the whole volume

Ever Yours affly John H Newman

C. Crawley Esqr

[1] Crawley had written on 26 February, 'In spite of the Gorham Judgment, and other events sufficiently lamentable in themselves, there is still I am happy to say unquestionable evidence of essential improvement in our Church since you left it.' On 12 March he said, 'I hope you did not think me too bold in what I ventured to say in my last.'

[2] *Essays and Reviews.*

To Charles Crawley

The Oratory Bm March 20. 1861

My dear Crawley

Thank you for your very kind letter. You may be sure, without my saying it, that I can have but one prayer for those whom I have known and love, and you and Mrs Crawley are among them. Our divisions are most mournful, certainly.

I don't think I said that 'the Bible, the Bible only etc' was the religion of the Church of England, but *of England*. And so I think it is, as far as there is religious feeling in England, and there is a good deal.

Of the historical Church of England, I always have contended, and still would contend, that Bull, Beveridge etc are the true doctors and representatives—

But the Church of England's religion is not the religion of England: and now for some time, and especially in the Gorham matter, we see that England is determined to *have* its *own* Church, and to make it *like itself*.

I write this, not at all in a controversial way, but merely lest I should leave you with the idea that I hold what I do not hold.[1]

God bless you—and believe me

Affectionately Yours John H Newman

C. Crawley Esqr

P.S. What I said was simply in reference to the 'Essays and Reviews'—The Catholic Church is not so much bound up with the plenary inspiration of the Bible as are the religion and the Church of England.

[1] Crawley on 21 March thanked Newman for his 'very kind reply', and continued the discussion.

To H. E. Manning

The Oratory Birmingham ⌐June 21. 1861

⌐Confidential⌐
My dear Manning

I find the Cardinal Archbishop (for Cardinal Antonelli is out of my field of sight) is taking strong measures on the question of the Temporal Power.

You will not, I know, fancy that I am capable of writing any thing in the shape of a threat; but I am obliged to write this; else you will say, when the event took place, 'You *should* have given me a hint before hand; *Why didn't* you tell me?'

I ought then to say what I am resolved on—but this is for you, not for the Cardinal

Should his Eminence put out any matter, bearing on the same question in the same way, in *his Inaugural Address on the 29th*, I certainly will not remain a member of the Academia.[1]

Ever Yours affectly John H Newman] of the Oratory[2]

⌈The Rt Revd Mgr Manning⌉

[1] Wiseman had just established an 'Academia of the Catholic Religion' on the model of the Roman Academies. It was to meet once a month, when a paper would be read on a theological, philosophical, or historical subject. Wiseman was to give the first lecture at his own house. Manning was the chief organizer. One purpose of the Academia was to rally support for the temporal power. See Newman's comments in a memorandum written on 22 May 1882 (*L.D.* XIX, pp. 561–2).

[2] Manning replied on 22 June, suggesting Newman might prefer to wait before joining, because it would be easier not to join than to withdraw. Newman did become a member of the Academia.

To Henry Bittleston

Cambridge. July 29/61

My dear Henry

Knowing your disputatious power, I am not sure you will not be able to deny that I *am* in Cambridge, in spite of the post mark—but you must let me assume that I am there, and it shall be a reserved point to discuss when I see you again.

On Friday, after seeing Badeley, whose torments seem to have been extraordinary,[1] we caught the train to Hampton Court, where we slept. Of course I am not going to write descriptions, but I will say that we were both enchanted with the place, and thought how great her majesty must be to have palaces such, as to enable her to chuck Wolsey's building to her servants and pensioners.

Well—I thought we should enjoy our incognito, and so we did during [a] good part of 24 hours—but at length we fell on Platner, who is so mighty in words, that I simply fell—and Wm [William Nevillle] making an excuse that just now I was unable to talk, picked me up and carried me off.[2]

Forthwith we fled; whither was a secondary question. We rowed to Kingston— the weather has been, and is, sometimes lovely, sometimes splendid. Then, after dining, we set off for Richmond through Ham. Thence at once by train to London, musing all the way where we should find ourselves at night fall. On getting to Waterloo Station we made for King's Cross, and by half past 9 PM behold us at Cambridge.

I have been here once before, for a quarter of a day, in 1832. Then, I recollect, my allegiance to Oxford was shaken by the extreme beauty of the place. I had forgotten this—but a second sight has revived the impression. Certainly it is exquisitely beautiful.[3]

We weathered Mr Q.[4] though we were so near capsizing, as to be asked by him to change our place, because we were in the way of his Confessional—And, as there was but one person, a stranger, at the Bull in the Coffee Room, we have been quite comfortable.

He has a strange distrait manner, and I took him for some enthusiastic parson, say a Drummondite or the like. I said but a few words to him, but he seemed absent— but, as he fidgetted about, and went in and out of the room, read the Bible, then sat where he could see me say office, and certainly followed our movements, we migrated to the other end of the room.

This was no annoyance to us; but what did annoy us was, that, when we were into King's College Chapel to hear the chanting and see the place, a little man at once fastened his eyes on us, whom William instantly jaloused as having been at the Oratory. William, who acts as a sort of Guardian Angel or Homeric god, instantly enveloped me in darkness, rustling with his wings, and flapping about with a vigor which for the time was very successful. But, alas, all through the day, wherever we were, this little man haunted us. He seemed to take no meals, to say no prayers, or elsewhere to know our times for these exercises with a preternatural exactness. William was ever saying, whether we were here or there, in garden or in cloister— 'Don't look that way—turn this way—there's the little man again.' His anxiety led him to make matters worse, for he boldly approximated him to be sure of the individual, but with too little caution, for the little man caught his hand and asked him how he was. However, his generalship kept me out of harm's way, and we dined peaceably at six. There was then no further danger—we lounged out at seven, and were tempted, by the merest accident to turn aside into PeterHouse. We were not two seconds in the Court, when William cried out, 'There's the little man— don't look.' But it would not do—he pounced upon his prey, and William turned quite red, whipping his finger as if it had been stung. He most civilly asked us, if we should like to see the Munich painted glass in the Chapel, and went at once for the Porter. Then he vanished—but William is now out paying him a call with my card; and I should certainly have done the same but that I am far from well this morning, very weak, because I have not had any sleep (from distress, it is not so much as pain) since 3. I heard 3 strike and every hour till I got up.

I have been hardly able to speak, certainly not to converse, with our fellow-occupant in the Coffee Room, who has left for the North just now—having never seen Cambridge before, and, like ourselves, having run down for the Sunday. He began talking this morning about Cambridge, which I agreed with him was most beautiful. He said he had been into the University Church for the evening service— and, after a word or two between us, he suddenly said 'I think I have heard *you* in the pulpit of St Mary's Oxford some thirty years ago.' 'Well', I answered rather bluntly, 'how *could* you know me? for my friends, who have seen me only half that time ago, don't know me, they think me so much changed.'

This led to some conversation, when at length we got on the Essays and Reviews. After which I started, proprio motu, a new subject, that of the movement for the alteration of the Liturgy. He said that was a religious movement, very different in spirit from the other. I agreed, but I said I had been much struck with the account of the effect, which I heard was produced by a book written by a lawyer, a Mr Fisher, whom the Bishops had noticed in their charges.[5] His book, they said, was a logical, candid work; but it was removing the veil from the eyes of a number of evangelicals, showing them that they could not honestly use the baptismal service, and demanding in consequence its alteration. I said, I thought this a remarkable movement and would gather strength. So we shook hands and parted.

I came down again, and he was not gone. It seemed to me rude not to have asked his name—So I said to him, 'Since you know me, pray do not let us part without my having the satisfaction of knowing with whom I have been conversing.'

He looked nervous, and distrait—and then said 'I am the Mr Fisher, of whom you have been talking'

Ever Yrs affly J H N

[1] Badeley had fractured his leg.

[2] Ferdinand Platner was the painter under whom Neville had studied at Rome in the early summer of 1856.

[3] See Newman's letter of 16 July 1832 to his mother.

[4] Canon Thomas Quinlivan, the priest at the Catholic church at Cambridge.

[5] John Cowley Fisher, *Liturgical Purity our Rightful Inheritance* (London, 1857; 2nd edn 1860). Phillpotts of Exeter was among the bishops who noticed the book.

To Sister Mary Gabriel Du Boulay

The Oratory. Bm Augst 18/61

My dear Child

Your letter was a great consolation to me. I could hardly get through it without tears. Especially am I touched by what you tell me of your dear Mother as regards me.[1] I am much better, but what has been so long coming on, will not easily go off.

I have not the faith, patience, and resignation which I ought to have—but this is another matter. My ailment is a physical effect, I may call it, on my mind. It is said that in a naval engagement, while the vessels near, and the men are standing quite still, the knees of the bravest shake. It is so bad to be simply passive in suffering. When we act as well as suffer, the effort alleviates the pain; in that case men are wounded without knowing it; but it is otherwise when you are hit, without hitting. It would have been better with me humanly and naturally, had I given as good as I took.

Now excuse my folly in speaking. Thirty years have passed since I have been a sort of target for a shot, when any one wished to try his hand, and had nothing better to do. I used as a Protestant, to say, that no one, except O'Connell was so well abused as I was. I have very seldom *replied*; if so, for the sake of others, or of our cause. My friends have sometimes defended me out of affection—but, not agreeing with me, they have taken grounds which were not mine, and which were sure ultimately to damage me. Gross misrepresentations remain of me to this day, and even now they bring up what I did 20 years ago, knowing that *they* can speak, and *I* cannot. At Brighton the other day I took up the Quarterly—Bishop Wilberforce says in it 'Why the Essayists are worse even than Dr Newman's Number 90' and then proceeds to assail, not them, but me. Then I take up the Edinburgh which writes against the said Sam Wilberforce, and Dr Stanley says in it 'Why, Dr Wilberforce is worse even than Dr Newman's Elucidations against Hampden,' and then proceeds not to abuse Dr W but me. These are little and ridiculous things taken separately, but they form an atmosphere of *flies*—one can't enjoy a walk without this fidget on the nerves of the mind. They are nothing in the eye of reason, but they weary.

For myself, 'obmutui'—I don't think I have called any one a bad name, or been ill natured. I never charged any one with any crime or fault except Achilli, and I suffered for that pretty considerably.

Then I have tried to do works for God year after year, and for thirty years, so far forth as they were *works*, they have all failed. My first sermon as an Anglican, was on the text 'Man goes forth to his work and to his labour until the evening;'[2] and now the evening is come and I have done nothing. I think of Keble's lines 'In disappointment Thou canst bless etc'—[3] and I know that it is better for me to seem to have done nothing—but still it is most difficult to go on working in the face of thirty years disappointment. And so it is—every thing seems to crumble under my hands, as if one were making ropes of sand.

I am speaking of the *physical* effects of such a trial. I suppose supernatural acts of whatever kind, are the destruction of flesh and blood. Do you think the sollicitudo omnium Ecclesiarum did not waste St Paul![4] 'By care' is meant that mental burden which consists in the perception of evil with the consciousness one cannot avert it. The wounds which one bears speechlessly, the dreadful secrets which are severed from the sympathy of others, the destruction of confidences, the sense of hollowness all around one, the expectation of calamity or scandal, this was a portion of St Paul's trial, and of all Bishops, as it is of all, in their degree, who have to work for God in this world. It is as real a penance as a hair shirt.

And as one man's skin endures a hair shirt better than another's—so it is with the effect of these trials on different minds respectively. For myself, I know I am deeply deficient in that higher life which lasts and grows in spite of the ills of mortality—but had I ever so much of supernatural love and devotion, I could not be in any different state from the Apostle, who in the most beautiful of his inspired epistles speaks with such touching and consoling vividness of those troubles, in the midst of which these earthern vessels of ours hold the treasure of grace and truth.[5]

Ever Yrs affly in J.C. John H. Newman

---

[1] Newman was moved to learn from Sister Mary Gabriel that Mother Margaret Mary Hallahan had for years been praying for him daily. Mother Margaret Mary Hallahan (1802–68) was a Dominican nun. She formed a friendship with Newman in 1846 that never faltered.

[2] *Psalm* 103:23. Newman's sermon is published in *John Henry Newman, Sermons 1824-1843*, v, ed. Francis J. McGrath (Oxford, 2012), pp. 17–24. On it he has written 'The first Sermon I ever wrote'. It was preached at St Clement's, Oxford, on the morning of 27 June 1824.

[3] *The Christian Year*, The Fifth Sunday after Trinity, last stanza.

[4] *2 Corinthians* 11:28. Newman's next sentences appear to refer to his anxieties over the Oratory School.

[5] *2 Corinthians* 4:7. Sister Mary Gabriel remarked on 7 September how often people were heard to say, 'We owe our souls to Dr Newman'.

To H. E. Manning

The Oratory Bm Jany 24/62

My dear Manning

I said Mass for you on St Charles's day, and was going to write you word of this, when I found you were gone. Your letter of the 10th was a great comfort to me.[1] Taking the matter from first to last, I never have had a severer blow—but I hope the proverb will be fulfilled as regards it, Si gravis, brevis. For never did matters right themselves so speedily—and, tho' we are not yet out of the wood, every thing promises well.

Suddenly, in one day (Friday St John's day), headmaster and all masters declared they would go at once, would accept no compromise, would not stay till their successors were appointed, unless I at once, without any delay, sent away, in winter, out of the place entirely, an infirm lady (Mrs Wootten), against whom they never had made complaint before, who had sacrificed herself for us, and was our bene-factress. Before our meeting was finished, when we had adjourned to the next day (Saturday), they wrote off by that very post to London and published in this place, that they were all gone. When I delayed my final answer to the Sunday, on the Sunday they published in this place that two Fathers had left the Congregation, and that they meant to set up an opposition school. On Monday morning the 30th I set off for the London train in the dark, carrying my travelling bag, never more sorrowful and desolate. But from the moment I got to London my prospects began to mend. I found all my friends on my side—and every day as it has passed, has brought an accession of hope, so that now, when we are on the eve of beginning the new term, we begin with full numbers and with a new staff, or rather partly new, and partly of old who have thought better of their acts, with great anxiety before us, but still with an expectation, correspondingly great, that, if we succeed, we shall be in a better state than we ever have been before.

All this I owe to the prayers of my friends, and I am encouraged to face the difficulties which I must meet in the months which lie before me by the thought that you do not forget me at the Holy Places.

The real wound, of course, is that in the Congregation itself, and the scandal among our people. This will not be lightly healed

Ever Yrs affly John H Newman

[1] Manning sent a letter of sympathy on 10 January from Rome because of the troubles in the Oratory School with which Newman was having to deal: 'I wished you to know that I share in anything that pains you ... It seems to me that our Lord must have a special love for you, and a special design over you: for you have had many trials: and after many years of great favour and help from Him our Lord has begun to purify you for a higher world by crosses.'

To W. G. Ward

The Oratory Bm ⌈April 22. 1862

(Copy)

My dear Ward

I shall be glad to see you at any time, and, as far as I know, shall be here or at Rednall for months.[1]

If things are to go as they have gone, I should anticipate our conversation would have this result: viz, you would begin by stating that I held something very different from, or the reverse of, what I really hold. I should undeceive you, and you would confess you were mistaken. Then we should branch off to some independent subject of theology, and you would be pleased to find that I agreed with you, when others did not. You would leave—and then, in a few weeks, you would write me word, that it pained you bitterly to think that we were diverging from each other in theological opinion more and more. If I then wrote to inquire what you could mean, you would answer that you really could not at the moment recollect the grounds on which you had been led to say so; but you would not withdraw it.

Thus I have to endure, in spite of your real affection for me, a never-dying misgiving on your part that I am in some substantial matter at variance with you— while I for my part sincerely think that on *no* subject is there any substantial difference between us, as far as theology is concerned.

As to Mr Green,[2] I should like nothing better than to have a long talk with you on the best mode of meeting his difficulties—but I fear it is a subject so large, that question would lead to question—and answers throw me back on the discussion of principles, till I had materials for a Volume. This would be, however, a real gain— but it must be presupposed as already done, before I could encounter Mr G.⌉ Again, when you contemplate my engaging with him in controversy, I really do not think you lay sufficient stress on what I said to you in my last, viz: that I am overworked, both as regards strength and time.

If I did not send you, Mrs Ward, and your family circle the best wishes of this sacred season in my last, let me do so now.

Ever Yrs affecly ⌈John H Newman⌉ of the Oratory

W G Ward Esqr

[1] There appears to be no record of a visit by Ward to Newman.
[2] Thomas Hill Green (1836–82), the philosopher, who was elected a Fellow of Balliol in 1860.

To The Editor of the Lincolnshire Express

The Oratory, Birmingham, June 17, 1862

Sir,

A friend has sent me, by this morning's post, an advertisement cut out from a recent number of your Paper, and signed 'G. Noel Hoare,' of 'Blatherwick Park.'[1]

It contains shocking untruths.

It asks, 'What has become of John Henry Newman?' Any Catholic could have answered the question.

I will enlighten the writer myself on this abstruse, mysterious point.

1. I am John Henry Newman, sometimes called Dr. Newman, sometimes Father Newman, but John Henry Newman still. *Egomet sum proximus mihi.*

2. I have been Superior of a Community of Priests in Birmingham ever since February 2nd, 1849.

3. Also, during the whole of that time I have had the spiritual charge of various large districts, called missions, in Birmingham and its neighbourhood.

4. Also, I have the charge of a school of seventy boys, sons of Catholic gentlemen up and down England and Ireland.

5. Also, I have been in these islands, and on this side of the British Channel, ever since February, 1856; and have only slept one night in Paris since September, 1846.

6. Also, I believe with all my heart and soul all that the Holy Roman Church teaches; and never have had one single doubt about any portion of her teaching whatever, ever since I became a Catholic.

7. Also, in the words of the Creed of Pope Pius IV, 'I freely profess and sincerely hold this true Catholic Faith, without which no one can be saved.'

Such is my account of myself; now for Mr. Hoare's account of me.

1. I am 'an unhappy individual.'

2. I have 'been lately residing in Paris.'

3. I have 'become utterly sceptical.'

4. I 'absolutely ridicule the Creed of Pope Pius IV. and the Romish persuasion altogether.'

5. 'The present phase of my mind' (i.e. scepticism), 'is as notorious as it is hopeless.'

According to Mr. Hoare, then, I am 'living *in Paris* the *unhappy* life of a *hopeless sceptic* and a *notorious* scoffer at the Catholic Religion.'

I can only repeat, What shocking untruths! Why, there is not one truth in his whole letter. I am tempted to ask in my turn, Who is this Mr. G. Noel Hoare? In an age of light, where in the world has the unfortunate man been living? Of what select circle is he the oracle? What bad luck has seduced him into print? What has ailed him to take up a position so false, that the Law might come down upon him, and every Englishman must cry shame upon him?

I am, Sir, your obedient servant, John H. Newman.

---

[1] On 16 June R. G. Macmullen sent Newman a letter addressed to the Editor of the *Lincolnshire Express*, and published there on 14 June, as an advertisement. Macmullen explained that the writer, G. Noel Hoare, was 'a person of some social position, but a busy muddling disciple of the "Reformation Society" school'. He was a cousin of Viscount Campden, the Catholic convert.

The letter was headed JOHN HENRY NEWMAN.
'Blatherwycke Park, June 9

Sir—In admitting controversial letters to the columns of your rising journal, you have acted impartially by inserting those of both sides. In reference, however, to a list of clerical perverts you allude to in your last number, let me suggest to any more of your readers that may wish to ascertain the fact more particularly than "Catholicus," perhaps, will explain, to enquire elsewhere, what has become of his great "giant" of intellect and sanctity—John Henry Newman. I have the authority of a clergyman of high-church caste, resident at Paris (where that unhappy individual has been lately residing), for saying he has become utterly *sceptical*; and as for believing, like "Catholicus," in the creed of Pope Pius IV. (that shibboleth of Romanism concocted in the 16th century), he absolutely ridicules it and the Romish persuasion altogether. I fear, Mr. Editor, the present phase of Mr. Newman's mind is as notorious as hopeless, and if "Catholicus" has no greater "giant" to produce, his list, after all, will prove but a *catena* of pigmies.

Your obedient servant, G. Noel Hoare.'

To The Editor of the Globe

The Oratory, Birmingham, June 28, 1862.

Sir,

A friend has sent me word of a paragraph about me, which appeared in your paper of yesterday, to the effect that 'I have left, or am about to leave, my Oratory at Brompton, of which I have been for several years the head, as a preliminary, in the expectation of my private friends, to my return to the Church of England.'[1]

I consider that you have transferred this statement into your columns from those of a contemporary, in order to give me the opportunity of denying it, if I am able to do so. Accordingly I lose not an hour in addressing these lines to you, which I shall be obliged by your giving at once to the public.

The paragraph is utterly unfounded in every portion of it.

1. For the last thirteen years I have been head of the Birmingham Oratory. I am head still; and I have no reason to suppose that I shall cease to be head, unless advancing years should incapacitate me for the duties of my station.

2. On the other hand, from the time that I founded the London Oratory, now at Brompton, twelve years ago, I have had no jurisdiction over it whatever; and so far from being its head, it so happens I have not been within its walls for the last seven years.

3. I have not had one moment's wavering of trust in the Catholic Church ever since I was received into her fold. I hold, and ever have held, that her Sovereign Pontiff is the centre of unity and the Vicar of Christ. And I ever have had, and have still, an unclouded faith in her creed in all its articles; a supreme satisfaction in her worship, discipline, and teaching; and an eager longing and a hope against hope that the many dear friends whom I have left in Protestantism may be partakers of my happiness.

4. This being my state of mind, to add, as I hereby go on to do, that I have no intention, and never have had any intention, of leaving the Catholic Church and becoming a Protestant again, would be superfluous, except that Protestants are always on the look-out for some loophole or evasion in a Catholic's statement of fact. Therefore, in order to give them full satisfaction,

if I can, I do hereby profess *ex animo*, with an absolute internal assent and consent, that Protestantism is the dreariest of possible religions; that the thought of the Anglican service makes me shiver, and the thought of the Thirty-nine Articles makes me shudder. Return to the Church of England! no; 'the net is broken, and we are delivered.' I should be a consummate fool (to use a mild term) if in my old age I left 'the land flowing with milk and honey' for the city of confusion and the house of bondage.

I am, Sir, your obedient servant, John H. Newman.[2]

[1] William Monsell copied out and sent to Newman a paragraph that appeared in the *Globe* of 27 June, stating that Newman was about to leave the Oratory and return to the Church of England. Monsell added, 'The Globe has great circulation and I suppose it might be well to contradict the lie.' Founded in 1803, the *Globe* was a leading Whig organ until 1866, when it came into Conservative hands.

[2] This letter was published in the *Globe* on 30 June. The rumours that Newman intended to return to the Church of England had been growing.

To W. J. Copeland

The Oratory, Birmingham July 6. 1862

My dearest Copeland,

Now you are not going to disappoint me.[1]

Except Ambrose St John, I have not spoken to any one so near to my heart and memory as you are, for near 17 years—and you are going to deny me what you promised!

I have been lately turning up letters of yours of untold antiquity.

How do I know that I shall ever see you again, if you don't come now? People are carried off so unexpectedly. There was Sir Robert Throckmorton last week, a hearty looking man, younger than I—and he is gone. Men drop as on a battlefield.

And I want to hear so much and to ask so many questions.

Ever Yrs affly John H Newman

[1] Copeland did not disappoint Newman. He visited him in Birmingham from 16 to 18 July.

To Charles Crawley

The Oratory. Bm July 21. 1862

My dear Crawley,

I am glad to find you thought me 'forbearing' in my letters to you last year.[1] I was so, because I love my old friends too deeply and tenderly to hurt them unnecessarily. If I have hurt them by my recent letter in the Globe, it was because I could not do my duty without hurting them. I rejoice to hear from you that there are those who go so far as 'still to retain' as much as 'a very sincere regard and respect for me.' I am obliged to them for it, though for seventeen years they have not shown it. I doubt whether, after so long a silence, they retain the right of expostulation.

341

When you asked me last year whether I should have left the Anglican Church, had the Anglican Church been in 1845, what it was in 1861, I marvelled to think, how little you understood why I left it. I waved [*sic*] the subject in my reply, for why should I have words with you? In a second letter, you could not keep from pressing me with the question, what I thought of your first? and had you given me pain? What strong words I *could* have uttered on the subject about which you were sounding me! but you know how I restrained myself.

Why should we correspond in order to quarrel? cur dextrae jungere dextram non datur?[2] For myself, my alienation from the Anglican system does not lessen my affection for its members, though they have put me into coventry, or my tender love for times and places now far away. Jacob found Laban a hard task master, and had to bear 'the drought by day and the frost by night'; but for the love of Rachel, the seven years which he served for her 'seemed to him but a few days'.[3] I served in order to gain the Pearl of great price, it was a pleasant labour, a pleasant suffering. I look back on it with pleasure; not on Laban, but on Rachel.

I suppose I never should have said a strong word against the Anglicanism which I had left, (and I have said many,) had I been let alone. But 'ye have compelled me.'[4] Ever since I have been a Catholic, the regard and respect you speak of has been shown (I am not speaking in irony) only in one way;—in reports that I was coming back. Vivid manifestations, on my part, of my real state of mind have been the only method by which I have been able to clear the air, and destroy the popular anticipation. They have succeeded for a time; and then I have enjoyed a little peace. But my silence has encouraged its revival, and then I have had to make new manifestations.

Hardly had I left Oxford, when the reports began. I had quarrelled with Dr Wiseman. I was suspended by ecclesiastical authority for my preaching. I had refused to be ordained. I had already come back to the Church of England, or at least my friends about me had done so. I had given up revealed religion altogether. I was an infidel. An Oxford friend of mine did not scruple in the Guardian to suggest this, that I was an infidel.

There was something of a lull in these reports between 1852 and 1859, when they could not well stand their ground in the face of what I was then suffering or doing in the Catholic cause. Then they revived, and with a plausible minuteness of detail. I have had letters from strangers assuming I was a Protestant, or asking whether I was not returning to Protestantism, or telling me that it was only pride that kept me from returning. Persons near conversion have been kept back by the assurance that I was on the point of returning; that I owned that Catholicism had its drawbacks as great as those of Protestantism; that I had recommended Protestants to stay where they were. It was stated that, if I did not return, yet I repented of going over, and was making the best of things; that I felt I never should have left the Established Church, if I had but waited; that I thought one religion as good as the other. All this so told upon some kind Protestants, that they wished to get me to their houses, by way of maturing and smoothing my change back again; and others have proceeded to discuss how I was to be treated, what was to be done with me, on my return.

At length Catholics began to believe the reports also; to their own distress, and to my grave dissatisfaction. I felt that, if I were to die, it was certain to be maintained by numbers of men, and to go down in history, that I had died a Protestant.

I could not, as a matter of conscience, allow such reports to continue without a decisive contradiction; nor could this be given, till they appeared in the Newspapers. At last they made their way into them; and the question then arose, what was the most effectual mode of contradiction.

There was but one real way of putting them down, and I adopted it. It was to show that I regarded Protestantism, not merely with disapprobation, but with aversion and scorn.

I had done this on former occasions, when the same reports were rife, and with success; and it is wonderful to me that the respect and regard for me, of which you speak, after weathering the passages, some of which I proceed to quote, should now take scandal at my letter to the Globe.

1. In 1846. I spoke of 'the Anglican system' as characterised by '*a dreariness which could be felt*, and which seemed the token of an incipient Socinianism,' with 'for orthodoxy, a frigid unelastic, helpless dogmatic, which could give no just account of itself, yet was *intolerant of* all teaching, which contained a doctrine *more* or a doctrine *less*'.[5]

2. In 1849 I said, in prospect, of the Anglican system, 'Twas a *palace of ice*, hard and cold as were they, and when summer came, it all melted away'.[6]

3. In 1850 I said (in strict correspondence with the feeling which I have been expressing above) of the years in which I especially knew you, 'When shall I not feel the soothing recollection of those dear years, which I spent in retirement, *in preparation for my deliverance from Egypt*, asking for light and by degrees gaining it?'[7]

What I have said then in my letter in the Globe about Protestantism and the Anglican system, was, like these former statements, the deliberately chosen and studied means of effecting a necessary end. It was intended to force Protestants to put out of their minds the hope of my ever coming back to them. Tastes, sentiments, affections, are deeper, more permanent, more trustworthy, than conclusions in logic. Convictions change: habits of mind endure. Had I mildly and courteously said that my reason was antagonistic to Protestantism, I should have said what was true, but I should not have obliterated the general anticipation and instinctive suspicion that I should return to it. It would have been said that my words were dictated, nay written by someone else; but I do not think that you yourself, however in your kindness to me you may wish to do so, will be able to cherish the secret hope any longer, now that you are acquainted, in expressions clearly my own, with the intensity and keenness of feeling, with which I regard the work of the Protestant Reformers.

> I am, My dear Crawley, Yours ever affectionately John H Newman

C. Crawley Esqr

---

[1] Writing from Littlemore on 15 July, about the letter of 28 June to the Globe, Crawley found it 'so painfully different' from Newman's letters to himself in the spring of 1861. These showed 'such a kindly forbearing spirit'. Crawley said of the *Globe* letter, 'do tell me that it is *not* yours:—and so relieve the minds of many who still retain a very sincere regard and respect for you'.

[2] *Aeneid* I, 408–9.

[3] *Genesis* 31:40; 29:20.

[4] 2 *Corinthians* 12:11.

[5] See 'John Keble, Fellow of Oriel', *Ess.* II, pp. 443–4.

[6] 'The Pilgrim Queen', *V.V.*, p. 282.

[7] *Diff.* I, p. 82.

To W. J. Copeland

The Oratory Bm Christmas Day 1862

My dear Copeland

So *you* sent the Turkey. I had the direction up, but I did not recognise your hand, for you wrote in a character intended for the benefit of the Railroad people. It is very kind of you. I am sure all here, myself imprimis et ante omnes, wish you all blessing and joy on this day—For myself, I have had a sad disappointment which quite weighs on me. I was taken ill in the night, and, instead of saying three Masses, on this day alone allowed, have said none. I was (as usual) to have sung the 5 o'clock Mass, the only solemnity of the kind in the whole year, and, alas, had to wake Edward Caswall out of a sound sleep to take it for me. How can I eat your Turkey with joy?—I think of Tobit ⟨(Tobias)⟩—whose feast was turned to mourning—and of my own former self at Malta, when on Christmas Day we had no religious act from first to last, but coaled in the morning, and had a portentous spread in the evening.[1]

I have been meditating a call on you these two months—some day or other I shall go to London for my teeth—and shall have to go to my Dentist twice. So I thought of running down to you one evening, and back the next morning. But of course I should write to get leave of you first.

You must come and look at my Letters—I only wish they were all in order. There are so many things I could talk to you about. And I want to show you, (Ambrose so suggests, and blames my omission when you were here) my Episcopal cross, ring, chain etc etc when they were going to make me a Bishop in 1854. The Pope did it—but Dr Cullen to my great joy put a spoke in the wheel, for which he is my great benefactor.

You could not be kinder to me than you are in telling me that persons whom I love have not forgotten me

Ever Yrs affly John H Newman

[1] See letter to Harriett Newman, 25 December 1832.

To Edmund S. Ffoulkes

The Oratory Bm March 20. 1863

My dear Mr Ffoulkes,

I will tell you just what my thoughts are on the anxious and interesting question which is the subject of your letter, though, as you will soon see, they are not worth much.[1]

The whole purpose and action of the Holy See of late years has been in the direction of what is called Unmixed Education, which in consequence must at Rome have been felt to be, not only the best and highest and most thorough mode of educating, but also the most expedient for religion at this time. I have heard of nothing to make me think that the Holy See has, down to this day, faltered ever so little in this course.

Again, though our Bishops perhaps have no very decided, and no very concordant view on the subject, if left to their own judgment by Propaganda, still, our laity, in spite of their thus being free to act as far as the Bishops are concerned, have at present very little thought, as far as I know, of using Oxford and Cambridge for what is so necessary, if we are to have any weight in England, places of University education of their sons.

As to ourselves at the Oratory, we should be guided, first, by the judgment of the Holy See, even though not formally expressed; therefore, we have no thought at all at present of connecting our School with Oxford or Cambridge, even if we could.

But, secondly, parents have a will of their own; and, as we should be obliged to follow their decision, did they propose Woolwich for their sons or the London University, or the Catholic University of Ireland, or Louvain, so we should do our best to prepare any youths for Oxford and Cambridge, did they wish it. Some have wished it, but not as yet any great many.

If they are to go to the two Universities, it is far better that they should go to a College of their own there, than to any of the existing ones. And I suppose, did many Catholic youths go to Oxford, whether from the Oratory, or from Oscott, or from Stonyhurst, the Bishops would feel themselves obliged to provide a Hall for them, unless they absolutely forbad their going at all. I am not certain that Propaganda would not urge upon them the latter course; but, if they did recognise their going, then, it is likely they would make their entrance at the Catholic Hall imperative. And if a Hall already existed, such as you are proposing to establish, they would naturally avail themselves of it; or, even if they set up one of their own, they could not refuse to license yours also. Perhaps, however, they would impose conditions on you.

However, you might have some difficulty also with the parents. They may wish their sons to go to Oxford for the very purpose of their mixing with the men of some particular College as Ch Ch [Christ Church]; and their purpose in sending them would be defeated, even though they sent them to Balliol, Oriel, or Merton, and à fortiori if they sent them to a Catholic Hall. Accordingly, if they were obliged by the Bishops to avail themselves of a Catholic Hall, or not think of Oxford at all, they might prefer to waive the University altogether.

Then again, I believe the Liberal party are, to say the least, quite as strong as the High Church, against allowing Catholics any recognition, such as granting a Hall would be. Indeed, putting all other reasons aside, such as their apprehensions of the polemical effects of a Catholic Society in Oxford, with its argumentative power and its ritual, it is simply against the principles of the Liberals to acknowledge any religious profession as such; and it would certainly be difficult to them to ignore successfully, even if they wished it, that, in admitting you, they were admitting the Catholic Head of a Catholic House.

Lastly, if you ask my own opinion on the matter, I can only answer, in perfect sincerity, that I am fairly puzzled. I see at present no issue of existing difficulties, and therefore am a waiter on events to come.

I rejoice to hear of the good news, which you tell me, so intimately interesting to yourself, and beg to offer you and Mrs Ffoulkes my best congratulations.[2]

I shall be glad to hear of the progress of your plans & am My dear Mr Ffoulkes,

Very sincerely Yours John H Newman of the Oratory

E. S. Ffoulkes Esqr

[1] Ffoulkes wrote on 19 March: 'I heard casually, though from no unusual personage, that you intend your pupils eventually going to Oxford or Cambridge, as the case may be. Now, it so happens that I have long had a scheme in my head, which I have been compelled to defer hitherto for various reasons, of going back to Oxford and setting up a Hall for Catholic students exclusively'.

[2] Ffoulkes's wife had become a Catholic.

To Mrs John Mozley

The Oratory, Bm ⌈May 18. 1863⌉

My dear Jemima

I take advantage of the recurrence of the 19th, of which I trust and pray you may have many happy returns, to get you to tell me how you are. Alas! as life goes on, one understands that it is almost a mockery to talk of many happy returns, if by 'happy' is meant as is commonly meant something temporal and external; for, if there are many returns, they cannot be happy ones.

I had looked out for you my Letters from abroad in 1832–3, as you wished; when the friend,[1] to whom I am to leave all my papers, happening to see them spread out, protested, on the ground that they contained the originals of my Poems in the Lyra Apostolica, and were intimately connected with the rise of the Oxford movement. The obvious solution of the difficulty would be to get copies made of them; but I doubt if you think them worth so much fuss. However, I will gladly do so, if you wish it, and you shall have the autographs. Any how, I should like, some time, to see the letters, which, during the same expedition, I wrote to *you*.

I wish I had any thing else to offer you instead. I would propose yours and my Mother's letters to me, if they were not of an ephemeral character necessarily, consisting of reference to what was going on either in the public or in their own world, or of matters of business. To be sure, they would vividly bring before you times gone by; yet to my own feelings the most pleasant memories of the past are painful. What one should like would be that a selection of some of them or parts of them could be made, which would interest a girl like Jane in her mother's early life and in her grandmother.[2] I have often regretted that I never asked my Mother any thing about her early life, her father of whom she was so fond, and her connections. Jane may be one day a grandmother herself; and, could any thing be preserved of my mother of a tangible nature, would thus be able to connect five generations, being the centre of them herself.

But I fear it is too probable that the warm affections and charities of the human heart, of which correspondence is both the stimulant and the expression, are evanescent in their exhibition, and fade away from the gaze of men as the ink in which they are recorded. Thackeray's Virginians opens very beautifully with a reference to a supposed collection of such letters, though *he* professes to have made a story out of them. And so too I was reading, a few days since, as for a last revision, my own books of Extracts, made in 1825, of my Letters received by me between 1804 and 1824; and it certainly reads like an interesting tale, with perfect unity of plot, yet sufficient variety of digression. But then, I am the hero of it; and moreover can from memory fill out and colour the outlines of which it is made up;—what would be *another's* judgment of it? Perhaps there are not half a dozen letters in the whole collection that are of any permanent value; yet I cannot tell myself, nor can any one else perhaps just now, what portions are important, and what are not; and under such circumstances I suppose I must leave it, as it stands, for the judgment of those who come after me.

What I really should covet, though I dare say it would give you much trouble, or rather would be impossible in you to grant till your strength is restored to you, would be the loan of my own letters to you between 1833 and 1845. If you numbered them, you should have them all back safely. ⌈It has ever been a hobby of mine (unless it be a truism, not a hobby) that a man's life lies in his letters. This is why Hurrell Froude published St Thomas a Beckett's Letters, with nothing of his own except what was necessary for illustration or connection of parts. It is the principle, I suppose, of the interest which attaches to such novels as Clarissa Harlowe, Evelina etc.[3] And it is exemplified in one of the popular novels of the day, the Woman in White, in which I cannot detect any merit except what lies in the narrative being a living development of events as exhibited in supposed letters, memoranda, and [[quasi-legal]] depositions.⌉[4]

A much higher desideratum than interest in Biography is met by the method, (as it may be called,) of Correspondence. ⌈Biographers varnish; they assign motives; they conjecture feelings; they interpret Lord Burleigh's nods;⌉[5] they palliate or defend. For myself, I sincerely wish to seem neither better nor worse than I am. I detest suppression; and here is the great difficulty. It may be said that to ask a biographer to edit letters is like putting salt on the bird's tail. How can you secure his fidelity? He must take care not to hurt people, make mischief, or get into contro-versy. Hence men, like Talleyrand, have forbade the publication of their corres-pondence till a thirty years have passed since their death, that the existing generation may have fairly died out. But party interests and party feelings never die out; and how can one promise oneself that men thirty years hence, whom one has never seen, into whose hands one's MSS come, will be above the influence of party motives, at a time when personal delicacies and difficulties are in their graves? It is very seldom that correspondence can be given *in extenso*, by reason of its prolixity. There must necessarily be a selection of passages; sometimes one half sentence alone is valuable in a whole letter, and that, very valuable: but it may tell on this side [of] a controversy, or on that: and whether it sees the light or not will depend upon the perspicacity or straightforwardness of an Editor.

However, I did not intend any such disquisition on biographical literature, when I began to write. The subject comes before me by fits and starts. When I have a little leisure, I recur to my pigeon-holes of letters, where they stand year by year from 1836 down to this date. I have digested them up to the former year. Thus from time to time I do a little work in the way of sifting, sorting, preserving, or burning. By the bye, one ought to write on good paper; some of my Mother's of 30 years since break under my hands like tinder, on the very opening of them

Ever Yours affectly John H Newman

Mrs John Mozley

P.S. I have found one or two child's letters of Herbert's—which I send you as a not unwelcome birthday gift. You will not treat them as before now other people have done, to whom I have sent letters I have found of theirs, and have got, not only no thanks, but no answer to show that they had arrived safely.[6]

---

[1] Ambrose St John.

[2] Jane Mozley (1844–91), Jemima's only daughter.

[3] Samuel Richardson's *Clarissa Harlowe*, 1747–8, and Fanny Burney's *Evelina*, 1778.

[4] Wilkie Collins's *The Woman in White* was published in *All the Year Round*, in 1860.

[5] Sheridan, *The Critic*, Act iii.

[6] Herbert was Jemima's eldest son. She replied on 19 May, 'It was a great pleasure to receive your two packets this morning. I shall be very glad indeed to receive Herbert's childish letters....I will remember your request about your letters, and get things out *by degrees*. As to those you have got (addressed to me)...keep them for the present. I have always thought your letters should be *together* as much as possible.'

To Emily Bowles

The Oratory Bm May 19. 1863

MOST PRIVATE

My dear Miss Bowles

Thank you for your most affectionate letter.[1] What you tell me is utter news to me. *I* never had any message from Fr St John. *I* never knew you had sent me a book. There is another thing which I do know, and perhaps you don't; that in a most cruel correspondence which we had in 1860, a letter of mine to you, perhaps a concluding one, was, as we found, mysteriously lost—I don't think *here*—but it was put into the post box, and did not get to you. I have so washed away the whole matter from my mind, that I know nothing but this fact. Perhaps its absence may have had some bearing on your impressions about my feelings, and have served (untruly) as a key to interpret other acts or non-acts of mine by.[2]

Don't think about *me*—God uses his instruments as he will. Hunc humiliat et hunc exaltat.[3] To myself I feel as full of thought and life as ever I was—but a certain invisible chain impedes me, or bar stops me, when I attempt to do any thing—and the only reason why I do not *enjoy* the happiness of being out of conflict is, because I feel to myself I could do much in it. But in fact I could not do much in it. I should come into collision with every one I met—I should be treading on every one's toes. From the very first an effort has been successfully made to separate all converts from me, and they are the only persons who would be likely to move aside of me without jostling. You told me that the Cardinal said that he had asked me to go to live in London. I said he never did. After you were gone, I asked Fr St John whether I could have forgotten it—but he answered with a distinctness and force which I did not use in speaking to you; 'No, no he never did.' (By the bye the last day or two Fr St John was in London, and tried to get at you, but could not get the time.) Well, I know what the Cardinal did say to Fr Faber, and what Fr Faber said to the world, viz 'that I had put myself on the shelf, and there was no help for it.'

But now to go to the root of the matter. This country is under Propaganda, and Propaganda is too shallow to have the wish to use such as me. It is rather afraid of such. If I know myself, no one can have been more loyal to the Holy See than I am. I love the Pope personally into the bargain. But Propaganda is a quasi-military power, extraordinary, for missionary countries, rough and ready. It does not understand an intellectual movement. It likes quick results—scalps from beaten foes by the hundred. Our Bishop once on his return from Rome, said pointedly to me what I am sure came as a quasi message from Propaganda, that at Rome 'they liked good news.'

True, the words were said with an implied antithesis—for I had lately been to Rome to complain. I suppose the issue of the Achilli matter must have made them despise me at Rome—but, whatever the cause of it was, two years after, Propaganda, without saying a word to me, appointed three Bishops to examine and report to it whether the Rule of the Birmingham Oratory could be, on a certain point, suspended to advantage. The news broke upon us in a message to the effect that a *Rescript* (which one, who was in the plot, said it would be mortal sin to disobey) was on the road from Rome, embodying the change. You may fancy the commotion it excited among us. Our Fathers wrote to me in Dublin, conjuring me to do something. I wrote an urgent letter to the Cardinal. He left it unanswered for a month. I wrote again, and then went up to London from Dublin—but effected nothing. Then, our Fathers prevailed on me to go to Rome about it. When I got there, I found to my great relief and gratitude, that at the last moment the dear Pope, when the matter necessarily came before him, simply asked, 'Has Dr Newman been consulted?' and would not give his assent to the act. Then, when I saw him, he asked me, *why* I wished to get him to make me head or general of the two Oratories! of which not even a dream had come into our minds here, more than that of making you a Father General of us;—showing what hidden tales against me were going on. When we saw Mgr Barnabò, he was very cross, and asked me why I had come to Rome, when, if I had remained quiet at home, the Pope would, as it turned out, have acted for me. When Monsell went to Rome shortly after, he came back with the remark that I had no friend at Rome. It was true:—but what had I *done*? *this* I had *not* done, and there was the rub, I had not preached sermons, made speeches, fussed about, and reported all my proceeding to Propaganda. I had been working away very hard in Ireland at the University, and saying nothing about it.

Well, immediately my Dublin engagement was over, at the Cardinal's and our Bishop's direct sollicitation, I interfered in the Rambler matter—and found myself in consequence, to my surprise and disgust, compelled to take the Editorship on myself. I not only made the best of it, but I really determined to make it *my work*. All those questions of the day which make so much noise now, Faith and Reason, Inspiration, etc etc would have been, according to my ability, worked out or fairly opened. Of course I required elbow room—but this was *impossible*. Our good Bishop, who has ever acted as a true friend, came after the publication of the first number, and advised me to give up the Editorship. He said I had caused dissatisfaction. I only edited two numbers; but I wrote enough to cause one of our Bishops formally to denounce one of the articles to Propaganda. What did Propaganda know of the niceties of the English language? yet a message came (not a formal one) asking explanations, and on the other hand dangling before my eyes the vision of a Bishoprick, if I explained well. It seems they fancied that I was soured because a Bishoprick was to be given me in 1854 (six years before) and Dr Cullen had stopped it. How little they knew of me! but I suppose they have to deal with low minded men. As what was said to me was very indirect and required no answer, I kept silence and the whole matter was hushed up. I suppose so—for I have heard no more of it—but I suppose it might (pel bisogno) be revived at any time.[4]

Don't you see that this, if nothing else, puts a great obex to my writing? This age of the Church is peculiar—in former times, primitive and medieval, there was not the extreme centralization which now is in use. If a private theologian said any thing free, another answered him. If the controversy grew, then it went to a Bishop, a theological faculty, or to some foreign University. The Holy See was but the court of ultimate appeal. *Now*, if I, as a private priest, put any thing into print, *Propaganda* answers me at once. How can I fight with such a chain on my arm? It is like the Persians driven on to fight *under the lash*. There was true private judgment in the primitive and medieval schools—there are no schools now, no private judgment (in the *religious* sense of the phrase,) no freedom, that is, of opinion. That is, no exercise of the intellect. No, the system goes on by the tradition of the intellect of former times. This is a way of things which, in God's own time, will work its own cure, of necessity; nor need we fret under a state of things, much as we may feel it, which is incomparably less painful than the state of the Church before Hildebrand, and again in the fifteenth century.

I am only speaking of it in its bearing on myself. There was some talk, when the Bishop put in his plea against me, of calling me to Rome. Call me to Rome! What does that mean? It means to sever an old man from his Home, to subject him to intercourse with persons whose languages are strange to him: it means to bring him to a climate, which is unhealthy to him—to food, and to floors, which are almost starvation on one hand, and involve restless days and nights on the other—it means to oblige him to dance attendance on Propaganda week after week and month after month—it means his death. (It was the punishment on Dr Baines in 1840–1 to keep him at the door of Propaganda for a year.)[5]

This is the prospect which I cannot but feel probable, did I say any thing, which one bishop in England chose to speak against and report. Others have been killed there before me. Lucas went of his own accord indeed—but when he got there, oh how much did he, as loyal a son of the Church and Holy See as ever was, what did he suffer because Dr Cullen was against him! He wandered, (as Dr Cullen *said* in a letter he published in a sort of triumph,) he wandered from Church to Church without a friend, and hardly got an audience from the Pope.[6] And I too should go from St Philip to our Lady, and to St Peter and St Paul, and to St Laurence and to St Cecilia, and, if it happened to me, as to Lucas, should come back to die.

We are not better than our Fathers. Think of St Joseph Calasanctius, or of Blessed Paul of the Cross, or of St Alfonso—or of my own St Philip, how they were misunderstood by the authorities at Rome. The Cardinal Vicar called Philip, to his face and in public, an ambitious party man, and suspended his faculties. It is by bearing these things that we gain merit, but has one a right to *bring it on one?*

I never wrote such a letter to any one yet, and I shall think twice before I send you the whole of it

Ever Yrs affly John H Newman

May 19/63

---

[1] Emily Bowles began her letter of 17 May, 'The sight of your most loved handwriting seemed to break a spell of silence which I thought would never end. You will say "Why did you not end it?" I wrote to Fr St John asking him to tell me if I might go on writing to you . . . No answer. I sent two little books, as he said you had never seen them he thought—Still a dead silence.'

[2] The 'cruel correspondence' was perhaps that about Emily's brother Frederick Bowles.

[3] *Psalm* 74:8. Emily Bowles wanted Newman to intervene in the controversies aroused by the Association for the Promotion of the Unity of Christendom and by the *Union Review*.

[4] When St John went to Rome in 1867 on Newman's behalf, the *Rambler* delation, 1859–60, was the first matter that arose.

[5] Peter Augustine Baines, Vicar Apostolic of the Western District, had issued a pastoral attacking what he considered indiscreet novelties in devotion.

[6] Frederick Lucas (1812–55), a friend of Newman's and MP for Meath from 1852, went to Rome in the winter of 1854–5, appealing on behalf of the Irish Tenant League. Cullen opposed him as a dangerous nationalist.

To Emily Bowles

The Oratory Bm May 29. 1863

My dear Miss Bowles,

I should have acknowledged your parcel of Lamps, which I was very glad to see, and your own contributions to its luminousness,[1] had not St Philip come in the way,[2] and given us a great deal of pleasant trouble, yet engrossing and absorbing, however pleasant, as is befitting, when the Master of a house comes to visit it. I was half tempted to ask you to come down to pay your homage to him, but doubted how far you were at liberty to do so, even had you leisure.

I send you the rest of my letter of ten days ago; and I do this principally because it strikes me you may fancy all sorts of miseries, which have no foundation, if I do not.

Sometimes I seem to myself inconsistent, in professing to love retirement, yet seeming impatient at doing so little; yet I trust I am not so in any very serious way. In my letter to the Bishop of Oxford, on occasion of Number 90, I said that I had come forward, because no one else had done so, and that I rejoiced to return to that privacy which I valued more than any thing else. When I became a Catholic, I considered I never should even write again, except on definite unexciting subjects, such as history and philosophy and criticism; and, if on controversial subjects, still not on theology proper. And when I came here, where I have been for 14 years, I deliberately gave myself to a life of obscurity, which in my heart I love best. And so it has been, and so it is now, that the routine work of each day is in fact more than enough for my thoughts and my time. I have no leisure. I have had to superintend two successive enlargements of our Church, to get the Library in order, to devote a good deal of pains to our music, and a great deal more to our accounts. Then, there was my Dublin engagement, and now there is the School. Just now too I am Sacristan, so hard up are we for hands. Things seem ordered for me, without my having a will in the matter.

And I am not only content, but really pleased that so things are. Yet there are three considerations which from time to time trouble me. First, lest my being where I am is my own doing in any measure, for then I say, 'Perhaps I am hiding my talent in a napkin.' Next, people say to me, 'why are you not doing more? how much you could do!' and then, since I think I could do a great deal, if I were let to do it, I become uneasy. And lastly, willing as I am to observe St Philip's dear rule that 'we should despise being despised,' yet when I find that scorn and contempt become the means of *my Oratory being injured*, as they have before now, then I get impatient.— Now observe, the letter of which I send you now the remainder is a freer one *than I ever wrote to any one before*

Ever Yrs affly J H N.

[1] The *Lamp*, a popular Catholic illustrated weekly, founded in 1850, to which Emily Bowles contributed.

[2] The feast of St Philip Neri is celebrated on 26 May.

To Isaac Williams

The Oratory, Birmingham, June 7. 1863.

My dearest Isaac

Your letter came an hour or two ago. I rejoiced to have it. Is it possible you should not have seen more of Oxford of late years than I have? I have not seen more than its spires in passing since February 22. 1846. I dined and slept at dear Johnson's, and left for good. I only heard lately that the cap and gown had gone out, and yet did not believe it, till you have confirmed it. Heu quantum mutatus ab illo![1] Of all human things perhaps, Oxford is nearest my heart—and some parsonages in the country— I cannot even realize to myself that I shall never see what I love so much again, though I have had time enough to do so in. But why should I wish to see what is no longer what I loved? All things change; the past never returns here. My friends, I confess have *not* been kind—I suppose this is what you allude to, as my having expressed it to Copeland. But really, I think I have a reason. I should not notice it, if *you* had not. If they act *on principle*, I should not say a word, but love them the better for it—If they said, as we used to say of Arnold, 'I cannot recognize you,' I understand it fully and am satisfied. But such cases are the exception. There is. . . .[2] That at least he could not do on principle. Well, well, if I spoke severely to Copeland, I am sorry for it,—but I don't think I did. I am *not* 'holy' in spite of you, but I think *I am* 'calm and loving,' though I wish there were more of supernatural grace and holiness in that calm and love. But to return. If any place in England will right itself it is Oxford; but I despond about the cause of dogmatic truth in England altogether. Who can tell what is before us? The difficulty is that the arguments of infidelity are deeper than those of Protestantism, and in the same direction, (I am using Protestantism in the sense in which you and Pusey would agree in using it.) and how can you bring back to something more primitive, more Christian, a whole nation, a whole Church? The course of everything is onwards, not backwards. Till Phaeton runs through his day, and is chucked from his chariot, you cannot look for the new morning. Every thing I hear makes me fear that latitudinarian opinions are spreading furiously in the Church of England. I grieve most deeply at it—The Anglican Church has been a most useful breakwater against scepticism—The time might come when you as well as I might expect that it would be said above, 'Why cumbereth it the ground?'[3]—but at present it upholds far more truth in England than any other form of religion would, and than the Catholic Roman Church could. But what I fear is that it is *tending* to a powerful establishment teaching direct error, and more powerful than it ever has been; thrice powerful, because it does teach error. It is what the Whig party have been at, all our time, not destroying the establishment, but corrupting it. Do you recollect little John Whitman? He is now a man of thirty and a shoemaker, living near us. He was calling on me an hour ago. He has just lost his mother. She broke a leg and died. She and Whitman live in St Clement's, he tells me. He is a nice fellow, but I neither liked, nor now like, father and mother, poor things. He was brought up by Mrs Small and Mrs Tombs, and never lived at home[4]

Ever Yours affly John H. Newman

---

[1] *Aeneid* II, 274.

[2] The copyist has left a gap of a line here. The letter to Copeland was that of 23 January 1863 (*L.D.* XX, pp. 399–400).

[3] *Luke* 13:7.

[4] They were inhabitants of Littlemore. Williams became Newman's curate in 1832.

To Cardinal Wiseman

The Oratory Bm July 14. 1863

My dear Lord Cardinal

I thank your Eminence for the feeling which dictated your Eminence's letter.[1]

I am perfectly aware of the hopeless state in which Fr Faber lies.

Your Eminence will be glad to know that Fr Faber has already been informed by me, not only of my wish to see him, but of the precise time when I hope to have that sad satisfaction

Your Eminence's obt Servt in Xt John H Newman

The Cardinal Wiseman

[1] Wiseman wrote in the afternoon of 14 July, after a visit to Faber, of the strong desire the latter had expressed of seeing Newman. 'He spoke of you with entire affection, and I am sure that a visit from you would shed a brightness over his death. He indeed expects this consolation; but you may not be aware how fast the end is approaching.' Newman visited him on 20 July.

To John Keble

The Oratory, Birmingham August 15. 1863

My dearest Keble,

I returned from abroad last night, and, among the letters on my table waiting my arrival, found yours. I answer it before any of the others.

Thank you very much for it, and for the books which accompany it, which I value first for your dear sake, next for their venerable and excellent subject. I am pleased too that you should tell me about your wife and brother—but how odd it seems to me that you should speak of yourself and of him as old! Did you ever read Mrs Sheridan's Tale of Nourjahad! such I think is the name. I have not read it since a boy.[1] I am like one of the seven sleepers awakened, when you so write to me, considering all my recollections of Hursley and of Bisley, which remain photographed on my mind, are of twenty five years ago, or thirty. I cannot think of little Tom but as of the boy I carried pick a back, when he was tired in getting from the steep valley to the table land of Bisley. And I recollect your Father, and your dear Sister, and your wife, as you cannot recollect them—at least the latter two—for in my case their images are undimmed by the changes which years bring upon us all. My great delight is to take up your Poetry Lectures—I only love them too well, considering my age, and that their subject is not simply a religious one. But what do *you* mean by saying that you are 'as if dying?' I have heard nothing of your being unwell; and I trust you will live long, and every year more and more to the glory of God.

I have not been abroad for pleasure till now, since I went with dear Hurrell. I went to St Germain's near Paris to see the Wilberforces. Then my dear and faithful friend, who went with me, Ambrose St John, insisted I should cut across to Treves, the place of sojourn of St Athanasius, St Ambrose, and St Jerome. Then we went down the Moselle and up the Rhine, which was all new to me, and we came back by Aix la Chapelle. I had a bad accident there, with (thank God and my guardian Angel) no harm whatever. I had a bag in one hand and clokes in the other, and turning round sharp at the top of a staircase, was sent down two flights headlong—but thank God I got nothing but a slight strain of the arm. Since then I have been stopping at Ostend to recruit.

I have said all this, knowing it will interest you. Never have I doubted for one moment your affection for me—never have I been hurt at your silence. I interpreted it easily—it was not the silence of men, nor the forgetfulness of men, who can recollect about me and talk about me enough, when there is something to be said to my disparagement. You are always with me a thought of reverence and love—and there is nothing I love better than you, and Isaac, and Copeland and many others I could name, except Him whom I ought to love best of all and supremely. May He Himself, who is the over abundant compensation for all losses, give me His own Presence—and then I shall want nothing and desiderate nothing—but none *but* He, *can* make up for the losses of those old familiar faces which haunt me continually.

Ever Yours most affectionately John H Newman

[1] Mrs Francis Sheridan (1724–66), was the mother of the playwright. Her *History of Nourjahad*, published in 1767, describes a sleeper who wakes every fifty years.

To J. D. Dalgairns

The Oratory Bm Septr 27/63

My dear Fr Bernard

Thank you for your telegram and letter. Stokes had prepared us for the event last week, for till then, all the accounts we heard were good. His long sufferings are over and bring him so much nearer, if not close, to his refrigerium and reward.[1]

Fr Ambrose and I propose to come to the Requiem on Wednesday. We shall present ourselves at eight a.m. under the hope that it will not be inconvenient for us to say Mass. I suppose the office and requiem will be at 10. After it we shall return to Birmingham.

Besides our three Masses here, we are having a Solemn Requiem. Various of our boys gave their communions with the same intention this morning.

Yours affectly John H Newman

The Revd Fr Dalgairns

[1] Faber died on 26 September.

To Miss Mary Holmes

The Oratory, Bm Novr 20. 1863

My dear Miss Holmes,

I was very glad to have your letters, and to find that for the present you are in peace. It is sad indeed that you are so much upon the rough sea.

I think I must have written to you since I returned from abroad—for that was such a time ago. I had not left England for pleasure since the year 1833, when I went with Hurrell Froude.

You ask about poor Fr Faber—I have nothing to tell. I saw him before he died—he suffered a good deal. His people are trying to make him a saint, and, depend on it, we shall soon have reports of miracles. It is very natural—he was a person of great natural gifts, and of high aspirations, and of an impulsive affectionateness. His great fault was that he was not the same man two days running—you never could be sure of him. He has devoted himself to religious writing, and has suffered a great deal of pain—but I had rather be in the shoes of one Dr Weedall than a dozen Father Fabers. You must not repeat this, please.[1]

Our school is flourishing—but the opposition made to it is so great that our hope is in nothing we see realized, but in St Philip, who seems to have taken us up. Hitherto, we have made progress against wind and tide.

I received the 2/

Ever Yours affectly John H Newman of the Oratory

Miss Holmes

[1] Newman had in the past written to Miss Holmes his admiration for Dr Weedall, and had more recently sent her the sermon he preached at his funeral, 'The Tree beside the Waters,' O.S., pp. 243–62. Weedall met with great adversities in his life. He was the founder of the New Oscott College, and was then supplanted by Wiseman. He also suffered physically. Cf. O.S., pp. 328–35.

The *Apologia* and the Oxford Mission
(1863–65)

At the end of December 1863 Newman received a copy of *Macmillan's Magazine* in the post, drawing his attention to a passing remark in a book review by Charles Kingsley. Kingsley, Anglican clergyman, Professor of Modern History, and novelist, had observed, 'Truth, for its own sake, had never been a virtue with the Roman clergy. Father Newman informs us that it need not, and on the whole ought not to be.' He could not have touched a rawer nerve. For many years, even before his reception as a Catholic, Newman had endured allegations of dishonesty. He had always remained silent, wondering whether he would ever have the chance to reply.

He wrote the same day to Macmillan's, drawing their attention to 'a grave and gratuitous slander, with which I feel confident you will be sorry to find associated a name so eminent as yours'. Further correspondence followed and Kingsley forwarded to Newman a letter of apology that was to appear in the next number of the *Magazine*. Newman regarded the apology as inadequate and in February he published their correspondence with a brief, but crushing commentary. Kingsley replied with a pamphlet of his own, *What, then, does Dr Newman Mean?*, and it was this salvo that led Newman to conclude that answering particular charges laid against him would not be enough. He had to tell the story of his religious opinions to show, whether people agreed with his views or not, that he had always acted honestly. He recognized that Kingsley was 'a furious foolish fellow', but he had a name, he was known. His pamphlet, 'a hodge podge of charges against me all about dishonesty', was a public challenge that had to be answered. 'I must speak,' Newman explained to Richard Church, 'and, unless I speak strongly, men won't believe me in earnest.'[1]

Writing his *Apologia* was for Newman both agony and relief. It was a relief at last to have the opportunity to explain himself, to show that in becoming a Catholic he had behaved honestly and honourably, but it was an agony to have to reveal his inmost thoughts and feelings. He was able to consult copies of his earlier letters and his memoranda, but papers for the crucial years were in disorder, and he needed to be accurate. His publisher insisted that his reply should not be delayed. He worked tirelessly, publishing seven parts weekly between April and June and calling on Anglican friends for criticism and corrections, especially those like Copeland, Church, and Rogers with whom he had made contact again in recent times. At one point he remarked to Church, 'Forgive my penmanship. My fingers have been *walking* nearly 20 miles a day.'[2] He felt he was

---

[1] 23 April 1864, *L.D.* XXI, p. 100. [2] 29 April 1864, *L.D.* XXI, p. 105.

speaking not only for himself, but also for the Catholic priesthood. The result was both a literary masterpiece and a personal triumph. Old friends, long separated, were able to realize the affection he still had for them and Catholic priests around the country paid him tribute. It was a turning-point for him, but not the end of his troubles.

One growing controversy concerned university education for Catholics. Should they be allowed to go to Oxford? If so, should they become members of the old colleges or should a Catholic college be erected for them? Newman was sceptical about the Catholic college. He believed that fathers would prefer their sons to follow in their footsteps. If they did so, however, pastoral care would need to be provided for them. With that in view he was encouraged by Bishop Ullathorne to establish a mission at Oxford and so he bought a plot of land. Letters at this time reveal Newman's shrewd business sense. There were others, however, completely opposed to the plan, who persuaded Rome to forbid Catholics access to Oxford. As Newman became aware of this opposition, he worked hard to safeguard what he had spent. He was supported by old friends, in this instance Edward Pusey and Mark Pattison, who helped him sell back the land. His exasperation is plain in a letter to Pattison: 'It is indeed marvellous that anyone should dream of enforcing a prohibition, when not one step is taken, nor hope held out, of any place of educating young Catholics *instead* of Oxford.'

One opponent was Manning. How influential he was at this stage is disputed, but, although they had never been close friends, the friendliness between them was now becoming strained. Newman had asked Manning's help when he was composing his *Apologia* and had thanked him for it warmly, in fact unawares he did so twice. But Manning already felt bruised by Newman when views of his on the temporal power of the papacy were criticized in the *Rambler*, although Newman was no longer editor when the article had appeared and had not seen it, while Newman was suspicious of Manning's rigid orthodoxy, which he called a 'dull tyranny'.[3] The trust between them was dwindling. When a rumour began circulating that Manning would succeed Wiseman as Archbishop, Newman commented to Pusey, 'I can't believe it'. When it happened, however, he wrote to accept the invitation he had received to Manning's episcopal consecration, but on the condition that Manning no longer attempt to have him too made a bishop. This was the third occasion when that possibility had threatened Newman. But he resisted it as a strategy that would seek to tame him. 'Such an honour', he declared, 'would be to me Saul's armour on David.'

During this intense period of Newman's life there are other memorable letters, personal, polemical, and philosophical. While absorbed in the *Apologia*, he found time to thank Jemima for marmalade she had sent, 'better than any other I ever ate'. Invited by George Talbot to preach to educated Protestants in Rome, he sent his famously withering reply, 'Birmingham people have souls; and I have neither taste not talent for the sort of work, which you cut out for me.' And in a letter to John Walker he illustrates how probabilities can bring certainty by using the image of a cable, 'which is made up of separate threads, each feeble, yet together as sufficient as an iron rod'. And early in 1865, Newman was writing *The Dream of Gerontius*.

[3] Letter to Sir John Acton, 18 March 1864, *L.D.* XXI, p. 84.

8

The *Apologia* and the Oxford
Mission (1863–65)

To Messrs Macmillan and Co.

The Oratory, Dec. 30, 1863.

Gentlemen,

I do not write to you with any controversial purpose, which would be preposterous; but I address you simply because of your special interest in a Magazine which bears your name.

That highly respected name you have associated with a Magazine, of which the January number has been sent to me by this morning's post, with a pencil mark calling my attention to page 217.[1]

There, apropos of Queen Elizabeth, I read as follows:—

'Truth, for its own sake, had never been a virtue with the Roman clergy. Father Newman informs us that it need not, and on the whole ought not to be; that cunning is the weapon which Heaven has given to the saints wherewith to withstand the brute male force of the wicked world which marries and is given in marriage. Whether his notion be doctrinally correct or not, it is at least historically so.'

There is no reference at the foot of the page to any words of mine, much less any quotation from my writings, in justification of this statement.

I should not dream of expostulating with the writer of such a passage, nor with the editor who could insert it without appending evidence in proof of its allegations. Nor do I want any reparation from either of them. I neither complain of them for their act, nor should I thank them if they reversed it. Nor do I even write to you with any desire of troubling you to send me an answer. I do but wish to draw the attention of yourselves, as gentlemen, to a grave and gratuitous slander, with which I feel confident you will be sorry to find associated a name so eminent as yours.

I am, Gentlemen, Your obedient Servant, John H. Newman.

---

[1] The sender of the copy of *Macmillan's Magazine*, which led to the writing of the *Apologia*, was William Pope. See letter of 27 February 1864.

To Charles Kingsley

The Oratory, Birmingham, January 7, 1864.

Reverend Sir,

I have to acknowledge your letter of the 6th, informing me that you are the writer of an article in Macmillan's Magazine, in which I am mentioned, and referring generally to a Protestant sermon of mine, of seventeen pages, published by me, as Vicar of St. Mary's, in 1844, and treating of the bearing of the Christian towards the world, and of the character of the reaction of that bearing upon him; and also, referring to my works *passim*; in justification of your statement, categorical and definite, that 'Father Newman informs us that truth for its own sake need not, and on the whole ought not to be, a virtue with the Roman clergy.'

I have only to remark, in addition to what I have already said with great sincerity to Messrs. Macmillan and Co., in the letter of which you speak, and to which I refer you, that, when I wrote to them, no person whatever, whom I had ever seen or heard of, had occurred to me as the author of the statement in question. When I received your letter, taking upon yourself the authorship, I was amazed.

I am, Reverend Sir, Your obedient Servant, John H. Newman.

To Alexander Macmillan

The Oratory, January 8, 1864.

Dear Sir,

I thank you for the friendly tone of your letter of the 5th just received, and I wish to reply to it with the frankness which it invites.[1] I have heard from Mr. Kingsley, avowing himself, to my extreme astonishment, the author of the passage about which I wrote to Messrs. Macmillan. No one, whose name I had ever heard, crossed my mind as the writer in their Magazine; and, had any one said that it was Mr. Kingsley, I should have laughed in his face. Certainly, I saw the initials at the end; but, you must recollect, I live out of the world; and I must own, if Messrs. Macmillan will not think the confession rude, that, as far as I remember, I never before saw even the outside of their Magazine. And so of the Editor: when I saw his name on the cover, it conveyed to me absolutely no idea whatever. I am not defending myself, but merely stating what was the fact; and as to the article, I said to myself, 'Here is a young scribe, who is making a cheap reputation by smart hits at safe objects.'[2]

All this will make you see, not only how I live out of the world, but also how wanton I feel it to have been in the parties concerned thus to let fly at me. Were I in active controversy with the Anglican body, or any portion of it, as I have been before now, I should consider untrue assertions about me to be in a certain sense a rule of the game, as times go, though God forbid that I should indulge in them myself in the case of another. I have never been very sensitive of such attacks; rarely taken notice of them. Now, when I have long ceased from controversy, they continue: they have lasted incessantly from the year 1833 to this day. They do not ordinarily come in my way; when they do, I let them pass through indolence. Sometimes friends send me specimens of them; and sometimes they are such as I am bound to answer, if I would not compromise interests which are dearer to me than life. The January number of Magazine was sent to me, I know not by whom, friend or foe, with the passage on which I have animadverted, emphatically, not to say indignantly, scored against.[3] Nor can there be a better proof that there was a call upon me to notice it, than the astounding fact that you can so calmly (excuse me) 'confess plainly' of yourself, as you do, 'that you had read the passage, and did not even think that I or any of my communion would think it unjust.'

Most wonderful phenomenon! An educated man, breathing English air, and walking in the light of the nineteenth century, thinks that neither I nor any members of my communion feel any difficulty in allowing that 'Truth for its own sake need not, and on the whole ought not to be, a virtue with the Roman Clergy;' nay, that they are not at all surprised to be told that 'Father Newman had informed' the world, that such is the standard of morality acknowledged, acquiesced in, by his co-religionists! But, I suppose, in truth, there is nothing at all, however base, up to the high mark of Titus Oates, which a Catholic may not expect to be believed of him by Protestants, however honourable and hard-headed. However, dismissing this natural train of thought, I observe on your avowal as follows; and I think what I shall say will commend itself to your judgment as soon as I say it.

I think you will allow then, that there is a broad difference between a virtue, considered in itself a principle or rule, and the application or limits of it in human conduct. Catholics and Protestants, in their view of the substance of the moral virtues, agree, but they carry them out variously in detail; and in particular instances, and in the case of particular actors or writers, with but indifferent success. Truth is the same in itself and in substance to Catholic and Protestant; so is purity: both virtues are to be referred to that moral sense which is the natural possession of us all. But when we come to the question in detail, whether this or that act in particular is conformable to the rule of truth, or again to the rule of purity; then sometimes there is a difference of opinion between individuals, sometimes between schools, and sometimes between religious communions. I, on my side, have long thought, even before I was a Catholic, that the Protestant system, as such, leads to a lax observance of the rule of purity; Protestants think that the Catholic system, as such, leads to a lax observance of the rule of truth. I am very sorry that they should think so, but I cannot help it; I lament their mistake, but I bear it as I may. If Mr. Kingsley had said no more than this, I should not have felt it necessary to criticize such an ordinary remark. But, as I should be committing a crime, heaping dirt upon my soul, and storing up for myself remorse and confusion of face at a future day, if I applied my abstract belief of the latent sensuality of Protestantism, on *à priori* reasoning, to individuals, to living persons, to authors and men of name, and said (not to make disrespectful allusion to the living) that Bishop Van Mildert, or the Rev. Dr. Spry, or Dean Milner, or the Rev. Charles Simeon 'informs us that chastity for its own sake need not be, and on the whole ought not to be, a virtue with the Anglican clergy,' and then, when challenged for the proof, said, '*Vide* Van Mildert's Bampton Lectures and Simeon's Skeleton Sermons *passim*;' and, as I should only make the matter still worse, if I pointed to flagrant instances of paradoxical divines or of bad clergymen among Protestants, as, for instance, to that popular London preacher at the end of last century who advocated polygamy in print;[4] so, in like manner, for a writer, when he is criticizing definite historical facts of the sixteenth century, which stand or fall on their own merits, to go out of his way to have a fling at an unpopular name, living but 'down,' and boldly to say to those who know no better, who know nothing but what he tells them, who take their tradition of historical facts from him, who do not know *me*—to say of *me*, 'Father Newman *informs* us that Truth for its own sake *need not be, and on the whole ought not to be,* a virtue with the Roman clergy,' and to be thus brilliant and antithetical (save the mark!) in the very cause of Truth, is a proceeding of so special a character as to lead me to exclaim, after the pattern of the celebrated saying, 'O Truth, how many lies are told in thy name!'

Such being the state of the case, I think I shall carry you along with me when I say, that, if there is to be any explanation in the Magazine of so grave an inadvertence, it concerns the two gentlemen who are responsible for it, of what complexion that explanation shall be. For me, it is not I who ask for it; I look on mainly as a spectator, and shall praise or blame, according to my best judgment, as I see what they do. Not that, in so acting, I am implying a doubt of all that you tell me of them; but 'handsome is, that handsome does.' If they set about proving their point, or, should they find that impossible, if they say so, in either case I shall call them *men*. But,—bear with me for harbouring a suspicion which Mr. Kingsley's letter to me has inspired,[5]—if they propose merely to smooth the matter over by publishing to the world that I have 'complained,' or that 'they yield to my letters, expostulations, representations, explanations,' or that 'they are quite ready to be convinced of their mistake, if I will convince them,' or that 'they have profound respect for me, but really they are not the only persons who have gathered from my writings what they have said of me,' or that 'they are unfeignedly surprised that I should visit in their case what I have passed over in the case of others,' or that 'they have ever had a true sense of my good points, but cannot be expected to be blind to my faults,' if this be the sum total of what they are to say, and they ignore the fact that the *onus probandi* of a very definite accusation lies upon them, and that they have no right to throw the burden upon others, then, I say with submission, they had better let it all alone, as far as I am concerned, for a half-measure settles nothing.

January 10.—I will add, that any letter addressed to me by Mr. Kingsley, I account public property; not so, should you favour me with any fresh communication yourself.

I am, Dear Sir, Yours faithfully, John H. Newman.

[1] Macmillan wrote that he had postponed his reply to Newman's letter of 30 December until after he had talked with Kingsley. 'The importance of the matter and the exceeding kindness and courtesy of your letter demanded that I should reply with care and with corresponding courtesy. Precious memories of more than twenty years since, when your Sermons were a delight and blessing shared and thereby

increased with a dear brother no longer here . . . would add strong weight to my desire to answer such a letter from you with peculiar care and reverence.

'I cannot separate myself in this case from whatever injustice, and your letter convinces me as indeed it apparently did himself that there was injustice, in Mr Kingsley's charge against you personally. I have read the passage, and I will confess to you plainly that I did not even think at the time that you or any of your communion would think it unjust. It is many years since I had intercourse with members of the Church that holds us heretics. My intercourse then was mainly with young men—some of them as noble and good as I have ever known. On the point alluded to in Mr Kingsley's article . . . I received an impression that it was generally true that their Catholic way of looking at these matters was what Mr Kingsley says it is. . . . While they were talking of English Christian gentlemen as wolves towards whom the combinations of serpentine wisdom and the innocence of the dove was the proper line of conduct, those who felt that they were not wolves but sought to live and think as Christian men ought, may have seen only the former quality without the redeeming one. . . . I am sure that Mr Kingsley and Mr Masson both will do all in their power to repair any wrong and print a full retraction of what you feel unjust.'

David Masson was editor of *Macmillan's Magazine* from its foundation, in 1859, until 1867.

[2] David Masson's name figured prominently on the cover of *Macmillan's Magazine* for January. In the table of contents on the cover, the review of J. A. Froude's *History of England* was attributed to 'Rev. Professor Kingsley'. This was in small print, and Newman evidently did not see that the offending review, with its author, was listed among the articles on the cover.

[3] See letter of 27 February 1864 to William Pope.

[4] This was Martin Madan (1726–90), a first cousin of Cowper the poet, who became a Calvinistic Methodist, and a follower of Lady Huntingdon. He was obliged to resign his chaplaincy of the Lock Hospital, near Hyde Park Corner, in 1780, after he published *Thelyphthora or a Treatise on Female Ruin*. In it he argued that polygamy was in accordance with the principles of Christianity properly understood, and a protection for those who would otherwise become prostitutes. Cf. *Ess.* I, 415–19.

[5] In his letter to Newman on 6 January, Kingsley had declared: 'I am most happy to hear from you that I mistook (as I understand from your letter) your meaning; and I shall be most happy, on your showing me that I have wronged you, to retract my accusation as publicly as I have made it' (see *L.D.* XXI, p. 10).

To Charles Kingsley

The Oratory, January 17, 1864

Reverend Sir,

Since you do no more than announce to me your intention of inserting in Macmillan's Magazine the letter, a copy of which you are so good as to transcribe for me, perhaps I am taking a liberty in making any remarks to you upon it. But then, the very fact of your showing it to me seems to invite criticism; and so sincerely do I wish to bring this painful matter to an immediate settlement, that, at the risk of being officious, I avail myself of your courtesy to express the judgment which I have carefully formed upon it.

I believe it to be your wish to do me such justice as is compatible with your duty of upholding the consistency and quasi-infallibility which is necessary for a periodical publication; and I am far from expecting any thing from you which would be unfair to Messrs. Macmillan and Co. Moreover, I am quite aware, that the reading public, to whom your letter is virtually addressed, cares little for the wording of an explanation, provided it be made aware of the fact that an explanation has been given.

Nevertheless, after giving your letter the benefit of both these considerations, I am sorry to say I feel it my duty to withhold from it the approbation which I fain would bestow.

Its main fault is, that, quite contrary to your intention, it will be understood by the general reader to intimate, that I have been confronted with definite extracts from my works, and have laid before you my own interpretations of them. Such a proceeding I have indeed challenged, but have not been so fortunate as to bring about.

But besides, I gravely disapprove of the letter as a whole. The grounds of this dissatisfaction will be best understood by you, if I place in parallel columns its paragraphs one by one, and what I conceive will be the popular reading of them.

This I proceed to do.

I have the honour to be, Reverend Sir, Your obedient Servant,
John H. Newman.

Mr. Kingsley's Letter.	Unjust, but too probable, popular rendering of it.
1. Sir,—In your last number I made certain allegations against the teaching of the Rev. Dr. Newman, which were founded on a Sermon of his entitled 'Wisdom and Innocence,' preached by him as Vicar of St. Mary's, and published in 1844.	
2. Dr. Newman has, by letter, expressed in the strongest terms his denial of the meaning which I have put upon his words.	2. I have set before Dr. Newman, as he challenged me to do, extracts from his writings, and he has affixed to them what he conceives to be their legitimate sense, to the denial of that in which I understood them.
3. No man knows the use of words better than Dr. Newman; no man, therefore, has a better right to define what he does, or does not, mean by them.	3. He has done this with the skill of a great master of verbal fence, who knows, as well as any man living, how to insinuate a doctrine without committing himself to it.
4. It only remains, therefore, for me to express my hearty regret at having so seriously mistaken him, and my hearty pleasure at finding him on the side of truth, in this or any other matter.	4. However, while I heartily regret that I have so seriously mistaken the sense which he assures me his words were meant to bear, I cannot but feel a hearty pleasure also, at having brought him, for once in a way, to confess that after all truth is a Christian virtue.

To Messrs Macmillan and Co

The Oratory, January 22, 1864.

Gentlemen,

Mr. Kingsley, the writer of the paragraph to which I called your attention on the 30th of last month, has shown his wish to recall words, which I considered a great affront to myself, and a worse insult to the Catholic priesthood. He has sent me the draft of a Letter which he proposes to insert in the February number of your Magazine; and, when I gave him my criticisms upon it, he had the good feeling to withdraw two of its paragraphs.

However, he did not remove that portion of it, to which, as I told him, lay my main objection.

That portion ran as follows:—

'Dr. Newman has by letter expressed in the strongest terms his denial of the meaning which I have put upon his words.'

My objection to this sentence, which (with the addition of a reference to a Protestant sermon of mine, which he says formed the ground of his assertion, and of an expression of regret at having mistaken me) constitutes, after the withdrawal of the two paragraphs, the whole of his proposed letter, I thus explained to him:—

'Its (the proposed letter's) main fault is, that quite contrary to your intention, it will be understood by the general reader to intimate, that I have been confronted with definite extracts from my works, and have laid before you my own interpretation of them. Such a proceeding I have indeed challenged, but have not been so fortunate as to bring about.'

In answer to this representation, Mr. Kingsley wrote to me as follows:—

'It seems to me, that, by referring publicly to the sermon, on which my allegations are founded, I have given, not only you, but every one, an opportunity of judging of their injustice. Having done this, and having frankly accepted your assertion that I was mistaken, I have done as much as one English gentleman can expect from another.'

I received this reply the day before yesterday. It disappointed me, for I had hoped that, with the insertion of a letter from him in your Magazine for February, there would have been an end of the whole matter. However, I have waited forty-eight hours, to give time for his explanation to make its full, and therefore its legitimate impression on my mind. After this interval, I find my judgment of the passage just what it was.

Moreover, since sending to Mr. Kingsley that judgment, I have received a letter from a friend at a distance, whom I had consulted, a man about my own age, who lives out of the world of theological controversy and contemporary literature, and whose intellectual habits especially qualify him for taking a clear and impartial view of the force of words. I put before him the passage in your January number, and the writer's proposed letter in February; and I asked him whether I might consider the letter sufficient for its purpose, without saying a word to show him the leaning of my own mind.[1] He answers:

'In answer to your question, whether Mr. Kingsley's proposed reparation is sufficient, I have no hesitation in saying, Most decidedly not. Without attempting to quote any passage from your writings which justifies in any manner the language which he has used in his review, he leaves it to be inferred that the representation, which he has given of your statements and teaching in the sermon to which he refers, is the fair and natural and primary sense of them, and that it is only by your declaring that you did not mean what you really and in effect said, that he finds that he had made a false charge.'

This opinion thus given came to me, I repeat, *after* I had sent to Mr. Kingsley the letter of objection, of which I have quoted a portion above. You will see that, though the two judgments are independent of each other, they in substance coincide.

It only remains for me then to write to you again; and, in writing to you now, I do no more than I did on the 30th of December. I bring the matter before you, without requiring from you any reply.

I am, Gentlemen, Your obedient Servant, John H. Newman

[1] Letter of 15 January to Edward Badeley, whose reply of 17 January Newman proceeds to quote. See also letter of 31 January to Badeley (*L.D.* XXI, pp. 18–19, 33–4).

To Mrs John Mozley

The Oratory, Bm Febry 23/64

My dear Jemima,

Thank you for your affectionate letter. I have now passed my great climacteric, and am older than my Mother when she died. Hitherto old age has come on me like the falling snow, so gently that I cannot realize it. I am better now than I have been for years, judging by any phenomena which I can detect. That I am getting thinner and thinner, is the exception, its outward indication, if it be one. I get up earlier than I used to do at Oxford—earlier perhaps than any time of my life, except when I was a boy at Alton, and used to read every morning at a spell from 5 till 9. The last two years I have, at my own suggestion, taken to the shower bath, which I used in Oriel—When I was an undergraduate, I used to bathe through the winter in the cold baths at Holywell—and indeed no medicine is like it. It requires indeed to be well to be able to stand it—that I am able to use the shower bath now, is a proof how substantially strong I am. I take it not later than six o'clock, and this is the second winter which I have gone through with it. It has done me wonderful good in various ways; and among others in preserving me from cold. I do not know whether you recollect, that, when I was young, I never used a great coat in winter, and used to go up to London outside the coach with nothing but my ordinary coat on. I could not do that now—I am very warmly clad from head to foot. There is a lady, whom I have never seen, who is ever throwing flannels and silks at me, in spite of my protesting, and sometimes sending them back.[1] I could not carry more clothes, without becoming a beast of burden, nor could I do with less. I go as far as I can go without passing the line of demarcation. Slender clothing then is not my boast—but the shower bath has wonderfully kept me from colds. I have not had a really bad one for all but two years—though I have had several bad threatenings and need to be very careful. I wish I heard from you a better account of yourself.

Ever Yrs affly J H N

[1] This was Jane Todd, a friend of Canon Walker, at Scarborough. She felt that she owed her spiritual life and peace to Newman.

To William Pope

The Oratory, Birmingham Feby 27. 1864

My dear Sir,

I thank you very much for your kind letter. It was a thoughtful and friendly act in you to send me the Number of Macmillan—and, though it entailed trouble on me, yet it was such trouble as it was a duty for me to incur.[1]

It is very kind in you to speak of my writings as you do. I heard years ago of the conversion of yourself and others of your family with great interest, as I think I am right in saying you are nearly related to those of your name with whom I was well acquainted when I was young.[2]

I have put your friend's name upon the Confraternity list—in return, since I am now an old man, let me beg you not to forget me in your good prayers.

Very sincerely Yours in Xt John H Newman of the Oratory

[1] Pope, who was at this time the priest at Yarm, Yorkshire, wrote on 24 February, 'Knowing how popular Mr. Kingsley had become in Cambridge, and knowing, too, that Macmillans is very much read, especially by men at Oxford and Cambridge, I took the liberty of sending the number containing the shameful passage to you.'
[2] Simeon Lloyd Pope, Newman's friend from his Trinity College days.

To Edward Badeley

To Oratory, Bm March 8/64

My dear Badeley

I have waited so long to answer you, that I forget everything I had to say—though there were several points I had to write about, and one point of criticism of yours which I had not answered.

But now I am expecting Kingsley's Pamphlet, on 'what does Dr Newman teach?' for which of course I have prepared myself from the first. I mean, I never have had an opening to defend myself as to various passages in my life and writings, and I have always looked forward to the possibility of that opening being presented to me. I have for a long time been attempting to arrange my letters and papers with a view to it—Unluckily I have not yet got further than 1836—and what I shall chiefly want is 1841–1845. However, I must take things as they come. Perhaps what he shall put together, when we see it, will seem hardly of a nature to admit or require a reply, but much as I shrink from the labour and the anxiety of it, my reason tells me I shall be glad of it afterwards. If I have to do it, you may conceive how solemn a thing it will be to me, and how I shall need the best advice of my friends. I shall try not to be overtroublesome to you, but I fear I shall have again to avail myself of your friendship.

I have just seen in the Times Mr K's advertisement. It is 'What, *then*, does Dr N. teach?'[1] Is not the 'then' significant? viz. as indicating that he is not going to bring distinct passages, in proof of what he has charged on me, but intending to *argue* from the context that I *must* have meant it, that I *could not* mean any thing else?—Now it is a great principle received on all hands now-a-days that one must not impute to a man inferences, which though possible from his words, he himself disclaims. Thus some doubt is thrown for the moment on the necessity of my writing again. It has been remarked to me, by the bye, that he can no longer directly say that 'I *teach* that truth is no virtue,' because he has *accepted my assurance* that I don't, and expressed his regret etc And hence again it follows that he must *infer* and *deduce* and nothing else.

Ever Yrs affly John H Newman

[1] The title of Kingsley's pamphlet was, ' *"What, then, does Dr. Newman mean?" A Reply to a pamphlet lately published by Dr. Newman'*. It does not seem to have been advertised in *The Times* of 8 March.

To Sir John Acton

The Oratory, Bm April 15/64

My dear Sir John,

Your letter is a very valuable one to me. I am writing from morning till night, and against time, which is not pleasant—this is the cause that I have not thanked you before, and why I do not write longer now. I get so tired.

As to the points you mention, you may be sure I shall go as far as ever I can[1]

Yours most sincerely John H Newman

Sir John Acton Bart M P

[1] See *Apo.*, Chapter v, 'Position of My Mind since 1845'. Acton had written about the strategy in the Church of avoiding scandal by 'proscribing truth and positively encouraging falsehood'.

To W. J. Copeland

The Oratory, Bm. April 19/64

I am very low—it is one of the most terrible trials that I have had. And I have to write against time, and to refresh my memory against time. Longman seemed to think an answer ought not to be delayed, if there was to be any—and people won't read a fat book—so the only way was to begin at once, and write as I printed. I do trust I shall be carried through it, but at my age it is a perilous toil. There will be at least five parts. The one on which I need your assistance is the fourth. It will be most kind if Keble looks at it too. The single point is, Have I made mistakes of fact, over-stated things, etc? or again left out important things? or can some point be strengthened? What I shall ask Keble (*as well* as you) to look at, is my sketch from (say) 1833 to 1840—but, mind, you will be disappointed—it is *not* a history of the movement but of *me*—it is an egotistical matter from beginning to end. It is to prove that I did not act *dishonestly*—I have doubts whether anyone could supply instead of me what I have to say—but, when you see it, you will see what a trial it is. In writing I kept bursting into tears—and, as I read it to St. John, I could not get on from beginning to end. I am talking of part 3. You can help me greatly, between 1840 and 1845. But Church could help me quite as much. Yet from the day he saw me off at Johnson's, he has been so dead to me, that I could not get myself to ask him.[1] I grieve at your account of your sister. You know how ill Henry Caswall is.

Ever yr afft John H Newman

P.S. I shall be *here* for a month to come. I cannot well ask you to come here on your return, even if you could—as I [am] writing from morning till night.

[1] Copeland replied on 21 April, that he had seen Keble, 'He bids me give you his "dear love" and say "he does not know how he may be able to help by memory, but will enter into all with deep sympathy."' Copeland also explained that he was partly to blame for Church's silence. The previous autumn Church had asked Copeland for news of Newman's whereabouts, hoping to visit him, and Copeland had never replied, because at the time Newman was travelling abroad.

To Mrs John Mozley

The Oratory Bm April 23/64

My dear Jemima

Thank you for the Marmalade which has just come. I had not eaten Marmalade for years and years, till you sent me some. Yours is better than any other I ever ate. And it has made me eat it again. But it is only a luxury, so you should not go on sending it.

I should have sent you my weekly Serial which is going on just now—except that I thought that it would excite you more than you would like. But you are very welcome to it, if you wish.

I have had a poor Easter—for a month I have been writing from morning to night—and this will go on for three weeks more,—till Whitsuntide.

Ever Yours affecty John H Newman

Mrs J. Mozley

To R. W. Church

The Oratory Bm April 26/64

My dear Church,

Your letter is most kind. But I am not going to take all the assistance you offer.[1]

As you say, it is almost an absurdity in me not to take more time. But I am not writing a history of the Movement, nor arguing out statements.

Longman agreed with me that, if I did any thing, I must do it at once. Also that a large book would not be read. For these two reasons I have done it, as it is. I heartily wish I had begun a week later. But L. particularly insisted that, when once I had begun, I should not intermit a week.

When you see it as a whole, you will not wonder at my saying, that, had I delayed a month, I should not have done it at all. It has been a great misery to me.

I only want to state things as they happened, and I doubt not that your general impressions will be enough.

The chief part I wanted you for, is the dullest part of the whole—the sort of views with which I wrote Number 90. I am not directly defending it; I am explaining my view of it.

Then again I fear you do not know my secret feelings when my unsettlement first began. But I shall state external generalized acts of mine, as I believe them to be— and you can criticize them.

I have no idea whatever of giving any *point* to what I am writing, but that I did not act dishonestly. And I want to state the stages in my change, and the impediments which kept me from going faster. Argument, I think, as such, will not come in— though I must state the general grounds of my change.

Your notion of coming to me is particularly kind. But I could not wish it now, even if you could. I am at my work from morning to night. I thank God, my health has not suffered. What I shall produce will be little—but parts I write so many times over.

Don't send your papers. You had better keep them to verify what I say. I change my mind; but don't give yourself trouble about them.

Ever Yours affly John H Newman

[1] Church wrote on 25 April from Whatley Rectory, Frome, 'I will most gladly do what you wish, or any thing else I can do, which may be of any use.'

To William Monsell

The Oratory Birmingham April 27/64

My dear Monsell

I am glad that you are back—and I should rejoice to have a talk with you. But I must delay your visit, I am sorry to say.

I am writing from morning till night with hardly time for my meals. I write this during dinner time. When you see it in print, you will lift up your eyes in astonishment. I could not write it, if I delayed it a month, yet for years I have wished to write it as a duty—yet it is a terrible trial. Give me some good prayers that I may get through it well

Ever affly Yours John H Newman

The Rt Honble Wm Monsell M P
P.S. I shall have to go on in this incessant toil for *at least* three weeks longer.

To R. W. Church

The Oratory Bm May 2/64

My dear Church

Many thanks for the trouble you have taken, the result of which is most satisfactory to me.[1] But, tell me, is the '*header*' too absurd, or may it stand? I had cut it out, and restored it, before it went to you. Perhaps you don't recollect it—n'importe.

Your letters will be of great use to me judging by the first I opened. I wish to write my sketch down as from my own memory first, and then I shall compare it with your letters. I have not begun Part 5 yet, which is from 1839 to 1845 (*except* the Number 90 matter)— If possible, I shall wish to trouble you with the slips on what *happened* upon Number 90—I mean, in order that you may say whether you have any thing to say against it.

I am in some anxiety lest I should be too tired to go on; but I trust to be carried through. I think I shall send you a slip of Part 4 tonight—but it is no great matter. It is in like manner,—I want your general impressions.

I shall not dream of keeping for good the letters which you have sent me. I want you to have them, that you may not forget me.

Don't suppose I shall say one word unkind to the Church of E. [England] at least in my intentions. My friends tell me that, as a whole, what I have written is unfavorable to Anglicanism—that may be, according to their notions—for I simply wish to state facts, and I can truly say, and never will conceal, that I have no wish at all to do any thing against the Establishment, while it is a body preaching dogmatic truth, as I think it does at present

Ever Yrs affly John H Newman

The Revd R. W. Church

[1] Church wrote on 30 April, 'I have no remark to make on the proofs. What you say entirely falls in with my recollections.'

To Isaac Williams

Rednall. June 17/64

My dear Isaac

I hope you have guessed why I did not answer your very kind letter from Oxford.[1] I never have had such a time. Under the lash of a printer, without any respite—and my matter growing under my hands, so that I thought it never would come to an end. And a dozen processes, efforts of memory, letter-hunting, planning, sketching, writing, correcting, transcribing, and correcting press, all going on at once. And then, it has affected and cut me up so cruelly, as no one can tell but those close about me.

And now I am come here for a little quiet—and have nothing to say but to thank you—and to thank your wife for her kind message

Ever Yours affectionately John H Newman

The Revd I. Williams

[1] Williams wrote on 13 May from Oxford and mentioned seeing Provost Hawkins more than once. Hawkins wrote to Newman on 6 June, 'I have read with the deepest interest your "Apologia", the first six parts at least; and I cannot forbear troubling you with a line to express my great pleasure in your expression of such very kind feelings towards myself and others among your old friends.'

To H. E. Manning

Rednal. June 22/64

My dear Manning

Thank you exceedingly for your very kind letter of May 6. I have been of necessity cut off from all letter writing by my late occupation—and now my hand is so tired that I can scarcely form a letter. However, I do not like yours to pass without some notice.[1]

It was very considerate in Mr Morison to send me the quotation from Kingsley's Sermon; and pray thank him for me for it—though it did not fall into the course of my writing to use it.

Ever Yours affectly John H Newman of the Oratory

The Rt Revd Mgr Manning

[1] In fact Newman had thanked Manning already on 8 May (*L.D.* XXI, p. 109).

To John Keble

The Oratory Bm July 4/64

My dear Keble

Your letter has been one of the great recompences which have come to me for a very great trial.[1] I cannot think how I have got through it. Sometimes I all but despaired. I was simply overwhelmed, if crying, profuse, frequent, and more at last than at first, be a token of it. However, now I am very thankful—it is done, and I trust I may dismiss it all from my mind.

Thank you for your allusion to the Article in the Guardian.[2] I cannot guess who it is better than you—there was not (to answer your question) any single sentence which seemed harsh to me; on the contrary, I thought it from beginning to end written with great consideration and forbearance, to say nothing of the positive praise which it gave me and which was far beyond my deserts.

It has been my great reward, (tho' I fear, if I boast some evil may come on me) to please readers in both communions. I have had, since the controversy began, addresses from London signed by 109 priests, from York signed by 70;—from this diocese signed by 123; besides one from a body of the chief gentry etc in London. My friends too in London and elsewhere bear witness to the general feeling in their own neighbourhood. I earnestly trust and pray that in some way or other it may turn to some Divine Purpose, and not be a barren fact ending with me.

Ever Yours most affectly John H Newman

The Revd John Keble

¹ Keble wrote on 28 June: 'My very dear Newman I will not wait any longer before thanking you with all my heart for your loving words *to* me and far too loving *of* me—If I wait till I write as I could wish, I should never write at all—for indeed dear friend the more and the more intently I look at this self drawn photograph (what a cruel strain it must have been to you) the more I love and admire the Artist— Whatever comes of controversial points, I see no end to the good which the whole Church, we may reasonably hope, may derive from such an example of love and candour under most trying circumstances.

You have said things which by the blessing of God will I trust materially help us in our sad weary struggle against Unbelief.'

² R. W. Church was the author of the review of *Apo.* in the *Guardian* (22 June 1864), pp. 609–10, reprinted in his *Occasional Papers* (London, 1897), II, pp. 379–97.

To J. Walker of Scarborough

The Oratory Bm July 6/64

My dear Mr Walker,

I thank you sincerely for the pains which you have taken to explain my passage, in which you have quite succeeded.¹ The best illustration of what I hold is that of a *cable* which is made up of a number of separate threads, each feeble, yet together as sufficient as an iron rod.

An iron rod represents mathematical or strict demonstration; a cable represents moral demonstration, which is an assemblage of probabilities, separately insufficient for certainty, but, when put together, irrefragable. A man who said 'I cannot trust a cable, I must have an iron bar,' would, *in certain given cases*, be irrational and unreasonable:—so too is a man who says I must have a rigid demonstration, not moral demonstration, of religious truth.

You have illustrated the point yourself most appositively.

Thus I thought as a Protestant; and I observe there are Catholic theologians of authority who go *further* in their estimate of the legitimate force of probability in creating certitude than I went,—maintaining that the *greater* probability is a sufficient, or rather the intended and ordinary, ground of certainty with men in general; or that that Religion, which is evidently more credible than the rest, is that very religion which is revealed by God, and therefore most certainly true, or demonstrated, for there is a way, by which the highest certainty of religion may be arrived at by fundamental articles which are only *more* probable.

For myself, I never, that I recollect, took this ground of 'the *more* probable,' but of a certitude which lay in an assemblage and accumulation of probabilities, which *rationally demanded* to be considered sufficient for certitude

Very sincerely Yours John H Newman of the Oratory

The Very Revd John Canon Walker

¹ Walker wrote on 4 July that he had received a letter of enquiry from Ushaw College, from someone who appeared to be startled by the passage in *Apo.*, p. 199, on probability. There Newman explained that in 1843–4 he believed in God, in Christianity, and in Catholicism on a probability, 'a cumulative, a transcendent probability, but still probability; inasmuch as He who made us has so willed, that in mathematics indeed we arrive at certitude by rigid demonstration, but in religious inquiry we arrive at

certitude by accumulated probabilities'. Walker had replied: 'Newman is not talking of probability in the popular sense in which it has *always* some uncertainty or misgiving about it, but in the philosophical sense in which it rises to the highest certainty in given cases equal to but differing from demonstration.'

To George Talbot

⌈July 25. 1864

Dear Monsignor Talbot

I have received your letter, inviting me to preach next Lent in your Church at Rome, to 'an audience of Protestants more educated than could ever be the case in England.'

However, Birmingham people have souls; and I have neither taste nor talent for the sort of work, which you cut out for me: and I beg to decline your offer

I am &c J H N⌉

To The Secular Clergy of the Dioceses of Liverpool and Salford

Birmingham, July 30th, 1864

My Very Rev. and Rev. Brethren,

I little thought when I entered the controversy which has given occasion to the letter you have sent me, what special rewards were in store for me in compensation for the trouble and anxiety in which I found myself involved.

One of the greatest earthly rewards which a Priest could name were he told to solicit some recompense for any exertions which he had made in the interest of religion, would be to have merited by them the praise of his brethren; and this is the very honour, so extraordinary and rare, which I now receive from your Reverences the Secular Clergy of the Dioceses of Liverpool and Salford.[1]

An address from two such large and important bodies of Clergy is indeed a great gratification to me, as giving me a warrant for believing without presumption that whatever be the shortcomings of my work it has been of service to the Catholic cause, and it is rendered doubly welcome and grateful to me by the tone of cordial personal kindness in which their approbation of me is conveyed.

I really do not know in what terms fittingly to express my gratitude to you for so friendly and considerate an act; I can but pray, as I do fervently, that the generous sympathy which you have shown towards me may be paid back in full measure to every one of you in such trials as the duties of the Christian ministry may at any time bring upon yourselves.

I am, my dear Very Rev. and Rev. Brethren,

Your affectionate servant in Christ,
John H. Newman, of the Oratory.

[1] This Address, drawn up at Preston on 27 July, and signed by Thomas Cookson, Provost and Vicar General of Liverpool, is printed at the end of *Apo.*, p.376.

To James Hope-Scott

The Oratory Birmingham ⌈August 29/64

My dear Hope Scott

Thank you for your munificent contribution. Gaisford is willing to go to £1000 also. And I suppose *we* too—that makes £3000. The Oxford Mission will go to £1000. That makes £4000. We could get, I suppose, nearly half the ground for that money. We should take the Walton Street frontage, above 400 ft—and give up the Little Clarendon Street frontage. Of this 2 acres and a bit, about half an acre with the frontage of 100 feet would belong to the Mission, i.e. the Bishop.

The Bishop has offered *us* the Mission—and is collecting money for a Church and Priests' house.[1] They would become, pro tempore, the Church and House of the Oratory. No *college* would be set up—but the Priest, i.e. the Fathers of the Oratory would take lodgers

So far, as far as a *plan goes*, is fair sailing—but now *can* the Oratory, *proprio motu*, (when once established in Oxford, for *this* I can do with nothing more than the Bishop's consent) can the Oratory, that is, I, *when once* set up, without saying a word to any one, make the Oratory a Hall? I cannot tell. I don't see why I should not. The *Oratory* is confessedly out of the Bishop's jurisdiction. Propaganda might at once interfere—perhaps would. Our Bishop left to himself would be for an Oxford Catholic College or Hall; but Propaganda would be against him—and my only defence would be *the support of the Catholic gentry.*

Further the old workhouse stands on the ground, (fronting Walton Street). It was built (of stone) about 90 years ago by ⟨Gwynne⟩ the architect of Magdalen Bridge[2]— it has a *regular* front of perhaps 220 ⟨(237)⟩ feet. I am writing for some information about it. Father Caswall went to see it, but could not get admittance. It holds 150 paupers. They *say* it will sell, i.e. the *materials*, for about £400. Perhaps it would admit of fitting up as a Hall or College. I dare say I could collect money for the specific purpose—perhaps Monteith, Scott Murray, Mr Waldron and others would give me £100 a piece—perhaps I might collect £1000 in that way, which might be enough. This plan would (might) be *independent* of any *Mission* plan—but it is a great point to come in under the Bishop's sanction and to be carrying out an idea of his. Also, it gives us an ostensible position quite independent of the College plan. We have our work in Oxford, though the College plan failed. And we can feel our way much better. It would not be worth while coming to Oxford to keep a mere lodging house—but *being* there already as Missioners, it is natural to take youths into our building, and many parents would like it.

But now per contra.

1. At my age—when I am sick of all plans—have little energy, and declining strength.
2. When we are so few, and have so many irons in the fire.
3. how could I mix again with Oxford men? how could I siccis oculis, see the monstra natantia,[3] when I walked the streets, who had made snaps at me, or looked torvè upon me in times long past—how could I throw myself into what

might be such painful reawakening animosities? how can I adjust my position with dear Pusey, and others who at present are my wellwishers?

4. Then all the *work* I might be involved in, do what I would!

5. And the hot water I might get into with Propaganda. Perhaps I should have to kick my heels at its door for a whole year, like poor Dr Baines.[4] It would kill me. The Catholic gentry alone could save me here.

6. Then again I ought to have *a view* on all those questions about Scripture, the antiquity of man, metaphysics, evidence etc etc which I have *not*—and which as soon as I got, I might get a rap on the knuckles from Propaganda for divulging.

7. Then, I have had *so much* disappointment and anxiety—the Irish University is such a failure—the Achilli matter was such a scrape—the School is such a fidget—that I once again quote against myself the words of Euripides in censure of οἱ περισσοί, or Lord Melbourne's 'Why can't you let it alone?'[5]

If we did it, we should have a resident curate—and a resident dean or the like; and should send one of our Fathers to and fro as 'Rector', which is the Oratorian name for a Vice-Superior and Vice-Provost.

Now I have put out all before you, and give me your opinion on the whole.][6] I have told Mr Ambrose Smith, I will give him his answer by the 8th September

Ever Yours affly John H Newman.

Jas R Hope Scott Esqr

[1] Ullathorne had visited Newman on 24 August and offered him the Oxford Mission.

[2] John Gwynne, who died in 1786, was the designer of a number of famous bridges, and built the Oxford Workhouse in 1772.

[3] Horace, *Odes* I, iii, 18.

[4] Peter Augustine Baines, Vicar Apostolic of the Western District, was summoned to Rome in 1840 to explain a pastoral letter alleged to attack converts and new 'devotions'. See letter to Emily Bowles, 19 May 1863.

[5] ἴτω. περισσοί παντες οὖν μέσῳ λόγοι. *Medea*, 819. 'Let it be. All further words are superfluous.' For Melbourne, see his remark in E. Jane Whately, *Life and Correspondence of Richard Whately* (new edn, London, 1868), p. 456: 'I say Archbishop, all this reforming gives a deuced deal of trouble, eh? eh? I wish they'd let it all alone.'

[6] Hope-Scott replied on 3 September, 'Catch me arguing your 7 points of objection! If you can get money enough to secure ground enough, go ahead—and let me know when you want my £1000.'

To Bishop Ullathorne

The Oratory Birmingham Septr 26. 1864

My dear Lord

We thank your Lordship very much for your most candid and instructive letter. I hope that in what I shall say in answer to it, I shall show that I understand its full drift, and shall meet your wishes.[1]

As regards then the Oxford matter I will say,

1. that we have no intention at present to do more than accept your Lordship's offer to put into our hands the Oxford mission.

2. that we do so with a view to the *future* foundation of an Oratory there; and for the same reason we buy ground.

3. that we have no intention in any way to co-operate with the University or with the Colleges of Oxford, whether by taking lodgers, or private pupils or in any other way.

4. that we propose to confine ourselves to the spiritual duties of the Mission, taking the cure of the present Catholics there, and doing our best to increase their numbers.

5. that neither now nor in time to come will we take part in any Catholic College there, or sell our ground for that purpose, without your Lordship's knowing our intention, so that you may write to Propaganda on the point, if you so wish.

6. that we feel the kindness of your offer to write for us to Propaganda, but we will not avail ourselves of it—nor write ourselves—for the simple reason, that, if we do, we shall give Propaganda the impression that we are contemplating something more than the performance of spiritual duties in Oxford.

7. that we contemplate, as our first step, to build a Church on such a site as we can best provide for it.

This is all that strikes me to say—I have put it down in a formal shape, that you may more easily see if I have left out any thing which it might be desirable to say[2]

Begging your Lordship's blessing and prayers especially, on this occasion

I am, My dear Lord, Your affte & obedient Servt in Xt
John H Newman of the Oratory

The Rt Revd the Bp of Birmingham
P.S. Thank you, I am very well—so well that I have not left home this year.

---

[1] Ullathorne's letter of 25 September describes his dilemma: Propaganda had cautioned him against ecclesiastical cooperation with the education of Catholics at Oxford, while being vague as to whether an individual bishop 'could act by accession to a Protestant University without direction from the Holy See'. Knowing that the matter was being considered in Rome, he did not wish to anticipate the decision of the Holy See.

[2] Ullathorne replied on 27 September, expressing his complete satisfaction with the position Newman had outlined.

To John Duke Coleridge

The Oratory, Birmingham, October 12, 1864.

My dear Mr Coleridge,

I do not know in what words to express my feeling of the kindness of the letter which I have just received from you. It has been the great mercy of God towards me, that a season of especial trial has had its especial compensation in the extreme personal sympathy shown towards me, by so many men, of such various characters of mind and shades of opinion. I have, indeed, had most equitable and lenient judges.[1]

You seem surprised that I should have been so much moved by Mr Kingsley—I will tell you how it came about.

I took him as representing large classes of men, who habitually thought as he spoke; and I found the effect of his pamphlet as authenticating a floating tradition, the tradition of thirty years. A sort of arraignment of me was made before the public, of a formal notion, and that, after ample opportunity, from a long lapse of time, for the termination of the first misunderstanding which encompassed the movement.

Slanders had not, as might have been hoped, died away—there was so much life in them, that Mr Kingsley, without an effort, was able to rekindle them. He brought them all together, with separate counts and a show of evidence. Such a formal trial of a man sometimes occurs on, or after, his death—sometimes in his life-time—generally only once. I felt that it might be now or never with me, and that I could not afford to be the last.

What I found in Birmingham seemed to me a sample of what probably was going on elsewhere. The Liberal Paper of the place, which had hitherto been fairly good-natured to me, turned round, on the publication of Mr Kingsley's pamphlet, and spoke of me as if I were, in point of reputation, irrecoverably damaged, or lost. The idea which it took of me was of a sharp clever writer, who might be expected to retort on Mr Kingsley with extreme adroitness, and run him through, perhaps. But this was a question of talent; as to high honour and conscience, I was nowhere.[2]

I had, for some years, had a sort of tacit understanding with myself, that, if ever I was publicly and formally confronted with those charges which from time to time, and in so many different ways, had drifted to my door, I would accept the challenge. I did not think I should ever have the opportunity; and the idea of it was so distasteful to me that I had not taken any step whatever—not so much as writing a line, or noting down one memorandum, or tying together any letters or papers—with a view to the chance of its occurring; so that I was absolutely unprepared for it, when it came. Therefore, when it did come, my actual method of reply arose out of the circumstances of the case, out of the provocation, and through the channel of those feelings, which the provocation excited.

Indeed, I felt that, unless I wrote with the keen feeling which I really had, though it is ordinarily one's duty not to show it, people would not believe me; they would say that my book was written for me, or corrected by revisers, or that I was not in earnest, but exerting myself in an intellectual fence. So that I might as well not write at all, if I didn't give out, as my thought, so my feelings.

And, besides, if I was making a manifestation, as I professed to do, I should not be doing this fully and consistently, if I did not manifest the deep sense, which possessed me, of that injustice which lay at the root of those charges, of which Mr Kingsley was the accidental spokesman.

Moreover, sensitive as I was of the misery of such a manifestation of myself as I was making, I felt it to be some excuse to myself, and some apology to the world for it, to bring out forcibly the gravity of the provocation which I had received, and the indignation which it was adapted to rouse in me.

If I do not apologize to you for all this egotism, it is from a hope that, in explaining myself to you, I am showing best the interest and grateful feeling with which I read your corroboration from your own recollection, of what I had related of myself in my narrative; and with which, especially, I read your kind testimony to such good effects as had followed my preaching at St Mary's. I am often led to call my life a history of failures. It is a great consolation to me to receive evidence, as I do from time to time, that all was not lost, when so much time and anxiety was expended.

I am, my dear Mr Coleridge, Very sincerely yours, John H. Newman.

J. D. Coleridge Esq.

[1] Coleridge wrote on 10 October, 'I cannot help thanking you with all my heart for the writing and publishing of your Apologia. I may humbly claim to be one of those men—no longer young I fear, who have never been in word or thought disloyal to you; and over whose life though I have sometimes been unable to follow you you have exercised ever since I first knew you by sight and as a preacher in 1840 an influence please God purely for good.'

[2] Newman is referring to the *Birmingham Daily Post* (23 March 1864), in its review of Kingsley's pamphlet *What then does Dr. Newman mean?*

To E. B. Pusey

The Oratory, Bm Nov 25/64

My dear Pusey

I assure you that controversy will not come from me, nor any one with whom I am associated.[1] You can hardly understand the sensation produced among my fellow-religionists by the admission of Catholic youth into Oxford. They are in a worse fright than any of you can be. They simply do not know what to do—and I never should be surprised if it came out, that the late condemnation of the 'Union' Association was connected with this new state of things at Oxford. To say that there are only a few Catholics at Oxford is not to the purpose, begging your pardon; the number may rapidly increase; and after all the soul of any one for whom Christ died is precious, and is worth keeping from liberalism.

Our Bishops are to meet at once and at an unusual time to form a judgment on the matter, and to send it to Rome, which reserves to itself the decision. Some persons go so far as to wish a prohibition issued against Catholics going to Oxford at all—others are against their going to the existing Colleges, and wish one erected for them. The Oratory going to Oxford is considered as a compromise, but whether it will be accepted as such, I know not. However, I hold it to be impossible that our youths will not find their way there in a year or two, if not now. So that no immediate decision would delay my movements.

The ground came to us in a most singular way—and the Mission was put into my hands most unexpectedly. We are selling again part of the land; that made me say, have I cut you out?[2]

I perfectly understand that there are persons who would think that my coming (ever so little) to Oxford would tend (so far forth) to weaken the dogmatic teaching of the Church of England—but I should not agree with them.

As to my meaning in the passage to which you allude,[3] I think that the only *body*, which has promises attached to it, is the Catholic Church—and if I think the Anglican Communion, as such, is not included in the Catholic Church, I think it has not any divine promise or power. Then I believe too Extra Ecclesiam nulla salus, and, as I think the head and heart of that Ecclesia is Rome, I think that to be in communion with Rome is to be united to the Church of the promises, of grace and of salvation. But then, as Manning has brought out in his Letter to you, till baptism is forfeited by deliberate conscious rebellion of thought, it remains, what it really is in itself, an introduction into the Catholic Church, that Church of which Rome is the head. God alone can tell who has thus rebelled, and who has not,—who is invincibly ignorant and who is not. In this respect I differ from Manning, because he attempts to define the classes, who are, and who are not.[4] But any how, when a man is united to the Communion which centres in the see of St Peter, I think the onus probandi that he is in the true Church and the Communion of Saints is, not with him, but with others—but if he is not, then the onus probandi is, not with others, but with him. Therefore, my dearest Pusey, in what I said in print, I meant to pray that you would be at some time in that normal condition and state, which is a pledge and token to all beholders, and to a man's self, that a man is Christ's. I hope I have not said anything which you would wish not said, or said in different words—excuse me, if I am rude. How can I undertake to judge any one, who have to be judged myself? but I cannot but say with St Jerome to Damasus, 'Ego nullum primum, nisi Christum sequens, Beatitudini tuae, id est cathedrae Petri communione consocior. Super illam Petram aedificatam Ecclesiam scio. Quicunque extra hanc domum agnum comederit pro-phanus est.'[5]

It seems an odd way of showing that I am not controversial, to make this quotation, but I should not have dreamed of doing so, had not you asked my meaning.

Ever Yours most affectionately, John H Newman

P.S. I cannot be sorry that Manning has brought out one or two points so clearly as he has—else, I should be sorry that he has written to you. Of course I do not see things on your side sufficiently to be able to say that you should not answer him—but I am tempted to ask, Why should you?[6]

---

[1] Pusey was anxious about the founding of the Oxford mission.

[2] Pusey and his friends were already contemplating the foundation which eventually took shape as Keble College.

[3] In *Apo.*, p.62, Newman spoke of Pusey's distance from the Catholic Church.

[4] *The Workings of the Holy Spirit in the Church of England*, pp. 10–21; reprinted in *England and Christendom* (London, 1867), pp. 91–104.

[5] *Epistola xv ad Damasum papam*: 'As I follow no leader save Christ, so I communicate with none save your blessedness, that is, with the chair of Peter. For this, I know, is the rock on which the Church is built. This is the house where alone the paschal lamb can be rightly eaten' (see Philip Schaff and Henry Wace, *Nicene and Post-Nicene Fathers* vi (New York, 1893)).

[6] Pusey soon began work on his *Eirenicon*, in reply to Manning.

To William Monsell

The Oratory Bm Jany 12/65

Private

My dear Monsell,

I have written so many letters lately, that I forget what I said to you in that letter which must have gone to you before Christmas day.

We are certainly under a tyranny; one or two persons, such as Manning seem to do everything. It is clear that our Bishop was not in the secret. He offered me the Mission of Oxford, before I dreamed of such a thing; he brought me forward; he gave me a strong letter of recommendation for getting money for a Church; he allowed me to tell me [him] in strong terms a month before I bought the land that my sole reason for going to Oxford was the fact that young Catholics were in the Colleges; and when, (to his surprise, I am sure, the order came for the Bishops to meet together) he allowed me to repeat distinctly that I went to Oxford for the Catholic youth there, and he assured me in writing that nothing that took place at the Episcopal meeting could interfere with the arrangement between him and meeting [*sic*]. That meeting, called so suddenly, and at so unusual a season, would not have been, I am sure, had I not bought the land and got the Mission.

But now where am I? with a property of £8000 or £9000 on my hand; and, if ever I were allowed to go on, (whereas the Bishop has already virtually taken the Oxford mission from me) how could I tell, that, before I have finished building my Church, but not before I had spent thousands on it, another letter would come from Propaganda, addressed perhaps to *me* to the effect of 'Pray, Fr Newman, why are you at Oxford? why are you not at Birmingham?' and how could I answer that my health would stand all these anxieties, pecuniary and ecclesiastical?

I must look out for myself—I have been left in the lurch many times—by the Cardinal in the Achilli matter—in my Dublin rectorship—in my Dublin church—in my translation of Scripture; and now I am left in the lurch again. I am selling, I hope I have sold, the land. This will give me some peace of mind, and a breathing time.

I cannot help saying, the English laity are in fault—they could do any thing, if they chose—but they do nothing. There was indeed a meeting last week at Lord Castlerosse's—it is well for a beginning. I shall rejoice if any thing really comes out of it. They ought to act on their own Bishops. I wish you could have been at the meeting, as well as have given your adhesion. Every thing must proceed from the laity—it is spoilt if priests interfere.

This is why I have not said, what I throw out to you as a private friend, that I think a (carefully weighed) pamphlet should be written by some prominent layman to state the *case* of the laity, in answer to the Dublin and other publications. It need not commit itself to a *plan*, but to stating the grievance. It is a multiform grievance— Why is there to be a prohibition, without any positive remedial measure to meet an acknowledged want? There was *once* a talk of an English Catholic University? Again, why is a privilege taken from Catholics which has not been *abused*? They have been allowed to go to Cambridge all along[1]—have the youths sent there become Prot-estants? Why is there to be a sudden restriction? Again—in Trinity College Dublin there have been apostasies to Protestantism among its Catholic members; and yet Catholics are allowed to go there—why are they to be prohibited Oxford, yet allowed Dublin? No one doubts, at least I don't, that the true normal condition of things would be a Catholic University for Catholic students—but in these matters you must go by what is practicable, and what you have not succeeded yet in doing for Ireland, a Catholic country, you cannot do in England, a Protestant. At least, the leave to go to Oxford and Cambridge should not be withdrawn, till an English Catholic University is actually provided. As to the question whether a Catholic college in Oxford or Catholics in Protestant Colleges, that is a point for subsequent consideration—but it is a strange act to forbid, yet not to compensate. Are Catholics to be worse educated than all other gentlemen in the country?

Of course my thoughts turned to you to write a pamphlet; but then comes the question whether you can establish your right to come forward. An Oxford man yourself you may well claim that your children should be there also. But I don't know whether your putting out this boldly, in detail and development, would not affect you in some ways which I do *not* know and you only *do*. How would it affect your political position in Ireland to quarrel with Dr Cullen and his Bishops? how could you thus pointedly abandon the Catholic University without explanations which would reflect upon it? I take it for granted that thus to come forward would not damage your local interests in your country at all. The pamphlet might of course contrast Catholic and quasi-Catholic Universities abroad with Oxford, to the advan-tage of Oxford. Also, it ought to draw special attention to the case of Bonn, where the Jesuits in the course of the last 20 years have done magnificently for Catholics there, what the Oratory might modestly hope to do in a measure for Catholics at Oxford. Baron Würzburg, a relation of the Norfolk (or rather Lyons) family, is my authority here.[2] He was here the other day, and his account is wonderful. Such a pamphlet ought to be addressed to some English peer, as Lord Herries.

As to the Encyclical and Syllabus,[3] I don't understand its meaning or its worth. Condemned propositions, as I have hitherto understood them, are propositions taken from the writings of *Catholics*. But what jurisdiction has the Church over statements which are made by the external world? Again, statements in books are concrete statements with a context and a drift, but who is to determine the sense of abstract propositions, such as those in the syllabus? Again, words must be defined to be understood; Gregory xvi speaking of 'Indifferentism' spoke definitely of La Mennais's theories—and further he *defined* the word in his Bull of August 15/32 'indifferentismum seu pravam illam opinionem, *qualibet fidei professione aeternam posse animae salutem comparari* etc', but who has defined 'interventus,' 'liberalismus,' 'progressus,' 'recens civilitas—' rather they are the newspaper cant of the day.— Now I wonder what a theologian, such as the Bishop of Orleans, would say on these points; for I am really perplexed *how* to view them. The only point of course which makes it interesting to *us*, is that the Encyclical is addressed to the whole Catholic world—there seems nothing else in it which looks like a theological decision—but, if it is urged against me as such, I should [be] obliged to fall back upon my liberty in opinion, *till* that liberty is *proved* to be taken away—and my liberty here is 'in possession,' for, even were it an ex cathedrâ enunciation, (which for the reasons I have mentioned I cannot see) still the infallibility of the Pope is not an article of faith.

However, when we come to the *matter* of the propositions condemned, at first sight I see little which would not be condemned by Archdeacon Denison, or by Keble, or the great body of the Anglican Church thirty years ago. The Pope deals with an abstract theory, with a normal state of things—not with what is prudent or expedient. The word 'expedit' hardly occurs in the whole document. The high church theory of Church and State may be true, but may be virtually suspended and in fact superseded. Again, take the case of Liberals themselves. Every now and then I hear a Liberal say, 'If all were to come over again, I would not grant Emancipation, Catholics have behaved so ill.' And is it not quite clear that Liberals *would* exclude us, if they could? Why is it that at this minute we cannot have a College in Oxford, till the law is altered? And so, looking through the whole syllabus, I don't think there is much that is really obstructive, rather, it is the *animus*—that is so alarming.

I *rejoice* that you think of getting something into the Times from a French Ecclesiastic.

I cannot say I am sorry for the Encyclical. Every thing is good which brings matters to a crisis. It is not the *matter* of the document, but the *animus* of its authors, and their *mode* of doing it, which is so trying.

Will not the next century demand Popes who are not Italians?

Ever Yrs affly John H Newman

[1] Subscription to the 39 Articles was required at Cambridge only before taking a degree, not as at Oxford on matriculation.

[2] The elder daughter of the first Lord Lyons married Philip Hartman Veit, Baron von Würtzburg, Bavaria, the younger married the fourteenth Duke of Norfolk.

[3] Pius IX's encyclical, *Quanta Cura*, attacking liberalism, to which the Syllabus of Errors was attached.

To Mark Pattison

The Oratory Birmingham Jany 20. 1865

My dear Rector,

I inclose a cheque for Mr Spearing, and thank you for the trouble you have taken in my matters. It seemed to me best to draw it in your favour, not in that of Mr Spearing.

Private The Papers have given you the outline of the course which the affair has taken. As I have reason to believe, Manning and W. G. Ward put up the Cardinal (who, they say, is dying) to oppose the Oxford scheme in every shape; and, when it became known that my Bishop had given me the Oxford Mission and that I had bought ground, a sudden and unusual meeting of the Bishops was called, which, without determining any thing, but remitting the matter to Propaganda, has availed to defeat *me*. In the conflict of opinion which has arisen, and the uncertainty of the issue, and the chance of a long suspense, I cannot succeed in raising the necessary funds for purchasing the land from Catholic gentlemen; and, as it is not possible to sell so large a property every day, I am committed to a heavy interest for borrowing money, and the probable eventual loss in the terms of the sale itself. Also, if things go well at Rome, still a second attempt might be made to change its decision, some time hence, perhaps when I have laid out money in buildings, and at my time of life I cannot run the risk of these superfluous anxieties. So I am making an attempt to sell the ground at once.

I am not complaining of those who take another view. They have a right to their opinion. On the other hand a great number of Catholic gentlemen, as might be supposed, are fierce the other way. It is indeed marvellous that anyone should dream of enforcing a prohibition, when not one step is taken, nor hope held out, of any place of education for young Catholics *instead* of Oxford. I should not wonder if we attempted to get another plot of ground, small and manageable, for the chances of the future.

Yrs affly John H Newman

To E. B. Pusey

The Oy Bm Febry 10/65

My dear Pusey

I am very glad to have got rid of the land, and thank you very much for your zeal in my behalf.[1]

For myself, I never thought to do more than to buy a fair sized plot of ground (when the 5 acres were offered me) for a College or Oratory at some future day; but to my surprise my Bishop wished me to undertake the mission of Oxford, and, when (in consequence of Mr A. Smith's death) it became a question of buying all or none, my friends here would not let me hesitate as to the alternative.

Then came, on the news of these steps, to my surprise the Episcopal meeting in December, gained by Manning, Ward and others acting on the Cardinal, and through him on Propaganda; and now a strong Address is on the point of being presented to Propaganda by an important body of Laity, indignant at their disappointment. In spite of the great influence of the Cardinal's entourage (the poor Cardinal is dying every day, and there is a great idea that Manning will succeed him, which I can't believe) they have got at least 150 names, most of them good names, such as Weld Blundell, Sir J. Gerard, Towneley, Throckmorton, Charlton, Scrope, Blount, Eyston, Cary, de Trafford, de Lisle, and Howard of Corby, and the Master of Lovat. A great number of gentlemen keep aloof, as not liking to commit themselves; but very few are distinctly hostile to the object.

For myself, of course, they rely on my still going to Oxford, but I don't think it will come to pass. The truth is, since the year 1855, influential converts have spread unfavourable reports about me at Rome; and I am told at this very time, that there would not be this unwillingness there to allow young Catholics to go to

Oxford, if I were not mixed up in the plan. My own Bishop, and other Bishops, are doing what they can to set this right; but of course I, for my part, should take higher ground, if I were asked again, than I have hitherto taken; nor shall I deem it consistent with my duty or my sense of propriety to go to Oxford without the express and direct sanction of Propaganda, and this I don't think there is a chance of my receiving[2]

Ever Yours affecty John H Newman

The Revd Dr Pusey

[1] Pusey wrote on 9 February that Convocation had agreed to purchase Newman's land at Oxford for £9,000.

[2] Pusey replied, 'It is a strange lot, but a great token of God's love, that you should be hidden and misunderstood now, as you were when here.'

To Charles Russell

The Oratory Bm March 2/65

My dear Dr Russell,

It is very kind of you to have proposed calling here—and I should have rejoiced to see you—but, as you don't mean to forget your purpose, it is pleasant to consider that your visit now will be made in a more genial time of the year.

The Cardinal has done a great work—and I think has finished it.[1] It is not often this can be said of a man. Personally I have not much to thank him for, since I was a Catholic. He always meant kindly, but his impulses, kind as they were, were evanescent, and he was naturally influenced by those who got around him and occupied his ear. In passing through London last St Charles's day, quite providentially (for I call it so) I called on him. He was then very ill—but he saw me for a ten minutes. I have not seen him above 6 or 7 times in the last 13 years. It was considerate in the parties, whoever they were, concerned in his funeral arrangements, that I was not asked to attend. I really should not have been able without risk, yet it would have been painful to refuse. What a wonderful fact is the reception given to his funeral by the Population of London! And the Newspapers remark that the son of that Lord Campbell, who talked of trampling on his Cardinal's Hat 14 years ago, was present at the Requiem Mass.

I have not forgotten that I have to send back to you the letters which you so kindly lent me. I have kept them to consult once more for my second edition—which will soon be out.

I am, My dear Dr Russell, Ever affectionately Yours in Xt

John H Newman of the Oratory

The Very Revd Dr Russell

[1] Cardinal Wiseman had died on 18 February 1865.

To Robert Whitty

The Oratory Birmingham March 19. 1865

My dear Fr Whitty

I thank you very much for your most kind letter; and thank you heartily for your prayers, which I value very much. It is very kind in you to be anxious about me, but, thank God, you have no need. Of course it is a constant source of sadness to me that I have done so little for Him during a long twenty years—but then I think, and with some comfort, that I have ever tried to act, as *others* told me—and if I have not done more, it has been because I have not been put to do more, or have been stopped when I attempted more.[1]

The Cardinal brought me from Littlemore to Oscott—he sent me to Rome—he stationed and left me in Birmingham. When the Holy Father wished me to begin the Dublin Catholic University, I did so at once. When the Synod of Oscott gave me to do the new translation of Scripture, I began it without a word. When the Cardinal asked me to interfere in the matter of the Rambler, I took on myself, to my sore disgust, a great trouble and trial. Lately, when my Bishop, proprio motu, asked me to undertake the Mission of Oxford, I at once committed myself to a very expensive purchase of land and began, as he wished me, to collect money for a Church. In all these matters I think (in spite of many incidental mistakes) I should, on the whole, have done a work, had I been allowed or aided to go on with them—but it has been God's Blessed Will that I should have been stopped.

If I could get out of my mind the notion, that I *could* do some thing and am *not* doing it, nothing could be happier, more peaceful, or more to my taste, than the life I lead.

Though I have left the notice of the Catechism to the end of the letter, be sure I value it in itself and as coming from you. Mr Pope will be very glad to hear the Author of it.[2]

Ever Yrs affly in Xt John H Newman

The Revd Fr Whitty

[1] Whitty had written affectionately to Newman on 14 March, hoping that his work would bear fruit and assuring him, 'whatever your trials you cannot but know that many—who can tell how many—are grateful and love you dearly tho' they have no means of showing it'.

[2] Whitty sent Newman 'a copy of the little Catechism on which I consulted you'. It was compiled by John George Macleod, a Jesuit who had formerly been Thomas Alder Pope's curate at Stoke Newington.

To Emily Bowles

The Oy Bm March 31/65

Confidential

My dear Child

I was going to write a long answer to your dear enthusiastic letter—but it is far too large and too delicate a subject to write about. If I ever had an hour with you,

I could tell you a great deal. No—you do not know facts—and know partially or incorrectly those which you know.[1] You say what you would do in my case, if you were a man; and I should rather say what I would do in my case, if I were a woman—for it was St Catharine who advised a Pope, and succeeded—but St Thomas of Canterbury and St Edmund tried and failed. I am too much of a philosopher too to have the keen energy necessary for the work on which you put me—Yet observe, Lacordaire, with whom I so much sympathize, was a fiery orator and a restless originator—yet he failed, as I have failed.

Look at the whole course of this Oxford matter. The Bishops have just brought out their sweeping decision, unanimously.[2] Unanimously, because Propaganda orders it— who directs Propaganda? What pains did they (the Cardinal) take in England to get opinions? As for myself, no one in authority has ever asked me. I never saw the questions (till afterwards)—few did—and what questions! leading questions and worse—arguments, not questions. The laity told nothing about it. The laity go to Propaganda. Cardinal Barnabò talks by the half hour, not letting any one else speak, and saying he knows all about it already, and wants no information, for Mgr Talbot has told him all about it. What chance should *I* have with broken Italian (they don't, can't talk Latin.)? I *know* what chance. I had to go to him nine years ago—he treated me in the same way—scolded me, before he knew what I had come about; and I went on a most grave matter, sorely against my will. No—we are in a transition time—and must wait patiently—though of course the tempest will last through our day

Ever Yours affly J H N

[1] Emily Bowles wrote on 26 March, impatient at the way Newman had been treated in general and wishing him to go to Rome to set matters right.

[2] On 24 March Ullathorne sent to his clergy a copy of the decision of the English bishops the previous day: 'The Bishops are unanimous in their disapproval of the establishing a Catholic College at any of the Protestant Universities. And they are further of opinion that Parents ought to be in every way dissuaded from sending their children to pursue their studies at such Universities.'

To Isaac Williams

The Oratory, Birmingham March 31. 1865

My dearest Isaac,

All last summer I was trying to get to you—but really I am tied by the leg here. In November I got away to the Sussex coast for a week—else, I was here almost the whole year. Copeland's account has saddened me very much—and I had been anxious before it. I don't forget, but remember with much gratitude, how for twenty years you are perhaps the only one of my old friends who has never lost sight of me—but by letters, or messages, or inquiries, have ever kept up the memory of past and happy days. How mysterious it is that the holiest ties are snapped and cast to the winds by the holiest promptings—and that they who would fain live together in a covenant of gospel peace, hear each of them a voice and a contrary voice, calling on them to break it! I cannot stir till Easter—but then I should like of all things to run down to you.

Ever Yours most affectionately, John H. Newman

The Rev. Isaac Williams

To Archbishop Manning

The Oratory Bm May 31. 1865

My dear Archbishop

On hearing of your appointment I said Mass for you without any delay. I will readily attend your consecration,—on one condition which I will state presently.[1] As I come as your friend, not as a Father of the Birmingham Oratory, I do not propose to bring any other Father with me. I am sure you will allow me to escape dinner or other meeting, as such public manifestations are so much out of my way. Nor do they come into the object of your asking me; which is, as you have said, to have my prayers at the function itself.

The condition I make is this:—A year or two back I heard you were doing your best to get me made a Bishop in partibus; I heard this from several quarters, and I don't see how I can be mistaken. If so, your feeling towards me is not unlikely to make you attempt the same thing now. I risk the chance of your telling me that you have no such intention, to entreat you not to entertain it. If such an honour were offered to me, I should persistently decline it, very persistently; and I do not wish to pain the Holy Father, who has always been so kind to me, if such pain can be avoided. Your allowing me then to come to your consecration I shall take as a pledge, that you will have nothing to do with any such attempt

I am, My dear Archbishop, Yours affectionately in Xt
John H Newman of the Oratory

The Most Revd Dr Manning
P.S. I suppose the *hour* of the Function will be advertised in Saturday's Papers.

[1] Manning wrote on 30 May, 'In calling to mind the old, and dear Friends who would pray for me at this moment your name arose among the first; and I can not refrain from writing to ask you to give me the happiness and consolation of your being with me on the 8th of June next at Moorfields. No one will better know than you how much I need your prayers.

I will give directions that places shall be reserved for you, and for Fr St John'.

To T. W. Allies

The Oratory Bm June 4./65

My dear Allies

I am glad you like Gerontius. You strangely misunderstood what I said about Manning, and treated it as if it denoted personal feeling on my part. What I said was, that I could not trust him—'confidence' is the word I used. Confidence is an intellectual habit, not a moral. When Sir Robert Peel was alive, I used to say, 'One can't trust him;' what was there 'Achillean' in that?[1] I never doubted Manning felt kindly to me. Only the other day I anticipated your words; I said to a friend, 'Now, you will see. M. [Manning] will wish to put me over some great scheme of education.' I repeat to *you*, what I should not say to every one, viz.—I never can trust he has not an arrière pensée, in any profession or offer he makes. It is not *my* feeling alone; I have long defended him: I am one of the last who have given into it; I thought that in your last, while you expressed 'penitence,' you had an arrière pensée, that you were indirectly trying to get me over. So I gave you open warning. Laterem lavas.[2]

Yours affly in Xt John H Newman of the Oratory.

[1] Allies had written about Manning to Newman, 'I knew the Achillean temperament', suggesting that Newman was sulking in his tent over the way he had been treated.

[2] 'You labour in vain,' literally 'you are washing a brick', Terence, *Phormio*, I, iv, 9.

To John Telford

The Oratory Bm June 16/65

My dear Sir

I thank you very much for your kind letter; but you do me too much honour, if you think I am to see in a dream every thing that *has* to be seen in the *subject* dreamed about.[1] I have said what I saw. Various spiritual writers see various aspects of it; and under their protection and pattern I have set down the dream as it came before the sleeper. It is not my fault, if the sleeper did not dream more. Perhaps something woke him. Dreams are generally fragmentary. I have nothing more to tell.

Yours very truly in Xt John H Newman

The Revd John Telford

[1] John Telford wrote on 15 June his praise of *The Dream of Gerontius*, but complaining that, although her name was mentioned, 'I should like to have seen our Dear and Blessed Lady appear . . . she must have a share . . . in the salvation of every predestined soul, in as much as she had her *very own* share in our Lord's Passion.'

To William Monsell

The Oy Bm June 18/65

Private

My dear Monsell,

One thing Ambrose told you *which you must not repeat*—viz. that I told Manning I wished him not to ask of the Pope a Bishoprick for me. Such an honour would be to me Saul's armour on David.

389

If Manning really wished to do us a service for our sakes, which (mind, 'for our sakes') I doubt,—he would simply speak a good word for our *School*. If he and, (by means of him) the Bishops, spoke in its favour, it would be all the difference of its being a success or not. If we had ten or twenty boys more, the two ends would meet, and we should require nothing more. Some one (I think Diogenes), when Alexander asked him what he should do for him, answered 'Stand out of my light.' Well, I suppose I am as surly as a Cynic—but this is all I want—a fair stage and no favour. But I don't think the Archbishop will give this. He will want to make use of me, as he wishes to make use of every one else. One great perplexity is, that we don't know what is coming—some great scheme of education perhaps, which I cannot stomach, and in which I must be somewhere, with the alternative, if I don't agree, of being no where any where. It is this suspicion which keeps us unsettled, and hinders us laying out any more money on our School. Things were awkward enough with the Bishops against us, the Cardinal especially; things are now more awkward still, with the uncertainty of some new schemes being in preparation. Therefore I say to him, Don't come to me with your mitres, but give the School fair play. Let us alone. I have reason to believe that his main opposition to the Oxford scheme was that it was my scheme—I believe he is afraid of any influence I might exert on the rising generation of Catholics, and that he would break up or transform our school, if he could. If I am wrong, I shall be too glad to find myself so—but any how, if he would do me personally a service, this is it—viz to get us 20 more boys.

Ever Yours affectly John H Newman of the Oratory

The Rt Honble Wm Monsell M P

To R. W. Church

July 11 [1865]

My dear Church,

I have delayed thanking you for your great kindness in uniting with Rogers in giving me a fiddle, till I could report upon the fiddle itself. The Warehouse sent me three to choose out of—and I chose with trepidation, as fearing I was hardly up to choosing well. And then my fingers have been in such a state, as being cut by the strings, that up to Saturday last I had sticking plaster upon their ends—and therefore was in no condition to bring out a good tune from the strings and so to return good for evil. But on Saturday I had a good bout at Beethoven's Quartetts—which I used to play with poor Blanco White—and thought them more exquisite than ever—so that I was obliged to lay down the instrument and literally cry out with delight. However, what is more to the point, I was able to ascertain that I had got a very beautiful fiddle—such as I never had before. Think of my not having a good one till I was between sixty and seventy—and beginning to learn it when I was ten! However, I really think it will add to my power of working, and the length of my life. I never wrote more than when I played the fiddle. I always sleep better after music. There must be some electric current passing from the strings through the fingers into the brain and down the spinal marrow. Perhaps thought is music.

I hope to send you the 'Phormio' almost at once.

Ever yrs. affly., John H Newman

To Thomas Joseph Brown, Bishop of Newport

The Oratory, Birmm Aug. 28. 1865

My dear Lord,

I have just received a letter, which, if I do not misread the signature, is from your Lordship. It is a great gratification to me to receive your Lordship's approbation on any thing which I have written.[1] Begging your Lordship's blessing, I am, My dear Lord,

Your faithful Servt in Xt John H. Newman of the Oratory

The Rt Revd The Bp of Newport

[1] Brown, who prefixed no '✠' to his signature, and addressed Newman as 'My dear very Reverend Brother', wrote from the Benedictine Priory at Colwich on 27 August. He expressed his admiration for *The Dream of Gerontius*, which he read aloud to the nuns, 'Many with myself shed tears ere we concluded it.' It was Brown who had delated Newman's 'On Consulting the Faithful in Matters of Doctrine' to Propaganda.

Answering Pusey and Anticipating the Vatican Council (1865–69)

Between 1865 and the opening of the First Vatican Council in 1869 Newman became involved in a debate with Pusey and responded to a further invitation to establish a mission at Oxford, while in 1867 Ambrose St John went to Rome on his behalf and managed more by chance than design to begin to unravel the confusion surrounding the *Rambler* affair. Otherwise in this period Newman's correspondence was more immediately personal than public, although after the success of the *Apologia* it displays a fresh confidence, for example, in his dealings with Manning and Barnabò and in his approach to the Oxford mission.

The debate with Pusey occurred following their meeting on 12 September in 1865 when Newman had finally called on Keble at his Hursley Parsonage. Discovering that Pusey would also be there, he almost decided to postpone the visit: the thought of seeing two such dear friends together for the first time after their ways had parted so long ago was almost too much for him. But then he made up his mind to go after all.

During the visit Pusey talked at length about his controversy with Manning and his forthcoming book, *An Eirenicon*. Manning, he felt, had taken delight over troubles in the Church of England and Pusey wanted to answer him. When the book appeared, however, Newman was disappointed: it seemed to present extreme Roman positions, for example, on the Virgin Mary, as normal. 'An Irenicon smooths difficulties', he commented to Pusey; 'I am sure people will think that you increase them.' Initially reluctant to take part in the dispute, he eventually decided to use his *Letter to Pusey* as an opportunity in particular to explain Catholic teaching on Mary in a way that steered a middle course between Protestant misconceptions, on the one hand, and Ultramontane excesses, on the other. Pusey was relieved that Newman had become involved and the episode is notable for the trust between them, in spite of their differences. And Keble supported them. Feeling the brunt of Newman's criticism, Ward and Manning were predictably less pleased.

The renewed attempt to set up an Oratory in Oxford was a tortuous affair. With the possibility of Catholics being able to attend the University, Bishop Ullathorne decided once again to invite Newman to establish a mission there. After his previous experience Newman's response was understandably cautious. He even observed specifically that the one thing he would find more trying than accepting the mission would be to discover that, having made all the preparations, Rome instructed him to retire. In the event that proved precisely to be the Roman plan: there was a secret instruction that Newman should not be allowed to reside in Oxford. Ullathorne had hoped to have that condition cancelled, but before he could act, Newman found out about it and saw no alternative but to withdraw.

Meanwhile Ambrose St John, who had travelled to Rome to vindicate Newman's position with regard to the Oratory School and its dealings with Oxford, discovered Barnabò's continued displeasure with Newman's failure (as he saw it) to respond to the charges against him arising from the *Rambler* controversy eight years earlier. St John astonished him by producing a copy of the letter that Newman had sent to Wiseman at the time, asking to know what the disputed issues were and offering to explain everything satisfactorily. It was exactly the reply that was required, but Barnabò declared he had never seen it before. After so many years, the air surrounding that matter was beginning to clear.

Newman's sense of the distorting effect on Catholic belief and practice of excessive Roman dominance surfaced again in letters lamenting the destruction of Europe's Catholic theological schools as 'a serious evil, as it throws us back on the Roman School, as nearly the only school in the Church'. It was a theme that would recur in his correspondence as extreme views about the papacy gathered force and preparations were being made for the Vatican Council. And it was illustrated from a different, more personal perspective in a letter to Ambrose St John in March 1867. Count de Torre Diaz, whom Newman admired and who had previously been friendly, was now criticizing him for his resistance to foreign influences on English Catholicism. '[It] is a charge against me', Newman told St John, 'of deliberately propagating a mutilated and crippled Catholicity.' What concerned Newman was the way 'allowable differences of opinion' were being identified as 'errors of faith'.

Another letter during these years contains an example of Newman's sensitivity to personal slight. In October 1865, he received an invitation from his sister, Jemima, inviting him to visit her in Derby while their brother Frank was staying for a few days. Newman refused. His reply must have taken her breath away. In difficult times she had been the one member of the family who had maintained contact with him, but now she received from him a torrent of criticism and pent-up self-pity, pouring forth from the sense of rejection that he had nurtured for years: 'None have so acted towards me [he meant 'acted so cruelly'] as my near relations and connexions.' It is a fierce letter, crackling with hurt. However, in spite of this blast, perhaps because of Jemima's good nature and because she knew her brother well, their relationship survived, and not too long after Newman did indeed visit her. And during this time as well, Manning made attempts both indirectly and directly to achieve a rapprochement with Newman. He did not succeed. Newman told him, 'I do not know whether I am on my head or my heels, when I have active relations with you.'

Other letters are more cheering. He asks Henry Wilberforce to send him some cider which he had been advised would be good for him. It seems that it was. And he discusses with William Copeland, his former Anglican curate, the possibility of republishing his Parochial Sermons. Elsewhere he remarks that Darwin's theory, whether true or false, need not 'be atheistical; it may simply be suggesting a larger idea of Divine Prescience and Skill'.

And throughout these years Newman was writing and finally about to complete his book that became *An Essay in Aid of a Grammar of Assent*.

9

Answering Pusey and Anticipating the Vatican Council (1865–69)

To Ambrose St John

⌈Buckland Grange Ryde Septr 13. 1865⌉

My dear A

⌈Here I am, very comfortable and, if I had my dear fiddle with me, I might sing and play recubans sub tegmine fagi[1] in full content. Scarcely had I left Birmingham, when it struck me that, since Pusey was to be at Keble's that evening, there was no manner of doubt that he would get into my train at Oxford and journey down with me.⌉ I was sure of this. When he did not get into my carriage at Oxford, I felt sure we should recognise each other when we were thrown off the train at Reading—⌈but no, he did not⌉ turn up—as it happened, he went by an earlier train. However, this expectation put me upon thinking on the subject—and ⌈I made up my mind to go to Keble's next morning and see him—and I did. I slept at the Railway Hotel at Southampton Dock—a very reasonable house, and good too—⌉ my bed only 2/6—⌈(they are building close by a grand Imperial Hotel) and then yesterday morning (Tuesday) I retraced my steps to Bishopstoke, left my portmanteau there, and went over to Hursley. I had forgotten the country and was not prepared for such beauty, in the shape of Woods. Keble was at the door, he did not know me, nor I him. How mysterious that first sight of friends is! for when I came to contemplate him, it was the old face and manner, but the first effect and impression was different. His wife had been taken ill again in the night, and at the first moment he, I *think*, and *certainly* I, wished myself away. Then he said, Have you missed my letters? meaning Pusey is here, and I wrote to stop your coming. He [[then]] said I must go and prepare Pusey. He did so, and then took me into the room [[where Pusey was]]. I went in rapidly, and it is strange how action overcomes pain. Pusey, as being passive, was evidently shrinking back into the corner of the room—as I should have done if he had rushed in upon me. He could not help contemplating the look of me narrowly and long—Ah, I thought, you are thinking how old I am grown, and I see myself in you—though you, I do think, are more altered than I am. Indeed, the alteration in him shocked me⌉ (I would not say this to every one)—⌈it pained and grieved me. I should have known him any where—his face is not changed, but it is as if you looked at him through a prodigious magnifier. I recollect him short and small—with a round head—smallish features—flaxen curly hair—huddled up together from his shoulders downward—and walking fast. This was as a young man—but comparing him even when last I saw him [[in 1846]], when he was slow in his motions and staid in his figure, still there is a wonderful change. His head and his features are half as large again—his chest is very broad ⟨⟨*don't say all this*⟩⟩—and he has, I think, a paunch—His voice is the same—were my eyes shut, I should not have been sensible of any lapse of time. As we three sat together at one table, I had as painful thoughts as I ever recollect, though it was a pain, not acute, but heavy. There were three old men, who had worked together vigorously in their prime. This is what they have come to—poor human nature—after 20 years they meet together round a table, but without a common cause, or free outspoken thoughts—but, though kind yet subdued, and antagonistic in their mode of speaking, and all of them with broken prospects. Pusey is full of his book [[Irenicon]] which is all but out—against Manning; and full of his speech on the relations between physical science and the Bible, which he is to deliver at the Church Congress at Norwich. He is full of polemics and of hope. Keble is as different as possible; he is as delightful as ever— and, it *seemed* to me as if he felt a sympathy and intimacy with me which he did not find with Pusey. At least he spoke to me of him—and I don't think in the same tone he would have spoken to him of me. I took an early dinner with them, and when the bell chimed for evensong at 4 o'clock, I got into my gig, and so from Bishopstoke to Ryde, arriving here between 7 and 8. Only three girls are here—Harry is away. Willie grown prodigiously,⌉ but as soon as ever he begins to look at a book, his headaches return—and he is only well in the open air.

⌈I have settled with Keble to go to him next Monday, if his wife is well enough.⌉ As to Lady C. [Chatterton][2] I have not yet heard—but I find I could not well have heard at Keble's—and there has not yet been time for any letter to have reached me here, sent on from Hursley. My love to all of you

Ever Yrs affly John H Newman

The Revd Fr St John

[1] Virgil, *Eclogue* I, 1: 'reclining under the covering of a broad beech tree'.

[2] Lady Georgina Chatterton (1806–75), whom Newman received into the Catholic Church the following week, on 20 September.

To John Keble

The Oratory Bm Octr 8. 1865

My dearest Keble

I do hope you will not think this letter requires any answer. If I did not rely on your understanding this, I should not write. It would be quite wicked in me to put any thing on you which had the resemblance of a duty or a call to exert yourself— and I write, not for an answer, but merely because I think you will really like to know the impression which Pusey's new book has upon my mind.[1]

Well then—I really marvel that he should have dreamed of calling it an Irenicon—it is said 'If he ask bread, will he give him a stone? or if he ask fish will he give him a serpent? or if he ask an egg, will he give him a scorpion?'[2] I grieve to use such an illustration—But so it is—if Pusey is writing to hinder his own people from joining us, well and good, he has a right to write as he has done—but how can he fancy that to exaggerate, instead of smoothing contrarieties, is the way to make us listen to him? I wish I were not obliged to say that his mode of treating with us is rhetorical and unfair. I will give one instance. The other day, when I was with you, he himself noticed the mistake of V. C. Wynter of Intercession for Invocation[3]—yet he seems to me to have fallen into the same. Our received doctrine is, after St Justin and St Irenaeus, as we interpret them, that as Eve had a secondary part in the fall, so had Blessed Mary in the redemption. And interpreting them still, it is our belief, that, whereas all the Saints intercede for us, through the merits and in the grace of Christ, she κατ' ἐξοχήν, is *the* Intercessor or Helper ⟨(Advocata, παράκλητος, St Irenaeus)⟩—that this is her distinct part in the economy of human salvation—so that, knowing the Will of our Lord most intimately, she prays *according* to His will, or thus is the ordained means or channel by which that will is carried out. Therefore 'every thing goes through the hands of Mary—' and this is a great reason for our asking her prayers.[4]

But there is all the difference in the world between saying that 'without her intercession no one is saved—' and 'without her invocation no one is saved—' whereas Pusey at page 102 passes from the one idea to the other, as if authors who said the one must necessarily say, may be taken and understood to say, the other. He quotes Suarez for the power of her Intercession—he quotes St Bernardine (or Eadmer) for the necessity of her Invocation, or of devotion to her—but Suarez is an authority quite in a different line of importance from St Bernardine—⟨(or rather Eadmer—)⟩ The former is a theologian, laying down doctrine—the latter is a devotional author,—and moreover writes for Italians, for those who already knew and held the doctrine of her Intercession, and were in a country where to neglect devotion to her would have been a rejection of a privilege which they *possessed.* I never can deny my belief that the Blessed Virgin prays efficaciously for the Church, and for individual souls in and out of it. Nor can I deny that to be devout to her is a duty *following* on this doctrine—but I never will say, even though St Bernardine said it, that no one is saved who is not devout to her, and (tho' I don't know St B's writings) I do not think *he* would have said it had he not been in his own Christendom, or had he known the history of the first centuries, or had he seen the religious state of things which we see ourselves. St B. again is not answerable for what *Faber* may have said; but even, if he agreed with him, Pusey has no right to put their doctrine under the sanction of Suarez, unless he produces from Suarez distinct passages, in which he speaks of invocation as well as intercession. As to Faber, I have not read his books—he is no authority—nor did I *ever hear* of the names of Oswald or de Montford, till I saw them in Pusey's book. Now this is a fact much to the point—for it proves that a man (like myself) may be a priest and in ecclesiastical station, may have had a DD degree given him, and set over a new University, without any knowledge whatever of those extreme views which are held by a particular party in the Church, and which they have a right to hold, (so that they don't force me to hold them,) while they keep clear of offending, in their devotional impulses, any doctrine of the Church. As soon as such views approach to such an offence, they are, they have been again and again, censured and beaten back by ecclesiastical authorities. I turned up a letter of mine the other day, (I *think* written to Christie between 1841–1845) in which I speak of the number of books, about our Lady, which Gregory xvi had censured.[5] Of *course* the devotions in question *tend* to superstition—there is no truth that may not be the occasion of error—but usum non tollit abusus—and Pusey's book looks far more like an argumentum ad hominem, because Manning charges *Anglicanism* with running into *infidelity*, than a calm view of the case.[6] Certain I am, that, as an Irenicon, it can only raise a smile—and I wish that were all it would raise. The first duty of charity is to try to enter into the mind and feelings of others. This is what I love so much in you, my dear Keble; but I much desiderate it in this new book of Pusey's—and I deplore the absence of it there—The instance I have given, is but one instance

Ever Yours affectly John H Newman

Revd John Keble.

P.S. Thank you for your account of Mrs Keble—Bournemouth is not such a banishment from home as Penzance must be.

P.S. Oct 19. I have kept this some days—hoping it might not be a duty to send it—but I am obliged unwillingly to say that it *is* a duty—I really think so.[7]

---

[1] *An Eirenicon.* It had the form of a letter to Keble.

[2] *Luke* 11:11–12.

[3] The Vice-Chancellor of Oxford University confused the two in 1843.

[4] On this and what follows see *A letter addressed to the Rev. E. B. Pusey, D. D., on occasion of his Eirenicon, Diff.* II, e.g. p. 105.

[5] This letter has not been traced.

[6] H. E. Manning, *The Workings of the Holy Spirit in the Church of England, a Letter to the Rev. E. B. Pusey,* pp. 27–37.

[7] Keble replied gently on 30 October, defending Pusey as intending precisely to bring out the actual devotional application of certain doctrines. Newman wrote back on 1 November, remarking that he would not have expressed himself to Pusey as freely as he had done to Keble (*L.D.* XXII, p. 91 n. 3).

To William Lockhart

The Oratory Bm. Octr 26/65

My dear Fr Lockhart,

As to your painfully interesting letter, you must bear in mind that the Dublin in great measure is but an answer to me.[1] *I have* spoken *already* in my Apologia—there is no reason why I should speak again. Our Bishop as soon as he read my 7th Portion (ch. 5 of second edition) wrote to me, to endorse the doctrine of it. Afterwards an attempt was made at Rome to criticize it—but the Jesuits (I understand) took it up and defended its correctness in all points. Since then, our Bishop has a second time given it his imprimatur. Were I to write something anew, I could not say more than I said last year; why will not that do for the purposes you name? why need I write again? It is not to be supposed that I could bring myself to enter into a personal controversy with Ward.

But further; I could not, if I would. It is impossible for a man to enter into such a controversy without reading up endless theology upon the subject of it—Suarez is but one of a host of divines, whom I must first master; and I have no time, not to say money, even had I strength, for such an occupation—And after all, it [I] could not get up theology in a day—and by the time I was fully furnished for the warfare, the whole scene of things might have been changed—and all my preparation thrown away. Indeed I trust that such a change will come, that what has risen in a night will perish in a night.

I resign myself to look out, or at least to look forward (for it may not be in my day) to such a termination of our present anxieties; and, if it cannot be expected in any other way, this arises from the circumstances under which the evil has found an outlet and made play and from the advantageous position which it occupies. And perhaps you will bear with me, if, in bringing out what I mean, I am obliged to be roundabout.

I think our great difficulty at present lies in this dilemma:

1. if we do not speak out, we let an exaggerated doctrine be mistaken for Catholic truth to the injury both of Catholics and Protestants; but there again,
2. if we *do* speak, then we create a great scandal, Protestants saying 'So, this is your unity of doctrine! here is the Dublin denying salvation to all Catholics such as yourselves, who will not hold its peculiar dogmas.'

Now how has this scandal originated? it has arisen out of the circumstance that the Dublin is in position and possession—that it has the first say—and that whoever protests against it is the first to break the peace. Thus e.g. it was urged on me last year by a Bishop that, if I said any thing [in] favour of youths going to Oxford, I should be violating the existing harmony among Catholics.

And how is it that the views opposed to the Dublin are not also in existing representative position, and possession; but have to maintain themselves at this disadvantage? It is because their organs, such as the Rambler and the Home and Foreign have been silenced.

And how is it that those organs have been silenced? It is because intemperate writers, such as X Y Z in the Rambler, shocked the Catholic public, and gave a handle to those who would suppress them. X.Y.Z. interfered with the education of the clergy; and now the Dublin etc. succeeds in interfering with the education of the laity.[2]

We have lost our position—we have got our heads under water—we cannot get ourselves into a position in which we might use our arms—and why? because we have been very extravagant, very high and mighty, very dictatorial, very provoking; and now we must patiently suffer the consequences

Patience, submission, faith in God's care of His Church, seem now our one course, our only means of righting ourselves. We do not mend matters by new imprudences, we have sowed the wind, and must reap the whirlwind. This seems to me the long and the short of the matter

J H N

¹ Lockhart had written, lamenting the influence of W. G. Ward, *The Dublin Review*, and extreme Ultramontanism, and wanting Newman to respond.

² X.Y.Z. was Henry Oxenham, writing in the *Rambler*, July 1860 (see *L.D.* XIX, Appendix 2).

To Mrs John Mozley

The Oratory Bm October 31/65

My dear Jemima

At the end of more years than I can count I have an invitation from you to Derby.¹ About two years ago indeed, when you were so ill, you half suggested, if I went from home, my coming your way, and that was all. Never an invitation from your husband. You have let your children grow up, and I not know them. They have ever been in my prayers. When you came here in 1853, I asked you why you had not brought one of them with you, and you repelled or evaded the question. When you came on that occasion, you pointedly refused to see Mrs Wootten or Mr St John, both of whom you knew. You said as plainly as possible, 'I come to see you, because you are my brother, but I will have none of your belongings.' It was the same when John (your husband) came here—he seemed afraid every minute that I was going to commit him to some recognition of me, as what I am. I turned up last year a copy of a letter of mine to you written (I think) in 1846. There I say to this effect, 'I have wished to write frankly, and tell you every thing about myself leaving the difference of religious sentiment on one side, but I can't, if you don't write naturally, and show interest yourself.'² I did not ignore the Church of England, but you persisted in ignoring my religion. Well, you wrote a sort of explanation—and I began to be full in my communications again. I wrote you detailed accounts of my goings on, when I was at Rome. On my return, you expressed interest in the descriptions in Loss and Gain. Accordingly I at once sent you the book. The way you thanked me was to write me word that 'I must not think that it would have any effect on your religious convictions,' as if I had said or thought any thing leading to such a remark. This sort of ignoring what I am, and antagonism to me, you continue down to this day. You never, down to the letter of this morning, direct to me as 'Dr Newman', or as at 'the Oratory.'

This being so, since you have let me alone so many years, since you have let all your family grow up and I not know them, it is not wonderful that I should be surprised at your wishing me to come to you now—surprised in a double way,—because you do so much, and because you don't do more—for who ever heard of an invitation except from the master of the House?

I know how this letter will pain you, but it is impossible I can write any thing else. It would not be honest, if I wrote otherwise. None have so acted towards me as my near relations and connexions. Did I wish to revive the past I could say a great

400

deal—and on some occasions, when I have appealed to you, and tried to get you to make matters better, you have declined to interfere.

Of course it much pleases me to have a change in you, however late—but you cannot bring back past years. I am old now I do not easily move about, never I may say by my will. I have been driven from home by my health. Twice this year I have been obliged to go away for definite reasons; on both occasions I got back quickly, lest I should be taken ill. I am well enough when I keep quiet.

As to the present moment, my duties keep me here—even were there no difficulties about my health. It is impossible I should come—but I am glad to have what I never have had for so long[3]

Yours ever affectly John H Newman

Mrs J. Mozley

[1] Jemima had written on 30 October, suggesting he visit, as their brother, Frank, had come to stay for a few days.

[2] See Newman's letter of 16 August 1846.

[3] Jemima and her husband visited Newman on 18 June 1867, and he stayed with them in May 1871.

To Henry Nutcombe Oxenham

Sent in substance

The Oratory Birmingham Novr 9. 1865

My dear Mr Oxenham,

By the Schola I mean a generalization, for the decisions of theologians throughout the world.[1] And as in all matters, and not the least in intellectual, there is a natural tendency to collect into centres, the Schola is in fact a generalized name for the bodies of theologians throughout the world, or for the Schools of the Church viewed as a whole. These Schools have for the most part a distinct character of their own, severally—but it may easily happen that a School may contain, and that to its great profit, able men of very different complexions of thought and of doctrine—as the old Universities did.

The first great schools were those of Alexandria, Antioch, and Rome. At present these are nearly all destroyed, in consequence of the Revolutions which ushered in this century. This has been a serious evil, as it throws us back on the Roman School, as nearly the only school in the Church. Nor is it enough to say, as it may be said with much truth, that various schools are represented at Rome—for still it is true also that many are not.

The Schola answers many purposes. It defends the dogma, and articulates it. Further than this, since its teaching is far wider and fuller than the Apostolic dogma which is de fide, it protects it, as forming a large body of doctrine which must be got through before an attack can be made on the dogma. And it studies the opinion of the Church, embodying tradition and hindering frequent changes. And it is the arena on which questions of development and change are argued out. And again, if changes of opinion are to come, and false interpretations of Scripture, or false

401

views of the dogma to be set right, it prepares the way, accustoming the mind of Catholics to the idea of the change, and preventing surprise and scandal.

It is a *recognised* institution with privileges. Without it, the dogma of the Church would be the raw flesh without skin—nay or a tree without leaves—for, as devotional feelings clothe the dogma on the one hand, so does the teaching of the Schola on the other. Moreover, it is the immediate authority for the practical working and course of the Church—e.g. what are mortal sins? what venial? what is the effect of the mass? What about indulgences? etc etc.

Yours very truly John H Newman

[1] Oxenham had asked Newman what he meant by 'the schola', scholastic theology or something wider.

To E. B. Pusey

The Oratory Birmingham In fest. Concept. Immac. 1865

My dear Pusey

You must not be made anxious that I am going to publish a Letter on your Irenicon. I wish to accept it as such, and shall write in that spirit. And I write, if not to hinder, for that is not in my power, but to balance and neutralize other things which may be written upon it. It will not be any great length. If I shall say any thing which is in the way of remonstrance, it will be, because, unless I were perfectly honest, I should not only do no good, but carry no one with me—but I am taking the greatest possible pains not to say a word which I should be sorry for afterwards[1]

I hope you found nothing to annoy you in Lockhart's second article

Ever Yours affectly John H Newman

The Revd E B Pusey D D

[1] Pusey replied at once, 'This discussion is taking too wide a range, for me to wish you to be silent.'

To W. G. Ward

The Oratory Bm Febry 18.1866

My dear Ward,

I thank you very much for the present of your volume, and for your kind letter—but far more of course for your prayers.[1] I do not feel our differences to be such a trouble, as you do; for such differences always have been, always will be, in the Church, and Christians would have ceased to have spiritual and intellectual life, if such differences did not exist. It is part of their militant state. No human power can hinder it; nor, if it attempted it, could do more than make a solitude and call it peace. And, thus thinking that man cannot hinder it, however much he try, I have no great anxiety or trouble. Man cannot, and God will not. He means such differences to be an exercise of charity. Of course I wish as much as possible to agree with all my friends; but, if, in spite of my utmost efforts, they go beyond me or come short of me, I can't help it, and take it easy.

As to writing a volume on the Pope's infallibility, it never so much as entered into my thoughts. I am a controversialist, not a theologian. And I should have nothing to say about it. I have ever thought it likely to be true, never thought it certain. I think too, its definition inexpedient and unlikely; but I should have no difficulty in accepting it, were it made. And I don't think my reason will ever go forward or backward in the matter.

If I wrote another pamphlet about Pusey, I should be obliged to have a few sentences to the effect that the Pope's infalliability was not a point of faith—that would be all

Ever Yours affectly in Xt John H Newman of the Oratory

W G Ward Esqr

[1] W. G. Ward had written on 17 February, thanking Newman for the kind references to him in his *Letter to Pusey* [*Diff.* II, pp. 22–3], but regretting that they were seen more and more as opponents. He also asked whether Newman was writing on infallibility.

To William Clifford, Bishop of Clifton

The Oratory Bm 17 March 1866

My dear Lord,

I have just read your Lordship's letter in the Tablet about me, and with extreme gratification.[1] You may easily understand with what anxious thought and care I wrote my letter to Dr Pusey; and, while I knew I should be offending various excellent persons any how, in things which I felt it a duty to say, I was very conscious also, that, whatever pains I took with my language and sentiments, I should come short of that exactness in statement and that tenderness for others, which was possible and desirable.

No one can do more than his best. I tried to do my best; and, having done so, felt myself willing to submit myself to whatever just criticism came on me for not doing better. When then I read a public expression of opinion, so favourable to me as that in today's Tablet, from a person such as your Lordship, a Bishop and a theologian, and so well acquainted both with Rome and with England, it is as great a relief and encouragement to me as could be granted to me.

This I say in the first place; but secondly, my special gratitude is due to your personal kindness to myself, in going out of your way so generously to defend me, when there was no direct call on you to put yourself to that inconvenience.

Begging your Lordship's blessing, I am, My dear Lord,

Your affecte servt in Xt John H Newman of the Oratory

The Rt Revd The Bp of Clifton

[1] Defending Newman, Clifford had denounced 'the practice which some people have of peremptorily setting down as un-Catholic, and anti-Roman, and contrary to this spirit of the Church, every practice and every teaching which does not coincide with their own views', *The Tablet* (17 March 1866), p. 165.

To Archbishop Manning

The Oratory Bm Easter Day 1866

My dear Archbishop

I thank you for your Easter greetings and return them with all my heart.[1]

I don't know how far you know the particulars of Keble's death. His wife had apparently only a few hours to live, so said the doctors, about a fortnight ago. He had nursed her till then; but then he was seized with fainting fits, which turned to erysipelas in the head, and he died in the early morning of Holy Thursday. His wife is still alive, but her death is constantly expected. He is to be buried at Hursley next Thursday. His brother and brother's wife are with them, viz. at Bournemouth. I heard some months ago, that his brother too was in bad health.

Yours affectionately in Xt John H Newman of the Oratory

The Most Revd The Archbp of Westminster

[1] Keble died on 29 March. Manning wrote two days later: 'I have just heard of dear Keble's death: and I feel as if it had put me back half my life to the days when we used to look to him and his Christian Year as the service of our happiest thoughts. Nobody can understand this as you, and I write to you almost instinctively.

I shall never forget the Long Vacation in 1830 when Saml Wood and I were together in Oxford before the term began and I dined with you after the Service at St. Mary's one Sunday. Memory is very sweet, but the hope before us is sweeter.

I hope you are well.

With Gaudia Paschalia believe me, always Affecly yours, ✠ H. E. Manning.'

To Bishop Ullathorne

The Oratory. ⌈St George's day. 1866. [[April 23]]

My dear Lord,

I hope you will not think us insensible to the great kindness and confidence shown us by your Lordship, in now renewing to the Oratory the offer of the Oxford Mission, if we venture to set before you several primâ facie difficulties,⌉ which stand in the way of our giving you an answer. It is the very importance of that offer, and our sense of our own insufficiency, which oblige us to do so.

1. We know that Catholics in Oxford are very eager to build a Church on a new site; and your Lordship has shared in their wish. With a view to it they have collected the sum of £187 which at present is in my hands; £300, I believe, is in your own, the contribution of a lady in Holywell Street; and Messrs Smith and Hanley have promised £200; that is, altogether £687. But this will go a very little way towards the expenses of ground and building, and these expenses would come upon us. Now, by the rule of the Oratory, one house cannot retain or govern another; each house must be distinct; as soon then as the Oxford Oratory is strong enough to go alone, the Birmingham Oratory must let it go. When that time comes, it will be found, that we have laid out time, trouble, and money at Oxford, which has been

just so much loss to Birmingham, or nearly so; and the Oxford Mission Church, which we should have built, would be the measure and the monument of our injustice to our own successors here. How is the Oxford Mission, small moreover as it is, ever to repay us? Then, I have a difficulty of my own in undertaking a new Mission Church. I have, in my time, built three, or rather four, Churches;[1] and I know the toil and anxiety which such a work involves. It would be too much for my strength, and would hinder me giving my attention to the proper interests of the Oxford Oratory, and to the state of religious parties in the University.

This is the difficulty,—but we do not say it cannot be overcome; and we propose the following method of doing so to your Lordship's consideration. We have, as you know, a piece of ground of our own, opposite Christ Church. I gave you the other day its dimensions. It is probable, if we had the means, we could increase it on three sides, with a frontage on two streets. If we could not, we should have ultimately to place ourselves elsewhere; and if so, from its situation, and from the building movement now going on in the University and likely to continue, we do not anticipate any difficulty in parting with it advantageously, even though buildings were upon it. Under these circumstances we should feel no difficulty in undertaking at once to build an Oratory Church upon it. This Church would be used by us for the strict purposes of an Oratory, for sermons and lectures, for popular services, according as there was an opening for them, for confessions, and for Catholic young men at the Colleges, the charge of whom is an especially Oratorian work. But we would also lend it to our Missioner (that is, to one of the Fathers,[2]) and to the Mission for the purposes of the Mission; that is, we would assign a certain number of sittings, and then charge the Mission a certain annual rent for the use of them. The Catholics of Oxford have already a sum in hand towards meeting this rent, viz. the £687 which I have mentioned above. They might put it out to interest for that purpose, and, if at length, years hence they thought it prudent in conjunction with the Oratory to build a new Church on a new site, it would be ready as a part of their contribution towards it. In the meanwhile, they would have the use of a Church without paying any thing for its erection; for the Oratory would build it from its own means and those of its friends. What rent the Oxford Catholics should pay to the Birmingham Oratory will be a future consideration.[3]

2. We are told that the Oxford Mission does not support a priest; this seems to me very unlikely. Your Lordship will be able to inform us on this point without trouble.[4]

3. A third and an obvious difficulty lies in the question, how we are to serve the Mission? We shall do so ourselves certainly, if it is possible; but our Fathers are so few, that we must at least contemplate the chance of having to obtain the services of a resident Curate. But if so, what would be his relations to your Lordship? would you look to me, as directly responsible to you for the Mission, and not recognise him except as our assistant and subordinate? or would you think it right to put him (to the exclusion of us) in direct and immediate relations with yourself, as Fr Flanagan was at Smethwick? We feel, if the latter was the case, that he would practically be the head authority, and not we. *We* should go there (say) once a week, and we

should find *him* at home there. And in consequence there might be collisions between him and us.[5]

4. We have a scruple arising from the course which Propaganda took in relation to Catholic youths at Oxford a year and a half ago. We did not expect it; and the Sacred Congregation may now again take some step which we do not anticipate, and thus accidentally derange our plans. Twice before that, Cardinal Barnabò had acted towards us with great abruptness, and on the latter of the two occasions had brought upon us much anxiety and considerable expense.[6] It would be imprudent in us not to guard ourselves now against a fourth mishap. Accordingly, we hope it is not too much to ask your Lordship to gain for us from the Sacred Congregation the necessary permission, that our House and Church at Oxford shall be considered an integral part of the Birmingham Oratory during my life time and for three years after it. We know Propaganda has great affairs to manage, and Cardinal Barnabò told me on one occasion with his own lips that the Oratory was of too little importance for me to have a right to petition (as I was doing) for a certain privilege in behalf of the London Oratory. This makes me feel so anxious on this point, that I do not see my way to incur any expense at Oxford in building or the like, till his Eminence makes the ground sure for us.

⌈5. This leads me to mention to your Lordship a last anxiety. My object in connecting myself with the Oxford Mission, is to be of such real and substantial service to the Catholic cause in Oxford, as God may permit. What shape that service may take, it is impossible to anticipate beforehand; but so far is clear, that the presence of Catholic young men in Oxford, be they many or few, will be of great use to us, as taking off the edge of the offence and irritation, which our going is likely to create there in many quarters, by suggesting an intelligible and reasonable motive for our taking that step. It is but natural and right, as all Protestants will feel, that the Catholic Bishop of the Diocese should protect the young members of his own communion; but it will be thought a simple aggression, if men who once belonged to the University, as ourselves, return thither as Catholics for no other assignable purpose than that of preaching Catholic doctrine in a Protestant place of education. Now we are quite content that things should remain as they are; that Catholics should be discouraged going to Oxford without being forbidden; for our purpose ten Catholics are as good as a hundred; nor do we wish, as we did wish a year and a half ago, before the Bishops had spoken, to start by publishing any advertisement to the effect that we were going there avowedly for the sake of Catholic students. So far we have no difficulty; but we have heard with great concern, that a præceptum has been promulgated in the Diocesan Synod of Westminster, making it necessary for all priests within its jurisdiction to preach, argue, and bring about by all means and to the best of their power, the eschewing of Oxford by all Catholics. This step seems to us much in advance of what was done by the Bishops last March year; and, if it were taken in other dioceses, would indirectly affect our position at Oxford seriously. Shall we then be going too far, if we ask your Lordship, whether there is any chance of other Bishops following the example of the Archbishop? or again, of his decision in his own diocese becoming a rule for English Catholics by some act of Provincial Synod.⁷

I hope you will excuse the anxiety which has dictated these inquiries; and, let me beg your Lordship's blessing especially at this moment, when we have such a momentous question under consideration.

Your Lordship's obedient & affte Servant in Xt
⌈John H Newman⌉ of the Oratory

The Right Revd The Bishop of Birmingham

¹ i.e. at Littlemore, at Alcester Street in Birmingham, the University church in Dublin, and at Edgbaston.

² In the draft Newman wrote here in pencil 'of the Oratory'.

³ Ullathorne acknowledged this letter on 28 April and replied on 22 May, and expressed gratitude for the proposal to build the church exclusively from means provided by the Birmingham Oratory. He thought the building of an Oratorian Church would satisfy the Roman authorities.

⁴ Ullathorne thought that the increasing number of Catholics in Oxford would enable a priest to be supported.

⁵ Ullathorne approved of Newman's proposals and explained that 'the relations of the Oxford House and mission to the Bishop can be settled upon the principles and rules in operation with respect to Churches served by regulars'.

⁶ The meeting of the English bishops at the request of Propaganda on 13 December 1864 led to the collapse of the first plan for an Oratory at Oxford. For the other episodes see letters of 24 and 25 November 1849 (*L.D.* XIII, pp. 306–10), and the correspondence in the autumn of 1855 and January 1856 (*L.D.* XVII).

⁷ Ullathorne replied, 'With respect to the education of Catholics at the University, I can only refer to the decision of the Bishops already promulgated, to the effect that they hold it their duty to discourage Protestant university education for Catholics, a decision which the Holy See approves as in conformity with its own views; and which was published for the guidance of the clergy. What future steps the Bishops might think it their duty to adopt it is impossible for me to say from my present information; but should the practice of sending Catholics to the University grow much more frequent than at present, it would of necessity force on a reconsideration of the whole subject, and that in the direction of discouragement, and of finding, as far as possible, a practical remedy against this frequentation.'

To William Neville

Champéry. Val d'Illiez Canton Valais August 12. 1866

My dear Wm

Thank you for your packet. I return the Bishop's letter with my answer.¹ I am going to give you the great trouble of copying my answer. You have already copied the Bishop's letter. Please send them both to him.

Ambrose put into this morning's box a letter for you. We had a most glorious walk this morning. The place is full of walks—but, alas, the weather is sad. This morning we took advantage of a few hours of comparative brightness—not that the sun came out. Now clouds float close around us—we have both been on, almost *in*, our beds, to get a little warmth after the exhaustion of our walk. I am sitting with three under garments on, a waistcoat, a coat, and my great rug over my shoulders, and my worsted cap on, and am just tolerably warm. The fare is fair here—the bread, butter, honey, cream, good. They won't give us cheese, though it is the pride of the country—the wine and brandy bad. I am very suspicious of the water, as having lime in it. The meat tolerable—dinner, alas, at one; a nice, clean house; about 40 inoffensive inmates, most of them women and children. The Church quite close by, we said Mass there this morning. Ambrose walks famously; has no asthma. I have done some certitude—little enough in quantity—but, (unless my whole theory be a maresnest, of which I am not sure) good in quality. I can do it when lying down, or travelling. It is a work of analysis, not of many words.[2] Ambrose thinks of taking up his sermons but work we both must have, for the weather keeps us indoors. It has been so for many weeks.

You will see I have been somewhat sharp in my answer to the Bishop—but I have written as carefully as I can—any one who likes can see your copy of my answer—not my own, lest it should get fingered

Love to all Ever Yrs affly John H Newman

Thank Austin for his letter. Tell him the Bankers only can suggest a remedy for my want of signature on the back of cheques. I will do what they tell me.

P.S. Your letter of the 9th just come with my nephew's letter.[3] Thank you.

P.S. 8 P M. pouring rain again.

[1] The letter to Ullathorne that follows, written the same day.
[2] This was preparation for *A Grammar of Assent*.
[3] The nephew was Henry Mozley.

To Bishop Ullathorne

Champery. Val d'Illiez Aug 12. 1866

My dear Lord

I feel very much obliged by your Lordship's letting me see your letter to the Cardinal, which I herewith return.[1]

Your kindness in showing it to me leads me to think that you will not be displeased at my making a remark upon one part of it

Your Lordship says, 'Itaque ad opus missionis simpliciter respectum habui, *cautelis interpositis* de non interveniendo in iis quae ad *educandos Catholicos in Universitate* spectant, quando propositum mihi factum fuerit pro ecclesiâ et Oratorio ibidem aedificandis.'

And then: 'Cum vero post aliquod tempus audirem, Patrem eundem litteras circulares ad subscriptiones pecuniarias invitandas paravisse, ubi non solum de missione, sed *aliquantulum de Catholicis in Universitate educandis tractavit*. Eum ergo adivi, et documentum, antequam in publicum deveniret, suppressum fuit.'

My own recollection of what passed on my part is as follows:—When I first thought of purchasing Mr Smith's five acres, it was with no intention at all of having in consequence any part myself in any work at Oxford of any kind. I entertained the idea of purchasing it, because I hoped to resell it to Bishops or laity, taking on myself the immediate responsibility of the purchase. Whether it was to be used at once, or some time afterwards, whether for an Academical College, or for an Oratory, or for both, or for a Monastic house, or for an inclosed nunnery, or for training schools, or for a Church and Mission, or for several of these, I left for the future. It did not come before me that I was to have a personal part in any plan.

To my surprise your Lordship called at the Oratory, and offered us the Mission; and thus for the first time my thoughts were turned to Oxford as a place in which I was personally concerned.

I wrote you word, after consulting with the Fathers, that, if I took the Mission, it would be solely for the sake of the young Catholics, then and in time to come at Oxford.[2] And in conversation afterwards I suggested that I might provide lodging for some of them within an Oratory, if erected there. This, according to my recollection, is the very whole of what I suggested as to any plan of educational work, if it so deserves to be called. Your Lordship replied, however, that to lodge undergraduates would be putting myself in relations with the University authorities.

In consequence I wrote to you a second letter, in which I said I would take it simply as a mission.[3]

These two principles, that I took it from your Lordship as a mission, and that, as my own personal motive, I undertook it for the sake of the Catholics in the University, actual or to be converted, I have never given up, nor hidden. I profess them now; and his Eminence should clearly apprehend that I feel no calling whatever to go to Oxford, except it be in order to take care of Catholic undergraduates or to convert graduates. Such care, such conversion, is at Oxford the chief and most important missionary work. If in future there are no undergraduates to care for, at least there will be graduates to convert.

It was in reference to the first of these two objects that I drew up the Circular which at your wish I suppressed before publication. It would have been very 'bellicose', (to use your Lordship's word of my recent one not yet circulated,)[4] to have referred *there* (unnecessarily) to the second.[5]

In the proposed circular I said *only* what I had *already* said to you, viz that I took the Mission of Oxford, especially for the sake of the Catholic youth there; this being at a time, when there was not only no discouragement from authority, but no talk of discouragement of their going there.

Not a word did I say in that circular, not a word did I mean to say, much less did I 'tractare de Catholicis in Universitate educandis.' What I did say, I will transcribe from a rough copy which I have here, which is (I know) substantially as I prepared it for the press.

'Father Newman, having been entrusted by his diocesan with the Mission of Oxford, has it in contemplation, with the blessing of God, to proceed to the establishment there of a Church and House of the Oratory.

Some such establishment is at this time especially required, as a provision in behalf of the Catholic youth, whom the *Colleges of the University*, in accordance with a kinder and more liberal policy than they have hitherto pursued, are beginning to admit *within their walls*.

It need scarcely be shown that a measure like this, conceived in however good a spirit, is nevertheless fraught with spiritual danger to the parties for whom it is designed, unless the inexperience incident to their time of life and the temptations of the place are met with some corresponding safeguard of *special religious superintendence*.

The Priests of St Philip Neri may attempt, it is hoped, without presumption to supply *this imperative need*, considering that the Oratory has ever made the care of young men its primary object, and that the English Congregation in particular, by virtue of the Apostolic letters constituting it, is sent to those classes of society above others to which the members of an Academical body necessarily belong.

Moreover, educated as they have been themselves at Oxford and Cambridge, they bring to their undertaking an intimate acquaintance with the routine and habits of University life, which furnishes a reasonable hope of their being able to discharge such duties as are involved in commencing such a work, without giving umbrage to the authorities of the place, ... '

So far my copy here allows me to go; but I am sure no words followed, suggestive of any educational plan, or work, ever so little. I guarded myself all through upon this point, keeping in view St Philip's Oratorium parvum as the type of the instrumentality by which we were to act upon the Catholics under education at Oxford, after the manner, (as we understood) of what the Jesuits have done at Bonn.

I will add, that, when after the December meeting of the Bishops (in that year 1864) I withdrew from the contemplation of any Oxford scheme, I did so on the avowed ground, which I got mentioned at Rome to a Cardinal (I think Cardinal Reisach) that the very fact of my going there would encourage parents to send their children to the University.

Moreover, I told every one, what I said to your Lordship in a letter of February 1865 (I think), that the Oxford scheme was, as far as I was concerned, entirely at an end.[6]

If I bought fresh land at Oxford, it was, as I both meant and said, for the future, not for any personal purpose.

I was not prepared for your Lordship's reviving the project of my having the Mission, as you did, in the spring of 1865, though I felt the kind confidence in me which it betokened. I have no anxious longing to be laden with so heavy a responsibility; though, if I was once engaged in it, certainly there would be no intention on my part, when the church was built, of keeping aloof from the practical working of the Mission.

It may surprise Cardinal Barnabo to master the fact, which your Lordship puts before him, that I am thus indifferent how the Holy See in its wisdom decides; but it is quite true, to use the words of one of your late letters to me, though his Eminence does not know it, that I undertake the Mission of Oxford with 'reluctance'.

There is only one thing which would be more trying to me than accepting it; viz. to be allowed to build the Church there, and, as soon as that preparatory work was over, to be told from Rome that I had now done my part, and might retire.

You have always allowed me to write so freely to you, that I have not been able to bring myself to disguise any feeling which has risen in my mind from the light which your Lordship's letter throws upon the Cardinal's view of the whole transaction.

I am, My dear Lord, begging your Lordship's blessing Your obt and affte Servt in Xt

John H Newman of the Oratory

The Rt Revd The Bishop of Birmingham

P.S. I should be much obliged to your Lordship to send me the proper form to enable me to say Mass in these parts. I am sorry to give you the trouble. Any letter, sent to Father Neville at the Oratory, would find me, wherever I am. We have sadly rainy weather.

[1] Ullathorne had sent Newman his letter to Cardinal Barnabò.
[2] See letter to Ullathorne, 23 September 1864, *L.D.* XXI, pp. 234–5.
[3] See letter to Ullathorne, 26 September 1864.
[4] See letter of 17 June to Ullathorne (*L.D.* XXII, p. 251).
[5] For the circular of 1864 see letter of 27 November 1864 to Ullathorne (*L.D.* XXI, p. 319).
[6] See letter to Ullathorne, 10 February 1865, *L.D.* XXI, pp. 412–13.

To T. W. Allies

The Oratory, Bm Oct. 21./66

My dear Allies

Of course I am very much gratified at what you say about Mr Dewar's conversion.[1]

As to my Sermon, I am publishing it, since so many reports are circulated about me, but I have seen nothing in the Papers about this sermon which was not *in the main* accurate.[2] The account of it in the Guardian (taken, I think, from the Daily News) was singularly fair. But of course I know nothing of what kind friends and enemies say about me privately without foundation.

Certainly, the tone of Dr Cullen, almost giving up the Church, if the temporal power went, shrieking as if he were on the edge of an abyss, and saying that it was all the Emperor of the French, did not recommend itself to me.[3] And, though I have no difficulty in saying that the temporal power is necessary, while it lasts, nothing can make me say that it is necessary, if it be clean taken away,—and I am quite as sure that, when it is clean gone, if that ever took place, no Pope would say that it was necessary, as I am sure no Pope will say that Our Lord is a mere man.

Ever yrs affly John H Newman

[1] Dewar had been influenced by Newman's *Letter to Pusey*.
[2] The sermon was 'The Pope and the Revolution', *O.S.* pp. 281–316. The *Pall Mall Gazette* (8 October 1866) thought that Newman's views on the temporal power 'appear to fall considerably short of those entertained by Dr. Manning and the Irish bishops'.
[3] In his pastoral letter read in the Dublin churches on 2 September Cullen spoke of how Napoleon III had allowed no other power than France to be the protector of the Holy See, and was now about to withdraw his troops. 'Thus Rome will be abandoned to the tender mercies of the infidel and excommunicated ministers of Victor Emmanuel.' *The Tablet* (8 Sept. 1866), p. 571.

To James Hope-Scott

The Oratory Bm ⌈Decr 6 1866

My dear Hope Scott

Charlie, the virtuous pony, which you gave us 14 years ago, has at length departed this life. He continued his active and useful habits up to last summer—bene meritus, but not emeritus. Then he fell hopelessly stiff, lame, and miserable. His mind was clear to the last—and, without losing his affection for human kind, he commenced a lively, though, alas, not lasting friendship with an impudent colt of a donkey—who insulted him in his stiffness, and teased and tormented him from one end of the field to the other. We cannot guess his age; he was old when he came to us. He lies under two sycamore trees, which will be by their growth and beauty the living monument, or even transformation of a faithful servant, while his spirit is in the limbo of quadrupeds. Rest to his manes! I suppose I may use the pagan word of a horse.⌉[1]

I hope you and Lady Victoria and your party are enjoying yourselves at Hyères.

Ever Yours affly John H Newman of the Oratory

⌈P.S. No news about Oxford.⌉

[1] Hope-Scott replied on 12 January, 'Bellasis brought me your lament over Charlie, which does credit to the feelings of your Congregation. Little did I think, when he left Abbotsford, that he would serve so long, and be so honourably remembered when he came to die.'

To Gerard Manley Hopkins

The Oratory 6 Dec 1866

I am glad that you are on easier terms than you expected with your friends at home. . . . I proposed your coming here because you could not go home—but, if you can be at home with comfort, home is the best place for you.[1]

Do not suppose we shall not rejoice to see you here, even if you can only come for Christmas Day. . . . As to your retreat, I think we have misunderstood each other . . . it does not seem to me that there is any hurry about it—your first duty is to make a good class. Show your friends at home that your becoming a Catholic has not unsettled you in the plain duty that lies before you. And, independently of this, it seems to me a better thing not to hurry [a] decision on your vocation. Suffer yourself to be led on by the Grace of God step by step.

[1] i.e. during the Christmas Vacation.

To Charlotte Wood

The Oratory Bm Dec 21/66

Most Private

My dear Miss Wood

We are now so close upon Christmas, that I may fitly send you and Mrs Wood by anticipation my best and kindest congratulations on the sacred season, as I do most heartily.

I don't think it would be any good saying any thing to others on the matters about which I write to you. It would only lead to correspondence which might leave things worse than they are.

There has been from the first an animus against me—why, I cannot tell, though I may conjecture. Not because I have been strong for a Catholic College at Oxford, for I have never advocated it, feeling more might be said against it than for it. My opinion, however, has never been asked by *any* one in authority from the first day that the subject of Catholics going to Oxford was mooted. All sorts of people were consulted—the written opinions of several of the London Oratorians were sent to Rome—but mine has never been even asked, though from my connexion with the Dublin Catholic University, it would have been natural to have consulted me among others.

It is now more than three years since Dr Manning put an article in the Dublin Review about a Catholic University for England—in the course of it he enumerated all the English Catholic Colleges and Schools, first rate and second rate except one—that one was ours, he simply left out our school altogether.

Two years ago (and since) at our Bishop's wish, I have thought of taking for the Oratory the Oxford mission. It has been carefully spread about in England and in Rome that I am contemplating *more* than an Oratory, namely a College. Manning is now opposing at Rome the Oratory's going there.

To strengthen this prejudice against the Oratory going there, they actually are now saying in London, by way of objection that, if I go there, I shall make too many converts, and create a row and so damage the Catholic cause. I have reason to think the Archbishop says this. It is not very long since it was objected to me that I was slow to make converts. Is it not a case of Dr Fell?[1]

When I published my Apologia, Dr Manning expressed his regret at it. Afterwards he qualified his reasons for it—he said he only meant my violence against Kingsley. Next, he wrote a pamphlet, which was mainly a covert attack on portions of it. One of the points I have mentioned in my letter to Dr Pusey—viz that I had said that the Anglican Church was a *bulwark* of the truth. That on this and another matter in it he was referring to me, I have the authority of a common friend to whom he showed the pamphlet either in MS or in the proof sheets.[2]

When I published the said letter to Pusey, he sent me two letters, one by his secretary, one in his own hand, expressing pleasure at it. Shortly after he secretly attempted to get parts of it *virtually* condemned by the Bishops. This fact I had from one of the Bishops to whom he applied.[3]

Two years ago, a lay friend of mine who was at Rome and saw various great people there said that he was sure Dr M, was more opposed to my going to Oxford than to Catholic youth going there, that *I* was the cause of his opposition.[4]

All this of course is in the strictest confidence.

If you ask my explanation of all this, I don't impute to him any animosity to me—but I think he is of a nature to be determined to *crush* or to *melt* every person who stands in his way. He has views and is determined to carry them out—and I must either go with him or be annihilated. I say this, because he long wished to get me made a Bishop (in partibus)—I believe because he knew it would be (as it were) putting me 'in the House of Lords'. When he found that I should not accept the offer, as feeling it would interfere with my independence, his only remaining policy is to put me out.

Now I have taken a great liberty with you. For I never wrote thus plainly and fully to any person yet

Ever Yrs most sincerely John H Newman

[1] 'I do not love you Dr. Fell,
    But why I cannot tell;
    But this I know full well,
    I do not love you, Dr Fell.'
    Thomas Browne's translation of Martial, *Epigrams*, I, 32, in *Works* 1719, IV, p. 113.
[2] See letters of 17 and 28 November 1864 to Walker, and notes there (*L.D.* XXI, pp. 298–9, 323–4).
[3] See first Memorandum of 26 March 1866 (*L.D.* XXII, pp. 189–91).
[4] This was Edward Bellasis.

To Mrs John Mozley

The Oratory Bm Febry 5/67

My dear Jemima

I am deeply concerned at what you tell me—it is quite tragical their leaving that house where they have so long lived. Of course what you tell me throws no light on the point, whether they will be well off and able to make another nice house for themselves, but nothing can make up for a place which from long familiarity is almost part of themselves. I have always in particular had a special liking for Anne. I like her as much as ever I did—and I sympathise with her most sincerely.[1]

You must not send me any more marmalade. My doctor won't let me eat it. He says the sugar is bad for me.

I don't like to boast—for a reverse comes with it—but I am thankful to say that this is the third season, in which I have had no cold whatever—tho' the third season is but begun, and March is to come. I attribute it to the shower bath, to which I have taken for 4 or 5 years—and to cod-liver oil.

Ever Yours affly John H Newman

[1] Anne Mozley and her sisters, on their mother's death, were leaving 'The Friary', their house in Derby.

To Ambrose St John

To the Revd Ambrose St John   March 16. 1867

My dear Ambrose

The message, which the Count de Torre Diaz, has sent me through you, has caused me the most serious concern. It has deeply moved me, that a person whom I so much respect, and who has on various occasions taken so friendly a part in matters in which I had an interest, should be so much changed in his feelings towards me, as to venture to say things of me, which I cannot, as a matter of conscience, pass over without formal notice. We are taught by holy men that any insult addressed to us may meritoriously be borne in silence, except such as has reference to our soundness in the Catholic faith; for, in allowing ourselves without remonstrance to be accused of misbelief, we are indirectly dishonouring Him from whom the matter of that faith proceeds. Such is the nature of the insult which the Count has directed against me.[1]

He imputes to me, to use his own words, 'a strong feeling, that, so far as England is concerned, it may be said of Catholicism, according as it is generally practised abroad, even by Bishops and Saints' teaching, what Paley said of Roman Catholicism in relation to Christianity, viz, that a weight has been laid upon it which sinks it for the English mind, and from which it must be relieved before the English mind takes to it—that this must be tried for—and that the Movement within a certain circle for University Education at Oxford, reprobated by Rome was, and now the Oratory, sanctioned certainly on an opposite understanding, is, intended to achieve that deliverance for Englishmen, which according to Paley Protestantism obtained for Christianity in the Infidel mind.'

It is here asserted, that I am attempting to eliminate from our present English Catholicism so much of it as is generally practised abroad; and that this foreign portion, which I wish to eliminate, is, when compared with our whole present English Catholicism, in extent and importance equal to the whole of Catholicism when viewed in comparison of Christianity. As then Christianity, as the Count would grant, is left in ruins, when Catholicism is withdrawn from it, so Catholicism itself will be left in ruins, when those elements of it are withdrawn from it, which he says I am actually aiming to withdraw.

His language, to my apprehension, admits of only this interpretation. In consequence, it is a charge against me of deliberately propagating a mutilated and crippled Catholicity; it is a charge against me of maintaining opinions, which are heretical, or very close upon heresy, or erroneous, or in some way or other opposed to the revealed word of God and the teaching of His Church. A charge like this, addressed to you, my subject, against me, your Superior, is certainly *contumelious*, and, as such, and on such a matter, an offence in its nature of a very grave character.

With the character indeed of the Count's personal acts, I have of course nothing to do; but I have much to do with their external bearing upon myself. Moreover, I have a right to remark upon their bearing on the Bishop of Birmingham, who is insulted in my person, seeing that his Lordship allows me, being such as the Count describes me, to remain in a very prominent position in his diocese, not only without rebuke, but with his positive sanction and approbation, nay is even employing me just now for an important service in a new sphere of action. And further still, I have undeniably serious cause to be offended with the language he uses about the Birmingham Oratory, as if it were a tool in my hands for carrying out my heterodox designs in that new missionary field.

I find it my duty then to ask of the Count an explanation of his words, such, as may relieve me of the painful course which I shall otherwise be obliged to pursue. That course is, to bring the matter formally before the Bishop, as my ecclesiastical Superior, who will advise me whether, as a Priest, and the Superior of a Religious House, and a Doctor in Theology, I cannot obtain ecclesiastical protection from assaults of this nature.

There are many theological questions, about which Catholics differ from each other, and differ with warmth and asperity; such warmth and asperity I lament, but I do not denounce; but there is a mode of religious warfare, of a far worse character, and abhorrent to every right minded man. It is, when Catholics, on account of allowable differences of opinion, to the great scandal both of their brethren and of Protestants, charge each other, without ecclesiastical warrant, with errors in faith.

I am sure the Count will agree with me in deprecating the scandal which I have indicated; and this feeling will lead him so to explain or modify what he has written, as to make it clear that he does not accuse me of any doctrinal error, and thereby to spare me the pain of giving his charges that publicity which will be involved in my making a formal complaint of them to my Superiors in the Church.

I beg you to send him a copy of this letter.[2]

JHN

[1] St John had written to Torre Diaz, inviting him to contribute to Newman's plans for Oxford. He had been friendly with Newman, but became increasingly an extreme ultramontane. He opposed deeply what Newman was trying to achieve. His reply to St John concluded, 'With all respect to Father Newman, and for all concerned I must say that want of sympathy with any thing approaching the view, which I have tried to explain is a very weak expression of my deepest feeling.'

[2] St John forwarded this letter with one of his own and the correspondence between him and Torre Diaz continued for a short while. Torre Diaz was unyielding in his criticism of Newman who eventually appealed successfully to Ullathorne to safeguard his position.

To Cardinal Barnabò

Given from our house of the Oratory at Birmingham,
the 21st day of March of the Holy Year 1867.

To the Most Eminent and most Reverend Prince, the Lord Alexander Cardinal Barnabò, Prefect of the Sacred Congregation of Propaganda.

Most Eminent Father,

The report which has reached the ears of your Eminence is founded on fact to this extent, that I have with me, close to our Oratory at Birmingham (amongst youths preparing for Army or Navy or other similar examinations), *one*, whom his father of his own accord is going to send to Oxford, and *one other*, sent to the same University from as far away as New Zealand, recommended to me by a letter of his Lordship Bishop Pompallier. Until he can be given rooms in his College at Oxford, and lest he should stay on as the guest of a certain Anglican minister, I took in this second one, very recently and for a short time, to live among my friends, receiving him into the bosom of the Catholic religion, providing him with the best opportunities of study and instruction.

All this I did because hitherto I had known of, I had heard of, nothing, absolutely nothing, that had been sent to this country either by the Sacred Congregation or by the Holy Father, whether as precept or as admonition, on the subject of Catholics going to Oxford;—on the contrary, our Bishops, who did not wish youths to go to that University, seemed to me to leave the whole matter to the prudent discretion of the parish priests and confessors under their jurisdiction, that is, that parish priests and confessors might treat with the parents in each case as it arose, in some cases dissuading, in others providing safeguards, sometimes reluctantly acquiescing, where they found parents rashly but obstinately determined in any case to send their sons to Oxford.

Moreover I have never heard, or hitherto ever suspected, that any Catholic youth at Oxford, at any time, either now or in the past, has lost his faith; nor would I now believe it, did I not have it on your Eminence's most weighty authority.

What I felt was, that if a number of youths were to go to Oxford, (with or without the approval of Ecclesiastical Superiors) it would be better if I, who knew well the dangers they would face, were to put forth my best endeavours to forearm them against those dangers with the weapons of faith and virtue.

And what I thought best and did, that I believe was thought best and done in other Colleges for Catholic boys in England, for example, at Oscott and at Stonyhurst, from which a number of boys are now being sent to Oxford, and have been in the past.

And now, when at last, and for the first time, I hear from your Eminence that it is the Sacred Congregation's desire that I should abstain from every deed and activity which might seem directly or indirectly to countenance the education of youths at Oxford, I promise the Sacred Congregation my ready and careful obedience.

For the rest, I will not conceal my surprise, most Eminent Father, that, after my twenty years of most faithful service, your Eminence reposes so little confidence in me in the matter:—but God will see to it.

With the deepest respect, and kissing the Sacred Purple, I am

> Your Eminence's most humble servant, John Henry Newman
> Priest of the Oratory of St Philip Neri.

To Bishop Ullathorne

Saturday April 6. 1867

(Copy)[1]

My dear Lord,

I am very glad to be informed by your Lordship of a condition, so intimately bearing on my being capable last Christmas to form a just and safe decision whether to accept or to decline your Lordship's offer to me of the Oxford mission.[2]

And now, on at length knowing it, I am obliged to say at once I cannot accept the mission with that condition. Nor am I likely to change my mind on this point. If I am missioner at Oxford, I claim to be there, as much or as little as I please.

Not that I have ever intended to leave residence in Birmingham; but such a condition would be a snare to my conscience, and if I stopped at Oxford for a few days in Term time, it would easily be construed by Propaganda into residence. No compromise is possible here.

But, even if the condition was withdrawn, how can I ever trust Propaganda again, after this instance thus brought to light of its secret instructions about me?

I hope you will not think me disrespectful if I refer you to two passages at the end of my letter to your Lordship from Switzerland under date of August 12. 1866.

'I have no anxious longing to be laden with so heavy a responsibility (as the Oxford mission) though, if I was once engaged in it, certainly there would be no intention on my part, when the Church was built, of keeping aloof from the *practical* working of the Mission.

There is only one thing which could be more trying to me than accepting it; viz. to be allowed *to build the Church* there, and, as soon as that preparatory work was over, to be told from Rome that I had now done my part and might retire.'

Begging your Lordship's blessing Your obt and affte Servt in Xt

John H. Newman.

[1] Newman wrote at the head of this copy of letter 'A': '(Shown to the Bishop by Fr Henry April 13 1867 and formally put into his hands August 18 1867)' [i.e. when Newman finally declined taking the Oxford Mission].

[2] The condition was that, were Newman likely to go into residence at the Oxford mission, he was to be gently dissuaded. He was to be forbidden to do so. Ullathorne, when first informed, understood the condition as addressed to himself and so kept it secret, not telling Newman. He hoped on a subsequent visit to Rome to have it rescinded. But the condition became more generally known and so he wrote to Newman to inform him.

To James Hope-Scott

The Oratory Bm ⌈April 13/67⌉

My dear Hope Scott

⌈I think it is now proved that what you called my 'sensitiveness' was not timidity, or particularity, or touchiness, but a true instinct of the state of the ecclesiastical atmosphere[1]—nor is it wonderful that I should know more than you of what threatened, and what did not, as you (I suspect) would know more than I could know about the temper of Parliamentary committees, and Gladstone more than myself about political parties. That neophyte, Mr Martin, is an index of the state of the weather at Rome, as the insects swarming near the earth is a sign of rain;[2]—and rash sayings in the Chronicle may be of as much danger indirectly to my influence in England, as an open window may avail to give me a cold.—The truth is, since Faber's matter in 1855, I have not had an atom of confidence in Propaganda. Faber and his friends and Barnabò treated me not less, or more, injuriously then, than my present opponents are treating me now—nay, I may say that my whole ecclesiastical life, since Mgr Palma's death in 1847 [*sic*], has been one long time of neglect and unkind usage.[3] I have come to think it my portion, and so it is—, it is my cross, and the easiest one I could have—how much easier than illhealth or bereavement, or poverty! I would not change it for any other—and somehow I don't think it will ever leave me. I have had it now for 34 years, ever since 1833. No one but myself knows how intensely anxious I have been, since I have been a Catholic, never to say any thing without good theological authority for saying it, and, though of course with the greatest care the human incuria is at fault, yet I have no reason to suppose that my mistakes are more than those which all writers incur;—yet there is no doubt that I am looked at with suspicion at Rome, because I will not go the whole hog in all the extravagances of the school of the day, and I cannot move my finger without giving offence.

I am going to make a stand on the following point, and some time, when Ambrose is writing [[to me]] you can tell him whether you think I am right, not only in my point, but in the reasons for it. Our Bishop has announced Ambrose at Rome for *his* messenger. Now we sent him *solely* on the school matters, not on the Oxford matter which has turned up since—all he was to do as to that was to thank the Cardinal [[Barnabò]] for what was granted us at Oxford (as we thought). Again, *we* have never corresponded with the *Cardinal* about Oxford, simply with the *Bishop*. He asked me to go to Oxford—I answered 'I won't unless you get me leave—' He then says 'I have got you leave.' But, if Ambrose says to the Cardinal a word about Oxford—*we* become *principals* in the matter instead of the Bishop. Moreover, the fact of Ambrose going to Propaganda implies that I have no quarrel there—that the whole difficulty is made up; *before* he goes, things must be set right—and how *can* they be set right?]

Ever Yrs affly John H Newman

[1] Hope-Scott was confident that all would be well for the Oxford enterprise, provided Newman 'doesn't let himself get too sensitive to what people say and if Catholics and especially Edgbaston boys don't lose their faith at Oxford'.

[2] Edwin Roper Martin, who had studied for Anglican orders, became a Catholic in 1864 and studied for the priesthood in Rome. He supported himself by acting as Rome correspondent for the *Tablet* and in that capacity circulated in Rome disparaging reports about Newman in 1866 in connection with the *Letter to Pusey* and in 1867 regarding plans for the Oxford Oratory. He was ordained in 1869 and died in 1877.

[3] G. B. Palma was shot through a window in the Quirinal Palace on 16 November 1848. He was Secretary to the Congregation of Propaganda and had arranged that Newman should adapt the Oratorian Rule for England. Newman regarded him as a great ally and benefactor (see letter to Henry Wilberforce, 30 November 1848).

To Emily Bowles

The Oratory Bm April 15. 1867

Private

My dear Child

Don't talk of giving your life—you are setting your heart on an object which, if gained, would certainly disappoint you.[1] I have no confidence I could do any thing at

Oxford—I have never wished to go, rather I have intensely wished not to go, and lately I have been even praying against going.

What you mean by 'going to Rome' last Autumn, I don't know. If you mean old Talbot's invitation, that was three years ago—and it was suggested by Dr Manning—the Pope had nothing to do with it—when Talbot left for England, he said among other things to the Pope, 'I think of asking Dr Newman to give a set of lectures in my Church—' and the Pope of course said, 'A very good thought,' as he would have said if Mgr T. had said 'I wish to bring your Holiness some English razors.' This was the whole of it—people now may make a story of it, as Ffoulkes, it seems, makes his stories about me; but the one is no more true than the other.

By the bye, what can you mean about Ffoulkes? He plagued me with some letters about Oxford two or three years ago—and I did nothing but contradict him in answer. Since that, he has, I believe, written against me in the Union Review, that in 1845 I betrayed the Anglican cause by not making terms with the Church before becoming a Catholic—and he has invented the charge, taken up by the high Anglican papers, that 'I fled away from the fight in cowardice.' That is all I know about him. (He has not subscribed to my undertaking). He was at Sir John Simeon's that night last June when I was there, and I recollect thinking it impudent in him, after that article, coming up to talk with me. I wish you would find out for me any thing he says, that I may contradict it

All this gossip would have been impossible, if Cardinal Wiseman, Archbishop Manning, or any one else, had ever asked my opinion about the Oxford matter, as others were asked—but I am the only one who has never been asked by any authority.

I don't mind Fr Coleridge under secrecy knowing the state of the case, which, as far as I know, is as follows:—It is plain that, as soon as the Bishops determined in December 1864 to discourage Catholic youths going to Oxford, it was a great inconsistency in any one of them to send me there. Accordingly I wrote to our Bishop to say so, and withdrew from the project—and I got a friend to say the same thing at Rome to Cardinal Reisach. Propaganda, however, did not *refuse* my going—and has therefore got into this dead lock, that it cannot so limit my residence there as at once to enable me to influence Protestants there and yet not to bring Catholics there. I say, it is impossible to influence Protestants without attracting Catholics. In this dilemma Cardinal Barnabò seems to have thrown the solution of the difficulty on our Bishop, and gave him a secret instruction to let me proceed, but, as soon as I attempted to reside there, 'blande et suaviter revocare Patrem Newman.' Though I am very indignant I can't help laughing—for such a direction, pace Eminentissimi Cardinalis, is as imbecile as it is crooked and cruel. Hope Scott has felt so much about it, that he has withdrawn his £1000, and says that I, 'as a gentleman,' can have nothing more to do with the Oxford scheme. He says in a word 'You can't trust them—' Well—our Bishop was much perplexed with this secret instruction, and not the less, because I (not dreaming of it) told him how Cardinal Barnabò had treated me in the matter of the Dublin Oratory—and still worse in the Faber matter, when he actually altered our rule here in a very important matter without telling us, and was on the point of sending us a rescript to that effect, when, on his taking it to the Pope, the Pope stopped it by asking, 'Does F. Newman know of it?' Accordingly our Bishop advised me to *wait* six months, that is, till he went to Rome, hoping then to get the secret instruction cancelled, as if it had never been, without my knowing about it. And so I should have left it, viz to wait six months, but our Fathers here, and friends in the country were so urgent with me not to delay that, against my own first judgment, I began collecting money and determined (since it *cost* nothing) to take the Mission on the 2nd week after Easter. Things were in this state, when Mr Martin at Rome got news of the secret condition, and, by the happy accident of a break in the Editorship of the W.R. [*Weekly Register*], got his letter into the Paper— and the Bishop, knowing *how* to interpret it, without any delay told me of the secret article, seeing that others knew it, and that therefore I ought to know it.

Well, now, if I go to Oxford, I shall not be safe there. I shall be clogged, perhaps recalled—and my days will be shortened in doing nothing.

Ever Yrs affly John H Newman

[1] Emily Bowles wanted to offer her life to God for the defeat of plots against Newman.

To Ambrose St John

The Oratory Bm April 17/67

My dear Ambrose

The Bishop has sent me up a letter today inclosing one from Bishop Brown—but it has miscarried. Accidentally I learn that Cardinal Barnabò is very angry with my letter to him. I am not at all sorry for it. By the time you get to him, he will have worked off his rage, and he will be more likely to treat me with respect. I hear too that Talbot, Vaughan, and Stonor besiege the Pope, and, if they can, will not let any one come near him. However, Dr Brown had an audience, and the Pope at once went to the Oxford question, and let Dr B. say all he would. And it seems Barnabò has said that the petition cannot be refused, when a considerable person, such as I, am the subject of it. But how am I to believe him henceforth—tho' I expect you, if you go, to become good friends with him, after a good explosion. Talbot or somebody says that Manning wished to take a more lenient view of the Oxford question and the Pope ⟨?⟩ would not let him.

The Bishop is very eager you should go, and before I send the letter I may know more about it—and perhaps it will be the only way of hindering my being forced to go. If you go, I think you must take it coolly; say you have come because Dr Ullathorne wished it; that you stayed on the road, because you did not see any cause for hurry, you knew that authorities at Rome were sure to wait to hear both sides—that you were an old man now and would not travel fast—and that I had been so overcome with grief at Cardinal B's duplicity, that I was in a stupor, and could not command myself sufficiently to order you on—so you remained at Hyères waiting for orders. You understand the sort of line I mean you to take.

Take every thing lightly and coolly except attacks on our faith, our honour, our loyalty, and the morality of the school. If the Pope asks you why you have come, answer, To refute the slanderers of Fr Newman. Say, we do not want any thing— you have come to ask nothing; if asked, confess boldly that my going to Oxford *would* tend to make certain parents send their sons to Oxford, you can't tell how many—don't explain the fact away, and don't over ride it with counter consider- ations, as if we were set upon our going to Oxford. As to the school, of course you must say that we will do nothing to promote boys going to Oxford. What I am thinking of is a line additional in our Prospectus to this effect:—'In consequence of a notice sent from Propaganda, boys intended for the Universities of Oxford and Cambridge cannot remain in the school longer than the age of fifteen.'

I recall of course the *instructions* I gave you on leaving this place, and the *letter* to Cardinal Barnabò; though you had better keep a copy of the Three Latin Proposi- tions in the Memorial. You cannot use that letter, or the instructions, as a base for talking or consulting. Your great business is to talk and nothing more. If you must have a letter of introduction, I think I shall say you go to Rome, as the great Solon went to Croesus θεωρίης εἴνεκα,[1] and with no practical purpose—but I don't see you need. You call on the Cardinal out of respect, since you are in Rome—ut valet? ut vescitur Aurâ etc etc.[2] The fear is, your getting yourself pledged in some way or other by what you may say to him. If I saw him, I should certainly let out, 'Decepisti nos Pater eminentissime.'

The Bishop's statement is in the press—it is very good, consisting simply of Propaganda's, his, and my letters—my Swiss letter in extenso[3] he sends it to the Bishops next Monday, so that they may have a week before the meeting to think over the facts of the case. I tell him he ought to put it into Italian.

April 18. This morning comes a letter from Mr Williams saying that the Lynch matter is at an end, with lawyers' correspondence. This is good news.[4] The Bishop's lost letter has come this morning. He urges earnestly that you should go on to Rome. I have answered that you shall go at the beginning of next (Easter) week. He says that Dr Brown and Neve are most unfairly tasked with *my* battles, and that you should be there as more authoritative than they. I have replied that, before you go, I wish you to do a matter for me with Hope Scott (i.e. I want to show him our School Accounts, which I hope to send by this post) and this may delay you a day or two, but then you shall go—but I said to him 'Fr St John goes to ask nothing but justice—no favours—he goes to clear my character and put down slanders; for nothing more.' You must expect to find Barnabò and the Pope angry, and must keep silence, and let them have their talk out. I suppose I must send a letter to the Cardinal, but it will be a very dry one. *By the bye would it not be best for you to leave all the letters* you can spare (including those which are superseded, such as the Letter to Barnabò) with Hope Scott—you could pick them up from him as you came back— or ask him to be so good as to take them to England. The table of accounts would be included in such.

I have not noticed Bellasis's letter—It is an excellent one and like him—but I cannot allow you to present it to Talbot.[5] I suppose he does not know Neve—

but he *does* know Cardinal Reisach. Could he not write to him? The nuisance is that it would give him the trouble of retranscribing it. Could not his daughter write it (in a lady's clearest hand) and he sign it? I send it you back as you wished, but you have scribbled on it.

I hope I am not mistaken in thinking, that I may now take a high tone with Barnabò, now I have so many 'Lordi', Baronets, and MP's at my back. As I have said before, you are to answer any questions about the School etc which Cardinal Barnabò asks, but not to *volunteer* any thing in the way of explanation to him. This is not inconsistent with your talking right and left with others persons

Ever Yrs affly J. H. N.

P.S. Your letter of the 16th has just come. April 18.

---

[1] τῆς θεωρίης ἐκδημήσας ὁ Σόλων εἵνεκεν. 'Solon travelled for the sake of seeing the sights.' Herodotus, *History* i, 30.

[2] 'How is he? Is he keeping well?' Cf. *Aeneid* I, 546, III, 339.

[3] i.e. letter of 12 August 1866 to Ullathorne.

[4] See letter of 20 February 1867, relating to a dispute about property in Oxford (*L.D.* XXIII, pp. 64–5).

[5] This was a long letter from Bellasis to Talbot, in defence of the Oratory School.

To W. G. Ward

The Oratory. Birmingham. May 9th 1867

My dear Ward,

Fr Ryder has shown me your letter to him, in which you speak of me; and though I know that to remark on what you say will be as ineffectual now in making you understand me, as so many former times in the last 15 years, yet, at least as a protest in memoriam, I will, on occasion of this letter and of your letter to myself, make a fresh attempt to explain myself.

Let me observe then, that, in former years *and now*, I have considered the theological differences between us as unimportant in themselves, that is, such as to be simply compatible with a reception, both by you and by me, of the whole theological teaching of the Church in the widest sense of the word 'teaching;' and again, now and *in former years too*, I have considered one phenomenon in you to be 'momentous,' nay portentous, viz. that you will persist in calling the said unimportant, allowable, inevitable differences (which must ever exist between mind and mind,) not unimportant, but of great moment.

In this utterly uncatholic, not so much opinion, as feeling and sentiment, you have grown in the course of years, whereas I consider that I remain myself in the same temper of forbearance and sobriety which I have ever wished to cultivate.

Years ago you wrote me a letter, in answer to one of mine, in which you made so much out of such natural difference of opinion between us, as exists, that I endorsed it with the words 'See how this man seeketh a quarrel against me!'[1]

Now you are running on, as it appears to me, into worse excesses. Pardon me if I say that you are making a Church within a Church, as the Novatians of old did within the Catholic pale,[2] and as, outside the Catholic pale, the Evangelicals of the Establishment. As they talk of 'vital religion' and 'vital doctrines,' and will not allow that their brethren 'know the Gospel' or are 'Gospel preachers' unless they profess the small shibboleths of their own sect, so you are doing your best to make a party in the Catholic Church, and in St Paul's words are *'dividing Christ'* by exalting your opinions into dogmas, and shocking to say, by declaring to me, as you do, that those Catholics who do not accept them are of a different religion from yours.

I protest then again, not against your tenets, but against what I must call your schismatical spirit. I disown your intended praise of me viz that I hold your theological opinions 'in the greatest aversion,' and I pray God that I may never denounce, as you do, what the Church has not denounced.

Bear with me. Yrs affecly in Xt
John H. Newman

[1] *2 Kings* 5:7. See second note to letter of 15 March 1862 to Ward (*L.D.* xx, p. 168).
[2] The Novatian schism arose in the third century. Though orthodox in doctrine, the Novatians were rigorists who were utterly severe with those who had compromised during times of persecution.

To Henry Wilberforce

The Oratory Bm May 14. 1867

My dear Henry

You can do me a service—and I hope with little trouble to yourself. My doctor here wishes me to try cyder as an experiment in the inconveniences I suffer. He thinks unadulterated cyder may be difficult to get in Birmingham, and he prefers for me Worcestershire or Herefordshire to Devonshire.

Can you order me from some safe hand a small cask? Not too much, since it is an experiment.

I hope Harry [Wilberforce] is as well as you wish. Love to all of you.

Ever Yrs affly John H Newman

P.S. I sent on your letter to F. Ward the other day

To George Talbot

St Philip's Day [26 May] 1867

Dear Monsignor Talbot,

I have received with much satisfaction the report which Father St John has given me of your conversations with him.[1]

I know you have a good heart; I know you did me good service in the Achilli matter—and you got me a relic of St Athanasius from Venice, which I account a great treasure; and for these reasons I have been the more bewildered at your having of late years taken so strong a part against me, without (I may say) any real ground whatever; or rather, I *should* have been bewildered were it not that, for now as many as thirty four years, it has been my lot to be misrepresented and opposed without any intermission by one set of persons or another. Certainly, I have desiderated in you, as in many others, that charity which thinketh no evil, and have looked in vain for that considerateness and sympathy which is due to a man who has passed his life in attempting to subserve the cause and interests of religion, and who, for the very reason that he has written so much, must, from the frailty of our common nature, have said things which had better not have been said, or left out complements and explanations of what he *has* said, which had better have been added.

I am now an old man, perhaps within a few years of my death, and you can now neither do me good nor harm. I have never been otherwise than well-disposed towards you. When you first entered the Holy Father's immediate service, I used to say a Mass for you the first day of every month, that you might be prospered at your important post; and now I shall say Mass for you seven times, beginning with this week, when we are keeping the Feast of St Philip, begging him at the same time to gain for you a more equitable judgment of us and a kinder feeling towards us on the part of our friends, than we have of late years experienced.

I am, dear Monsignor Talbot, Yours sincerely in Xt
John H Newman of the Oratory[2]

[1] St John had written from Rome on 2 May (see *L.D.* XXIII, pp. 208–9).

[2] Talbot replied on 31 May, thanking Newman for his kind letter, and hoping that they might resume correspondence. He declared his unwavering love and affection for Newman, but acknowledged his opposition to those views of his that seemed contrary to the wishes of the Holy See and he affirmed as well his hostility to the liberal Catholics who wished to place Newman at their head.

To Mrs John Mozley

The Oratory Bm June 29/67

My dear Jemima

I have received from Rednall your letter, and the other of yesterday. I have no doubt I began that sonata too fast, out of nervousness. The one in 3 flats is the grandest. I see Sharp's name is over all three, and begin to wonder whether I stole them, and they are really his. Poor man, I wonder whether he is alive or dead. By the bye, I meant to have asked you whether Mrs Ostrehan is still alive, and Mr Ostrehan, and still near Cheltenham—also whether Augusta and Mary Withy are alive. Mary was 20 in 1813—so she is 74, if alive. I don't recollect seeing her after that date, though I suppose I did in 1821. I almost think I saw Mrs Rodney's death in the Papers some time back.[1]

I am glad you liked my violin—yet I think the one which Rogers and Church gave me two years ago is a much better one—and, if I came to you, I should bring *it*. But I have *ever* been puzzled by violins—they *suddenly* go harsh. I think it must be from the temperature, yet I cannot reduce it to rule. For weeks they will be as easy as possible to play upon—then, you do not know why, you cannot bring out a note.

The effect is, as if the finger-board gave way a bit, and the strings were at an impossible distance from the wood.

I have told John [Mozley] the state of things here—not pleasant.[2]

Ever Yours affectly John H Newman

[1] Anne Withy (1797–1870), Newman's second cousin, married Joseph Duncan Ostrehan in 1822. He died in 1870, aged 71. Mary and Augusta Withy were sisters of Anne.

[2] This refers to the anti-Catholic riots provoked by William Murphy.

To Marianne Bowden

The Oratory Bm July 15. 1867

My dearest Child

Your letter of this morning brought tears into my eyes—first because you spoke so affectionately of me, and said, that, wherever you are, you will not forget me.[1] When God brings you to His Blessed Presence, then at length you will know how weak I am, though so old, and how I need your prayers, and what good you can do me by them. You are one of my most faithful friends—I have ever said Mass for you under that title—and you will not cease to be faithful to me, though God calls you to Himself. Meanwhile, if He gives me grace, I will try to do what I can to merit your remembrance of me, by keeping you and your present necessities in mind.

You are one of those to whom God has been most good—He has shielded you from evil all your life long—He has brought you into His Holy Church, and then made you one of His own elect children and spouses and now if it is His blessed will to take you hence, it is in order to bring you to Himself for all eternity. Oh how much better will you understand this, than poor human words can say it, when it has taken place. May our Lord Jesus and His dear Mother and St Joseph be with you, when ever that solemn change comes.

I like of course to hear from you, and it is very kind in you to write—but don't trouble yourself with writing—for I know you will think of me, as I shall think of you

Ever Yours most affectly in Jesus & Mary
John H Newman of the Oratory

[1] Marianne Bowden wrote on 14 July, 'I get worse by steady degrees, though with no marked symptoms. Thank God I feel very calm and peaceful, and though I have no idea whatever what I shall find in Eternity, still I feel most happy to go, for I know that God loves me . . . I need not say dear Father that wherever I am I can never forget you, and if God shows me mercy as I trust, I hope you will feel the effects of my prayers.'

To Bishop Ullathorne

[The Oratory Bm August 18. 1867

My dear Lord,

I do not think you will feel any surprise, if I at length act on the resolve which I formed on the very day that I heard of the restriction placed on my presence in

Oxford, which I have cherished ever since, and only not carried out because of the dissuasion of friends here and elsewhere.

That dissuasion has now ceased, and accordingly I now ask your permission to withdraw from my engagement to undertake the Mission of Oxford, on the ground that I am not allowed by Propaganda the freedom to discharge its duties with effect.

Thanking you for all your kindness, and with much regret for the trouble I have caused you,] I am,

My dear Lord, Your Lordship's obt and affte Servt in Xt
John H Newman of the Oratory

The Rt Revd The Bp of Birmingham

[P.S. I inclose a copy of my Letter written to you, on receipt of the news of the restriction, April 6, held back by my friends, lest I should be acting on impulse, and shown to your Lordship by Fr Bittleston April 13. You have already a letter of mine to the same effect dated April 12.][1]

[1] Ullathorne replied on 19 August, 'Your letter reached me this morning from Stone. I am not at all surprised that you have renounced the project of the Oxford mission. Were I in the same position, I should do the same. And yet I receive the announcement of your decision with a sense of pain both acute and deep.

I have no hesitation in saying it, as my complete conviction that you have been shamefully misrepresented at Rome, and that by countrymen of our own.

When I went thither, I had some hope of being able to put this affair more straight. But when I got there, I plainly saw that the time had not come for an impartial hearing. Preoccupations in the quarters where alone representation is effectual was [sic] still too strong, and minds were too much occupied with the vast multitude of affairs brought to Rome by so many Bishops there assembled.

On the other hand, the closing sentence of your letter to Cardinal Barnabò [of 21 March 1867] which, the moment I read it, I felt would be interpreted in a much stronger sense than you could have intended, made so unpleasant an impression, that I believe that sentence stood as a considerable obstacle in the way of those explanations which were proffered by your own representatives. Indeed I have good evidence that it was so from those who took your part with cordiality. You will quite understand that I am not making a reflection, but pointing to a fact.

I still trust that the time will come when the facts of the case will be better understood at Rome, and when justice will be done to you.'

To Mrs J. W. Bowden

The Oratory Bm Octr 13. 1867

My dear Mrs Bowden

The news from Westbury after all took me by surprise.[1] She has no need of our prayers—but I shall say many masses for her, please God, and name her in my daily Memento. How joyful you must be amid your grief—and Emily too, and John and Charles. May we all die such deaths, and leave such memories behind us

Ever Your affectly in Xt John H Newman of the Oratory

Mrs Bowden

P.S. Since writing the above, I have received your letter. Of course I shall not forget you all.

[1] Marianne Bowden died on 10 October.

To *A Student at Maynooth*

The Oratory, Birmingham. March 2nd 1868

Dear Sir,

I would gladly serve you by answering the question which you ask had I anything to say which would be materially of use to you.

Also I know what able instructors you have at Maynooth, and I should shrink from interfering in a matter which requires an experience of young men which the Maynooth Professors have, and I have not. Besides, while I thank you heartily for the compliment you pay to my own mode of writing, and am truly glad if you and others have received pleasure from it, you must recollect that those who are expert in any work are often the least able to teach others; and for myself I must simply say that I have followed no course of English reading, and am quite at a loss to know what books to recommend to students such as yourselves.

As to the writing or delivery of sermons to which you refer, the great thing seems to be to have your subject distinctly before you; to think over it till you have got it perfectly in your head; to take care that it should be one subject, not several; to sacrifice every thought, however good and clever, which does not tend to bring out your one point, and to aim earnestly and supremely to bring home that one point to the minds of your hearers.

I have written some pages on the subject of preaching in a volume upon 'University Subjects' which I published when I was in Dublin.[1] It is unfortunately out of print or I would have sent it to you. One great difficulty in recommending particular authors as models of English arises from the Literature of England being Protestant and sometimes worse—Thus Hume is a writer of good English, but he was an unbeliever. Swift and Dryden write English with great force, but you can never be sure you will not come upon coarse passages. South is a vigorous writer, but he was a Protestant clergyman, and his writings are sermons. All this leads me to consider that everyone must form his style for himself, and under a few general rules, some of which I have mentioned already. First, a man should be in earnest, by which I mean, he should write, not for *the sake of writing*, but to bring out his *thoughts*. He should never aim at being eloquent. He should keep his idea in view, and write sentences over and over again till he has expressed his meaning accurately, forcibly and in few words. He should aim at being understood by his hearers or readers. He should use words which are most likely to be understood—ornament and amplification will come to him spontaneously in due time, but he should never seek them. He must creep before he can fly, by which I mean that humility, which is a great Christian virtue, has a place in literary composition—He who is ambitious will never write well. But he who tries to say simply and exactly what he feels or thinks, what religion demands, what Faith teaches, what the Gospel promises, will be eloquent without intending it, and will write better English than if he made a study of English literature. I wish I could write anything more to your purpose, and am, dear Sir,

Faithfully Yours in Christ, John H Newman of the Oratory

[1] *Idea*, pp. 405–27.

To J. M. Capes

The Oratory, Birmingham, March 16. 1868

My dear Capes,

I have seen your article on my Verses in the Fortnightly, and hope you will take my words as kindly as they are meant, when I say I sincerely thank you for it.[1]

Some parts of it struck me as very just. I have often been puzzled at myself, that I should be both particularly fond of being alone, and particularly fond of being with friends. Yet I know both the one and the other are true, though I can no more reconcile them than you can. You are the first, as far as I know, who have noticed an apparent inconsistency to which I can but plead guilty.[2]

I have said above that some parts of your review struck me as just, because I hardly know how to take to myself the special encomiums contained in other parts, which read more like the composition of a friend than of a critic.

I am, my dear C., Most sincerely Yours, John H Newman

J.M. Capes Esq.

[1] *Fortnightly Review* (1 March 1868), pp. 342–5.
[2] Capes replied that what Newman called 'an apparent inconsistency' he on the contrary regarded as 'indicating a completeness of character'.

To W. J. Copeland (I)

The Oratory Bm April 24/68

My dear Copeland

I have unfortunately mislaid the copy you sent me of the projected passage in your Preface.[1] I hope you have got one, for I thought it very good.

As the first volume is now near publication, is it not well to get it ready? Perhaps you have no need of a Preface at all, but, if you mean to have one, one ought to have before one the *whole*, in order to judge of the effect of the particular passage.

As I have read the Sermons already in print, (for the first time since I last published them,) I have been agreeably pleased with many of them—but many of them, which I used to think some of the best, I have been disappointed in—and especially in this way, that I could not understand what they were aiming at or what parties they were describing. Things are so different now from what they were. But if *I* do not recognize their truth, how will a younger generation? So that I have thought perhaps that Rivington will find it a bad bargain

Ever Yrs affly John H Newman

P.S. How it was you did not receive till March 26 what I put into the post on March 15 is to me a great mystery.

[1] Copeland was republishing Newman's *Parochial and Plain Sermons*.

To *W. J. Copeland (II)*

April 24/68 Evening

My dear C

Your letter has just come, since the inclosed was written.

1. It is good your talking of *my* trouble with the sheets, when you have so much, and all out of love.
2. Nothing will be better than for you to draw up something *without* me, if you will take the trouble. I do hope you have a copy of your Paper. I can't fancy where it has got to.
3. I have no opinion about Parochial *or* Plain—'Parochial and Plain' connects them all together—and Rivington is the better judge.
4. As to *my feeling* about the republication put it at the lowest, it is this, which even fierce Anti-Anglicans would understand. When certain persons think the Sermons would do good to the cause of religion (if they do, which I assume) I should act like the dog in the manger if I barked when they were about to be re-published, considering that in my heart that [*sic*] on the whole I think their effect will be good, and can thank God that I feel I can think this. If the alternative is put to me, had you rather *all* printed or *none* printed? I should think myself right in saying, *of the two* alternatives, the former. I say this to make you master my feeling.
5. About your name appearing only in the Preface, not in the Title Page, I leave it quite to you.
6. The Preface should not be long, and if it is all as good as the two sentences you sent me, it will be very good.
7. I shall be here all next week with this chance, viz a very holy person is dying at Stone—a remarkable woman—who has raised up something like 80 nuns, being herself a nobody—simply a servant originally.[1] And I may be suddenly called to her Funeral. They wished me to preach the Funeral Sermon, but this I declined.

I grieve about your brother.

Ever Yours affly John H Newman

The *type* of the Reprint is very keen and good.

[1] Mother Margaret Mary Hallahan who died on 11 May.

To Gerard Manley Hopkins

The Oratory Bm May 14. 1868

My dear Hopkins

I am both surprised and glad at your news.[1] If all is well, I wish [to] say a Mass for your perseverance. I think it is the very thing for you. You are quite out, in thinking that when I offered you a 'home' here, I dreamed of your having a vocation for us. This I clearly saw you had *not*, from the moment you came to us. Don't call 'the Jesuit discipline hard', it will bring you to heaven. The Benedictines would not have suited you.

We all congratulate you

Ever Yrs affly John H Newman

[1] Hopkins had decided to become a Jesuit. He had wondered whether he should become a Benedictine.

To J. Walker of Scarborough

The Oratory Bm May 22/68

My dear Canon Walker

I got Smith on the Pentateuch at once on your suggestion, and have been much interested in what I have read of it—but have not read enough to get into it as a whole.[1] Mr Beverley's work too has come, but with no supplemental chapter. Pray convey my acknowledgement to the *unknown* author.[2] It is a careful and severe examination of the theory of Darwin—and it shows, as is most certain he would be able to do, the various points which are to be made good before it can cohere. I do not fear the theory so much as he seems to do—and it seems to me that he is hard upon Darwin sometimes, which [*sic*] he might have interpreted him kindly. It does not seem to me to follow that creation is denied because the Creator, millions of years ago, gave laws to matter. He first created matter and then he created laws for it—laws which should *construct* it into its present wonderful beauty, and accurate adjustment and harmony of parts *gradually*. We do not deny or circumscribe the Creator, because we hold he has created the self acting originating human mind, which has almost a creative gift; much less then do we deny or circumscribe His power, if we hold that He gave matter such laws as by their blind instrumentality moulded and constructed through innumerable ages the world as we see it. If Mr Darwin in this or that point of his theory comes into collision with revealed truth, that is another matter—but I do not see that the *principle* of development, or what I have called construction, does. As to the Divine *Design*, is it not an instance of incomprehensibly and infinitely marvellous Wisdom and Design to have given certain laws to matter millions of ages ago, which have surely and precisely worked out, in the long course of those ages, those effects which He from the first proposed. Mr Darwin's theory *need* not then be atheistical, be it true or not; it may simply be suggesting a larger idea of Divine Prescience and Skill. Perhaps your friend has got a surer clue to guide him than I have, who have never studied the question, and I do not like to put my opinion against his; but at first sight I do not [see] that 'the *accidental* evolution of organic beings' is inconsistent with divine design—It is accidental to *us*, not to *God*

Most sincerely yours in Xt John H Newman

[1] W. Smith, *The Book of Moses or the Pentateuch in its Authorship, Credibility, and Civilisation* (London, 1868).

[2] *The Darwinian Theory of the Transmutation of Species examined by a Graduate of the University of Cambridge* (2nd edn, London, 1868). The author was Robert Mackenzie Beverley, then aged about 70, who, as a young man, had published attacks on what he called the corrupt state of the Church of England. He lived at Scarborough.

To W. J. Copeland

Rednall June 25/68

My dear C

We have been greatly concerned to hear of your serious illness—and now my only fear is that you will go to work too eagerly for your safety. It is unfortunate that, instead of pushing on Volume 4, they have nearly finished Volume 6. I can't think why— whereas Volume 4 wants a good 100 or 150 pages. I am still astonished they should make plain Sermons 2 volumes not 1. It will be not more than 440 pages altogether— which is only 40 more than volume 2, whereas two volumes of 220 each will be ghosts.

I heard of your illness from Crawley, and your letter, tho' bad, was a great relief. But rheumatic fever has sequels, and you must, as of course you know, be very cautious. I wish you took care of yourself, half as much as I am careful for Number 1.

Ambrose and I went suddenly to Littlemore—I wanted to see it once before I died. We went straight to Abingdon—then by fly to Sandford—Walked about the place— and back from Littlemore straight to Birmingham. We did not go through Oxford. We had 5 hours there, but not time for every thing. It was a most strange vision—I could hardly believe it real. It was the past coming back, as it might in the intermediate state.

I was rejoiced to see Littlemore so green—tho' very few of my *street* trees remain—I wonder any have lived through the dangers of road commissioners and boys' knives. Crawley's is a really pretty place—the Church is greatly improved— and the Vicarage is very nice.

We saw Mrs Palmer, young Humphries and his second wife (a Boswell)—old Mrs Humphries and her daughter—Martha King—Charles Pollard's nephew—Mr Whitlock—We could not walk about much—the day was so hot. We did it all between 7 and 7 o'clock.[1]

Now do *take care* of yourself, for that is the point.

Ever Yrs affly John H Newman

[1] Mrs. Palmer was the schoolmistress. Boswell had brought Newman's library from Littlemore to Maryvale. Martha King he had prepared for confirmation.

To Edward Bellasis

Aug 1/68

I have my own subject, one I have wished to do all my life, one which I fear would not interest you and—at all, one, which, if I did, I should of course think it the best thing I have done, being on the contrary perhaps the worst. I have the same fidget about it, as a horseman might feel about a certain five feet stone wall which he passes by means of a gate every day of his life, yet is resolved he must and will some day clear—and at last breaks his neck in attempting. It is on 'Assent, Certitude, and Proof' I have no right to look to having time to do anything—but if I have, it must be this.[1]

[1] Newman's description of his desire to work on what would become *A Grammar of Assent*.

To Bishop Ullathorne

The Oratory. Oct 15. 1868

My dear Lord,

I thank you for your letter and for the sight of the Cardinal's, which I now return.[1]

I hope you will understand the deep sense I have of the Holy Father's condescension in thinking of me as one of the Consultors previous to the Council, and also of the delicacy towards me of the Cardinal in the mode of his reporting to you that most gracious thought of his Holiness.

I say the delicacy, because by the words, 'Quatenus nihil observatu dignum habeas,' and 'Sit [Si] velit Newman oblatum honorem acceptum habere,' he allows your Lordship privately to consult me, and anticipates the chance of my declining, without any direct communication being made from me to his Eminence in answer.

I have then availed myself of his, and indeed your Lordship's, permission to consider the matter carefully on its own merits by my best lights; and the result of my deliberation has been to decline the honour (which I hereby do) wishing to do so in the way most expressive of my true and humble gratitude for so great an act of favour on the part of his Holiness.

I decline it 1. because of the state of my health, which requires at present a careful and continual watching which I could not observe except at home. 2. And next, because, though health and life are of course not to be thought of in comparison of a great religious end, still no great religious end would be promoted by my presence at Rome for an august and momentous solemnity, for which I am not fitted either by my talents or by my attainments.

No one would gain by my being there, and I am not at all sure I should not lose my life.

I am, my dear Lord, begging your Lordship's blessing, Yr affte & obt Servt in Xt

John H Newman of the Oratory

The Rt Revd The Bp of Birmingham

[1] Cardinal Prospero Caterini, Prefect of the Congregation of the Council, had written to Ullathorne expressing the Pope's wish that Newman should attend the Vatican Council as a consultor of one of the commissions that was preparing its business. Newman would have had to be in Rome by the end of 1868.

To John Hayes

The Oratory, Birmingham. April 13, 1869.

My dear Sir,

I saw the article you speak of in the 'Times', and felt flattered by the passage which referred to myself.[1]

The writer must have alluded in the sentence which leads to your question, to my 'Lectures and Essays on University Subjects,' which is at present out of print. In that volume there are several papers on English and Latin composition.[2]

It is simply the fact that I have been obliged to take great pains with everything I have written, and I often write chapters over and over again, besides innumerable corrections and interlinear additions. I am not stating this as a merit, only that some persons write their best first, and I very seldom do. Those who are good speakers may be supposed to be able to write off what they want to say. I, who am not a good speaker, have to correct laboriously what I put on paper. I have heard that Archbishop Howley, who was an elegant writer, betrayed the labour by which he became so by his mode of speaking, which was most painful to hear from his hesitations and alterations—that is, he was correcting his composition as he went along.

However, I may truly say that I never have been in the practice since I was a boy of attempting to write well, or to form an elegant style. I think I never have written for writing sake; but my one and single desire and aim has been to do what is so difficult—viz. to express clearly and exactly my meaning; this has been the motive principle of all my corrections and re-writings. When I have read over a passage which I had written a few days before, I have found it so obscure to myself that I have either put it altogether aside or fiercely corrected it; but I don't get any better for practice. I am as much obliged to correct and re-write as I was thirty years ago.

As to patterns for imitation, the only master of style I have ever had (which is strange considering the differences of the languages) is Cicero. I think I owe a great deal to him, and as far as I know to no one else. His great mastery of Latin is shown especially in his clearness.

Very faithfully yours, John H. Newman.

The Rev. John Hayes

P.S. Thank you for what you so kindly say of me in old times.[3]

---

[1] 'The English Language', *The Times* (10 April 1869), p. 4, included this passage: 'If we were asked to name the three greatest masters of English style in the generation which is just closing we should point to De Quincy, Macaulay, and Dr. Newman. Their styles are very different, but each is superb in its way, and we believe that they are all the result of severe and laborious training, though they give the impression of innate and effortless grace. Dr. Newman at all events, has related in an interesting and instructive essay the various steps of that mental discipline which has made him such a consummate master of his native tongue.'

[2] *Idea*, pp. 331–80.

[3] Hayes spoke of 'the cherished remembrance of having listened to your teaching from the Pulpit of St Mary's in my old undergraduate days'. He was matriculated at Magdalen Hall on 2 July 1834, aged 19, and was Vicar of Coalbrookdale, Salop, 1854–78.

To Charles Meynell

The Oratory Bm July 2/69

Private

My dear Dr Meynell

At length, on an auspicious day, I send you my sheets.[1] The printers have only sent the second this morning.

Your experienced eye will see if I have run into any language which offends against doctrinal propriety or common sense. Thanking you for your trouble,

Very sincerely Yours John H Newman

[1] Feast of the Visitation. Newman had asked Meynell to criticise the sheets of *G.A.*

To Bishop Ullathorne

The Oratory Nov 1. 1869

I know nothing, and never have had, nor have, nor can have, the slightest suspicion, of Dr Manning ever at any time having suppressed any letter of mine written to Cardinal Wiseman, and containing matter which had an ulterior destination.[1]

John H Newman

[1] On 31 October Manning wrote to Ullathorne that he had just heard a statement that Newman had written Wiseman a letter that would have cleared him in the matter of the *Rambler* delation, and that he, Manning, had intercepted it.

To Archbishop Manning

Nov. 3 1869

My dear Archbishop

Thank you for your kind letter—I can only repeat what I said when you last heard from me.[1] I do not know whether I am on my head or my heels, when I have active relations with you. In spite of my friendly feelings, this is the judgment of my intellect

Yours affectionately in Christ, John H Newman

The Most Revd Dr Manning

[1] Ullathorne showed Manning Newman's letter of 1 November and Manning had written to Newman warmly. Newman's previous letter had been on 2 September 1867 (*L.D.* XXIII, pp. 328–9).

To Charles Meynell

Novr 17/69

My dear Dr Meynell

Thank you for your two very good letters.

I have put a note on the passage, in consequence of one of them, in which I boldly say that 'If it isn't A, it must be B' is not reasoning, except materially.[1]

I quite agree with you that the deepest men say that we can never be certain of any thing—and it has been my object therefore in good part of my volume to prove that there is such a thing as *unconditional* assent.

I have defined certitude, a conviction of what is *true*. When a conviction of what is not true is considered as if it was a conviction of what is true, I have called it a false certitude.

You will be sadly disappointed in my 'illative sense'—which is a grand word for a common thing.

Ever Yrs most sincerely John H Newman

P.S. I send a number of slips

[1] G.A., p. 287, footnote.

To Mrs William Froude

The Oratory Nov 21/69

My dear Mrs Froude

I have ever held the Pope's Infallibility as an opinion, and am not therefore likely to feel any personal anxiety as to the result of this Council. Still I am strongly opposed to its definition—and for this reason. Hitherto nothing has been ever done at Councils but what is *necessary*; what is the necessity of this? There is no heresy to be put down. It is a dangerous thing to go beyond the rule of tradition in such a matter. In the early times the Nicene Council gave rise to dissensions and to confusions which lasted near a century. The Council of Ephesus opened a question which it took three centuries to settle. Well, these Councils were NECESSARY—they were called to resist and condemn opposition to our Lord's divinity—heresies— They could not be helped. But why is the Pope's infallibility to be defined? even, if denying it were a heresy, which no one says, how many *do* deny it? do they preach their denial? are they making converts to it? Let us look to it lest a judgment come down upon us, if we do, *though we have a right to do*, what we ought not to do. We must not play with edged tools.

I am against the definition, because it opens a long controversy. You cannot settle the question by a word—whatever is passed, must be a half, a quarter measure. Archbishop Manning himself only aims at *condemning two propositions*, i.e. at a *negative* act. How will that *decide* the question? No—it only opens it. At Nicæa, and Ephesus, great questions were opened, only opened—they had, as I have said, been opened by heretics first. *Now*, the Bishops of the Church are called upon to take the first step in opening a question as difficult, and not as justifiable, as the question which those early Councils were obliged to discuss. This question will lead to an alteration of the *elementary constitution* of the Church. Our *one* doctrine, in which all doctrines are concluded, is, 'The Church's word is to be believed—' Hitherto 'the Church's decision' means that of the Pope and the Bishops; now it is proposed to alter this for 'the Pope's word.' It is an alteration in the fundamental dogma. Hitherto, I *personally* may be of *opinion* that the Pope is infallible by himself—*but I have never been called to act* upon it—no one has—and what is the consequence? that *the Pope* cannot act upon it. Hitherto, the Pope has always acted, (for greater caution,) with the Bishops—he has not gone to the extent of what he might do, supposing him infallible. But, define his infallibility, and he will act alone. Well— God will direct him—but what is this but throwing away one of the human means *by* which God directs him? It is making the system more miraculous—and it is like seeking a bodily cure by miracle, when human means are at hand.

I say, any decision will be a half or quarter measure—as the Councils of Ephesus and Chalcedon were such. It opens a very large question. Suppose you pass Dr Manning's condemnation—still the *positive* question will be left open—and a new controversy set open—first, what *is* the implied positive force of these negatives?—let this be settled, then comes the question in *what matters* is the Pope infallible?—after this—when, under what conditions, is the Pope infallible? when e.g. he writes a letter? Councils are formal things—and there is no need of drawing the line between their acts, or not much need, but a Pope is a living man, ever living, and it will be a great work to go through this question well. You have to treat it doctrinally—and then again historically, reconciling what you teach with the verdict of history.

Then again recollect that this doctrine is a retrospective doctrine—it brings up a great variety of questions about *past* acts of Popes—whether their decrees in past ages are infallible, or whether they were not, and which of them, and therefore whether they are binding on *us*.

If any thing could throw religion into confusion, make sceptics, encourage scoffers, and throw back inquirers, it will be the definition of this doctrine. This I shall think, even if it passes—because, though then the doctrine must be inwardly received as true, its definition may still be most unseasonable and unwise. I do not know that the Church is protected against inexpedient acts—though of course God overrules them—and also, when they are once passed, there is no good, and much disrespect and highmindedness, in finding fault with them. Paul iii alienated England. I don't think he acted wisely; yet in one sense it is God's act, because it was done

Ever Yrs affly John H Newman

P.S. Keep this; I may want it. I have never before put my thoughts on paper

To Edward Bellasis

The Oratory Dec 15/69

My dear Serjeant

I should have written before, had I not been so desperately busy. Thank you for all you say so kindly about the school, as you always do. Did we get to 70 boys we should be right—but we have not come to that yet.[1]

Tell me your style and title 'Edward Bellasis Esqr, Serjeant-at-Law'? You will still let me put your name, won't you, to the beginning of my book? I suppose it will be my last. I have not finished it. I have written in all, (good or bad) 5 constructive books—My prophetical office (which has come to pieces)—Essay on Justification—Development of Doctrine—University Lectures (Dublin) and this. Each took me a great deal of time and tried me very much. This, I think, has tried me most of all. I have written and re-written it more times than I can count. I have now got up to my highest point—I mean, I could not do better did I spend a century on it—but then, it may be 'bad is the best.'

Your two boys have been ill, I am sorry to say, as well as yourself—but trust the South will at once set you up. Thank you for your pleasant account of William [Bellasis]

Ever Yrs affectly John H Newman

[1] Bellasis wrote on 9 December that he heard from his son Richard, at Edgbaston, 'that your book is "in the Press"'. Newman dedicated *A Grammar of Assent* to Bellasis.

Vatican I and Answering Gladstone (1870–75)

Newman's *Essay in Aid of a Grammar of Assent* was published on 15 March 1870 and was sold out the same day. It was unique among his works as the only one not prompted by some particular call or occasion. The relationship between faith and reason had fascinated Newman throughout his life and the book marked the culmination of years of reflection. He had dedicated it to his friend, the lawyer Edward Bellasis, and, when close to death, Bellasis remarked to his wife that no event in his life had given him more pleasure than that dedication. 'I don't know what I can have done to deserve such an honour', he told her. He died on 24 January 1873, one of many of Newman's friends who died in these years, including his brother-in-law John Mozley, James Hope-Scott, and Henry Wilberforce. But for Newman the most painful loss of all came on 24 May 1875 with the sudden death of Ambrose St John, the most loyal of all his friends for the previous thirty-two years.

St John's health had been undermined by overwork and the final straw that had broken him was his translation of Joseph Fessler's *The True and False Infallibility of the Pope*, undertaken to support Newman's answer to Gladstone's pamphlet on the Vatican decrees. Gladstone had lost the General Election in 1874 and attributed his misfortune in part to papal influence on the Irish bishops. He was led to declare that Roman Catholics had forfeited their moral and mental freedom and had placed their civil loyalty and duty under the Pope. Many people turned to Newman for an answer, and he saw here an opportunity once again, as with his *Letter to Pusey* on Mariology, to offer an account of Catholic teaching on papal infallibility that followed a middle way between Gladstone's anti-papalism and the ultra-papal views of Catholics like Ward. This reply was contained in his *Letter to the Duke of Norfolk*. Gladstone wrote to thank him for 'the genial and gentle manner' in which he had treated him. His more significant target, of course, was the Catholic extremism that had been a preoccupation of his for years.

In January 1870, while the Council was in session, Newman wrote one of his most famous letters. It was confidential and sent to his bishop, Ullathorne, protesting at the behaviour of those who were seeking relentlessly to force through the definition of papal infallibility at the Council. He described them as an 'aggressive insolent faction'. His letter captures vividly the anxiety many people felt when the terms of the definition had yet to be drawn up, and their fear of what might be imposed upon them if that faction had its way. Ullathorne showed the letter to Bishop Clifford who was sympathetic and made a copy. Others saw it. Before long Newman's protest became known. When his reference to the 'aggressive insolent faction' appeared in the press, he disowned it at first. But later, looking more closely at his much corrected draft, he acknowledged that he had indeed used the expression. He also acknowledged to a friend, Sir John Simeon, that he was pleased by the turn of events: his letter to his bishop had been confidential; he was in no way responsible for its publication; but he was glad to have been able to make his view known.

Many letters in the years immediately following the Council were concerned with infallibility. Newman was counselling and reassuring Catholics who had been disturbed by the definition. His advice revealed his sense of history and his far-sightedness: 'Let us be patient, let us have faith, and a new Pope, and a re-assembled Council may trim the boat.' And to his friend, Bishop David Moriarty of Kerry, he displayed his anger at the way some priests were forcing the definition on people without allowing them time to consider: 'I rise in indignation against such cruelty.' And there is a characteristically penetrating letter to Isy Froude, not only on infallibility, but also on the importance of the *schola theologorum*: 'there are no words, ever so clear, but they require an explanation'.

Then there is an intriguing letter, written in July 1871, in which Newman says that, had he remained in the Anglican Church till that time, he probably would not have become a Catholic, but only because it would mean he had not responded to the grace offered to him: 'God gives grace, and if it is not accepted He withdraws His grace'. He wrote with humour to his friend Richard Church, describing how he had been turned out of St Paul's Cathedral. Church was by then the Dean of St Paul's. And there is a brief entertaining letter to Mrs Sconce in 1874, thanking her for the gift of a metal pen, but explaining, 'a metal pen in my hands is nothing else than a skewer'. He used a quill pen all his life.

And in 1875 there was another death, that of Charles Kingsley, aged 55. Newman was shocked by the news. He declared that he had never felt anger towards him, not least because he had never seen him. And he went on, 'much less could I feel resentment against him when he was accidentally the instrument in the good Providence of God, by whom I had an opportunity given me, which otherwise I should not have had, of vindicating my character and conduct in my Apologia'.

10

Vatican I and Answering Gladstone (1870–75)

To W. J. Copeland

Feast of the Holy Name of Jesus [16 January] 1870

My dear Copeland

Rejoice with me. I have written the last sentence of my book.[1] But, though I have ended, I have not finished it. There is much to correct and re-write. And I have a month or six weeks work still.

I hope I wished you all the blessings of the past season

Ever Yrs affly John H Newman

P.S. I was sorry to see Mr Parsons's death in the paper.

[1] *An Essay in Aid of a Grammar of Assent.*

To Bishop Ullathorne

The Oratory. [Jany 28. 1870]

My dear Lord

I thank your Lordship very heartily for ⌈your most interesting and seasonable letter. Such letters, if they could be circulated, would do much to re-assure the many minds which are at present distressed when they look towards Rome.[1] Rome ought to be a name to lighten the heart at all times, and a Council's proper office is, when some great heresy or other evil impends, to inspire the faithful with hope and confidence; but now we have the greatest meeting which ever has been, and that at Rome, infusing into us by the accredited organs of Rome and its partizans (such as the Civiltà, the Armonia, the Univers, and the Tablet,) little else than fear and dismay.

When we are all at rest, and have no doubts, and at least practically, not to say doctrinally, hold the Holy Father to be infallible, suddenly there is thunder in the clear sky, and we are told to prepare for something we know not what to try our faith we know not how. No impending danger is to be averted, but a great difficulty is to be created. Is this the proper work for an Ecumenical Council? As to myself personally, please God, I do not expect any trial at all; but I cannot help suffering with the various souls which are suffering, and I look with anxiety at the prospect of having to defend decisions, which may be not difficult to my private judgment, but may be most difficult to maintain logically in the face of historical facts. What have we done to be treated, as the faithful never were treated before? When has definition of doctrine de fide been a luxury of devotion, and not a stern painful necessity? Why should an aggressive insolent faction be allowed to 'make the heart of the just to mourn, whom the Lord hath not made sorrowful?' Why can't we be let alone, when we have pursued peace, and thought no evil? I assure you, my dear Lord, some of the truest minds are driven one way and another, and do not know where to rest their feet; one day determining to give up all theology as a bad job, and recklessly to believe henceforth almost that the Pope is impeccable; at another tempted to believe all the worst which a book like Janus says;[2] others doubting about the capacity possessed by Bishops, drawn from all corners of the earth, to judge what is fitting for European society, and then again angry with the Holy See for listening to the flattery of a clique of Jesuits, Redemptorists, and converts.

Then again, think of the store of Pontifical scandals in the history of 18 centuries, which have partly been poured out, and partly are still to come. What Murphy inflicted upon us in one way, M. Veuillot indirectly is bringing on us in another.[3]

And then again, the blight which is falling upon the multitude of Anglican ritualists etc who themselves perhaps, at least their leaders, may never become Catholics, but who are leavening the various English denominations and parties (far beyond their own range) with principles and sentiments tending toward their ultimate absorption in the Catholic Church

With these thoughts before me, I am continually asking myself whether I ought not to make my feelings public; but all I do is to pray those great early Doctors of the Church, whose intercession would decide the matter,⌉ Augustine and the rest, ⌈to avert so great a calamity. If it is God's will that the Pope's infallibility should be defined, then it is His blessed Will to throw back 'the times and the moments'[4] of that triumph which He has destined for His Kingdom; and I shall feel I have but to bow my head to His adorable, inscrutable Providence. You have not touched upon the subject yourself, but I think you will allow me to express to you feelings, which for the most part I keep to myself.⌉

As to my book I have attempted it three or four times in the last 20 years, and could not get on. And I have in consequence felt that till it was actually *ended*, it really was not *begun*; I have had no confidence that I should be able to complete it. I have done so—but now that it is done, I think it will disappoint most people. It is not written against writers of the day, Mr Huxley or Professor Tindall, or Sir C. Lyell, or any one else. It is on a dry logical subject, or semi-logical, Assent. Of course, unless I thought the book had its use, I should not have made so many attempts to write it—but I am no judge of its worth.

Pray convey my best respects to the Bishop of Plymouth and ask his blessing for us.[5] I know well how much I owe to the kindness and sympathy of the American Bishops, and hope they are aware of the gratitude I feel towards them in consequence.

Thank you for what you say about St Girolamo and the Chiesa Nuova[6]

Begging your Lordship's blessing, I am Yr obedient & affte Servt in Xt

⌈John H Newman⌉[7]

[1] This was Ullathorne's letter of 20 January to Newman, printed in Cuthbert Butler, *The Vatican Council: The Story Told from Inside in Bishop Ullathorne's Letters* (London, 1930), I, pp. 209–12. Ullathorne, who took an optimistic view, described the setting of the Council and the attitudes of the different nationalities among the bishops. He went on, 'You will hear a good deal of movements outside of the Council, and indeed I wish there was less of them; but they certainly began on what may be called the *ultra* side, which naturally led to efforts at counter organisation.' Ullathorne said that he was refusing to join any party or to sign petitions on one side or the other, and quoted the saying of Pius IX, 'You will find the Holy Ghost inside the Council, not outside of it.'

Ullathorne concluded: 'Be assured of this, that Rome itself is learning a great deal about the state of the Church and of the position of the faithful in their diverse countries, and that the very freest speech is used consistent with that mutual respect which the Authorities of the Church owe to each other. One great result of the Council must necessarily be the widening of knowledge and experience on the part of Rome as well as on that of the Universal Episcopate. For the rest, even the strongest adversaries in so far as questions of ecclesiastical polity are concerned, are full of kindness and courtesy towards each other, even to great edification.'

[2] Janus was the pseudonym of Döllinger (and others) for their letters attacking the Papacy and Ultramontanism in the Augsburg *Allgemeine Zeitung*, in the earlier part of 1869. The letters were published in book form, and in English translation as *The Pope and the Council*, later in the year.

[3] Murphy was the violent Protestant whose scandalous lectures against Catholics caused riots in Birmingham and the Midlands. See letter to Jemima Mozley, 29 June 1867.

[4] *Acts* 1:7.

[5] William Vaughan, an inopportunist, uncle of Herbert Vaughan.

[6] Ullathorne wrote, 'My best regards and blessings to all the fathers. I have an habitual intention of giving my Mass for you at St Philip's Altar which I will fulfil, and always think of you passing St Jerolimo, or the Oratory.' San Girolamo, opposite the English College, was the church where St Philip lived and founded the Oratory. From there he moved to the Chiesa Nuova, where he is buried.

[7] This, which Newman described on 27 March to Sir John Simeon, as 'one of the most passionate and confidential letters that I ever wrote in my life', became public. See the correspondence from 14 March onwards.

To Mrs John Mozley

The Oratory Febr 21 1870

My dear Jemima

Thank you for your affectionate letter. Birthdays now are like strokes of a passing bell. I am so wonderfully well, that one fancies it may be the rapids before the fall. This cold weather I have used a severe shower bath with nothing but good effect. I have had no cold—and I sleep like a top. This book has given me such trying work, that I was quite frightened lest it should damage my brain, yet apparently no harm has come of it. The only remaining trouble is the state of my teeth—but that in a few months must come to a crisis—at present I have no pain.

As to my book, it will disappoint every one—and I advertised it under the title you saw in order to prepare people for a balk. The truth is the rumour that I was writing a book on Rationalism was spread ill naturedly by those who do not love me. I have been writing it (it is not against Rationalism) this thirty or forty years, and never succeeded. I attempted it in my Oxford University Sermons—stopped after the first of these upon it in 1832, managed to get a little further in 1839 or thereabouts, and did no more. I have attempted it again more times than I can count, and have a pile of MS on the subject, in 1846, in 1850, in 1853, in 1859, in 1861, in 1865—but I could not get on—it was like tunnelling through the Alps. Therefore I have long said 'I have not begun till I have ended.' This made me very angry with the report about 'Rationalism;' the more so, that it was not true. The beginning of my success dates from 1866—when in Switzerland. We went up to Glion, and then suddenly the idea came into my head, which have [sic] been a clue to the treatment of my subject; and my first pages stand pretty much as I wrote them in August 1866. However, the work was not less like tunnelling than before, though I had found the point from which to begin.

However, it is done—done for my own pleasure, for people in general, I think, won't see the meaning of it—and will be disappointed. The title I have given it rightly describes it so far, viz that it will seem to them dry and humdrum—and they will say, what is it all about?

It touches on a number of subjects, on which there has been much written in this day—but I have carefully kept myself from reading what any one else has published, because I wished to bring out my own view, and I was sure that, if once I began to read, I should so get confused in the terms and language of others, so mixed up in their controversies, and carried away with the views which they opened, that my own work would vanish. Of course I have the consequent inconvenience that I may be saying what others have said before me, and saying what others have disproved—but it was a choice of difficulties, and I think I have done what is best.

I am glad you have mentioned about Louisa Deane—and I wonder whether she has mentioned my name from something of a bad conscience. At the end of 1867, I wrote her a letter which as far as I recollect was to the following effect—that she would be surprised to hear from me, but that I was about to publish a volume of Verses, and that I could not help, for auld lang syne, not to send it to her;—that I did not know her direction (you will recollect I asked you, and I forgot what you said) and therefore she must be so good as to inform me of it—I added, alluding to the Catholic poems in it, that there would be some perhaps which would displease her, but others would not. I directed the letter to her under cover to the 'Revd J. Deane, Bath,' being sure that that direction to a clergyman would find him, though so imperfect. And it certainly did find him, for the letter did not come back to me from the Dead letter office. However, I got no answer at all—and consequently, even had I wished it ever so much, could not send the book, not knowing how to direct it.[1]

I am glad to hear your various informations from Sydenham. John has been answering me a question some months since, on a point I wanted to know as regards the subjects of my book; he did me a service.[2]

Our violin boys are vanishing, for time with boys is not stationary—as it is with old men.

I am very sorry to hear what you say of Janie—you should take her to the Alps, the Bel Alps or St Moritz for two or three months in the summer—and it would set her up.

Ever Yours affecly John H Newman

P.S. Thank A. and E. Mozley for their invitation. I should like it very much.[3]

---

[1] Louisa Elizabeth Deane had not received Newman's letter.

[2] See letter of 21 October 1869 to J. R. Mozley, who was married and living at Sydenham (*L.D.* XXIV, p. 357).

[3] Anne and Elizabeth Mozley, Jemima's sisters-in-law, who lived at Barrow, near Derby. Newman visited them on 15 June 1871.

To Bishop Ullathorne

The Oratory March 14. 1870

My dear Lord

I lose no time in sending you a line, in order to assure you that the following passage in today's Standard has neither directly nor indirectly come from this House. No one saw my letter to your Lordship but Fr St John—and neither he nor I have opened our mouths to any one about its contents.

The passage runs thus:—

'It will interest many people to know that Dr Newman has written to his Bishop at Rome, stigmatizing the promoters of Papal Infallibility as an insolent, aggressive faction, praying that God may avert this threatened peril from the Church, and affirming his conviction that, if He does not see fit to do so, it is because He has chosen to delay the Church's ultimate triumph for centuries.'

I am, Yr Lordship's obedient & affecte Servant John H Newman[1]

---

[1] Ullathorne replied on 18 March:

'I am much distressed at your letter to me having got out into other hands, though without my concurrence, and proceed by return of Posts to explain all that I know about it. I showed your letter to some four of the English Bishops, all your friends, and all having strong feelings of difficulty, greater indeed than I have, about the definition. One of these was Bishop Clifford the only one to whom I parted with it out of my sight, he living in another part of Rome, promising he would let no one see it, and that he would return it me next morning, after reading it. We were at the moment leaving the Council in opposite directions. To my surprise, on returning it next morning, he told me he had taken a copy of it. On my expressing my annoyance at this, he solemnly promised that no one should see it without my express permission, and I was satisfied, though not altogether so.

... it was Archbishop Errington and Bishop Moriarty, who came to me and asked if I would consent to have your letter to me translated, and put into the hands of Cardinal Barili, etc. I asked if they had seen the letter, for I had not shown it to them or authorised its being shewn. Archbishop Errington replied that he had not, but that from what they had heard of it, it seemed fuller and clearer than the one addressed to Bishop Moriarty [to whom Newman had also written on 28 January]. For the purpose of making my refusal more emphatic I replied that I would answer them after the Congregation was over. They then came to me in company with Bishop Clifford, and I replied that it would be very inexpedient, that it would be sure to be misunderstood, and that individual passages would be certain to be taken hold of and used to do you an injury. With this they expressed themselves satisfied....

About a week or so after this reports reached me through a friend, that a copy of your letter to me was in the hands of a lady, and had been shewn about. I went to Dr Clifford, and told him of what I had heard, and expressed my conviction that he, and he alone, could have let it out. He answered me in the most solemn terms that no one could have seen or taken a copy of his copy. This is all I know about it. I cannot possibly see Bishop Clifford before post time, and so I send off this statement without delay. At this distance I do not see, after consulting Dr Northcote to whom I have shewn your letter, that I can do anything more. But of course you are free to take whatever course you think most prudent.'

In a letter of 25 April to his Vicar General, Michael O'Sullivan, Ullathorne wrote that he learned from Bishop Clifford that Archbishop Errington made a copy of Clifford's copy of Newman's letter. When the matter was mentioned by Newman, in 1875, in *A Letter to the Duke of Norfolk, Diff.* II, p. 300, Ullathorne told St John that one of the bishops to whom he had shown Newman's letter was Archbishop Connolly of Halifax. According to Neville's memorandum of this conversation with St John on 29 January 1875, Ullathorne 'in a way admitted having allowed its publication'. 'He did not hinder it but professed that it was not his own act.' See also letter of 22 March to Sir John Simeon (*L.D.* xxv, p. 62).

To The Editor of the Standard

The Oratory, March 15. [1870]

Sir,

I am led to send you these few lines in consequence of the introduction of my name, in yesterday's *Standard*, into your report of the 'Progress of the Oecumenical Council.'[1] I thank you for the courteous terms in which you have, on various occasions, as on the present, spoken of me; but I am bound to disavow what you have imputed to me, viz.—that I have 'written to my bishop at Rome, Dr. Ullathorne, stigmatising the promoters of Papal Infallibility, as an insolent, aggressive faction.'

That I deeply deplore the policy, the spirit, the measures of various persons, lay and ecclesiastical, who are urging the definition of that theological opinion, I have neither intention nor wish to deny; just the contrary. But, on the other hand, I have a firm belief, and have had all along, that a Greater Power than that of any man or set of men will over-rule the deliberations of the Council to the determination of Catholic and Apostolic truth, and that what its Fathers eventually proclaim with one voice will be the Word of God.—[2]

I am, Sir, your obedient servant, John H. Newman.

[1] 'Progress of the Oecumenical Council', an article in the *Standard* (14 March 1870), p. 5, contained the following sentence: 'The letter of M. de Montalembert, though the utterance of a dying man, expresses the sentiments of many Roman Catholic laymen of high distinction; and it will interest many people to know that Dr. Newman has written to his bishop at Rome, Dr. Ullathorne, stigmatising the promoters of Papal Infallibility as an insolent, aggressive faction, praying that God may avert this threatened peril from the Church, and affirming his conviction that if He does not see fit to do so, it is because He has chosen to delay the Church's ultimate triumph for centuries.'

[2] This letter was published in the *Standard* on 17 March. See letter of 22 March to the editor.

To The Editor of the Standard

March 22. [1870]

Sir,—

In answer to the letter of 'The Writer of the Progress of the Council,' I am obliged to say that he is right and I am wrong as to my using the words 'insolent and aggressive faction' in a letter which I wrote to Bishop Ullathorne. I write to make my apologies to him for contradicting him.

I kept the rough copy of this private letter of mine to the bishop, and on reading the Writer's original statement I referred to it and did not find there the words in question.

This morning a friend has written to tell me that there are copies of the letter in London, and that the words certainly are in it. On this I have looked at my copy a second time, and I must confess that I have found them.

I can only account for my not seeing them the first time by my very strong impression that I had not used them in my letter, confidential as it was, and from the circumstance that the rough copy is badly written and interlined.

I learn this morning from Rome that Dr Ullathorne was no party to its circulation.

I will only add, that when I spoke of a faction I neither meant that great body of bishops who are said to be in favour of the definition of the doctrine nor any ecclesiastical order or society external to the Council. As to the Jesuits, I wish distinctly to state that I have all along separated them in my mind as a body from the movement which I so much deplore. What I meant by a faction, as the letter itself shows, was a collection of persons drawn together from various ranks and conditions in the Church.—I am, Sir, your obedient servant,

John H. Newman

To Sir John Simeon

The Oratory March 27. 1870

My dear Sir John

As my confidential letter to the Bishop shows, I have been anxious for some time that an opportunity of speaking out, which I could not make myself, should be made for me.

I could not make it myself, for, as I said to you before, I am bound to act in my own place as a priest under authority, and there was no call, nor excuse for my going out of it.

One thing I could do without impropriety,—liberare animam meam to my Bishop, and that I did. I did so with great deliberation in one of the most passionate and confidential letters that I ever wrote in my life.

I am glad I have done it; and moreover, I am not sorry that, without any responsibility of my own, which I could not lawfully bring on me, the general drift of what I wrote has been published.

Every thing hitherto has happened well. It was very lucky that I was so firmly persuaded I did not use in the letter the words imputed to me. My persuasion being such, I felt it to be a simple duty to disown them; and I could not in fairness disown them without avowing at the same time, as I did in my letter to the Standard, that, though I did not use the words, I thought them in my heart. If I had recognized my own words from the first, I should have had no opportunity of explaining their meaning, or against whom they were directed. My two letters to the Standard have given me two such opportunities.

Now, however, this is done, and I feel quite easy, and need do nothing more.

There were two reasons which might be urged upon me for making my views known, viz in order that they might act as a means of influencing some of the Bishops in the Council, and as a protest against the action of a certain party. What I have already done, is all that I can, all that I need, do. Would any thing more on my part move a single Bishop? Would any thing more make my mind on the matter more intelligible to the world? I think not.

I will add one thing. I do not at all anticipate any ultimate dissention. Like a jury, they will sit till they agree. I have full confidence in the French and German Bishops.

Ever Yours affectionately John H Newman

P.S. Certainly I rejoice to hear from you that an Address protesting against the definition of Infallibility would, if started, be largely signed; but what have I to do with such measures, beyond giving my opinion, which I have done?[1]

---

[1] Simeon said it was proposed to organize an address to Bishop Clifford, which would be a counter-weight to the various petitions on the other side.

To William Ewart Gladstone

The Oratory March 30. 1870

My dear Mr Gladstone

I am quite ashamed to think, that, in your great kindness, you have considered it necessary even to look into my new book, not to speak of your explaining why you have not taken it in hand.[1]

I ventured to send it to you for the pleasure it gave me to think I had done so, even though you gave me no opinion upon it; not that I do not prize your opinion, but because I would not, by occupying your time, 'in publica commoda peccare.'

There are, I am sure, (if it is not impertinence to say so) very many, who, much as they value words from you, would shrink from eliciting them at the cost of depriving you of those moments of mental rest which are all that are allotted to a Prime Minister.

I will bear in mind your question about a history of Priesthood. What is a puzzle to me, and bearing both on this subject, and your remark about Davison's view, is, how sacrifices came into Mahometanism. I had fancied it had no priests or altars. Perhaps sacrifices are retained merely as private acts of worship. If they are simply an innovation, does not that show, that, whether originally a divine institution or not, they are so natural to the human mind that a widely spread religion cannot on the long run do without them?[2]

Most sincerely Yours John H Newman

The Rt Honble W. E. Gladstone

[1] Gladstone wrote on 27 March to thank Newman for *A Grammar of Assent*, although he had scarcely been able to begin reading it.

[2] In his letter Gladstone had wondered whether sacrifice was a divine institution and had also wished for 'a thorough and careful history of Priesthood'.

To Louisa Elizabeth Deane

The Oratory, Birm March 31. 1870

My dear Louisa

I have not for a long while had a letter which has so delighted me as yours of this morning.[1] I love you as much as ever I did, and always have loved you—and it pained me exceedingly to think you should not have answered the very kind letter which I addressed to you at the close of 1867.

Of course I did not keep any copy of the letter which I sent you—but I recollect quite well its contents—that I wanted to send you a book of verses which I was publishing—but did not know your address—that I begged you to tell me what your address was—and that, though I knew there were sets of verses, in which you would not concur, there were others which you would not be unwilling to see. As I knew you were somewhere in Bath, and was sure that a clergyman would be known anywhere, I sent the letter in a cover addressed to 'the Rev. J. B. Deane, Bath'. It did not come back to me from the dead letter office.

My Parochial Sermons are not in my hands, and I have not got a single copy to send you—but I hope by this post to send you a copy of my Verses.[2]

Ever yours most affectionately John H. Newman

P.S. Say every thing kind from me to James [Fourdrinier]. I did not know you had grandchildren! I never move—but, if ever I got as far as Bath, I should certainly find you out.[3]

I have no more to do with Oscott, which is 6 or 7 miles off, than with the Moon. Your letter has travelled.

Mrs Deane

[1] Mrs Deane wrote on 28 March:

'My dear Cousin, In a letter I lately received from Jemima she mentions your kind remembrance of me, in writing to offer to send your book of Verses [see letter of 21 February to Mrs John Mozley]. I need hardly say, I did not receive your letter or I should surely have answered it. I felt so great a desire to see it that I bought it, and how many and affecting remembrances it brought to my mind of those who have gone before us.'

² Mrs Deane wrote, 'You once gave me a volume of your Parochial Sermons, if they are still in your hands I should much prize another. I never forget how much I owe to you and yours in helping a very young and unformed mind, do not forget me in your prayers.'

³ Mrs Deane wrote, 'My brother James lives with us which is a great comfort to me, and I have a large number of children round me and am a grandmother in two branches.'

To Thomas Joseph Brown, Bishop of Newport

The Oratory, Birmingham April 8. 1870

My dear Lord,

I am very happy to have your Lordship's approbation, and thank you for the letter which I have just received from you.¹

My letter to Dr Ullathorne was one of the most confidential ones that I ever wrote in my life. It has got abroad by no fault of his; but since it is neither his fault nor mine, and I felt it a sacred duty to write it, I trust it has got about for some good. I will not believe that the Pope's Infallibility will be defined by the Council till it is actually done and over—when this is so, then of course, with every Catholic, I will accept it.

Begging your Lordship's blessing, I am, Your faithful Servt in Xt
John H. Newman of the Oratory

The Rt Rev. The Bp of Newport.

¹ Bishop Brown, who was too infirm to go to the Council, wrote on 7 April, a letter marked 'Private': 'I cannot resist my desire of thanking you for the admirable letter you wrote to Dr Ullathorne, and am rejoiced at finding it in print. With every word of it my feelings and judgment fully coincide—though it would not be prudent in me to give them publicity. Yet in regard to the Tablet I have not hesitated to express loudly my disapproval, also my apprehension of the serious evil likely to ensue from the course pursued by Herbert Vaughan and his party in England—as by the Univers and Monde in France.' Although Newman's confidence had been betrayed, 'Yet out of evil good is brought; and though you feel annoyed, the interests of religion will be promoted'

To J. Walker of Scarborough

The Oratory [April 8 1870]

My dear Canon Walker

I am truly glad to have your letter, though I was not waiting for one.

What you say of my book is perfectly true. Unless it had already grown so fat, and I was so desperately tired of the whole subject, I had intended to sum up in a last chapter.

You see I called it an *Essay*, as it really is, because it is an analytical inquiry—a Grammar ought to be synthetical. But to put it in synthetical form, had I after all attempted it, would have been to write a new book. And it would, to my own feelings, have been bumptious. Let thoughtful minds first determine whether it is worth putting into didactic form; it is enough for me to have attempted an investigation, and I cannot hope that there will be no weak points found in it. What is the good of building a house with girders which have not previously been tested?

⌈As to my letter, I was very much startled to find it known to the Correspondent of the Standard. He told me in a private letter that it was so long and so widely known that he could not consider it any more a private one—and therefore he felt at liberty to quote from it. Then a friend wrote me word that there were copies in London, and that it had been read by a great number of people. Then other passages were quoted in the Augsburgh Gazette—and not correctly quoted, and I could not deny what *was* incorrect without stating what was *not* incorrect. Also, I feared the whole would get into print, as a whole, in an incorrect form, which it would [[be]] impossible to set right. So on the whole I found myself obliged to publish it myself.⌉ The beginning and ending [of] the letter (of which I wrote no rough copy) had reference to the letter to which it was an answer

Most sincerely Yours John H Newman

To Aubrey De Vere

The Oratory Aug 31. 1870

My dear Aubrey de Vere,

It is a great pleasure to hear your commendations of two publications of mine[1]— As to my Essay on Assent it is on a subject which has teazed me for this 20 or 30 years. I felt I had something to say upon it, yet, whenever I attempted, the sight I saw vanished, plunged into a thicket, curled itself up like a hedgehog, or changed colours like a chameleon. I have a succession of commencements, perhaps a dozen, each different from the other, and in a different year, which came to nothing. At last four years ago, when I was up at Glion over the Lake of Geneva, a thought came into my head as the clue, the 'Open Sesame', of the whole subject, and I at once wrote it down, and I pursued it about the Lake of Lucerne. Then when I came home, I began in earnest, and have slowly got through it.

Now you must not think, in consequence of my thus speaking, that I am sure myself that I have done any great thing—for I have felt very little confidence in it— though words like yours, and you are not the only person who have used such, are a very great encouragement to me—but I could not help feeling that I had something to give out, whatever its worth, and I felt haunted with a sort of responsibility, and almost a weight on my conscience, if I did not speak of it, and yet I could not. So that it is the greatest possible relief, at length to have got it off my mind—as if I heard the words 'he has done what he could' and, while I say this, I really am not taking for granted that your favorable criticism is the true one—and I recollect that what a man thinks his best work is often his worst, but then I think too that sometimes a man's failures do more good to the world or to his cause than his best successes—and thus I feel as if I could die happier, now that I have no Essay on Assent to write, and I think I shall never write another work, meaning by work a something which is an anxiety and a labour, 'Man goeth forth to his work and to his labours until the evening—'[2] and my evening is surely come—though not my night

Ever Yrs affly John H Newman

[1] De Vere had written enthusiastically to Newman about *A Grammar of Assent* and the *Letter to Pusey*.
[2] *Psalm* 104:23.

To David Moriarty, Bishop of Kerry

The Oratory Nov 1. 1870

My dear Lord,

I heard what a continued anxiety you had had and have, I believe, still, as regards your brother, ever since last Lent, when you wrote to me from Rome[1]—and I feared that, together with other anxieties of an ecclesiastical nature, they would have affected your health, but I was told the other day by one who has seen you that, in spite of all this, and in spite of the Roman climate, you really had benefited from your absence from home, which is good news indeed.

When you are likely to come here, do, if you possibly can, give me notice. I have been most unlucky, once or twice, or thrice, when you have come suddenly.

The definition, if we are to suppose it legitimately passed, is producing most untoward effects, as far as I have experience of it—and, when poor people ask me categorically 'Is it binding?' I don't know what to say. That 'securus judicat orbis terrarum,' I am sure—but time has not been given yet to ascertain this, and the very cruelty of certain people, of which I complain is, that *they will not let people have time*. They would come round quietly if you gave them time—but, when you hold a pistol to their heads and say, 'Believe this doctrine, however new to you, as you believe the Holy Trinity, under pain of damnation,' THEY CAN'T. Their breath is taken away—they seem to say 'Give me time, give me time—' And their confessors all about the country, say 'No, not an hour—believe or be damned—we want to sift the Catholic body of all half Catholics.'

I assure you this so pierces my heart, I do not know what to do—and I rise in indignation against such cruelty.

And then comes the grave retort either from themselves or from third persons, which increases the unsettlement of those whose treatment is the occasion of it 'At least you Catholics are as much divided in opinion as we Anglicans—you are divided in a question of faith. We thought certainty your special boast.' On this I assure you I feel quite ashamed, and know not what to say—Pudet hæc opprobria nobis Et dici potuisse, et non potuisse refelli.[2]

How I wish your opinion had been followed on that last day, and not the Bishop of Orleans's. Surely it was *not* a free council, if the Pope *lectured each Bishop* so sharply as he did.[3] He lectured you, as you told me

Ever Yrs affly in Xt John H Newman

[1] Moriarty's brother was ill.

[2] Ovid, *Metamorphoses*, I, 758–9: 'It shames us that these reproaches can be cast upon us and cannot be repelled.'

[3] Moriarty had written: 'I hear some yet complaining of want of liberty. This is not fair. The whole conduct of business was not what some of us had wished; but it was what the immense majority of the Council wished, and the Council can not complain of its own acts. If there was any restraint it was self-imposed. Even our absence on the last day—to which I was vehemently opposed—was the free act of the minority, and was advised, and effected by the persuasion of Mgr Dupanloup.'

To Lady Simeon

The Oratory Nov 18. 1870

My dear L[ady Simeon]

It is very kind in you to have written to me so fully. I have had your letter before me ever since it came, but I thought it might worry you, if I answered it at once.

God has certainly brought upon you a dreadful weight of suffering, but He will enable you to bear it, and will bless you in it and after it. The day will come when you will look back upon it, and praise Him for it, though it is so difficult to feel this before that day comes.

As to the immediate subject of your letter what comes upon myself with most painful force is the scandal which is involved in the whole proceeding. The Archbishop only does what he has done all along—he ever has exaggerated things, and ever has acted towards individuals in a way which they felt to be unfeeling.[1] I am speaking from the various letters I have had from strangers, since nothing has happened between him and me. And now, as I think most cruelly, he is fearfully exaggerating what has been done at the Council. The Pope is not infallible in such things as you instance. I enclose a letter of our own Bishop, which I think will show you this. I must trouble you to let me have it back.[2] Therefore, I say confidently, you may dismiss all such exaggerations from your mind, though it is a cruel penance to know that the Bishop, where you are, puts them forth. It is an enormous tyranny.

For myself, I think that a new world is coming in, and that the Pope's change of position (which in spite of any temporary re-action which may come, is inevitable) will alter matters vastly. We have come to a climax of tyranny. It is not good for a Pope to live 20 years. It is [an] anomaly and bears no good fruit; he becomes a god, has no one to contradict him, does not know facts, and does cruel things without meaning it. For years past my only consolation personally has been in our Lord's Presence in the Tabernacle. I turn from the sternness of external authority to Him who can immeasurably compensate trials which after all are not real, but (to use a fashionable word) sentimental. Never, thank God, have I had a single doubt about the divine origin and grace of the Church, on account of the want of tenderness and largeness of mind of some of its officials or rulers. And I think this will be your experience too. Bear up for a while and all will be right. What you tell me that you have ever held about the Pope's Infallibility is, I am sure, enough now. Recollect men like the Archbishop and Mr Ward said all the strong things they now say, *before* the Council. Such sayings did not trouble you then, why should they trouble you now? They certainly spoke without authority, before the Council was held; is it wonderful that (however little the Council has said) they should persevere now? Do not let such phantoms frighten you or make you sad. God bless you. I will not forget you.

Yours affly J. H. Newman

The Honble Lady [Simeon]

[1] In October Manning issued *The Vatican Council and its Definitions: Pastoral Letter to the Clergy*, which gave an impression of unlimited claims for papal infallibility.

[2] This was probably Ullathorne's letter of 13 November to the *Birmingham Daily Post*, (14 Nov. 1870), p. 5, in which he said that papal infallibility 'as defined by the Vatican Council, is limited to "faith and morals;" and, I may add, to faith and morals as they are taught in Scripture, and in the constant traditional teaching of the Catholic and Roman Church'.

To Sir Frederic Rogers

The Oratory, February 18th. 1871

My dear Rogers,

I guessed the sad intelligence of your letter from its outside. Someone told me, I think Wilson, that your dear mother was sinking gradually. One can but once lose a Mother. I don't forget, I never have, how kind you were to me, when I lost mine.[1] How many years have passed, how many events, since then, but it seems to me like yesterday. What a dream life is! It does not make it a less sorrow to you that you must have all expected it so long. The freshness of her mind and the continuance of her strength, for so long, which will be so pleasant to look back upon, perhaps have made the gradual changes of the last year more sad to your sisters. I hope to say Mass for her on Monday morning.

You know that on Tuesday I am 70. By fits and starts I realize it; but usually it seems incredible to me.

Ever yours affectionately, John H. Newman.

[1] Rogers's mother died on 16 February. Mrs Newman died on 17 May 1836.

To Emily Bowles

The Oratory March 19. 1871

My dear Child

I write to those who exact letters, not to those who deserve them. That is the reason why I am so benevolent to strangers, and so ungrateful to friends. Really I have been oppressed with letters since I heard from you—and when I don't answer almost by return of post, the chance is that I don't answer at all.

This must be my excuse for not thanking you for your affectionate letter, and for the Chartreuse. I was 'vexed', to use your word, not that I received it, but that you gave it. It was very good, and the Fathers drank my health in it, when it was you who merited that return[1]

I am very glad that you can do us so great a service as to stop such absurd reports, as that was, whatever it was, I know, about young Monsell.[2] It will be a thousand pities if he does not go to a school, where he may get rubbed both by the discipline itself and by his schoolfellows—he is just the boy whom it will much prejudice to have nothing but a home life—but I fear his Mother thinks that he is already so formed and complete, that whatever change school can make in him will be for the worse. But keep this, of course, to yourself.

I am busy republishing my British Critic Articles—with some notes, refuting or defending what I have said in them. I don't want it known, till the work is published. It will consist of two volumes. All this is part of my winding up—on which I shall employ myself continually.

Ever Yrs affly John H Newman

[1] Emily Bowles sent Newman a bottle of Chartreuse on his birthday, for which the Father Minister at the Oratory sent thanks. In a letter of 20 February she wrote, 'I hope you will not be vexed about the chartreuse.'

[2] There were unfounded rumours that Monsell was taking his son away from the Oratory School.

To Lady Simeon

Rednall April 26. 1871

My dear Lady Simeon

I had half heard of your new affliction—and grieve much to hear from you how great it is.[1] Also you and the children have the whooping cough! What great trials have come on you—but I cannot doubt you will have consolations at length to equal them. Who can but feel distressed about Döllinger?[2] but it is very hard you have no one you can talk with about these things—it is a great trial to be shut up in oneself. I firmly believe that all this will work for good, tho' not perhaps in my day. If you look into history, you find Popes continually completing the acts of their predecessors, and Councils too—sometimes only half the truth is brought out at one time—I doubt not a coming Pope, or a coming Council, will so explain and guard what has been now passed by [the] late Council, as to clear up all that troubles us now. As to Dollinger, I think his case is only a portion of the long conflict between the Italians and the Tedeschi. Each wishes to put the other down.

But as to your question. Your inscription seems to me very natural and sober.[3] I would not alter any part of it. I have thought it might be made a little clearer at the end—whether I have suggested what will make it so, you must judge—but I am not confident in my suggestions myself. Don't make any excuse for writing to me, pray:—I only feel so little able to do any thing serviceable.

Most sincerely Yours John H. Newman

The Hon. Lady Simeon

P.S. 'Sacrificed in the fulfilment of duty'—should it not be 'public duty'?

[1] Lady Simeon's younger sister died on 18 March.

[2] Ignaz von Döllinger had been excommunicated by the Archbishop of Munich for rejecting papal infallibility.

[3] For a memorial to her husband, Sir John Simeon, who had died on 21 May 1870.

To Mrs Houldsworth

The Oratory July 3rd. 1871

My dear Mrs. Houldsworth

As to your question, suggested by your friends, it is not at all the case that I left the Anglican Church from despair—but for two reasons concurrent, as I have stated in my *Apologia*—first, which I felt *before* any strong act had been taken against the Tracts or me, namely, in 1839, that the Anglican Church *now* was in the position of the Arian Churches of the fourth century, and the Monophysite Churches of the fifth, and this was such a shock to me that I at once made arrangements for giving up the editorship of *The British Critic*, and in no long time I contemplated giving up St. Mary's. This shock was the *cause* of my writing Number 90 which excited so much commotion. Number 90 which roused the Protestant world against me, most likely never would have been written except for this shock. Thus you see my condemnation of the Anglican Church arose *not* out of despair, but, when everything was hopeful, *out of my study of the Fathers*. Then, as to the second cause, it began in the autumn of 1841, six months after Number 90, when the Bishops began to charge against me. This brought home to me that *I had no business in the Anglican Church*. It was not that I despaired of the Anglican Church, but that their opposition *confirmed* the interpretation which I had put upon the Fathers, that they *who loved the Fathers, could have no place in the Church of England*.

As to your further question, whether, *if* I had stayed in the Anglican Church *till now*, I should have joined the Catholic Church at all, at any time now or hereafter, I think that most probably I should *not*; but *observe, for* this reason, because God gives grace, and if it is not accepted He withdraws His grace; and since, of His free mercy, and from no merits of mine, He then offered me the grace of conversion, if I had not acted upon it, it was to be expected that I should be left, a worthless stump, to cumber the ground and to remain where I was till I died.

Of course you are endlessly bewildered by hearing and reading on both sides. What I should recommend you, if you ask me, is to put aside controversy and close your ears to advocates on both sides for two months, and not to open any controversial book, but to pray God to enlighten you continually, and then at the end of the time to find where you are. I think if you thus let yourself alone, or rather take care that others let you alone, you will at the end of the time see that you ought to be a Catholic. And if this is the case, it will be your duty at once to act upon this conviction. But if you go on reading, talking, being talked to, you will never have peace. God bless you and keep you and guide you, and bring you safe into port.

Yours most sincerely John H. Newman

To Emily Bowles

The Oratory June 8. 1872

My dear Child

You may say from and for me three things to any one you please—[1]

1. That I never have by word or act advocated the scheme of a Catholic College at Oxford, though many have attributed such a scheme to me. What alone I took part in was the establishment of an Oratory there to protect Catholic youths residing in Protestant Colleges.

2. And what I advocated then I advocate now. In a bad matter and in a choice of difficulties, I would rather have Catholic youths in Protestant Colleges at Oxford with a strong Catholic Mission in the place, than a Catholic College.

3 And I thought and think that the Bishops took an unadvisable step, and brought the whole Catholic body in England into a great difficulty, when on March 23, 1865 they discountenanced, to the practical effect of a prohibition, the residence of Catholics at Oxford.

Moreover, since the Archbishop or Dr Ward may maintain that I have now softened what I said in my private letter to a friend, part of a sentence of which was shown to the Archbishop, I here quote the whole sentence unmutilated, as it stood in my letter, that you may have your answer pat.

'If I were upon the rack, and forced to name some scheme or other for Catholic University education, when nothing satisfactory is possible, I should not propose a Catholic University, for I think our present rulers would never give us a real one, nor a Catholic College at Oxford, for such a measure at the present moment would be challenging controversy and committing Catholic theologians most dangerously in the religious difficulties of the day; but I should say that the Bishops ought to have let things alone seven years ago, and that, in our present straits, they will do best to undo their own work, and to let Catholics go to Protestant Colleges (without their formal sanction) and to provide a strong Mission worked by theologians, i.e., a strong Jesuit Mission, to protect the Catholic youth from the infidelity of the place.'[2]

As to Fr St John, he has advocated in his late remarks a Catholic College at Oxford;[3] but he adds, (I believe, for he may have some trouble in finding his paper) that no youths had gone to Oxford lately who did not lose by the absence of a strong ecclesiastical superintendence[4]

I rejoiced to see you and Louisa Simeon.

Ever Yours affecty John H Newman

Miss Bowles

[1] On 7 June Emily Bowles wrote out for Newman passages in a letter she had just received from W. G. Ward: 'The following was told me directly by the Archbishop and is no secret. Fr Newman wrote a letter to be shown the bishops, in which he said that the changed condition of Oxford led him *directly to reverse* his former opinion. He now strongly thinks that great evils would result from any connection with Oxford.'

Emily Bowles remarked:

'As the Archbishop's words (and I suppose he never knew the whole) are spreading what is directly contrary to the truth, will you not tell *the whole* publicly . . . ? For you have in truth urged a "connection with Oxford" as strongly as you have deprecated a Catholic Hall.

May this be said if the thing really is "no secret"—I mean by me and true friends?

I find considerable sub-irritation among the Jesuits—*even Fr Coleridge*—about your opposition to the Hall—"playing into the hands of the Archbishop and Ward"—'

[2] See letter of 9 April 1872 to J. Spencer Northcote, (*L.D.* XXVI, p.61).

[3] Emily Bowles also quoted W. G. Ward as saying: 'I have it on indubitable authority that Fr St John, who advocated a Catholic College at Oxford, stated in his evidence that he believed *no one Catholic student* had yet gone to Oxford without more or less spiritual evil resulting.' Emily Bowles asked, 'Did Fr Ambrose say that? Of Henry Stourton, Charles Thynne, Horace Gaisford, Richard Ward, Froudes?'

[4] Newman made a memorandum: 'June 9, 1872: Ambrose has it and had it clearly in his mind that in 1864 I was in favour of a Catholic College at Oxford. This, as far as I can make out, is a great mistake. The question of a Catholic College was not before us, but of Catholics belonging to Protestant Colleges, and our supplying their religious needs as an Oratory' (*L.D.* XXVI, pp. 110–11).

To Miss M. R. Giberne

Abbotsford Melrose July 20/72

My dear Sister Pia

My dear friend, Hope Scott, asked me to visit him here—and, as he has been and is anxiously ill, and I am as anxiously old, I have come for some days. It is 20 years since I was here, during the Achilli matter, and now the young heiress of Abbotsford and representative of Sir Walter Scott is grown up. She has just been presented at Court, and had her first season in London.

This Presbyterian region has now several lights set upon high candlesticks. This Abbotsford is one of them. Then, Lord and Lady Henry Kerr are two miles off—then there is Mr Monteith of Carstairs, who came in 1846 to Maryvale to find by personal inspection whether or not I was mad, as people said—and when he found I really wasn't, he went on to Oscott and was received. And then there is the Duchess of Buccleugh [*sic*].[1] Hope Scott has established three Church[es] or Chapels here, at Galashiels and at Selkirk. Mr Monteith two. I am going to see him (Mr M) next week in my way back home. Before, however, I get to Edgbaston, I shall spend one night at Derby. I have had a sad letter from Derby, not unexpected, about John Mozley's health. Jemima is at least aware in what a serious state it is. I saw it two years ago, and told young John, but I don't think those who saw him daily, realized his state, as I did, who was unprepared for it.

Fr Edward Caswall has got a bad knee, which will confine him to his room for some time. Fr H. Bittleston has never quite got right, after his attack last year. He is going now for his holidays. We are all getting old—I saw Rogers in London, who is Lord Blachford now; and Church who is Dean of St Paul's. I don't suppose either of them has a chance of being a Catholic, humanly speaking, but we are very good friends. What a strange world this is, and how full of vanity! That is the conclusion of the whole matter. God grant we may be as prepared for the next world, as we are out of joint with this.

I leave Fr William to tell you what news is to be told about the Oratory. I ought to have added to my Catholic information of this neighbourhood, old Traquair house—the oldest inhabited house in Scotland, which is up the Tweed, and where lives Lady Louisa Stewart, a Catholic lady aged 96. We lunched with her the other day. You would say she was between 70 and 80—deaf, but not very. Else, very much alive[2]

Ever Yrs affly John H Newman

[1] Lady Charlotte Anne Thynne, widow of the fifth Duke of Buccleuch, became a Catholic in 1855. She lived at Bowhill, Selkirk, where Newman visited her on 22 July.

[2] The eighth and last Earl of Traquair died in 1861. His sister Lady Louisa Stuart died on 6 December 1875 in her hundredth year.

To Richard Frederick Littledale [?]

The Oratory Sept 17. 1872

My dear Sir,

Without implying that I am necessarily opposing your view of our doctrine, I will say this:—

Infallibility is not a *habit* in the Pope, or a state of mind—but, as the decree says, that infallibility which the Church has. The Church when in Council and proceeding by the strictest forms enunciates a definition in faith and morals, which is certainly true. The Church is infallible *then, when* she speaks ex cathedrâ—but the Bishops out of Council are fallible men. So the Pope is infallible *then, when* he speaks ex cathedrâ—but he has no habit of infallibility in his intellect, such that his *acts cannot but* proceed from it, *must* be infallible *because* he is infallible, *imply, involve,* an infallible judgment. He is infallible *pro re natâ* [according to the circumstances], *when* he speaks ex cathedra—not except at particular times and on grave questions.

Nay further than this, even on those grave questions the gift is negative. It is not that he has an inspiration of truth, but he is simply guarded from error, circumscribed by a divine superintendence from transgressing, extravagating beyond, the line of truth. And his definitions do not come of a positive divine guidance, but of human means, research, consulting theologians etc etc. It is an 'adsistentia' not an 'inspiratio—' an aid *eventual,* in the event, and does not act till the event, not in the *process*—and an adsistentia, as I have said, *pro re natâ.* His words would be infallible one moment, not the next. 'Numquam Catholici docuerunt,' says Perrone, 'donum infallibilitatis à Deo Ecclesiæ tribui per modum inspirationis.' 'Nec enim sive Romani Pontificis sive Concilii Œcumenici infallibilitas (est) per modum *infusi* doni, sed per modum præsidii sive adsistentiæ.'[1] It is an external not internal aid

Very truly Yours John H Newman

[1] J. Perrone, S. J. *Praelectiones Theologicae* (Rome, 1841), II, *De Locis Theologicis,* I, pp. 253, 541.

To Mrs John Mozley

The Oratory Oct 15. 1872

My dear Jemima

It is very kind in you to write so long a letter—I only hope it is not a fatigue to you to do so. I have been and am very anxious lest your necessary watchfulness and strain of mind, which John's illness involves, should simply knock you up. It is a most cruel suffering so to be separated from him, as you describe, while you are close to him. And yet what help is there for it, but to put yourself into God's Hands?[1]

You say nothing about Janie's health, which I take to be a good sign. And it must be a real comfort to her, and I should think really good for her, to find herself useful in the business matters, which are so great a perplexity.[2]

I have no pleasant news from the friends I am anxious about. Mr Hope Scott has gone back—and is in a very anxious state—and Henry Wilberforce is wheeled from room to room. I don't think they well know what is the matter with him—they talk of a congestion of blood upon the spine—but the question is whether saying so brings them one step nearer to a cure, or an alleviation of symptoms.

Ever Yours affectly John H Newman

[1] John Mozley died on 23 October.
[2] Newman's niece, Jane, was helping in the work of the Mozley family publishing business.

To Anne Mozley

The Oratory Octr 29. 1872

My dear Anne Mozley

It is very kind in you to write to me. I supposed you would form a large party, and rejoice indeed at what you tell me about Tom [Mozley]. You have had, I can feel, a very great loss, which cannot be made up—and of which perhaps you will be more sensible as time goes on—but it will be a great consolation to you always to look back on yesterday—as a time, when the last sad duties and offices towards one you loved so much, in themselves so soothing as well as so sorrowful, were sealed and consecrated by a reconciliation.[1]

How strangely festivity and mourning are woven together here! This day a daughter of my friend, the late Sir John Simeon, is to be married. She asked me to marry her. I declined, for various reasons. It happened well I did—how could I have been in a marriage party, when Jemima's husband had only just been taken away, and my most dear Hope Scott lay dying! What a great contrast, your brother's life and his! Your brother had a long course of (as far as I know) happy and uneventful years—he lived to see five sons started in life—he lost no children—Hope Scott has had a brilliant public career as a barrister. He married first Walter Scott's heiress, then a Duke's daughter. The upshot is, he dies a widower a second time—has lost 4 children—leaves one girl, the heiress of Abbotsford, just entering into life, and four little children under ten. I dwell on all this, because it is not selfish to do so—for, if I think of myself, I lose one of those whom I love most in the world, one who has gone out of his way to know me, who has ever been faithful to me, who stood by me in great difficulties, who has aided me in great needs, and who is one of the sweetest-tempered, gentlest, most religious-minded men I ever knew. He fell off just a day or two after I left Abbotsford in the summer, and has gradually sunk ever since—and I rejoiced to find that he wrote to his people in England that my being with him had been a fortnight of sunshine to him. I have strangely digressed—I end by asking whether Jemima ought not to have some perfect rest which she cannot have at Derby—You know best

Yrs affly John H Newman

[1] The reconciliation was between Tom Mozley and his sisters. His father had bequeathed his house in Derby to him, and on his mother's death he sold it, with the result that his unmarried sisters had to leave their home.

To R. W. Church

St Stephen's day 1872

My dear Dean

I hope to send you the book this evening. ⟨Perhaps I shall be obliged to delay⟩

Yes, I was morally turned out and I told you at the time, I did nothing but what you might have done at Chester or Carlisle, where you might not be known. I stood just inside the door listening to the chanting of the Psalms, of which I am so fond. First came Verger one, a respectful person, inquiring if I wanted a seat in the choir, half a mile off me. No, I said—I was content where I was. Then came a second, not respectful, with a voice of menace—I still said No. Then came a third, I don't recollect much about him, except that he said he could provide me with a seat. Then came Number 2 again, in a compulsory mood, on which I vanished.

I am sure if I was a dissenter, or again one of Mr Bradlaugh's people, nothing would attract me more to the Church of England than to be allowed to stand at the door of a Cathedral—did not St Augustine while yet a Manichee, stand and watch St Ambrose? No verger turned him out.

Of course, knowing the nature of those men, I was amused, and told you and Blachford in the evening. You were annoyed, and said it was just what you did *not* wish, and that you would inquire about it

I have not a dream how it got into the Papers—as mine is a Somersetshire one, I thought the paragraph had trickled out from Whatley[1]

Ever Yrs affly J H N

All Christmas blessings to you and yours.

[1] Church had been Vicar of Whatley in Somerset before becoming Dean of St Paul's.

To Mrs Edward Bellasis

The Oratory Purification, 1873

My dear Mrs Bellasis

How can I thank you enough for your two beautiful letters? I hope you got my answer to your first. I wrote it on receiving yours, but forgot, in directing it, to add the department.

You have had the greatest of losses and the greatest of gains.[1] For myself, though I have felt greater pain than I have felt ever since we lost Father Joseph Gordon in 1853, still I could not really grieve—and though I have said Mass for the dear Serjeant's soul and hope to say more Masses, yet I cannot say them as really believing in my heart that he needs them, any more than I could say them from my heart for dear Mary Anne Bowden, whom I had known from a child, and who died a few years ago a Nun at Westbury. Fr Ambrose feels the same and I am sure it is the feeling of all of us; so deeply impressed is our imagination with the conviction of his fitness for the heavenly Paradise.

In like manner, when I wrote to Mamo [Hope-Scott], fearing her father might be thrown back by the tidings of his great loss, she answers to the same effect, that the Serjeant's beautiful death has overcome all his natural grief and dejection at his bereavement.

What you tell me of his feeling about my Dedication is, as you may suppose, very grateful to me, and most surprising.[2] It does but show how true and thorough a friend he was to me, and I bless God for putting it into my heart to do a simple natural act of gratitude towards him in memory of his many, many services to me, which I little thought, when I did it, would receive from him so great a reward as he has bestowed upon me in the words he used in conversing with you.

May God's Mercy grant that I may be prepared to go, when my time comes, at least with some measure of the hope, love, and peace which have so remarkably shown forth in him!

Henry [Bellasis] desires his love. He has been in our house during the past week— and he has something of a cold but it is better than it was

Ever Yrs My dear Mrs Bellasis Most sincerely John H Newman

[1] Edward Bellasis died on 24 January.

[2] In her letter of 29 January Mrs Bellasis described how she asked her husband seven weeks previously, when he was looking over some notes, what event in his life had given him greatest pleasure. He replied, 'Well! Indeed. I *do-not-know*—⟨(slowly)⟩ ANYTHING that ever gave me the gratification that Newman's dedication of his book [G.A.] to me gave rise to—I consider it raised me to a great height in the English Catholic world. I don't know what I can have done to deserve such an honor.'

To Mrs John Mozley

The Oratory April 5. 1873

My dear Jemima

I send you a Pall Mall Gazette (let me have it back), in which you will see a report of F W N's letter. It is strange, they call this licensed suicide 'Euthanasia', 'a good death.'[1]

I have been to H W W [Henry Wilberforce] for a night this week . . . that is, I had two good days, getting to him by 11 AM, and leaving him next day at 7 PM.

It was a beautiful day, last Wednesday, and he was sitting out in the garden. He looked inexpressibly like his Father—most strangely so—in every feature in the shape and colouring of his features. It is close upon 40 years when his father died, and he then was the only son on the spot and represented him when it was settled that he was to be buried in the Abbey. Certainly you might have fancied him 80. He is very weak, sleeps a great deal—is deaf—and has the feebleness of a very old man. It seems to me simply a matter of time, when he is taken. I know people last longer than all one's expectations—but he has all the signs of approaching death. He has a wife and two daughters about him—and has, as you may suppose, every wish anticipated. I suppose they all in their hearts think his case hopeless—but they do not say so. He inquired particularly after you.

He has given over reading—has a great disgust of eating. I believe he sleeps well at night and is best in the morning. I saw no signs of a clouded mind—except that, when he is drowsy, he cannot think and talk. The future is always before him—his one idea is the thought of meeting his God. He took leave of me, and I of him, as if we were never to meet again here. I said Mass in his room, and gave him communion

Ever Yours affly John H Newman

[1] See letter of 6 March to Mrs John Mozley (*L.D.* xxvi, p. 270), and the *Pall Mall Gazette* (22 Feb. 1873), p. 9, 'Professor Newman writes to the *Spectator* that . . . suicide may be a duty', 'if Euthanasia were legalised' the registrar would 'interrogate the patient'.

To Wilfrid Wilberforce

The Oratory, April 23, 1873

My dear Wilfrid

Your telegram told me what I had expected to hear.[1] I sent on its tidings to Father Ambrose, who is in London.

There never was a man more humble than your dear father—never one who so intimately realised what it was to die—and how little we know, and how much we have to know about it. Now he knows all: he knows all that we do not know. He has the reward of all his prayers; there is an end of all his fears. He has served God with a single aim all through his life, and he now understands how good it has been to have done so. I have known him most intimately for forty-seven years and he has always been the same.

Of course I shall say Masses for his soul; but I wish and pray that each of us, when our time comes, may as little need them as I think he does. None of us are fit to enter God's Holy Presence, but he has been preparing himself for it all through his life.

May God sustain your dear mother and all of you—but I don't doubt they will have abundant strength and consolation in their trial.

Ever yours affectionately, John H Newman

¹ The death on 23 April of Henry Wilberforce.

To Miss Hope-Scott

The Oratory April 30. 1873

My dear Child

You alone can know what it is to be bereaved of such a Father.¹ You never can have a heavier blow, because you are so young and so untried in suffering. But God is more than enough to make up all to you, and He will. You will look back with tender affection, not only on happy past days, but on this long sad time, when hope rose and fell again, and you felt weary of the changes.

May you be as great a blessing to all around you, as he has been.

For me, his departure is a memento that my day must come. May I be as well prepared as he.

We shall have high Mass for him as one of our benefactors, for whom we say a weekly Mass. I shall say many Masses for him besides, not excluding you and your need of strength and consolation

This of course requires no answer

Ever Yours affectionately John H Newman

¹ James Hope-Scott died on 29 April.

To Henry James Coleridge

The Oratory May 4. 1873

My dear Fr Coleridge

I am to attempt to preach at your Church tomorrow at Hope Scott's Requiem Mass. I take it for granted that the Duke or Lord Henry Kerr has asked the leave of your Fathers, and, if necessary in your case, of the Archbishop. But I don't write on this account—but, because I am told there is a garden way from Number 111 to the Sacristy of your Church, and I wish to ask your Fathers' leave to avail myself of it.

I come to Town tomorrow morning, and expect to get to Mount Street at latest by half past eleven. The Mass begins at eleven, and I take it for granted that the Sermon is after it.

I am sadly down, and have not a dream how I shall get through it—I go down again by the first available train

Yours affecty John H Newman

You must say a prayer for me

To John Hungerford Pollen

The Oratory July 23. 1873

My dear Pollen

At length I return your most interesting and precious memorial of a wonderful trial and a wonderful and heroic conduct under it, and, I may add of a wonderful Providence blessing that trial and that conduct.[1]

What a strange number of deaths of friends has marked this year! at least to me. Sam Wilberforce is the last—I call him Sam, because it recalls old days.[2] I never knew him well, but I have before me quite clearly the vision of his coming up to residence at Oriel in 1823, leaning on Robert's arm. Ah me, what an age ago! it is a new world; yet to the great Creator of worlds it is but yesterday.

There is something inexpressibly sad in the picture of a man going out on a beautiful Saturday, with a few friends, in a beautiful country, with every thing calm and joyous and heavenly around him, and suddenly being carried off to the awful darkness of the other world.

What a strange contrast the lives of Sam and Henry! When I first knew Henry, he used to say, 'I hope you will never know my brother Sam: if you do, you will love him so much more than you love me—and I shall lose you.'

Ever Yours affecty John H Newman

[1] Pollen had sent Newman a narrative written by his sister-in-law that, however, has not been traced.
[2] On 19 July Bishop Samuel Wilberforce fell from his horse and was killed instantly, while riding with Earl Granville, the Foreign Secretary, from Burford Bridge to Abinger Hall, Dorking, the residence of T. H. Farrer.

To Archbishop Manning

Novr 24 1873

(Copy)

My dear Archbishop,

I beg you will have the kindness to convey to the Bishops my most respectful and sincere thanks for the honour they have done me in thinking of me first, when they were forming a list of those who are to serve on the Senate of their new College of Higher Studies.

I have read the Prospectus which you sent me with great and careful interest; and I hope their Lordships and yourself will not deem it a presumption in me to say, that I feel an unsurmountable difficulty in giving my name to it. I hope they will so far throw themselves into my history and my life-long opinions as to understand, that I could not without a great inconsistency take part in an Institution, which formally and 'especially' recognizes the London University, a body which has been the beginning, and source, and symbol of all the Liberalism existing in the educated classes for the last forty years.[1]

I am &c J H N

To the Archbp of Westminster

[1] The final paragraph of Manning's Prospectus for the proposed Kensington College said: 'The course of studies will be so ordered as to enable the students to present themselves for the Civil Service and other examinations, and especially to obtain such degrees of the London University as confer advantages in the practice of certain professions.' For Newman's lifelong opinions see especially letter of 25 January 1859 to Henry Weedall, 'I am not a fair person to judge of the position of the Catholic Colleges towards the London University—so intense is the antipathy which now for 30 years and more, since its commencement, I have felt towards it' (L.D. XIX, p. 29).

To Miss Hope-Scott

The Oratory 9 June 1874

My dear Mamo

You may think, without my telling you, how your letter rejoiced me.[1] Francis Kerr (who, by the bye, is to call here with his wife this evening) told me how well Algiers had suited you, but no one but yourself could answer me that question, which, since this time year, has been silently on my mind,—what was to be your future.

Now then, with great thankfulness, I find you know it and can tell me of it—and I congratulate you upon it with all my heart.

Tell me when the time approaches, that I may say some Masses for you.[2] How sorrow and joy go together in this life, a joy in our deepest sorrow, a sorrow in our most abounding joy! But both joy and sorrow are well, if they lead us on towards heaven[3]

Ever Yours affectionately John H Newman

[1] Miss Hope-Scott wrote from Arundel Castle on 8 June to announce her engagement to Joseph Maxwell, third son of Lord Herries.

[2] She was married on 21 July 1874.

[3] Miss Hope-Scott had just visited Hyères, where her father used to winter, and she wrote 'it was a sad pleasure'.

To Mrs Sconce

The Oratory, Aug. 21st. 1874

My dear Mrs. Sconce,

How kind it is in you to think of me and my wants. The pen is most ingenious, and that to a very useful end. But alas! a metal pen in my hands is nothing else than a skewer. And, while it is beyond my mastery, it is proportionately fatiguing—and knocks my fingers up. However, your gift will not be lost, for others will benefit by it, though I cannot.[1]

Of course I should not forget your most kind suggestion as to Florence, did I go to Rome—but I am too old to travel It was very good in you proposing to come here, but, as you have found, we are as far off from Liverpool pretty much as from London.

> With the kindest good wishes and prayers, I am,
> My dear Mrs. Sconce, Sincerely Yours John H. Newman.

[1] Newman continued to use quill pens until the end of his life.

To J. Spencer Northcote

The Oratory Sept. 20. 1874

My dear President

It is most natural and becoming in the holy Community at Westbury to be zealous in behalf of their great Saint; and gladly would I do any thing in my power to further the object about which they write to you.[1] Moreover, as far as my own personal feelings go, nothing would rejoice me more than to find that the Holy Father had pronounced St Francis a doctor of the Church. But it seems to me that the Holy See alone has the means of judging who they are who have by their writings merited that high honour.

In the Canonization indeed of Saints it is intelligible to appeal even to the popular voice, because sanctity can be apprehended, not only by good Catholics, but by bad, nay, by those who are not Catholics at all. But none except the learned can judge of learned men, and none but the Ecumenical Doctor of the Church, the Holy Father himself, can pronounce about doctors.

For myself, and of myself your letter makes it necessary for me to speak, I cannot understand why the existing assemblage of doctors is just what it is in quantity and quality. It is easy to understand why St Gregory Nazianzen or St Augustine, St Leo or St Thomas are doctors; but why should St Peter Chrysologus, St Isidore, or St Peter Damian be on the list, and St Antoninus or St Laurence Justinian not? I cannot make out by my own wit why St Alfonso has lately been put upon the level of St Athanasius and St Jerome. I do not even clearly understand why a woman has never been pronounced a doctor; for though St Paul says they are to 'keep silence in the Churches,' he is speaking of ecclesiastical and formal teaching, not of the supernatural gifts and great works, of such a one as St Catherine of Sienna.[2]

The conclusion I draw from this is plain. If I should have made such mistakes, left to myself, in determining who are doctors and who are not having in view the existing list, how can I possibly tell that I be correct, if I pretended to judge whether that great and beautiful Saint, St Francis of Sales, has or has not upon him the notes of a Doctor? No—these things are matters of faith. What the Holy Father holds,

I hold;—I follow, I do not go before him, in so deep and sacred a matter. I am sure Revd Mother will sympathize, even though she may not agree with me.

Ever Yours very sincerely John H Newman

[1] The Visitation Nuns at Westbury were pressing for the inclusion of St Francis of Sales among the Doctors of the Church. This was done in 1877.

[2] St Catherine of Siena and St Teresa of Avila were declared Doctors of the Church in 1970, St Thérèse of Lisieux in 1997, and St Hildegard of Bingen in 2012.

To Lord Emly

The Oratory Nov 7. 1874

My dear Emly
   Confidential.
   Your letter has just come. I *could not* have answered Gladstone's parenthetic, sweeping declamation. It had no points. And Ireland became a great difficulty—But his today's pamphlet, I can answer—at least I shall try and will tell you when I fail, or else go to press[1]

Yrs affly John H Newman

[1] Gladstone's initial attack on converts to Rome was diffuse and Newman could not answer it to his satisfaction. But on 5 November Gladstone published a more general popular pamphlet, *The Vatican Decrees in their bearing on Civil Allegiance: a Political Expostulation*, to which Newman was able to offer his reply.

To Malcolm MacColl

The Oratory. January 4. 1875

My Dear Mr MacColl,
   On Mondays I have no proofs from London, so I take up my pen to wish you a very happy new year, and to try to make up, as far as a few words can do so, for my silence hitherto.
   As to Mr Ward you can tell me nothing more extravagant about his view of me than I know already. He has told my friends that I am in material heresy, that he would rather not have men made Catholics than have them converted by me, and that he accounts it the best deed of his life that he hindered my going to Oxford by the letters he sent to Rome etc. He is so above board, and outspoken, that he is quite charming. It is the whisperers, and I have long suffered from them, whom (as Dickens says) I 'object to'. But both whisperers and outspeakers had received a blow over the knuckles from Fessler's pamphlet, which has the Pope's approbation, and simultaneously with its being known in this country I have been afforded an opportunity, at the earnest wishes of my friends and strangers, by answering Mr Gladstone to break a silence I have so long observed.
   In saying this, you must not suppose that my direct reason for writing was to protest against men like Ward—Time will answer them without me—but it so happens, that the intense indignation, which Mr Gladstone has excited among

Catholics, has led to their being very pressing with me to come forward, as otherwise I should never have done. Of course I may make mistakes as well as others, but it is well for the world to be told that those wild views, which have been put forward as the sole and true Catholic ones, are not what they pretend to be.

As to Mr Gladstone's letter I think it quite shocking. I should not have thought it possible that a statesman could be so onesided. With you I agree most fully that 'he wears his heart upon his sleeve' but that does not seem to me an excuse for charges so serious, so inaccurate, and so insulting.

I suppose I shall be out in a week or ten days.

Very sincerely yours, John H. Newman.

P.S. I cannot agree with what you say in the Pamphlets you were so kind as to send me.[1]

[1] MacColl had sent Newman his pamphlets, including *Papal Infallibility and its Limitations*, reprinted from the *Church Review*.

To *William Ewart Gladstone*

The Oratory Birmingham Jany 16. 1875

My dear Mr Gladstone

I thank you for your forbearing and generous letter. It has been a great grief to me to have had to write against one, whose career I have followed from first to last with so much (I may say) loyal interest and admiration. I had known about you from others, and had looked at you with kindly curiosity, before you came up to Christ Church, and, from the time that you were launched into public life, you have retained a hold on my thoughts and on my gratitude by the various marks of attention which every now and then you have shown me, when you had an opportunity; and I could not fancy my ever standing towards you in any other relation than that which had lasted so long.

What a fate it is, that, now when so memorable a career has reached its formal termination, I should be the man, on the very day on which it is closed, to present to you, amid the many expressions of public sympathy which it elicits, a controversial pamphlet as my offering:—but I could not help writing it. I was called upon from such various quarters; and my conscience told me, that I, who had been in great measure the cause of so many becoming Catholics, had no right to leave them in the lurch, when charges were made against them as serious as unexpected.

I do not think I ever can be sorry for what I have done, but I never can cease to be sorry for the necessity of doing it.[1]

I am, My dear Mr Gladstone, Most truly Yours John H Newman

P.S. I ventured to send you a copy of my pamphlet on Wednesday It was directed, I believe to Hawarden

[1] Newman's reply to Gladstone coincided with the day Gladstone had retired as leader of the Liberal Party. He wrote to thank Newman 'for the genial and gentle manner in which you have treated me' (*L.D.* XXVII, p. 192).

To Emily Bowles

The Oratory Jany 24. 1875

My dear Child

My success would not be complete without a letter from you, which I am very glad to have, though I don't deserve, I know, all that you say.[1] I call it success because I have had such satisfactory letters from St Beuno's, the Bishop of Plymouth, from Maynooth, from Archbishop Errington etc. It has been, as you may suppose, a great anxiety to me, because I felt bound in duty to speak out, yet thought I might be putting myself in opposition to influential people, if I did. At Stonyhurst too they are satisfied with it. I don't see that the Archbishop can say any thing against it; but the chance is he will engage himself chiefly with Lord Acton.[2]

I wrote to Ward, saying how I wished he would live in peace with me and others—he answered that he desired it of all things, but that faith was a greater thing than peace, and it was a great grief to him that I would not take his views. Every thing would go right, if I did.[3]

Ever Yrs affly John H Newman

[1] Emily Bowles wrote her thanks on 23 January for *A Letter to the Duke of Norfolk*, which had lifted a burden off her mind, and made Infallibility and the Syllabus of Errors understandable to Protestants.

[2] Manning wrote to Rome on 9 February, maintaining that 'The substance of the recent pamphlet is sound', and emphasising how disastrous any censure of it would be. See *L.D.* XXVII, Appendix 1, pp. 401–11.

[3] Emily Bowles wrote, 'I never can be glad enough that you have spoken and that strongly about those who have made Our Lord's yoke heavy on His little ones—crushing and trampling on them, without the least remorse—nay with joy. The last time I saw Mr [W.G.] Ward and I said something to him about the sufferings of some (which I had witnessed) about the Vatican Decrees—he said he *rejoiced*—and always should rejoice that such non-believers should be cut off. He is in a terrible state about the Letter—and yet I agree with Louy Ward that if he met you face to face he would burst into tears and you would come to more understanding than now seems possible.'

To Sir William Henry Cope

The Oratory Febr. 13. 1875

My dear Sir William

I thank you very much for the gift of your sermon. The death of Mr Kingsley, so premature, shocked me.[1] I never from the first have felt any anger towards him. As I said in the first pages of my Apologia, it is very difficult to be angry with a man one has never seen. A casual reader would think my language denoted anger—but it did not. I have ever felt from experience that no one would believe me in earnest if I spoke calmly, when again and again I denied the repeated report that I was on the point of coming back to the Church of England. I have uniformly found that, if I simply denied it, this only made newspapers repeat the report more confidently—but, if I said something sharp, they abused me for scurrility against the Church I had left, but they believed me.[2] Rightly or wrongly, this was the reason why I felt it would not do to be tame, and not to show indignation at Mr Kingsley's charges—Within the last few years I have been obliged to adopt a similar course towards those who said I could not receive the Vatican Decrees. I sent a sharp letter to the Guardian, and of course the Guardian called me names, but it believed me—and did not allow the offence of its correspondent to be repeated.[3]

As to Mr Kingsley, much less could I feel any resentment against him when he was accidentally the instrument in the good Providence of God, by whom I had an opportunity given me, which otherwise I should not have had, of vindicating my character and conduct in my Apologia. I heard too a few years back from a friend that she chanced to go into Chester Cathedral, and found Mr K. preaching about me kindly though of course with criticisms on me.[4] And it has rejoiced me to observe lately that he was defending the Athanasian Creed, and, as it seemed to me, in his views generally nearing the Catholic view of things—I have always hoped that by good luck I might meet him, feeling sure there would be no embarrassment on my part, and I said Mass for his soul, as soon as I heard of his death.

Most truly Yours John H Newman

[1] Charles Kingsley, who died in his fifty-sixth year, was buried on 28 January at Eversley, where he was rector. The following Sunday, 31 January, Sir William Cope, who was patron of the living and himself a clergyman, preached a memorial sermon, of which he sent Newman a copy.

[2] cf. letter of 28 June 1862 to the editor of the *Globe*.

[3] See letter of 12 September 1872 (*L.D.* xxvi, pp. 166–8).

[4] See letter of 27 January 1875 to Geraldine Fitzgerald (*L.D.* xxvii, pp. 206–7).

To Cardinal Manning

The Oratory Easter Eve [27 March] 1875

My dear Lord Cardinal

I beg you to accept the congratulations of myself and this house on your recent promotion.[1] It must be a great gratification to you to receive this mark of the confidence placed in you by the Sovereign Pontiff. And it must be a source of true pleasure to your brother and his family and your other relatives and friends.

And as regards the Protestant world it is striking to observe the contrast between the circumstances under which you return invested with this special dignity and the feelings which were excited in England twenty five years ago on occasion of the like elevation of your predecessor, Cardinal Wiseman.

That the temporal honours, to which you have attained may be the token and earnest of those which come from God above, is the sincere prayer of

Yours affectly John H Newman

His Eminence the Archbp of Westminster

[1] Manning was created Cardinal on 15 March. When he returned to London on 5 April, Newman's was the first letter he answered, expressing his 'affectionate thanks' and referring to 'the memories of many happy days, and of the many benefits I owe to you'.

To Lord Blachford

The Oratory Ap. 11. 1875

My dear Blachford

I sent you my P.S. mainly to elicit a letter from you, not on its subject, but for the sake of a letter.[1] As to my Pamphlet, what you say of its success agrees, to my surprise as well as my pleasure, to what I hear from others. What surprises me most is its success among my own people. I had for a long time been urged by my friends to write—but I persisted in saying that I would not go out of my way to do so. When Gladstone wrote, I saw it was now or never, and I had so vivid an apprehension that I should get into a great trouble and rouse a great controversy around me, that I was most unwilling to take up my pen. I had made a compact with myself, that, if I did write, I would bring out my whole mind, and especially speak out on the subject of what I had in a private letter called a 'violent and aggressive faction'[2]—So that I wrote and printed, I may say, in much distress of mind. Yet nothing happened such as I had feared. For instance, Ward is unsaying in print some of his extravagances,[3] and a priest who with others has long looked at me with suspicion and is a good specimen of his class, writes to me 'I hope everybody will read it and re-read it. . . . I may also congratulate you that you have carried with you the Catholic mind of England, and made us feel but one pulse of Ultramontane sympathy beating in our body— May God give you length of days etc.'[4] In Ireland Cardinal Cullen spoke of me in the warmest terms in his Lent Pastoral, read in all the Churches of his Diocese, and my friend Dr Russell of Maynooth, who had been frightened at the possible effect of some of my pages, wrote to me, after being present at a great gathering of Bishops and priests from all parts of Ireland, on occasion of Archbishop Leahy's funeral, that I had nothing to fear, for there was but one unanimous voice there, and that was in my favour.

Of course as time goes on 'the clouds may return after the rain'[5]—but anyhow I have cause for great thankfulness—and I trust that now I may be allowed to die in peace. Old age is very cowardly—at least so I find it to be.

As to Canon Neville's passage, you must recollect what a strong thing it is to tell the party spirit, and the enthusiasm, and the sentiment unreasoning and untheological, of Catholics, that the Pope is *ever* to be disobeyed[6]—not to speak of the political partizans of his cause and the tyranny of newspaper Editors. To quote a Maynooth Professor who could say the Pope need not be obeyed in the critical case of an English war against him, that his command was to be resisted on *any* motive, for *any* reason, that this was the *rule* in such a case, was to possess a great ally, who would block any attack, any annoyance, which my words might have caused. Recollect the contract under which soldiers are bound, holds as soon as it is found to be lawful. And Canon Neville's argument secures its legality. Nor did I at all mean, as the Saturday thinks to *withdraw* my *own* ground.

The Jesuits, as usual, have stood my friends. One of them only, Fr Botalla, without the sympathy of the body, has made in a Liverpool Paper, five charges against me—but we have stood to our guns, and all but silenced him.

I don't forget you have done all in your power to get me to Devonshire, but an old man is a coward in physical action as well as in moral; I am afraid of accidents. During that week last September when I was away from home I had or nearly had two. In the dark, getting out of the rail carriage my foot dived into the space between the carriage and the platform—and on getting out of a chaise I fell and barely escaped its wheel. And besides, why I don't know, I am always well at home, scarcely ever when I leave it.

I am so grieved at what you say of your sister. She is before me as she was near forty years ago, when I last saw her. What a dream life is!⁷

This is bad weather for your bronchitis, if you are not better off in that article (the weather) just now than we are. I had a touch in January.

Ever yours affly John H. Newman

¹ Newman had sent Lord Blachford the fourth edition of *A Letter to the Duke of Norfolk* which included the postscript. Lord Blachford replied on 9 April, 'The pamphlet seems to have been a great success. And I hope matters are resting a good deal where you have placed them—at least among Anglicans.'

² Letter of 28 January 1870 to Ullathorne.

³ Ward now allowed Newman's views on the Syllabus and on the extent of infallibility.

⁴ Letter of 7 April from Canon Thomas Longman, who was living at Bishop's House, Birmingham.

⁵ *Ecclesiastes* 12:2.

⁶ Lord Blachford wrote: 'On one point I do not know that you mend matters much. I would rather have you as a soldier than Canon Neville, who, as I infer, would in the case he puts, think himself bound to run away the moment he could do so without "grave inconvenience" to himself—à fortiori if the inconvenience was in standing fast.' In his *Letter*, Newman had stated that if in a war he could not see to be unjust, the Pope were to order all Catholics to leave the army, he would not obey him (see *Diff.* II, p. 242). In his postcript he supported this with a quotation from Canon Henry Neville, Professor of Theology at Maynooth from 1852 until 1869, who said, 'It is a trite principle, that mere ecclesiastical laws do not bind, when there would be a very grave inconvenience in their observance' (*Diff.* II, p. 358).

⁷ Newman stayed with Frederic Rogers and his sisters at Blackheath in July 1836.

To Miss M. R. Giberne

The Ravenhurst May 22. 1875

My dear Sister Pia,

You must not be alarmed that we have had a great fright about Fr Ambrose. He had a sort of sunstroke; and it brought on a kind of fever. We knew you always prayed for him, and God knew your intention, and would direct your prayers according to dear A's need.

So, while things were uncertain, we thought we should be needlessly making you anxious, by writing. Now I trust our suspense is over—of course he will have a long illness, but the danger I trust is over. At least our Doctor believes he will recover.

Of course you may fancy what a trial [it] is to me

I hope you will give me a good account of yourself.

Let me tell you in confidence, that my nephew John [Mozley] is in that state of mind, that he may be slowly led on into the Church—or may give up the thought of it once for all

Ever Yours affly John H Newman

To Miss M. R. Giberne

The Ravenhurst May 25. 1875

My dear S. Pia

I little thought when I wrote to you a day or two ago, what my news was to be to you as now.

Dear Ambrose has been taken away from us—by exhaustion. Last night at 11.15 he fainted away and died—Every thing is pleasant we have to tell—but I am too much overcome to write more

Ever Yrs affly John H Newman

To Lord Blachford

The Oratory. May 31. 1875

My dear Blachford

I cannot use many words, but I quite understand the kind affectionateness of your letter just come. I answer it first of the large collection of letters which keen sympathy with me and deep sorrow for their loss in Ambrose St John have caused so many friends to write of [sic] me. I cannot wonder that, after he has been given me for so long a time as 32 years, he should be taken from me. Sometimes I have thought that like my Patron Saint, St John I am destined to survive all my friends.

From the first he loved me with an intensity of love, which was unaccountable. At Rome 28 years ago he was always so working for and relieving me of all trouble, that being young and Saxon looking, the Romans called him my Angel Guardian. As far as this world was concerned I was his first and last. He has not intermitted this love for an hour up to his last breath. At the beginning of his illness he showed in various ways that he was thinking of and for me. That illness, which threatened permanent loss of reason, which, thank God, he has escaped, arose from his over-work in translating Fessler, which he did for me to back up my letter to the Duke of Norfolk. I had no suspicion of this overwork of course, but W N. [Neville] reminds me, that, at that time, startled at the great and unexpected success of my Pamphlet, I said to him, 'We shall have some great penance to balance this good fortune.'

There was on April 28 a special High Mass at the Passionists two miles from this. He thought he ought to be there, and walked in a scorching sun to be there on time. He got a sort of stroke. He never was himself afterwards. A brain fever came on— after the crisis, the doctor said he was recovering—he got better every day—we all saw this. On his last morning he parted with great impressiveness from an old friend, once one of our lay brothers, who had been with him through the night.[1] The latter tells us, that he had in former years watched, while with us, before the Blessed Sacrament, but he had never felt our Lord so near him, as during that night. He says that his (A's) face was so beautiful; both W. N. and myself had noticed that at different times and his eyes, when he looked straight at us, were brilliant as jewels.— It was the *expression*, which was so sweet, tender, and beseeching. When his friend left him in the morning, Ambrose smiled on him and kissed his forehead, as if he was taking leave of him. Mind, we all of us, thought him getting better every day. When the doctor came, he said the improvement was far beyond his expectation. He said 'From this time he knows all you say to him,' though, alas he could not speak. I have not time to go through that day, when we were so jubilant. In the course of it, when he was sitting on the side of his bed, he got hold of me and threw his arm over my shoulder and brought me to him so closely, that I said in joke 'He will give me a stiff neck'. So he held me for some minutes, I at length releasing myself from not understanding, as *he* did, why he so clung to me. Then he got hold of my hand and clasped it so tightly as really to frighten me, for he had done so once before when he was not himself. I had to get one of the others present to unlock his fingers, ah! little thinking what he meant. At 7 p.m. when I rose to go, and said 'Goodbye, I shall find you much better tomorrow', he smiled on me with an expression which I could not and cannot understand. It was sweet and sad and perhaps perplexed, but I cannot interpret it. But it was our parting. W. N. says he called me back as I was leaving the room, but I do not recollect it.

About midnight I was awakened at the Oratory, with a loud rapping at the door, and the tidings that a great change had taken place in him. We hurried off at once, but he had died almost as soon as the messenger started. He had been placed or rather had placed himself with great deliberation and self-respect in his bed—they had tucked him up, and William N. was just going to give him some arrowroot when he rose upon his elbow, fell back and died.

I dare say Church and Copeland, and Lord Coleridge will like to see this—will you let them.[2]

Ever yours affectionately John H. Newman

---

[1] Thomas Godwin.

[2] Lord Blachford sent this letter in addition to Newman's sister Mrs John Mozley, and to Bloxam.

To Emily Bowles

The Oratory June 3. 1875

My dear Child

Don't be surprised that I have written to some others before you—this is because I love you so much and trust you so well, that I have wanted to send you a longer letter than I could now. But I send a few lines.

I wanted to have written to your brother[1] to tell him, but I am overpowered with letters, most kind to me, and written as a relief to sorrow. I cannot bear not to answer them—but they are between 80 and 90

Ever Yours affly John H Newman

[1] Frederick Bowles, formerly an Oratorian.

To Miss M. R. Giberne

The Oratory Jun. 4. 1875

My dear Sister M. Pia

Great as our trial is, yours in some respects is greater. You indeed have not lost as we have a face and a voice always present—but then you have no partner nor confidant in your sorrow, and have no relief as having no outlet of it. This feeling of solitariness must be very oppressive—especially the very fact of *one* English friend being taken away, seems almost a commencement of the operation of that awful law which sooner or later must take us *all* away from this visible scene.

William is rather afraid you must be ill by your not writing—but I do not see that that is a sufficient reason for his thinking so. But any how write, if you have stamps.

This has come upon us as a great shock, but think how much worse it would have been, had he been subjected to a chronic derangement. As it was, his reason had returned enough, though he could not speak, for him to think, and he knew he was going, though we did not know it.

What a faithful friend he has been to me for 32 years! yet there are others as faithful. What a wonderful mercy it is to me that God has given me so many faithful friends! He has never left me without support at trying times. How much you did for me in the Achilli trial, (and at other times), and I have never thanked you, as I ought to have done. This sometimes oppresses me, as if I was very ungrateful. You truly say that you have been [seen?] my beginning, middle, and end. Since his death, I have been reproaching myself for not expressing to *him* how much I felt *his* love—and I write this lest I should feel the same about you, should it be God's will that I should outlive you. I have above mentioned the Achilli matter, but that is only one specimen of the devotion, which by word and deed and prayer, you have been continually showing towards me most unworthy. I hope I don't write too small for your eyes

Ever Yrs affly John H Newman

To Miss Mary Holmes

The Oratory June 13. 1875

My dear Miss Holmes

I thank you heartily for your sympathetic letter. This is the greatest affliction I have had in my life, and so sudden. Pray for him and for me.

Yours affectly John H Newman

To Lady Henry Kerr

The Oratory June 18. 1875

My dear Lady Henry

Thank you for your affectionate letter, and your and Lord Henry's most kind sympathy.

I praise God for having given me for 32 years not merely an affectionate friend, but a help and stay such as a guardian from above might be, as making my path easy to me in difficulties, and cheering me by his sunny presence, as Raphael took the weight upon him of Tobias. I cannot think how I could have done anything without him, and, as knowing how timorous and unready I am, therefore doubtless God gave him to me. Just when all friends Protestant and Converts were removed from me, and I had to stand alone, he came to me as Ruth to Naomi. How I should ever in 1846 have gone to Oscott and then to Rome—how I should have negociated with the authorities there about an English Oratory, how I should have journeyed to and fro, without him, I do not know and cannot fancy. At that time being young and fair he was even called by the Romans my Angel Guardian—and so on, when I came to Birmingham, it was still he who acted for me. Never would he let me undertake any work without doing his part to save me the burden or the pain of it, as when he insisted on coming to Town with me on the day of your dear Brother's Requiem Mass.[1] And so to the last, while his senses remained to him, his last thoughts were on a plan for my comfort; and, when he had lost them, he still knew *me* and flung his arms about my neck, and except one day when his fever was at its height, he obeyed whatever I ordered him, and on the last day, when his senses were restored to him though he could not speak, again flung his arms over my neck and drew me tightly to him, he knowing he was near death, though we were exulting in the prospect of his recovery.

As I have said, from the first, he knew he was to die. He not only gave me his will, but dictated to [me] memoranda connected with it, made over to me his account in the Bank, showed me his private drawers, went through to me the history of his whole life, expressed his hope that during his whole priestly life he had not committed one mortal sin, and gave me his crucifix, blessed by the Pope, which he had brought from Rome in 1847.

We, however, though fully aware how serious his illness was, did not think it would terminate in death and our experienced physicians assured us again and again that of sudden death there was no chance at all.

We were told he would be much better when they came to see him next, but at 11 o'clock at night he suddenly fell back and died.

Yours affectly in Xt John H Newman

---

[1] On 5 May 1873, for Hope-Scott's funeral.

To Isy Froude

Rednall July 28. 1875

My dear Isy

I have owed you a letter a long time, and when you write to me, shall want you to tell me a good deal about you all, especially about your own health. This you must not forget, if you find I have not answered your two questions as you wish them to be answered, and have need to say to me more upon them.

I am not sure that you apprehend my answer to your first which was, I think, to this effect. 'Did not the Pope exert his infallible voice in early times? but if so, must he not have known himself infallible, and did he?' I think I answered thus—He never acted by himself—he acted in General Council, or in Roman Council, or with the concurrence or co-operation of some local Council, or with his own counsellors and theologians, never by himself—nor to this day has he acted by himself—Now in cases of this kind, the question always arises, what was, and in what lay, the *essence* of the act—for instance, the Holy Eucharist is a *sacrifice*—but to this day it is an open question, *what* is the act of sacrifice, what is the *constituting* act, which *is* the sacrifice. The common opinion is that the act of consecration is the act of sacrifice—but Bellarmine, I think, held that it is the Priests communion—While another opinion is that the whole action from the consecration to the communion is sacrificial. I believe also it is allowable to consider that it cannot be determined, but that the whole canon, must be viewed as one indivisable act, (per modum unius is the theological phrase) and that we *cannot* analyze it, as schoolmen wish to do.

The condemnation of Nestorius illustrates what I would say—his doctrine is first condemned by the Alexandrians—then by his own people of Syria—then the Pope sends round to the principal sees of Christendom who do the same—Upon this the Pope sends him notice he must recant within ten days or he will excommunicate him— After this the General Council is called and his condemnation passed—on which the Emperor banishes him. Now where in what lay the infallible voice? if they had been asked, I suppose they could not have told—viz whether it lay in the whole process as being the result of it, or in the Council or in the Pope, or again, taking the Pope by himself, while they would understand that an infallible decision followed on his voice. Still they would not be able to say whether he spoke by his own intrinsic absolute authority, or as the voice and organ of the whole Church, who spoke through him.

This too must be considered—that the *infallibility* of the Church (or of the Pope) is, as far as I know, a novel phrase. The infallibility of the Church has never been defined as a dogma (except indirectly in the late Vatican Council). The form which the doctrine took was to say that the point in dispute, when once decided, was 'irreformable', it was settled once for all—it was part of the Catholic faith— Therefore attention was centred in the *thing* not in the person—and, though of course it could not be settled for good in one certain way, *unless* the parties settling it were infallible, this view of the subject did not prominently come before the Pope or the Bishops. This is what I have meant to say on your first question.

Your second, I think, was this:—'If the *Schola* Theologorum decides the meaning of a Pope or a Council's words, the Schola is infallible, not *they* or *he*'.

In answer to this I observe that there are no words, ever so clear, but require an interpretation, at least as to their extent. For instance, an inspired writer says that 'God is love'—but supposing a set of men so extend this as to conclude '*Therefore* there is no future punishment for bad men?' Some power then is needed to determine the general sense of authoritative words—to determine their direction, drift, limits, and comprehension, to hinder gross perversions. This power is virtually the *passive infallibility* of the whole body of the Catholic people. The active infallibility lies in the Pope and Bishops—the passive in the 'universitas' of the faithful. Hence the maxim 'Securus judicat orbis terrarum.' The body of the faithful never can misunderstand what the Church determines by the gift of its active infallibility. Here on the one hand I observe that a *local* sense of a doctrine, held in this or that country, is not a 'sensus universitatis'—and on the other hand the schola theologorum is one chief portion of that universitas—and it acts with great force both in correcting popular misapprehensions and narrow views of the teaching of the active infallibilitas, and, by the intellectual investigations and disputes which are its very life, it keeps the distinction clear between theological truth and theological opinion, and is the antagonist of dogmatism. And while the differences of the School maintains the liberty of thought, the unanimity of its members is the safeguard of the infallible decisions of the Church and the champion of faith

I wonder whether I have made myself clear.

Ever Yours affly John H. Newman

Honorary Fellow of Trinity
and Cardinal (1876–81)

After Newman's controversy with Gladstone, there was a period of relative calm. More of his friends died, among them Frances Wootten who had been Matron of the Oratory School that Newman had founded and who had been a staunch ally in demanding times, and a little later Mary Holmes to whom he had been a wise spiritual guide, even when she was at her most exasperating. Letters at this time, informing other friends of deaths or reacting to the news, reveal the tenderness and affection he felt for those he was recalling. And in January 1878 Edward Caswall, his fellow Oratorian in Birmingham and renowned hymn writer and translator, also died. He was, Newman told Caswall's sister, 'one of my dearest friends, and is a great loss to us all, for he was loved far and wide round about the Oratory'.

During this time he was continuing to work on the uniform edition of his writings and in 1877 he produced a piece as discreet as it has been influential. In preparing for republication his *Lectures on the Prophetical Office*, the book that had expounded his position as an Anglican, he decided to add, besides a range of qualifying footnotes, an extended Preface in which he spoke of the priestly and political offices in the Church, as well as the prophetical, and of the relationship between them. He was in effect writing a reply to his former self. He drew out the system of checks and balances that taken together these three offices create. He was not the first to speak of this Triple Office in the Church, but what he wrote has since that time often been quoted, adopted, and developed by others.

Then before the year had ended Newman received a letter from Samuel Wayte, President of Trinity College, Oxford, where he had been an undergraduate, inviting him to become the first Honorary Fellow of the College. He could not have been more pleased. He recognized the compliment that was being paid him and was eager to accept. However, he felt he needed to consult the other members of his community before doing so and he wanted as well to receive his bishop's permission and ask his advice: he did not wish his acceptance of the honour to appear inconsistent, given his lifelong resistance to non-religious education. He was also anxious at his age not to be incurring further duties. When these possible difficulties melted away, he wrote to accept 'with a full heart an honour which is as great a surprise to me as it is a pleasure'. So after thirty-two years he went back to Oxford in February 1878, called on Pusey at Christ Church, and visited Keble College. He returned home to Birmingham delighted and to show his gratitude, as he had nothing else, dedicated the new edition of his *Essay on Development* to Wayte, who received the gesture graciously.

What happened next was even more unexpected than the Fellowship. He became aware of a startling rumour that the new Pope, Leo XIII, wanted to make him a Cardinal. He was dismissive of the notion. Nevertheless it persisted. The Catholic laity, led by the Duke of Norfolk, wished to have his contribution to the Catholic Church in England recognized and to see him honoured so that suggestions that he was only half a Catholic and his writings untrustworthy would be demolished. A Cardinal's hat seemed the ideal way to achieve that end.

Months passed. When Newman was finally approached by his bishop in February 1879 to see whether he would accept the honour, he was grateful, but also uncertain how to respond. It was very rare for a cardinal who was not a diocesan bishop to live away from Rome. He was 78 and felt he could not move from his Oratory, but he did not wish to appear to be negotiating the terms of his acceptance with the Pope. Bishop Ullathorne assured him that residence in Rome would not be the Pope's intention and suggested a way to proceed. He advised Newman to write a letter to him as his bishop, expressing his gratitude for the honour, but explaining his reluctance to leave Birmingham, while Ullathorne would himself write a letter as well to accompany Newman's, so that there could be no misunderstanding, making clear Newman's acceptance, but also his desire to remain at the Oratory. These two letters were then entrusted to Cardinal Manning who was about to leave for Rome in any case. Manning, however, did not enclose Ullathorne's explanation, but only forwarded to Rome Newman's letter which, read on its own, could seem ambiguous and like a refusal of the honour. Perhaps that was what Manning hoped. Moreover, he told the Duke of Norfolk, even before Newman's letter could have reached Rome, that the honour had been declined. When that became known, there was uproar. Letters shuttled back and forth between Newman, Ullathorne, Manning, Norfolk, and others. When Manning realized he had miscalculated, he hurried to see the Pope and put the matter right. The formal news of Newman's elevation was then sent to Birmingham and he was created a Cardinal in Rome on 15 May. There was great rejoicing, but for most of the time he was there he was unwell and, because of his ill-health, he had a trying journey back to England. Bad weather in France even made it impossible for him to visit his old friend, Maria Giberne, now Sister Pia, at her convent in Autun, as he had hoped. They were never to meet again.

Before leaving for Rome and in spite of the preparations that had to be made, Newman wrote a valuable letter to William Froude on faith and reason, but never sent it, as Froude died in South Africa on 4 May. Although he was ageing, he remained active. At this time he was re-arranging his translation of his *Select Treatises of St Athanasius* for inclusion in the uniform edition of his writings. They appeared in 1881.

And the hammer blows of deaths kept falling. On Christmas Day in 1879 Jemima died. On the Epiphany he wrote to Anne Mozley, 'What I miss and shall miss Jemima in is this—she alone, with me, had a memory of dates . . . e.g. yesterday was the anniversary of [their sister] Mary's death—my mind turned at once to Jemima, but she was away.'

11

Honorary Fellow of Trinity and Cardinal (1876–81)

To R. W. Church

The Oratory Jany 11. 1876

My dear Dean

Dear Mrs Wootten was taken from us on Sunday night. She had been ill for some months, but her mind was her own to the last—and through last term, tho' confined to her sofa, she saw our school boys as usual, so that they would not believe that she was on her death bed. She died most peaceably so that we did not know when her end came. Nothing can make up to us for her loss—except the prayers she gives us in heaven

I hear that you and the Archbishop of York (to say nothing of Cardinal Manning etc) are going to let Professor Huxley read in your presence an argument in refutation of our Lord's Resurrection. How can this possibly come under the scope of a Metaphysical Society? I thank my stars that, when asked to accept the honour of belonging to it, I declined. Aren't you in a false position? Perhaps it is a ruse of the Cardinal to bring the Professor into the clutches of the Inquisition.

How does Mary [Church] go on?

Ever Yours affly John H Newman

To Miss Mary Holmes

The Oratory June 3. 1876

My dear Miss Holmes,

I wish your letters gave a better account of yourself—and the cold wind still continues. I have not had, thank God, one cold through the winter—and tomorrow evening am going to London for a day or two, for Lady Coleridge to finish her likeness of me.

Talking of Trollope, I don't think it fair of him to be charging 5/ a part for his scanty new novel.[1] You may say that George Eliot (for what I know) does the same—but George Eliot may do what he likes for me, who am no great admirer of his, whereas Trollope's writings are the best of their kind

Yours affectly John H Newman

---

[1] *The American Senator* was serialised in *Temple Bar* from May 1876 to July 1877.

483

To J. R. Bloxam

The Oratory March 8. 1877

My dear Bloxam

What a shame you should have allowed such a suspicion to come into your mind. I never was more astonished than when I found how it was. If you knew what a burden of letters I have upon me, and how it wearies my hand to write, you would find a better reason for my not writing. I always recollect September 22 and you are kind enough to write upon it to me—but I never have been punctual in answering you

Now don't do it again[1]

Ever Yrs affly John H Newman

[1] Bloxam evidently misinterpreted Newman's failure to answer his letter of 19 September 1876. Littlemore Church was consecrated on 22 September 1836.

To Isy Froude

The Oratory March 12 1877

My dear Isy

While I am lamenting I have not answered your and Mama's letters, your second most amusing as well as serious letter comes. I write a line that you may not think me for certain a stick or a stone—and to say I will write to you in a few days Tell Mama this

Ever Yours affly John H Newman

To W. J. Copeland

The Oratory Easter Day 1877

My dear Copeland

Thank you for your welcome congratulations on the Season, which I heartily return. I inclose a bit of a letter which I find I have kept from Miss Gooch. I had destroyed the rest upon receiving it as being too private to keep Let me have it back.

I don't like to hear of your rheumatism, but the spring will carry it off

I am glad Rivington is consulting you. If you will select your fifty, I will show them to some Catholic friend. I don't want any notice inserted, to signify that they have passed a censorship—and not a word is to be altered—So I don't think they will be less acceptable than before to Church of England readers[1]

Edward has changed his room today, and thank you for your inquiries. This is a great step, but I can't forget that the twice when he almost died have been sudden attacks

Ever Yours affectly John H Newman

[1] Copeland wrote on 31 March that Rivington had consulted him about the selection from *Parochial and Plain Sermons*.

To J. R. Bloxam

The Oratory July 24. 1877

My dear Bloxam

I have never been to Oxford since I left it in February 1846. I went to Littlemore from Abingdon with Father Ambrose St John on June 16, 1868. I saw many of my old parishioners, the Crawleys, and the then incumbent. Of course, when I saw my Mother's monument, I could but cry.

Yours affectly John H Newman

To Arthur Sandes Griffin

Rednall Octr 4. 1877

Dear Canon Griffin

Your telegram followed me here.[1] It was very kind and considerate in you to send it, and I thank you for it—but it was very heavy tidings. I owe very much to dear Bishop Moriarty—now for thirty years he has been a constant and true friend to me—and the news was so great a surprise. I had not heard of his having any such seizure before, and by his working on on Saturday it would seem as if he had no suspicion or dread of the complaint which in fact carried him off. I have said Mass for his soul, and hope to do so again tomorrow

Yours very faithfully John H Newman

The Very Revd Canon Griffin

[1] It announced the death of Bishop Moriarty on 1 October and explained that in spite of being unwell on 29 September he had continued to work until struck by paralysis. Griffin had been the bishop's secretary for many years.

To W. J. Copeland

The Oratory Oct 22. 1877

My dear Copeland

I have plucked some of the Sermons you have selected, not many—and marked others as doubtful.

Among the doubtful, are some which I shall try to spare, as I shall explain.

1. Not a few have only this difficulty, viz 'Lord's Supper' for Eucharist—or 'Sacrament of communion'—communion is *not* a sacrament—or 'Comforter' for Paraclete. Now, since the words Eucharist and Paraclete *are* found in the Sermons, I wonder whether Rivington would consent to this correction in the text, it being noticed in the Preface

2. The other difficulty is a bit of heresy or what is proximum hæresi, on the subject of original sin. I thought at first it simply plucked the sermons which contained it—(as I have said in the accompanying paper) but on further thought

and consulting theologians I think all may be explained and allowed but one and that in a good sermon, viz Volume V, Sermon 9. This, I fear must be plucked

The received doctrine with us is that original sin, as such, is a privation, and does not in itself incur eternal damnation (else, unbaptised infants would incur that suffering) but I have asserted what in the notes I send you I say is equivalent to this tenet.[1] And I thought it had been positively condemned by the Church, but, I suppose, out of reverence for St Augustine, it has been spared. It is contained in the Anglican 9th Article. I have spoken of original sin as an infection of our nature, as *sin in the baptized* after baptism tho' baptism really washes it away—(This, I suspect, goes *beyond* St Augustine) and as meriting eternal damnation

vid	Vol ii Serm 19	p 223	
	vol v Serm 4	p 52	these *may* be allowed
	„ „ 7	p 90	
	„ „ 9	p 120	this cannot be whitewashed[2]
	vol vi Serm 6	p 76	this may be allowed

But, though I might let some of these pass, as involving an open question, I could not give my sanction to it. I could not *profess* St Austin's tenet—and therefore I have come to the conclusion that I had better not put any Preface with my name to it. I think this extreme view, cursorily expressed in the Sermons, is not enough to hinder Catholics reading them, but, in a *preface* such as I contemplated, I should commit myself to saying that there was nothing uncatholic in the Sermons selected, but I do consider this tenet uncatholic in spite of St Augustine. Will Rivington accept my withdrawal of the Preface as a compensation for the withdrawal of 'Lord's Supper' and 'Comforter'?

What I propose then is this. To say in the Title page 'Selection of Sermons from the eight Volumes of the Revd J H Newman arranged according to the course of the Christian year ⟨seasons⟩.'

Will you think over this?

Ever yrs affly John H Newman

[1] These are the notes which Newman wrote on 15 October and enclosed with this present letter.

[2] Newman was criticizing his reference to the power of sin that remains in spite of baptism and called his words 'the worst bit of heresy I have as yet met—"the body of death which infects us, . . . sins because it *is* sin"'. The sermon was nevertheless included in the volume *Selection from the Parochial and Plain Sermons of John Henry Newman* (London, 1895), p. 99.

To Henry James Coleridge

The Oratory Nov 5. 1877

My dear Fr Coleridge

I write to thank you for the favorable critique, which you have admitted in the Month, of my Preface in the Via Media.[1] And I am pleased that you *could* admit it. I mean, I have been so bullied all through life for what I have written, that I never publish without forebodings of evil. And, though I know that, besides the necessary differences of opinion, which ever will be between man and man, there always must be that in what I write which really deserves criticism, yet I am more pleased when people are kind to me than when they are unjust.

What, you will ask, has come of the project of a Catholic Selection of my sermons? Well, I fear it has broken down, though from very slight causes. E.g. I may generally indeed have spoken of the 'Eucharist' yet perhaps in one Sermon, desirable, and not otherwise objectionable, may have once, towards the end, when all danger was passed, as it appeared, used the 'Lord's Supper—' etc etc

So I suppose the Selection will be all but Catholic—but without any imprimatur.

Have you any thing to say in the way of criticism on my Essay on Development of doctrine, which is now going to the Printers?

Yours affectly John H Newman

[1] The *Month* (Nov. 1877), pp. 372–3, called the Preface 'one of the most important papers which have proceeded from the pen of its illustrious author for many years', and explained that it was 'intended to meet many difficulties... with regard to alleged inconsistencies between doctrine and practice, as to the acts of Popes in the government of the Church, the toleration of excesses in devotion... the policy of the Holy See in temporal matters, and the like'.

To Samuel William Wayte

Dec 15. 1877

Private

My dear President

No compliment could I feel more intimately, or desire more eagerly at once to seize and appropriate than that which is the subject of your letter just received.[1] Trinity College is ever, and ever has been, in my habitual thoughts. Views of its buildings are at my bed side and bring before me morning and evening my undergraduate days, and those good friends, nearly all now gone, whom I loved so much during them, and my love of whom has since their death ever kept me in affectionate loyalty to the college itself. But I am obliged to reflect before I accept the honour you wish to do me and I understand from the wording of your letter that you have written to me as a first step for the purpose of enabling me to do so.

First I suppose I should have to replace my name on the University Books—also I take for granted that I should [have] a right to do so, if I pleased, or what is equivalent to a right.

Next I could not accept the honour without leave from my own dear brothers here, the Fathers of the Oratory. Our Rule forbids 'ne nostrorum aliquis sese obliget aut dedat... Seminariis, Collegiis, Congregationibus, Societatibus, aut aliis Universitatibus;' and, when I went to Ireland as Rector of the Catholic University twenty five years ago, it was upon a written leave from the Pope, and that only for three years. Our Oratory here then must have a voice in the matter, though I don't at all myself consider that an Honorary Fellowship is contemplated in the Rule, as one of the forbidden offices.

Further I have for years and years been most keenly opposed to the abolition of religious profession in places of education, and have not long ago declined any formal connexion with Mgr Capel's College on the ground of its refusal to engage to keep clear of the London University.[2] I can be no judge myself whether it would or would not be in consequence inconsistent in me to take the step of replacing my name on the books of the University, and must take advice before I do so.

Again, such advice should most suitably come from my own Bishop, Dr Ullathorne, not that in this matter I am under his jurisdiction, but as of a friend with whom I have acted for near thirty years, and who has stood by me on various occasions. He has lately in a pastoral spoken against Catholics writing in the Magazines open to contributions of unbelievers, and has thereby stopped my writing in them; and I cannot tell whether he would feel strong enough on the point to express an opinion against your offer.[3]

Then lastly, I ought to ask you if an Honorary Fellowship involves any duties tho' I don't suppose it does. You know I am close on 77, and, though wonderfully well, I am not equal to going from home, but am at once run off the rails, cannot sleep, cannot talk or otherwise exert myself, and feel myself only a burden to others on whom I am thrown. This may seem a little thing, but it is not so, when one feels a desire to show gratitude to those who have been extraordinarily kind to one[4]

I am &c J H N

[1] Wayte wrote on 14 December, inviting Newman to become an Honorary Fellow of Trinity. He was the first person to receive such an offer since the power to elect honorary fellows had been established in 1857.

[2] Letter of 24 November 1873 to Archbishop Manning.

[3] Ullathorne's pastoral letter, read in the churches of his diocese on 25 November, was a denunciation of the attacks of unbelievers on the Christian faith and Church. When Newman wrote to him, however, Ullathorne congratulated him on the honour being paid to him (*L.D.* XXVIII, p. 284 n.1).

[4] Wayte replied on 17 December 1877, 'It will at all events be very pleasing to the Fellows of the College to know that whatever may be your final determination you feel so much good will towards our society. I think I may venture to state to the Fellows so much of the purport of your letter as will enable them to see that in making the proposal which was so gratifying to themselves they have not done anything distasteful to your feelings'. Wayte added that Newman could replace his name on the University books, but that this was not necessary.

To Samuel William Wayte

The Oratory, Birmingham Decr 20. 1877

My dear President,

It has been a singular gratification to me to receive your letter, informing me of the proposal of your Society to make me an Honorary Fellow of Trinity, it being the first instance of their exercising the power given them of making such an appointment, and I accept with a full heart an honour which is as great a surprise to me as it is a pleasure.

It is indeed a most strange good fortune, after a long sixty years and more, to become again a freshman of my first and dear College.

This, however, at least I can say in my behalf, that, if a lifelong affection for Trinity is a reason for my being singled out for such a kindness, I am pleased to think that I am not altogether unworthy of being made the subject of it.

Begging you to convey this answer to your Fellows I am, My dear President,

Most truly Yours John H Newman[1]

The Revd the President of Trinity.

[1] Wayte replied on 22 December: 'I have received this morning your letter of the 20th, and I shall lose no time in announcing to the Fellows the fact, which will please them so much, that your name will be again connected with the College.'

To Lord Emly

The Oratory Dec 26. 1877

My dear Emly

All best blessings for the Sacred Season on you and yours—but I think I sent you my Christmas greetings in my last.

Now I write to tell you, what you will be glad to hear that my dear old first College, Trinity, has made me an honorary Fellow of their Society. My affections have ever been with my first College, though I have more and more intimately personal Oriel friends. There was too much painful at Oriel, to allow of its remembrances being sweet and dear;—hence I rejoice that it is Trinity, not Oriel, that has reclaimed me.[1] But College feeling and College loyalty will become things of the past, if the present influences go on to triumph at Oxford, which aim at mashing up into one great pudding all that is individual.

Ever Yours affectly John H Newman

[1] In his letter of congratulation on 22 December Copeland wrote: 'How is it that Trinity has been beforehand with Oriel, of which I heard a whisper of the sort some year or two ago?'

To Miss Caswall

The Oratory Jany 2. 1878

Dear Miss Caswall

You may guess why I write to you.

And I cannot doubt, so long an illness has prepared you for what I have to tell you about your dear Brother.

He suddenly fell off about seven this evening, and was taken from us, in a quarter of an hour, so peacefully, that we could not fix the time when he went. Nor did we pronounce that he was no more, though he had gone for some minutes, till the medical man, Dr Jordan, who has been unremitting in his attentions, came and assured us that we are not mistaken.

He seems to have felt that he was drawing to his end, for in the middle of the day he began to express his sense of God's mercies in having been so tender and careful of him all through his life, and having kept him from pain during his last illness.

He was one of my dearest friends, and is a great loss to us all, for he was loved far and wide round about the Oratory.

That God may comfort you and your Sister under this great grief is the sincere prayer of

Yours most truly John H Newman

To Anne Mozley

The Oratory Febr. 13. 1878

My dear Anne Mozley,

Thank you for your letter.[1] I can't deny that I am very anxious about Jemima. Any illness at her age is serious—and it is impossible that such pain as she has, and such compulsory abstinence, should not tell upon her. I should never be surprised, if her ailments took some definite and pronounced shape, or if she suddenly fell off in strength.

This is a wonderful time for deaths. You may have seen by the Papers that Pickering, my publisher, is just dead.[2] He was very useful to me—and I ever found him upright and religious. He lost his wife last December year—two children in the next month. This quite upset him. He declined all through the year 1877, took to his bed at the end of it and now is dead, leaving some young children. A tragedy not yet ended is going on among the Froudes—but don't mention it, except as far as it relates to accomplished facts, for no one likes to have sorrowful events anticipated. Hurrell Froude, my godson, married a very nice girl, George Ryder's daughter. He took her to India; last summer she suddenly died, her husband being a fortnight's journey off, and mahometan servants (very kind in their way) all around her, leaving two children, one of whom has died since. His sister went out to India to take care of him and the remaining child. Meanwhile grief at loss of her daughter-in-law is killing dear Mrs Froude, my great friend, and the brother and sister are abruptly called back to England, in order, as it would appear, to attend the deathbed of their mother. Of course what is only in prospect should not be talked about.

Then Henry Wilberforce's widow has died suddenly—and William his elder brother has had another stroke.

Amid this whirl of sad events I have to go to Oxford to inaugurate my second entrance at Trinity

I am glad you have got James's papers. You will be able to do full justice to them, and it must be a very grateful occupation, tho' all legacies are sorrowful[3]

Yours affly John H Newman

P.S. As James's name is mentioned in the inclosed, I send it to you, wishing to have it back. It is the last I received from dear Mary Wilberforce. She died January 27, 16 days after.[4]

---

[1] On 11 February when sending news of Jemima's health, Anne Mozley liked 'the *excuse* of sending my report to keep up the privilege of now and then writing a few lines. Many things in these days make me anxious to keep hold of all ties that are left.'

[2] B. M. Pickering died on 8 February.

[3] Anne Mozley edited *Letters of the Rev. J. B. Mozley* (London, 1885).

[4] In her letter of 11 January Mary Wilberforce wrote of James Mozley, 'Some friends of ours became acquainted with him at Malvern, and were much struck with his goodness'.

To Helen And Mary Church

The Oratory February 21. 1878

My dear Helen and Mary,

How shall I best show kindness to you on your birthday?[1]

It is by wishing and praying that year by year you may grow more and more in God's favour and in inward peace,—in an equanimity and cheerfulness under all circumstances which is the fruit of faith, and a devotion which finds no duties difficult, for it is inspired by love.

This I do with all my heart, & am, My dear Children very affectionately yours,

John H. Newman

[1] Helen and Mary Church were twins, born in 1858.

To Mrs William Froude

The Oratory Mar. 4. 1878

My dear Mrs Froude,

My visit to Oxford has been very successful, tho' it was a trial both to my host and to me. I did a good deal in two days, tho' not near so much as there was to be done.

I have not much or any thing to say over what the Papers say of me.[1] Every one was abundantly kind, and consulted for my comfort in every way—and I was much drawn in kind feeling to the Fellows. I saw there my old Tutor, Short, in the same Rooms in which he had encouraged and rowed me as an Undergraduate, in which he had been my opportune bottle holder when I was standing at Oriel and much discouraged. That was 58 years ago. He is now almost blind and could not see me. He is 87, and has three Oxford friends older than himself.

I called on Pusey, and found him much older since I last saw him in 1865—as I suppose he found me.

And I went over Keble College—This is nearly all I did. Various friends came from London to see me—one from Durham—others from the country.[2] The weather was wet, and this alone was sufficient to keep me from seeing the new buildings (except Keble) but I have no expectation of their pleasing me.

My love to William and Eddy,[3] and trusting the weather suits you, I am

Ever Yours affectly John H Newman

[1] See *Apo.*, p. 390.

[2] Alfred Plummer came from Durham, and brought with him a letter from W. C. Lake, Dean of Durham, 'May I ask you to give him [Newman] (I may almost venture to say) my *tender* regards'.

[3] Robert Edmund Froude.

To Robert Whitty, S. J.

March 24. 1878

To Dr Whitty

Perhaps you have seen in the Papers a wild article about me in relation to the Holy Father.[1] I have reason to believe it was not Roman news but composed in London; and that in consequence of the action of some very kind friends and well-wishers of mine, persons known or unknown to me. But I trust nothing will come of it, I am far from making light of dignities, but under the example and shadow of St Philip, I may be allowed to decline them. They are much to be prized, both when they open on a man opportunities and channels of serving God, and again when they are a means of recommending ⟨sanctioning⟩ and rewarding his past attempts at service. Now I am too old to do any thing new, and wish only to have time to set my house in order before I go; so that honours would not be in my case any means of usefulness. And as to their being a sanction of my past attempts, it would be a more simple, easy, and to me acceptable act on the part of superiors, if I was fortunate enough to deserve and obtain a few lines such as I believe have been vouchsafed to the Universe newspaper and the Dublin Review, to the effect that my books ⟨writing⟩ had done service to the Catholic cause.

JHN

[1] Pope Pius IX had died on 7 February and been succeeded by Pope Leo XIII on 20 February. On 21 March the *Standard*, p. 5, had a report from its correspondent in Rome: 'Intelligence has reached this city that a report is being widely circulated in England to the effect that the Pope intends to present a Cardinal's hat to Dr. John Henry Newman. I am enabled to give a contradiction to this on high authority, and to state that no such idea has been hitherto entertained.' But the Duke of Norfolk and the Marquis of Ripon soon became active in this cause. See *L.D.* xxix, Appendix 1.

To William Ewart Gladstone

The Oratory April 26. 1878

My dear Mr Gladstone

I must write a few lines, however inadequate, to tell you of the gratification, as well as the surprise, with which I have read in to-day's Times your notice of me yesterday at Keble College.[1]

Not that I can think of appropriating myself all that you say of me—but, leaving that matter alone, I can thank you for it, and am reminded by it to pray, now I am so near my end, that, when at length it comes, my long account may not be found inconsistent with my profession and preaching

I am, My dear Mr Gladstone, Very sincerely Yours John H Newman

This of course requires no answer.[2]

[1] In a speech at the luncheon after the opening of the hall and library of Keble College on 25 April, Gladstone said, after referring to the Oxford Movement, Keble, and Pusey: 'But there is a name which, as

an academical name, is greater than either of those—I mean the name of Dr. Newman. (Cheers.) When the history of Oxford during that time comes to be written, the historian will have to record the extraordinary, the unexampled career of that distinguished man in the University. He will have to tell, as I believe, that Dr. Newman exercised for a period of about ten years after 1833 an amount of influence, of absorbing influence, over the highest intellects—over nearly the whole intellect, but certainly over the highest intellect of this University, for which perhaps, there is no parallel in the academical history of Europe, unless you go back to the twelfth century or to the University of Paris. We know how his influence was sustained by his extraordinary purity of character and the holiness of his life. (Cheers.) We know also the catastrophe—I cannot call it less—which followed. (Cheers.) We know that he who held the power in his hand found himself compelled by the action of conscience to carry his mind and gifts elsewhere', *The Times* (26 April), p. 6.

² Gladstone replied on 28 April from Hawarden, 'Your note supplies one of the instances rather rare in life—I have received thanks, where I rather felt myself to owe apology. What I said at Keble was meant for a piece of history faithfully rendered; but it is taking a liberty with the living, at any rate outside the world of politics, to use them for such a purpose, nor would I have done it but for the feeling that it was important to state the case fully, when there are so many inclined or tempted to misunderstand.'

To Anne Mozley

The Oratory July 6. 1878

My dear Anne Mozley

In answer to your letter of this morning, I will say that in my own opinion you will be hardly fair to your dear Brother's memory or to the cause of truth, if you do not publish or get published his review of my 'Development of doctrine.'¹ I have myself the fullest confidence in my argument—I have never doubted it—my faith in it has been rekindled by my recent perusal of it—I should really like a good answer given—by good I mean clever—as your brother's would be. I never heard of it ⟨his⟩—and, when I set about the new Edition, having heard Mr Archer Butler's spoken of, I sent for it,² but it was a deplorable disappointment—*that* I should not find your brother's, if at my age I found myself up to studying it. Mr Butler wrote amid the duties of a parish and in a Newspaper. How could it be worth any thing?— your brother's will be nothing of this kind.

I never have minded my friends writing against me—what I have complained of is their imputing motives, or bringing in other personalities. Your brother pained me, because in his first writings against me, he said what he never could have said without private knowledge of me, intimate conversations with me.³ Pusey pained me, for in print he attributed my conversion to 'oversensitiveness—' this is what in another connexion I have called 'poisoning the wells.'⁴ I don't think I have myself ever imputed motives—or at least my principle has been not to do so. As to my Volume, I don't doubt at all that so acute a mind as James's has found blots in it, or defects, or omissions—when I say I have confidence in it, and no fear, I am speaking of its substance.⁵

Tom [Mozley] said he never should have time to read my letters to him—so he sent me all in a heap. I have burned some—given him one or two back—sent you some and interleaved the rest with his letters to me. Of course I have kept no secrets.

My 'Selection' of Sermons (as Rivington knows, tho' he would not like it talked) is of such as, without alteration of text, are consistent with the doctrines of the Holy Roman Catholic Church

Just now I think I have *no* photograph

Yrs affly J H N

[1] This was J. B. Mozley's 'Newman on Development', *Christian Remembrancer* (January 1847), pp. 117–265.

[2] See letter to B. M. Pickering, 5 November 1877 (*L.D.* XXVIII, p. 64).

[3] See letters of 8 January 1846 to Ambrose St John and 27 January 1846 to Henry Wilberforce, on J. B. Mozley's article in the *Christian Remembrancer* (January 1846), pp. 167–218.

[4] See Pusey's letter to the *English Churchman* of 16 October 1845, reprinted in H. P. Liddon's *The Life of Edward Bouverie Pusey* (4 vols, London, 1893–7), II, pp. 460–3, after Newman had become a Catholic. Towards the beginning of it Pusey said, 'One cannot trust oneself to think, whether his keen sensitiveness to ill was not fitted for these troubled times.' In the first edition of *Apo.*, p. 22, Newman described Kingsley's method of disputation as the infusing by anticipation in the public mind of suspicion and distrust of everything he might say in reply, and called it '*poisoning the wells*'.

[5] Anne Mozley followed Newman's advice, and J. B. Mozley's *The Theory of Development: A Criticism of Dr. Newman's Essay on the Development of Christian Doctrine*, reprinted from the *Christian Remembrancer*, was published at once, London 1878.

To William Froude

The Oratory July 22. 1878

My dear William

You have sent me very heavy tidings, but your letter months ago prepared me. How long have I known you and her!—and what good faithful friends you have both been to me! May God be with her.[1]

Ever Yours affectly John H. Newman

[1] Mrs William Froude died at 7 p.m. on 24 July.

To Mrs Brackenbury

The Oratory Octr 2. 1878

Dear Mrs Brackenbury,

Your news was a great shock to me—the more so, because I felt I had not given to the accounts which Miss Holmes gave me of herself that weight which the event shows that I ought to have given.[1] I knew she suffered greatly, especially from shortness of breath—but I did not understand how serious her case was. Alas—I should have written to her oftener and interested myself more in her state of health, had I fancied she was so near death. I suppose she had not been at Church for a long while—and perhaps she had had no priest to see her.[2]

It is very kind in you writing to me, and I thank you much. Dear Miss Holmes has had a very hard life; and I have for a long course of years been anxious about the prospect which lay before her, when she got old. It is in this point of view, that I am led to thank God, while I grieve that He has taken her. She has had several good friends; you have done more for her than any; but she had no reason for wishing to live longer, and she had had a long time of illness, which was a long preparation for death And she used it most religiously. I mean to say Mass for her tomorrow morning, and so will Mr Neville, whom she knew.

Yours faithfully John H Newman

[1] Mary Holmes died on 1 October.
[2] In a letter of 4 October to John Henry Wynne, who was the priest in charge at Bournemouth where Mary Holmes died, Newman expressed his 'great relief to find she had been in such spiritually good hands' (*L.D.* XXVIII, p. 405).

To Isy Froude

The Oratory Novr 24. 1878.

My dear Isy

I ought to have acknowledged your welcome letters before this, but you will excuse me.

I am very glad of Papa's cruize—it is the very thing to do him good—but it must be forlorn for you two to be left alone.[1] If Mr Ryder is still on visit to you—pray say everything kind from me to him.

As to Eddy I meant to have written to him about Mr Mallock's article—which is very clever and very useful. The prodigious cockiness of certain philosophers deserves to be met with satire, and his is very effective. Ridicule is, not the test of truth quite, but the proper physic for pomposity and sublime self conceit, and, tho' parts of the Desert Island were too strong for me, e.g. the cruel attack upon the harmless curates, yet his various papers have done very good service.[2]

And this is all I have to say and so I conclude with assuring you that I am your ever affte

John H Newman

[1] William Froude was taken ill after his wife's death, and went on a cruise to South Africa. There he caught dysentery and died on 6 May 1879 at Simon's Town.
[2] W. H. Mallock's articles were collected to form *The New Paul and Virginia, or Positivism on an Island* (London, 1878).

To Edward Hayes Plumptre

The Oratory. Dec.9.1878

My dear Dr Plumptre

Thank you for your letter, which I feel to be very kind.[1] Certainly there are very few men whose life has been tried by such afflictions, I mean their true life, their domestic, as your Archbishop. That the great calamity of his son's death should in consequence carry off his wife, is a tragical climax of his various bereavements.[2]

Some one, I forget who, told me years ago, that Mrs Tait thought kindly of me; and of course it touched me much to be told that words of mine were used at her funeral. It shows me that even those who have found it their duty to be hard upon me have at bottom a feeling towards me of respect and good will[3]

I am, dear Dr Plumptre, Sincerely Yours John H. Newman[4]

[1] Plumptre wrote that on 7 December at the funeral of Catherine Tait, wife of the Archbishop of Canterbury, one of the hymns sung had been 'Lead Kindly Light'.

[2] Five daughters of the Taits died of scarlet fever between 6 March and 8 April 1856. On 29 May 1878 their only son, Craufurd Tait, died in his 29th year.

[3] A. C. Tait had been one of the four tutors who denounced *Tract* 90. He had attacked Newman at the time of 'Papal Aggression' in 1850, and remained the opponent of Pusey and the ritualist party.

[4] On 24 December Plumptre wrote: 'I hope you will not think that I have acted wrongly in letting the Archbishop see your last note to me. His son-in-law [Randall Thomas Davidson, later Archbishop of Canterbury] thanks me warmly for doing so—and says that he was much touched by it—and that it was a real comfort and pleasure to him.'

To Bishop Ullathorne

Birmingham, 2 February, Feast of the Purification B.V.M. 1879

To the Right Reverend Lord, William Bernard, Bishop of Birmingham

My Right Reverend Father

I trust that his Holiness and the most eminent Cardinal Nina will not think me a thoroughly discourteous and unfeeling man, who is not touched by the commendation of Superiors, or a sense of gratitude or the splendour of dignity, when I say to you, my Bishop, who know me so well, that I regard as altogether above me the great honour which the Holy Father proposes with wonderful kindness to confer on one so insignificant, an honour quite transcendent and unparalleled, than which his Holiness has none greater to bestow.

For I am, indeed, old and distrustful of myself; I have lived now thirty years 'in my little nest'[1] in my much loved Oratory, sheltered and happy, and would therefore entreat his Holiness not to take me from St Philip, my Father and Patron.

By the love and reverence with which a long succession of Popes have regarded and trusted my St Philip, I pray and entreat his Holiness in compassion of my diffidence of mind, in consideration of my feeble health, my nearly eighty years, the retired course of my life from my youth, my ignorance of foreign languages, and my lack of experience in business, to let me die where I have so long lived. Since I know now and henceforth that his Holiness thinks kindly of me, what more can I desire?[2]

Right Reverend Father, your most devoted

John H Newman

[1] This was the traditional description of the room of an Oratorian.

[2] On 3 February Newman went to Oscott, and took with him this letter, addressed to Bishop Ullathorne, but intended for Cardinal Nina. After consultation with Ullathorne, it was agreed that it should be sent by Ullathorne, with his covering letter of 3 February addressed to Manning, but also

intended for Cardinal Nina, which would make clear Newman's mind. It was practically unheard of for a Cardinal who was not a diocesan bishop to reside out of Rome. But, as Ullathorne explained, Newman was unwilling to say 'anything that would look like hinting at any kind of terms with' the Pope. Manning replied that he would forward the enclosure to Cardinal Nina, which made Ullathorne suspicious that his covering letter would not be included, leaving Newman's letter on its own apparently declining the honour. His suspicion was to prove correct. He wrote again therefore the following day to Manning more explicitly and a week later, when rumours were filtering through that Newman had in fact declined, he wrote directly to Cardinal Nina explaining the situation so that there could be no mistake. See *L.D.* xxix, pp. 24–5.

To The Duke of Norfolk

The Oratory Febr 20. 1879

My dear Duke

I have heard from various quarters of the affectionate interest you have taken in the application to Rome about me, and I write to thank you and to express my great pleasure at it.

As to the statement of my refusing a Cardinal's hat, which is in the Papers, you must not believe it, for this reason

Of course it implies that an offer has been made me, and I have sent my answer to it. Now I have ever understood that it is a point of propriety and honour to consider such communications *sacred*. The statement therefore cannot come from me. Nor could it come from Rome, for it was made public before my answer got to Rome—It could only come then from some one who, not only read my letter, but, instead of leaving the *Pope* to interpret it, took upon himself to put an interpretation upon it, and published that interpretation to the world. A private letter, addressed to Roman authorities, is *intercepted* on its way and *published* in the English Papers. How is it possible than [that] any one can have done this?

And besides, I am quite sure that, if so high a honour was offered me, I should not answer it by a blunt refusal

Yours affectly John H Newman

To The Marquis of Ripon

Oratory 21. 2. 79

My dear Lord Ripon

Your letter is exceedingly kind and a great comfort to me.[1]

First let me thank you for your notice of my birthday.

Next, does not the grave fact involved in this anniversary, viz my great age, explain my unwillingness to accept the honour so kindly offered me?

One cannot have half of a dignity. It is not only a reward for what one has tried to do but a claim for doing more.

If it were only a gracious mark of approbation who would refuse it? But am I to leave my 'nido' (as St Philip calls it) all the habits of life which I have grown into since I went into Oxford in 1817? live in London, solitarily or in society? be engaged in rebus gerendis which are quite foreign to my education and my experience? Was it not Caligula who made his horse a Consul, and would not the Pope be reviving by his proceeding the memory of that extravagance?

And now let me take the liberty of saying to you what I have said to no one else, for I have considered the communication sacred. I was to give in my answer by the 5th (for Cardinal M—[Manning] to take to Rome) having received the offer on the 1st. I thought I would compromise thus—by accepting it, on condition I remained at my Oratory. But I could not bargain with a Pope—so I wrote, showing (as I hope) my keen sense of his graciousness by begging him not to tear me from St Philip:— and thus shirking yes or no—One ecclesiastical authority saw it—and thought what I asked possible and would be granted—and besides letters went to Rome interpreting my letter in that sense.[2]

Most sincerely yrs &c J. H. N

[1] The Marquis of Ripon wrote on 20 February, his 'extreme satisfaction' at the offer of the Cardinalate. 'Those who like myself owe to your teaching, more than any other earthly cause, the blessing of being members of the Catholic Church, must rejoice with a very keen joy at this recognition on the part of the Holy See of your eminent services to the Church and to so many individual souls.

I do not venture to question the wisdom of your refusal to accept the dignity of Cardinal, though I cannot but regret that you should have felt bound to decline it.'

Lord Ripon noted in his diary next day, 21 February, 'Lilly came to me in the evening to say that he had received information from Sir R. Blennerhassett, which seems to show that D Newman did not intend absolutely to refuse the Cardinalate.' 'The Ripon Diary', *Recusant History* (Jan. 1973), p. 31.

[2] This refers to Ullathorne's letter of 3 February to Manning, intended for Cardinal Nina, but not sent on by Manning.

To Francis William Newman

[28 February 1879][1]

My dear Frank

Every thing has two sides. Of course my accepting would disappoint these men, but declining would disappoint those. And just for the same reasons would their feelings be contrary viz because my accepting would show the close adherence of my mind to the Church of Rome, and my declining would seem an evidence of secret distance from her. Both sides would say 'You see he is not a Catholic in heart.'

Now this has riled me this thirty years; men won't believe me. This act would force them to do so. So that to a man in my mental position your argument just tells the *other* ⟨contrary⟩ way to what you anticipate

But again as to what you kindly call my 'post of deep moral value' this must be viewed relatively to Unitarians Theists and Sceptics on the one side, and Catholics and Anglicans on the other. I wish to be of religious service, such as I can, to both parties—but, if I must choose between Theists and Catholics, 'blood is thicker than water.' You forget that I believe the Catholic Religion to be true, and you do not. It is not that I am insensible to and ungrateful for the good opinion of Theists etc, but that Catholics are my brethren and I am bound to consult for them first.

[1] F. W. Newman wrote on 27 February, 'Do not think me intrusive, if I now give you a piece of advice. *Persevere in your refusal of the Cardinalate. Decisive* refusal is the simplest way. If I argue that it is more for your honour (*as it is*) to refuse, ingenuity may urge that it is your duty to choose what is less honourable and more troublesome. I should expect you to be soon killed by vexation. New habits are dangerous in age. But one thing is certain. You cannot help the Pope, nor (what is more important) do good to men's souls, by such an elevation; but you will lose a post of deep moral value, in which you are (I believe) a valuable counsellor to numbers. The pressure of friends must not be yielded to.

Affectionately yours F W Newman'

To *Anne Mozley*

The Oratory March 1. 1879

My dear Anne Mozley

I quite understood your silence. The Papers were no Authority. I have this very day learned that the offer of a Cardinal's Hat is to be made to me with the privilege of living still here as before. So great a kindness, made with so personal a feeling towards me by the Pope, I could not resist, and I shall accept it.

It puts an end to all those reports that my teaching is not Catholic or my books trustworthy, which has been so great a trial to me so long.

Refusal too would have created a suspicion that it was true that I was but a half and half Catholic, who dared not commit himself to a close union with the Church of Rome, and who wished to be independent.

It would have unsettled some Catholics, and would have thrown back inquirers.

It would [have] disheartened so many zealous well-wishers, who had so rejoiced or so laboured personally, that my fair fame should be vindicated, and who felt that a refusal would be most ungracious to the Pope, nay, as it was expressed to me, 'a snub and no mistake to him,' and would be shrinking from aiding him in my place when he was pursuing the very line of policy which for so many years I had desiderated at Rome.[1]

And now I thank you for your most kind letter and am

Yours affectly John H Newman

[1] Anne Mozley replied on 3 March: 'I feel the unanswerable force of all the reasons you have given My first thought on hearing the announcement was that this was the most decided and noble step taken by the present Pope and one may feel sure that nothing but your acquiescing in his wish would make the opposite party receive it as a fact beyond dispute

I do not understand how anyone who has heard your conversation or read your works since 1845 could entertain the idea of the "half a Catholic"'.

To The Duke of Norfolk

The Oratory March 1. 1879

My dear Duke

I hope these lines will save the Post to tell you that a letter from Cardinal Manning has just come to me to the effect that the Pope has granted all I petitioned for about my place in the Oratory etc. in the kindest way, and that letters will come to me offering me, I suppose, the Hat

Ever Yours affly John H Newman

To Cardinal Manning

The Oratory Bm March 4. 1879

Dear Cardinal Manning

I hardly should have thought it became me, since no letter has been addressed to me, to write to any one at Rome myself, on the gracious message of the Holy Father about me.

Since, however, the Bishop of Birmingham recommends me to do so, I hereby beg to say with much gratitude and with true devotion to His Holiness I am made acquainted with and accept the permission He proposes to me in his condescending goodness to keep place within the walls of my Oratory at Birmingham.

I am, sincerely Yours kissing the Sacred Purple

John H Newman

To Cardinal Manning

The Oratory March 5. 1879

Dear Cardinal Manning

Wishing to guard against all possible mistake I trouble you with this second letter

As soon as the Holy Father condescends to make it known to me that he means to confer on me the high dignity of Cardinal, I shall write to Rome to signify my obedience and glad acceptance of the honour, without delay.

I write this thinking that the impression which existed some fortnight since, that I had declined it, may still prevail

Yours very sincerely John H Newman

P.S. This second letter is occasioned by something which has come to my knowledge since my letter of yesterday.[1]

[1] Lady Herbert of Lea wrote on 3 March, asking Newman not to persist in his refusal of the red hat. And so he wrote to Manning again.

From Cardinal Manning

English College. March 8. 1879

My dear Newman,

Your letter[1] reached me last night; and I took and repeated it to the Holy Father this morning.

He charged me to say that the official letter will be sent to you: and that he gives full permission that you should continue to reside at your home at the Oratory.

He told me to say to you that in elevating you to the Sacred College he intends to bestow on you a testimony to your virtues and your learning: and to do an act grateful to the Catholics of England, and to England itself for which he feels an affectionate interest.

It gives me much happiness to be the bearer of this message to you.[2]

Believe me to be always Yours affectly H. E. Card: Archbp.

[1] That of 4 March.
[2] Newman replied on 11 March.

To R. W. Church

The Oratory March 11. 1879

Private

My dear Church

I did not like to write to you till I had something like official notice of my promotion. This comes within this half hour. Yet not so much official as personal, being a most gracious message from the Pope to me.

He allows me to reside in this Oratory, the precedent for the indulgence being Cardinal de Berulle, Founder of the French Oratory in the 17th century

Hæc mutatio dexteræ Excelsi! all the stories which have gone about of my being a half Catholic, a liberal Catholic, under a cloud, not to be trusted, are now at an end. Poor Ward can no longer call me a heretic, and say (to H. Wilberforce) he 'would rather a man should not be converted than be converted by me—' and another writer give it as a reason why I was not allowed to go to Oxford.

It was on this account that I dared not refuse the offer. A good Providence gave me an opportunity of clearing myself of former calumnies in my Apologia—and I dared not refuse it—And now He gave me a means, without any labour of mine, to set myself right as regards other calumnies which were directed against me—how could I neglect so great a loving kindness?

I have ever tried to leave my cause in the Hands of God and to be patient—and He has not forgotten me

Ever Yours affly John H Newman

To The Duke of Norfolk

The Oratory March 12. 1859 [1879]

My dear Duke

I have said all my life, and I repeat to myself now 'Never had a man such good friends.' Thanks for the letter.[1]

Cardinal Manning has been to the Pope, and has got me a personal message for me from him quite as good as an official, and removes all my suspence.

Also he has been so good as to explain all that took place at the time of his leaving England, and you will be glad to hear me say that I wish it all swept out of every one's mind and my own—and shall be sorry if it is not so. I wish it known that I am quite satisfied, and am grateful to him for the trouble that he has taken in my matters

Yours affly John H Newman

[1] The Duke of Norfolk wrote on 11 March that he had convened a small meeting in London at which the Marquis of Ripon had proposed and Lord Petre had seconded a Resolution, 'That His Holiness the Pope having intimated his intention to create the Very Rev. John Henry Newman, D.D., a Cardinal of the Holy Roman Church, a subscription be opened for the purpose of providing a Fund to be presented to Dr Newman as a mark of affection and respect.'

To Cardinal Nina

[20 March 1879]

My Lord Cardinal

Were I to delay my answer to the very generous communication your Eminence deigned to make to me on the part of his Holiness, until I could write what seems to be befitting and adequate to express all the feeling of my heart, I fear that I should never write at all. For the longer I think of it, the more generous and gracious the condescension of the Holy Father seems to me, and the more deeply I feel that I am altogether unworthy of it.

I am overpowered, first of all, by the weight of the high dignity to which the Holy Father deigns to raise me, and still more by the words he has used to announce to me his intention, words breathing a goodness so fatherly, and implying an approval the more touching and precious that it is the Vicar of Christ who awards it.

I venture to hope that the Holy Father will allow me, as soon as the weather becomes milder, and the journey less toilsome, to present myself before his sacred person, that I may try to tell him how deeply I feel his immense goodness, and may receive his apostolic blessing.

I cannot close this letter, my Lord Cardinal, without begging you to accept the homage of my profound respect and my deep-felt gratitude for the kind courtesy with which you have condescended to discharge the commission of his Holiness.

I have the honour to kiss the Sacred Purple and to be

Your Eminence's most humble and devoted servant, John H. Newman

To The Provost and Canons of Hexham and Newcastle

The Oratory. March 22. 1879

My dear Right Rev. Provost of Hexham,

I do not know how adequately to express the great pleasure with which I have received the congratulations of yourself and your Chapter on occasion of the singular honour which the Holy Father proposes to confer on me.[1]

That honour is the highest that I could receive at his hands. I should be utterly heartless, if it did not touch me and gratify me deeply. But it is no want of due appreciation of it or ingratitude to the Giver, if I say, how greatly it adds to my happiness to find his condescension on my behalf so warmly welcomed, nay hailed with so generous an impulse, by my brethren in the Priesthood and by Ecclesiastics so highly placed as yourselves.

I have no fear, lest, so speaking, I should be mistaken by him who has been so good to me; for I have reason to know that, with an affectionate thought not only of me, but of his children in these parts generally, and as realizing my antecedents and my present circumstances in my own country, it has been his express intention, in bestowing on me this high dignity, to do an act which will be grateful to the Catholic body, and even to England itself.

You will understand how proud I am, that what in you has been a spontaneous kindness towards me should have been in the Holy Father a sure anticipation of it.

I take for granted that those who have been so considerate towards me in other ways do not forget how old I am and the needs of old men.

I am, My dear Provost of Hexham Sincerely yours in Xt,

John H. Newman of the Oratory

The Very Revd Provost Consitt.

[1] Edward Consitt, the Provost, wrote on 20 March, 'You have not more loyal and devoted friends than the clergy of this Diocese, and I am sure it will please you to know that many of us are indebted to your writings for a deeper appreciation of the beauty and truth of our Holy Faith.

We rejoice, therefore, exceedingly that your most valuable services to the Clergy and the Church have met with their fitting recognition and recompense.

It is a special subject of congratulation to us that you, whom we have always looked upon as our Champion and defender, should be the first amongst the second order of the English Clergy to be made a Prince of the Church.'

To W. J. Copeland

The Oratory Mar 26. 1879

My dear Copeland

I am really overcome with kindness and with the labour of writing answers to addresses and congratulations.[1]

But what is painful is the great confusion into which it is throwing my new edition of Athanasius, which, considering its subject and its author I am deeply grieved to anticipate a failure

Excuse a short letter

Ever Yours affly John H Newman

Have I received proof of the Lyra beyond 120? have you?[2]

[1] On 25 March Copeland sent his congratulations, which he had held back knowing how occupied Newman was.

[2] Newman had asked Copeland to proof read some poems of Keble's and Isaac Williams's for the Lyra.

To William Froude

Rome April 29. 1879

I have been much touched by your consideration for me in writing to me, when you would put into shape your thoughts upon religion, thus putting me in your affection and regard, on a level with dear Hurrell; and I wish I had just now leisure enough and vigour of mind enough to answer your letter so thoroughly as I think it could be answered, and as its delicacy and tenderness for me deserves. But I will set down just as it strikes me on reading, having no books, and depending mainly on my memory.

My first and lasting impression is that in first principles we agree together more than you allow; and this is a difficulty in my meeting you, that I am [not] sure you know what I hold and what I don't; otherwise why should [you] insist so strongly on points which I maintain as strongly as you?

Thus you insist very strongly on knowledge mainly depending upon the experience of facts, as if I denied it; whereas, as a general truth and when experience is attainable, I hold it more fully than you. I say 'more fully,' because, whereas you hold that 'to *select*, square, and to fit to materials which experience has supplied is the very function of the intellect,' I should [not] allow the intellect to select, but only to estimate them.

I will set down dicta of mine, which I think you do not recollect, which are to be found in my University Sermons, Essay on Development of Doctrine, and Essay on Assent.

'No one can completely define things which exist externally to the mind, and which are known to him by experience.'[1]

'Our notions of things are never simply commensurate with the things themselves.'[2]

'It is as easy to create as to define.'[3]

'This distinction between inference and assent is exemplified even in mathematics.'[4]

'Argument is not always able to command our assent though it be demonstrative.'[5]

'Concrete matter does not admit of demonstration.'[6]

'It is to me a perplexity that grave authors seem to enunciate as an intuitive truth, that everything must have a cause'[7]

'The notion of causation is one of the first lessons which we learn from experience.'[8]

'Starting from experience, I call a cause an effective will.'[9]

'There are philosophers who teach an invariable uniformity in the laws of nature; I do not see on what ground of experience or reason they take up this position.'[10]

'Gravitation is not an experience any more than is the mythological doctrine of the presence of innumerable spirits in physical phenomena.'[11]

'Because we have made a successful analysis of some complicated assemblage of phenomena, which experience has brought before us, in the visible scene of things, and have reduced them to a tolerable dependence on each other, we call the ultimate points of this analysis and the hypothetical facts in which the whole mass of phenomena is gathered up by the name of causes, whereas they are really only formulae under which these phenomena are conveniently represented' etc. and so on.[12]

You say 'I doubt whether it is really possible to give a blind man a common idea of a star.' I have drawn out elaborately in one of my University Sermons the necessity of experience from the case of a blind man attempting to write upon colours, how he might go on swimmingly at first—but before long, in spite of his abstract knowledge would be precipitated into some desperate mistake.[13]

I cannot think you would write as you have written had you recollected in my volumes passages such as these. Therefore you must let me state what[,] according to my own view of the matter, I consider to be our fundamental difference, and it is certainly so considerable and accompanied with so [much that is] simply à priori and personal, that, if you really hold firmly all you say, I must with great grief think ⟨consider⟩ I shall have done all that I can do, when I have clearly stated what I conceive it to be

We differ in our sense and our use of the word 'certain.' I use it of minds, you of propositions. I fully grant the uncertainty of all conclusions in your sense of the word, but I maintain that minds may in my sense be certain of conclusions which are uncertain in yours.

⟨April 30, Rome⟩

Thus, when you say that 'no man of high scientific position but bears in mind that a residue of doubt attaches to the most thoroughly established scientific truths,' I am glad at all times to learn of men of science, as of all men, but I did not require their help in this instance, since I have myself laid it down, as I had already quoted my words, 'Concrete matter does not admit of demonstration.' That is, in your sense of the word 'doubt,' viz a recognition and judgment that the proof is not wholly complete, attaches to all propositions; this I would maintain as well as you. But if you mean that the laws of the human mind do not command and force it to accept as true and to assent absolutely to propositions which are not logically demonstrated, this I think so great a paradox, that all the scientific philosophers in Europe would be unable by their united testimony to make me believe it. That Great Britain is an island is a geographical, scientific truth. Men of science are certain of it; they have in their intellects no doubt at all about it; they would hold and rightly that a residuum of defectiveness of proof attaches to it as a thesis; and, in consequence they would admit some great authority, who asserted that it was geographically joined to Norway, tho' a canal was cut across it, to give them his reasons, but they would listen without a particle of sympathy for the great man or doubt about ⟨as to⟩ his hallucination, and all this while they allowed it had not been absolutely and fully proved impossible that he was right.

Then I go on to say, ⟨that, [it is] just this, which⟩ what scientific men believe of Great Britain, viz that its insularity is an absolute truth, that we believe of the divinity of Christianity; and, as men of science nevertheless would give a respectful attention and a candid and careful though not a sympathetic hearing to any man of name and standing who proposes to prove to them that Great Britain is not an island, so we too, did men in whom we confide come to us stating their conviction that Christianity was not true, we should indeed feel drawn to such men as little as professors of science to the man who would persuade them that Great Britain was joined to the continent, but we should, if we acted rightly, do our utmost, as I have ever tried to do, in the case of unbelievers, to do justice to their arguments. Of course it may be said that I could not help being biassed, but that may be said of men of science too.

I hold then, and I certainly do think that scientific philosophers must, if they are fair, confess too, that there are truths of which they are certain, tho' they are not logically proved; which are to be as cordially accepted as if they were absolutely proved, which are to be accepted beyond their degree of probability, considered as conclusions from premises. You yourself allow that there are cases in which we are forced and have a duty to act, as if what is but possible were certainly true, as in our precautions against fire; I go further so much, not as to say that in merely possible, or simply probable cases, but in particular cases of the highest probability, as in that of the insularity of Great Britain, it is a law of thought ⟨the human intellect⟩ to accept with an inward assent as absolutely true, what is not yet demonstrated. We all observe this law; science may profess to ignore it; but men of science observe it every day of their lives, just as religious men observe it in their own province.

In opposition then to what you assume without proved [sic], which you don't seem to know that I have denied, even to throwing down the gauntlet in denying, I maintain that an act of inference is distinct from an act of assent, and that the strength does not vary with the strength of the inference. A hundred and one eye witnesses adds strength to the inference drawn from the evidence of a hundred, but not to the assent which that evidence creates. There is a faculty in the mind which I think I have called the inductive sense, which, when properly cultivated and used, answers to Aristotle's φρόνησις,[14] its province being, not virtue, but the 'inquisitio veri,' which decides for us, beyond any technical rules, when, how, etc to pass from inference to assent, and when and under what circumstances etc etc not. You seem yourself to admit this faculty, when you speak of the intellect, not only as adjusting, but as selecting the results of experience. Indeed I cannot understand how you hold certain opinions with such strength of conviction—as you[r] view of divine justice, of the inutility, if not worse, of prayer, ('it seems to me *impossible* that I should *ever*' etc) against eternal punishment, against the Atonement, unless you were acting by means of some mental faculty (rightly or wrongly used) which brought you on to assents far more absolute than could be reached by experience and the legitimate action of logic upon its results

I am led to conclude then that you grant or rather hold two principles most important to my view of this great matter:—first that there is a mental faculty which reasons in a far higher way than that of merely measuring the force of conclusions by the force of premises; and next, that the mind has a power of determining ethical questions, which serve as major premises to syllogisms, without depending upon experience. And now I add a third, which is as important as any; the gradual process by which great conclusions are forced upon the mind, and the confidence of their correctness which the mind feels from the fact of that gradualness.

This too you feel as much as I should do. You say, 'the communication of mind with mind cannot be effected by any purely abstract process.' I consider, when I sum up the course of thought by which I am landed in Catholicity, that it consists in three propositions: that there has been or will be a Revelation; that Christianity is that Revelation; and that Catholicity is its legitimate expression; and that these propositions naturally strengthen the force of each. But this is only how I should sum up in order to give outsanders an idea of my line of argument, not as myself having been immediately convinced by abstract propositions. Nothing surely have I insisted on more earnestly in my Essay on Assent, than on the necessity of thoroughly subjecting abstract propositions to concrete. It is in the experience of daily life that the power of religion is learnt. You will say that deism or scepticism is learnt by that experience. Of course; but I am not arguing, but stating what I hold, which you seem to me not to know. And I repeat, it is not by syllogisms or other logical process that trustworthy conclusions are drawn, such as command our assent, but by that minute, continuous, experimental reasoning, which shows badly on paper, but which drifts silently into an overwhelming cumulus of proof, and, when our start is true, brings us on to a true result.

Thus it is that a man may be led on from scepticism, deism, methodism, anglicanism, into the Catholic Church, God being with him all through his changes, and a more and more irresistible assent to the divinity of the Catholic Church being wrought out by those various changes; and he will simply laugh and scoff at your doctrine that his evidence is necessarily defective and that scientific authorities are agreed that he can't be certain. And here I must digress a moment to give expression to a marvel that you should think I do not hold with [Hurrell] ('There is another point in which etc. etc. he used to feel) that, whoever was heartily doing his best to do God's will, as far as he knew it, would be divinely guided to a clear knowledge of theological truth.' Why, this is what I have enunciated or implied in all that I have written:—but to return.

You continue:—'The consciousness that they mean the same thing by the same words is a consciousness growing out of experience or daily experiment.' This I have virtually insisted on in a whole chapter in my Essay on Assent, in which, among other instances in point, I refer to the difference of the aspects under which the letters of the alphabet present themselves to different minds, asking 'which way does B look? to the right or to the left?'[15] Moreover, it is the principle of my Essay on Doctrinal Development, and I consider it emphatically enforced in the history of the Catholic Schools. You must not forget that, though we maintain the fact of a Revelation as a first principle, as firmly as you can hold that nature has its laws, yet, when the matter of the Revelation (given) comes to be considered, very little is set down as the original doctrine which alone is *de fide*, and within which the revealed truth lies and is limited.

As Newton's theory is the development of the laws of motion and of the first principles of geometry, so the corpus of Catholic doctrine is the outcome of Apostolic preaching. That corpus is the slow working out of conclusions by means of meditation, prayer, analytical thought, argument, controversy, through a thousand minds, through eighteen centuries and the whole of Europe. There has been a continual process in operation of correction, refinement, adjustment, revision, enucleation, etc, and this from the earliest times, as recognised by Vincent of Lerins. The arguments by which the prerogatives of the Blessed Virgin are proved may be scorned as insufficient by mechanicians, but in fact they are beyond their comprehension, and I claim for theologians that equitable concession that they know their own business better than others do which you claim for mechanical philosophers. Cuique in arte suâ credendum: I do not call your friends 'technical' in their mechanics, because ⟨tho'⟩ you do call me 'technical' in my theology; but I go so far as to take for my own friends what I grant to yours, and this I will ever do; I have long thought your great men in science to be open to the charge of superciliousness, and I will never indulge them in it ⟨so far will never give way to them⟩. Our teaching, as well as yours, requires the preparation and exercise of long thought and of a thorough imbuing in religious ideas. Even were those ideas not true, still a long study would be necessary for understanding them. ⟨When such a study is given⟩ what you call the random reasonings of theologians will be found to have as clear a right to be treated with respect as those proceedings of mechanical philosophers who you say are microscopic in their painstaking. ⟨Rome May 1⟩ But words are but the symbols of ideas, and the microscopic reasoner, who is not only so painstaking, but so justly successful in his mechanics, is simply an untaught child in questions of theology.

Hence it is that we, as well as you, make such account of authority, even though it be not infallible. Anthanasius, Gregory, Augustine, Leo, Thomas Aquinas, Suarez, Francis de Sales, Petavius, Lambertini, and a host besides have, from ⟨our estimation of⟩ their theological instincts, that honour with us, which, on account of their mechanical and physical instincts, you accord to your men of material science. You say that an ordinary man would think it his duty to listen to any great mechanical philosopher who should bring reasons for even so great a paradox as the possibility of perpetual motion; why should such personal reverence be reserved for mechanicians alone? why not for theologians? To none indeed of the opinions of the schools, nor to the reasonings even of Councils and Popes, are we bound; none are *de fide*; none but may be changed. I think there was a day when the whole body of divines was opposed to the doctrine of the Immaculate Conception; two great men, St Bernard and St Thomas, threw back the reception of it for 600 years. The Jesuits have reversed the long dominant opinion of St Augustine of absolute predestination, and have been confirmed by two saints, St Francis de Sales and St Alfonso. On the other hand, sometimes a doctrine of the schools has been made a dogma, that is, has been pronounced a portion of the original revelation, but this, when it has occurred, has been no sudden extempore procedure, but the issue of long examination and the controversy of centuries. There were circumstances in the mode of conducting the Vatican Council which I could not like, but its definition of the Pope's Infallibility was nothing short of the upshot of numberless historical facts looking that way, and of the multitudinous mind of theologians acting upon them.

What then you say of mechanical science, I say emphatically of theology, viz that it 'makes progress by being always alive to its own fundamental uncertainties.' We may allowably argue, and do argue, against every thing but what has been ruled to be Apostolic; we do ⟨thus argue⟩, and I grant sometimes with far less temper, and sometimes with far less freedom of mind than mechanical philosophers ⟨argue⟩ in their own province, and for a plain reason, because theology involves more questions which may be called burning than physics; but if you [who] are modest before Newton and Faraday may be fierce with tableturners, and the schola astronomicorum with that poor man who some years ago said ⟨maintained⟩ that the moon did not rotate, I think it no harm to extend an indulgence towards the prejudicium or the odium theologicum in religious writers.

And now I go on to the relation of the will to assent, in theological matters, as to which, perhaps from my own fault, I have not made my doctrine quite clear to you in the passage in Loss and Gain. You seem to think that I hold that in religion the will is simply to supersede the intellect, and that we are to force ourselves to believe against evidence, or at least in some way or other not to give the mind fair play in the question of accepting or rejecting Christianity. ⟨May 2. 1879⟩ I will say then what I really meant.

Now, as far as I recollect, Reding says, 'I see the truth as tho' seen thro' clouds. I have real grounds for believing, and only floating imaginations against it; is this enough for faith?'[16]

First of all, then, I had fancied that every one granted that in practical matters our wishes were ever apt to bias our judgments and decisions; how then is it strange that a Catholic Priest, as in that story, who was quite sure that there was but one truth and that he possessed it, should be urgent with a youth who was within grasp of this pearl of great price, lest, under the strong secular motives against his acting, he might through faintheartedness lose ⟨miss⟩ it? But he would hold, and I hold most distinctly that, tho' faith is the result of will, the will itself ever follows ⟨on nothing short of an act [of] a conscious⟩ *intellectual judgment*.

But again; it must be recollected, that, since nothing concrete admits of demonstration, and there is always a residuum of imperfection in the proof, it is always also possible, perhaps even plausibly to resist a conclusion, even tho' it be one which all sensible men consider beyond question. Thus, in this day especially, new lights are thrown upon historical events and characters, sometimes important, sometimes, as the world agrees, clever, ingenious, but not likely to have a permanent value. Now here it is the common sense, good judgment, φρόνησις, which sweeps away the aggressive theory. But there are cases in which judgment influences the will. Thus a tutor might say to his pupil, 'I advise you not to begin your historical studies with Niebuhrism[17] or you will end by knowing nothing; depend upon it the world is not mistaken in the grand outline of events. When objections come before you, consider them fairly, but don't begin with doubting,' and his pupil might, simply by an act of the will, put from his mind, at least for the time, real difficulties.

Still more [does this apply] to the cases, not a few, in which excited, timid, narrow, feeble, or over-sensitive minds have their imaginations so affected by a ⟨one⟩ single difficulty connected with a received truth that [it] decides for them their rejection of it against reason, evidence, authority, and general reception. They cannot get over what so distresses them, and after a thousand arguments for the truth, return with full confidence to their objection. Thus if a man said he was fully convinced of the divinity of the Catholic Church, if he judged her by her rites, her doctrines, her history or her fruits, but that he could not get over the fact that in the Apocalypse the dragon was red and red was the colour of the Cardinals' cassocks, I should [say] it would be the duty of a friend to tell him to put this difficulty aside by a vigorous act of the will, and to become a Catholic.

This is an extreme case; there are others more intelligible and to the point. Wives may be unfaithful, but Othello ought by a strong act of the will to have put aside his suspicions. Do you mean to say that a man can feel any doubt whatever of the truth and affection of an old friend? is he not in his inward heart fully confident and certain of him, while he will willingly own that there is a residue of doubt looking at the fact as a matter of inference and proof? Will it be any thing to him that a stranger who has not his experiences does not feel the force of them, when put into words; that stranger will of course disbelieve, but that is not reason against his own believing. You will say that cases of perfidy are possible, and a man may at length be obliged to pronounce against his friend; certainly, and (false) arguments may overcome the Christian and he may give up his faith, but, till such a strong conclusion has overtaken him, he will by an act of the will reject, it will be his duty, as well as his impulse to reject, all doubts, as a man rejects doubts about his friend's truth. And if it be said that his friend is visibly present, and the object of faith invisible, there the action of supernatural grace comes in, which I cannot enter upon here. It is ⟨brings us into⟩ ⟨leads us to a⟩ question of premisses, not of proof. I have said much on this point in my Essay on Assent.[18]

May 10. To conclude, in my last words I mention the great difference which separates us and to which I referred above. I believe that the Moral Governor of the world extends a supernatural aid to the efforts of nature to find religious truth, which He does not accord to inquirers in the theory of Natural Science. That φρόνησις which in every branch of inquiry is required for obtaining knowledge, is guided and enlightened by Him to right conclusions in religion, as it is not prospered supernaturally in the arts and sciences. And the conditions of obtaining this aid are faith, dependence on him and a spirit and habit of prayer. This dependence on God is, I conceive, as really an attribute of the mind and a primary element in the sense of duty as justice, or benevolence.

As to dear Hurrell's opinions. I don't pretend to determine what would have been his ultimate convictions. As, in accordance with him, I should have had no difficulty in going by experience not by abstract thought in proving the principle of the lever, or the power ⟨action⟩ of gravitation without contacts. I do not see that such words of his as you quote show that he would eventually have adopted the system of thought which you advocate in your letter. Again, when he said, 'When Keble and Newman [differ], you will have a call to choose for yourself,' he plainly meant 'choose for yourself in those matters in which you differ'; but he and I agreed intensely to the last day of his life in antagonism to the opinion in your letter, and in every point of Catholic doctrine, except that of the necessity of being in communion with the Pope. You would have very little liberty to differ from either [of] us, if you could only differ where we differ from each other. Again, rightly or wrongly, I think he judged of opinions specially by the upshot of them. I think if a principle he held led to the conclusion that prayer was wrong or absurd, he would rather give up the principle ⟨he would have thought it a reductio ad absurdum⟩ than suffer the conclusion. Again he allowed to the Turk a tyrany [sic] over Christians, rather than give up the principle that we might keep under dissenters and Catholics. I had more to say about him, but have mislaid my notes. J H N[19]

---

[1] This is a statement in Froude's letter to which Newman is replying. See Dev., p. 35.

[2] G.A., p. 49.

[3] 'but it were as easy to create what is real as to define it.' U.S., p. 332.

[4] G.A., p. 169.

[5] G.A., pp. 169–70.

[6] G.A., p. 160.

[7] G.A., p. 66.

[8] G.A., p. 66.

[9] 'Starting, then, from experience, I consider a cause to be an effective will.' G.A., p. 68.

[10] G.A., p. 70, abbreviated.

[11] G.A., p. 68.

[12] G.A., p. 67.

[13] U.S., p. 341.

[14] 'Practical wisdom'.

[15] G.A., p. 374.

[16] ' "I am not denying, God forbid! the objectivity of revelation, or saying that faith is a sort of happy and expedient delusion; but really, the evidence for revealed doctrine is so built up on probabilities that I do not see what is to introduce it into a civilized community, where reason has been cultivated to the utmost, and argument is the test of truth. Many a man will say, 'Oh that I had been educated a Catholic!' but he has not so been; and he finds himself unable, though wishing, to believe, for he has not evidence enough to subdue his reason. What is to make him believe?"

His fellow-traveller had for some time shown signs of uneasiness; when Charles stopped, he said, shortly, but quietly, "What is to make him believe! the will, his will." ' L.G., pp. 383–4.

[17] Barthold Georg Niebuhr (1776–1831) the historian of Ancient Rome, held to be the first writer of scientific history, preferred inference to tradition.

[18] See Chapters IV and V, 'Notional and Real Assent' and 'Apprehension and Assent in the matter of Religion'.

[19] William Froude died on 4 May 1879 at Simonstown, South Africa, and so this letter was never sent. Isy Froude wrote the news of his death to Ignatius Ryder, leaving him to break it to Newman.

To Henry Bittleston

Via Sistina No 48 May 2. 1879

My dear Henry

Your letter came safe and thank you for it. I have been laid up with a bad cold ever since I have been here. Yesterday and today I have been in bed. It has seized my throat and continues hard. I have had advice, but it does nothing for me. The weather is so bad—I think it will not go till spring weather comes. It pulls me down sadly. Here great days are passing, and I a prisoner in the house. It answer[s] to my general experience of Roman weather.

The Holy Father received me most affectionately—keeping my hand in his.[1] He asked me 'Do you intend to continue head of the Birmingham House?' I answered, 'That depends on the Holy Father' He then said 'Well then I wish you to continue head;' and he went on to speak of this at length, saying there [was] a precedent for it in one of Gregory xvi's cardinals.

He asked me various questions—was our house a good one? was our Church? how many were we? of what age? when I said, we had lost some, he put his hand on my head and said 'Don't cry.' He asked 'had we any lay brothers'? 'how then did we do for a cook?' I said we had a widow woman, and the kitchen was cut off from the house. He said 'bene.' Where did I get my theology? at Propaganda? etc etc When I was leaving he accepted a copy of my four Latin Dissertations, in the Roman Edition. I certainly did not think his mouth large till he smiled, and then the ends turned up, but not unpleasantly—he has a clear white complexion his eyes somewhat bloodshot—but this might have been the accident of the day. He speaks very slowly and clearly and with an Italian manner.

William has had a letter to Austin on the stocks for some days. I hope it went a day or two ago.

Love to all

Ever Yours affly John H Newman

[1] This audience was at midday on Sunday 27 April.

To John Norris

Roma 48 Via Sistina May 11. 1879

My dear John

I have been going to write to you for several days, but my great weakness has hindered me—and now you anticipate me by your affectionate letter about me and Thomas.[1]

Only fancy my having been a fortnight and more in Rome, and having only said *one* Mass, and been into *one* Church, St Peter's! It is a heavy trial, and is sent to me to teach me patience. The first week in May I have always thought a golden time; and to be in Rome, and to have nothing of its blessings!

But I am getting much better, thank God, and all in time for the trying days next week from Monday to Thursday inclusive.[2] Nothing can exceed the thoughtfulness of the Holy Father for me, and he inquires after my health daily.

My first difficulty I have in answering your letter is the uncertainty when I shall [be] back. We have got these rooms till the 27th but I should aim at getting off by the 21st—yet I despair of it. The Pope [says] you so to go that you may celebrate Pentecost in your church in Birmingham; but, even, if I cut of [f] Mrs Sconce at Florence, the Priest at St Catherine's at Bologna,[3] the Archbishop at Turin,[4] and the Blounts at Paris[5]—I *must* go to Miss Giberne at Autun—and then when I got to London, I could not help accepting the Duke's invitation, who, in making it, did not forget the claims of Birmingham.[6] How could I get off without calling etc on Lord Ripon, the Cardinal Archbishop etc etc? and, if it was Pentecost week, I should have perhaps to end it by going to Oxford for Trinity Monday the 9th. Moreover, in expectation of these fatigues, I have thought of resting a day or two at Dover by way of recruiting.

Thus I am led to say despairingly, When shall I ever be at Edgbaston? and I seem incapable of forming any plan except I should like to go straight from the Station to our Church, and have a Te Deum.

I shall be quite content with any arrangement you all make for St Peter and Paul or any other day. CC, [Corpus Christi] June 12, is I suppose, too soon.

If a scene in the Phormio is taken, it should be one without women among the characters.[7]

The question on which I had meant to write to you, was a broader one, and intended for all the Fathers, viz what ceremonial rules you wish to observe towards me, and for me to observe.[8] It seems as if I might take just as much of the strict ceremonial as I chose. I must have an Altar, and it may be under a bedroom, and I should ask leave to take the room next me for that purpose, and I would pay rent for it. Whether I need a reception room the event alone can show. As far as I see, I shall have to give up hearing confessions—for I could not be allowed to do so in church. You spoke, when I was at home, as if the Cardinalate was a card which might be worked for the benefit of the Congregation—I wish you to settle how. E.g. I should think it a good thing if we worked the Peter's pence.

The post is impatient. I have not time to read this over. We grieve over Jenico[9]

Yrs affly J H N

Arthurs letter to Paul has come.

---

[1] On 6 May Norris wrote to Thomas Pope about plans for the reception of Newman in the church and by the Oratory School on his return, which, it was hoped, would be before the end of June.

[2] On Monday morning 12 May Newman went to the Palazzo della Pigna, the residence of Cardinal Howard, to receive there the *biglietto* from the Cardinal Secretary of State informing him that at a

Consistory that same morning the Pope had raised him to the rank of Cardinal. He then delivered his Biglietto Speech, which is printed in *Add.*, pp. 61–70, and *Ward*, II, pp. 459–63. On Tuesday morning 13 May he went to the Vatican to receive the Cardinal's biretta from Leo XIII and on Wednesday morning 14 May there was the address and presentation of vestments from the English-speaking Catholics of Rome, at the English College. *Add.*, pp. 71–4. Finally, on Thursday 15 May there was the Public Consistory, at which the Cardinals' hats were presented, and the new Cardinals embraced the Pope and their brother Cardinals. There were six new Cardinals appointed who were diocesan bishops, and three others besides Newman who were not bishops, Joseph Pecci, Leo XIII's brother, Joseph Hergenröther and Thomas Zigliara, O.P.

[3] This priest has not been identified.

[4] Lorenzo Gastaldi, a Rosminian, who had worked for many years in England.

[5] Edward Charles Blount and his wife had invited Newman to stay with them at 6 Rue de Courcelles on his way back to England.

[6] The Duke of Norfolk hoped that Newman would hold a reception in London.

[7] There was to be a reception on Newman's return to Birmingham for parents and old boys of the Oratory School, at which the boys were to provide music and to act one of the scenes from Terence's *Phormio*.

[8] Norris in his letter of 6 May had spoken of the liturgical ceremonies that would have to be observed in the church now that Newman was a Cardinal.

[9] Norris wrote that Jenico John Preston, who had been a boy at the Oratory School and was serving in the Afghan War, died of fever on 30 April at Jellalabad.

To Cardinal Manning

Leghorn June 5. 1879.

My dear Lord Cardinal,

I am sure I shall be pardoned by your Eminence, and their Lordships present with you at the annual Episcopal meeting, for my delay in replying sooner to your and their most acceptable letter of May 16. in consideration of the serious illness which came upon me on the very day on which you wrote, and which can hardly yet be said to have left me.[1]

Now that I am well enough to have left Rome, my first duty is to express to your Eminence both the gratification and the gratitude which I felt on reading your letter. I know well how, on becoming a Catholic thirty years and more ago, my foremost wish was to approve myself, as to the Sovereign Pontiff, so also to the then Bishops of the Catholic body in England. I at once presented myself to them one by one, and was pleased to find the interest which they took in me. Now then when the Bishops pay me the high honor of assuring me that for the last thirty years they and their predecessors have regarded me 'with so true a friendship and veneration' I have the gratification of learning that my honest pains to please them have not been taken in vain; and I have nothing more to desire.

No such encouragement indeed did I need from some of their Lordships, since I made their acquaintance when they were young, almost as soon as I was received into the Catholic Church, and through that long interval they have allowed me to feel sure that they were personally attached to me; much less from your Eminence, whom I knew even in your early college days; but it is a great satisfaction to be told, and told in so formal an address, that even when there was not such a bias in my

514

favour, equally as when there was, I have through so many years, and under such varying circumstances, and by such men, been so tenderly and considerately regarded.

Thanking then, your Eminence and them with all my heart for your most gracious and most welcome congratulations, and for your good wishes in my behalf.

I am, My dear Lord Cardinal Your Eminence's faithful friend & Servant

John H. Card. Newman

June 14. I hope you will excuse my using an amanuensis, as I have been confined to my bed for the last week.[2]

---

[1] Cf. letter of 19 May to Manning (*L.D.* XXIX, p. 127), who wrote, on 16 May, at the annual meeting of the English bishops: 'In their name, and in my own I write to express the joy we feel in your elevation to the Sacred College.' See *Add.*, pp. 88–9.

[2] From 'faithful friend' onwards is in Newman's hand.

To Miss M. R. Giberne

Hotel Anglo Americain Livourne June 9. 1879

My dear Sister M. Pia

Fever, pneumonia, and diarrhea are pretty well for an old man. I dictate to William from my bed but I am gaining strength.

In consequence my friends in England have insisted on my being taken home by a doctor. Accordingly I am like a prisoner in chains moved to and fro at his word of command.

Think of my being at Rome six weeks at such a festive season and with such great saints days and having said mass only three times and having been into not more than half a dozen churches What a disappointment

Ever yours affectionately John H Card Newman[1]

---

[1] Only the signature is Newman's.

To The Duke of Norfolk

Copy of letter sent

June 18. 1879
Confidential

My dear Duke

In the Coffee Room of the Westminster Hotel, I said I wanted to talk to you about the London Oratory. I will do so now.

As soon as I knew I was to be a Cardinal, I felt that my position towards the London Oratory was quite changed, and that I might put myself in relations to them, from which, while I was a lesser man, I abstained

I felt I had an opportunity of returning good for evil.[1]

If it would please them that I should give Benediction in their Church, I would do so. In that case the initiative should come from them, and they should write and ask me.[2]

Or, again, it has struck me whether they would like me to hold my Reception in their house. Protestant friends would come to me there, who would not go to the Cardinal Archbishop's. But perhaps you will say I *must* go to the Archbishop's.[3]

I cannot comfortably write a long letter, but I have said enough to enable you to form a judgment on what I have thrown out. As I move tomorrow or next day, you cannot send me an answer.

JHN

[1] Although the London Oratory was from 1850 legally independent, Newman stood in a moral relation to it as being its founder. After the breach of 1855–6 when he had been accused of trying to exercise control over the London House, he had taken care not to give any excuse for a renewal of the charge. Now he could visit them as an Oratorian Cardinal without implying any special claim, in a way that was not possible when he was a mere Oratorian Superior.

[2] Newman preached and gave Benediction at the London Oratory on 9 May 1880. On 13 May he held a reception there for the Clergy.

[3] Newman stayed at Norfolk House in London from 9 to 15 May 1880 and held receptions there. Cardinal Manning was absent in Rome at the time.

To Miss M. R. Giberne

The Oratory July 3. 1879

My dear Sister Pia

We must subject ourselves to the Will of God. What is our religion, if we can't?

When I got to Macon, it was almost determined we should cut across to you next morning. I went to bed with this expectation—but next morning we rose in heavy rain, and my doctor had a great fear that the waiting at the various stations, and change of carriages, with the damp, drafts, and worry which accompanied it would bring on fever etc—for you would hardly believe how weak I am, and what very slight imprudences had caused a relapse already. So he felt, as having the charge of me, that he could not leave the direct road to Paris in which there were no stoppages, no changes of carriage.

The season is so exceptional.

Ever Yours most affly John H Card. Newman

To Henry Williams Mozley

The Oratory July 25. 1879

Private

My dear Harry

Thank you for your frank letter and your kind congratulations. You are right on the whole.

Tho' the chance of a Roman residence was the main anxiety I felt at the notion of my being Cardinal, it was the dignity, publicity, and ceremonial state which mainly and directly distressed me; for it would be, I felt, such a new life—and this led to my protesting against the efforts of my friends to bring me before the Pope, last year. However, they persisted, and the Pope was more than willing—rather, as I make it out, it was his act, and he only used the English applications as a suitable introduction to his moving.[1] Then he sent me a letter in which he said he wished to give me 'a solemn and public testimony' of his great opinion of me, using strong words. When I came, he showed me such wonderful attention, that I don't like to mention it, but it astonished all there. It was this attitude, so to speak, of the Pope, which obliged me to sacrifice my own feelings. For 20 or 30 years ignorant or hot-headed Catholics had said almost that I was a heretic. I knew well that the theology of Rome, and the theologians of Rome, were on my side, i.e. either as sanctioning me or as allowing me.

I knew and felt that it was a miserable evil that the One True Apostolic Religion should be so slandered as to cause men to suppose that my portrait of it was not the true—and I knew that many would become Catholics, as they ought to be, if only I was pronounced by Authority to be a *good* Catholic. On the other hand it had long riled me, that Protestants should condescendingly say that I was only a half Catholic, and too good to be what they were at Rome. I therefore felt myself constrained to accept. As to Dollinger's saying that the Pope did not know what he was doing, it is a good joke[2]

Yours affly John H Newman

P.S. I should be much grieved, if any part of this letter got into the Papers.[3]

[1] Leo XIII said to Lord Selborne in 1888 about Newman, 'I always had a cult for him. I am proud that I was able to honour such a man', Lady Laura Ridding, *Sophia Matilda Palmer de Franqueville 1852–1915 a Memoir* (London, 1919), p. 190.

[2] Döllinger had observed that Newman could only have been made a Cardinal because the Romans had not understood his views. It was a comment that pained Newman. See letter of 28 May to an unknown correspondent (*L.D.* XXIX, pp. 132–3).

[3] According to a note by Neville, Newman remarked of this letter, 'I have been writing to my nephew; it is one of the gravest and most important letters I ever wrote.'

To William Bright

The Oratory Oct. 18. 1879

Dear Dr Bright

Please, thank your friend for his corrections, which are quite valid. I wish to have, and yet dread to ask for, such acts of kindness. I say 'dread' for my journey to Rome has so put my head and my work into confusion, that the volume which I meant to have made for Athanasius's sake my most perfect will be to all appearance my most disgracefully slovenly. I dread even the number of false prints—but there is no help for it. I know that translation can never be done to the translator's satisfaction, and when I say 'perfect' I mean according to the captus of translation and captus meus— but it will be sadly open to just criticism—but it is no good to go on waiting.

I have been coming to Oxford every day this six weeks, and meant to take the liberty of seeing whether you were there, in order to thank you for all the corrections you sent me some time ago.

Most truly Yours John H Card Newman

To R. W. Church

The Oratory Oct. 29. 1879

My dear Dean

I must take you by surprise. I have just learned that I go to London tomorrow Thursday. A Dentist gives the omnipotent word. I hope to lunch with you not later than 2 P.M. and then to return to this place.

Ever yrs affly J.H.N.

To Miss M. R. Giberne

New Years Day 1880

My dear Sister M. Pia

I hope you will excuse my not writing to you sooner about dear Jemima, but such events put one out, and I cannot recall things.[1]

For myself I have been frightened a long time, but they got accustomed to her pain and weakness at Derby—and at last by a telegram the sudden news came to me.

She had fallen off at the beginning of December from the cold, and had had a great deal of pain. And the pain hindered her eating. At length she had erysipelas—and then she got a little better; then she fell off, and, though they sent letters to me, she declined faster, and the telegram anticipated the letters

All her children were around her at her death, which was very peaceful. She could not speak, but was herself almost to the last.

Ever Yours affly in Xt John H. Card. Newman

P.S. I fear the pictures must not be even an inch larger than the measure sent to you; else, they will not get in.[2]

[1] Jemima Mozley died on Christmas Day 1879.

[2] See letter of 13 November 1879 to Miss Giberne (*L.D.* XXIX, p. 196). She had drawn scenes from the life of St Francis de Sales that are still in Newman's private chapel.

To Anne Mozley

The Oratory Jan 6. 1880

My dear Anne Mozley

I am sorry to hear you have a cold. Thank you for telling me that Harry and Jane have the care of what dear Jemima left.

All I have to say is, what I dare say she told Jane, that about the date of 1850 I sent her (nothing of which I wish back) my sister Mary's copy of the Xtian Year (I think I gave it Mary, it was once mine, I know, it had the mark of her gloves on some of the pages, it was the first edition) my small Bible, which I had had from about the year 1807, miniatures back to back of my Father and my Mother's Father, and some other small things—one, a red morocco prayer book given me by my Mother in 1815. I only mention them, that Jane may know what to look for.

What I miss and shall miss Jemima in is this—she alone, with me, had a memory of dates—I knew quite well, as anniversaries of all kinds came round, she was recollecting them, as well as I—e.g. my getting into Oriel—now I am the only one in the world who know a hundred things most interesting to me. E.g. yesterday was the anniversary of Mary's death[1]—my mind turned at once to Jemima, but she was away.

Yours affecty John H Card. Newman

[1] Mary Newman died on 5 January 1828.

To An Unknown Correspondent

The Oratory Mar. 17. 1880

Dear Sir

It is very kind of you to send me the photographs of my dear Brother—and I thank you for them[1]

As I have not seen him for close on 43 years, they are valuable to me as bringing before me his present likeness—and if, as I doubt not, they are as successful in that respect as they are, when considered as works of art, their value is very great

Very truly Yours John H. Cardinal Newman

[1] The photographs were of Charles Robert Newman at Tenby.

To Alfred Plummer

The Oratory April 17. 1880

My dear Mr Plummer

You must not fancy I have forgotten your kind notice of Febr 21, because I have not thanked you for it.[1] My silence was owing to an accident I had at midnight on the 19th, my falling out of bed and breaking two ribs. If I was to have an accident, I could not have it with less pain and inconvenience—but it interfered with my letter writing and I am not considered well yet. And moreover, at my age, the shock must be considered as well as the breakage.

I shall read with great interest your volume on St John, and I see no difficulty at first sight in the use you are making of any thing I said to you—but I should like first, if you will let me, to cast my eye over it.[2]

I don't know what your politics are, but I suppose, whether with pleasure or disappointment, you must have been taken by surprise at the catastrophe which has overtaken Disraeli. For myself, at the risk of differing from you, I must confess to an extreme joy that Disraeli is gone I hope never to return[3]

Yours most sincerely John H Card. Newman

[1] Plummer had sent Newman birthday wishes on 20 February.

[2] Plummer wanted to quote a letter he had received from Newman on 15 July 1878 (*L.D.* XXVIII, pp. 384–5).

[3] Plummer's reply on 19 April shows that he fully shared Newman's view of Disraeli who had just lost the General Election. Disraeli died the following year.

To His Holiness, Pope Leo XIII (I)[1]

Birmingham 2 May 1880

Most Blessed Father

It has been committed to record that St Philip Neri—if a son may speak of a Father—on meeting some young Englishmen in Rome who were living in the Papal College for the sake of their studies, used no other greeting than that which Holy Mother Church addresses to Innocent Martyrs. *Hail the flower of the Martyrs.*[2] Nor were they called the flowers of the Martyrs in vain who professed that they would work in that country where, if anyone was found to be a priest, or to have attended mass, was executed without mercy on a charge of alleged treason.

Wherefore, as if in my own right, I offer my prayer to your Holiness, asking and beseeching more urgently, most urgently, that you permit the cause of the English Martyrs to be introduced.

I prostrate myself at the feet of your Holiness, and humbly beg for your Apostolical Blessing.

Your Holiness's most humble, most devoted, and most obliged
Servant and creature + John H. Card. Newman.

Given at Birmingham, 2 May 1880.

[1] These two letters of Newman to Pope Leo XIII were included in the Positio for the Cause of the English and Welsh Martyrs.

[2] St Philip Neri lived for more than thirty years at the Church of San Girolamo della Carità, opposite the Venerable English College, Rome, and according to tradition used to greet the students with the words, '*Salvete flores martyrum*'.

To His Holiness, Pope Leo XIII (II)

Birmingham 2 May 1880

Most Blessed Father

How many people have I received asking me in these days to write a letter to your Holiness that you may deign to look kindly on the cause of our Martyrs and to bestow on them such honour as shall seem good upon careful examination, I judged that, like others, I ought not to conceal. For it is by a double chain that I find myself linked to these servants of God. For well-nigh first among them is John Fisher,[1] Cardinal Priest of the Holy Roman Church, on which most lofty peak it recently seemed good to your Holiness to place my unworthiness, that of the least of Englishmen. And then I glory in being recorded amongst the sons of St Philip Neri, and to none other than the Congregation of the London Oratory has it been entrusted duly to attend to and institute the Ordinary Process by the authority of the Most Eminent Metropolitan.[2]

By which redoubled title I urgently beg and pray you, Most Blessed Father, not to disdain my prayers, and to sign the Cause of our Martyrs at the first opportunity.

Prostrate at your feet, Most Blessed Father, I earnestly beg for your Apostolical Blessing.

Your Holiness's most humble, most devoted, and most obliged

Servant and creature + John H. Card. Newman

Given at Birmingham, 2 May 1880

[1] The trial of John Fisher took place and sentence was pronounced on 17 June 1535. He was beheaded five days later. He was 66 years old.

[2] Henry Edward Manning, Archbishop of Westminster from 1865.

To Edward Stuart Talbot

[20 May 1880]

My dear Warden of Keble,

I am writing in much anxiety. I found I could not come to the Gaudy at Trinity without preaching in the Catholic Church near you, where I have never preached as yet, and there is just a chance of my doing acts unpleasing to the authorities of Keble.

If I were one of those authorities I should feel that parents of undergraduates had shown me a great confidence in putting their sons' souls into my hands, and therefore any order which you think right to issue on this occasion I shall take as on your part simply an act of duty. On the other hand I can conceive a youth of 18 and upwards having a right to an opinion of his own upon religion, and feeling it a duty, whatever happened, as he might say 'to obey God rather than men,'[1] and how could I in such a case, believing that the Catholic Roman Religion is the Truth, throw him back into doubt and perplexity?

I do not know, I am not thinking of any particular case; but what I desire, what I write for is, that we may preserve the bond of charity which now unites us; that you may not think it a duty to take that stern course in my respect, which I myself took towards Father Spencer, when I was at Oriel,[2] and which from 1845 to 1864 was taken towards me by nearly all my friends.

Very sincerely yours, John H. Card. Newman.[3]

[1] Acts 5:29.

[2] See letter to Francis Newman, 11 April 1840 and Apo., pp. 124–5.

[3] Talbot replied warmly and appreciatively from Keble College on 21 May, but expressed as well his regret because Newman's preaching, he felt, coloured the character of his visit. He was fearful that Newman's standing would be an influence on young and uninstructed minds.

To Mother Mary Imelda Poole

May 26 1880

My dear Mother Provincial

I wish I had time or strength to tell you how well you and yours have carried me through London and Oxford At least every one tells me each of the two was a great success

I was very much down, and it was like going to execution. All was so out of keeping with my life-long habits. I look out towards next February the 21st, as a sort of heaven, for surely I shall be excused such exhibitions of myself when I am 80. But we are in God's hands, and must do what He would have us do

I saw Dr Pusey at Oxford, he is as mild and loving, and as full of work as ever— quite deaf, and looking much older. I thought I might never see him again.

I have been greatly touched by Mother F. Raphael's beautiful verses. Pray thank her for me, for them. They suggest many thoughts and much wonder and thanks-giving towards the tender mercy of Him who has so dealt with me.[1]

I have looked at the passage in Loss and Gain. I had quite forgotten it and was much amused.[2]

[1] The verses of Mother Francis Raphael, Augusta Theodosia Drane, were called 'Oxford Revisited', and consisted of three sonnets, 'The Past', 'The Present', and 'The Future'. They are printed in *A Memoir of Mother Francis Raphael*, ed. Bertrand Wilberforce (London, 1895), pp. cxiv—cxv (2nd edn, pp. 107–8).

[2] The conclusion is missing. The nuns at Stone had reminded Newman how he made Charles Reding in *L.G.* return to Oxford and be kindly received. *L.G.* III, Chapter V.

To Miss M. R. Giberne

The Oratory Nov 1. 1880

My dear Sister Pia

I was looking, apropos of this great feast, (of which I wish you all the blessings) looking last night into my wardrobe for a festal cassock, and I felt a rattling of paper. I got at the pocket—and to my surprise and satisfaction I found in it an unopened letter of yours. On opening it, I found it dated 'July 15', and found, as I had anticipated on the first sight of your handwriting on the envelope, the letter which you rightly accused me of not answering.

It strikes me as a very curious coincidence that I should have found it so soon after your information about your sending it.

Your last letter destroys the necessity of answering the one of July. I rejoice you are so much reconciled, and I doubt not that He who has done so much for you will do still more. As to the letter, depend upon it, it was brought to me when I was engaged in some function or other duty, and then I forgot to open it and recollected nothing about it, which is one of my growing infirmities.

Allies's book is a most interesting one, though rather sharp.[1] Perhaps you have got it by this time—If you tell me you have not, I will send it to you.

As to William, you can't expect he can have the heart and spirit to write, much as he may wish it, after that dreadful letter of yours to him which he showed me.[2]

Ever Yrs affly John H Card. Newman

[1]   *A Life's Decision.*
[2]   William Neville plainly could not cope with Maria Giberne's letters. See letter on 17 September 1883.

To The Duke of Norfolk

Birmingham April 8. 1881

My dear Duke

It would be most ungracious in me not to accept with much gratitude the kindness and honour done me by yourself and the other friends who wish to have my portrait painted by Millais, and I readily answer their request in the affirmative.

Equally kind to me is the invitation which accompanies it from you and the Duchess. I am sure you know already how deeply I have felt your affectionate welcome and sollicitude, as bestowed on me last May, and the singular observance and consideration with what [sic] for the Holy Father's sake, you received a Cardinal. And indeed what a wonderful, though silent, recognition was it, on the part of so many and such great persons, not Catholic, of the presence of the Old Religion in England, and of the House of Norfolk as its hereditary head and representative.

But now, instead of at once accepting your new kindness, I am going to make a proposal which I think will not be unpleasing to you. Would it not be well if I took the opportunity, which will not occur again, of asking the London Fathers whether they could receive me into their house for the time I am to be in London?

I am sanguine you will like this suggestion and I have another reason for making it. I know, that, if there is a house in which a man of 80 can be at home, and be allowed to take care of himself and live by rule, it is yours, but I have other friends who do not know how wanting in strength I am and I should be unable to resist what I feel to be the real kindness of the invitations which they urge upon me, without seeming disrespectful to them, if they found me making no difficulty in accepting yours. Yet, on the other hand, if I accept theirs, it would involve much personal inconvenience, which I do not think it wrong to wish to avoid.

I think these are good reasons, and I hope you will feel their force[1]

Your Grace's affectionate Servant John H Card. Newman

His Grace The Duke of Norfolk E M

[1]   The Duke had written on 6 April about the proposal for the John Everett Millais portrait and inviting Newman to stay with him, but wrote again on 13 April, accepting Newman's plan.

To William Philip Gordon

The Oratory April 14. 1881

My dear Fr Superior,

I have to come to London for a week in the course of May and June. The Duke of Norfolk encourages me to think, that, during my stay there, your Fathers will receive me into their house.

My own object, in asking the favour, being that of saving myself, as far as possible, by being in a religious house, from publicity which naturally accompanies the presence of a Cardinal, is, I trust, a guarantee, how little I intend or contemplate giving you any trouble, more than such as necessarily follows from the ordinary requirements of hospitality.[1]

I am, My dear Father, Affectly Yours
John H. Card. Newman

[1] Gordon replied on 15 April accepting warmly Newman's proposal.

To John Everett Millais

Birmingham June 1. 1881

Dear Sir

I am to have the honour of sitting to you for my portrait. And my friend, Mr Lilly, has conveyed to me a message from you that I am to call on you for that purpose on Monday, June 27

This I will do—but I should like to know from you whether I am right in thinking besides, that I shall have to go to you the days succeeding the 27th, up to the following Saturday inclusive, and not further.

I hope you will not think me unreasonable in asking this question—but I am of a great age now, and am obliged to take it into account

Your faithful Servant John H. Card. Newman

To William Philip Gordon

Birmingham June 19. 1881

Dear Fr Gordon

I would gladly preach, but I have great difficulty in pledging myself. I cannot reckon on my strength, and, when that goes, my head goes, and I am fit for nothing but to come down the pulpit steps. And then it is a continual tease to me that people are *looking forward* to my preaching, and brings about the very incapacity which I fear. And yet I don't like to say No. Sunday, as being an ordinary day, would be easier for me.[1]

Are you having any devotions for the Jubilee, and have you had any sermons upon it? Don't say I ask this question.[2]

I am obliged to be somewhat troublesome in my food. I have been told to dine in middle of the day—and with such benefit to me that I don't like to leave it off. As it takes about 25 minutes, it may well be synchronous with your luncheon. I should sit at table with your Fathers (*as I do here*) at their dining time, and have some slight refection, nothing out of the way.

I gather from your letter that there is no particular reason for my taking part in any function, over and above *assisting* in red cassock, rochet etc at Mass or Benediction. This would be what I should prefer, as the least fatigue, the least baggage to bring to Town, and the least chance of injury to delicate things ⟨mitre etc⟩ not to say that it would be pleasanter to me in the Cardinal Archbishop's diocese to make little show—but if you *wish* it, I will not carry this out.

Yrs affly J. H. Card. Newman

[1] Newman preached in the London Oratory church on Sunday 26 June.

[2] Leo XIII in March proclaimed a Jubilee that was to last until the end of 1881.

Final Years
(1881–90)

Advancing years meant inevitably declining powers. While Newman's health in general held up well, he was now over eighty. As he remarked to one correspondent with possibly a touch of humour, 'it is with difficulty that I walk, eat, read, write or talk—my breath is short and my brain works slow'. All the same, he added that, apart from minor lapses of memory, 'I am not conscious that my mind is weaker than it was'. But more and more frequently in his letters he refers to finding writing difficult. He was losing the use of his fingers. Towards the end of his life he was dictating.

Nevertheless these letters cover a wide range of topics, from Home Rule which he thought likely, though damaging to English power, to a proposal to build a Channel Tunnel which he opposed. He also wrote articles at this time on the inspiration of Scripture, arguing that God's word as inspired need not necessarily extend to specific secular facts. These articles were prompted by the challenges to biblical Christianity that arose from developments in science and historical research. It was characteristic of Newman to want to leave open questions that need not be closed down. And in an exchange with the Congregationalist, A. M. Fairbairn, he set out again his view on the relationship between faith and reason, explaining that reason in this context was not abstract and disembodied. It could not be considered independently of the first principles and assumptions from which it proceeded, or of the moral character of the person making use of it.

These final years, however, were the time he was particularly concerned to put his papers in order. He had been so impressed by the way Anne Mozley had edited the letters of her brother James that he asked her to perform a similar service for him, preparing an account of his life as an Anglican from early journals, a memoir he had written, and from his correspondence. He supplied her with materials and was happy for her to consult Lord Blachford and Dean Church, as they were his friends, his contemporaries, and they were Anglicans; those three qualifications were invaluable; but he wanted no one else to be involved, and he had no wish to see for himself what she had produced. She was to be independent. As to his Catholic life, he felt any account of that would be premature, because it would need to refer to people still alive and would be likely to stir up controversy. All the same, he had papers prepared and set aside in case some dispute arose and his own position needed to be explained.

And he could still be sharp. In October 1881 he was delighted to hear that his brother-in-law, Tom Mozley, was going to write a memoir. 'My dear Tom,' he began, 'I am sure that no one is in a better position to write an account of the Oxford Movement than yourself.' But when it appeared the following year, he was appalled.

'My dear Mozley,' he now wrote after he had read two chapters, 'I shall not have the courage to read a line more.' He found it littered with mistakes.

In 1884 a more painful episode occurred that revived and revealed past hurt. Newman remained unyielding when he believed a principle to be at stake. The occasion arose because the Fathers of the London Oratory wished to invite him to attend the opening of their new Church. As founder of the Oratory in England, their invitation was natural enough and in fact, since he had been made a Cardinal, relations between the two houses had been much eased. The London Fathers were aware, however, that the matter was delicate. So their Superior, William Gordon, wrote informally to the Duke of Norfolk about inviting Newman, but the Duke then took the initiative and at once approached Newman. Newman was not pleased. 'Why could you not have sounded me, before you let the Duke write to me?' he asked Gordon. What they wanted was more than he felt he could grant. While he had appreciated the hospitality the London House had shown him in more recent times, the breach between them in 1855 and 1856, created by misunderstanding and their mistaken belief that he had sought to exercise authority over them in a way that was contrary to the Oratorian spirit, had never been healed. He had never received an apology for the charge they had laid against him or the damage they had done by spreading it abroad in other Oratories. That injustice still disturbed him. He could not bring himself to overlook it. His presence, he felt, could be interpreted as acquiescence in their behaviour. In the event, no great harm was done. None of this exchange was public and his absence, he told Gordon, could be attributed to his great age.

And all the while, people whom he had known and loved were dying. Pusey died in September 1882 and Provost Hawkins two months later. Newman wrote to his widow, 'Your dear husband has never been out of my mind of late years'. In 1884 he visited another old friend, Mark Pattison, Rector of Lincoln College, shortly before he too died. He was hoping even at the last to revive Pattison's Christian faith. And that same year his brother Charles died, and then the following year both Copeland and Maria Giberne. In November 1889 Newman heard that Blachford too had died, 'nearly the dearest as well as the oldest of my early friends'.

During these years Newman was corresponding as well with the Evangelical, George Edwards, and affirming in February 1887 how the 'great and burning truths' that he had learned as a boy from evangelical teaching, he had found 'impressed upon my heart with fresh and ever increasing force by the Holy Roman Church'. It is a late claim to the enduring consistency of his thought.

Newman's last letter was to his niece, Grace Langford, the daughter of his estranged sister Harriett, who had died in 1852, and Tom Mozley. He had not seen her since 1843. Grace had married and emigrated to Australia, but was visiting England and wished to call on him. She saw her uncle two days before he too died.

Final Years (1881–90)

To Thomas Mozley

The Oratory Bm Oct. 21. 1881

My dear Tom

I am sure no one is in a better position to write an account of the Oxford Movement than yourself.[1] Perhaps you know that Copeland has long been collecting materials with the same purpose, but I think he would rather aim at a documentary history (if even a writer's self can prophesy the outcome of his intentions) whereas yours would be the narrative of your own experience. Few men could bring to the work such literary power, such observation such a command of detail, such memory as yourself. I think you are likely to be caustic, and wanting in tenderness—(I am not thinking of myself, for I have full confidence in your affection for me, but of such as Blanco White and Tony Buller, (supposing him alive)) and what I *fear* is *controversy*[2] Recollect how very sore people may be on points one least suspects—For instance, as to Sidney Herbert—his widow is still alive, and, as I cannot guess what you are to say of him, so you cannot guess what will afflict his near relatives.[3]

The only exception I observe to my above remark about your writing from *experience*, is your first chapter, 'Newman, London and Trinity.' What can you know of me accurately before 1825–6?

I welcome with great pleasure and full trust your anticipation that as to your *whole* work 'I shall find your intention kind and the result at least harmless.' I know how very interesting your book will be, but you are so powerful a writer that against your wish your little finger can wound.

I hope I have said nothing to trouble you

Yours affectionately John H Card. Newman

---

[1] Mozley wrote on 20 October from 7 Lansdown Terrace, Cheltenham: 'I am writing "Reminiscences of Oriel College, and of the Oxford Movement," and the MS nearly complete is in Longman's hands . . . I need not say that you are inevitably the most prominent, and central figure in it. Now I know that you have perfect confidence in my affection, and some confidence in my truth and justice; but you certainly have good reason not to repose too confidently in my discretion. So I have only to say that I feel very sure there is not a line, or a word to give you pain.' See letter of 9 June 1882 to T. Mozley for Newman's remarks on reading the published work.

[2] Anthony Buller died on 13 August 1881. Chapter lxxxviii was devoted to him, and Chapter vii to Blanco White.

[3] Sidney Herbert appeared in Chapter xcvi. His widow was Lady Herbert of Lea.

To William J. Walsh

Birmingham Dec 19. 1881

Confidential

Dear Dr Walsh,

I want to ask you as an Irish theologian, whether you think the following position is tenable. I do not know enough of Irish history or Irish opinion to be able to say that it *is* tenable, but I am not at all sure it is *not*.[1]

It is a probable opinion and therefore may be acted on by an individual, that the Irish people has never recognized, rather have and continuously since the time of Henry ii protested against and rejected the sovereignty of England, and have seemingly admitted it only when they were too weak to resist; and therefore it is no sin to be what would be commonly called a rebel.

I will beg you to burn this, and, if you are good enough to answer it I will in turn burn your letter[2]

J H N

[1] Walsh, who was President of St Patrick's College, Maynooth, had given his support to the Land Act and was a strong Home Ruler.

[2] Newman presumably burned Walsh's reply. His own letter survives only in a draft.

To W. J. Copeland

Bm Dec 21. 1881

My dear Copeland

Your annual remembrance of us has come right—and we all return you our best thanks and kindest greetings on this sacred tide, which is close upon us. They wish me here to sing Mass at 5 a m on Christmas day in full Pontificals, with Mitre and Staff which I have never done and doubt whether I am strong enough to do, though I am very well.

Why have you not written to me this long time? I have supposed you were buried in Cornwall or had been carried off by a balloon, and had no address, or I should have tried to elicit a letter from you.

Myself, I am busy in composing a Volume of William Palmer's Russian etc travels—which will be to his contemporaries, I think, interesting, but I can't answer for the new generation.

Now do give me some sign, over and above the turkey, that you are in rerum natura

I fear your Sister is still very ill

Ever Yours affecty John H Card. Newman

To Miss M. R. Giberne

The Oratory Bm Jan 5. 1882

My dear Sister Mary Pia

This is the anniversary of my dear Mary's death in 1828, an age ago; but she is as fresh in my memory and as dear to my heart, as if it were yesterday; and often I cannot mention her name without tears coming into my eyes.

I have nothing to say, except to wish you the best blessings on the season. I should have written earlier, were I not half drowned by correspondence, and find it difficult to handle my pen without pain. My best good wishes of the season to all your community, and to M. Antoine.

I do not like what you say of yourself. If you have not teeth, you *cannot* eat hard substances without danger. Unchewed meat is as dangerous to the stomach as brick and stone, or a bunch of keys. You are not an ostrich. I am *very serious*. As to myself I have for years lived mainly on soup and milk. Any doctor would recommend you such a diet—and peas pudding very well boiled, and eggs in the shape of omelet—but not with the white in lumps. I dare say, you think of all this, but perhaps you don't. Talk to Mgr Place about this—and, when you see him, give him from me a kind and respectful message.

I grieve about your tooth ache, having experience of it, and I wish I was sure that you were attending properly to that more serious complaint

Ever Yrs affly J H Card. Newman

Have you got *spectacles* which suit you?

To Lord Blachford

Birmingham, April 1st. 1882

My dear Blachford,

I am very much tempted by my own fears and feelings to put my name to the protest made against the Channel Tunnel. But am held back by my utter ignorance of political and military matters, and that in such an act I run the risk of its being refracted, like a stick in water, by being poked into a medium of which I have no experience and which I do not understand e.g., it may be fraternizing with some party or other—or fairly mean something which I have no intention of its meaning.

Among those who have given their names to it are Lord Bath, Lord Lytton, Lord Halifax, Lord Bury, Cardinal Manning, Sir James Paget, Mr. Tennyson, Professor Huxley, Mr. Hutton, Mr. Knowles and Mr. Holyoake.[1]

I suppose *you* have reason against it—or does a Private Bill come before the House of Lords.[2]

A Happy Easter to you and Lady Blachford.

Ever yours affectionately, J. H. Card: Newman.

[1] The protest against the proposed Channel Tunnel appeared in the *Nineteenth Century* for April. Lord Blachford seems to have written about Newman's feelings to the editor, James Knowles, because on 3 April the latter sent him a copy of the protest, and asked for his signature to it. In the event Newman signed.

[2] There were two private bills about the Channel Tunnel before the House of Commons.

To The Hon. Mrs Pereira

Birmingham April 17, 1882

Dear Mrs Pereira,

I feel with you that it does George much credit to wish to go to Oxford, and that it would be a permanent advantage in many ways to him and especially enable him to enter the army as a man, and not as a mere boy, as many do.

But I have great difficulties in advising you. It is now near 20 years, since the frightful evil of infidelity or agnosticism has been epidemic in Oxford. And about the same time a general feeling arose among our Catholic laity to send their sons to one of the two great seats of education, originally belonging to the Catholic Church.

My own notion was to meet the difficulty, not by forbidding Catholic youths to go to Oxford—but by establishing (by the powers which I possessed from the Holy See) an Oratory there, which might be the protection of the Catholic students from the intellectual dangers of the place.

But the Bishops judged otherwise—and not only brought out a serious warning against Catholic youths going to Oxford, but prevailed at Rome to hinder my beginning an Oratory there. In consequence there has been no effectual safe-guard; for the Jesuits, though they have had very able Fathers there, have not put forth their whole strength, or acted on a plan; and not only this, but what I have called an epidemic has increased in virulence, intensity and extent for the last ten years.

Thus I have two reasons against advising you letting George go to Oxford, first the actual warning of the Bishops, and secondly, the very alarming state of Oxford itself.

I don't like to delay my acknowledgement of your letter—and therefore I write this—but I must think more and inquire more, before I make up my mind what to advise you.[1]

You must excuse my mistakes in writing. It is one way in which old age is telling upon me. I am forgetting how to spell.

Very sincerely Yours John H. Card. Newman

[1] George Pereira, aged seventeen, did not go to a university, but in 1884 became an officer in the Grenadier Guards.

To Thomas Mozley

Birmingham, June 9. 1882

My dear Mozley

I have just received your volume, and chapter 2 has so knocked me down, that I shall not have courage to read a line more. It is full of small misstatements and I must take it as a specimen of the whole.[1]

It is not true that my Father was a clerk in Ramsbottom and Co. He was first a Partner in Harrison, Prickett and Newman; the partners of which retiring from business, another firm was formed.

It is not true that my Mother knew any of the authors you mention. She would be called an Arminian and Remonstrant. The only Sermons she seemed to know were 'Tillotson's'.

I never dreamed of being 'converted' and had no lasting religious thoughts till I knew Mr Mayers.

My Father's bank never failed. It stopped—but paid by the end of the month its creditors in full.

Henry Bowden should be John William Bowden.

I could notice other mistakes—but all that you have said is so uncalled for, that I am almost stupefied.

Yours affly J. H. Card. Newman

[1] This was a copy of Mozley's *Reminiscences chiefly of Oriel College and the Oxford Movement* (London, 1882).

To E. B. Pusey

Rednall. June 29. 1882

My dear Pusey,

Your kind and considerate letter has just come here.

I opened Mozley's book, and was so much offended by what I saw in it (offended, because it was so incorrect in what it stated or suggested,) that I put it down, and have not opened it since. What was the use, when I could not condescend to answer it? Some time, if I have leisure, I shall note down its serious mistakes. All that I have seen of it since, has been, when, on looking into newspapers, my eye has been caught by some quotations of it; and every where, in little things as well as great, I find him loose and inaccurate. When a man aims at gossip, he is obliged to dress up facts in order to make his story stand upright.

I did not see what he says about the Oriel election; as usual, from what you say, his story will not run on all fours—nor does any one page, I think, of his book. I recollect your own words in your Sermon perfectly well.[1]

I am at a volume of W. Palmer's Visit to Russia, and meant to send it to you when done. It seems to me exceedingly interesting, as bringing out the genius and position of the Russian Church. He makes the Filioque question somewhat more difficult than I hoped it would have proved.

Ever yours affectionately J. H. N.

P.S. I ought to have added that though *you* did not in your Sermon say that I was one of Hawkins's advocates, I *was*—and Jenkyns, who at first said he feared Hawkins would not get on with the Fellows, and so was against him, was turned round and voted for Hawkins (so, I think, did Awdry) on finding three residents, Dornford, you and me all for him—I recollect making Jenkyns laugh by saying in defence of my vote 'You know we are not electing an Angel, but a Provost. If we were electing an Angel, I should, of course vote for Keble, but the case is different.' I voted, however, for Hawkins from my great affection for, and admiration of him. I have never ceased to love him to this day.

I certainly was sorry I had helped in electing Hawkins—but I cant say I ever wished the election undone. Without it, there would have been no movement, no Tracts, no Library of the Fathers—I could go on at great length, had I time for it.

[1] Pusey wrote on 27 June about a passage in T. Mozley's *Reminiscences chiefly of Oriel College and the Oxford Movement*, II, p. 139, stating that Newman was 'much surprised and *concerned* when he read in a sermon preached by P. [Pusey] at the consecration ⟨(opening)⟩ of the chapel at K.C. [Keble College on 25 April 1876] that Newman had lived to regret the part which he had taken in Hawkins' election to the Oriel Provostship.'

To Miss M. R. Giberne

Bm July 3. 1882

My Dear Sister Pia,

I did not forget you on the Visitation, but said Mass for you on two other days instead, because I heard that William George Ward was dying.[1] How it was that his serious state of health was not known generally before, I cannot tell. His principal complaint is that of which Fr Joseph Gordon died, and that was three years upon him.

It will be still some time before Palmer's Journal will issue from the Press. I shall send it to you. It seems to me very interesting—but 40 years is more than a generation, and I can't prophesy how it will strike most people. The Czar does not appear in it, though afterwards he had Palmer to dine with him. I think the book shows the impossibility of the union of Greece with Rome. As for the Russian ecclesiastics, he found that they had all but given up the idea of unity, or of the Catholicity of the Church. So far they were behind the Anglicans, who at least profess belief in One Catholic Church.

I am very well, as far as health goes—but I am more and more infirm. I am dimsighted, deaf, lame, and have a difficulty in talking and writing. And my memory is very bad.

I fear the enemies of the Church are all but effecting its absolute fall in France.[2] The first and second generation after us will have a dreadful time of it. Satan is almost unloosed. May we all be housed safely before that day!

Yours affectly in Xt J. H. Card. Newman

Are you not 80 now?[3]

[1] The feast of the Visitation of our Lady was on 2 July. W. G. Ward died on 6 July. Miss Giberne replied in a letter of 4–6 July, 'I hope Mr Ward has asked pardon for all the hard and unjust things he has said and written about you if not—may God have mercy on him'.

[2] This refers to the secularizing laws against religion in schools, hospitals, and elsewhere, and the expulsions of religious orders.

[3] Miss Giberne replied that she would be 80 on 13 August.

To Emily Fortey

The Oratory Birmingham July 6, 1882.

Dear Miss Fortey

Your letter has interested me very much, and has led me to entertain great hopes that God is calling you by His grace into His Church, and of course it is your duty to attend to that call, and that you may duly attend to it, I earnestly pray.[1]

So much I have no difficulty in saying; but, when you come to the question, what your duty is at this time, my answer is not so easy. I consider that a stranger to you cannot give you satisfactory advice. You should have recourse to some priest on the spot, put your whole case before him, and go by his judgment. The Father Jesuits, for instance are sure to be careful and experienced priests, and they would, on talking to you decide whether, *young* as you are, and dependent, I suppose, on your Father, it would be advisable for you at once to undergo the great trial of breaking with him. Our Lord tells us to 'count the cost'[2]—the change of religion is a most serious step— and must not be taken without great preparation by meditation and prayer. The Jesuit Fathers are to be found at the Catholic Church on the Quay, Bristol.

Do not doubt that our Lord will guide you safely and happily if you place yourself unreservedly into his hands.[3]

Yours sincerely J. H. Card. Newman

[1] Emily Fortey wrote on 4 July from 7 Vyvyan Terrace, Clifton: 'I do not want to trouble you with my opinions and my affairs, but I do need your help *so* much and you could give it me by your advice. I am 16 years old and am entirely a Catholic at heart and have been so for about four years. I have lately read the "Characteristics of Your Writings" by Lilly and also "Loss and Gain" which have of course much influenced me. My parents are—nothing in the way of Religion. I have only a step-mother and my father has only been home from India a short time so I do not know either of them well and could certainly *never* tell them my opinions, or talk at all on the subject. I go to the Clifton High School and one of the mistresses is a great friend of mine. She is an Anglican and if any thing could keep me from joining the Church it would be love for her. But that seems so wrong. Do you think I ought to join the Church now, or wait till I am of age? I am sure my Father would never give his consent. And if I stay in the Anglican Church ought I to go to Communion? I have always believed in Transubstantiation in the Anglican Church, but after reading your books it seems to me impossible. And then do you think I am wrong in going to Catholic services? That I do without my father's knowledge. I could not tell him. I never talk about these things to him. . . . It is because I feel sure that the Catholic Church is the "Ark of Salvation" that I dare do any thing that may lead me to it.'

[2] *Luke* 14:28.

[3] See letter of 3 October 1884 to Emily Fortey.

To E. B. Pusey

Birmingham. Aug. 4. 1882

My dear Pusey,

If the words you quote in p. 24 of your Sermon are Mozley's, they are in keeping with all other statements which have been reported to me from his book; they contain a reckless untruth.[1]

I never expressed, I never felt any surprise whatever, any concern whatever, at your words about me, including me with yourself in what you said about Hawkins's election.

What I did feel on reading it was, that your saying it on so public an occasion implied that you were not now on such familiar terms with Hawkins as you were up to the time of my leaving Oxford.

That I had any personal feeling about your paragraph is a simple untruth. It is a specimen of all M.'s statements, as far as I know them. To answer him, would require a book as long as his.

I fear that I must have written you a misleading letter the other day from my not having seen M.'s words.[2] It is infamous to make me complain of you, who have always been so careful in your words about me.

Yours affectly J. H. Card. Newman

P.S. I hope you will have Palmer's Journal in a few weeks now.

[1] On 31 July Pusey wrote about the reprint of his 1876 sermon at the opening of Keble Chapel (see letter of 29 June 1882).

[2] Letter of 29 June to Pusey.

To Henry Acland

[21 September 1882]

My dear Dr. Acland

Your and your daughter's kindness to me two years ago will never leave my mind, and your present offer is like it.[1]

I have from the first felt that, as a Cardinal, I represent the Holy See of the Pope so directly, that I had no right to indulge my private feelings by coming to Oxford and taking part in today's solemnities.[2] Nor was I sure that I should be welcome to dear Pusey's immediate relatives; even Mrs Brine, who wrote me a most kind letter, took it for granted that I should not come. No hint came to me, implying such a wish, on occasion of the funerals of Isaac Williams and Keble; and, as regards Williams's, the first of the two, Sir George Prevost wrote to me to say that he was sorry he could *not* ask me. I thought then, and think, that even were I *not* a Cardinal, there would be a technical or ecclesiastical difficulty in (say) a Bishop of Oxford receiving me, both on my side and on his, in what *must* be public.

One of our Fathers is going from this place, and, since this house is mainly made up of converts, I and others make him their representative.[3] One thing struck me just now that I might have done. I might have asked to go to see him, before the coffin was closed; but on Monday, I had arranged to go on a matter of private duty to Tenby, returning last night, and my mind was so occupied with the anxieties connected with it, that such a thought did not occur to me.[4]

I have sent your name some weeks ago to my publishers, with the hope you will accept from me William Palmer's *Russian Journal*, but the publication has been unavoidably delayed.

Most truly Yours John H. Card. Newman.

[1] See letter of 31 May 1880 to Acland (*L.D.* XXIX, pp. 277–8). Pusey died on 16 September and Acland had asked Newman to stay at his house in Oxford for Pusey's funeral.

[2] The day of Pusey's funeral at Oxford, during which 'Lead, Kindly Light' was sung.

[3] This was A. W. Hutton.

[4] On Monday 18 September Pusey's body was brought from Ascot, where he died, to Oxford. On that day Newman went to see his brother Charles, now a complete invalid. Dr Chater the local doctor wished him to change his lodgings, where he had lived for years, on grounds of health, but he was unwilling to do so. The Rector of Tenby, George Huntington, thought it wiser to leave him in the surroundings to which he was accustomed, where he was well cared for by the daughter of his former landlady.

To Anthony Trollope

Birmingham Oct 28, 1882

My dear Mr Trollope

I should not have ventured to trouble you with any so-called remedy for the attacks from which Lord Emly he said you suffered [*sic*], had not what he happened to say of your case been so parallel to that of a very dear friend of mine, now departed. I have seen enough of the caprice and subtle nature of asthma, hastily to suggest a relief.

My friend, Mr Hugh Rose, whose name I dare say you recollect, could not sleep in Kings College, but was safe at his parsonage house of St Thomas' hospital over the water. But my friend *here* had no difficulty in sleeping in any town, here or abroad, nor any part of the country—but was simply debarred from going to a cottage on the slope of a well wooded hill, where he had bought land, and laid out a garden, after numberless trials, suffering on the 2nd or 3rd night most cruelly.[1]

I am sorry Lord Emly took from hence a specimen of the paper; it was at least seven years old, and was not to be depended upon.

It is very kind of you to express pleasure at hearing of my admiration of your novels. Many of them I read again and again. I have just been re reading one for the third time, (which I first read about 1865 when) I was at our Cottage [*sic*].

Excuse my mistakes in writing. It is old age.

Your faithful servant John H. Card. Newman.

[1] This refers to Ambrose St John and Rednal. Hugh James Rose was Perpetual Curate of St Thomas's, Southwark.

To Lord Braye

Birmingham Oct 29. 1888

My dear Lord Braye

I thank you for your most touching letter which I think I quite understand and in which I deeply sympathise.[1]

First, however, let me say a word about myself, for I think I was not exact in what I said to you, to judge by your letter. I am thankful to say that I am at present quite free from any complaint, as far as I know—but I am over eighty, and it is with difficulty that I walk, eat, read, write or talk—my breath is short and my brain works slow—and, like other old men, I am so much the creature of hours, rooms, and of routine generally, that to go from home is almost like tearing off my skin, and I suffer from it afterwards. On the other hand, except in failure of memory, and continual little mistakes in the use of words, and confusion in the use of names, I am not conscious that my mind is weaker than it was.

Now this is sadly egotistical—but I want you to understand why it is that I do not accept your most kind invitations, any more than I have Lord Denbigh's. I decline both with real pain: and thank you both. But I have real reasons, which friends sometimes will not believe, for they come and see me, and say 'How well you are looking!'

Now what can I say in answer to your letter? First, that your case is mine. It is for years beyond numbering—in one view of the matter for these 50 years—that I have been crying out 'I have laboured in vain, I have spent my strength without cause and in vain: wherefore my judgment is with the Lord, and my work with my God.'[2] Now at the end of my days, when the next world is close upon me, I am recognized at last at Rome. Don't suppose I am dreaming of complaint—just the contrary. The Prophet's words, which expressed my keen pain, brought, *because* they were his words, my consolation. It is the rule of God's Providence that we should succeed by failure; and my moral is, as addressed to you, Doubt not that He will use you—be brave—have faith in His love for you—His everlasting love—and love Him from the certainty that He loves you.

I cannot write more today . . . and, since, it is easier thus to write, than to answer your direct questions, I think it is better to write to you at once, than to keep silence.

May the blessings from above come down upon you—and they will.

I am, my dear Lord Braye Yours, (may I say?) affectionately
John H Card. Newman.

[1] Lord Braye had become a Catholic in 1868 and took great interest in higher education for Catholics.
[2] *Isaiah* 49:4.

To Mrs Edward Hawkins

Birmingham Nov. 21. 1882

My dear Mrs Hawkins,

What wonderful kindness it is in you to write to me in your present deep distress; it has touched me greatly.[1]

I thought of writing to *you*, when I heard yesterday of your loss, but on second thoughts I did not dare. Now by your own letter you give me leave, or rather invite me. Your dear husband has never been out my mind of late years. When the first snow came down some weeks back, I thought what the effect of it might be upon him, and only last week, I quoted to a friend with reference to him (thinking at the same time of my own case) a Greek poet's words, 'A light stroke puts to sleep aged men'[2]

I have followed his life year after year as I have not been able to follow that of others, because I knew just how many years he was older than I am, and how many days his birthday was from mine. These standing reminders of him personally sprang out of the kindness and benefits done to me by him close upon sixty years ago, when he was Vicar of St Mary's and I held my first curacy at St Clement's. Then, during two Long Vacations, we were day after day in the Common Room all by ourselves, and in Ch Ch [Christ Church] meadow.[3] He used then to say that he should not live past forty; and he has reached, in the event, his great age. I never shall forget to pray for him, till I too go, and have mentioned his name in my Obituary book, which dear Mrs Pusey made for me in her last illness.

May God be with you, and make up to you by His grace this supreme desolation

Most truly Yours John H Card. Newman

[1] Edward Hawkins died on 18 November.

[2] σμικρὰ παλαιὰ σώματ᾽ εὐνάζει ῥοπή. Sophocles, Oedipus Tyrannus, 961.

[3] Cf. Apo., p. 8. The long vacations were those of 1824 and 1825. Hawkins was elected Provost of Oriel on 31 January 1828. He was born on 27 February 1789.

To William Clifford, Bishop of Clifton

Birmingham Jany 7. 1883

My dear Lord

I hope I am giving you the trouble of nothing more than a few lines. The inclosed contains an Article from a man of great consideration, and it seems clear that before long his argument must be met.[1]

Can you tell me, are we bound to the titles of the books of Scripture more than to the notices of time and place at the end of some of St Paul's Epistles, which are found in the Protestant version and left out in the Catholic?

I believe we are not bound to consider that St Paul wrote the Epistle to the Hebrews, though of course the writer, whoever he was, was inspired.

The Council of Trent altered, I think, the title 'the Psalms of David' into the vaguer form 'Psalterium Davidicum'.

Is it necessary to hold that Solomon wrote Ecclesiastes?

I am not proposing to you to answer all these questions but can you refer me to any theologian who treats of them?

As you have entered upon this grave subject by the very interesting Paper which appeared lately in the Dublin Review, I am sanguine that you can help me[2]

I am, with all kind wishes to you for the New Year

Your Lordship's very faithful servant John H Card. Newman[3]

The Rt Revd The Bishop of Clifton

[1] This article appears to have been a reply to an article said to be called 'History, Criticism and the Roman Catholic Church', which commented on the English edition, just published, of Ernest Renan's *Recollections of my Youth*. This unidentified article Newman now sent to Bishop Clifford. Newman was preparing to write on the inspiration of Scripture.

[2] 'The Days of the Week, and the Works of Creation', *Dublin Review* (April 1881), pp. 311–32.

[3] Bishop Clifford replied on 9 January and promised to obtain information from Archbishop Errington.

To R. W. Church

March 28, 1883

I said Mass for Helen and her husband elect this morning. So did Fr Neville. Of course it is, however glad an event, a very trying one for all of you, and not least for Mary.[1]

I don't suppose she will find a fiddle make up for Helen, but it has struck me that you and Blachford will let me give the beautiful instrument you and he gave me, to Mary. I don't think she will refuse it; I hear much of her proficiency.

You gave it me in 1865—and I had constant use and pleasure in the use till lately—but I find now I have no command of it; nay, strange to say, I cannot count or keep time. This is a trouble to me; one gets an affection for a fiddle, and I should not like to go without getting it a good master or mistress. My friends in this house have instruments of their own. So has Mary doubtless—but this would come with associations in its history

[1] Helen, twin sister of Mary Church, was married to Francis Paget on 28 March.

To Miss M. R. Giberne

Rednall 17 Sept. 1883

My dear Sister

I cannot let the pictures of the witnesses go.[1] They are historical, and are placed for ever in our Congregation Room.

As to the elastic stockings, I have used them these 29 years—ever since I broke a tendon at Dorkey [Dalkey] by running up hill.

So the Holy Father has called on all his children to unite their prayers for the deliverance of the Church from her enemies. I wonder what was the last time such an exhortation came from the Holy See. The bicentenary of the victory of John Sobieski over the Turks seems to have suggested it to him. I trust it will be a great demonstration.[2]

Fr William showed me one of your last letters to him, and I am obliged to say that it was so intolerable in its skits and jibes, as almost to make me start as if a gnat stung me, and I saw it was impossible he could do more than he actually did, that is, attend to all your wants, as far as he knew them[3]

Yrs ever affecty J H Card Newman

[1] These were Maria Giberne's portraits of witnesses for the Achilli trial, painted gradually, to keep them occupied, while waiting for the trial to begin. See letter of 24 February 1852 to Miss Giberne (*L.D.* XV, p. 43).

[2] Leo XIII's Encyclical Letter on the Rosary, urging that it should be said for the deliverance of the Church, was issued on 1 September. This was to be done publicly each day during the month of October. Sobieski relieved the Turkish siege of Vienna on 12 September 1683.

[3] Miss Giberne wrote on this letter, 'I cannot think what he means I wrote an easy friendly letter and nothing more How wonderful dear Father you never understand me now—Is it Fr Willm who has changed your ideas about me?'

To Mark Pattison

Bm Dec 27. 1883

My very dear Pattison,

I grieve to hear that you are very unwell. How is it that I, who am so old am carried on in years beyond my juniors?

This makes me look back in my thoughts forty years, when you, with Dalgairns and so many others now gone, were entering into life.

For the sake of those dear old days, I cannot help writing to you. Is there any way in which I can serve you? At least I can give you my prayers, such as they are,

Yours affectionately John H Card. Newman

To Mark Pattison

Jany 8. 1884

My dear Pattison

As you only said 'no' to my coming to see you on *Monday*, but implied I might come to you some other day, I will make a call tomorrow, Wednesday.

You need not see me, if it is too much for you—but my coming will not be *sudden* now, as it would have been then.[1]

Yrs affecty J. H. Card Newman

[1] Pattison wrote at once to Newman after his visit, a letter which Neville acknowledged on 10 January, saying that Newman had borne the journey well.

On 28 January Pattison wrote his account to Meta Bradley, in the last volume of his letters to her, among the Pattison Papers at the Bodleian Library: 'Surely I told you all the particulars of Newman's visit, if I did not it was a strange omission, as it was the most remarkable event of this winter's illness, and has been the object of general wonder and curiosity here. After he had accepted, or acquiesced in my put off for the reasons I gave, on the Wednesday morning I got a note saying he would be here at 12 o'clock. I need not say how flurried I was by this, for other reasons, but also now my invalid routine of hours was upset. He came at 12 and left at 2.15 to return to Birmingham and out of that short time had to be taken lunch. The interview was most affecting. I was dreadfully agitated, distressed even. On the one hand I felt what a proof of affection he was giving, to one who had travelled so far, from what he regarded as important—On the other, I felt that it was not all personal regard which had brought him, but the hope, however slight, that I might still be got over in my last moments. And I could not tell in what proportion these two motives might have influenced N. to undertake a fatiguing journey. The conversation at first turned on old times and recollections. It gradually slid into religious discourse, when I found as I expected, that he had not realized the enormous distance at which I had left behind the stand-point of 1845. More than this he did not seem to apprehend more than any ordinary Catholic would have done, that there is such a space to travel, or that one can look back upon the ideas of those days as the ideas of childish ignorance. Of course I could not set about trying to put things in this light to a man of 84, let alone a Cardinal. On the other hand I did not feel it right to leave him under the illusion in which he evidently was that I was still hesitating about my road and doubting as we were in 1845 as to where the true church was to be found. In this dilemma having to be true and on the other hand having to avoid the futile attempt to explain to him, what it was evident could not be explained, I was in great embarrassment as to how to express myself. N. did not of course attempt the vulgar arts of conversion, nor was there anything like clerical cant, or affection of unction like a parson's talk by a deathbed. He dwelt upon his own personal experiences since he had been reconciled to the Church, the secret comfort and support which had been given him in the way of supernatural grace under many great trials; that he had never been deserted by such help for a moment; that his soul had found sweet peace and rest in the bosom of the Church. Then we got for a moment, but only for a moment, on more controversial matter. Here he had nothing to say, but the old argument of the Apologia which I need not repeat to you. I said in answer three hypotheses each less probable than the one before it. After I had said this I regretted it, but was relieved to find that he had not taken the scope of the remark, so it passed harmless. We very soon changed the conversation; he allowing me to ask him several questions about Oriel before I became a member of it. This last conversation I should have liked to have prolonged as it interested me much more than the other, but I felt that that was not what he had come for and was therefore shy of pursuing it

There I have given you an outline of what took place; considering the busy life you are now leading it is probably more than you will care for. But it is the fullest account I have yet written and as you are so careful to keep my letters I consider that I have placed it upon record in as permanent a way as I could.'
Pattison died on 30 July.

To Edward Bellasis, Junior

Private   Birmingham February 4. 1884.

My dear Edward,

Thank you for the letters. The chief thwarters I had at Rome were Ward and Vaughan—and Manning did his part. I tell you this in confidence. I never intended this to be known, and at least of all *now*, when my Cardinalate, so wonderfully conferred on me washes me quite clean. I have carefully kept all the documents, *meaning never to use them* or *letting them* be used except in a case of necessity.

To use them would be a great scandal which I never would bring about, except it was a duty. That is, I cannot be quite sure that, after I am gone, false statements may not be confidently put forward against me (e.g. as maintained at Rome in 1867 that I had set up the Oratory School to feed Oxford, a simple falsehood) and in that case from my papers a brief answer might be given, reaching no further than the occasion required.

Hence I have thought and think that no account of my *Catholic* life can ever be given, for it would involve the saying things which would be disadvantageous to the reputation of men who for their writings (and or) their works are in merited esteem.

To John Rickards Mozley

March 14. 1884

My dear John

You are quite right in thinking I should be deeply interested in your letter, and grateful to you for writing it. It is that which all these scientific men need, and which is hid from them, the experience of the religious soul. . . . [1] Of course what are called 'experiences' involve often much that is enthusiastic and wild, but usum non tollit abusus.

For myself, now at the end of a long life I say from a full heart that God has never failed me—never disappoint[ed] me—has ever turned evil into good for me. When I was young, I used to say (and I trust it was not presumptuous to say it) that our Lord ever answered my prayers. And what He has been to me, who have deserved His love so little, such He will be, I believe and know, He will be to every one who does not repel Him and turn from His pleading.

And now I believe He is visiting you, and it rejoices me to think He will gain you.

Yours very affectionately John H. Card. Newman

[1] J. R. Mozley had written to his uncle about his conviction, gained from his own experience, of the 'personal help of Jesus Christ for our permanent welfare' as indispensable.

To William Philip Gordon

March 19. 1884

Dear Father Superior

What a pity I should be asked for more than I can possibly grant![1]

Three years ago, I was the first to move towards you, before any one had said a word to me, in order that we might end well with acts of grace on both sides; and, in the first page of the memorial which your Community accepted from me, I spoke of myself solely as a Cardinal.[2]

Both then, and the year before, I was indebted to you for acts of hospitality.[3]

Thus things seemed well settled: now all is reversed. I am appealed to in the name of St Philip to renew a tie which he broke thirty years ago; and am asked to take part in an act, which concerns intimately and solely the London Oratory. Thus we shall end with a recognized disruption.[4]

Why could you not have sounded me, before you let the Duke write to me? Why did you so little consult for me as not to hinder his making a request to me, which

543

I am obliged for so many reasons not to entertain? Have I shown anything but kindness to you personally?

I have delayed my answer to the Duke for several days. If you wish to be kind to me, prepare him in the interval for what that answer will be. It will, alas, be a disappointment to him, and to the kind hearts which surround him. But that is all you can do now.

God bless you

Yours affectionately John H Card. Newman

The Very Rev. Fr Gordon

[1] The Duke of Norfolk wrote to Newman on 18 March that Father William Gordon wished to invite him to the opening of their new church.

[2] See at 2 July 1881 the dedication in the first volume of the set of Newman's works, which he presented to the Fathers of the London Oratory (*L.D.* XXIX, p. 390).

[3] See letter of 18 June 1879 to the Duke of Norfolk and letter of 14 April 1881 to Gordon, as well as Appendix 3, *L.D.* XXIX, pp. 429–30.

[4] Here the clash between Newman and the London Oratorians emerged again. Had relations between them been normal, the invitation to him as founder would have been quite in order, but after the relationship between the two Oratories had broken down in 1855–6, because of the false and damaging report, spread by the London house and never withdrawn, that Newman claimed formal power over them, he refused to act as if nothing had happened. As Cardinal, he sought to be gracious, but as founder he refused to condone the past. The 'recognised disruption' was the impairing of pacific relations by recalling that past, which moreover could hardly be done without the reasons for it becoming to some extent public.

To The Duke Of Norfolk (Draft)[1]

Mar 21/84

My dear Duke

There are few wishes of yours to which I should not at once accede; and when I make your present proposal one of those exceptions my only consolation in my real pain in not complying with it is that the very earnestness with which you urge it upon me shows that you are partly prepared for its being very difficult for me to grant.

And indeed it is impossible for many and various reasons, among which I will only note this that I have been represented, at Rome and elsewhere as well as at home to my great disadvantage, as claiming formal power over the London Oratory, and that to participate in an act so simply internal to it as that to which you invite me ⟨under past circumstances⟩ would seem to justify ⟨countenance⟩ a charge as injurious to me as unfounded. This is not said in the spirit of controversy but because I was bound out of respect and love towards Your Grace not to send ⟨leave⟩ you a blank or a bald refusal You must kindly believe that my words mean more than they say.

I am sure you will trust me as writing seriously and deliberately, as being Your Grace's affectionate Servant

JHN

P S Thank you kindly[?] for your offer, had I come to London to take me in at N. [Norfolk] House.

[1] This is the draft of Newman's reply to the Duke of Norfolk's letter of 18 March referred to in note to that of 19 March to W. P. Gordon. It is given in full for the sake of the explicit second paragraph, which Newman omitted in the letter as sent.

To Anne Mozley

March 23. 1884

My dear Anne Mozley

I write a line to tell you that my poor brother Charles died yesterday. He must have had some curious natural gifts, for eccentric, violent and self-willed as he was, he attached to him the mother and daughter with whom he lodged and, the mother having died, the daughter has refused a nurse and has nurst him day and night through his last illness.

It is more than sixty years that he embraced and acted on the principles of Owen the Socialist.

He was past 80. I believe you just saw him once.[1]

Yours affecly John H. Card. Newman

[1] George Huntington, the Rector of Tenby, wrote on 23 March that Charles Robert Newman died 'without a struggle and apparently without pain'.

To William Philip Gordon

March 25. 1884

My dear Fr Superior

I thank you for your letter received yesterday, and in turn I sincerely withdraw any thing I have said which was unnecessary and inconsiderate towards you, for which I am very sorry, but it is most difficult to say just what one means, and nothing else.[1]

No one here, as far as I know, had, or has, any thought of my being asked to the opening of your Church, (so no harm is done,) or, as far as I have heard, has wished it. Rather, they have thought that a building on so grand a scale implied that *they* at Birmingham were very rich, and that impression in various ways has been a disadvantage to us.

I have for 30 years enlarged to every one who asked, what little intimacy, according to my experience, there is between the Italian Oratories: and kept a strict silence about any deeper cause in our case. I don't think then any remark will be made, especially considering my age, on my absence from your opening

Yours affectly John H Card. Newman

---

[1] Gordon wrote on 23 March: 'I can only again express my great sorrow at having most unintentionally displeased your Eminence. I regret very much having spoken to the Duke before I had written to your Eminence but it was in my mind a very preliminary step and I had no idea that the Duke would act upon it.

I could hardly have had a greater mortification than to have seemed wanting in appreciation of your Eminence's past kindness, and to have actually caused you annoyance by my want of tact and judgment.'

To Emily Fortey

Birmingham Oct 3. 1884

My dear Child

I thank God with my whole heart for His goodness to you, and gladly send you my blessing. I will not forget you on Saturday.[1]

I think your Father has been very good to you. It was right you should have a trial, but he has not opposed your convictions, as some parents have in their dealings with their children.

You must not suppose your present state of peace and joy will always continue. It is God's mercy to bring us over difficulties. As time goes on, you may be cast down to find that your warmth of feeling does not last as it once was, and instead of it you may have trials of various kinds. Never mind; be brave; make acts of faith, hope, and charity; put yourself into God's hands, and thank Him for all that he sends you, pleasant or painful. The Psalms and Saint Paul's Epistles will be your great and abiding consolation.

'Rejoice with trembling'.[2] I say all this, not as dissuading you from enjoying your present joy and peace, but that you may enjoy them religiously.

I repeat, God bless you, keep you, and direct you. Through His grace you have begun life well. May he give you perseverance.[3]

Yours most sincerely John H. Card. Newman

---

[1] On 2 October 1884 Emily Fortey wrote: 'Nearly two and a half years ago, when I was feeling rather in a muddle, I wrote to you and you were kind enough to write a very beautiful letter to me. [That of 6 July 1882]. Then, following your advice, I went to see a Priest, and I have never been in a muddle since. All this time I have not been allowed to go to a Catholic Church or see Priests, but my father found that it made no difference to me; I was still at heart a Catholic, so lately he has given me permission to do as I like. So I have been instructed and on Saturday, the Feast of S. Francis, a day specially chosen by me, I am going to be received into the Church. And now I am writing to thank you *very* much for your kindness to me more than two years ago. Perhaps if you had not written to me I might never have become a Catholic'.

[2] *Psalm* 2:11.

[3] Emily Fortey visited Newman on 8 August 1887. When he died, she wrote from 11 Orchard Gardens, Teignmouth: 'Dear Father Ryder, May my flowers be put somewhere near his feet?'

To Anne Mozley

Bm Octr 20. 1884

Confidential

My dear Anne Mozley

I think your volume, not only singularly interesting and valuable, for so it must be to *me*, but well done as a sample of clear and careful putting together and of good judgment in literary work.[1] James [Mozley] would have reason to say with Queen Catharine, 'After my death I wish no other herald, But such an honest chronicler as Griffith',[2] and that, because you have let him speak for himself.

This leads me to speak of myself. Many years ago, at two separate independent times, I came to the conclusion, that, if a memoir was to be published of me, a Protestant Editor must take the Protestant part, and a Catholic the Catholic. When I went down at a later date, 1876 to Blachford, I was struck by Lord B. volunteering the same judgment As to the Catholic part, it does not concern me. It cannot be written for many years. I never could take part in it myself; it would involve a criticism on various persons. My representatives have instructions only to answer misrepresentations to my disadvantage from curious persons wishing to elicit secret history, if they can

What I thought could be done, and what only, was a sketch of my life up to 1833, which with the Apologia from 1833 to 1845 would finish my Protestant years. With this view in 1874 I wrote a brief memoir of my life up to 1833.[3] This, I think, of printing so as to have it ready almost upon my death in order to break, as much as I can, the sale and the gossip of catch penny publications.

Though I am open to the criticism and advice of friends, that is not my special desideratum just now—but the following. I have a number of letters of my own, and of my mother and sisters, and memoranda, and while I know they afford illustrations of my Memoir, yet in a matter so personal I cannot go by my own judgment.

The only persons (besides Fr Neville) who have seen the Memoir are Jemima and Jane [Mozley].

What I venture to ask of you is to read the Memoir, when I have got it copied, and to say whether it needs illustration and where[4]

Yours affectly John H Card. Newman

---

[1] *Letters of J. B. Mozley* (London, 1885), 'edited by his sister.' Anne Mozley's Advertisement at the beginning is dated 'September 1884'.

[2] Shakespeare, *King Henry the Eighth*, IV, ii.

[3] A.W., pp. 29–107. See also *Moz.* I, between pp. 26 and 160.

[4] Anne Mozley thanked Newman on 21 October, 'Your most kind judgment of the work as a whole has set up my spirits' and added, 'the book has already brought a lasting satisfaction—your entrusting me with the MS. you tell me of. I have been feeling that my work of this sort was quite over and here comes a task of all others most interesting to me.'

To Anne Mozley

Jany 16. 1885

My dear Anne Mozley

I see I have completely puzzled you, and I am puzzled myself. One thing I ask of you not to send my MS back at once as you propose Think better of this by thinking longer. I am much gratified to have your praise, but I wanted from you something else, but I hardly know what I wanted, and time is going.

I am very well at present—but no one can reckon on his life at my age. Lord Blachford, as an independent witness confirmed me on my own idea that a Memoir of me up to 1845 should be written by an Anglican.[1] I doubt whether my Catholic Life can ever be written without causing much controversy, which ought not without strong reason to be allowed.

Then I thought how few there are now among Anglicans who know any thing about me, or would care to bother themselves with my collections of letters etc This led me in 1874 to write, as a specimen, the MS I have sent you, of what I should like This I sent to Jemima, but, tho' I dare say she felt, she showed, no interest in it, and I had it back.

As time has gone on, I have got more reconciled to the idea of its being not a mere specimen, but, as far as it goes, the memoir itself; but I should ask of the friend or well wisher into whose hands it came to exercise a judgment on every part of it, and omitting or inserting accordingly

And I speculated on his doing his work, (whether from my papers or from other informations in my life time,) and *that I should never see what he had done.*

If you look back on my letters already written to you, perhaps they will become clearer to you now.

Now, if you consent to keep MS a while, perhaps suggestions may occur, and may lead me to explain more fully my difficulties and wishes

Yours affecty John H. Card. Newman

[1] See letter of 20 October 1884 to Anne Mozley.

To Anne Mozley

Febr. 10. 1885

My dear Anne Mozley

First let me say that I wish you quite to understand that I am to have no part in any thing you write. I am neither to *see* nor to *suggest* knowingly any thing which you pen. This does not mean that neither you nor I am at liberty to introduce into your work *bodily* and with an *open profession* remarks or statements of mine, which you may wish to have, e.g. the whole of the memoir which I sent you to read, but you would not make yourself answerable for one word of it.

And I should say that I sent that Memoir to you for quite a distinct reason—viz to set before you what *I* thought the *best* way of writing a memoir, viz. to be brief, not to pad, not to digress etc. etc, but not for me to *bind* you even to this. I consider you ought to pursue your own ideal of a Memoir, not mine, and that I should never see what would in fact be after my death. At the same time it is plain that I should not have taken the step of asking of you a great favour, if I did not believe that your ideal would not be very different from my own. And in particular, I should say I do not object to footnotes, if the possible evils, which I pointed out are kept in mind.

If you think it best to begin with the autograph Memoir I sent you, you can; and you can add to it, if you wish so that you *profess* to be adding. On this supposition your own independent work would commence in 1832, when I had just given up the Tutorship. At this time the influence of Hurrell Froude upon me was fully developed, and my University Sermon of December 2 1832, preached the day before I set out for Gibraltar is worth looking at, and then you are launched on your own work. The documents I should send you are my letters home and to my Sisters from 1815 to 1845, my Mother's to me from 1817 to 1836; perhaps some private memorandums from 1816 to 1828; my letters from abroad 1832–3 a number of notes on particular points, such as 'Number 1, Number 2, Number etc' spoken of in a recent letter,[1] none of them yet written;—my letters to Bowden, Keble etc Hurrell Froude for a long course of years—This is enough for the present.

You would find many letters of mine 1839–45 in Hope Scott's life. Vid. also Froude's Remains volume 1 and 2 ⟨?⟩

I am so very busy, that I must ask you to bear with some delay[2]

Yours affectly John H Card. Newman

[1] Letter of 14 January to Anne Mozley (*L.D.* XXXI, pp. 11–12).

[2] Anne Mozley replied on 11 February and remarked, 'my aim would be in my selection of letters etc to show a *character*'. Then she went on, 'Every letter of yours that I have seen—with thought or character in it—all tells the same way, is as it were a representative letter, as coming from the same mind and hand and *heart*. No one can help the book being interesting that has such letters in it'.

To Mary Murphy

April 7. 1885

Dear Mrs Murphy

Your letter and its contents took away my breath. I was deeply moved to find that a book of mine had been in General Gordon's hands, and that, the description of a soul preparing for death.[1]

I send it back to you, with my heartfelt thanks, by this post in a registered cover. It is additionally precious, as having Mr Power's writing in it[2]

Most truly Yours John H. Card. Newman[3]

[1] Mary Murphy wrote on 6 April from 10 Upper Mount Street, Dublin: 'Seeing that you are a large subscriber to the "Memorial Fund" for General Gordon, it strikes me, that you would be pleased to see the enclosed little book It was given to my brother the late Mr Frank Power by General Gordon soon after his

arrival in Khartoum. As you will see by the front page the pencil marking through the book is done by General Gordon himself I need not say how highly I prize it, for many reasons so I will feel obliged if you will return it to me at your earliest convenience.' This was a copy of the small edition of *The Dream of Gerontius*. Power was *The Times* correspondent at Khartoum, which General Gordon reached on 18 February 1884. On the same day he gave this marked copy to Power, who sent it to his sister. Gordon received the copy in Egypt and must have read it on his way to the Sudan. See end of letter of 19 May 1885 to Lord Blachford. His friend E. A. Maund wrote on 30 January 1888 to Miss Gordon: 'It may interest you to know how it was that General Gordon had this little Roman Catholic poem with him in Khartoum.

'The day he left, your brother related to me how his spiritual life was changed by what he experienced at his father's death-bed, as, gazing on his lifeless form, he thought: "Is this what we all come to?" This led to a long discussion of death, when I remarked that some of his ideas reminded me of Dr. Newman's little Book, *The Dream of Gerontius*. Whereupon he said he should like to read it; and I promised to send it after him to Egypt. Your brother in a postcard, dated from Khartoum, 7 March, 1884, acknowledging the book says: "My Dear Mr. Maund,—Your letter 25 January arrived today . . . , Thanks for the little book . . . "' *General Gordon's Letters to his Sister* (London, 1888), pp. 402–3.

[2] Gordon wrote in the fly leaf: 'Frank Power with kindest regards of C G Gordon 18 Feby 84.' Power wrote below this:

'Dearest M
    I send you this little book which General Gordon has given me. The pencil marking thro' the book is his Frank Power Khartoum'.

On 10 September 1884 Power steamed down the Nile to try to hasten the relieving force. His ship struck a rock and on 18 September he was murdered.

[3] Neville made several transcriptions of Gordon's markings into copies of the Dream. The first was sent to Dean Church, who wrote to Newman on 10 April: 'You are indeed kind in letting me have a copy of the book with the pencil notes and marks. . . . All our party are alive to the interest of the book—one result was that they all went to get copies of the small edition'.

To Lord Blachford

May 19. 1885

My dear Blachford

You have escaped a long letter by my difficulty of writing, and perhaps a short one will not unsuitably stand as a mode of thanking you for yours.

I wonder you don't go back further for our present leap in the dark—a leap which, coinciding with our foreign difficulties, is a most grave event.[1]

Why don't you go back to 1832? since which I personally have felt that I was not clever enough to have any politics. That so called Reform (tho' a Reform was necessary) was a party move in favour of Whiggism—and has not Reform been shamefully used, or shamelessly, by both parties as a party weapon since? Some years, I think, before Disraeli's and Gladstone's handling of it, I recollect an occasion when Lord John [Russell] shed tears in the House, when he found his Bill was not to pass,[2] he who had indirectly called the Act of 1832 scarcely less than a Revolution. Disraeli in 1865 ⟨?⟩ had this excuse, that he with many Tories thought that to lower the Franchise would be to increase the Aristocratic power, but what excuse has poor Gladstone for helping on the Radicals? How well it would be for him if he had carried out his resolution in 1874 ⟨?⟩ to give his last years to something giving more satisfaction than Radicalism, initiating his new career with a wanton attack upon the

Catholic Church! We have been accustomed to say that Lord John never prospered after he attacked the Catholic Church. How truly this is said I cannot tell; but it certainly has struck me that perhaps it can be said of Gladstone. This is quite consistent with my acknowledgment of what is so admirable and high in Gladstone's character and conduct.

Well, I have done pretty well, considering what I said about short and long letters when I began. I will but say a word about Gordon.

What struck me so much in his use of 'The Dream etc' was that in St Paul's words he 'died daily'—he was always on his death bed, fulfilling the common advice that we should ever pass the day, as if it was to be our last[3]

Ever Yrs affectly John H Card. Newman

[1] This refers to Gladstone's Franchise Act, passed at the end of 1884.
[2] When withdrawing his Reform Bill on 11 April 1854.
[3] See letter of 7 April to Mary Murphy.

To Anne Mozley

Sept. 7. 1885

My dear Anne Mozley

Thank you for your sympathy. Dear Copeland was one of the faithfullest of friends, and a great loss.[1] I write with such difficulty, that I write as little as I can—but I have managed to write out my letters to Keble. I think you would like to see them. I should propose to send you only the Anglican—they reach to May 1843, when I told him I was likely to be a Catholic I should not wonder if that date would be found to be the best that could be taken for the termination of your undertaking

Yours affectly John H. Card Newman

[1] W. J. Copeland died on 26 August.

To Miss M. R. Giberne

Septr 8. 1885

My dear Sister Pia,

I had your letters in my hands only the other day. I shall be sure to find them—and wish you to determine whether I should send them to you or to burn them. Recollect, I have made use of them in the Apologia.[1]

Mr Copeland, as you know is gone. My oldest living friends are, besides you, Rogers and T. Mozley—is it not so?

I have finished my article.[2] I don't think people will *like* it—but I am *satisfied* with it. My trouble with it has been very great. My memory goes before I have set down what I have in my mind, and I have been fagging six hours and more every day to find by next morning that it won't do—and I must do it over again When I was once atop of the embankment all was right—but how should I get there

Ever Yours affectionately J H Card. Newman[3]

[1] Miss Giberne had asked for Newman's letters to her to be returned to her. She wrote again on 10 September 1885, 'it is my great and fervent wish for years to possess them once more before I die. Why, *they* with your published writings were the making of me'. She promised they would be returned to Newman after her death, if he wished.

[2] See next letter.

[3] This letter seems to have been the last Newman wrote to Maria Giberne.

To Percy William Bunting

Sept 9. 1885

Dear Sir

I ask to be allowed to insert in the Contemporary Review an answer to Principal Fairbairn's criticism of me in your number of last May.[1] The Article will take from 8 to 10 of your pages. The copy is printing—I have done this for my own convenience; it will not interfere with your printer

I hope you will allow me to make two conditions 1. that I should not receive any payment for the Article and 2. that I retain the copy right of it.[2]

I am, Dear Sir, Yours faithfully
J H Card Newman

[1] A. M. Fairbairn's article was 'Catholicism and Modern Thought', *Contemporary Review* (May 1885), pp. 652–74, reprinted in *Catholicism: Roman and Anglican* (3rd edn, London, 1899), pp. 94–140. He accused Newman of philosophical scepticism and of withdrawing the proofs of religion from the region of reason into the realm of conscience and imagination.

[2] On 10 September John Rae replied on behalf of Bunting, editor of the *Contemporary Review*, 'Of course we assent to your conditions', and asked for Newman's article in time for the next number, where it appeared as 'The Development of Religious Error', *Contemporary Review* (Oct. 1885), pp. 457–69, reprinted separately in 1886 by Burns and Oates, and in *S.E.*, pp. 69–89, also in *The Theological Papers of John Henry Newman on Faith and Certainty*, Oxford 1976, pp. 140–9.

To Lord Blachford

Sept. 14. 1885

My dear Blachford

You know how very sensitive I am, more so because I am older—but let me say a word apropos of Miss Mozley's great kindness towards me. I wanted all my papers (down to *May 1843*, when I told Keble I was likely to be a Catholic) to be left on my death for the inspection of some contemporary of mine (they will be the property of Fr William Neville.) I mean, not only a contemporary, but an Anglican and a friend. I felt I could not escape the chance of the book making by strangers which pays so well, if I did not succeed in my own attempt. I thought that the three conditions of a friend, an Anglican and a contemporary, *if possible*, would give the prospect of a true account of what otherwise would be sure to be full of errors. Ah, if 'possible'—for there is another condition still. It would not be published till after my death. I could not let it be written with the chance, the opportunity of my seeing any part of it—yet every year takes away contemporaries.

Under these circumstances I read Miss M's volume of James Mozley's Letters—and it struck me, I should be fortunate, if she would receive my papers with a view to using them in her own way. I wanted her to accept the full leave and discretion to use just what of them she would, making on my part two conditions, that it should not be published till after my death, and that I should not see any part of it, or hear about it in prospect.

Now I am come to my sensitiveness. I could not be in better hands than yours and Church's. I should be more than contented. You would not in all things agree with me—who would? but I should perfectly trust you both, as well as Miss M. I should be grateful. But let me be dead to it—don't speak about it to me—don't say whether it is 'interesting' or not. There is just this one thing I can't help having [hoping] and should be pleased to find—that my papers had come back to Wm Neville (tho' I am in no hurry for them) This would show the work was done, but I can't expect this will come to pass in my life time.[1]

Ever Yrs affly J. H. Card. Newman

[1] On 5 October Anne Mozley wrote to Newman: 'I have had letters lately from Lord Blachford and the Dean *very* satisfactory to me.'

To Lord Blachford

September 17th. 1885

My very dear Blachford,

I don't like to be seeming to be striving for the last word—and I assure you I had nothing of any feeling you would wish away in noting the word 'interesting'—but the long and the short is that I am as if my skin was torn off (metaphorically) by the number of Memoirs written of me (written in kindness). Within this week I hear that one of my Catholic life is coming out[1]—I do feel gratitude—and so I should to a surgeon who performed an operation upon me—But, besides this, in Miss Mozley's matter came the additional imagination lest I myself should have part in a work which I professed (however truly) so hugely to dislike; and 'interesting' was the first touch of my having a partnership in it. Forgive me if I have hurt you.

Yours affectionately, John H. Card: Newman.

P.S. I know well how anxious I was about the Oriel Election in 1833, but had quite forgotten it came into my letters.[2]

[1] Wilfrid Meynell wrote on 13 September that he was about to publish 'a record of your Eminence's Catholic Life' in *Merry England* (October 1885), under the pseudonym of 'John Oldcastle'. In fact it was

described as 'Cardinal Newman Number', and was occupied entirely with him during the forty years after October 1845, except for a dedication at the beginning to Cardinal Manning.

[2] This refers to the Oriel Fellowship election, when Frederic Rogers (Lord Blachford), and Charles Marriott were elected. See *A.W.*, p. 134, and letters to John Frederic Christie, 6 April 1833, and Mrs Newman, 9 June 1833.

To *William Barry*

The Oratory Nov 4. 1885

Dear Dr Barry

I thank you sincerely for your article about me in the Contemporary of this month. It is in form an answer to Dr Fairbairn, but from its impartiality and fairness it is really a defence of me.[1]

I require and desire no better defence, for it would be a great mistake in me, to suppose that any thing I have written, with whatever care, was not in some way or other open to criticism.

There is only one point to which I will call your attention. In an Oxford Sermon, preached in 1839, which Dr Fairbairn confuses with my 'Grammar of Assent' I have expressed a doubt whether the argument from *final causes* is, as facts stand, sufficient to prove the being of God[2] (vid. also 'the Idea of a University' p 219) but that is not all one with denying that the *physical universe* was sufficient to prove it. On the contrary, I should maintain that the very fact of the world's existence implies an Almighty, intelligent, personal Creator. And again, the same great truth is proved from what I should call the argument from *design*, that is, from the wonderful order, harmony, unity, and beautifulness of the Universe as dwelt on in the Psalm 'Caeli enarrant'.[3]

I am, Dear Dr Barry Very truly Yours
John H Card Newman

P.S. Since writing this, Fr Ryder has given me your message.

[1] 'Catholicism and Reason', *Contemporary Review* (Nov. 1885), pp. 656–75. After explaining that no individual could be taken as in all things the spokesman of the Catholic Church, Barry defended Newman's teaching on reason and on conscience.

[2] 'Faith and Reason, contrasted as habits of mind', *U.S.*, p. 194.

[3] *Psalm* 18:2.

To *Richard Stanton*

Decr 6. 1885

My dear Fr Stanton

Sister Mary Pia, had been in retreat and had renewed her vows.[1] She was very happy, and took part in the recreation with much gaiety, to use the Bishop's word. Then she wrote a letter to Mr Fullerton, and went either to her work room or to her cell. She was found on the floor with her face downward insensible and bleeding.

This was about 4 o'clock. She remained in that state till 7 o'clock next morning, the 2nd, when she died.

Her letter to Mr F. was like any other letter, without any appearance of illness, of weakness and confusion. I think she spoke of some pictures which she was engaged upon and her handwriting was quite as usual.[2]

You kindly ask after my health. I have nothing the matter with me, but I am feeble. My eyesight is failing me, and my organs of speech, and my hearing, and my writing fingers, my knees and my ankles; so that at any time some part of me might give way, or have an accident. I have had several falls—I walk, read, write, speak at a snail's pace, and my mind gets soon confused, especially my memory. Thus I may call myself emphatically in God's hands, unable to move day by day except He wills it.

I pray for all your Fathers the best and fullest blessings of the coming Sacred Season and am,

My dear Fr Stanton Yours affecty
John H Card. Newman

The Rev Fr Stanton

[1] Stanton thanked Newman for a telegram announcing Miss Giberne's death on 2 December.

[2] Newman had also sent a telegram to Alexander Fullerton, who in return forwarded Miss Giberne's last letter. This had reached him only an hour or so before Newman's telegram.

To The Superior of the Visitation Convent at Autun

[15 December 1885]

I write to you, Reverend Mother, to condole with you and your Community on the loss you have sustained in the death of your dear Sister Mary Pia This at the moment is an extreme trial, especially when we consider the shock which was caused and its suddenness and other circumstance. Bearing this in mind, I have offered the Holy Sacrifice on this morning, the Octave of the Immaculate Conception for you all, feeling a great sympathy for you invoking in your behalf the powerful intercession of the Blessed Virgin, so dear to you and to her

But I trust your 'sorrow will soon be turned into joy'. Heaviness endures for a night, but joy comes in the morning.[1] You have another Sister in heaven to pray for you, and to aid you in your journey to the land of rest and gladness. You have for 25 years given her a shelter and a home, while she was on earth, and she will not be ungrateful to you for your [care], but will do her part in securing you an eternal habitation and home for you in heaven

I cannot close this letter without thanking you for the great care you have taken to inform me without delay of the death of one in whom I was so much interested, and for whom I had so true and deep an interest.

I send you and all the inmates of your Monastery my fullest blessing and am

[1] *John* 16:20; *Psalm* 30:5.

To J. Spencer Northcote

June 2. 1886

Dear Provost Northcote

I do indeed, with all my heart, join in the Address of congratulation, which, I believe, you are sending to the dear Bishop on the completion of the 40th year of his episcopate, and I hope that the chapter and clergy will allow me to unite my name to theirs in their pleasant and dutiful act.[1]

I recollect the day of consecration well. His Lordship had most kindly invited me and my intimate friends to the sacred rite, and after it he did me the special favour of making me acquainted with that holy woman, Mother Margaret Halloran [*sic*].

Not long after the Oratory took its start in England, and special relations were created by the Holy Father's Brief between its Fathers and the Bishop of Birmingham, and the experience of the long series of years which have followed has filled me, as you may well understand, with the affectionate and grateful recollections, which so holy and kind a Superior could not fail to impress upon me.

This letter but feebly expresses what I would say—but I am losing the use of my fingers, and, strange to say, this confuses and impedes my use of words

I am, My dear Provost, Yours most sincerely
John H Card. Newman

The Very Rev Provost Northcote

---

[1] There was no formal Address from the Clergy. In the middle of June Newman called on Ullathorne at Oscott College. The latter wrote: 'He came alone, was very feeble, and glad of an arm along the gallery; but cheerful, gentle, and affectionate.' Butler, *The Life and Times of Bishop Ullathorne*, II, p. 277.

To Lord Blachford

October 5. 1886

My dear Blachford,

When our Cook first saw your partridges, she cried out 'O how lovely' What will happen, when the first fruits of October makes its appearance!

I had not heard of the death of young Wilson.[1] Such sad events inflict upon one what I hope is not a wrong pessimism. In 2 of his plays Terence introduces the fear 'ne aut filius alserit aut usquam ceciderit,' 'peregre rediens aut filii peccatum, aut uxoris mortem, aut morbum filiae.'[2] Of course this carried our powers too much, for we cannot with Timon[3] leave human kind—but at times it is a keen and irresistible thought. I recollect, on the loss of my dear sister[4] shortly before I knew you, how my mother would not leave off gazing on her portrait—and I always have thought that she was going in fancy through the prospective sorrows and trials of her life, had she lived.

As to hobbies, doubtless I have mine as well as another, but you have not quite hit on mine. On publishing my Apologia, strangers asked me for a list of my publications. I think I attempted one in the second edition, and I soon found I could not stop short of some arrangement, yet the greater part of what I have written, is caused by *occasions* which needed putting together—and one hobby I will confess to is a love of order, good in itself, but excessive.

But I don't go on; in order to spare your eyes and to mortify my egotism.

I will but say about Athanasius that my second edition arose from my wish to make it as different from that in the Library of the Fathers as I could to meet Pusey's generosity, and that my plan was spoiled by my being called to Rome for the Cardinalate. I have stated and apologised for this in my Advertisement.[5] I shall not live for the proof sheets of edition 3.[6]

Yours affectionately, J. H. Newman

The pheasant is come. My Greek friend was Linwood.

P.S. Thank your sister for her most welcome letter.

[1] Blachford, thinking of the man's father, R. F. Wilson, wrote, 'Certainly paternity has a good deal of suffering to set against the blank of childlessness', which was his own state.

[2] *Adelphi*, I, i, 11–12; *Phormio*, II, i, 13–14.

[3] The Cynic philosopher.

[4] Mary Newman died on 5 January 1828.

[5] Lord Blachford wrote on 4 October, 'I am amused at your taking refuge in Athanasius as a light relaxation.'

[6] This was published in 1887.

To Nicholas Darnell

Nov 12th 1886.

My dear Fr Nicholas

I am not a good scribe just now, but I have been thinking of you ever since I heard so poor an account of you from R Bellasis, that you had left your work in the North and were constrained to be all but idle at Clifton.[1]

I can fancy how this may try you and have been setting my brains to work to find how I could show you my sympathy. I can find nothing better than to ask your acceptance from me of my publication of Mr Palmer's Russian Journal which it is possible you have not seen and which will at least show I do not forget you.[2]

Yours affectionately John H Card: Newman

[1] Darnell had retired from his parish at Haydon Bridge, Northumberland, and was living at the Clifton Wood Convent.

[2] Darnell, whose actions as headmaster of the Oratory School in 1861 had been such a trial to Newman, replied on 15 November, 'how utterly unworthy I feel myself of your great condescension and goodness in admitting me to occupy a place in your thoughts for a single moment—one who has been worse than unfaithful to S. Philip and yourself, and so long estranged from your salutary influence and your happy home.'

On 18 November Darnell acknowledged William Palmer's *Notes of a Visit to the Russian Church*, in which was written 'With the affectionate regards of John H Card. Newman'.

To Alfred Henry Spurrier

Dec. 11. 1886

I wish the state of my fingers allowed me to write a sufficient, or at least a readable answer to your question. I must be abrupt, because I must be short.

Who can have *dared* to say that I am disappointed in the Church of Rome? 'dared,' because I have never uttered, or written, or thought, or felt the very shadow of disappointment. I believe it to be a human institution as well as divine, and so far as it is human it is open to the faults of human nature; but if, because I think, with others, that its rulers have sometimes erred as fallible men, I therefore think it has failed, such logic won't hold; indeed, it is the wonderful anticipation in Our Lord's and St Paul's teaching, of apparent failure [and real] success in the times after them which has ever been one of my strong arguments for believing them divine messengers.

But I can't write more. One word as to your next page. Faith is a divine gift. It is gained by prayer. Prayer must be patient and persevering. I have not strength to explain and defend this here. God bless you.[1]

[1] Spurrier wrote in February 1887 to say that he had prayed as Newman told him, and was about to be received into the Church. He seems to have begun studying for the priesthood, since he was at the Gregorian University in Rome, but then went to the London Hospital, and eventually became Health Officer of Zanzibar.

To George T. Edwards

Febr. 24. 1887

My dear Mr Edwards

My difficulty in writing breaks my thoughts and my feelings, and I not only can't say what I wish to say, but also my wishes themselves fare as if a dish of cold water was thrown over them.

I felt your letter, as all your letters, to be very kind to me and I feel very grateful to you. I don't know why you have been so kind, and you have been so more and more.[1]

I will not close our correspondence without testifying my simple love and adhesion to the Catholic Roman Church, not that I think you doubt this; and did I wish to give a reason for this full and absolute devotion, what should, what can, I say, but that those great and burning truths, which I learned when a boy from evangelical teaching, I have found impressed upon my heart with fresh and ever increasing force by the Holy Roman Church? That Church has added to the simple evangelicism of my first teachers, but it has obscured, diluted, enfeebled, nothing of it—on the contrary, I have found a power, a resource, a comfort, a consolation in our Lord's divinity and atonement, in His Real Presence, in communion in His Divine and Human Person, which all good Catholics indeed have, but which Evangelical Christians have but faintly But I have not strength to say more.

Thank you for the beautiful edition of the New Testament. I have a great dislike to heavy books

Very sincerely Yours, John H Card. Newman

[1] Edwards sent a New Testament, Authorised Version, in large print, and divided into four parts, to make each lighter to handle. He had visited Newman a fortnight before, and on 19 February wrote: 'I venture also to hope that amid the sad divisions of our English Christianity you regard the English Bible as a not unimportant bond of Union among a large number of those, whom, though you cannot regard as fellow Churchmen, yet I know you regard as fellow Christians. William Wilberforce once said, "if we cannot reconcile all opinions, at least let us try and unite all hearts", and your Eminence, living in the loving regard of many English Christians has shown how practicable it is to have much of the latter, where corporate unity is unattainable'.

To Miss Emmeline Deane

March 3/87

My dear Emmeline

It would be a great pleasure and favour to me to be painted by you. These are not idle words, and I should rejoice to see you. But my time is not my own. It is not now my own, as if I were young—and I have much to do, and have no certainty when the supply of time will cease, and life end.

You may recollect the histories of St Bede and St Anselm. They were each of them finishing a great work, and they had to run a race with time. Anselm did not finish his—but Bede just managed to be successful. Anselm was 76—but Bede was only 62. I, alas, alas, am 86.

What chance have I of doing my small work, however much I try? and you lightly ask me, my dear child, to give up the long days, which are in fact the only days I have!

The only days I have, because it is my misfortune not to be able to read by candle-light, and at this very time though March has begun, I am anxiously waiting day by day, though as yet in vain, for the morning light to be strong enough to enable me to say Mass without the vain attempt to use a candle.

I must add that now for two years I have lost the use of my fingers for writing, and am obliged to write very slowly in order to form my letters.

It is all this which hinders my saying categorically 'yes' to your kind, and, to me, welcome question

But I will say this—I am labouring to carry two volumes of St Athanasius through the press—I fear this will take at least half a year—this must be—but I know no excuse, if it suits you, why you should not write again to me then, if I am then alive.[1]

Yours affecty John H. Card. Newman

Miss Emmeline Deane.

[1] Emmeline Deane painted Newman's portrait in oils during March 1888.

To Gerard Manley Hopkins

March 3. 1887

Dear Fr Hopkins,

Your letter is an appalling one—but not on that account untrustworthy. There is one consideration however, which you omit. The Irish Patriots hold that they never have yielded themselves to the sway of England and therefore never have been under her laws, and never have been rebels.[1]

This does not diminish the force of your picture—but it suggests that there is no help, no remedy. If I were an Irishman, I should be (in heart) a rebel. Moreover, to clench the difficulty the Irish character and tastes is [sic] very different from the English.

My fingers will not let me write more

Very truly Yrs J. H. Card. Newman

[1] See letter of 19 December 1881 to William Walsh. Hopkins was in Dublin, Professor of Classics at the Catholic University College, which was under the care of the Irish Jesuits.

To Lord Blachford

April 2. 1887

My dear Blachford,

Some weeks ago you were amused at learning from me that I was engaged on a third Edition of the Treatises of St. Athanasius; and you were led in consequence to enquire whether it was not possible to suggest a philosophical reason for my act by putting me and the Bishop of Chester into one category, as lovers of Printers Proofs.[1]

As to the Bishop, in his case 'habes confitentem reum',[2] as to me, I send you the Advertisement to my second, and now to be reprinted in the forthcoming 3rd. edition of my volume, if you won't mind the trouble of it.

I am going through the work again from a deep sense of its imperfection. I am writing against time. St. Bede and St. Anselm both wrote against time, in a like case. St. Bede was granted his wish; St. Anselm, I think, was not. St. Bede was a little past 60. St. Anselm a little past 70. What prospect have I at 86? However, the new Edition has gone to Press.

Sometimes I think I am slowly going downhill but I can't tell. My liability to fall is my great danger. I began in 1880 with breaking my ribs. In the last year I have lost 2 inches in my height, without counting loss of uprightness.

The Duchess of Norfolk is dying. It will be a grievous blow to the Duke. He is a specially domestic man, and his wife has been his life. I have known him since he was a child of 5 years old at Abbotsford.[3]

Yours affectionately, John H. Card: Newman.

[1] Answering Newman's letter of 1 October 1886 (see *L.D.* XXXI, p.165), Lord Blachford wrote on 4 October, 'I am amused at your taking refuge in St Athanasius as a light recreation.

Have you seen ... the Bishop of Chester's (Stubbs') Lectures on Medieval and Modern history?—The first sentence of his preface caps pretty well your story of the Ch. Ch. [Christ Church] scholar.

"If I am asked" he says "what is my reason for printing these lectures I might be at a loss for an answer.... It may be that they owe their present form to the fact that the *love of correcting proof sheets* has become a leading passion with the author."'

² Cicero, *Pro Ligario* I, i.

³ The young Duchess of Norfolk died on 11 April 1887.

To Charles Gore

The Oratory, Birmingham, Novr [14] 1888

Dear Mr Gore,

In the prospect of the Feast of St Edmund King and Martyr. Amen

I am bold to ask you to accept from me a picture of Keble made sacred by a relic of a Saint and Martyr.[1]

As the likeness of a very dear Friend, I welcomed it when received from dear Mr Richmond, and have gladly guarded it since that time. But in spite of my personal affection for the original I have not thought I could consistently leave it to my brothers of St Philip Neri.

It has struck me from your own relation to my other and equally dear friend Pusey, that I may gain in your House in St Giles's place for the picture, and thus in our Lord's words you will be receiving 'the just in the name of the just, and a disciple in the name of a disciple.'[2]

Excuse me if I have said anything rude or unacceptable in this request.[3]

Believe me dear Mr Gore Most truly Yours
John H. Card. Newman

[1] The portrait of Keble was 'framed in oak from the tree in Oakley Park traditionally associated with the martyrdom of St. Edmund. So much confirmation of the tradition exists as that when the tree fell, in 1849, an arrowhead was found embedded in it.' G. L. Prestige, *The Life of Charles Gore* (London, 1935), p. 80.

[2] *Matthew* 10:41–2.

[3] Gore replied from Pusey House on the 'Eve of St Edmund', 15 November, 'However great the value which the picture of Mr Keble would in any case have had for us, it is increased tenfold by its having belonged to you and been prized by you and coming from you—and by its having attached the sacred relic of which you speak.'

To George T. Edwards

The Oratory, Birmingham Jan 7, 1889

Dear Mr Edwards

God has never failed me. He has at all times been to me a faithful God. I trust your prayers will do me good. They will carry me on to the end.

Yours most truly J. H. Newman

Geo. T. Edwards Esqre

To Wilfrid Ward

The Oratory Birmingham Jany 7. 1889

My dear Wilfrid

I grieve to read your letter, and as far as lies in our power we will join our prayers with yours.

My blessing on Josephine and the little child.[1]

Yours affectionately J H N

Wilfrid Ward Esqre.

[1] This was Maisie Ward, born on 4 January and not expected to live. She was out of danger by 9 January and died in 1975.

To Lord Blachford

The Oratory, Birmm Sept. 28. 1889

My dear Blachford,

Your letter of this morning added of course to the griefs which for a long course of years have gathered heavily upon my mind. And though I knew all along what must take place any how some day or other to the destruction of my tenderest memories, yet, I was not the more prepared for your very kind and distinct announcement when it came to me[1]

Yours J.H.N.

[1] Lord Blachford wrote on 27 September, 'I ought to tell you that within the last two days, my doctors have told me plainly that I am not to recover.'

To Lady Blachford

The Oratory, Birmm Nov. 24/89

My dear Lady Blachford,

It was very kind in you to write your words so directly though on so sad a matter.[1]

I do not know why, but, as coming from you, it gave me a feeling of comfort which I needed. I pray that the blessing of God may come upon you and him and all dear to him. He is nearly the dearest as well as the oldest of my early friends.

Yours most sincerely John H. Cardinal Newman

[1] Lady Blachford wrote on 21 November that her husband died in his sleep at 6 a.m. that day.

To R. W. Church

The Oratory, Birmingham December 9, 1889

My dear Dean,

You have had domestic sorrows which I have not had, yet I rival you in many ways which equal yours. My memory runs back as yours cannot into a grave memento which comes vividly home to me. Do you recollect our walking together in 1841 to see the last from the top of the coach at Carfax of Hope-Scott when he was on his passage to Rome. I then felt strangely that in seeing Blachford I was seeing the last of a dear friend leaving me after a long friendship. I was losing in him the dear friend whom I had known so long. I never quite recovered that loss, but I think we have loved each other to the end in spite of serious obstacles. Your kindness will excuse these reminiscences.[1]

Ever yours affly J H N

The Very Revd The Dean of St Paul's

[1] Dean Church, who had kept Newman informed of the stages of Lord Blachford's illness, replied on 12 December, 'I knew what he was to me, and I knew that he must have been very much more to you, and that you had in a way lost him twice.' For the renewal of Newman's friendship with Lord Blachford see letter of 26 August 1863 to Ambrose St John, *L.D.* xx, 512–13.

To Mrs William Langford

The Oratory, Birmm Aug 2/90

My dear Grace,

Thank you for your wish to see me.[1] I embrace it readily and I will see you whatever day next week suits you for that purpose.[2]

Yours affectionately, J.H.N.

P.S. I am sometimes engaged with the doctor.[3]
Mrs Langford.

[1] Grace Mozley, the only child of Newman's sister Harriett, had married in 1864 and emigrated with her husband to Australia. She was born in 1839 but Newman had not seen her since 1843, when his sister had broken off relations as he became more Catholic. Grace was now on a visit to England, staying with John Rickards Mozley and his wife Edith, who wrote on 1 August that 'she would like very much to try and see you before she goes back to Australia. She is rather shy of proposing it'.

[2] Grace Langford replied on 5 August:

'My dear Uncle—

It is very kind of you to be willing to see me—I am staying at the Lakes with John and Edith Mozley and return to Cheltenham [where her father Tom Mozley lived] on Friday—but break the journey at Birmingham and hope to be with you some time on Saturday morning [9 August]— should this be convenient to you.

My time is short in England as I sail for Australia in October.

Believe me Yours affectionately Grace Langford'

[3] Mrs Langford wrote a long account of her visit, 'He was very kind, holding my hand in his all the time. I was sorry I had kept my glove on. But I could not quite understand all he said to me. . . . He told me he had once seen me at the Oxford Observatory when I was three years old . . . He said Willie (my son) had gained good opinions and everyone had spoken well of him. He asked about my father's books. . . . At last he gave me, as he does to all visitors, a blessing'.

Afterwards Mrs Langford told Neville that she had 'met Maria Giberne at Rome and that she had nursed me through an illness, and had been one of the pleasantest recollections of my Roman visit'. As she left Neville gave her 'a small volume nicely bound of the Cardinal's earlier poems with his and my initials in his own hand'. He also gave her Newman's last message that 'I had touched him deeply by the way I had spoken of Maria Giberne'.

This was in the afternoon of Saturday 9 August. At 1 a.m. on Sunday 10 August Newman was taken ill. He died of pneumonia in the evening on Monday 11 August 1890.

Index of Newman's Correspondents

*with notes derived largely from the information supplied in the published
volumes of Newman's Letters and Diaries*

Acland, Sir Henry Wentworth (1815–1900), educated at Harrow and Christ Church, Oxford, he was elected a Fellow of All Souls in 1840. During this time he saw much of Newman. He became Regius Professor of Medicine from 1857 to 1894 and transformed the teaching of medicine in Oxford.

Acton, Sir John Dalberg (1834–1902), created first **Baron Acton** in 1869, was educated at Oscott and in Germany, where he laid the foundations of his immense learning, developing his passionate devotion to freedom and his liberal Catholicism. He sat in Parliament from 1859 to 1865 and was also proprietor of the *Rambler* and its editor after Newman resigned. He opposed the definition of papal infallibility. In 1895 he was appointed Regius Professor of Modern History at Cambridge.

Allies, Thomas William (1813–1903), Fellow of Wadham and for two years Chaplain to C. J. Blomfield, Bishop of London. He was greatly influenced by Newman and became a Catholic in 1850, but with little means to support his family. Newman appointed him Lecturer in History at the Catholic University in Dublin in 1855 and from 1853 to 1890 he was Secretary of the Catholic Poor School Committee.

Badeley, Edward (1803–68), only met Newman around 1837, but they became close friends. He was one of the leading Tractarian lawyers, was counsel for the Bishop of Exeter in the Gorham case in 1850, and assisted Newman during the Achilli trial. He became a Catholic in 1852.

Bagot, Richard (1782–1854), Bishop of Oxford from 1829 to 1845, and so was Newman's bishop throughout his Tractarian years. He then became Bishop of Bath and Wells.

Barberi, Dominic (1792–1849), the youngest son of a peasant farmer, he joined the Passionist Order and was ordained in 1818. He felt a special call to work in England. He met Newman in 1844 and received him into the Catholic Church the following year. He was beatified, the final step before canonization, in 1963.

Barnabò, Alessandro (1801–74), appointed Secretary to the Roman Congregation of Propaganda in 1846 and its Cardinal and Prefect in 1856. He was a rough and ready administrator of whom Newman was critical when he had dealings with him in 1856 with regard to the breach between the Oratories and in 1867 over the Oxford scheme.

Barry, William (1849–1930), priest of the Birmingham Diocese and for a while a professor at Oscott. He wrote many articles, novels, and historical work, including *Newman* (London, 1904).

Bellasis, Edward (1800–73), a distinguished parliamentary lawyer who met Newman in 1839 and began a lifelong friendship. He became a Catholic in 1850 and stood by Newman during the Achilli trial.

Bellasis, Edward (1852–1922), second son of Edward Bellasis.

Bellasis, Eliza Jane, **Mrs Edward** (1815–98), married Edward Bellasis in 1835 and became a Catholic in 1851, three months after her husband.

Bittleston, Henry (1818–86), educated at St John's College, Oxford, he was ordained as an Anglican, but came to Birmingham in 1849 and was received into the Catholic Church by Newman. He joined the Oratory the following year, but left in 1879, perhaps because of some financial impropriety. He continued to work as a secular priest.

Blachford, Lord, see **Rogers, Sir Frederic**.

Blachford, Lady, wife of Lord Blachford.

Bloxam, John Rouse (1807–91), for a time was a Fellow of Magdalen, Newman's curate at Littlemore, and later Vicar of Upper Beeding in Sussex. He never became a Catholic, but remained always on friendly terms with Newman, visiting him regularly at the Oratory.

Bourne, Henry (1826–70), father of Cardinal Francis Bourne who was Archbishop of Westminster from 1903 to 1935.

Bowden, Elizabeth (1805–96), married Newman's great friend from his undergraduate days, John Bowden. She became a Catholic in 1846 and attended Newman's funeral.

Bowden, John Edward (1829–74), elder son of John and Elizabeth Bowden, educated at Eton and Trinity College, Oxford. He became a Catholic in 1848, joining the English Oratory the following year. He was one of those sent to start the London House and lived to be F. W. Faber's biographer.

Bowden, John William (1799–1844), Newman's close friend from their days as undergraduates together at Trinity College, Oxford. After leaving Oxford he was Commissioner of Stamps from 1824 to 1840. He was an important member of the Oxford Movement.

Bowden, Marianne (1831–67), delicate elder daughter of John and Elizabeth Bowden. She became a Visitation nun at Westbury.

Bowles, Emily (1818–1904?), met Newman in 1840 and became a Catholic in 1843. She was for a time a nun in the Society of the Holy Child Jesus, but she later quarrelled with the founder, Cornelia Connelly. She and Newman corresponded very freely.

Brackenbury, Mrs, a friend of Mary Holmes.

Braye, Lord, **Edgell, Alfred Wyatt** (1849–1928), educated at Eton and Christ Church and became a Catholic in 1868. He succeeded his mother Baroness Braye in her own right as fifth Baron Braye in 1879. He took great interest in higher education for Catholics.

Bright, William (1824–1901), educated at Rugby School and University College, Oxford. In 1868 he was appointed Regius Professor of Ecclesiastical History and a Canon of Christ Church. He was a friend and supporter of Pusey.

Brown, Thomas Joseph (1798–1880), a Benedictine monk who became the first Bishop of Newport. He delated Newman to Rome for his article on consulting the faithful. He later wished to have him as his theologian at the First Vatican Council.

Bunting, Percy William (1836–1911), editor of the *Contemporary Review* from 1882 till his death.

Capes, John Moore (1812–89), educated at Westminster and Balliol College, Oxford, he was initially opposed to the Tractarians and wrote against Newman. He was ordained as an Anglican. Doubts about the state of the Church of England led him to seek Newman's advice in 1845 and he was received as a Catholic in June that year. He taught at Prior Park and founded the *Rambler*. In 1870 he returned to the Church of England, but by 1882 had become a Catholic once more.

Caswall, Edward (1814–78), educated at Brasenose College, Oxford, he took Anglican Orders in 1839, but was received into the Catholic Church in Rome in 1847 in Newman's presence. He had married in 1841 and his wife too became a Catholic, but after her death in 1849, he joined the Oratory and remained always with Newman in Birmingham. He is remembered especially as a writer and translator of hymns.

Caswall, Miss, sister of Edward Caswall.

Christie, John Frederic (1808–60), a Fellow of Oriel from 1829 to 1848 and a friend of the leaders of the Oxford Movement.

Church, Helen Beatrice (1858–1900), twin sister of Mary Church, and daughter of R. W. Church. In 1883 she married Francis Paget who became Bishop of Oxford the year after her death.

Church, Mary (1858–1954?), twin sister of Helen Church, and daughter of R. W. Church.

Church, Richard William (1815–90), met Newman in 1836 and their friendship became close when he was elected a Fellow of Oriel in 1838. As a proctor he vetoed the proposal to censure *Tract 90*. Newman and he renewed their friendship in 1864 and Church was appointed Dean of St Paul's in 1871.

Clerke, Charles Carr (1798–1877), a Student of Christ Church, he was appointed Archdeacon of Oxford in 1830.

Clifford, William (1823–93), served Newman's first mass and preached his funeral sermon. He was ordained in 1850 and appointed Bishop of Clifton in 1857. He did not favour the defining of papal infallibility in 1870. He was always Newman's staunch friend.

Cockburn, Sir Alexander (1802–80), educated privately and at Trinity Hall, Cambridge. He was a distinguished QC and liberal MP for Southampton. He was Newman's barrister during the Achilli trial. He served as Solicitor-General and later as Attorney General. In 1859 he was appointed Lord Chief Justice.

Coleridge, Henry James (1822–93), educated at Eton and Trinity College, Oxford, he became a Fellow of Oriel in 1845, but left in 1848 to become a curate at Alphington in Devon. He was received as a Catholic in 1852, studied in Rome and was ordained in 1856. He joined the Jesuits the following year. He became a close friend and frequent correspondent of Newman's.

Coleridge, John Duke (1820–94), brother of Henry James Coleridge, was a Fellow of Exeter College from 1843 to 1846. He was called to the bar and sat as a Liberal MP from 1865 to 1873, when he was appointed Lord Chief Justice. He was created Baron Coleridge in 1874. He had known Newman at Oxford and became an admirer and close friend after the *Apologia*.

Cope, Sir William Henry (1811–83), was an officer in the Rifle Brigade, but took Orders in 1840. He was a follower of the Tractarians and collected all Newman's writings.

Copeland, William John (1804–85), a Fellow of Trinity, a Tractarian, and a great friend of Newman. He was his curate at Littlemore in 1840 and later brought out an edition of Newman's *Parochial and Plain Sermons*. After a break of sixteen years he met Newman by chance in London in 1862 and then brought Keble, Rogers, and Church back into touch with him.

Crawley, Charles (1788–1871), after being a merchant in Spain, he built a house at Littlemore in 1842. He was a parishioner and admired Newman. They resumed correspondence in the sixties.

Cullen, Paul (1803–78), after being Vice-Rector and then Rector of the Irish College in Rome, he was appointed Archbishop of Armagh in 1849, and translated to Dublin in 1852. He invited Newman to found the University there in 1851, but they had different ideas about what was intended and in practical terms Newman found him impossible to work with. He was the first Irish bishop to be made a Cardinal.

Dalgairns, John Dobrée, or **Bernard** (1818–76), one of the younger Tractarians, he brought Dominic Barberi to Littlemore, when Newman was to be received as a Catholic. He joined Newman in the Oratorian novitiate in Rome and was a member of the Birmingham community before going to London. He took the name Bernard. He came back to Birmingham for a while, but he and Newman were no longer in sympathy. He returned to London and succeeded Faber as Superior.

Darnell, Nicholas (1817–92), educated at Winchester and Oxford, becoming a Fellow of New College. He resigned his fellowship when he became a Catholic in 1847 and joined Faber's Wilfridians. With them he became an Oratorian in 1848 and was ordained a priest the following year. He was the first headmaster of the Oratory School in 1859, but resigned in 1861 with all the other masters, when Newman insisted that the school was under the control of himself and the Oratory. He worked for a time as a private tutor and later as a priest in Northumberland.

Deane, Emmeline (1858–1944), daughter of Louisa Elizabeth Deane. She painted Newman's portrait.

Deane, Louisa Elizabeth (1811–92?), was Newman's cousin.

Du Boulay, Susan, Sister Mary Gabriel (1826–1906), was received into the Catholic Church by Newman in 1850. After travelling for a year, she then entered Mother Margaret Hallahan's convent at Clifton.

Edwards, George T., secretary of the London Evangelisation Society,

Emly, Lord, see **Monsell, William**.

Estcourt, Edgar Edmund (1816–84), educated at Exeter College, Oxford, and was working as a clergyman in 1845, but was received that year into the Catholic Church. He was ordained in 1848 and became Bishop Ullathorne's secretary and the treasurer of the Birmingham Diocese.

Faber, Francis Atkinson (1804–76), the elder brother of F. W. Faber, was a Fellow of Magdalen College, Oxford, from 1834 to 1845, and' rector of Saunderton, Bucks, till his death. He adopted Tractarian views and admired Newman.

Faber, Frederick William (1814–63), a Fellow of University College, Oxford, met Newman in 1837 and was ordained as an Anglican in 1839. He was drawn to Rome more and more and introduced its practices into his parish at Elton in Huntingdonshire. He was received as a Catholic in November 1845 and founded a community, the Brothers of the Will of God. In 1846 he moved his community to St Wilfrid's, Cotton, near Alton Towers, and so they were known as Wilfridians. On Newman's return to England, the community became Oratorians. When the London Oratory was founded, Faber was put in charge and, when it became independent, he was its Superior.

Ffoukles, Edmund Salusbury (1819–94), educated at Shrewsbury School and Jesus College, Oxford, he became a Catholic in 1855, returning to the Church of England in 1870. He was Vicar of St Mary's, Oxford, from 1878. As a Catholic he had wanted to open a hall for Catholics in Oxford.

Fortey, Emily, a schoolgirl who in 1882, when she was sixteen, wrote to Newman about her wish to become a Catholic. His private letter in reply was printed in *The Times* six months later. She was received in 1884, once her father had given his consent. She visited Newman in 1887.

Froude, Eliza Margaret (1840–1931), always known as Isy, was the eldest daughter of William and Catherine Froude. She became a Catholic in 1859 and married Baron Anatole von Hugel, the brother of Friedrich, in 1880. She was always a faithful friend of Newman.

Froude, Richard Hurrell (1803–36), Fellow of Oriel and one of Newman's closest friends who had a great influence on the Oxford Movement.

Froude, William (1810–79), Hurrell Froude's brother, who gained a First in mathematics at Oriel. He worked as a railway engineer and later became a celebrated naval architect. He and Newman were good friends and corresponded at length. This friendship was not impaired by his wife and family becoming Catholics. Newman was drafting him a long letter when he heard of his death.

Froude, Mrs William, Catherine née Holdsworth (1809 or 1810–78), had known Newman before her marriage to Hurrell Froude's brother, William. She became a Catholic in 1857, as did most of her children, but not her husband, William, who remained a close friend of Newman.

Giberne, Maria Rosina (1802–85), a friend of Newman's family and his enthusiastic disciple, she was also a loyal friend. She moved from Evangelicalism to Tractarianism, before being received as a Catholic in 1845, shortly after Newman. She collected witnesses for his defence when he was accused of libel in 1851 and was professed as a Visitation nun at the convent in Autun in 1863. She kept up her correspondence with him till she died.

Gillow, John (1814–77), went to Ushaw in 1828 and stayed there for the rest of his life. He was ordained in 1842. He taught first philosophy, then dogmatic theology, and later moral theology. His cast of mind was satisfied only with what he conceived to be authoritative, Scripture, tradition, infallible teaching, formal reasoning, and the incontrovertible conclusions of physical or mathematical science.

Gladstone, William Ewart (1809–98), four times Prime Minister. He was a friend of Manning and Hope-Scott, and adopted Tractarian opinions. He was also friendly with Newman and admired him.

Golightly, Charles Portales (1807–85), had a fanatical hatred of Roman Catholicism. In spite of his earlier friendly relations with Newman, he became a bitter opponent of the Tractarians and was largely responsible for the outcry against *Tract 90*.

Gordon, John Joseph (1811–53), joined the Indian Army, but was invalided home in 1831. He went to Trinity College, Cambridge, and was ordained as an Anglican in 1837. Having been an Evangelical, he became Tractarian and increasingly High Church. He was received as a Catholic in 1847 and offered himself to Newman at the end of the year, joining the Oratory with his brother in February 1848. He went to Italy in 1852 to find witnesses for the Achilli trial and died of pleurisy the following year. Newman dedicated *The Dream of Gerontius* to him.

Gordon, William Philip (1827–1900), the brother of John Joseph Gordon, was received as a Catholic in 1847 and joined the Oratory the following February. He was one of the group sent to London in 1849 and was Superior of the London Oratory four times.

Gore, Charles (1853–1932), educated at Harrow and Balliol, was elected as a Fellow of Trinity College, Oxford. He was the first Principal of Pusey House, and successively Bishop of Worcester 1902, of Birmingham 1905, and Oxford 1911.

Grant, Anthony (1806–83), a Fellow of New College from 1825 to 1839, and later Archdeacon of St Albans and then of Rochester. He was renowned as an administrator.

Grant, Thomas (1816–70), educated at Ushaw and the English College in Rome, where he was Rector from 1844 to 1851, when he was appointed the first Bishop of Southwark.

Griffin, Canon Arthur Sandes, secretary to Bishop Moriarty of Kerry.

Hampden, Renn Dickson (1793–1868), had been a Fellow of Oriel before Newman's time. The Tractarians were critical of his orthodoxy and in 1836 there was controversy, led by Newman, on his appointment as Regius Professor of Divinity. His appointment as Bishop of Hereford in 1847 was also controversial.

Hawkins, Edward (1789–1882), Fellow of Oriel and from 1828 Provost. He was an early influence on the young Newman and, although he opposed Newman's plans to develop the tutor's role in the College and was opposed to Tractarianism, his relations with Newman remained cordial.

Hawkins, Mrs Edward, wife of Provost Hawkins.

Hayes, John, was matriculated at Magdalen Hall on 2 July 1834, aged 19, and was Vicar of Coalbrookdale, Salop, 1854–78.

Holmes, Mary (1815?–78), a Tractarian who had Newman as her director for two years till she became a Catholic in 1844. She was well read and knew both Thackeray and Trollope. She was a governess, but never stayed in one place for long. She corresponded with Newman till the end of her life.

Hope-Scott, James Robert (1812–73), a fellow of Merton who took up Tractarian views. He made a great deal of money as a parliamentary lawyer for the railway companies and was very generous to charities. He became a Catholic with Manning in 1851. In 1847 he had married

Charlotte Lockhart, Sir Walter Scott's granddaughter, and subsequently took the name Hope-Scott. He was always a loyal friend to Newman.

Hope-Scott, Mary Monica (1852–1920), known as Mamo, the only surviving child of James Hope by his first marriage.

Hopkins, Gerard Manley (1844–89), the poet, at first a disciple of Pusey and H. P. Liddon, he came to doubt the Anglo-Catholic position. He read Newman's works, visited him, and was received by him into the Catholic Church in 1866. After taking a double First at Oxford in 1867, he taught briefly at the Oratory School before leaving to become a Jesuit in 1868. He went to Dublin as Professor of Classics in 1884, but remained in touch with Newman.

Houldsworth, Mrs of Craigforth, Stirling, was drawn to the Catholic Church and wrote to Newman about her inquiries and difficulties. She was anxious about telling her husband of her intention of becoming a Catholic. She was received at the Birmingham Oratory on 1 July 1872.

Jager, Abbé Jean-Nicholas (1790–1868), a French Church historian who engaged Newman in controversy between 1834 and 1836. The letters helped contribute to Newman's *Lectures on the Prophetical Office*.

Jubber, a Baptist who lived in St Mary's parish.

Keble, John (1792–1866), Fellow and Tutor of Oriel and a leader of the Oxford Movement. Newman regarded his Assize Sermon in 1833 as the start of the Movement. In spite of a long silence shortly after Newman's conversion, the bond between them remained strong and was renewed in 1863.

Kenrick, Francis Patrick (1796–1863), born in Dublin, he studied in Rome and was ordained there in 1821. He became Archbishop of Baltimore in 1851.

Kerr, Lady Henry, Louisa Dorothea (1811–84), the sister of James Hope-Scott, she married Lord Henry Kerr in 1832 and became a Catholic shortly after her husband in 1852.

Kingsley, Charles (1819–75), whose religious doubts were resolved by reading the works of F. D. Maurice and others, reacted strongly against the Oxford Movement. He took Orders in 1842. He became a Christian Socialist and his first novels were written under their influence. He was an advocate of muscular Christianity. He became Chaplain-in-Ordinary to Queen Victoria in 1859 and was appointed Regius Professor of Modern History at Cambridge the following year. He had more than one breakdown from overwork and, after resigning his Professorship in 1869, he was appointed a Canon of Chester and then of Westminster in 1873.

Langford, Grace, née **Mozley** (1839–1908), Newman's niece, only child of Harriett and Thomas Mozley. She married William Langford in 1864 and emigrated to Australia. She published two novels and was an excellent pianist.

Leo XIII, Pope (1810–1903), Gioacchino Pecci, ordained priest in 1837, was Papal Nuncio in Brussels, 1843–6, when he was nominated as Archbishop of Perugia. He was elected Pope in 1878.

Littledale, Richard Frederick (1833–90), educated at Trinity College, Dublin, where he obtained a First in Classics. He held various curacies in England till forced to retire through ill-health in 1861. He was a leading Anglo-Catholic controversialist.

Lockhart, William (1819–92), was at Exeter College, Oxford, and joined Newman at Littlemore in 1842. Drawn to Catholicism, though restrained by Newman, he promised to make no move for three years, but in 1843 he went to consult the Rosminian, Fr Luigi Gentili, at Ratcliffe College, and was received three days later. His defection prompted Newman to resign as Vicar of St Mary the Virgin and to preach his final Anglican sermon, 'The Parting of Friends'. Lockhart became an exemplary Rosminian and remained a loyal disciple of Newman.

Lynch, Patrick Nelson (1817–82), emigrated to America at the age of one, was ordained in Rome in 1840, and became Bishop of Charleston in 1858.

MacColl, Malcolm (1831–1907), received Orders in the Episcopalian Church in Scotland, but owing to his support of Catholic teaching found himself obliged to leave Scotland. He was licensed in London and in 1884 became a residentiary Canon of Ripon.

MacHale, John (1791–1881), Archbishop of Tuam from 1834. He was opposed to mixed education and was a committed Irish nationalist. He resisted Cullen over the University in Dublin, accusing him of exercising too independent a control over it, and, while personally respectful, was against Newman's appointment as Rector because he was English.

Maclaurin, William Cowper Augustine, became an Episcopalian clergyman and the Dean of Moray and Ross. Newman dissuaded him initially from becoming a Catholic, but he and his family were eventually received in 1850. He suffered financially from the move.

Macmillan, Alexander (1818–96), took employment with the publisher, E. B. Seeley, in 1839, and became a bookseller and publisher with his brother Daniel, in 1843. They moved to Cambridge, but returned their headquarters to London in 1863.

Manning, Henry Edward (1808–92), an undergraduate at Balliol and a Fellow of Merton, he became Archdeacon of Chichester and rallied the Tractarians after Newman's conversion to Rome. He became a Catholic himself in 1851 and was ordained a priest of the Westminster Diocese. In 1865 he was appointed Archbishop of Westminster and was created a Cardinal in 1875. His extreme views on the temporal power of the Pope, on papal infallibility, and on mixed university education for Catholics placed him at odds with Newman in later life.

Mayers, Walter (1790–1828), an evangelical clergyman who was the Senior Classical Master at Ealing School where he had a significant influence on Newman.

Meynell, Charles (1828–82), from an old Catholic family, he was ordained in Rome in 1856 and taught at Oscott until 1870. Newman consulted him over *A Grammar of Assent*. After three years at St Chad's Cathedral in Birmingham, he went to the small mission of Caverswall in Staffordshire.

Millais, Sir John Everett (1829–96), one of the most successful British painters of his time. In 1848, with W. Holman Hunt he founded the Pre-Raphaelite Brotherhood.

Miller, Charles (1796–1885), who entered Worcester and was a Demy of Magdalen, or **John** (1787–1858) of Worcester. Both were clergymen and John and Keble were good friends from their undergraduate days.

Mills, Henry Austin (1823–1903), was received into the Catholic Church in 1846, joined Faber's Wilfridians, and with them became an Oratorian. He remained in the Birmingham community for the rest of his life.

Monsell, William (1812–94), educated at Winchester and Oriel, he became MP for Limerick in 1847, until created Lord Emly in 1874. He held various offices in Liberal governments. He was received into the Catholic Church in 1850 and became one of Newman's close friends and correspondents.

Monteith, Robert (1812–84), son of a rich Glasgow cotton merchant, he called on Newman in 1844 and became a Catholic two years later. He was a generous benefactor of the Church in Scotland.

Moriarty, David (1814–77), educated in Boulogne and then at Maynooth, was ordained in 1839. He met Newman in Birmingham in 1849 and became a lifelong friend. He was consecrated Coadjutor to the Bishop of Kerry in 1854 and succeeded him two years later. He did not favour the need to define papal infallibility at the First Vatican Council.

Mozley, Anne (1809–91), sister-in-law of Newman's sisters who lived almost her entire life in her family circle at or near Derby. She was a writer and in touch with the Oxford Movement. Newman was fond of her and appreciated her skills as an editor. He invited her to edit the letters of his Anglican years which she completed within weeks of his death.

Mozley, Henry Williams (1842–1919), third son of Newman's sister, Jemima.

Mozley, John Rickards (1840–1931), second son of Newman's sister, Jemima.

Mozley, Thomas (1806–93), came to Oriel in 1825, was Newman's pupil, and was elected a Fellow in 1829. In 1836 he married Harriett, Newman's eldest sister, and became Vicar of Cholderton in Wiltshire. He was an ardent Tractarian and nearly converted to Rome in 1843, but Newman restrained him. Harriett blamed her brother for his Romanizing and the estrangement between them began. In 1882 he produced his *Reminiscences of Oriel College and the Oxford Movement*, which Newman criticized severely for its many mistakes and inaccuracies.

Munro, Miss G. (*c.*1822–*c.*1913), was received into the Catholic Church by Wiseman in 1845. She had money of her own and thought of becoming a nun, but never did. Newman was her director. His last known letter to her was written in 1882.

Murphy, Mary, sister of Frank Power, *The Times* correspondent who was with General Gordon in Khartoum.

Neville, William Paine (1824–1905), educated at Winchester and Trinity College, Oxford. He was received as a Catholic by Newman in 1851. He joined the Birmingham Oratory later that year, but being a rather hesitant, indecisive person, was not ordained until 1861. After the death of Ambrose St John he attended on Newman more and more, becoming his secretary and nurse. After Newman had died, he tirelessly collected and copied Newman's letters and papers.

Newman, Charles Robert (1802–84), the older of Newman's two brothers. He was able, but restless, and quarrelled with his family on his father's death, breaking off relations. Nevertheless for some time he relied on Newman for financial support.

Newman, Elizabeth Good (1765–1852), Newman's aunt to whom he owed part of his early religious instruction. Newman was devoted to her and she was distressed by his conversion, but softened by his letters and visits.

Newman, Francis William (1805–97), Newman's younger brother. Newman supported him when he went up to Worcester where he took a double First. He was then elected a Fellow of

Balliol, but resigned in 1830 on account of his nonconformist views. He was appointed Professor of Classical Literature at Manchester and later of Latin at University College, London. He abandoned Christianity for Unitarianism and, although he and Newman drifted apart, they kept in touch and met from time to time.

Newman, Harriett (1803–52), Newman's eldest sister who married Thomas Mozley. She had no sympathy with Newman's developing religious opinions and became estranged from him even before his conversion.

Newman, Jemima (1808–79), Newman's second sister who married John Mozley, printer and publisher at Derby. Although she was far from approving of Newman's conversion, they remained on friendly terms.

Newman, John (1767–1824), a banker, Newman's father.

Newman, Mrs John, Jemima, née Fourdrinier (1772–1836), Newman's mother.

Newman, Mary (1809–28), Newman's youngest sister.

Nina, Lorenzo (1812–85), created a Cardinal in 1877, becoming Secretary of State in 1878. He retired owing to ill health in 1880.

Norfolk, Henry Fitzalan Howard, fifteenth Duke of (1847–1917), succeeded his father in 1860 and was sent to the Oratory School from 1861 to 1864. He was a devoted and active Catholic to whom Newman addressed his *A Letter to the Duke of Norfolk* on papal claims in answer to Gladstone. He played the chief part in securing from Leo XIII Newman's cardinalate.

Norris, John (1843–1911), was from a Lancashire Catholic family and went to Ushaw to study for the priesthood, but his health broke down. He came to the Birmingham Oratory in 1864 and joined the following year. He succeeded Ambrose St John as headmaster of the Oratory School and continued in office till February 1911. He was Superior from 1905 till his death in October 1911.

Northcote, James Spencer (1821–1907), was greatly influenced by Newman and a close friend of Pusey. He was appointed a curate at Ilfracombe in 1840 and married his cousin, Susannah Spencer Ruscombe Poole, two years later. She became a Catholic in November 1845 and he followed her in January 1846. He travelled in Italy, becoming an expert on Christian antiquities, and was editor of the *Rambler* from 1852 to 1854. After his wife's death in 1853, he studied for the priesthood and was President of Oscott from 1860 to 1876, and from 1885 he was Provost of the Birmingham Chapter.

Oxenham, Henry Nutcombe (1829–88), educated at Harrow and Balliol, he was ordained by Samuel Wilberforce. He was one of the founders of the Association for the Promotion of the Unity of Christendom and was received into the Catholic Church by Manning in 1857. He tried his vocation at the London Oratory and then at St Edmund's, Ware, but he attacked the seminary system and was not ordained. He taught at the Oratory School in 1861 and became involved in the crisis when members of the staff resigned. He also remained friendly with Anglicans.

Pattison, Mark (1813–84), went up to Oriel in 1832 and came under Newman's influence, adopting Tractarian views for a while. He became a Fellow of Lincoln College in 1839, took

Orders, and in 1861 was elected Rector of Lincoln. He and Newman remained friendly and he helped Newman over the negotiations for the Oxford Oratory site. Newman visited him when he lay dying.

Pereira, Mrs Edward, Margaret Ann Stonor (1839–94), sent her three sons to the Oratory School. Two became generals and the third joined the Birmingham Oratory and became headmaster of the Oratory School.

Phillipps, Ambrose Lisle (1809–78), who, on the death of his father in 1862, assumed the name of de Lisle, becoming Ambrose Phillipps de Lisle. He became a Catholic at 15 and went up to Cambridge, but left after two years because of ill health. An enthusiast and supporter of the architect, Pugin, he also worked hard for the reunion of the Anglican and Catholic Churches. He was one of the founders of the Association for the Promotion of the Unity of Christendom in 1857, from which Catholics were ordered to withdraw in 1864.

Plummer, Alfred (1841–1926), was a Fellow of Trinity College, Oxford, and from 1874 was Master of University College, Durham.

Plumptre, Edward Hayes (1921–91), elected to a Fellowship of Brasenose College, Oxford, in 1844, which he resigned on marrying in 1848. He was Rector of Pluckley 1869–73 and Bickley 1873–81, while he held various chairs successively at University College, London, from 1847 to 1881, when he was appointed Dean of Wells.

Pollen, John Hungerford (1820–1902), a Fellow of Merton who was ordained as an Anglican. He was received into the Catholic Church in 1852 and decided to devote himself professionally to art and architecture. In 1855 he came to Dublin as Newman's Professor of Fine Arts and built the University Church. Two years later he settled in London and was one of Newman's most devoted and faithful friends.

Poole, Maria Spencer Ruscombe (1815–81), was directed first by Pusey, but was received into the Catholic Church in September 1845. In 1849 she entered St Catherine's Convent at Clifton, taking the name Sister Mary Imelda, and succeeded Mother Margaret Hallahan as Provincial in 1868. She was a devoted friend of Newman.

Pope, Simeon Lloyd (1802–55), entered Trinity College, Oxford, in 1820, where he and Newman became great friends. He was ordained as an Anglican. Newman was godfather to his son, Henry Edmund.

Pope, William (1825–1905), a nephew of Richard Whately's who became a Catholic in 1853 and later was the priest at Harrogate. He sent Newman the copy of Macmillan's Magazine that led to his writing his *Apologia*.

Pusey, Edward Bouverie (1800–82), after his election as a Fellow of Oriel in 1823, he was appointed Regius Professor of Hebrew and so became a Student of Christ Church. His personal religious practice was austere. He became a leader of the Tractarians and their undisputed leader after Newman's departure. His and Newman's friendship never faltered.

Pusey, Maria, née Barker (1801–39), a vivacious attractive personality with whom Pusey fell deeply in love. She came to follow his strict religious way of life and died from consumption.

Ripon, George Frederick Samuel Robinson, first Marquis of (1827–1909), held various political posts in the House of Commons and then in the Lords as a younger man. Brought up a strict Evangelical, he was attracted to Catholicism when only seventeen, but through family opposition he lost interest until 1870 when his brother was assassinated by Greek brigands. He then read Newman extensively and, at risk of excluding himself from political life, was received as a Catholic in 1874. When Gladstone became Prime Minister in 1880, he was appointed Viceroy of India for four years and on his return fully supported Gladstone over Irish Home Rule. He was first Lord of the Admiralty in 1886, Colonial Secretary from 1892 to 1895, and in the great Liberal Government of 1905 he was Lord Privy Seal and Leader of the House of Lords. He resigned in 1908.

Rogers, Sir Frederic (1811–89), inherited the baronetcy in 1851. He was a pupil of Newman's and became one of his dearest friends. There was a break in their relationship that lasted for twenty years as Newman was moving towards Rome, but, once their friendship was renewed in 1863, it continued more warmly than ever. He was Permanent Under-Secretary of State for the Colonies from 1860 to 1871, when he was created Lord Blachford.

Rose, Hugh James (1795–1838), a friend of Newman's from Trinity College, Cambridge. He invited Newman to write a history of Church Councils, a book that became *The Arians of the Fourth Century*.

Russell, Charles (1812–80), was President of Maynooth, and a friend of Newman. One of the first Catholics Newman came to know, he influenced him by his understated manner.

Ryder, George Dudley (1810–80), one of Newman's pupils at Oriel, who was influenced by the Oxford Movement. He became an Anglican priest, but was received into the Catholic Church with his family in 1846. His eldest son joined the Birmingham Oratory.

St John, Ambrose (1815–75), a Student of Christ Church who joined Newman at Littlemore in 1843 and thereafter was Newman's loyal friend, becoming an Oratorian with him and settling at the Birmingham Oratory. He supported him tirelessly in any way that he could.

Sconce, Mrs, widow of Robert Knox Sconce who went up to Brasenose College, Oxford, and later had been Rector of St Andrew's, Sydney. He died in 1852. She and her husband had been received into the Catholic Church in Sydney by Archbishop Polding in 1848.

Shrewsbury, John Talbot, sixteenth Earl of (1791–1852), completed Alton Towers. Faber's Wilfridians undertook the mission for him at Cotton which then created problems for Newman.

Simeon, Lady Catherine Dorothea (d.1904), second wife of Sir John Simeon, who became a Catholic when she married him in 1861.

Simeon, Sir John (1815–70), educated at Christ Church, Oxford, and succeeded as third baronet in 1854. He had been Liberal MP for the Isle of Wight from 1847 to 1851, when he resigned on being received into the Catholic Church. He returned to Parliament in 1865. He became a friend of Newman, sought his advice, and supported his plan for the Oratory School and his effort to found an Oratory in Oxford.

Simpson, Richard (1820–76), educated at Oriel, he took Orders as an Anglican, but became a Catholic in 1844. He was one of the ablest of the converts, a linguist and a Shakespearean scholar, while also being deeply interested in theological matters. He collaborated with Acton over the *Rambler* and the *Home and Foreign Review*. He was a devout and also a liberal Catholic, whose extravagances Newman tried to moderate.

Sparkes, William Prescott, appears to have been a confidence trickster (see *L.D.* IX, p. 461 n.1).

Spurrier, Alfred Henry (1862–1935), became a Catholic in 1887 and was later Health Officer in Zanzibar.

Stanton, Richard (1820–1901), educated at Oxford and ordained as an Anglican deacon, but then joined Newman at Littlemore and was received with him. He went to Rome for his Oratorian novitiate in 1847 and was one of the original English Oratorians. He was sent by Newman to London in 1849, where he stayed for the rest of his life.

Talbot, Edward Stuart (1844–1934), became the first Warden of Keble College, Oxford, in 1870. He was later successively Bishop of Rochester, 1895, of Southwark, 1905, and of Winchester, 1911. He resigned in 1923.

Talbot, George (1816–86), the fifth son of Baron Talbot of Malahide, after Oxford took Anglican Orders. He was received into the Catholic Church by Wiseman in 1842 and ordained in 1846. In 1847 Newman politely refused his request to join the Oratory and, after working in London, he returned to Rome through Wiseman's influence and was made a Canon of St Peter's and a Papal Chamberlain. For the last eighteen years of his life he lived and worked near Paris, avoiding the intense heat of Rome for health reasons.

Telford, John, probably the priest at Ryde on the Isle of Wight who was friend of Mrs and Miss Wood.

Thompson, Edward Healy (1813?–91), after being at Emmanuel College, Cambridge, and holding several curacies, he became a Catholic under Newman's influence in 1846. Newman put him forward as Lecturer in English Literature at the Catholic University in Dublin in 1853, but he never acted upon it.

Trollope, Anthony (1815–82), novelist.

Ullathorne, William Bernard (1806–89), was a Benedictine who helped organize the Church in Australia. He became Vicar Apostolic of the Western District in 1846, was transferred to the Central District in 1848, and was appointed the first Bishop of Birmingham in 1850.

Vere, Aubrey de (1814–1902), educated at Trinity College, Dublin, he visited Newman at Oxford in 1838. His experience of the Irish famine greatly affected him, and in 1851 he became a Catholic. Newman appointed him Professor of Political and Social Science at the Catholic University in Dublin in 1855.

Walker, John (1800–73), educated at Ushaw and ordained there in 1826. He became one of Newman's major correspondents.

Walsh, William J. (1841–1921), was at the Catholic University of Ireland while Newman was Rector, and was then at Maynooth as Professor of Theology 1867, as Vice-President 1878, and President 1880, before becoming Archbishop of Dublin in 1885. He was a Nationalist and supporter of Sinn Fein, but opposed to violence.

Ward, Catherine (*c.*1813–97), felt drawn to Catholicism and corresponded with Newman in 1848 and 1849. She was received in June 1849. In 1857 she married George Tylee who had retired from the Army with the rank of Major-General; after his death in 1865 she lived on at Clifton.

Ward, Wilfrid (1856–1916), son of William George Ward and writer of the first major biography of Newman.

Ward, William George (1812–82), a gifted mathematician and man of extreme views, both as a Tractarian and as a Catholic. He was a Fellow of Balliol and became a Catholic in 1845. In spite of their disagreements, Newman liked him because he was open and straightforward. He taught philosophy and then theology at the seminary at St Edmund's, Ware, and from 1863 to 1878 he edited *The Dublin Review* and made it an organ of extreme ultramontanism.

Wayte, Samuel William (1819–98), was successively a Scholar, 1838–42, a Fellow and tutor, 1842–66, and then from 1866 President of Trinity College, Oxford. He invited Newman to become the first Honorary Fellow of the College in December 1877.

Westmacott, Richard (1799–1872), the sculptor and a friend of Newman's since their days together at Ealing School. He executed a well-known bust of Newman.

Whately, Richard (1787–1863), Fellow of Oriel from 1811 to 1821 and Principal of St Alban Hall, Oxford, from 1825 to 1831, when he became Archbishop of Dublin. He brought the young Newman out of his shy shell, but shunned him later.

Whitty, Robert (1817–95), was born and prepared for the priesthood in Ireland, but ordained in England in 1840. He showed real sympathy for the converts and tried his vocation as an Oratorian, but then joined the Diocese of Westminster before eventually becoming a Jesuit. As a Jesuit he held a number of important positions. He always remained attached to Newman.

Wilberforce, Henry (1807–73), the fourth and youngest son of William Wilberforce the philanthropist. He was first Newman's pupil and then his long-standing friend. He took Orders and married in 1834. With his wife and family he was received into the Catholic Church in 1850. He later took up religious journalism.

Wilberforce, Mary Frances (1800–80), wife of William Wilberforce, the eldest son of the philanthropist. Newman dissuaded her from becoming a Catholic in 1834 and she did not take the step till 1852. Her husband followed her in 1863.

Wilberforce, Robert Isaac (1802–57), the second son of William Wilberforce, the philanthropist. He was a Fellow and Tutor of Oriel with Newman. He left Oxford in 1831 and in 1841 became Archdeacon of the West Riding. He was a leading Tractarian theologian and became a Catholic in 1854.

Wilberforce, Samuel (1805–73), the third son of William Wilberforce, the philanthropist. He remained a devoted Anglican and became Bishop of Oxford in 1845 and Bishop of Winchester in 1869. He died in a horse riding accident.

Wilberforce, Wilfrid (1850–1910), son of Henry Wilberforce.

Williams, Isaac (1802–65), educated at Harrow and Trinity College, Oxford, where he became a Fellow. He was a poet and retiring by nature. His failure to succeed Keble as Professor of Poetry was seen as a serious defeat by the Tractarians. He had been Newman's curate at Littlemore and they continued to correspond occasionally after Newman's conversion, but did not meet again until Newman visited him when he was dying. Newman had real affection for him.

Wiseman, Nicholas (1802–65), was Rector of the English College, Rome, from 1828 to 1840 and met Newman first when Newman visited Rome in 1833. When he returned to England as Rector of Oscott and Coadjutor Bishop for the Midland District in 1840 he encouraged the Tractarians, and after 1845 advised Newman to consider his vocation as an Oratorian. In 1847 he moved to London and in 1850 became the first Archbishop of Westminster and a Cardinal.

Wood, Charlotte, daughter of William and Charlotte Wood. Her father had died, but she and her mother were received as Catholics together in 1845 and remained close friends of Newman.

Wynter, Philip (1793–1871), was a Fellow and then Master of St John's College, Oxford. He was Vice-Chancellor from 1840 to 1844, which were critical years for the Oxford Movement. Though tending to be a High Churchman, he had little sympathy for Newman and the Tractarians.

Index